Sixth Edition

SOCIOLOGY

Exploring the Architecture of Everyday Life

DAVID M. NEWMAN

DePauw University

SAGE Publications
Thousand Oaks ■ London ■ New Delhi

For information:

Pine Forge Press
An imprint of Sage Publications, Inc.
2455 Teller Road
Thousand Oaks, California 91320
E-mail: order@sagepub.com

Sage Publications Ltd.
1 Oliver's Yard
55 City Road
London EC1Y 1SP
United Kingdom

Sage Publications India Pvt. Ltd.
B-42, Panchsheel Enclave
Post Box 4109
New Delhi 110 017 India

Printed in the United States of America

Library of Congress Cataloging-in-Publication Data

Newman, David M., 1958-
Sociology: Exploring the architecture of everyday life / David M. Newman—6th ed.
    p. cm.
Includes bibliographical references and index.
ISBN 1-4129-2814-1 (pbk.)
  1. Sociology. I. Title.
HM585.N48 2006
301—dc22

                                                    2005026713

This book is printed on acid-free paper.

06   07   08   09   10   10 9 8 7 6 5 4 3 2 1

Acquiring Editor:	Benjamin Penner
Associate Editor:	Margo Beth Crouppen
Editorial Assistant:	Annie Louden
Production Editors:	Diana E. Axelsen, Astrid Virding
Copy Editor:	Jamie Robinson
Typesetter:	C&M Digitals (P) Ltd.
Indexer:	Mary Mortensen
Cover Designer:	Michelle Lee Kenny

Brief Contents

Detailed Contents

PART I
THE INDIVIDUAL AND SOCIETY   1

PART II
THE CONSTRUCTION OF SELF AND SOCIETY   53

8   Constructing Difference: Social Deviance   248

About the Author

David M. Newman (Ph.D., University of Washington) is Professor of Sociology at DePauw University. In addition to the introductory course, he teaches courses in research methods, family, social psychology, and deviance. He has won teaching awards at both the University of Washington and DePauw University. His other written work includes *Identities and Inequalities: Exploring the Intersections of Race, Class, Gender, and Sexuality* (McGraw-Hill).

Preface

It was the first day of the fall semester in 1994. I had just finished making the final adjustments to the first edition of this book, which was due to be published the following January. I felt good, like I'd just accomplished something monumental. Even my two children were impressed with me (although not as impressed as the time we went to a professional hockey game and I leaped out of my seat to catch an errant, speeding puck barehanded). I walked into the first meeting of my Contemporary Society class eager to start teaching wide-eyed, first-year students a thing or two about sociology.

In my introductory comments to the class that day I mentioned that I had just written this book. The panicked look in their eyes—a curious combination of awe and fear—calmed when I told them I wouldn't be requiring them to read it that semester. I assured them that the process of writing an introductory text helped me immensely in preparing for the course and that I hoped to pass on to them the knowledge I had accumulated.

The next day after class one of the students—a bright, freshly scrubbed 18-year-old—approached me. The ensuing conversation would leave a lasting, humbling impression on me:

Student: Hi. Umm. Professor Newman . . . I called my parents last night to, like, tell them how my first day in college went. I think they were, like, more nervous than I was. You know how parents can be.

Me: Yes, I sure do. I'm a parent myself, you know.

Student: Yeah, whatever. Anyway, I was telling them about my classes and my professors and stuff. I told them about this class and how I thought it would be pretty cool. I told them you were writing a book. I thought that would impress them, you know, make it seem like they were getting their money's worth and everything.

Me: Well, thanks.

Student: So, they go, "What's the book about?" [He laughed sheepishly.] I told them I didn't know, but I'd find out. So that's what I'm doing . . . finding out.

Me: Well, I'm glad you asked. You see, it's an introductory sociology textbook that uses everyday experiences and phenomena as a way of understanding important sociological theories and ideas. In it I've attempted to . . .

Student: Wait, did you say it was a *textbook*?

Me:	Why, yes. You see the purpose of the book is to provide the reader with a thorough and useful introduction to the sociological perspective. I want to convey . . .
Student:	[quite embarrassed now] Oh . . . Professor Newman, I'm really sorry. I misunderstood you. I thought you had written a *real* book.

Real book. *Real* book. *Real* book. Those words rang in my head like some relentless church bell. At first I tried to dismiss the comment as the remarks of a naïve kid who didn't know any better. But the more I thought about it, the more I realized what his comment reflected. The perception that textbooks aren't *real* books is pervasive. I recently heard a radio ad for a local Red Cross book drive asking listeners to donate any unused or unwanted books *as long as they weren't textbooks.* Torn copies of *The Cat in the Hat?* Fine, they'll take 'em. Grease-stained owners' manuals for 1976 Ford Pintos? Sure, glad to have 'em. Textbooks? No way!

Sadly, these sorts of perceptions are not altogether unwarranted. Textbooks hover on the margins of the literary world, somewhere between respectable, intellectual tomes on trailblazing research and Harlequin romance novels. Historically they've been less than titillating: thick, heavy, expensive, and easily discarded for a measly five bucks at the end-of-semester "book buy-back."

My goal from the start has been to write a textbook that reads like a *real* book. In the first five editions I tried to capture simultaneously the essence of my discipline and the reader's interest. From what reviewers, instructors, and students who've read and used the book over the years have said, I think I've been fairly successful. People seem to like the relaxed tone and appreciate the consistent theme that ties all the chapters together. Many instructors have commented on how the book enables students to truly understand the unique and useful elements of a sociological perspective.

Features of the Sixth Edition

To my younger son—who believes that I have nothing relevant to say about anything anyway—continually revising this book is a sure sign of my incompetence. "Why do you keep writing the same book over and over? My English teacher once made me rewrite my book report on *To Kill a Mockingbird* because I answered a few questions wrong. Is that what's going on here? Is your publisher making you write the book over because you've put too much wrong stuff in it?" I told him no and that I'd make him read the book—cover to cover—if he continued to criticize it. He stopped.

Despite his concerns, sociology textbooks do need to be revised regularly and frequently. No book can be of lasting value if it remains static, locked into a particular style and content. I constantly keep my ears and eyes open, always looking for some new example or current issue to include in the book. My office overflows with boxes of newspaper articles, photocopied journal articles, and shreds of paper napkins containing scribbled notes that I write to myself at the breakfast table when I hear something interesting on the radio.

When an author revises a book, it's easier to paste on new material than it is to cut out the old stuff. But simply adding on bits and pieces, here and there, tends to make books fat, messy, and unwieldy. So I've tried to streamline the book wherever possible. I've replaced outdated material with new material where appropriate, revised all the statistical information, condensed or moved some sections, and changed the order of certain sections.

Here are some of the specific changes I've made in this sixth edition to enhance the features that worked so well in previous editions.

Updated Examples and Statistical Information

As in the first five editions, each chapter is peppered with anecdotes, personal observations, and accounts of contemporary events. Many of the examples you will read come from incidents in my own life; others are taken from today's news headlines. For instance, since I wrote the last edition we have experienced increased military actions in Afghanistan and Iraq that have altered the course of international relations and have endured a major hurricane that will leave its mark on domestic economics and politics for years to come. It would be impossible to write an introduction to the discipline of sociology without accounting for these life-altering occurrences. So I've made a special effort to provide some sociological insight into these events throughout the book. Such striking examples, as well as smaller ones taken from everyday life, are meant to show you the pervasiveness and applicability of sociology in our ordinary experiences in a way that, I hope, rings familiar with you.

Throughout the book I've also tried to provide the most current statistical information possible. I've updated all the graphic exhibits and, in the process, changed many from statistical tables to more readable charts, making trends and relationships more obvious. Most of the new statistical information is drawn from the most recent data from the U.S. Census Bureau, the Population Reference Bureau, the Bureau of Labor Statistics, and the Department of Justice.

New and Improved Visual Essays

This edition includes some changes in the visual component. Most textbooks contain photographs, comic strips, and other types of pictures. But rarely does this material go beyond simply filling up space. I wanted the visual images in this book to serve a purpose: to paint detailed, informative sociological portraits. To that end, Doug Harper, Eric Margolis, Becky Smith, and Liz Grauerholz have produced the unique, vivid, and provocative visual essays that appear in this edition. The visual essays are now embedded in most chapters instead of placed at their ends. These essays—focusing on such diverse social phenomena as baseball games, funeral rituals in the Netherlands, fashions in body ornamentation, "family friendly" public facilities, tramps, global vegetable markets, Indian schools, images of social class, the immigrant experience, and coal miners' strikes—provide a wonderful opportunity for you to "see" many of the concepts and ideas I've written about in the book. As you study the visual essays, you will become a much more visually astute observer of and participant in your own social world.

New *Sociologists at Work* and *Micro-Macro Connections*

In the first five editions I provided many in-depth features that focused either on a specific piece of sociological research or on some issue that illustrates the connection between the everyday lives of individuals and the structure of their society. These extended discussions link social institutions to personal experiences and provide insight into the methods sociologists use to gather information and draw conclusions about how our world works.

Instructors and students alike have found these features very useful in generating classroom discussion. The features that I've updated from the previous edition focus on such topics as suicide, parents' rights, the language of war, the news media, obesity, dual-earner couples, the cultural impact of antidepressant drugs, the U.S. health care system, media images of social class, racial profiling, and the shifting politics of immigration. I've also added several new features about the economics and politics of food, cell phones, unequal childhoods, human trafficking, the intellectual demand of low-wage jobs, the global health divide, wealthy white men's perception of race, sexual inequality in medical care, and the pressures of childhood sports. Many other topics that I didn't have room to include appear on the study site for the book at www.pineforge.com.

Increased Focus on Globalization

This edition also contains many more cross-cultural examples and discussions of globalization than did the previous editions, showing how our lives are linked to, and affected by, our increasingly global society. One of the most profound trends in the world today is the linking of heretofore disconnected societies and cultures. It is difficult, if not impossible, to provide a complete picture of sociology and social life without examining how our lives are intertwined with global events and processes.

New Articles in the Companion Reader

Jodi O'Brien, a sociologist at Seattle University, and I have carefully edited a companion volume to this book consisting of short articles, chapters, and excerpts written by other authors. These readings are provocative and eye-opening examples of the joys and insights of sociological thinking. Many of them vividly show how sociologists gather evidence through carefully designed research. Others are personal narratives that provide firsthand accounts of how social forces influence people's lives. The readings examine common, everyday experiences, important social issues, and distinct historical events that illustrate the relationship between the individual and society. We've taken great pains to include readings that show how race, social class, gender, and sexual orientation intersect to influence everyday experiences.

Of the 36 selections in this edition of the reader, 14 are new. Four others are articles that appeared in earlier editions, were taken out, but are now back "by popular demand." To improve their applicability and usefulness, we have also moved several of the readings to chapters different from where they were located in the previous edition. The new selections touch on such important and relevant sociological issues as the unique problems faced by gay evangelicals, cultural standards of female thinness, the balance of work and family, immigrant nannies, racial imbalances in prison, the development of municipal smoking bans, how hospital nurses deal with horror and trauma in their jobs, media portrayals of social class, the sociology of whiteness, sexual desire of teen girls, intergenerational conflict, and the effect of migration on Latin American coffee farmers.

Teaching Resources and Web Site to Accompany the Book and Companion Reader

The *Teaching Resources Guide* is available for instructors from Pine Forge Press in hard copy or on a disk. The manual provides comprehensive, thorough coverage of the material in both the text and the companion reader, including the following:

- ◆ Chapter Summaries
- ◆ Class Exercises and Discussion Topics. Suggestions for writing exercises, discussion topics, and student assignments to use both in and outside of class. This section also provides suggestions for how to use this book's Your Turn activities.
- ◆ Literary and Visual Resources
- ◆ Selected Internet Resources
- ◆ Testing Materials: Multiple-choice, short-answer, and essay questions. The test bank was developed to test students' understanding of the material, so instructors can encourage students to move beyond basic memorization of materials toward application and critique. The multiple-choice questions are organized as recall questions and application questions. Recall questions are based more directly on the information presented in the textbook, and application questions assess students' comprehension of the material and their ability to apply concepts, theories, and research findings.
- ◆ Summaries of Classic Sociological Studies
- ◆ Teaching Resource Materials: Annotated Bibliography. An annotated bibliography of resources useful in preparing for and designing classes, suggestions for how to manage teaching interactions and elicit and evaluate student performance, and techniques for handling any challenges that arise in class.

Students can also access an Internet study site for this book at www.pineforge.com. This site includes additional material not included in the book as well as test questions that can be used to gauge understanding of the book's contents.

A Word About the "Architecture of Society"

I have chosen the image of architecture in the subtitle to convey one of the driving themes of this book: Society is a human construction. Society is not "out there" somewhere, waiting to be visited and examined. It exists in the minute details of our day-to-day lives. Whenever we follow its rules or break them, enter its roles or shed them, work to change things or keep them as they are, we are adding another nail, plank, or frame to the structure of our society. In short, society—like the buildings around us—couldn't exist were it not for the actions of people.

At the same time, however, this structure that we have created appears to exist independently of us. We don't usually spend much time thinking about the buildings we live, work, and play in as human constructions. We see them as finished products, not as the processes that created them. Only when something goes wrong—the pipes leak or the walls crack—do we realize that people made these structures and people are the ones who must fix them. When buildings outlive their usefulness or become dangerous to their inhabitants, people must renovate them or, if necessary, decide to tear them down.

Likewise, society is so massive and has been around for so long that it *appears* to stand on its own, at a level above and beyond the toiling hands of individual people. But here too when things begin to go wrong—widespread discrimination, massive poverty, lack of affordable health care, escalating crime rates—people must do something about it.

So the fascinating paradox of human life is that we build society, collectively "forget" that we've built it, and live under its massive and influential structure. But we are not "stuck" with society as it is. Human beings are the architects of their own social reality. Throughout this book, I examine the active roles individuals play in planning, maintaining, or fixing society.

A Final Thought

One of the greatest challenges I face as a teacher of sociology is trying to get my students to see the personal relevance of the course material, to fully appreciate the connection between the individual and society. The true value of sociology lies in its unique ability to show the two-way connection between the most private elements of our lives—our characteristics, experiences, behaviors, and thoughts—and the cultures, groups, organizations, and social institutions to which we belong. The "everyday life" approach in this book uses real-world examples and personal observations as a vehicle for understanding the relationship between individuals and society.

My purpose is to make the familiar, unfamiliar—to help you critically examine the commonplace and the ordinary in your own life. Only when you step back and examine the taken-for-granted aspects of your personal experiences can you see that there is an inherent, sometimes unrecognized organization and predictability to them. At the same time, you will see that the structure of society is greater than the sum of the experiences and psychologies of the individuals in it.

It is my conviction that this intellectual excursion should be a thought-provoking and enjoyable one. Reading a textbook doesn't have to be boring or, even worse, the academic equivalent of a trip to the dentist (although I personally have nothing against dentists). I believe that part of my task as an instructor is to provide my students with a challenging but comfortable classroom atmosphere in which to learn. I have tried to do the same in this book. Your instructor has chosen this book, not because it makes his or her job teaching your course any easier, but because he or she wants you, the student, to see how sociology helps us to understand how the small private experiences of our everyday lives are connected to this thing we call society. I hope you learn to appreciate this important message, and I hope you enjoy reading this book as much as I enjoyed writing it.

Have fun,

David M. Newman
Department of Sociology and
Anthropology
DePauw University
Greencastle, IN 46135
E-mail:DNEWMAN@DEPAUW.EDU

Acknowledgments

A book project such as this one takes an enormous amount of time to develop. I've spent thousands of hours on this book, toiling away at the computer, holed up in my isolated third-floor office. Yet as solitary as this project was, it could not have been done alone. Many people provided invaluable assistance to make this book a reality. Without their generous help and support, it wouldn't have been written, and you'd be reading some other sociologist's list of people to thank. Because I have revised rather than rewritten this book, I remain indebted to those who have helped me at some point during the writing of all five editions.

First, I would like to thank the former publisher and president of Pine Forge Press, Steve Rutter. Early on, he pushed, prodded, and cajoled me into exceeding my expectations and overachieving. The numerous suggestions he offered over the years made this book a better one. Likewise, the former staff at Pine Forge—Sherith Pankratz, Paul O'Connell, Kirsten Stoller, Jean Skeels, and Rebecca Holland—must be thanked for helping me through the maze of details and difficulties that cropped up during the earlier editions of this book.

I would also like to extend my sincere gratitude to copyeditor Jamie Robinson and to Jerry Westby, Ben Penner, Margo Crouppen, Annie Louden, Astrid Virding, and Diana Axelsen at Pine Forge for their insight and guidance in putting together this newest edition. Having already written five editions, I was definitely an old dog with absolutely no desire to learn any new tricks when this team became involved. To their credit, they let me write as I have always written. For that, I am eternally grateful.

I want to especially thank my long-time developmental editor Becky Smith for her years of patience and insightful guidance. She has been directly involved in all six editions of this book. Other than me, she is more familiar with this book than anyone on the planet. As trite as it may sound, I simply couldn't have written it without her.

I would also like to express my thanks to Liz Grauerholz, Denise Simon, Eric Margolis, and Becky Smith for constructing provocative visual essays in the book, to Lisa A. Pellerin, Ellen Berg, and Norman Conti for creating an excellent instructor's manual and an impressive Web site, and to Karen Wiley and Kassie Graves for securing copyright permissions.

I appreciate the many helpful comments offered by the reviewers of the six editions of this book:

Sharon Abbott, Fairfield University

Deborah Abowitz, Bucknell University

Stephen Adair, Central Connecticut State University

Rebecca Adams, University of North Carolina, Greensboro

Ron Aminzade, University of Minnesota

Afroza Anwary, Carleton College

George Arquitt, Oklahoma State University

Carol Auster, Franklin and Marshall College

Ellen C. Baird, Arizona State University

Ellen Berg, California State University, Sacramento

David Bogen, Emerson College

Frances A. Boudreau, Connecticut College

David L. Briscoe, University of Arkansas at Little Rock

Todd Campbell, Loyola University, Chicago

Wanda Clark, South Plains College

Thomas Conroy, St. Peter's College

Norman Conti, Duquesne University

Doug Currivan, University of Massachusetts, Boston

Jeff Davidson, University of Delaware

Kimberly Davies, Augusta State University

Tricia Davis, North Carolina State University

James J. Dowd, University of Georgia

Laura A. Dowd, University of Georgia, Athens

Charlotte A. Dunham, Texas Tech University

Donald Eckard, Temple University

Charles Edgley, Oklahoma State University

Rachel Einwohner, Purdue University

June Ellestad, Washington State University

Shalom Endleman, Quinnipiac College

Rebecca Erickson, University of Akron

Kimberly Faust, Winthrop University

Patrick Fontane, St. Louis College of Pharmacy

Michael J. Fraleigh, Bryant University

Sarah N. Gatson, Texas A&M University

Barry Goetz, University of Dayton

Lorie Schabo Grabowski, University of Minnesota

Valerie Gunter, University of New Orleans

Roger Guy, Texas Lutheran University

John R. Hall, University of California, Davis

Charles Harper, Creighton University

Douglas Harper, Duquesne University

Peter Hennen, University of Minnesota

Max Herman, Rutgers University

Christine L. Himes, Syracuse University

Susan Hoerbelt, Hillsborough Community College

Amy Holzgang, Cerritos College

W. Jay Hughes, Georgia Southern University

Gary Hytreck, Georgia Southern University

Valerie Jenness, University of California, Irvine

Kathryn Johnson, Barat College

Richard Jones, Marquette University

Tom Kando, California State University, Sacramento

Steve Keto, Kent State University

Peter Kivisto, Augustana College

Lisa Konczal, Barry University

Marc LaFountain, State University of West Georgia

Sharon Melissa Latimer, West Virginia University

Joseph Lengermann, University of Maryland, College Park

Linda A. Litteral, Grossmont Community College

Julie L. Locher, University of Alabama, Birmingham

David G. LoConto, Jacksonville State University

D. A. Lopez, California State University, Northridge

Fred Maher, Temple University

Kristen Marcussen, University of Iowa

Benjamin Mariante, Stonehill College

Joseph Marolla, Virginia Commonwealth University

Michallene McDaniel, University of Georgia

James R. McIntosh, Lehigh University

Jerome McKibben, Fitchburg State University

Ted P. McNeilsmith, Adams State College

Melinda Milligan, Sonoma State University

John R. Mitrano, Central Connecticut State University

Susannne Monahan, Montana State University

Kelly Murphy, University of Pittsburgh

Elizabeth Ehrhardt Mustaine, University of Central Florida

Daniel Myers, University of Notre Dame

Anne Nurse, College of Wooster

Marjukka Ollilainen, Weber State University

Toska Olson, Evergreen State College

Lisa A. Pellerin, Ball State University

Larry Perkins, Oklahoma State University, Stillwater

Bernice Pescosolido, Indiana University, Bloomington

Mike Plummer, Boston College

Edward Ponczek, William Rainey Harper College

Tanya Poteet, Capital University

Sharon E. Preves, Grand Valley State University

Kennon J. Rice, North Carolina State University

Judith Richlin-Klonsky, University of California, Los Angeles

Robert Robinson, Indiana University, Bloomington

Mary Rogers, University of West Florida

Sally S. Rogers, Montgomery College

Wanda Rushing, University of Memphis

Michael Ryan, University of Louisiana, Lafayette

Scott Schaffer, Millersville University

Aileen Schulte, SUNY New Paltz

Dave Schweingruber, Iowa State University

Mark Shibley, Southern Oregon University

Thomas Shriver, Oklahoma State University

Toni Sims, University of Louisiana, Lafay

Kathleen Slevin, College of William and Mary

Lisa White Smith, Christopher Newport University

Eldon E. Snyder, Bowling Green State University

Nicholas Sofios, Providence College

George Spilker, Clarkson College

Melanie Stander, University of Washington

Kandi Stinson, Xavier University

Richard Tardanico, Florida International University

Robert Tellander, Sonoma State University

Kathleen Tiemann, University of North Dakota

Steven Vallas, George Mason University

Tom Vander Ven, Indiana University, South Bend

John Walsh, University of Illinois, Chicago

Gregory Weiss, Roanoke College

Marty Wenglinsky, Quinnipiac College

Stephan Werba, Catonsville Community College

Cheryl E. Whitley, Marist College

Norma Williams, University of North Texas

Janelle Wilson, University of Minnesota, Duluth

Mark Winton, University of Central Florida

Judith Wittner, Loyola University, Chicago

Cynthia A. Woolever, Hartford Seminary

Don C. Yost, Mountain State University

Ashraf Zahedi, Stanford University

Stephen Zehr, University of Southern Indiana

I also want to express my appreciation to the colleagues and friends who offered cherished assistance throughout the production of all six editions of this book and who put up with my incessant whining about how hard it all was. Some offered invaluable advice on specific topics; others provided general support and encouragement that helped me retain my sanity; and still others helped remind me that there's more to life than writing a book. In particular, I'd like to thank Nancy Davis, Rob Robinson, Matthew Oware, Tom Hall, James Mannon, Eric Silverman, Rebecca Upton, Nathan Lauster, Rebecca Bordt, Krista Dahlstrom, Kelley Hall, Bruce Stinebrickner, Wayne Glausser, Jodi O'Brien, Judy Howard, and Peter Kollock.

I would like to express special gratitude to my students who, throughout the years, have kept me curious and prevented me from taking myself too seriously. And finally, I want to thank my wife Elizabeth and my sons Zachary and Seth for putting up with the frequent late nights, long faces, and crises of confidence.

PART I

The Individual and Society

What is the relationship between your private life and the social world around you? Part I introduces you to the guiding theme of this book: Our personal, everyday experiences affect and are affected by the larger society in which we live. Chapters 1 and 2 discuss the sociological perspective on human life and the ways in which it differs from the more individualistic approaches of psychology and biology. You will read about what society consists of and get a glimpse into sociologists' attempts to understand the two-way relationship between the individual and society.

As you read on, keep in mind a metaphor that will be used throughout the book to help explain the nature of society: *architecture*. Like buildings, societies have a design discernible to the alert eye. Both are constructed by bringing together a wide variety of materials in a complex process. Both, through their structure, shape the activities within. At the same time, both change. Sometimes they change subtly and gradually as the inhabitants go about their lives; other times they are deliberately redecorated or remodeled. As you make your way through this book, see if you can discover more ways in which buildings and societies are alike.

Taking a New Look at a Familiar World

Sociology and the Individual

The Insights of Sociology

The Sociological Imagination

André graduated from college in 2003. He had been a model student. When not studying, he found time to help kids read at the local elementary school and actively participated in student government at his own school. He got along well with his professors, his grades were excellent, he made the dean's list all four years, and he graduated Phi Beta Kappa. As a computer science major with a minor in economics, André thought his future was clear: He would land a job at a top software company or perhaps a stock brokerage firm and work his way up the ladder so that he'd be earning a six-figure income by the time he was 30.

But when André entered the job market and began applying for jobs, things didn't go exactly according to plan. Despite his credentials, nobody seemed willing to hire him full time. He was able to survive only by taking temporary freelance programming jobs here and there and working nights at The Gap. Some of his friends from college had similar difficulties. Nevertheless, André began to question his own abilities: "Do I lack the skills that employers are looking for? Am I not trying hard enough? What the heck is wrong with me?" His friends and family were as encouraging as they could be, but some secretly wondered if André wasn't as smart as they had thought he was.

Michael and Carole were both juniors at a large university. They had been dating each other exclusively for the past two years. By all accounts, the relationship seemed to be going quite well. In fact, Michael was beginning to imagine them getting married, having children, and living happily ever after. Then one day out of the blue, Carole dropped a bombshell. She told Michael she thought their relationship was going nowhere and perhaps they ought to start seeing other people.

Michael was stunned. "What did I do?" he asked her. "I thought things were going great. Is it something I said? Something I did? I can change."

She said no, he hadn't done anything wrong, they had simply grown apart. She told him she just didn't feel as strongly about him as she used to.

After the breakup, Michael was devastated. He turned to his friends for support. "She wasn't any good for you anyway," they said. "We always thought she was a little unstable. She probably couldn't be in a serious relationship with anybody. It wasn't *your* fault, it was *hers.*"

In both these stories notice that people immediately try to explain an unhappy situation by focusing on individual characteristics and attributes. André blames himself for not being able to land a job; others question his intelligence and drive. Michael wonders what he did to sour his relationship with Carole; his friends question Carole's psychological stability. Such reactions are not uncommon. We have a marked tendency to rely on **individualistic explanations**, attributing people's achievements and failures to their personal qualities.

Why can't André, our highly intelligent, well-trained, talented college graduate, land a permanent job? It's certainly possible that some personal flaw is making André unemployable: lack of drive, laziness, bad attitude, and so on. Or maybe he doesn't come across as particularly capable during job interviews.

But by focusing exclusively on such personal "deficiencies," we overlook the broader societal trends that affected André's job prospects. For instance, the corporate downsizing of the early 2000s made it difficult for new college graduates to find high-paying jobs right out of college. In fact, graduates in André's group faced the worst hiring slump since the early 1980s. As one individual put it, "we definitely picked the wrong time to be graduating from college" (quoted in Leonhardt, 2003b, p. A1).

The employment situation for college graduates like André was merely part of a broader economic trend that has been affecting all corners of the job market for several years. In 2005, roughly 5.2% of American adults (close to 8 million people) were officially unemployed. That figure didn't include several million other out-of-work people who didn't meet the government's official definition of "unemployed" because they hadn't been actively seeking employment in the past month (U.S. Bureau of Labor Statistics, 2005a). Between March 2001 and June 2004, because of a weak stock market, global instability, fear of terrorism, and a variety of other economic factors, 1.4 million U.S. jobs disappeared entirely. Even after an economic recovery, 36 states had fewer jobs than they did three years earlier (Mishel, Bernstein, & Allegretto, 2004).

Furthermore, college degrees are no longer the guarantee of employment they once were. One in five Americans who suffer long-term unemployment—that is, who have been unemployed for at least 27 weeks—is a college graduate (National Public Radio, 2005b). Even for graduates who do land a job, the "wage premium"—the taken-for-granted assumption that a college degree will bring higher wages—has lost steam in recent years. College graduates still earn nearly 45% more, on average, than people with high school diplomas. But the education-based wage gap has leveled off and has shown signs of shrinking further (Uchitelle, 2005).

Industries that require higher education and advanced skills—including technology and financial services—were hit especially hard by the economic downturn of the early 2000s. In the collapse of the dot.com industry a few years ago, many Web-based and telecommunications companies went bankrupt and disappeared. Other high-tech companies, seeking to cut costs, severely downsized their staffs, put a freeze on new hiring, or outsourced many of their entry-level positions to overseas facilities.

But according to the Collegiate Employment Research Institute, job opportunities are starting to improve for college graduates. After several years of very limited hiring, many employers in business, information technology, marketing, and several other areas are slowly expanding their workforce (P. D. Gardner, 2005). Indeed, according to the National Association of Colleges and Employers (2005), employers increased their college hiring in 2005 by 13% over 2004. So you see, André's employability was as much a result of the economic forces operating at the time he began looking for a job as of any of his personal qualifications. Had he graduated a few years later, when the economy was doing a little better, his prospects might have been much brighter.

And what about Michael and Carole? It seems perfectly reasonable to conclude that something about either of them or the combination of the two caused their breakup. We tend to view dating relationships—not to mention marriages—as situations that succeed or fail solely because of the traits or behaviors of the two people involved.

But how would your assessment of the situation change if you found out that Jason—to whom Carole had always secretly been attracted—had just broken up with his longtime girlfriend and was now available? Like it or not, relationships are not exclusively private entities; they're always being influenced by outside forces. They take place within a larger network of friends, acquaintances, ex-partners, coworkers, fellow students, and people as yet unknown who may make desirable or, at the very least, acceptable dating partners. Web sites and blogs where people can post word of their breakups are becoming as popular as the more traditional places where people announce their weddings. As one columnist put it, "What good does it do to know that Joe and Jane are getting married? The news we really need is who's breaking up—so we can go and . . . hit on them" (quoted in Soukup, 2004, p. 15).

When people believe they have no better alternative, they tend to stay with their present partners, even if they are not particularly satisfied. When people think that better relationships are available to them, they become less committed to staying in their present ones. Indeed, people's perceptions of what characterizes a good relationship (such as fairness, compatibility, affection) are less likely to determine when and if it ends than the presence or absence of favorable alternatives (Felmlee, Sprecher, & Bassin, 1990). That is, couples may endure feelings of dissatisfaction until one partner sees a more attractive possibility elsewhere. Research shows that the risk of a relationship ending increases as the supply of potential alternative relationships increases (South & Lloyd, 1995).

In addition, Carole's decision to leave could have been indirectly affected by the sheer number of potentially available partners—a result of shifts in the birth rate 20 years or so earlier. For a single, heterosexual woman like Carole, a surplus of college-age men would increase the likelihood that she would eventually come across a better alternative to Michael. A shortage of such men, in contrast, would make Michael look a lot better. The number of available alternatives can even vary from state to state. For instance, Michael's attractiveness would have improved if he lived in New York (where there are 80 men for every 100 women) but worsened if he lived in Alaska (where there are 114 men for every 100 women) (Kershaw, 2004). In sum, Michael's interpersonal value, and therefore the stability of his relationship with Carole, may have suffered not because of anything he did but because of population forces over which he had little if any control.

Let's take this notion beyond Carole and Michael's immediate dating network. For instance, the very characteristics and features that people consider desirable (or undesirable) in the first place reflect the values of the larger culture in which they live.

Fashions and tastes are constantly changing, making particular characteristics (for example, hairstyles, physiques, clothing), behaviors (smoking, drinking, exercising), or life choices (occupation, political affiliation) more or less attractive.

The moral of these two stories is simple: To understand phenomena in our personal lives, we must move past individual traits and examine broader societal characteristics and trends. External features beyond our immediate awareness and control often exert more influence on the circumstances of our day-to-day lives than our "internal" qualities. We can't begin to explain why relationships work or don't work without addressing the broader interpersonal network and culture in which they are embedded. We can't begin to explain an individual's employability without examining current and past economic trends that affect the number of available jobs and the number of people who are looking for work. By the same token, we can't begin to explain people's ordinary, everyday thoughts and actions without examining the social forces that influence them.

Sociology and the Individual

Herein lies the fundamental theme of sociology and the theme that will guide us throughout this book: Everyday social life—our thoughts, actions, feelings, decisions, interactions, and so on—is the product of a complex interplay between societal forces and personal characteristics. To explain why people are the way they are or do the things they do, we must understand the interpersonal, historical, cultural, organizational, and global environments they inhabit. To understand either individuals or society, we must understand both (C. W. Mills, 1959).

Of course, seeing the relationship between individuals and social forces is not always so easy. The United States is a society built on the image of the rugged, self-reliant individual. Not surprisingly, it is also a society dominated by individualistic understandings of human behavior that seek to explain problems and processes by focusing exclusively on the personality, the psychology, or even the biochemistry of each individual. Consequently, most of us simply take for granted that what we choose to do, say, feel, and think are private phenomena. Everyday life seems to be a series of free choices. After all, we choose what to major in. We choose what to wear when we go out. We choose what and when to eat. We choose our lifestyles, our mates, and so on.

But how free are these decisions? Think about all the times your actions have been dictated or at least influenced by social circumstances over which you had little control. Have you ever felt that because of your age or gender or race, certain opportunities were closed to you? Your ability to legally drive a car or drink alcohol or vote, for instance, is determined by society's prevailing definition of age. When you're older, you may be forced into retirement despite your skills and desire to continue working. Some occupations, such as bank executive and engineer, are still overwhelmingly male, whereas others, such as nurse and administrative assistant, are almost exclusively female. In the United States, African Americans are conspicuously underrepresented in the highest management positions in professional team sports like football and basketball, despite their overrepresentation as players.

Likewise, the doctrines of your religion may limit your behavioral choices. For a devout Catholic, premarital sex or even divorce is unlikely. A strict Muslim is required to pause five times a day to pray. An Orthodox Jew would never drink milk and eat meat at the same meal.

Then there's the matter of personal style, your choices in hairstyle, dress, music, and the like. Large-scale marketing strategies can actually create a demand for particular products or images. Would Britney Spears or Ashlee Simpson or Lil' Romeo have become so popular without a tightly managed and slickly packaged publicity program designed to appeal to adolescents and preadolescents? Your tastes, and therefore your choices as a consumer, are often influenced by decisions made in corporate boardrooms. Furthermore, what you wear is dictated in part by the organizational setting in which you find yourself. For instance, appropriate attire for a stockbroker is very different from that for a college student.

Broad economic trends also influence your everyday life. You may lose your job or, like André, face a tight job market as a result of economic fluctuations brought about by increased global competition or a recession. Or, because of the rapid development of certain types of technology, the college degree that may be your ticket to a rewarding career today may not qualify you even for a low-paying, entry-level position in 10 years. And if you don't get a good job right out of college, you may have to live at home for years after you graduate—not because you can't face the idea of living apart from your beloved parents but because you can't earn enough to support yourself.

Certainly government and politics affect our personal lives too. A political decision made at the local, regional, national, or even international level may result in the closing of a government agency you depend on, make the goods and services to which you have grown accustomed either more expensive or less available, or change the amount of taxes you pay. Workplace leave policies established by the government may affect your decision whether and when to have a baby. If you are homosexual, the government can determine whether or not you can be covered by your partner's insurance policy and file a joint income tax return, whether or not you can inherit jointly acquired assets, or whether or not you can be fired from your job because of your sexual orientation. In the United States, decisions made by the U.S. Supreme Court can increase or limit your options for controlling your fertility, suing an employer for discrimination, using your property however you please, buying certain products, or keeping the details of your life a private matter.

People's personal lives can also be touched by events that occur in distant countries:

♦ In 2003, fear over the spread of severe acute respiratory syndrome (SARS) in Asia and Canada dramatically reduced international travel, thereby affecting tourism and airline jobs in the United States and elsewhere.

♦ Fallout from the war in Iraq and turmoil elsewhere in the Middle East affects foreign trade, international migration, university enrollments, and tourism. Many American companies became skittish about opening new stores abroad because of security concerns after the attacks in the United States on September 11, 2001

(Eichengreen, 2001), helping to slow the U.S. economy and limiting entry-level job opportunities around the world.

♦ In 2005, Hurricane Katrina killed thousands of people, rendered hundreds of thousands homeless and unemployed, contaminated local waterways, and decimated Gulf Coast industries such as tourism and steel, lumber, and oil production. Its economic effects were felt immediately in the rest of the country where, for instance, gasoline prices skyrocketed. It will no doubt have a staggering impact on U.S. exports and on the travel industry—both nationally and internationally—in years to come.

♦ The technologically interconnected nature of the world has made the effects of international events almost instantaneous. In 2004, a computer virus known as MyDoom took less than a day to infect individual computers as well as corporate, university, and governmental computer networks in Asia, Europe, and the United States. At its peak, it infected one out of every 12 e-mails worldwide ("MyDoom virus," 2004) and cost organizations $250 million in lost productivity and technical support expenses ("Microsoft offers," 2004). In 2005, a brief reference in *Newsweek* magazine to a story about American interrogators at Guantánamo Bay flushing a copy of the Koran down a toilet instantly incited anti-American violence in several Muslim countries. The story was quickly retracted, but not before scores of people were killed or injured in the ensuing riots. These are only some of the ways that events in the larger world can affect individual lives.

The Insights of Sociology

Sociologists do not deny that individuals make choices or that they must take personal responsibility for those choices. But they are quick to point out that we cannot fully understand things happening in our lives, private and personal though they may be, without examining the influence of the people, events, and societal features that surround us. The structure of our lives often is not immediately apparent. By showing how social processes can shape us, and how individual action can in turn affect those processes, sociology provides unique insight into the taken-for-granted personal events and the large-scale cultural and global processes that make up our everyday existence.

Other disciplines study human life, too. Biologists study how the body works. Neurologists examine what goes on inside the brain. Psychologists study what goes on inside the mind to create human behavior. These disciplines focus almost exclusively on structures and processes that reside *within* the individual. In contrast, sociologists study what goes on *among* people as individuals, groups, or societies. How do social forces affect the way people interact with one another? How do people make sense of their private lives and the social worlds they occupy? How does everyday social interaction create "society"?

Personal issues like love, poverty, sexuality, aging, and prejudice are better understood within the appropriate societal context. For instance, we may believe that we marry purely for love, when in fact society pressures us to marry people from the same social class, religion, and race (P. L. Berger, 1963). Sociology, unlike other disciplines, forces us to look outside the tight confines of individual personalities to understand the phenomena that shape us. Consider, for example, the following situations:

- ◆ A young high school girl, fearing she is overweight, begins systematically starving herself in hopes of becoming more attractive.
- ◆ A 55-year-old stockbroker, unable to find work for three years, sinks into a depression after losing his family and his home. He now lives on the streets.
- ◆ A 36-year-old professor kills herself after learning that her position at the university will be terminated the following year.
- ◆ The student body president and valedictorian of the local high school cannot begin or end her day without several shots of whiskey.

What do these people have in common? Your first response might be that they are all suffering or have suffered terrible personal problems—eating disorders, homelessness, suicidal depression, alcoholism. If you saw them only for what they'd become—an "anorexic," a "homeless person," a "suicide victim," or an "alcoholic"— you might think they have some kind of personality defect, genetic flaw, or mental problem that renders them incapable of coping with the demands of contemporary life. Maybe they simply lack the willpower to pick themselves up and move on. In short, your immediate tendency may be to focus on the unique, perhaps "abnormal," characteristics of these people to explain their problems.

But we cannot downplay the importance of their *social* worlds. The circumstances just described are all linked to larger phenomena. There is no denying that we live in a society that praises a lean body, encourages drinking to excess, and values individual achievement and economic success. Some people suffer under these conditions when they don't measure up. This is not to say, however, that all people exposed to the same social messages inevitably fall victim to the same problems. Some people overcome wretched childhoods; others withstand the tragedy of economic failure and begin anew; and some people are immune to narrowly defined cultural images of beauty. But to understand fully the nature of human life or of particular social problems, we must acknowledge the broader social context in which these things occur.

The Sociological Imagination

Unfortunately, we often don't see the connections between the personal events in our everyday lives and the larger society in which we live. People in a country such as the United States, which places such a high premium on individual achievement, have difficulty looking beyond their immediate situation. Someone who loses a job, gets divorced, or flunks out of school in such a society has trouble imagining that these experiences are somehow related to massive cultural or historical processes.

The ability to see the impact of these forces on our private lives is what the famous sociologist C. Wright Mills (1959) called the **sociological imagination**. The sociological imagination enables us to understand the larger historical picture and its meaning in our own lives. Mills argued that no matter how personal we think our experiences are, many of them can be seen as products of society-wide forces. The task of sociology is to help us view our lives as the intersection between personal biography and societal history, to provide a means for us to interpret our lives and social circumstances.

Getting fired, for example, is a terrible, even traumatic private experience. Feelings of personal failure are inevitable when one loses a job. But if the unemployment rate in a community hovers at 25% or 30%—as it does in many places around the world and in many inner-city neighborhoods in the United States over the past several decades—then we must see unemployment as a social problem that has its roots in the economic and political structures of society. Being unemployed is not a character flaw or personal failure if a significant number of people in one's community are also unemployed. Nor can we explain a spike in the unemployment rate as a sudden increase in the number of incompetent or unprepared individual workers in the labor force. As long as the economy is arranged so that employees are easily replaced or slumps inevitably occur, the social problem of unemployment cannot be solved at the personal level (Lekachman, 1991; C. W. Mills, 1959).

The same can be said for divorce, which people usually experience as an intimate tragedy. But in the United States, close to one out of every two marriages will eventually end in divorce, and divorce rates are increasing in many countries around the world. We must therefore view divorce in the context of broader historical changes occurring throughout societies: family, law, religion, economics, and the culture as a whole. It is impossible to explain significant changes in divorce rates over time by focusing exclusively on the personal characteristics and behaviors of divorcing individuals. Divorce rates don't rise simply because individual spouses have more difficulty getting along with one another than they used to, and they don't fall because more husbands and wives are suddenly being nicer to each other.

Mills did not mean to imply that the sociological imagination should debilitate us— that is, force us to powerlessly perceive our lives as wholly beyond our control. In fact, the opposite is true. An awareness of the impact of social forces or world history on our personal lives is a prerequisite to any efforts we make to change our social circumstances. Indeed, the sociological imagination allows us to recognize that the solutions to many of our most serious social problems lie not in changing the personal situations and characteristics of individual people but in changing the social institutions and roles available to them (C. W. Mills, 1959). Drug addiction, homelessness, sexual violence, hate crimes, eating disorders, suicide, and other unfortunate situations will not go away simply by treating or punishing a person who is suffering from or engaging in the behavior.

❖❖
Émile Durkheim
A Sociological View of Suicide

Several years ago a tragic event occurred at the university where I teach. On a pleasant night a few weeks into the fall semester, a first-year student shot and killed himself in his dorm room. The incident sent shock waves through this small, close-knit campus. As you would expect in such a situation, the question on everyone's mind was, Why did he do it? Although no definitive answer could ever be obtained, most people simply concluded that it was a "typical" suicide. People assumed he must have been despondent, hopeless, unhappy, and unable to cope with the demands of college life. Some students said they heard that he was failing some of his courses. Others said that no one really knew much about him, that he was a bit of a loner. In other words, something was wrong with him.

As tragic as this incident was, though, it was not and is not unique. Between the 1950s and the 1990s, the U.S. suicide rate (the percentage of people who die through suicide) more than doubled for people between the ages of 15 and 24 (National Center for Health Statistics, 2005). Although the rate has dropped a bit since then, suicide is still the third leading cause of death among young Americans, behind accidents and homicides (U.S. Bureau of the Census, 2004a). In one national survey, about 19% of high school students admitted to having seriously considered suicide, and 9% have actually attempted it (National Center for Health Statistics, 2005).

Focusing on individual feelings such as depression, hopelessness, and frustration doesn't tell us why so many people in this age group commit suicide, nor does it tell us why rates of youth suicide increase—or for that matter decrease—from decade to decade. So, to understand "why he did it," we must look beyond the student's private mental state and examine the social and historical factors that may have affected him.

Clearly, life in contemporary developed societies is focused on individual achievement—being well dressed, popular, and successful—more strongly than ever before. Young people face almost constant pressure to "measure up" and define their identities, and therefore their self-worth, according to standards set by others (Mannon, 1997). Although most adjust well, others can't. In addition, as competition for scarce financial resources becomes more acute, young people are likely to experience heightened levels of stress and uncertainty about their own futures. The quest for success begins earlier and earlier, and the costs for not succeeding increase. Such changes may explain why suicides among young African American men (ages 15–24), once quite rare and still relatively low compared to other ethnic groups, increased from 4.1 deaths per 100,000 people in 1960 to 15.1 deaths in 1990 (see Exhibit 1.1). The rate has since fallen but is still almost triple what it was four decades ago (National Center for Health Statistics, 2005). Some experts blamed the increase on a growing sense of hopelessness and a long-standing cultural taboo against discussing mental health matters. Others, however, cited broader social factors brought about, ironically, by a growing economy. As more and more black families moved into the middle class at the end of the 20th century, they felt increasing pressure to compete in traditionally white-dominated professions and social environments. In fact, black teenagers who committed suicide were more likely to come from higher socioeconomic backgrounds than black teenagers in the general population (cited in Belluck, 1998).

You'll also notice in Exhibit 1.1 that the suicide rate among young African American men dropped in the early 2000s. Can you think of a sociological reason to account for this trend? Is it less stressful being a black teenager today than it was a few years ago?

In other societies, different types of social changes may account for increases in suicide rates. In the late 1990s, Japan saw its unemployment and bankruptcy rates rise to record levels as companies grappled with a severe economic recession that continues to this day. Since then, suicide rates have risen steadily, reaching an all time high in 2003. According to Japan's National Police Agency, over 25% of suicides are caused by financial problems such as difficulty paying bills, finding a job, and keeping a

Exhibit 1.1 Increasing Rates of Suicide Among Black Teens

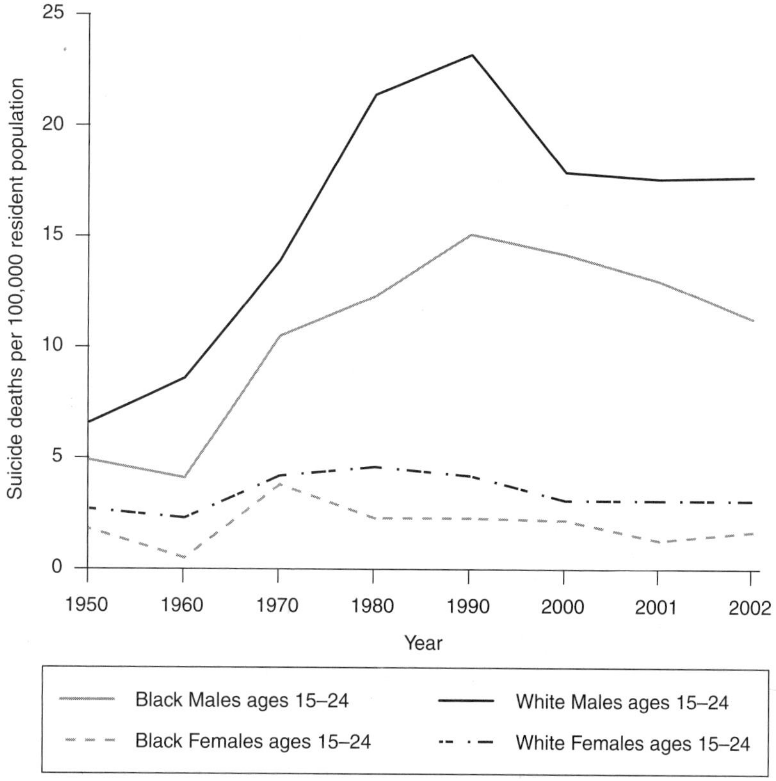

Suicide deaths per 100,000 resident population
25
20
15
10
5
0
1950
1960
1970
1980
1990
2000
2001
2002
Year
Black Males ages 15–24
Black Females ages 15–24
White Males ages 15–24
White Females ages 15–24

Source: National Center for Health Statistics, 2005.

business going (cited in Curtin, 2004). Though the elderly make up the largest segment of suicides in Japan, rates have increased dramatically among elementary-, middle-school, and college students. A veritable suicide subculture has arisen among Japanese youth, reflected in the dramatic growth of "suicide sites" on the Internet. One such site rates various methods of suicide in terms of "pain," "chance of success," and "annoyance to other people" (Brooke, 2004, p. 11).

The stress of change due to rapid development has been linked to increased suicide rates in China too, particularly among rural women, who are most likely to be displaced from their villages (Rosenthal, 2002). In Ireland, which has the fastest-growing rate of suicide in the world, one in four suicides occur among those aged 15 to 24 (Clarity, 1999). Experts there attribute much of this increase to a weakening of religious prohibitions against suicide and to an alteration of gender roles that has left many men unsure of their place in Irish society.

Sociology's interest in linking suicide to certain processes going on in society is not new. In one of the classic pieces of sociological research, the famous French sociologist Émile Durkheim (1897/1951) argued that suicide is more likely to occur under particular social circumstances and in particular communities. He was the first to see suicide as a manifestation of changes in society rather than of psychological shortcomings.

How does one go about determining whether rates of suicide—perhaps the most private act one can commit—are due to the structure of society? Durkheim decided to test his theory by comparing existing official statistics and historical records across groups, sometimes called the **comparative method**. Many sociologists continue to follow this methodology, analyzing statistics compiled by governmental agencies such as the U.S. Bureau of the Census, the FBI, and the National Center for Health Statistics to draw comparisons of suicide rates among groups.

For about seven years Durkheim carefully examined the available data on rates of suicide among various social groups in Europe—populations of countries, members of religions or ethnic groups, and so on—looking for important social patterns. If suicide were purely an act of individual desperation, he reasoned, one would not expect to find any noticeable changes in the rates from year to year or from society to society. That is, the distribution of desperate, unstable, unhappy individuals should be roughly equal across time and culture. If, however, certain groups or societies had a consistently higher rate of suicide than others, something more than individual disposition would seem to be at work.

After compiling his figures, Durkheim concluded that there are actually several different types of suicide. Some suicides, what he called anomic suicide, occur when people's lives are suddenly disrupted by major social events, such as economic depressions, wars, and famines. At these times, he argued, the conditions around which people have organized their lives are dramatically changed, leaving them with a sense of hopelessness and despair.

But he also discovered that suicide rates in all the countries he examined tended to be consistently higher among widowed, single, and divorced people than among married people; higher among people without children than among parents; and higher among Protestants than among Catholics. Did this mean that unmarried people, childless people, and Protestants were more unhappy, depressed, or psychologically dysfunctional than other people? Durkheim didn't think so. Instead, he felt that something about the nature of social life among people in these groups increased the likelihood of what he called egoistic suicide.

Durkheim reasoned that when group, family, or community ties are weak, people feel disconnected and alone. If a person lacks family ties and close friends or lives in a community that stresses individual achievements and de-emphasizes ties to a larger group, then that person is likely to lack a supportive network that could be a buffer against personal difficulties. Durkheim pointed out, for instance, that the Catholic Church emphasizes salvation through community and binds its members to the church through elaborate doctrine and ritual; Protestantism, in contrast, emphasizes individual salvation and responsibility. This religious individualism, he believed, explained the differences he noticed in suicide rates between Catholics and Protestants. Self-reliance and independence may glorify one in God's eyes, but they become liabilities if one is in the throes of personal tragedy.

Durkheim feared that life in modern society tends to be individualistic and dangerously alienating. A century later, contemporary sociologists have found evidence supporting Durkheim's insight (for example, Bellah, Madsen, Sullivan, Swidler, & Tipton, 1985; Riesman, 1950). Many people in the United States today don't know and have no desire to know their neighbors. Strangers are treated with suspicion. In the pursuit of economic opportunities, we have become more willing to relocate, sometimes to regions far from family and existing friends and colleagues. As we spread out we become more separated from those who could and would offer support in times of need. One study found that membership in voluntary organizations (PTA, Elks Club, Red Cross, League of Women Voters, and the like) has steadily declined in the United States over the past several decades (Putnam, 1995). Over the same period the average number of hours a day that people watch television by themselves has increased (cited in S. Roberts, 1995).

The structure of our communities discourages the formation of bonds with others, and not surprisingly, the likelihood of suicide increases at the same time. In the United States today, the highest suicide rates can be found in Alaska and in the sparsely populated mountain states of Nevada, Montana, New Mexico, and Wyoming (U.S. Bureau of the Census, 2004a). Exhibit 1.2 shows this pattern. These states tend to have a larger proportion of new residents who are not part of an established community. People tend to be more isolated, less likely to seek help or comfort from others in times of trouble, and therefore more susceptible to suicide than people who live in more populous states. It's also worth noting that sparsely populated rural areas also have higher rates of gun ownership than other areas of the United States. Over 70% of suicides committed in rural counties in the United States are committed with firearms (Butterfield, 2005).

Durkheim also felt, however, that another type of suicide (what he called altruistic suicide) can become more likely when the ties to one's community are too strong instead of too weak. He suggested that in certain societies individuality is completely overshadowed by one's group membership; the individual literally lives for the group, and personality is merely a reflection of the collective identity of the community. Some religious sects, for example, require their members to reject their ties to outside people and groups and to live by the values and customs of their new community. When members feel they can no longer contribute to the group and sustain their value within it, they may take their own lives out of loyalty to group norms.

A terrible example of the deadly effects of overly strong ties occurred in 1989 when four young Korean sisters, ranging in age from 6 to 13, attempted to kill themselves by ingesting rat poison. The three older sisters survived; the youngest died. The eldest provided startling sociological insight into this seemingly senseless act. Their family was poor—the father supported everyone on a salary of about $362 a month. The girl told the authorities that the sisters had made a suicide pact to ease their parents' financial burden and leave enough money for the education of their 3-year-old brother. Within the traditional Korean culture, female children are much less important to the family than male children. These sisters attempted to take their lives not because they were depressed or unable to cope but because they felt obligated to sacrifice their personal well-being to the success of their family's male heir ("Korean Girls," 1989).

Just as the suicide pact of these young girls was tied to the social system of which they were a part, so, too, was the suicide of the young college student at my university.

Exhibit 1.2 A Population density and suicide rates in all 50 states (suicides per 100,000 residents)

State	Suicides per 100,000 residents	Persons per square mile	State	Suicides per 100,000 residents	Persons per square mile
United States	*10.8*	*82.2*	Missouri	12.9	82.8
Alabama	11.5	88.7	Montana	19.3	6.3
Alaska	16.1	1.1	Nebraska	10.9	22.6
Arizona	14.5	49.1	Nevada	18.4	20.4
Arkansas	14.2	52.3	New Hampshire	13.3	143.6
California	8.2	227.5	New Jersey	6.9	1164.6
Colorado	16.3	43.9	New Mexico	19.8	15.4
Connecticut	8.2	719.0	New York	6.6	406.5
Delaware	13.6	418.5	North Carolina	12.1	172.6
District of Columbia	7.0	9175.6	North Dakota	12.4	9.2
Florida	14.1	315.6	Ohio	10.7	279.3
Georgia	11.1	150.0	Oklahoma	14.8	51.1
Hawaii	11.1	195.8	Oregon	14.5	37.1
Idaho	15.9	16.5	Pennsylvania	10.4	275.9
Illinois	9.1	227.6	Rhode Island	8.3	1029.9
Indiana	11.7	172.7	South Carolina	11.5	137.7
Iowa	10.4	52.7	South Dakota	13.8	10.1
Kansas	10.8	33.3	Tennessee	12.4	141.7
Kentucky	12.2	103.7	Texas	10.4	84.5
Louisiana	11.0	103.2	Utah	14.1	28.6
Maine	12.5	42.3	Vermont	11.7	66.9
Maryland	8.4	563.6	Virginia	11.1	186.6
Massachusetts	6.7	820.6	Washington	11.9	92.1
Michigan	10.5	177.5	West Virginia	15.9	75.2
Minnesota	9.6	63.6	Wisconsin	11.8	100.8
Mississippi	11.5	61.4	Wyoming	16.8	5.2

Exhibit 1.2 B   States with highest and lowest suicide rates

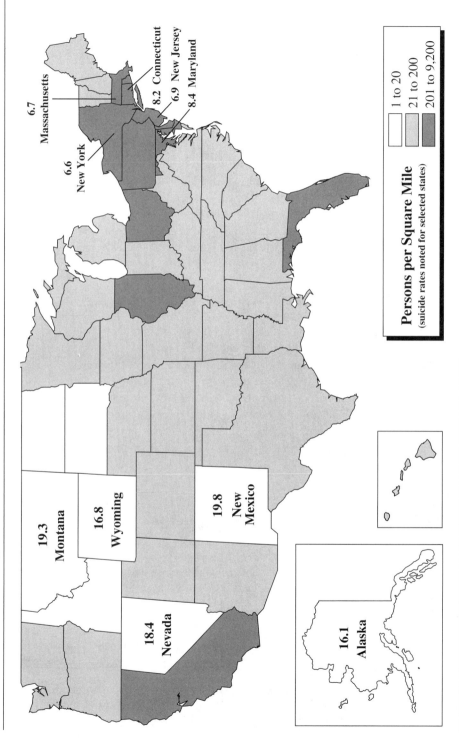

Massachusetts
6.7

New York
6.6

8.2 Connecticut
6.9 New Jersey
8.4 Maryland

19.3
Montana

16.8
Wyoming

19.8
New
Mexico

18.4
Nevada

16.1
Alaska

Persons per Square Mile
(suicide rates noted for selected states)

1 to 20
21 to 200
201 to 9,200

Source: U.S. Bureau of the Census, 2004a.

His choices and life circumstances were also a function of the values and conditions of his particular society. No doubt he had serious emotional problems, but these problems may have been part and parcel of his social circumstances. Had he lived in a society that didn't place as much pressure on young people or glorify individual achievement, he might not have chosen suicide. That's what the sociological imagination helps us understand.

Conclusion

In the 21st century, understanding our place within cultural, historical, and global contexts is more important than ever. The world is shrinking. Communication technology binds us to people on the other side of the planet. Increasing ecological awareness opens our eyes to the far-reaching effects of environmental degradations. The changes associated with colossal events in one country (political revolutions, terrorist attacks, natural disasters, economic crises, cultural upheavals) often quickly reverberate around the world. The consequences of such events often continue to be felt for years.

When we look at how people's lives are altered by such phenomena—as they sink into poverty or ascend to prosperity; stand in bread lines or work at a job previously unavailable; or find their sense of ethnic identity, personal safety, or self-worth altered—we can begin to understand the everyday importance of large-scale social change.

However, we must remember that individuals are not just helpless pawns of societal forces. They simultaneously influence and are influenced by society. The next chapter provides a more detailed treatment of this theme. Then, in Part II, I examine how society and our social lives are constructed and ordered. I focus on the interplay between individuals and the people, groups, organizations, institutions, and culture that collectively make up our society. Part III focuses on the structure of society, with particular attention to the various forms of social inequality.

YOUR TURN

The sociological imagination serves as the driving theme throughout this book. It's not a particularly difficult concept to grasp in the abstract: Things that are largely outside our control affect our everyday lives in ways that are sometimes not immediately apparent; our personal biographies are a function of social history. Yet what does this actually mean? How can you see the impact of larger social and historical events on your own life?

One way is to find out what events were going on at the time of your birth. Go to the library and find a newspaper and a popular magazine that were published on the day you were born. It would be especially useful to try to find a newspaper from the town or city in which you were born. What major news events took place that day? What were the dominant social and political concerns at the time? What was the state of the economy? What was considered fashionable in clothing, music, movies, and so forth?

Ask your parents or other adults about their reactions to these events and conditions. How do you think those reactions affected the way you were raised and the values in your family? What have been the lasting effects, if any, of these historical circumstances on the person you are today?

In addition, you might want to check newspapers and magazines and the Internet to determine the political, economic, global, and cultural trends that were prominent when you entered high school. The emergence from adolescence into young adulthood is a significant developmental stage in the lives of most people. It often marks the first time that others—including parents and other adults—take us seriously. And it is arguably the most self-conscious time of our lives. Try to determine how these dominant social phenomena will continue to influence your life after college. Imagine how different your life might have been had these social conditions been different—for instance, a different political atmosphere, a stronger or weaker economy, a more tolerant or restrictive way of life, and so on.

CHAPTER HIGHLIGHTS

- The primary theme of sociology is that our everyday thoughts and actions are the product of a complex interplay between massive social forces and personal characteristics. We can't understand the relationship between individuals and societies without understanding both.

- The sociological imagination is the ability to see the impact of social forces on our private lives—an awareness that our lives lie at the intersection of personal biography and societal history.

- Rather than study what goes on within people, sociologists study what goes on between people, whether as individuals, groups, organizations, or entire societies. Sociology forces us to look outside the tight confines of our individual personalities to understand the phenomena that shape us.

KEY TERMS

altruistic suicide Type of suicide that occurs where ties to the group or community are considered more important than individual identity

anomic suicide Type of suicide that occurs when the structure of society is weakened or disrupted and people feel hopeless and disillusioned

comparative method Research technique that compares existing official statistics and historical records across groups to test a theory about some social phenomenon

egoistic suicide Type of suicide that occurs in settings where the individual is emphasized over group or community connections

individualistic explanation Tendency to attribute people's achievements and failures to their personal qualities

sociological imagination Ability to see the impact of social forces on our private lives

2 Seeing and Thinking Sociologically

In 1994, ethnic violence erupted in the small African nation of Rwanda. The Hutu majority had begun a systematic program to exterminate the Tutsi minority. Soon gruesome pictures of the tortured and dismembered bodies of Tutsi men, women, and children began to appear on television screens around the world. When it was over, close to a million Tutsi had been slaughtered—half of whom died within a three-month period. Surely, we thought, such horror must have been perpetrated by bands of vicious, crazed thugs who derived some sort of twisted satisfaction from committing acts of unspeakable cruelty. Or maybe these were the extreme acts of angry soldiers, trained killers who were committed to destroying the enemy as completely as possible.

Actually, much of the responsibility for these atrocities lies elsewhere, in a most unlikely place: among the ordinary, previously law-abiding Rwandan citizens. Some of the participants in the genocide were the least likely brutes you could imagine. Two Benedictine nuns and a University of Rwanda physics professor stood trial in 2001 for their role in the killings. The nuns were accused of informing the military that Tutsi refugees had sought sanctuary in the church and of standing by as the soldiers massacred them. One nun allegedly provided the death squads with cans of gasoline used to set fire to a building where 500 Tutsis were hiding. The professor was accused of drawing up a list for the killers of Tutsi employees and students at the university and then killing at least seven Tutsis himself (Simons, 2001).

A report by the civil rights organization African Rights provides evidence that members of the medical profession were deeply involved as well—conceiving, planning, and executing much of the brutality ("Doctors Implicated," 1996). The report details how doctors joined with militiamen to hunt down Tutsis, turning hospitals into slaughterhouses. Some helped soldiers drag sick and wounded refugees out of their beds to be killed. Others took advantage of their position of authority to organize road blocks, distribute ammunition, and compile lists of Tutsi colleagues, patients, and neighbors to be sought out and slaughtered. Many doctors who didn't participate in the actual killing refused to treat wounded Tutsis and withheld food and water from refugees who sought sanctuary in hospitals. In fact, the president of

Rwanda and the minister of health were both physicians who were eventually tried as war criminals.

Ordinary, well-balanced people—teachers, nuns devoted to the ideals of charity and mercy, and physicians trained to heal and save lives—had changed, almost overnight, into cold-hearted killers. How could something like this have happened? The answer to this question lies in the sociological claim that individual behavior is largely shaped by social forces and situational contingencies. The circumstances of large-scale ethnic hatred and war have the power to transform well-educated people with no previous history of violence into cruel butchers. Tragically, such forces were at work in many of the 20th and 21st centuries' most infamous examples of human brutality, such as the Nazi Holocaust during World War II and, more recently, ethnic massacres in Cambodia, Iraq, Bosnia, Kosovo, and Sudan, as well as Rwanda.

Conversely, social circumstances can also motivate ordinary people to engage in astounding acts of heroism. The 2004 film *Hotel Rwanda* depicts the true story of Paul Rusesabagina, a hotel manager in the Rwandan capital, Kigali, who risked his own life to shelter over a thousand Tutsi refugees from certain death. Rusesabagina was a middle-class Hutu married to a Tutsi and the father of four children. He was a businessman with an eye toward turning a profit and a taste for the finer things in life. But when the genocide began, he used his guile, international contacts, and even water from the swimming pool to keep the refugees alive.

In this chapter, I examine the process by which individuals construct society and the way people's lives are linked to the social environment in which they live. The relationship between the individual and society is a powerful one—each continually affects the other.

How Individuals Structure Society

Up to this point, I have used the word *society* rather loosely. Formally, sociologists define **society** as a population living in the same geographic area that shares a culture and a common identity and whose members are subject to the same political authority. Societies may consist of people with the same ethnic heritage or of hundreds of different groups who speak a multitude of languages. Some societies are highly industrialized and complex; others are primarily agricultural and relatively simple in structure. Some societies are very religious; others are distinctly secular. Some societies are self-sufficient and produce most of the goods and services their people need; others rely mostly on trade with foreign countries for survival.

According to the 19th-century French philosopher Auguste Comte, all societies, whatever their form, contain both forces for stability, which he called "social statics," and forces for change, which he called "social dynamics." Sometimes, however, people use the term *society* only to mean a "static" entity—a natural, permanent, and historical structure. They frequently talk about society "planning" or "shaping" our lives and describe it as a relatively unchanging set of organizations, institutions, systems, and cultural patterns into which successive generations of people are born and socialized.

As a result, sociology students often start out believing not only that society is powerfully influential (which, of course, it is) but also that it is something that exists "out there," completely separate and distinct from us (which it isn't). It is tempting to view society simply as a "top down" initiator of human activity, a massive entity that methodically shapes the lives of all individuals within it, like some gigantic puppeteer manipulating a bunch of marionettes. This characterization is not altogether inaccurate. Society does exert influence on its members through certain identifiable structural features and historical circumstances. The concept of the sociological imagination discussed in Chapter 1 implies that structural forces beyond our direct control do affect our personal lives.

But this view is only one side of the sociological coin. The sociological imagination also encourages us to see that each individual has a role in forming a society and influencing the course of its history. As we navigate our social environments, we respond in ways that may modify the effects and even the nature of that environment (House, 1981). As one sociologist has written,

> No [society], however massive it may appear in the present, existed in this massivity from the dawn of time. Somewhere along the line each one of its salient features was concocted by human beings. . . . Since all social systems were created by [people], it follows that [people] can also change them. (P. L. Berger, 1963, p. 128)

To fully understand society, then, we must see it as a human construction made up of people interacting with one another. It consists of everyday *microsituations*—what we do, say, feel, and think when we're alone, in pairs, or in groups. When enough people alter their behavior, the nature of society changes (Collins, 1981).

Communication plays an important role in the construction of society. If we couldn't communicate with one another to reach an understanding about society's expectations, we couldn't live together. Through day-to-day communication, we construct, reaffirm, experience, and alter the reality of our society. By responding to other people's comments and gestures in the expected manner and by talking about social abstractions as real things, we help shape society (Shibutani, 1961).

Imagine two people sitting on a park bench who strike up a conversation. Their talk eventually turns to the "war on terrorism." One person is convinced that the actual threat to individual citizens, following the attacks of September 11, 2001, does not warrant the erosion of civil rights and personal privacy through such measures as the recently extended USA Patriot Act, which allows the government to gain access to citizens' tax records, credit records, library records, bookstore records, and medical records without probable cause, consent, or knowledge. The other person counters that more recent terrorist attacks, such as those on transportation services in Madrid and London, show that we're always potential targets and that any means of preventing American deaths at the hands of foreign terrorists is worthwhile, even if it means sacrificing some freedoms. The debate becomes heated: One thinks that our nation's founding principles are the best protection for individual liberty; the other feels that individual liberty is irrelevant if people's lives are in danger. These two people obviously don't agree on the need for or the effectiveness of a "war on terrorism." But merely by discussing it, they are agreeing that such a thing exists. In talking about such matters, people give shape and substance to society's ideals and values (Hewitt, 1988).

Even something as apparently unchangeable as our collective past can be shaped and modified by individuals. We usually think of history as a fixed, unalterable collection of social events that occurred long ago; only in science fiction can one "go back" and change history. No one would question that the Declaration of Independence was signed in 1776, that the Civil War ended in 1865, that John F. Kennedy was assassinated on November 22, 1963, that hijackers flew passenger jets into the Pentagon and the World Trade Center on September 11, 2001, or that Hurricane Katrina made landfall on August 29, 2005.

Although such historical events themselves don't change, their meaning and relevance can. Consider the celebration in 1992 of the 500th anniversary of Columbus's voyage to the Americas. For generations, American schoolchildren have been taught that Columbus's 1492 "discovery" represented a triumphant step forward for Western civilization. However, increasing sensitivity to the social value of all racial and ethnic groups and the acknowledgment of their past persecution forced many people to reconsider the historical meaning of Columbus's journey. In fact, some historians now consider it and what it led to one of history's most dismal examples of wanton and deadly prejudice. So you see society might best be regarded as a work in progress, a succession of events, a flow of interchanges among people (Shibutani, 1961, p. 174).

When we view society this way, we can begin to understand the role each of us has in maintaining or altering it. Whenever we modify the expectations or behaviors associated with a social position we occupy, we are simultaneously modifying a part of our society. Individuals who occupy highly visible and influential positions are particularly effective. It is often argued, for instance, that Franklin D. Roosevelt's terms as U.S. president forever changed the nature of the presidency and the role of the federal government in people's lives (House, 1981). However, not only powerful, influential people are able to modify society. Sometimes the actions of ordinary individuals mobilize larger groups of people to collectively alter some aspect of social life.

Consider the story of a young Canadian named Craig Kielburger. About a decade ago, when he was 12, Craig was searching through his local newspaper for the comics. A front-page article caught his eye. It described a Pakistani boy about his age who was sold into bondage as a carpet weaver, escaped, and was eventually murdered for speaking out publicly against child labor. Upset by the story, Craig gathered up a few friends and formed an organization he called (Kids Can) Free the Children (KCFTC). Craig traveled throughout Canada and other countries addressing business groups, government bodies, educators, unions, and students on the plight of children worldwide.

Since then the organization, which now has over 100,000 young volunteers in 35 countries, has built more than 400 primary schools providing education to 35,000 children a day (Free the Children, 2005). In addition, KCFTC has donated more than $8 million worth of medical supplies to needy families in 13 countries. It also supports clean water projects, health clinics, and alternative income cooperatives in 21 developing nations. Before Craig had even completed his college education, he had written a book, had met world leaders such as the late Pope John Paul II and the Dalai Lama, and was nominated for the 2002–2003 Nobel Peace Prize. He now co-chairs the Commission on Globalization along with such international dignitaries as former U.S. Senator Bill Bradley and former Nobel Prize winners Mikhail Gorbachev and Desmond Tutu.

We live in a world in which our everyday lives are largely a product of macro-level societal and historical processes. Society is an objective fact that coerces, even creates, us (P. L. Berger, 1963). At the same time, we are constantly creating, maintaining, reaffirming, and transforming society. Hence society is part and parcel of micro-level human interaction (Collins, 1981). But although we create society, we then collectively "forget" we've done so, believe it is independent of us, and live our lives under its influence.

Throughout the remainder of this book, you'll see brief features called *Micro-Macro Connections* that examine this interrelationship between macro-level societal forces and many of the everyday phenomena we experience at the individual level.

Social Influence: The Impact of Other People in Our Everyday Lives

We live in a world with other people. I know that's not the most profound statement you've ever read, but it is key to understanding the sociology of human behavior. Our everyday lives are a collection of brief encounters, extended conversations, intimate interactions, chance collisions, and superficial contacts with other people. In our early years we may have our parents, siblings, uncles, aunts, and grandparents to contend with. Soon we begin to form friendships with others outside our families. Our lives also become filled with connections to other people—classmates, teachers, coworkers, bosses, spiritual leaders, therapists—who are neither family nor friends but who have an enormous impact on us. And, of course, we have daily experiences with total strangers: the clerk at the supermarket, the server at the restaurant, the people who sit next to us on airplanes or in doctors' waiting rooms.

If you think about it, understanding what it means to be alone requires that we know what it's like to be with other people. As I discuss in Chapters 5 and 6, much of our private identity—what we think of ourselves, the type of people we become, and the images of ourselves we project in public—comes from our contact with others.

Sociologists tell us that these encounters have a great deal of *social influence* over our lives. Whether we're aware of their doing so or not, other people affect our thoughts, perceptions, and behaviors. Before acting, we take into account their feelings and concerns. Perhaps you've decided to date someone, only to be stopped dead in your tracks by the question, What would my mother think of this person? The others who influence us may be in our immediate presence or hover in our memories. They may be real or imagined, loved or despised. And their effects on us may be deliberate or accidental. We spend our lives forming or dissolving attachments to other people; we may seek them out one moment, avoid them the next.

Imagine for a moment what your life would be like if you had never had contact with other people (assuming you could have survived this long!). You wouldn't know what love is, or hate or jealousy or compassion or appreciation, for that matter. You wouldn't know if you were wealthy or poor, bright or dumb, witty or boring. You'd also lack some important and basic information. You wouldn't know what day it is, how much a pound weighs, where Belgium is, or which plants and animals are edible. Furthermore, you'd have no language, and because we use language to think, imagine, predict, plan, wonder, and reminisce, you'd lack these abilities as well. In short, you'd lack the key experiences that make you a functioning human being.

Contact with people is essential to a person's social development. But there is more to social life than the mere fact that it involves bumping into other people from time to time. We act and react to things and people in our environment as a result of the meaning we attach to them. At the sight of a dog barreling toward it, a squirrel instinctively runs away. A human, however, does not have such an automatic reaction. We don't have very many instincts. We've learned from past experiences that some animals are approachable and others aren't. So we can think, "Is this dog friendly or mean? Does it want to lick my face or tear me limb from limb?" and respond accordingly. In short, we usually interpret events in our environment before we act.

The presence of other people may motivate you to improve your performance—for example, when the quality of your opponent makes you play the best tennis match of your life. But their presence may at other times inhibit you—as when you forget your lines in the school play because your little brother's making faces at you and your mother's videotaping the whole thing. Other people's presence is also essential for the expression of certain feelings. Have you ever noticed that it's impossible to tickle yourself? Being tickled is the product of a *social* interaction. Indeed, according to one study of laughter, people are about 30 times more likely to laugh when they are around other people than when they're alone (Provine, 2000).

Other people can also have a direct and purposeful effect on our behavior. I'm sure you've been in situations in which people have tried to persuade you to do things against your will or better judgment. Perhaps someone convinced you to steal a candy bar, skip your sociology class, or disregard the speed limit. On occasion, such social influence can be deadly.

❖
❖
Stanley Milgram
Ordinary People and Cruel Acts

If a being from another planet were to read the history of human civilization, it would probably conclude that we are tremendously cruel, vicious, and evil creatures. From countless wars and crusades to ethnic genocides and terrorist attacks, from backwater lynchings and violent crimes to schoolyard bullying and bum fights, humans have always shown a powerful tendency to ferociously turn on their fellow humans.

The curious thing is that people involved in such acts often show a profound capacity to deny responsibility for their actions by pointing to the influence of others: "My friend made me do it" or "I was only following orders" or "That's what the audience wants to see." Can an ordinary, decent person be pressured by another to commit an act of extreme cruelty? Or do cruel actions require inherently cruel people?

In one of the classic pieces of social research, social psychologist Stanley Milgram (1974) set out to answer this question. He wanted to know how far people would go in obeying the commands of an authority. He set up an experimental situation in which a subject, on orders from an authoritative figure, flips a switch, apparently sending a 450-volt shock to an innocent victim.

Subjects were told they would be participating in a study of the effects of punishment on learning. On a specified day, each subject arrived at the laboratory with another person who, unknown to the subject, was actually an accomplice of the experimenter. Each subject was told he or she would play the role of "teacher," and the other person would be the "learner." The teacher was taken to a separate room that held an ominous-looking machine the researchers called a "shock generator." The learner was seated in another room out of the sight of the teacher and was supposedly strapped to an electrode from the shock generator.

The teacher read a series of word pairs (for example, *blue–sky, nice–day, wild–duck*) to the learner. After reading the entire list, the teacher then read the first word of a pair (for example, *blue*) and four alternatives for the second word (for example, *sky, ink, box, lamp*). The learner had to select the correct alternative. Following directions from the experimenter, who was present in the room, the teacher flipped a switch and shocked the learner whenever he or she gave an incorrect answer. The shocks began at the lowest level, 15 volts, and increased with each subsequent incorrect answer all the way up to the 450-volt maximum.

As instructed, all the subjects shocked the learner for each incorrect response. (Remember, the learner was an accomplice of the experimenter and was not actually being shocked.) As the experiment proceeded and the shocks became stronger, the teacher could hear cries from the learner. Most of the teachers, believing they were inflicting serious injury, became visibly upset and wanted to stop. The experimenter, however, ordered them to continue—and many did. Despite the tortured reactions of the victim, 65% of the subjects complied with the experimenter's demands and proceeded to the maximum, 450 volts.

Milgram repeated the study with a variety of subjects and even conducted it in different countries, including Germany and Australia. In each case about two thirds of the subjects were willing, under orders from the experimenter, to shock to the limit. Milgram showed that out of deference to authority, ordinarily nice people would do terrible things that they wouldn't do under other circumstances.

Milgram's research raises questions not only about why people would obey an unreasonable authority but also about what the rest of us think of those who do. A contemporary study of destructive obedience in the workplace—investigating such actions as dumping toxic waste in a river or manufacturing a defective automobile—found that the public is more likely to forgive those who are responsible when they are believed to be conforming to company policy or obeying the orders of a supervisor than when they are thought to be acting on their own (Hamilton & Sanders, 1995).

Milgram's study has generated a tremendous amount of controversy. For three decades, this pivotal piece of research has been replicated, discussed, and debated by other social scientists (Miller, Collins, & Brief, 1995). Since the original study, other researchers have found that in small groups people sometimes collectively rebel against what they perceive as unjust authority (Gamson, Fireman, & Rytina, 1982). Nevertheless, Milgram's findings are discomforting. It would be much easier to conclude that the acts of inhumanity we read about in our daily newspapers are the products of defective or inherently evil individuals. All society would have to do then is identify, capture, and separate them from the rest of us. But if Milgram is right, if most of us could become evil given the "right" circumstances or influences, then the only thing that separates us from evildoers is our good fortune and our social environment.

❖ ❖

Societal Influence: The Effect of Social Structure on Our Everyday Lives

Social life is more than just individual people affecting one another's lives. Society is not just a sum of its human parts; it's also the way those parts are put together, related to each other, and organized (Coulson & Riddell, 1980). Statuses, roles, groups, organizations, and institutions are the building blocks of society. Culture is the mortar that holds these blocks together. Although society is dynamic and constantly evolving, it has an underlying *macro-level* structure that persists.

Statuses and Roles

One key element of any society is its collection of **statuses**—the positions that individuals within the society occupy. When most of us hear the word *status,* we tend to associate it with rank or prestige. You might hear someone say that an army general has more status than a corporal. But here we're talking about a status as any socially defined position that a person can occupy: cook, daughter, anthropologist, husband, student, alcoholic, computer nerd, electrician, shoplifter, and so on. Some statuses may, in fact, be quite prestigious, such as president. But others carry very little prestige, such as gas station attendant. Some statuses require a tremendous amount of training to enter, such as physician; others, such as ice cream lover, require little effort at all.

We all occupy many statuses at the same time. I am a college professor, but I am also a husband, son, nephew, uncle, father, brother, friend, coworker, consumer, swimmer, vegetarian, occasional poker player, runner, homeowner, neighbor, and author. My behavior at any given moment, of course, is dictated to a large degree by the status that's most important at that particular point in time. When I am jogging, my status as professor is not particularly relevant. But if I decide to run in a half-marathon race instead of giving a final exam in my sociology course, I may be in trouble!

Sociologists often distinguish between ascribed and achieved statuses. An **ascribed status** is a social position that we acquire at birth or enter involuntarily later in life. Our race, sex, ethnicity, and status as someone's child or grandchild are all ascribed statuses. As we get older, we enter the ascribed status of teenager and, eventually, old person. These aren't positions we choose to occupy. An **achieved status**, in contrast, is a social position we take on voluntarily or acquire through our own efforts or accomplishments, such as being a student or a spouse or an engineer.

Of course, the distinction between ascribed and achieved status is not always so clear. Some people become college students not because of their own efforts but because of their parents' influence. Chances are the religion with which you identify is the one your parents belong to. However, many people decide to change their religious membership later in life. Moreover, as we'll see later in this book, certain ascribed statuses (sex, race, ethnicity, and age) influence our access to lucrative achieved statuses.

Statuses are important sociologically because they all come with a set of rights, obligations, behaviors, and duties that people occupying a certain position are expected or encouraged to perform. These expectations are referred to as **roles**. For instance, the role of a "professor" includes teaching students, answering their questions, being impartial, and dressing appropriately. Any out-of-role behavior may be met with shock or suspicion. If I consistently showed up for class in a thong and a tank top, that would certainly violate my "scholarly" image and call into question my ability to teach.

Each person, as a result of her or his own skills, interests, and interactional experiences, defines roles differently. Students enter a class with the general expectation that their professor is going to teach them something. Each professor, however, may have a different method. Some professors are very animated; others remain stationary behind a podium. Some do not allow questions until after the lecture; others demand constant discussion and probing questions from students. Some are meticulous and organized; others spontaneous and absent-minded.

People engage in typical patterns of interaction based on the relationship between their roles and the roles of others. Employers are expected to interact with employees in a certain way, as are dentists with patients and salespeople with customers. In each case, actions are constrained by the responsibilities and obligations associated with those particular statuses. We know, for instance, that lovers and spouses are supposed to interact with each other differently from the way acquaintances or friends are supposed to interact. In a parent-child relationship, both members are linked by certain rights, privileges, and obligations. Parents are responsible for providing their children with the basic necessities of life—food, clothing, shelter, and so forth. These expectations are so powerful that not meeting them may constitute the crime of negligence or abuse. Children, in turn, are expected to abide by their parents' wishes. Thus interactions within a relationship are functions not only of the individual personalities of the people involved but also of the role requirements associated with the statuses they occupy.

We feel the power of role expectations most clearly when we occupy two conflicting statuses simultaneously. Sociologists use the term **role conflict** to describe situations in which people encounter tension in trying to cope with the demands of incompatible roles. People may feel frustrated in their efforts to do what they feel they're supposed to do when the role expectations of one status clash with the role expectations of another. Someone may have an important out-of-town conference to attend (status of sociologist) on the same day her 10-year-old son is appearing as a talking pig in the school play (status of parent). Or a teenager who works hard at his job at the local ice cream shop (status of employee) is frustrated when his buddies come and expect him to give them free ice cream (status of friend).

In 1998, Barry Elton Black, the leader of a branch of the Ku Klux Klan in Pennsylvania, was arrested for burning a cross at a Klan rally. Although the owner of the property had given the Klan permission to hold the rally on his private land, the burning cross was about 30 feet tall and clearly visible from a nearby state highway. Local police testified that the sight of the burning cross caused a car with black passengers to flee the area and some white residents to seek protection from sheriff's deputies (Holmes, 1998). Believing that cross burning was a form of free speech protected by the U.S. Constitution, Mr. Black contacted the American Civil Liberties Union to defend him. The attorney who agreed to represent Mr. Black was David Baugh, a black man. In doing so, Mr. Baugh had to choose between the conflicting role expectations associated with his ascribed racial status (fighting cross burning out of the belief that it is an act designed to terrorize and intimidate and that one should not assist an organization committed to one's destruction) and those of his achieved occupational status (a lawyer committed to defending the belief that all Americans, no matter how distasteful their actions are, have a constitutionally guaranteed right to free expression). Mr. Black was found guilty and sentenced to five years in prison. The important point for us here is the role conflict raised by a black lawyer's decision to represent a white Klan member. What would you have done if you were Mr. Baugh?

Groups

Societies are not simply composed of people occupying statuses and living in accordance with roles. Sometimes individuals form well-defined units called groups. A **group** is a set of people who interact more or less regularly with one another and who are conscious of their identity as a group. Your family, your colleagues at work, and any clubs or sports teams to which you belong are all social groups.

Groups are not just collections of people who randomly come together for some purpose. Their structure defines the relationships among members. When groups are large, enduring, and complex, each individual within the group is likely to occupy some named position or status—mother, president, treasurer, supervisor, linebacker, and so forth.

Group membership can also be a powerful force behind one's future actions and thoughts. For instance, a girl who is not a member of the popular clique at school, but wants to be, is likely to structure many of her daily activities around gaining entry into that group. In addition, like statuses and roles, groups come with a set of general expectations. A person's actions within a group are judged according to a conventional set of ideas about how things ought to be. For example, a coworker who always arrives late for meetings or never takes his or her turn working an undesirable shift is violating the group's expectations and will be pressured to conform.

The smallest group, of course, is one that consists of two people, or a **dyad.** According to the renowned German sociologist Georg Simmel (1902/1950), dyads (marriages, close friendships, and so on) are among the most meaningful and intense connections we have. The problem, though, is that dyads are inherently unstable. If one person decides to leave, the relationship completely collapses. Hence, it's not surprising that for society's most important dyads (that is, marriages), a variety of legal, religious, and cultural restrictions are in place that make it difficult for people to dissolve them.

The addition of one person to a dyad—forming what Simmel called a **triad**—fundamentally changes the nature of the group. Although triads might appear more stable than dyads because the withdrawal of one person needn't destroy the group, they develop other problems. If you have two siblings, you already know that triads always contain the potential for **coalitions**—when two individuals pair up and perhaps conspire against the third.

Groups can also be classified by their influence on our everyday lives. A **primary group** consists of a small number of members who have direct contact over a relatively long period of time. Emotional attachment is high in such groups, and members have intimate knowledge of each other's lives. Families and networks of close friends are primary groups. A **secondary group**, in contrast, is much more formal and impersonal. The group is established for a specific task, such as the production or sale of consumer goods, and members are less emotionally committed to one another. Their roles tend to be highly structured. Primary groups may form within secondary groups, as when close friendships form among coworkers, but in general secondary groups require less emotional investment than primary groups.

Like societies, groups have a reality that is more than just the sum of their members; a change in a group's membership doesn't necessarily alter its basic structure. Change in primary groups, though, perhaps through divorce or death, produces some dramatic effects on the nature and identity of the group, although the group itself still exists. Secondary groups, however, can endure changing membership relatively easily even if some, or even all, individuals leave and new ones enter—as for example, when the senior class in a high school graduates and is replaced in the school the following year by another group of students.

Although social groupings based on race, gender, ethnicity, and religion are not social groups in the strictest sense of the term, they function like groups in that members share certain characteristics and interests. They become an important source of a person's identity. For instance, members of a particular racial or ethnic group may organize into a well-defined unit to fight for a political cause. The feelings of "we-ness" or "they-ness" generated by such group membership can be constructive or dangerous, encouraging pride and unity in some cases, and anger, bitterness, and hatred toward outsiders in others.

Organizations

At an even higher level of complexity are social units called **organizations,** networks of statuses and groups created for a specific purpose. Honda Motors, the International Brotherhood of Teamsters, Oxford University, Microsoft, the Federal Emergency Management Agency, the National Organization for Women, and the Methodist Church are all examples of organizations. Organizations contain groups as well as individuals occupying clearly defined statuses and taking on clearly defined roles.

Some of the groups within organizations are transitory, some are more permanent. For instance, a university consists of individual classes that disband at the end of the semester as well as more permanent groups such as the faculty, administration, secretarial staff, maintenance staff, and alumni.

Large, formal organizations are often characterized by a *hierarchical division of labor.* Each person in an organization occupies a position that has a specific set of duties and responsibilities, and those positions can be "ranked" according to power and importance. At General Motors, for instance, assembly line workers typically don't make decisions about personnel or budgetary policies, and the vice president in charge of marketing doesn't spray-paint the underbodies of newly assembled Chevrolets. In general, people occupy certain positions in an organization because they have the skills to do the job that is required of them. When a person can no longer meet the requirements of the job, he or she can be replaced without seriously affecting the functioning of the organization.

Organizations are a profoundly common and visible feature of everyday social life, as you'll see in Chapter 9. Most of us cannot acquire food, get an education, pray, undergo life-saving surgery, or earn a salary without coming into contact with or becoming a member of some organization. To be a full-fledged member of modern society is to be deeply involved in some form of organizational life.

Social Institutions

When stable sets of statuses, roles, groups, and organizations form, they provide the foundation for addressing fundamental societal needs. These enduring patterns of social life are called **social institutions**. Sociologists usually think of institutions as the building blocks that organize society. They are the patterned ways of solving the problems and meeting the requirements of a particular society. Although there may be conflict over what society "needs" and how best to fulfill those needs, all societies must have some systematic way of organizing the various aspects of everyday life.

Key social institutions in modern society include the family, education, economics, politics and law, and religion. Some sociologists add health care, the military, and the mass media to the list.

Family: All societies must have a way of replacing their members, and reproduction is essential to the survival of human society as a whole. Within the institution of family, sexual relations among adults are regulated; people are cared for; children are born, protected, and socialized; and newcomers are provided an identity—a "lineage"—that gives them a sense of belonging. Just how these activities are carried out varies from society to society. Indeed, different societies have different ideas about which relationships qualify for designation as family. But the institution of family, whatever its form, remains the hub of social life in virtually all societies (J. H. Turner, 1972).

Education: New members of a society need to be taught what it means to be a member of that society and how to survive in it. In small, simple societies, the family is the primary institution responsible for socializing new members into the culture. However, as societies become more complex, it becomes exceedingly difficult for a family to teach its members all they need to know to function and survive. Hence, most modern, complex societies have an elaborate system of schools—preschool, primary, secondary, college, professional—that not only create and disseminate knowledge and information but also train individuals for future careers and teach them their "place" in society.

Economy: From the beginning, human societies have faced the problems of securing enough food and protecting people from the environment (J. H. Turner, 1972). Today, modern societies have systematic ways of gathering resources, converting them into goods and commodities, and distributing them to members. In addition, societies provide ways of coordinating and facilitating the operation of this massive process. For instance, banks, accounting firms, insurance companies, stock brokerages, transportation agencies, and computer networks don't produce goods themselves but provide services that make the gathering, producing, and distributing of goods possible. To facilitate the distribution of both goods and services, economic institutions adopt a system of common currency and an identifiable mode of exchange. In some societies, the economy is driven by the value of efficient production and the need to maximize profits; in others, the collective well-being of the population is the primary focus.

Politics and Law: All societies face the problem of how to preserve order, avoid chaos, and make important social decisions. The legal system provides explicit laws or rules of conduct and mechanisms for enforcing those laws, settling disputes, and changing outdated laws or creating new ones (J. H. Turner, 1972). These activities take place within a larger system of governance that allocates and acknowledges power, authority, and leadership. In a democracy, the governance process includes the citizens, who have a say in who leads them; in a monarchy, kings or queens can claim that their birthright entitles them to positions of leadership. In some societies, the transfer of power is efficient and mannerly; in others, it is violent.

Religion: In the process of meeting the familial, educational, economic, and political needs of society, some individuals thrive whereas others suffer. Hence all societies also face the problem of providing their less successful members with a sense of purpose and meaning in their lives. Religion gives individuals a belief system for understanding their existence as well as a network of personal support in times of need. Although many members of a given society may actively reject religion, it remains one of the most enduring and powerful social institutions. Although religion provides enormous comfort to some people, it can also be a source of hatred and irreparable divisions.

Health Care: One of the profoundly universal facts of human life is that people get sick and die. In some societies, healing the sick and managing the transition to death involves spiritual or supernatural intervention; other societies rely on science and modern technology. Most modern societies have established a complex system of health care to disseminate medical treatments. Doctors, nurses, hospitals, pharmacies, drug and medical equipment manufacturers, patients, and others all play an active role in the health care institution.

Military: To deal with the possibility of attack from outside and the protection of national interests, many societies maintain an active military defense. However, militaries are used not only to defend societies but also, at times, to attack other countries in order to acquire land, resources, or power. In other cases, the military is used for political change, as when the U.S. military was mobilized to overthrow the government of Saddam Hussein in Iraq in 2003.

Mass Media: In very small, relatively close-knit societies, information can be shared through word of mouth. However, as societies become more complex the dissemination of information requires a massive coordinated system. The modern mass media—radio, newspapers, television, and the Internet—provide coverage of important societal events so individuals can make informed decisions about their own lives. But the media do more than report events of local, national, and international significance. They also actively mold public opinion and project and reinforce the society's values.

From these very brief descriptions you can see that the social institutions within a society are highly interrelated. Debates over the state of the U.S. health care system make people aware of its links to the economy and politics. Although much of the information we need to survive we learn in schools, religion and politics can play a major role in what gets taught there. For instance, in 2005 the Kansas Board of

Education, in response to pressure from anti-evolution religious organizations, held hearings to determine if it would require public school science classes to give equal time to religiously based ideas about the origins of life.

To individual members of society, social institutions appear huge, natural, and inevitable. Most of us couldn't imagine life without a family. Nor could most of us fathom what society would be like without a stable system of government, a common currency, schools to educate our children, or an effective military. It is very easy, then, to think that institutions exist independently of people.

But one of the important themes that will be revisited throughout this book is that we each have a role to play in maintaining or changing social institutions. For instance, in 1999 people in 11 European nations voted to adopt a common form of currency, the euro. Planning proceeded to add more nations to the European Union and to create a constitution that would override national constitutions on certain issues. That plan met with considerable resistance in public elections in France and the Netherlands in 2005. Still, travel, trade, and politics among the countries that adopted the euro, as well as the options available to their individual workers and consumers, look different than they did 10 years ago. Although the effects of these changes are felt at the organizational and institutional level, they are ultimately initiated, implemented, or rejected, and, most importantly, experienced by individual people.

Marion Nestle
The Economics and Politics of Food

Institutional influence is sometimes not so obvious. For instance, we usually think of nutrition as an inherent property of the foods we eat. Either something is good for us or it's not good for us, right? We rarely consider the economic and political role that food companies play in shaping our tastes and our dietary standards.

Marion Nestle (2002), a professor of Nutrition and Food Studies, wanted to examine the institutional underpinnings of our ideas about health and nutrition. She faced an interesting methodological dilemma, however. No one involved in the food industry was willing to talk to her "on the record." So she compiled information from government reports, newspapers, magazines, speeches, advocacy materials, conference exhibits, and supermarkets. She also used information that she'd previously received from lobbying groups and trade associations representing such diverse interests as the salt, sugar, vitamin, wheat, soybean, flaxseed, and blueberry industries.

Despite alarming levels of food hunger among the world's population (see Chapter 10), Americans overall have so much food that we could feed all our citizens twice over. Most people can afford to buy more food than they actually need (hence, the popular "doggy bag"). The food industry is therefore highly competitive. But like all major industries, companies are beholden to their stockholders rather than the consuming public. Marketing foods that are healthy and nutritious is a concern as long as it can increase sales.

Food marketers have long identified children as their most attractive targets. According to Nestle, the attention paid to children has escalated in recent years because of their increasing responsibility for purchasing decisions. Children between 6 and 19 are estimated to influence upwards of $500 billion in food purchases each year (cited in Nestle, 2002). By age 7, most children can shop independently, ask for information about what they want, and show off their purchases to other children.

Soft drink companies have become especially adept at targeting young people with diverse marketing strategies. Soft drinks are not simply occasional snacks. They have replaced milk as the primary beverage in the diets of American children as well as adults. Between 1985 and 1997, American school districts decreased the amount of milk they bought by 30%; during that same period, they increased their purchases of carbonated sodas by 1,100% (cited in Nestle, 2002). The typical American teenage boy now derives about 9% of his daily caloric intake from soft drinks, and about a fifth of one- and two-year-olds now regularly drink soda (Schlosser, 2001).

One of the most controversial marketing strategies in the soft drink industry is the "pouring rights" agreement, in which a company buys the exclusive right to sell its products in all schools in a particular district. For instance, one 53-school district in Colorado signed a 10-year, $8 million pouring rights agreement with Coca-Cola. In financially strapped districts, a pouring rights contract often supplies a significant part of the district's annual funding. It may be the only thing that allows a school system to buy much needed resources like computers and textbooks.

Besides the lump sum agreed to in the contract, companies frequently offer school districts cash bonuses if they exceed certain sales targets. Hence it is in the district's financial interest to encourage students to consume more soft drinks. In light of such incentives, ethical implications and health concerns become secondary. Indeed, many school districts justify these agreements by saying that soft drinks pervade the culture and students will drink them anyway, so why not get some benefit?

In addition to the long-term health effects of heavy soft drink consumption, however, Nestle points out that students learn a somewhat cynical lesson: that school officials are willing to compromise nutritional principles (and the students' physical well-being) for financial gain. Pouring rights contracts can also have a serious impact on long-term school funding. While they may solve short-term financial needs, they may also hamper efforts to secure adequate federal, state, and local funding for public education. Taxpayers may come to the conclusion that raising taxes to support public schools is unnecessary if the bulk of a district's operating budget comes from these commercial contracts.

In pouring rights contracts we can see how a child's food choices in school are linked deeply and profoundly to broader educational, political, and economic needs, often with little, if any, attention paid to nutritional considerations and individual health.

Culture

The most pervasive element of society is **culture**, which consists of the language, values, beliefs, rules, behaviors, and physical artifacts of a society. Think of it as a society's "personality." Culture gives us codes of conduct—the proper, acceptable ways of doing things. We usually don't think twice about it, yet it colors everything we experience.

Human societies would be chaotic and unlivable if they didn't have cultures that allow people to live together under the same set of general rules. But culture can also sometimes lead to tragedy. In 2005, a high-speed Japanese commuter train crashed, killing close to 100 passengers. The most immediate cause of the accident was human error. The driver was going too fast when the train jumped off the tracks on a curve and crashed into an apartment building. However, upon closer inspection we can see that the root cause of the accident rested in the harmful effects of culture. The train was 90 seconds behind schedule, which wouldn't be a big deal in the United States where a train is considered "late" only when it is 5 or 6 minutes behind schedule. But in Japanese culture, where efficiency and punctuality take on vital importance, trains are considered late when they are a mere 60 seconds behind schedule. A 90-second delay was unacceptable and the driver knew it. Everyday life in Japan is so tightly scheduled that it leaves little room for casual or slow-paced travel (Onishi, 2005a)—or even in some cases, for safety.

Culture is particularly apparent when someone questions or violates it. Those who do not believe what the majority believes, value what the majority values, or obey the same rules the majority obeys are likely to experience punishment, psychiatric attention, or social ostracism. I discuss the power of culture in more detail in Chapter 4, but here we should look at two key aspects of culture that are thoroughly implicated in the workings of social structure and social influence: values and norms.

Values

Perhaps no word in the English language carries more baggage than *values*. People throw around terms such as *moral values, traditional values,* and *homespun American values* with little thought as to what they actually mean. Sociologically speaking, a **value** is a standard of judgment by which people decide on desirable goals and outcomes (Hewitt & Hewitt, 1986). Values represent general criteria on which our lives and the lives of others can be judged. They justify the social rules that determine how we ought to behave. For instance, laws against theft clearly reflect the value we place on personal property.

Different societies emphasize different values. Success, independence, and individual achievement are seen as important values in U.S. society. In other societies, such as Vietnam, people are more likely to value group obligation and loyalty to family.

Values within a society sometimes come into conflict. The value of privacy ("stay out of other people's business") and the value of generosity ("help others in need") may clash when we are trying to decide whether to help a stranger who appears to require assistance. Similarly, although the value of cooperation is held in high esteem in contemporary U.S. society, when someone is taking a final exam in a sociology class, cooperation is likely to be defined as cheating. When the key values that characterize a particular social institution come into conflict, the result may be widespread legal and moral uncertainty among individuals.

❖

Micro-Macro Connection
Family Privacy Versus Children's Welfare

One such conflict involves the cultural value of family privacy. Contemporary U.S. life is built on the assumption that what a family does in the privacy of its home is or at least should be its own business. Family life, many people believe, is best left to family members, not to neighbors, the government, the courts, or other public agencies. Consequently, American families are endowed with significant autonomy—the right to make decisions about their future or about treatment of their members (see Chapter 7).

Privacy has not always characterized American families. Before the 19th century people felt free to enter others' homes and tell them what to wear or how to treat their children. The development of the value of family privacy and autonomy emerged with the separation of home and work and the growth of cities during the late 19th century (Parsons, 1971). Innovations in the amenities available within the home—indoor plumbing, refrigerators, telephones, radios, televisions, central heating and air conditioning, backyard swimming pools, video players, and computers—have all increased the privacy and isolation of American households. Our need to leave home for entertainment, goods, or services has been considerably reduced. Air conditioners, for instance, allow us to spend hot, stuffy summer evenings inside our own homes instead of on the front porch or at the local ice cream parlor. Today, with the Internet and home shopping TV networks, a family can purchase all it needs, including groceries and medicine, without ever leaving home. The institution of family has become increasingly self-contained and private.

But the ability to maintain family privacy has always varied along social class lines. In poor households, dwellings are smaller and more crowded than more affluent homes, making privacy more difficult to obtain. Thin walls separating cramped apartments hide few secrets. Mandatory inspections by welfare caseworkers and housing authorities further diminish privacy. And poor families must often use public facilities (health clinics, laundromats, public transportation, and so on) to carry out the day-to-day tasks that wealthier families can carry out privately.

Moreover, the value we place on the well-being of children has come into direct conflict at times with the value of family privacy. At what point should a state agency intervene and violate the privacy of the family to protect the welfare of a child? Does it better serve society's interests to protect family privacy or to protect children from harm?

Parents have never had complete freedom to do as they wish with their children. We're horrified at the thought of a parent beating his or her child to the point of injury or death. But we're equally horrified, it seems, at the thought of the state intruding on parents' right to raise or treat their children as they see fit. In the United States, parents have the legal right to direct the upbringing of their children, to determine the care they receive, and to use physical means to control their children's behavior. From a sociological perspective, injuring children is simply the extreme outcome of the widely practiced and accepted belief that parents have the right to use physical punishment to discipline their children.

Concern with parents' privacy rights is often framed as a freedom of religion issue. Forty-eight states currently allow parents to refuse immunizations for their children on religious grounds; 39 states and the District of Columbia allow parents to use religion as a defense against charges of criminal abuse, endangerment, and neglect if they physically injure their child. Delaware, West Virginia, Arkansas, and Oregon allow defenses on religious grounds in cases where parents kill their children (CHILD, Inc., 2005).

Nevertheless, the government does sometimes violate the privacy of a family when that family's religious or cultural beliefs conflict with the values of the larger society. For instance, in 2005, a Superior Court judge in Indiana issued a divorce decree to prevent the two estranged parents from exposing their 9-year-old child to "non-mainstream religious beliefs and rituals" (Corcoran, 2005, p. 1). The ex-spouses were both followers of Wicca, a pagan religion that emphasizes a balance in nature and respect for the earth. That same year, a Johnson County, Indiana couple was convicted of reckless homicide for refusing to seek medical treatment and instead relying on prayer for their fatally ill newborn daughter. The baby died of sepsis, a blood infection that doctors testified could have been easily cured (Bird, 2005).

Ironically, concern over increases in juvenile violence has led some cities and states to enact laws that make parents more responsible for disciplining their children (Applebome, 1996). For instance, if their child associates with a convicted felon, drug dealer, or members of a street gang, Louisiana parents can be found guilty of "improper supervision of a minor" and fined up to $1,000 and imprisoned for up to 6 months. In 2005, a jury in Ohio determined that the parents of a 17-year-old boy who assaulted a young girl didn't do enough to stop him and were therefore responsible for paying the victim 70% of the damages she was awarded ($7 million) (Coolidge, 2005).

All the cases described here illustrate the profound effects of cultural and political values on the everyday lives of individuals. Situations such as these pit the privacy and autonomy of families against society's institutional responsibility to protect children and create new citizens.

Norms

Norms are culturally defined rules of conduct. They specify what people should do and how they should pursue values. They tell us what is proper or necessary behavior within particular roles, groups, organizations, and institutions. Thousands of norms guide the minor and the grand details of our lives, from the classroom to the boardroom to the bedroom, from how we should act in elevators to how we should address our boss. You can see, then, that norms serve as the fundamental building blocks of social order.

Norms make our interactions with others reasonably predictable. Americans expect that when they extend a hand to another person, that person will grasp it and a brief handshake will follow. They would be shocked if they held out their hand and the other person grabbed it and spit on it or wouldn't let go. In contrast, people in some

(Text continues on page 44)

The Old Ball Game

Douglas Harper

To watch a professional baseball game is to experience the world both as an individual and as a member of a larger social structure. A baseball game offers a good example of how individuals participate in creating social life and, conversely, how social structure shapes our everyday experience. This essay features photographs from several ballparks. They take the perspective of a sociologist rather than a typical spectator or sports photographer.

❖ When we watch a baseball game as fans, we're likely to focus on the interactions of the people on the field, what sociologists call a micro-level of analysis. In this photo several individuals carefully coordinate their actions, hoping to achieve different ends. The umpire, symbol of social control, defines actions as good or bad, successful or unsuccessful. The batter wants to drive the approaching ball into the outfield; the catcher wants the ball in his mitt after it crosses the strike zone. The game of baseball, seen from this perspective, consists of individuals acting on their interpretations of the actions of others. These interpretations require that people agree on the meaning of certain symbols, including words, gestures, and material objects such as uniforms.

❖ This photograph was taken from roughly the same vantage point as the micro-level photo but with a different camera lens. The perspectives created by these lenses may be viewed as metaphors for different sociological perspectives. If the micro-level photo suggests an interactional level of analysis, this one suggests a middle-range level of analysis. Typical units of analysis at this level are statuses, roles, and norms.

Here we can see the coordination of several statuses within the realm of baseball, including first baseman, base runner from the opposing team, first base coach, and two umpires. The roles that these people play in the game—their actions—are aligned with their statuses: The pitcher has the role of throwing the ball to the catcher, the first base coach of guiding the base runner's actions, and so on. The positions of the players are determined by norms, or rules of behavior. Even an argument between an umpire and a player is socially choreographed: Only certain words, gestures, and forms of touch are allowed.

In what sociologists might call a macro-level, structural view of baseball, we would look at the way that various social institutions—such as the economy, government, and the media—influence the way the sport is conducted. It's difficult to observe these large-scale influences, but we can observe the setting of the game and some of the elements that give the game meaning in a larger social context.

For instance, baseball, like other professional sports, is sustained and driven by corporate sponsorship. This influence shows up in the advertisements that plaster scoreboards and fences around the outfield but is especially obvious in the names of stadiums these days. Gone are the days when stadiums were simply named after the team that played there (Tiger Stadium, Astrodome), the location (County Stadium, Cleveland Stadium), features of the local physical landscape (Three Rivers Stadium, Candlestick Park), or influential individuals in the community (Comiskey Park, Forbes Field). Today, stadium names are sold to the highest corporate bidder and are more likely to reflect commercial investments than anything evoking the flavor of baseball (Comerica Park, PacBell Park, Safeco Field, Bank One Ballpark, Network Associates Coliseum, Petco Field, Edison International Field). To some sociologists, this trend indicates a shift from baseball as a micro-level, personal experience to a sport that seems overly impersonal and profit-driven.

❖ Such a conclusion is reinforced by the perception that today's baseball players, in the quest for ever-higher salaries, have lost any sense of team loyalty—a concept that seems quaint today. And it's certainly true that players have always given top priority to their personal financial interests over the organization's. But in general, in the past, a fan could count on a favorite player remaining with the hometown team for years. Today, players come and go so frequently that a team's roster might be virtually unrecognizable from one year to the next. Cal Ripken, Jr., pictured here, was one of the very few exceptions in that he played with the same team, the Baltimore Orioles, for his entire 21-year career.

A macro-level analysis of baseball can also be enhanced by a critical look at the history of professional baseball. Baseball was originally played in a narrow band of cities, such as New York, Pittsburgh, Chicago, and St. Louis. But it soon expanded to both the north and the south, to such cities as Minneapolis, Montreal, Houston, and Tampa, and the season lengthened well into autumn. Because of more extreme weather conditions in these areas, it became difficult to play the game outdoors all season long. The solution was to build many of the stadiums with permanent or retracting roofs and to replace the grass field with plastic carpet. The new parks, built from the mid-1960s through the 1980s, were dual-purpose facilities that often also accommodated football. However, these stadiums have been a failure. Most of them have been torn down and replaced or are in the process of being replaced by single-use facilities that are designed to evoke the more intimate ballparks of the past.

The extension of baseball into regions where it cannot easily be played, and the creation of stadiums to fit both baseball and football, can be seen as an example of something that the 19th-century sociologist Max Weber warned us about: focusing so much on rationality and efficiency that we lose sight of our real goals. It may seem quite practical to build a facility for both baseball and football and to cover a facility to keep out the weather. But the main point of baseball—a pleasurable fan experience—is diminished by these decisions. Similarly, plastic carpet may be more economically rational than grass, but it is ugly and changes the way the game is played.

Baseball began where the seasons invited outside activities from April to October. Because the pace of a baseball game is leisurely, it is a perfect summer event. The extension of major league baseball to more extreme climatological regions (whether it can be played and viewed in the way the game was intended or not) is a clear attempt to transform a leisure activity into an economic enterprise. Major league baseball (as well as other national-level sports) is a huge financial concern. It will likely continue to expand to new regions as long as it can be financially viable, whether this expansion makes sense for the game or for fans.

❖ This is Olympic Stadium, home of the now defunct Montreal Expos. The stadium was originally built for the 1976 Summer Olympics. It has artificial turf and a retractable roof and seats well over 50,000 people. It is considered by many baseball aficionados to be one of the least appealing ballparks in the major leagues. This game, with only a few thousand spectators on hand, was played in early April. At that time of the year, watching a game in an uncovered stadium in Montreal would be an unattractive experience for a fan.

The simple act of watching a baseball game might seem like a highly individual experience, far from the concerns of sociologists, but consider the differences between attending a game in a stadium and viewing the game on television. If we watch the game on television, TV personalities direct us to notice one set of events rather than another. The photographic style used to broadcast the game (especially the close-up) emphasizes the individual players and their accomplishments. We do not get as broad a view of the game experience or even see the way that several players participate on a given play. Because the televised event emphasizes the individual player-as-hero, we often overlook the social context—namely the team—that gives his heroic actions meaning. The home run glorifies the batter and is exciting to witness, but the sacrifice fly may allow a run to score that is just as meaningful to the team.

If we attend a game in person, however, we become actively involved in constructing the "fan experience." We watch carefully to keep track of the players and the progress of the game; perhaps we keep inning-by-inning records, using the arcane symbols of scoring. We may even be able to affect the outcome of the game, through vocally encouraging the home team and actively distracting the visiting team. Indeed, in some ballparks, the fans are given the honorary title of "tenth man" to symbolize their contributions to the team. In short, the actions of all the players, all the other members of the crowd, and all the stadium personnel (hot dog vendors, security guards, announcers, and so on) become part of our experience of the game.

❖ Being part of a collective event also has strong appeal. This photograph shows how thousands upon thousands of people can be drawn to crowd together to take part in an experience. Order is maintained through well-understood expectations and norms. Ironically, this was the last game at Three Rivers Stadium in Pittsburgh, October 2000. It drew a sold-out crowd of 54,000. Fans gathered to say goodbye to a stadium that was still functional but about to be torn down to be replaced with a park resembling the park that Three Rivers replaced in 1970.

❖ Although TV viewers get close-ups and biographical notes about players, they can't experience the thrill of interacting personally with the players. For an hour before the game, fans who can talk their way past the ushers who guard the passageway to the hitting area can watch the players practice and can call greetings and good wishes to their heroes. The players seldom look up as they trot back and forth to the dugout, but sometimes a player will toss a ball to a fan or meander to a designated area where the fan and player can intersect—the end of the dugout—to sign autographs. Note, though, that the early birds can occupy these most desirable seats only temporarily, because they are increasingly owned by corporations and given as favors to business partners.

❖ General disillusionment with the sport, along with hard economic times and security concerns, have forced many teams to try to further enhance the fan experience. Baseball teams now regularly stage "fan friendly" events, such as live music, in an attempt to bolster sagging attendance. Here a fan dances with an even younger fan, on whom the typical barrage of beer advertising is wasted.

Luckily, the sport has a lot going for it. To be a baseball fan is to internalize some more heroic messages about the history of the game. Symbols communicate some of this history.

❖ For Pittsburgh Pirate fans, few if any heroes can compare with Roberto Clemente, who is poised, larger than life, outside the Pirates' stadium.

❖ Inside New York's Yankee Stadium, one of the great old stadiums, the greatest player of all time, Babe Ruth, needs only a photograph and a neon sign to evoke a heroic tradition.

❖ Fans also claim symbols as part of their own identity. Wearing a copy of the uniform of a hero is certainly a common form of fan behavior. But here we see an unusual degree of fan dedication: a tattoo indicating loyalty to the game of baseball itself.

Another important cultural element of the fan experience is the repeated events—called rituals—that define the audience experience in the park. They link the individual with the history of baseball and with all the fans who have attended ballgames before. For example, at Yankee Stadium the groundskeepers groom the infield while marching in unison to the song "YMCA." These rituals help define what it means to be an audience and contribute to the overall experience of the game.

Among the formal rituals of all games are the singing of the National Anthem at the beginning of the game and the "seventh-inning stretch," where all fans stand and rock back and forth while singing "Take Me Out to the Ballgame." Like all rituals, these must be performed correctly. All men are instructed to remove their hats before singing the National Anthem, and everyone must stand. But there is some flexibility in the ritual as well: At Camden Yards, for example, home of the Baltimore Orioles, the crowd yells out a resounding "O" at the beginning of the phrase: "Oh say does that star spangled banner yet wave . . ." It was startling to a visiting fan until I realized that the faithful were calling out for their home team, the Orioles.

❖ In the 1970s fans began a strange ritual called "the wave." To start a wave, a group of fans stand simultaneously and throw their hands into the air. If they are successful, the wave moves around the stadium as adjoining sections take their turn. One watches the wave move around the stadium and then engulf one's own section. Here young girls are trying unsuccessfully to initiate a wave.

❖ A more compelling ritual is the singing of "Take Me Out to the Ballgame" during the seventh-inning stretch. Projecting the words of the song onto a screen, as at Camden Yards, home of the Baltimore Orioles, gives the ritual an "official" imprint that encourages participation.

societies commonly embrace or kiss each other's cheek as a form of greeting, even when involved in a formal business relationship. A hearty handshake in those societies may be interpreted as an insult. In Thailand, people greet each other by placing the palms of their hands together in front of their bodies and slightly bowing their heads. This greeting is governed by strict norms. Slight differences in the placement of one's hands reflect the social position of the other person—the higher the hands, the higher the position of the person being greeted. Norms like these make it easier to "live with others" in a relatively harmonious way (see Chapter 4).

Social Structure in Global Context

A discussion of social structure would not be complete without acknowledging the fact that statuses, roles, groups, organizations, social institutions, and culture are sometimes influenced by broad societal and historical forces in today's world. One broad societal force with deep implications for contemporary society is **globalization**, the process through which people's lives all around the world become increasingly interconnected—economically, politically, environmentally, and culturally (see Chapter 9 for more detail).

For instance, international financial institutions and foreign governments often provide money to support the building of hydroelectric dams in poor countries. According to the World Commission on Dams, 1,600 such dams in 40 countries were under construction in 2000 (Bald, 2000). These projects are meant to strengthen societies by providing additional energy sources in areas where power is dangerously deficient. However, they frequently transform individual lives, social institutions, and indigenous cultures in a negative way. A dam built along the Moon River in Thailand destroyed forests that for centuries were villagers' free source of food, firewood, and medicinal herbs. With the flooding created behind the dam, local farmers not only lost their farmland but also lost the value of their knowledge of farming methods that had developed over centuries to adapt to the ebb and flow of the river. A multi-dam project along the Narmada River in India displaced over 200,000 people and led to violent protests there. The Manantali Dam in Mali has destroyed the livelihood of downstream farmers and has resulted in the spread of waterborne diseases (Fountain, 2005). None of these dams would have been built without the funding and political clout of global financial organizations and foreign corporations.

Cultures have rarely been completely isolated from outside influence, because throughout human history people have been moving from one place to another, spreading goods and ideas. What is different today, though, is the speed and scope of these changes. Several decades ago, overnight mail service and direct long-distance telephone dialing increased the velocity of cross-national interaction. Advances in transportation technology have made international trade more cost-effective and international travel more accessible to ordinary citizens. And recently the Internet has given people around the world instantaneous access to the cultural artifacts and ideals of other societies. Through search engines like *Google, Yahoo,* and *MSN Search,* children in Beijing, Beirut, or Baltimore can easily and immediately mine unlimited amounts of the same information on every imaginable topic.

Although some aspects of regional culture are likely to survive, some sociologists believe that the outcome of today's globalization will be a "global culture," where traditional geographic, economic, political, and cultural boundaries gradually fade away:

> Once I started looking for them, these moments were everywhere: That I should be sitting in a coffee shop in London drinking Italian espresso served by an Algerian waiter to the strains of the Beach Boys singing "I wish they all could be California girls. . . ." Today we are in the throes of a worldwide reformation of cultures, a tectonic shift of habits and dreams called . . . "globalization." (Zwingle, 1999, p. 12)

Clearly, societies are more interdependent than ever, and that interdependence matters for individuals around the world. Sometimes the effects are positive. Pharmaceutical breakthroughs in the United States or Europe, for instance, can save lives around the world. Globalization gives us a chance to learn about other societies and learn from them. Other times, however, global influence can have disastrous consequences. Many of today's most pressing societal problems—widespread environmental devastation, large- and small-scale wars, economic crises, viral epidemics, and so on—are a function of globalization. Closer to home, the establishment of a toy factory in Southeast Asia or a clothing factory in Mexico may mean the loss of hundreds of manufacturing jobs in Kentucky or California.

In short, it is becoming increasingly difficult, if not impossible, to consider ourselves members of a single society unaffected by other societies. It's like sitting in the nonsmoking section of a restaurant that allows smoking elsewhere. We may want to believe that the barriers in the restaurant set us apart and protect us from unhealthful air. But the smoke knows no such boundaries and inevitably some of it will reach our lungs. The point is that all of us are simultaneously members of our own society and citizens of a world community.

Three Perspectives on Social Order

The question of what holds all these elements of society together and how they combine to create social order has concerned sociologists for decades. Sociologists have three major intellectual orientations that they often use to address this question: the structural-functionalist perspective, the conflict perspective, and symbolic interactionism (see Exhibit 2.1 on page 49). Each of these perspectives has its advantages and shortcomings. Each is helpful in answering particular types of questions. For instance, structural-functionalism is useful in showing us how and why large, macro-level structures, such as organizations and institutions, develop and persist. The conflict perspective sheds light on the various sources of social inequality that exist in this and other societies. And symbolic interactionism is helpful in explaining how individuals construct meaning to make sense out of their social surroundings. At times the perspectives complement one another; at other times, they contradict one another.

Throughout the remaining chapters of this book, I will periodically return to these three perspectives—as well as several other specific perspectives—to apply them to specific social phenomena, experiences, and events.

The Structural-Functionalist Perspective

According to sociologists Talcott Parsons and Neil Smelser (1956), two theorists typically associated with the **structural-functionalist perspective**, a society is a complex system composed of various parts, much like a living organism. Just as the heart, lungs, and liver work together to keep an animal alive, so, too, do all the elements of a society's structure work together to keep society alive.

Social institutions play a key role in keeping a society stable. All societies require certain things to survive. They must ensure that the goods and services people need are produced and distributed; they must provide ways of dealing with conflicts between individuals, groups, and organizations; they must provide ways to ensure that individuals are made a part of the existing culture.

Institutions allow societies to attain their goals, adapt to a changing environment, reduce tension, and recruit individuals into statuses and roles. Economic institutions, for instance, allow adaptation to dwindling supplies of natural resources or to competition from other societies. The family controls and regulates reproduction. Likewise, educational institutions train people for the future statuses they will have to fill to keep society going. Religions help maintain the existence of society by reaffirming people's values and maintaining social ties among people (Durkheim, 1915/1954).

Sociologist Robert Merton (1957) distinguishes between manifest and latent functions of social institutions. **Manifest functions** are the intended, obvious consequences of activities designed to help some part of the social system. For instance, the manifest function of going to college is to get an education and acquire the credentials necessary to establish a career. **Latent functions** are the *unintended,* sometimes unrecognized, consequences of actions that coincidentally help the system. The latent function of going to college is to meet people and establish close, enduring friendships. In addition, college informally teaches students how to live on their own, away from their parents. It also provides important lessons in negotiating the intricacies of large bureaucracies—registering for classes, filling out forms, learning important school policies—so that students figure out how to "get things done" in an organization. These latent lessons will certainly help students who enter the equally large and bureaucratic world of work after they graduate (Galles, 1989).

From the structural-functionalist perspective, if an aspect of social life does not contribute to society's survival—that is, if it is *dys*functional—it will eventually disappear. Things that persist, even if they seem to be disruptive, must persist because they contribute somehow to the survival of society (Durkheim, 1915/1954). Take prostitution, for example. A practice so widely condemned and punished would appear to be dysfunctional for society. But prostitution has existed since human civilization began. Some structural-functionalists suggest that prostitution satisfies sexual needs that may not be met through more socially acceptable means, such as marriage. Customers can have their physical desires satisfied without having to establish the sort of emotional attachment to another person that would destroy a preexisting marriage, harm the institution of the family, and ultimately threaten the entire society (K. Davis, 1937).

Structural-functionalism was the dominant theoretical tradition in sociology for most of the 20th century, and it still shapes sociological thinking to a certain degree today. But it has been criticized for accepting existing social arrangements without examining how they might exploit or otherwise disadvantage certain groups or individuals within the society.

The Conflict Perspective

The **conflict perspective** addresses the deficiencies of structural-functionalism by viewing the structure of society as a source of inequality, which always benefits some groups at the expense of other groups. Conflict sociologists are likely to see society not in terms of stability and acceptance but in terms of conflict and struggle. They focus not on how all the elements of society contribute to its smooth operation and continued existence but on how these elements promote divisions and inequalities. Social order arises not from the societal pursuit of harmony but from dominance and coercion. The family, government, religion, and other institutions foster and legitimate the power and privilege of some individuals or groups at the expense of others.

Karl Marx, perhaps the most famous scholar associated with the conflict perspective, focused exclusively on economic arrangements. He argued that all human societies are structured around the production of goods that people need to live. The individuals or groups who control the means of production—land in an agricultural society, factories in an industrial society, computer networks and information in a postindustrial society—have the power to create and maintain social institutions that serve their interests. Hence, economic, political, and educational systems in a modern society support the interests of those who control the wealth (see Chapter 10).

Marx believed that when resources are limited or scarce, conflict between the "haves" and the "have-nots" is inevitable and creates a situation in which those in power must enforce social order. He said this conflict is not caused by greedy, exploitative individuals; rather, it is a by-product of a system in which those who benefit from inequality are motivated to act in ways that maintain it.

Contemporary conflict sociologists are interested in various sources of conflict and inequality. One version of the conflict perspective that has become particularly popular among sociologists in the last several decades is the **feminist perspective**. Feminist sociologists focus on gender as the most important source of conflict and inequality in social life. Compared with men, women in nearly every contemporary society have less power, influence, and opportunity. In families, especially in industrialized societies, women have traditionally been encouraged to perform unpaid household labor and child care duties whereas men have been free to devote their energy and attention to earning money and power in the economic marketplace. Women's lower wages when they do work outside the home are often justified by the assumption that their paid labor is secondary to that of their husbands. But as women in many societies seek equality in education, politics, career, marriage, and other areas of social life, their activities inevitably affect social institutions (see Chapter 12 for more details). The feminist perspective helps us understand the difficulties men and women face in their everyday lives as they experience the changes taking place in society.

Because the conflict perspective focuses so much on conflict, it tends to downplay or overlook the elements of society that different groups and individuals share.

In addition, its emphasis on inequality has led some critics to argue that it is a perspective motivated by a particular political agenda and not the objective pursuit of knowledge.

Symbolic Interactionism

The structural-functionalist and the conflict perspectives differ in their assumptions about the nature of society, yet both analyze society mostly at the *macro-* or structural level, focusing on societal patterns and the consequences they produce. In contrast, **symbolic interactionism** attempts to understand society and social structure through an examination of the *micro*-level, personal, day-to-day interactions of people as individuals, pairs, or groups.

These forms of interaction take place within a world of symbolic communication. A **symbol** is something used to represent or stand for something else (Charon, 1998). It can be a physical object (like an engagement ring standing for betrothal), a characteristic or property of objects (like the pink color of a triangle standing for gay rights), a gesture (like a thumb pointed up standing for "everything's ok"), or a word (like the letters *d-o-g* standing for a particular type of household pet).

Symbols are created, modified, and used by people through their interactions with others. We concoct them and come to agree on what they should stand for. Our lives depend on such agreement. Imagine how chaotic automobile travel would be, for example, if we didn't all agree that green stands for go and red stands for stop.

Symbols don't bear any necessary connection to nature. Rather, they're arbitrary human creations. There's nothing in the natural properties of "greenness" that automatically determines that it should stand for "go." We could have decided long ago that purple meant go. It wouldn't have mattered as long as we all learned and understood this symbol.

Most human behavior is determined not by the objective facts of a given situation but by the symbolic meanings people attach to the facts (Weber, 1947). When we interact with others, we constantly attempt to interpret what they mean and what they're up to. A gentle pat on the shoulder symbolizes one thing if it comes from someone with whom you are romantically involved but something quite different if it comes from your mother or your boss.

Society, therefore, is not a structure that exists independent of human action. It is "socially constructed," defined by people's interactions. It emerges from the countless symbolic interactions that occur each day between individuals. Each time I refer to "U.S. society," "the school system," "the global economy," "the threat of terrorism," or "the Newman family" in my casual conversations with others, I am doing my part to reinforce the notion that these are real things. By examining how and why we interact with others, symbolic interactionism reveals how the everyday experiences of people help to construct and maintain social institutions and, ultimately, society itself.

This perspective reminds us that for all its structural elements, society is, in the end, people interacting with one another. But by highlighting these micro-level experiences, symbolic interactionism runs the risk of ignoring larger social patterns and structures that create the influential historical, institutional, and cultural settings for people's everyday interactions.

Exhibit 2.1   Sociological Perspectives at a Glance

Sociological Perspective	Key Concepts	Main Assumption
Structural-Functionalist Perspective	Manifest and latent functions Dysfunctions Social stability	Social institutions are structured to maintain stability and order in society.
Conflict Perspective	Power Inequality Conflict Dominance	The various institutions in society promote inequality and conflict among groups of people.
Symbolic Interactionist Perspective	Symbolic communication Social interaction Subjective meaning	Society is structured and maintained through everyday interactions and people's subjective definitions of their worlds.

Conclusion

Living with others, within a social structure, influences many aspects of our everyday lives. But we must be cautious not to overstate the case. Although the fundamental elements of society are not merely the direct expressions of the personalities of individuals, we must also remember that people are more than "robots programmed by social structure" (Swanson, 1992).

The lesson I hope you take from this chapter—and, in fact, from this book—is that the relationship between the individual and society is reciprocal. One cannot be understood without accounting for the other. Yes, this thing we call "society" touches our lives in intimate, important, and sometimes not altogether obvious ways. And yes, this influence is often beyond our immediate control. But society is not simply a "forbidding prison" that mechanically determines who we are and what we do (P. L. Berger, 1963). We as individuals can affect the very social structure that affects us. We can modify role expectations, change norms, create or destroy organizations, revolutionize institutions, and even alter the path of world history.

◆

YOUR TURN

Alcohol occupies an important but problematic place in many societies. We decry its evils, yet we are encouraged to turn to it in times of leisure, celebration, despair, disappointment, anger, and worry.

Behavior "under the influence" is a biological consequence of the presence of alcohol in the body. Among the physical effects are vomiting, hangovers, and liver damage. When a person's blood alcohol level reaches a certain point, that person will have trouble walking and talking; at a higher level he or she will pass out.

But is the social behavior we see in drunken people reducible to a chemical reaction in the body? The traditional explanation for drunken behavior is that the chemical properties of alcohol do something to the brain that reduces inhibitions. If this were true, though, drunken behavior would look the same everywhere. The fact is, social behavior under the influence of alcohol can vary from culture to culture. The way people handle themselves when drunk "is determined not by alcohol's toxic assault on the seat of moral judgment, conscience, or the like, but by what their society makes of and imparts to them concerning the state of drunkenness" (MacAndrew & Edgerton, 1969, p. 165).

Ask people who grew up in a culture different from yours (for example, students who grew up in a different country or in a different socioeconomic class or geographic region) how people behaved when drunk. Do these behaviors differ from those you've observed? Have them describe their first drunken experience. Are there similarities or differences in how people are introduced to alcohol?

Also ask the same questions of people from different sexes, races, ethnic groups, and ages. Are there variations in the "drunken experience" within a society? What do these differences illustrate about the norms and values of these different groups? You might also ask some young children to describe how drunk people act. Are there any similarities in the images they have of drunkenness? Do you consider their ideas about drunkenness accurate? Where do you think their ideas about alcohol come from?

Use the results of these interviews to explain the role of social and societal influence on people's personal lives. Do you think your conclusions can be expanded to other private phenomena, such as sexual activity or religious experiences? Why or why not?

CHAPTER HIGHLIGHTS

♦ Although society exists as an objective fact, it is also created, reaffirmed, and altered through the day-to-day interactions of the very people it influences and controls.

♦ Humans are social beings. We look to others to help define and interpret particular situations. Other people can influence what we see, feel, think, and do.

♦ Society consists of socially recognizable combinations of individuals—relationships, groups, and organizations—as well as the products of human action—statuses, roles, culture, institutions, and broad societal forces such as globalization.

♦ There are three major sociological perspectives. The structural-functionalist perspective focuses on the way various parts of society are structured and interrelated to maintain stability and order. The conflict perspective emphasizes how the various elements of society promote inequality and conflict among groups of people. Symbolic interactionism seeks to understand society and social structure through the interactions of people and the ways in which they subjectively define their worlds.

KEY TERMS

achieved status Social position acquired through our own efforts or accomplishments or taken on voluntarily

ascribed status Social position acquired at birth or taken on involuntarily later in life

coalition Subgroup of a triad, formed when two members unite against the third member

conflict perspective Theoretical perspective that views the structure of society as a source of inequality, which always benefits some groups at the expense of other groups

culture Language, values, beliefs, rules, behaviors, and artifacts that characterize a society

dyad Group consisting of two people

feminist perspective Theoretical perspective that focuses on gender as the most important source of conflict and inequality in social life

globalization Process through which people's lives all around the world become economically, politically, environmentally, and culturally interconnected

group Set of people who interact more or less regularly and who are conscious of their identity as a unit

latent function Unintended, unrecognized consequences of activities that help some part of the social system

manifest function Intended, obvious consequences of activities designed to help some part of the social system

norm Culturally defined standard or rule of conduct

organization Large, complex network of positions, created for a specific purpose and characterized by a hierarchical division of labor

primary group Collection of individuals who are together over a relatively long period, whose members have direct contact with and feel emotional attachment to one another

role Set of expectations—rights, obligations, behaviors, duties—associated with a particular status

role conflict Frustration people feel when the demands of one role they are expected to fulfill clash with the demands of another role

secondary group Relatively impersonal collection of individuals that is established to perform a specific task

social institution Stable set of roles, statuses, groups, and organizations—such as the institution of education, family, politics, religion, health care, or the economy—that provides a foundation for behavior in some major area of social life

society Population of people living in the same geographic area who share a culture and a common identity and whose members fall under the same political authority

status Any named social position that people can occupy

structural-functionalist perspective Theoretical perspective that posits that social institutions are structured to maintain stability and order in society

symbol Something used to represent or stand for something else

symbolic interactionism Theoretical perspective that explains society and social structure through an examination of the *micro*-level, personal, day-to-day exchanges of people as individuals, pairs, or groups

triad Group consisting of three people

value Standard of judgment by which people decide on desirable goals and outcomes

❖

STUDY SITE ON THE WEB

Don't forget the interactive quizzes and other learning aids at www.pineforge.com/newman6study. In the Resources File for this chapter, you'll also find more on seeing and thinking sociologically, including:

Social Researchers at Work

- ◆ Solomon Asch: Social Pressures and Perception
- ◆ Bibb Latane and John Darley: Why Don't People Help?
- ◆ Philip Zimbardo: The Psychology of Imprisonment

Micro-Macro Connection

- ◆ Family Care for Elderly Parents

PART II

The Construction of Self and Society

Part II examines the basic architecture of individual identities and of society: how reality and truth are constructed; how social order is created and maintained; how culture and history influence our personal experiences; how societal values, ideals, and norms are instilled; and how we acquire our sense of self. The tactical and strategic ways in which we present images of ourselves to others are also addressed. You will see how we form relationships and interact within small, intimate groups. The section closes with a look at how we define "acceptable" behavior and how we respond to those who "break the rules."

Building Reality
The Social Construction of Knowledge

The year was 1897. Eight-year-old Virginia O'Hanlon became upset when her friends told her that there was no Santa Claus. Her father encouraged her to write a letter to the *New York Sun* to find out the truth. The editor's reply—which included the now famous phrase "Yes, Virginia, there is a Santa Claus!"—has become a classic piece of American folklore. "Nobody sees Santa Claus," the editor wrote, "but that is no sign that there is no Santa Claus. The most real things in the world are those that neither children nor men [sic] can see" ("Is There a Santa Claus?" 1897).

In his book *Encounters with the Archdruid,* John McPhee (1971) examines the life and ideas of David Brower, who was one of the most successful and energetic environmentalists in the United States. McPhee recalls a lecture in which Brower claimed that the United States has 6% of the world's population and uses 60% of the world's resources and that only 1% of Americans use 60% of those resources. Afterward, McPhee asked Brower where he got these interesting statistics:

> Brower said the figures had been worked out in the head of a friend of his from data assembled "to the best of his recollection." . . . [He] assured me that figures in themselves are merely indices. *What matters is that they feel right* [emphasis added]. Brower feels things. (p. 86)

What do these two very different examples have in common? Both reflect the fickle nature of "truth" and "reality." Young Virginia was encouraged to believe in the reality of something she could and would never perceive with her senses. She certainly learned a different sort of truth about Santa Claus when she got older, but the editor urged the young Virginia to take on faith that Santa Claus, or at least the idea of Santa Claus, exists despite the lack of objective proof. That sort of advice persists. A survey of 200 child psychologists around the United States found that 91% of them advised parents not to tell the truth when their young children asked about the existence of Santa Claus (cited in Stryker, 1997).

Likewise, David Brower is urging people to believe in something that doesn't need to be seen. What's important is that the information "feels right," that it helps one's cause even if it is not based on hard evidence.

Such precarious uses of truth may appear foolish or deceitful. Yet much of our everyday knowledge is based on accepting as real the existence of things that can't be seen, touched, or proved—"the world taken-for-granted" (P. L. Berger, 1963, p. 147). Like Virginia, we learn to accept the existence of things such as electrons, the ozone layer, black holes in the universe, love, and God, even though we cannot see them. And like David Brower, we learn to believe and use facts and figures provided by "experts" as long as they sound right or support our interests.

How do we come to know what we know? How do we learn what is real and what isn't? In this chapter, I examine how sociologists discover truths about human life. But to provide the appropriate context, I must first present a sociological perspective on the nature of reality. How do individuals construct their realities? How do societal forces influence the process?

Understanding the Social Construction of Reality

In Chapter 2, I noted that the elements of society are human creations that provide structure to our everyday lives. They also give us a distinctive lens through which we perceive the world. For example, because of their different statuses and their respective occupational training, an architect, a real estate agent, a police officer, and a firefighter can each look at the same building and see very different things: "a beautiful example of Victorian architecture," "a moderately priced fixer-upper," "a target of opportunity for a thief," or "a fire hazard." Mark Twain often wrote about how the Mississippi River—a waterway he saw every day as a child—looked different after he became a riverboat pilot. What he once saw as a place for recreation and relaxation, he later saw for its treacherous currents, eddies, and other potential dangers.

What we know to be true or real is always a product of the culture and historical period in which we exist. It takes an exercise of the sociological imagination, however, to see that what we ourselves "know" to be true today—the laws of nature, the causes and treatments of certain diseases, and so forth—may not be true for everyone everywhere or may be replaced by different truths tomorrow (Babbie, 1986). For example, in some cultures the existence of spirits, witches, and demons is a taken-for-granted part of everyday reality that others might easily dismiss as fanciful. On the other side of the coin, the Western faith in the curative powers of little pills—without the intervention of spiritual forces—might seem far-fetched and naïve to people living in cultures where illness and health are assumed to have supernatural causes.

Ideas about reality also change over time. In 1900 a doctor might have told a patient with asthma to go to the local tobacconist for a cigarette; people with colds may have been told to inhale formaldehyde. Tuberculosis was treated with strychnine; diabetics received a dose of arsenic (Zuger, 1999). Early 20th-century child development experts offered parents such advice as "Kissing a baby after it's eaten will likely cause vomiting" or "Never let a baby sit on your lap" (Cohen, 2003). In the 1950s, obstetricians encouraged pregnant women to have a martini or glass of wine each night to calm their nerves. In the 1960s, doctors believed that alcohol prevented premature labor; women arriving at the hospital in labor were often handed vodka or even given alcohol intravenously (Hoffman, 2005).

In 2003, a government-appointed committee of medical experts lowered the definition of what constitutes normal blood pressure. This sudden redefinition meant that 45 million Americans—who were once normal—now weren't normal ("'Normal' Blood Pressure," 2003). Likewise, in 2004 federal health officials in the United States lowered the threshold level for harmful cholesterol (Kolata, 2004a). Millions of people who went to bed one night thinking that their cholesterol was in the "healthy" range woke up the next day with cholesterol levels that are now considered "unhealthy" and "risky." According to one researcher, about a third of major medical studies are eventually contradicted by further research (Ioannidis, 2005). Quite possibly people 100 years from now will look back at the beginning of the 21st century and regard some of our taken-for-granted truths as mistaken, misguided, or downright laughable.

The process through which facts, knowledge, truth, and so on are discovered, made known, reaffirmed, and altered by the members of a society is called the **social construction of reality** (P. L. Berger & Luckmann, 1966). This concept is based on the simple assumption that knowledge is a human creation. Ironically, most of us live our lives from a different assumption—that an objective reality exists, independent of us, and is accessible through our senses. We are quite sure trees and tables and trucks don't exist simply in our imagination. We assume this reality is shared by others and can be taken for granted as reality (Lindesmith, Strauss, & Denzin, 1991).

At times, however, what we define as real seems to have nothing to do with what our senses tell us is real. Picture a 5-year-old child who wakes up in the middle of the night screaming that monsters are under her bed. Her parents comfort her by saying, "There aren't any monsters. You had a nightmare. It's just your imagination." The next day the child comes down with the flu and wants to know why she is sick. The parents respond by saying,

> "You've caught a virus, a bug."
>
> "A bug? You mean like an ant or a beetle?"
>
> "No. It's the sort of bug you can't see—but it's there."

Granted, viruses can be seen and verified with the proper equipment, but without access to such equipment the child has to take the parents' word for it that viruses are real. In fact, most of us accept the reality of viruses without ever having seen them for ourselves. The child learns to accept the authoritative claims of her parents that something that was "seen" (the nightmare monster) is not real, although something that was not seen (the virus) is real.

Hence, reality often turns out to be more a matter of agreement than something inherent in the natural world. Sociologists, particularly those working from the conflict perspective and symbolic interactionism, strive to explain the social construction of reality in terms of both its causes and its consequences. Their insights help explain many of the phenomena that influence our daily lives.

Laying the Foundation: The Bases of Reality

Think of society as a building constructed by the people who live and work in it. The building's foundation, its underlying reality, determines its basic shape and dimensions. And the foundation is what makes that building solid and helps it stand up through time and weather. For students of architecture as well as sociology, the first thing to understand is the way the foundation is prepared.

Symbolic interactionism encourages us to see that people's actions toward one another and interpretations of situations are based on their definitions of reality, which are in turn learned from interactions with those around them. What we know to be real we share with other members of our culture. Imagine how difficult it would be to believe in something no one else around you thought existed. Psychiatrists use such terms as *hallucination* and *delusion* to describe things experienced by people who see, hear, or believe things others don't.

The social construction of reality is a process by which human-created ideas become so firmly accepted that to deny them is to deny common sense. Of course, some features of reality are grounded in physical evidence—fire is hot, sharp things hurt. But other features of reality are often based not on sensory experiences but on such forces as culture and language, self-fulfilling prophecies, and faith.

Culture and Language

As I mentioned in Chapter 2, we live in a symbolic world and interact chiefly through symbolic communication—that is, through language. Language gives meaning to the people, objects, events, and ideas of our lives. In fact, language reflects and often determines our reality (Sapir, 1949; Whorf, 1956). Thus language is a key tool in the construction of society.

Consider, for instance, the difference between "spit" (mouth moisture located outside the mouth) and "saliva" (mouth moisture located inside the mouth). In terms of their chemical properties, these substances are identical. Yet everybody knows we define them and treat them quite differently. We are perfectly willing to swallow our own saliva, and we probably swallow gallons of the stuff during the course of a day. But once it leaves our mouths—even if only for a second or two—it becomes something distasteful, even disgusting, to ingest (Brouillette & Turner, 1992). Such a reaction shows that the act of "swallowing saliva" has been socially transformed into the act of "drinking spit." The socially constructed reality is that these two substances are socially and linguistically distinct (even though they're chemically identical), so much so that even the thought of treating one as the other can make us physically sick.

Within a culture, words evolve to reflect the phenomena that have practical significance. The Solomon Islanders have nine distinct words for "coconut," each specifying an important stage of growth, but they have only one word for all the meals of the day (M. M. Lewis, 1948). The Aleuts of northern Canada have 33 words for "snow" that allow them to distinguish differences in texture, temperature, weight, load-carrying capacity, and the speed at which a sled can run on its surface (E. T. Hiller, 1933). The Hanunóo people of the Philippines have different names for 92 varieties of rice, allowing them to make distinctions all but invisible to English speakers, who lump all such grains under a single word: *rice* (Thomson, 2000). Yet a traditional Hanunóo coming to this country would be hard-pressed to see the distinction between the vehicles called *Ford* and *Toyota* or *sedan* and *station wagon*.

Language is such a powerful filter that it can even influence sensory perception. All human beings with normal eyesight see the same spectrum of colors because all colors exist in the physical world. Color consists of visible wavelengths that blend imperceptibly into one another (Farb, 1983). No sharp breaks in the color spectrum distinguish, say, red from orange. But when Americans look at a rainbow they see six different colors: red, orange, yellow, green, blue, and purple. Not everyone in the world sees those same colors, though. As Exhibit 3.1 shows, the Shona of Zimbabwe divide the spectrum into three colors and the Bassa of Liberia have only two color categories (Gleason, 1961). These basic categories provide convenient labels from which people of these cultures can describe variants of color that matter in their lives. When a Shona says *citema*, others know immediately that she is referring to a color we would consider either green or blue. For the Bassa, purple, blue, and green are different shades of *ziza*, just as aquamarine and Navy are different shades of blue in English.

Exhibit 3.1   Cross-Cultural Differences in Color Terms

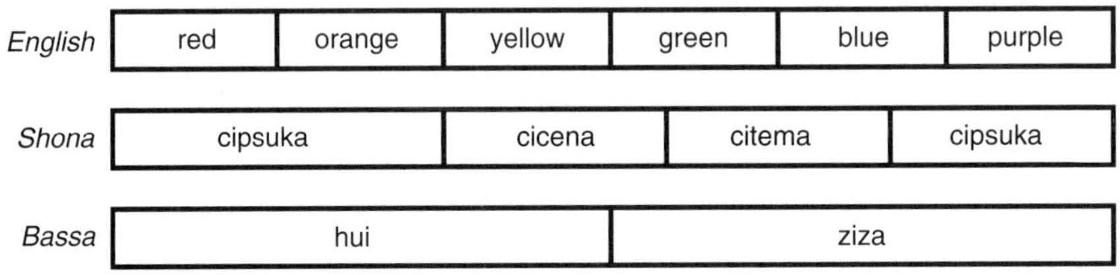

English	red	orange	yellow	green	blue	purple
Shona	cipsuka		cicena		citema	cipsuka
Bassa	hui			ziza		

In addition to affecting perceptions of reality, language reinforces prevailing ideas and suppresses conflicting ideas about the world (Sapir, 1929). In a highly specialized market economy such as the United States, for example, the ability to distinguish linguistically between "real" work and "volunteer" work allows us to telegraph our attitudes about a person's worth to society. In small, agricultural societies, where all people typically perform tasks to provide the basic necessities and to ensure the survival of their tight-knit community, work is work whether you're paid to do it or not.

Language can pack an enormous emotional wallop. Words can make us happy, sad, disgusted, angry, or even incite us to violence. Racial, ethnic, sexual, or religious slurs can be particularly volatile. Among heterosexual adolescents, for example, homophobic name-calling (*queer, fag, dyke*) is one of the most common modes of bullying and coercion in school (Thurlow, 2001). The word *nigger* has been called the "nuclear bomb" of racial epithets. In 2004, a white public safety commissioner in Minnesota was forced to resign after admitting that he had used the word once 12 years earlier in a court deposition (B. Williams, 2004).

Within a culture, certain professions or groups sometimes develop a distinctive language, known as *jargon,* which allows members of the group to communicate with one another clearly and quickly. Surfers, snowboarders, and techies each have a specialized vocabulary (not understandable to most outsiders) through which they can efficiently convey to others information about wave quality, snow conditions, or the latest innovations in microprocessors. Teenagers must keep up with a constantly evolving vocabulary to avoid falling out of favor with their peers. At the same time, jargon can sometimes create boundaries and therefore mystify and conceal meaning from outsiders (Farb, 1983). For instance, by using esoteric medical terminology when discussing a case in front of a patient, two physicians define who is and who isn't a member of their group, reinforce their image as highly trained experts, and keep the patient from interfering too much in their decision making.

Language is sometimes used to purposely deceive as well. A *euphemism* is an inoffensive expression substituted for one that might be offensive. On the surface, such terms are used in the interests of politeness and good taste, such as saying "perspiration" instead of "sweat" or "no longer with us" instead of "dead." However, euphemisms also shape perceptions. Political regimes routinely use them to cover up, distort, or frame their actions in a more positive light. Here are a few examples of euphemisms, followed by their real meanings:

- Pre-owned—used
- Seasoned—old
- Underachiever—failing student
- Inventory shrinkage—theft
- Ethnic cleansing—deportation and massacre of the people of one culture by those of another culture
- Economically nonaffluent—poor
- Biological changes over time—evolution
- Revenue enhancement—tax increase
- Urban camper—homeless person
- Postconsumer waste material—garbage
- Negative pay raise—pay cut
- Deselected, involuntarily separated, downsized, nonretained, given a career change opportunity, vocationally relocated, streamlined, or dehired—fired

In sum, words help frame or structure social reality and give it meaning. Language also provides people with a cultural and group identity. If you've ever spent a significant amount of time in a foreign country or even moved to a new school, you know you cannot be a fully participating member of a group or a culture until you share its language.

Micro-Macro Connection
The Language of War

The governmental or political use of language illustrates how words can determine the course of people's everyday lives both at home and abroad. We all know what the word *war* means. It's when two opposing forces wage battle against one another, either until one side surrenders or both agree to a truce. The vocabulary of war is vast, containing words such as *troops, regiments, ammunition, artillery, innocents* and *enemies, heroes, battles, casualties,* and so forth. Wars usually begin with some sort of declaration. In wartime, there is good and evil, us and them. The language of war contains euphemisms too, such as "collateral damage" (civilian deaths during military combat) and "friendly fire" (accidental shooting at fellow soldiers, not the enemy).

Once a situation is framed as a "war," people's lives are subjected to a different set of rules and expectations. "War" rallies people around their collective national identity and a common objective, creating obligatory expressions of patriotism and a willingness to fight and make sacrifices (Redstone, 2003). The interpretation of people's behavior dramatically changes as well. For example, some characterized the atrocities that occurred during the conflict in Bosnia-Herzegovina in the 1990s as the normal consequences of war. However,

> Is wide-scale sexual violence, including the rape of women and the forced oral castration of men, neighbors burning down their neighbors' homes, the murder and targeting for murder of civilians—men and women, children, the elderly, and infirm—"normal" simply because it takes place within the context of something we call "war"? (Wilmer, 2002, p. 60)

Immediately after the attacks of September 11, 2001, President Bush unofficially declared a "war" on terrorism (which the dictionary defines as a group of actions that create an atmosphere of threat or violence) that continues to this day. But the administration later opted for the term "War on Terror" rather than "War on Terrorism," evoking both violent actions of terrorists and the fear they're trying to create:

> "The war on terror" . . . suggests a campaign aimed not at human adversaries but at a pervasive social plague. At its most abstract, terror comes to seem as persistent and inexplicable as evil itself, without raising any inconvenient theological qualms. And in fact, the White House's use of "evil" has declined by 80 percent over the same period that its use of "terror" has been increasing. (Nunberg, 2004, p. 7)

Whether this is a war on terror or on terrorism, it is—in the traditional sense of the word—a linguistically impossible war. This war has no geographically or nationally identifiable enemy and no achievable end. Technically, a nation can no more declare war on "terror" or "terrorism" than it can declare a war on guns or bombs or drunk driving. In 2005, the administration shifted its language and began testing a new slogan, "a global struggle against violent extremism," in an attempt to convey the impression that the war is as much an ideological battle as it is a military mission (Schmitt & Shanker, 2005).

Whether the enemy is "terror," "terrorism," or "violent extremism," invoking the vocabulary of war has some practical advantages—among them, justifying actions that would not be acceptable in any other context. By continually using wartime terms and expressions, the administration framed the expansion of government powers and the limitation of civil liberties as steps we need to take to protect freedom, bring "enemies" and "evildoers" to justice, and avoid another catastrophe. Consider some of the steps taken since September 11 that directly challenge long-standing protections guaranteed by the U.S. Constitution and federal legislation ("It Can't Happen Here," 2002; Jackman & Eggen, 2002; National Public Radio, 2005a):

♦ Law enforcement officials have broader power to use wire tapping and Internet surveillance techniques to gather information about citizens.
♦ Noncitizens can be detained indefinitely on minor visa violations.
♦ The FBI can demand access to sensitive business records without a court order or demonstration that a crime has been committed.
♦ Law enforcement officials can monitor communications between lawyers and their clients.
♦ The U.S. attorney general can order a secret search of a U.S. citizen's home and, based on the information discovered, secretly declare him or her an "enemy combatant." Enemy combatants can be investigated, jailed indefinitely, interrogated without legal representation, tried, punished, or deported by a military tribunal.

And, of course, the vocabulary of war became the justification for invading two countries, Afghanistan and Iraq, though we're technically not "at war" with either country.

Governments must also try to control language during wartime. In the spring of 2004, we all saw the horrible pictures of Iraqi prisoners being mistreated by American soldiers at the Abu Ghraib prison. Some were shown being attacked by dogs; others were stripped naked and forced to simulate sexual acts to the laughter of their American captors; still others were hooded and attached to electrical wires. The ensuing battle over words was as heated as the battle to determine criminal responsibility for these acts. The International Committee of the Red Cross charged that the treatment of these prisoners as well as suspected terrorists detained at the U.S. Marine base in Guantánamo Bay, Cuba, was "tantamount to torture" (Lewis, 2004). Liberal journalists and critics of the administration used the term "torture" freely and frequently. A popular conservative radio talk show host, however, encouraged his listeners to see the incidents as no worse than "fraternity pranks." The administration itself went to great pains to avoid using the word "torture," arguing instead that the prisoners were the victims of "abuse" and "humiliation." The Secretary of Defense said that they weren't prisoners at all but were "unlawful combatants" and therefore didn't have any rights to be treated humanely (Sontag, 2004).

In a wartime mode, even though concerns with national security are warranted and fears of attack are very real, the system, according to one prominent law professor, "by definition sweeps very broadly and ends up harming hundreds if not thousands of people" (quoted in Liptak, 2003, p. A1). As in other times of war, otherwise unacceptable actions taken as part of the "War on Terror" occur largely without debate or opposition, reflecting the power of language in shaping the social reality of everyday life.

Self-Fulfilling Prophecies

As you will recall from Chapter 2, we do not respond directly and automatically to objects and situations; instead, as the symbolic interactionist perspective points out, we use language to define and interpret them and then we act on the basis of those interpretations. By acting on the basis of our definitions of reality, we often create the very conditions we believe exist. A **self-fulfilling prophecy** is an assumption or prediction that, purely as a result of having been made, causes the expected event to occur and thus confirms the prophecy's own "accuracy" (Merton, 1948; Watzlawick, 1984).

Every holiday season we witness the stunning effects of self-fulfilling prophecies on a national scale. In September or so, the toy industry releases the results of its annual survey of retailers indicating what toys are predicted to be the top sellers at Christmas. Usually one toy in particular emerges as the most popular, can't-do-without, hard-to-get gift of the year. In the 1980s it was Cabbage Patch Dolls; in the early 1990s Mighty Morphin Power Rangers and Ninja Turtles; more recently, Beanie Babies, Furbies, SpongeBob SquarePants toys, Razor scooters, Halo 2 X-Box games, Robosapiens, Bratz dolls, and poker paraphernalia. By around November we begin to hear the hype about unprecedented demand for the toy and the likelihood of a shortage. Powerful retail store chains—such as Toys "R" Us and Wal-Mart—may announce the possibility of rationing: one toy per family. Fueled by the fear of seeing a disappointed child's face at Christmas, thousands of panicked parents and grandparents rush the stores to make sure they're not left without. Some hoard extras for other parents they know. As a result, supplies of the toy—which weren't perilously low in the first place—are severely depleted, thereby bringing about the predicted shortage. The mere belief in some version of the reality creates expectations that can actually make it happen.

Self-fulfilling prophecies are particularly powerful when they become an element of social institutions. In schools, teachers can subtly and unconsciously encourage the performance they expect to see in their students. For instance, if they believe their students are especially intelligent they may spend more time with them or unintentionally show more enthusiasm when working with them. As a result, these students may come to feel more capable and intelligent and actually perform better (Rosenthal & Jacobson, 1968).

Self-fulfilling prophecies can often affect people physically. For years, doctors have recognized the power of the "placebo" effect—the tendency for patients to improve because they have been led to believe they are receiving some sort of treatment even though they're not. For instance, in one study, 42% of balding men taking a placebo drug either maintained or increased the amount of hair on their heads. Doctors in Texas studying knee surgery found similar levels of pain relief in patients whether the surgery was real or faked (cited in Blakeslee, 1998). Researchers estimate that in studies of new drugs, between 35% and 75% of patients benefit from taking dummy pills (Talbot, 2000b). In 1999, a major pharmaceutical company halted development of a new antidepressant drug it had been promoting, because studies showed placebo pills were just as effective in treating depression (Talbot, 2000b).

The inverse of the placebo effect is the creation of expectations that make people worse, sometimes referred to as the "nocebo" effect. Anthropologists have documented numerous mysterious and scientifically difficult-to-explain deaths that follow the pronouncement of curses or evil spells (Watzlawick, 1984). Recently, medical researchers have begun to examine this phenomenon. For instance, in Japan, researchers carried out an experiment on 13 people who were extremely allergic to poison ivy. The experimenters rubbed one of each of the subjects' arms with a harmless leaf and told them it was poison ivy; the experimenters rubbed the other arm with poison ivy and told the subjects it was a harmless leaf. All 13 broke out in a rash where the harmless leaf had touched their skin; only 2 reacted to the real poison ivy leaves (cited in Blakeslee, 1998). In another study, patients with asthma were given a bronchodilator (a drug that widens air passages, making breathing easier) but were told it was a bronchoconstrictor (a drug that narrows air passages, making breathing more difficult). Half of them experienced difficulty breathing after the treatment (cited in Harvard Mental Health Letter, 2005). In other words, in many cases when people expected to get worse, they did. Once again, we see how reality is shaped by human beings, as much as reality shapes them.

Faith and Incorrigible Propositions

David Blaine is a New York street performer who combines sophisticated magic tricks with a hint of comedy. He's been called "The Michael Jordan of Magic" and "The New Houdini." In one of his more astounding stunts, he appears to rise up and float several inches off the ground for a few seconds. Suppose you saw him perform such a feat. He looks as if he were levitating, but you "know better." Even though your eyes tell you he is floating in mid air, you have learned that it's just not possible. Rather than use this experience to entirely abandon your belief that people can't float in mid air, you'll probably come up with a series of "reasonable" explanations: "Maybe it's an optical illusion, and it just appears like he's floating." "Perhaps there are wires holding him up." To acknowledge the possibility that he is literally floating is to challenge the fundamental reality on which your everyday life is based. It is an article of faith that people aren't capable of levitating.

Such an unquestionable assumption, called an **incorrigible proposition,** is a belief that cannot be proved wrong and has become so much a part of common sense that one continues to believe it even in the face of contradictory evidence. By explaining away contradictions with "reasonable" explanations, we strengthen the correctness of the initial premise (Watzlawick, 1976). In the process, we participate in constructing a particular version of reality. For instance, if an incorrigible proposition for you is that women are inherently less aggressive than men, seeing an especially violent woman might lead you toward explanations that focus on the peculiar characteristics of *this particular* woman. Maybe *she's* responding to terrible circumstances in her life; maybe *she* has some kind of chemical imbalance or neurological disorder. By concluding she is an exception to the rule, the rule is maintained.

Even belief systems most of us might consider unconventional can be quite resilient and invulnerable to contradiction (Snow & Machalek, 1982). For instance, practitioners of Scientology strive to attain a perfect level of mental functioning called "clear." Yet there is no evidence any Scientologists have ever achieved such a state. Does this historical failure contradict the group's claims? No. Instead, individual members focus on their individual deficiencies: They have not yet attained the "appropriate mental level" necessary to reach clear. Note how such an explanation allows practitioners to maintain the belief that such a mental state really exists while at the same time reinforcing the hope that someday they may be able to achieve it.

Sociologists Hugh Mehan and Houston Wood (1975) furthered our understanding of incorrigible propositions by examining the research of the anthropologist E. E. Evans-Pritchard (1937). Evans-Pritchard described an elaborate ritual practiced by the Azande, a small African society located in southwestern Sudan. When faced with important decisions—where to build a house, whom to marry, and so on—the Azande consulted an oracle, or a powerful spirit. They prepared for the consultation by following a strictly prescribed ceremony. A substance was extracted from the bark of a certain type of tree and prepared in a special way during a seancelike ritual. The Azande believed that a powerful spirit would enter the potion during this ceremony. They then posed a question to the spirit in such a way that it could be answered either yes or no and fed the substance to a chicken. If the chicken lived, they would interpret the answer from the spirit as yes; if the chicken died, the answer was no.

Our Western belief system tells us the tree bark obviously contains some poisonous chemical. Certain chickens are physically able to survive it, others aren't. But the Azande had no knowledge of the bark's poisonous qualities or of chicken physiology. In fact, they didn't believe the tree or the chicken played a part in the ceremony at all. The ritual of gathering bark and feeding it to a chicken transformed the tree into the spirit power. The chicken lived or died not because of a physical reaction to a chemical but because the oracle "hears like a person and settles cases like a king" (Evans-Pritchard, 1937, p. 321).

But what if the oracle was wrong? What if an Azande was told by the oracle to build a house by the river and the river overflowed its banks, washing away the house? Evans-Pritchard observed several cases of Azande making bad decisions based on incorrect "advice" from the oracle. How could they reconcile these sorts of inconsistencies with a belief in the reality of the oracle?

To us the answer is obvious: There was no spirit, no magic, just the strength of the poison and the health of the chickens. We see these bad decisions as contradictions, because we view them from the reality of Western science. We observe this ritual to determine if in fact there is an oracle, and of course we're predisposed to believe there isn't. We are looking for proof of the existence of something of which we are highly skeptical.

For the Azande, though, the contradictions were not contradictions at all. They *knew* the oracle existed. This was their fundamental premise, their incorrigible proposition, just like our fundamental premise that people can't float in mid air. It was an article of faith that could not be questioned. All that followed for the Azande was experienced from this initial assumption. The Azande had ways of explaining contradictions to their truths, just as we do. When the oracle failed to give them proper advice, they would say things like, "A taboo must have been breached" or "Sorcerers must have intervened" or "The ceremony wasn't carried out correctly."

Protecting incorrigible propositions is essential for the maintenance of reality systems. By explaining away contradictions we are able to support our basic assumptions and live in a coherent and orderly world.

Building the Walls: Conflict, Power, and Social Institutions

We, as individuals, play an important role in coordinating, reproducing, and giving meaning to society in our daily interactions. But our ability to define social reality is limited. We are certainly not completely free to create whatever version of social reality we want to create. We are, after all, born into a preexisting society with its norms, values, roles, relationships, groups, organizations, institutions, and so forth. Just as the walls of a building constrain the ability of the inhabitants to move about, directing them through certain predetermined doorways and corridors, these features of society influence our thoughts and deeds and consequently constrain our ability to freely construct our social world (Giddens, 1984). As Karl Marx wrote, "[People] make their own history, but they do not make it just as they please; they do not make it under circumstances chosen by themselves, but under circumstances directly encountered, given and transmitted from the past" (Marx, 1869/1963, p. 15).

As the conflict perspective points out, certain people or groups of people are more influential in defining reality than others. In any modern society—where socioeconomic classes, ethnic and religious groups, age groups, and political interests struggle for control over resources—there is also a struggle for the power to determine or influence that society's conception of reality (Gans, 1971). Those who emerge successful gain control over information, define values, create myths, manipulate events, and influence what the rest of us take for granted. Conflict theorists therefore argue that people with more power, prestige, status, wealth, and access to high-level policymakers can make their perceptions of the world the entire culture's perception. In other words, "He who has the bigger stick has the better chance of imposing his definitions of reality" (P. L. Berger & Luckmann, 1966, p. 109). That "bigger stick" can be wielded in several ways. Powerful social institutions and the people who control them play a significant role in shaping and sustaining perceptions of reality for everybody else. But if you wish to develop the sociological imagination, you need to understand the role of not only these larger forces in shaping private lives but also private individuals who struggle to shape public reality.

The Economics of Reality

Definitions of reality frequently reflect underlying economic interests. Consider, for instance, the story of a very successful contemporary painter named Marla Olmstead. Marla's paintings have been compared in style and spirit to the work of Jackson Pollock and currently sell for about $6,000 a piece, though one gallery owner thinks they could easily sell for $50,000 ("Marla Olmstead," 2004, p. 1). Her work has appeared at some of New York's finest art galleries. Critics note that her pieces are rhythmic, beautiful, and magical. They rave about her depth and understanding of colors, which combine in unique ways and blossom across the canvases. She has been featured on *The Today Show* and *60 Minutes* as well as in the *New York Times* and *Time* magazine. There's even a DVD—available for purchase on her Web site—that depicts her creating one of her paintings.

Marla has garnered all this attention not because of the quality of her work alone but because of who she is. When she first burst onto the artistic scene, Marla was 4 years old—and she'd already been "painting" for two years.

Marla uses bright acrylic paints, which she splatters and scrapes on large 6' × 6' canvases. She sometimes works on one piece for days at a time, and her parents never know exactly when she's done. When she decides she's finished, she gives her paintings titles, prints her name at the bottom (sometimes with the "r" backwards), and goes on to the next thing that interests her—a TV show, a doll, a swim in the pool.

Is Marla an "artist?" Is her work the expression of creative, artistic vision, or is it the result of a child playing around with paint? More importantly, who gets to decide if her work is defined as "art" or as "childish doodles"? The investors and collectors who pay thousands of dollars for each of her paintings clearly define it as art. But what if she had never come to their attention and never sold a single piece? Would she have simply remained a child who goofed around with paint? For something to be considered art, does it have to have some economic exchange value? And how do you think all the thousands and thousands of struggling artists who never sell anything their entire lives feel about Marla's instant and apparently effortless success? Would they be less inclined to define her as an "artist" than the investors who buy her work? These questions are not trivial. They reflect a deeper issue regarding the role of economics in shaping the way social reality is defined.

The key concerns from the conflict perspective are who benefits economically and who loses from dominant versions of reality. Take mental illness, for example. The number of problems officially defined by the American Psychiatric Association (APA) as mental disorders and defects has now reached nearly 400 (Horwitz, 2002). In defining what constitutes a mental disorder, the APA unwittingly reflects the economic organization of U.S. society. In the United States individuals seldom pay the total costs of medical services out of their own pockets. Most of the money for health care services comes from the federal and state governments or from private insurance companies. Only if problems such as alcoholism, gambling, depression, anorexia, and cocaine addiction are formally defined as illnesses is their treatment eligible for medical insurance coverage.

Similar economic considerations affect the general health care system. In 2004, the federal Medicare program abandoned its long-standing policy against defining obesity as a disease, which had allowed it to routinely deny coverage for weight loss therapies (Stein & Connolly, 2004). Such a policy shift has enormous economic consequences. For instance, in Pennsylvania alone, private insurance companies paid 85% of the cost of weight loss surgeries in one year, an amount that exceeded $205 million (Kolata, 2004b).

Another example of how economics affects the social construction of reality is our society's history of attempts to protect people with disabilities. Approximately 50 million Americans are estimated to have some type of disability (Freedman, Martin, & Schoeni, 2004), which the 1990 Americans with Disabilities Act (ADA) defines as "a physical or mental impairment that substantially limits one or more of the major life activities of such individual" (U.S. Department of Labor, 2004a, p. 1). Under this law, employers are required to accommodate employees who have a documented disability and are forbidden to fire them simply because of their disability. For instance, a company that has wheelchair-bound employees must have ramps or elevators that give these workers access to all areas of the building. Ironically, the added cost of employing disabled workers may actually work to their disadvantage by making them less attractive to potential hirers in the first place. One study found an 11% drop in the employment rate of people with disabilities after the ADA was enacted (De Leire, 2000). Moreover, highly publicized stories of employees with questionable disabilities seeking accommodations—like an office worker allergic to artificial fragrances demanding that her or his employer install an expensive new air filtration system—give the impression that the ADA is placing an excessive economic burden on companies. Although powerful businesses and industries were not able to prevent this act from being passed in the first place, they have been able to create a reality that still works in their interest.

The Politics of Reality

The institution of politics is also linked to societal definitions of reality. To a great extent, politics is about controlling public perceptions of reality so people will do things or think about issues in ways that political leaders want them to. During important political campaigns, we can see such attempts to influence public perception. Mudslinging, euphemistically called "negative campaigning," has become as common an element of the U.S. electoral process as speeches, debates, baby kissing, and patriotic songs. Most politicians know that if you say something untrue or unproven about an opponent often enough, people will believe it. Ironically, constant public denials by the victim of the charges often reinforce the reality of the charges and keep them in the news. The actual validity of the claims becomes irrelevant as the accusations are transformed into "fact" and become solidified in the minds of the voting public.

However, the relationship between politics and reality goes beyond the dirty campaigns of individual candidates. The social construction of reality itself is a massive political process. All governments, both national and local, live or die by their ability to manipulate public opinion so they can reinforce their claims to legitimacy. Information is selectively released, altered, or withheld in an attempt to gain public approval and support for their policies. Over the past five years, at least 20 different federal agencies, including the Department of Defense and the Census Bureau, have produced and distributed hundreds of suspect "news" reports to local television networks. The reports look like actual journalistic reports but are in fact prepackaged productions designed not just to inform but to build public support for governmental policy objectives, such as Medicare reform or Social Security reform (Barstow & Stein, 2005). For instance, in 2004, the Department of Health and Human Services distributed fake news (in the form of video news releases in which actors played the parts of reporters) to hundreds of local television stations in support of administration prescription drug policies (Alter, 2005). And in 2005, it was discovered that this department as well as the Department of Education had paid several sympathetic journalists and television commentators between $10,000 and $240,000 to present government policies in a favorable light in their writings and broadcasts.

When the lives of thousands of citizens are at stake and public opinion is crucial, such information control becomes particularly tight. Between September 2001 and March 2003, the Bush administration worked diligently to foster a belief that Iraq and its then-dictator Saddam Hussein played a direct role in the September 11 attacks and had stockpiles of weapons of mass destruction. They were quite successful. Immediately after the attacks, national opinion polls showed that only 3% of Americans mentioned Iraq or Saddam Hussein when asked who was responsible. But by January 2003, 44% of Americans reported that either "most" or "some" of the hijackers were Iraqi citizens. In fact, none were (Feldman, Marlantes, & Bowers, 2003). Two years after the attacks, 69% of Americans said in a *Washington Post* poll that they thought it at least likely that Hussein was involved in the attacks, even though the link between Iraq and al Qaeda was never established (Milbank & Deane, 2003). Nevertheless, these beliefs provided the kind of public support necessary to justify the military invasion of Iraq that began in March 2003 and continues to this day. Such a molding of public perception is accomplished most notably through the media.

The Medium Is the Message

The mass media—television, radio, books, newspapers, magazines, the Internet—are the primary means by which we are entertained and informed about the world around us. But the messages we receive from the media also reflect dominant cultural values (Gitlin, 1979). In television shows and other works of fiction, the way characters are portrayed, the topics dealt with, and the solutions imposed on problems all link entertainment to the prevailing societal tastes in consumption and the economic system.

The media also play a key role in any political system. They are our primary source of information about local, national, and international events and people. News broadcasts and newspapers tell us about things we cannot experience directly, making the most remote events meaningful (Molotch & Lester, 1974). The way we look at the world and define our lives within it is therefore shaped and influenced by what we see on the news, hear on the radio, and read in our daily papers.

Because the news is the means by which political realities are disseminated to the public, it is an essential tool in maintaining social order (Hallin, 1986; Parenti, 1986). In many societies, most news sources don't even try to hide that they are mouthpieces of one faction or another. In repressive societies, the only news sources allowed to operate are those representing the government. In North Korea, for instance, the flow of news information is clearly controlled by the government. People who live in societies with a cultural tradition of press independence, in contrast, assume that news stories are purely factual—an accurate, objective reflection of the "world out there" (Molotch & Lester, 1975). Like everything else, however, news is a constructed reality.

Hundreds, perhaps thousands of potentially newsworthy events occur every day. Yet we'll see maybe 10 of them on our favorite evening broadcast. These events exist as news not because of their inherent importance but because of the practical, political, or economic purposes they serve. The old newsroom adage "If it bleeds, it leads" attests to the fact that events with shocking details—which appeal to the public's fondness for the sensational—are the ones most likely to be chosen. At its most independent, the news is still the product of decisions made by reporters, editors, network executives, and corporation owners, all of whom have their own interests, biases, and values (Molotch & Lester, 1974).

The manipulation of events for political gain is such an expected part of the cultural landscape that it's become institutionalized, with its own term: *spin.* To put a spin on an event is to give it a particular interpretation, often one that is to the speaker's advantage. Spin is a valuable political resource. Every U.S. president, whether Republican or Democrat, has spun the facts to put his policies in the best possible light, often by withholding information from the public, fudging statistics, or exaggerating the progress or benefits of particular actions and policies (Stolberg, 2004).

Spin has become a profession in its own right. Immediately following a televised presidential debate, for instance, a gaggle of trained supporters (the "spin doctors") for both candidates situate themselves in a specified area—called "spin alley"—where they creatively provide television viewers with a version of the outcome that benefits their candidate. Top aides are dispatched to cable news programs; local party officials visit news studios; teams of researchers send dozens of messages to reporters covering the debate, accusing the other candidate of misstatements or lies.

In a wired world, spin isn't just practiced by professional media pundits. For each debate during the 2004 presidential campaign, representatives of both candidates called on millions of their supporters to flood online polls, chat rooms, and discussion boards as soon as the debate ended with instant declarations that their candidate had won. What's interesting is that these instructions went out days before the debates actually took place (Rutenberg, 2004). These tactics continue between elections as groups seeking to influence policy making send e-mails to supporters requesting that they sign petitions and contact their legislators. In addition, Web blogs are a continuing source of spin as they mix fact with the blogger's opinion, much of it selected and phrased to present a clearly one-sided version of reality.

Although "freedom of expression" and "freedom of the press" are core American values, official censorship has been not only tolerated but encouraged in some situations. Take the media coverage of the Persian Gulf War in 1991. This was the first war covered in a live, around-the-clock format, and it was a truly global media event (Barker, 1997). But the most striking feature of the coverage of this war was the reliance on studio-based coverage and stage-managed events. Journalists were permitted to cover the war in the traditional sense only if they were in organized "pools" escorted by military personnel (Pratkanis & Aronson, 1991). Military officials decided which army units could be visited by reporters, which reporters could make the visits, which soldiers they could talk to, what the television cameras could show, and what could be written (Cummings, 1992). Any journalist who attempted to operate independently was subject to arrest. Reporters were completely dependent on official statements and government-issued videotapes. The public was told that such tight restrictions were necessary to ensure the physical safety of the war correspondents, protect the well-being of our soldiers, and promote the war effort. Not surprisingly, media reports during this war focused on the low number of Allied casualties, the spectacular success of the air campaign and ground attacks, the effectiveness of U.S. high-tech weaponry, the carefully calibrated pressure that kept the Iraqis from unleashing chemical weapons, and so on. Only 1% of the visual images on television were of death and injury (Barker, 1997).

In contrast, the press coverage of the initial stages of the current war in Iraq seemed to be relatively open. The Pentagon decided to allow hundreds of reporters to accompany fighting forces and transmit their stories from the front lines throughout the war. According to one study, 61% of their reports during the first three days of the war were live and unedited (Project for Excellence in Journalism, 2005). By granting such unprecedented access, Pentagon officials hoped that these "embedded" reporters would convey the "heroism and hard work" of American soldiers to a worldwide audience and in the process discredit Iraqi propaganda (Getlin & Wilkinson, 2003). Some media critics, however, were concerned that the reporters still became a tool of the military, especially given their often close attachment to the soldiers with whom they were traveling. For instance, 80% of early embedded reports included no commentary at all from soldiers (Project for Excellence in Journalism, 2005). In addition, there is some evidence that military personnel and news organizations fabricated stories to present the war in a favorable light. For instance, the famous scene of freed Iraqis toppling a statue of Saddam Hussein as well as footage of the dramatic rescue of captured U.S. soldier Jessica Lynch from a hospital were at least partially staged for dramatic effect.

❖
Micro-Macro Connection
Missing From the News

For everyday news stories, even in societies that restrict the press, official censorship is usually unnecessary. Because of the economic pressures to attract audiences and keep their attention, TV networks and newspapers usually censor themselves (Bagdikian, 1991). Reporters pursue stories that are relatively easy to research and that have immediate interest to audiences. Less exciting, more complicated stories don't get enough journalistic resources or are cut in the editing process. We usually have no way of knowing which events have *not* been selected for inclusion in the day's news or which plausible alternatives are kept out of the public eye.

Hence, the main problem with the daily distillation of information is not so much what is false but what is missing (Bagdikian, 1991). Each year Project Censored, a media watchdog group, publishes its list of the top news stories that never made the news in the United States and hence never came to the public's attention (Jensen & Project Censored, 1995; Phillips & Project Censored, 1997, 2000; Project Censored, 2003, 2005). Here are some recent stories the mainstream media never covered:

♦ The Food and Drug Administration refused to take steps to protect consumers from known carcinogens found in some personal care products, such as toothpaste, shampoo, sunscreen, and makeup.

♦ According to scientists from the Uranium Medical Research Center, civilian populations in Afghanistan and Iraq, as well as American troops, were contaminated with radiation from uranium that was between 400% and 2000% higher than normal levels.

♦ American scientists have developed ways to make pox viruses significantly more deadly. These new strains are immune to the most powerful antiviral drugs.

♦ All around the country, legal ordinances known as TRAP (Targeted Regulation of Abortion Providers) laws attempt to regulate the medical practices or facilities of doctors who perform abortions by imposing burdensome requirements that are different and more stringent than regulations applied to comparable medical practices. These restrictions make it difficult for women to exercise the legal right to choose an abortion.

♦ The U.S. Justice Department rejected a study, which it had originally commissioned, finding that the most popular school-based drug prevention program in the country—Drug Abuse Resistance Education (DARE)—was an extremely expensive failure.

The economic and political motivation for such selectivity becomes apparent when we consider who owns the media. For instance, one company, Clear Channel, owns more than 1,200 radio stations in all 50 states, reaching more than 110 million listeners every week (Clear Channel Communications, 2003). Another, the Sinclair Broadcast Group, owns and operates 61 television stations in 38 markets and reaches an estimated 24% of the viewing population (Sinclair Broadcast Group, 2005). In 1983, 50 companies controlled over half of all U.S. media outlets; by 2000, six companies—General Electric, Viacom, Disney, Time Warner, Bertelsmann, and Rupert Murdoch's News Corporation—controlled over half of all media outlets (Bagdikian, 2000).

Many media observers fear that corporation-owned news outlets will twist certain stories to promote the parent company's economic or political interests. For instance, in 2001 *NBC Nightly News* aired an enthusiastic story about a "revolutionary" new airplane being manufactured by Boeing called the Sonic Cruiser. The story left out any mention of strong criticisms by aviation experts about the plane's technical flaws or by environmentalists about the plane's poor fuel efficiency. NBC's parent company, General Electric, had invested over $1 billion in the creation of the proposed jet's engine (Jackson & Hart, 2001).

As the viewing and listening public, our recourse is difficult. To criticize faulty government policies and consider solutions to difficult social problems, we need solid information, which is frequently unavailable or difficult to obtain. The recent growth in popularity of podcasting, video-on-demand, Internet-protocol television, and subscription satellite radio networks may be a sign that some citizens are growing weary of the filtered and sometimes partisan information they receive from traditional news sources. In addition, a bill in Congress would increase the number of low-power FM radio stations, thereby expanding the number of radio outlets owned by smaller independent companies.

Nevertheless, the challenge we face in our own private lives is to recognize the processes at work in the social construction of reality and to take them into account as we "consume" the news. A critical dimension of the sociological imagination is the ability to "read silences"—to be attentive to what the mass media *don't* say. Fortunately, one of the purposes of sociology is to scientifically amass a body of knowledge that we can use to assess how our society really works.

Moral Entrepreneurs

Individual efforts to control the construction of reality are difficult. But we are not consigned to meekly accept the reality presented to us by powerful organizations and institutions. Individuals banding together in interest groups have managed time and again to contribute to the construction of social reality. For instance, they have created new understandings of the rights of ethnoracial minorities, brought environmental degradation to the public's attention, and changed our attitudes toward particular crimes.

Although economic and political power have been the motivating concerns of many of these groups, certain groups have had moral concerns they passionately want

(Text continues on page 80)

Personal Billboards

Liz Grauerholz and Rebecca Smith

Virtually everything we experience in our lives is mediated through language and symbols. At times, we sit back and passively accept the linguistic reality that others create. At other times, through our selective use of language, we actively attempt to construct, or at least influence, others' perceptions of reality. Bumper stickers and T-shirts are powerful forms of this sort of communication, pithy and to the point.

These "personal billboards" communicate messages cheaply and are available to any group or individual with a vehicle or a wardrobe. They are not reserved solely for powerful people or those whom the media deem worthy of coverage. In fact, personal billboards are some of the most powerful "voices" for underprivileged groups. No matter who uses them or what their messages are, they advertise a reality to others about who we are, what we stand for, and what we consider important.

❖ The messages on T-shirts cover the cultural spectrum . . .

❖ ...As do the messages on bumper stickers.

Personal billboards are often used as a means of communicating group pride and identity. They reinforce the reality and vitality of the groups they represent.

Such communicative displays are especially prominent during crises, though different cultures might present very different realities. In the days immediately following the terrorist attacks of September 11, 2001, Americans and people living in southern Asia felt a similar need to express solidarity but with very different messages.

❖ This Pakistani Muslim cleric displays a T-shirt lauding Osama bin Laden as Hero of Islam.

T-shirts and bumper stickers can also provide greater awareness of oppressed groups and their causes. Certain classes, ethnic and religious groups, age groups, sexual minority groups, and political interest groups struggle for control over resources and for the power to determine or influence society's conception of reality.

Oppressed Americans are not unique in displaying messages on their cars or clothing.

❖ In Australia . . .

❖ In Vietnam . . .

❖ In England . . .

Certain groups, referred to as moral entrepreneurs, have social concerns they passionately want translated into law. Often, their personal billboards are designed to dramatize the emotional impact of the underlying message.

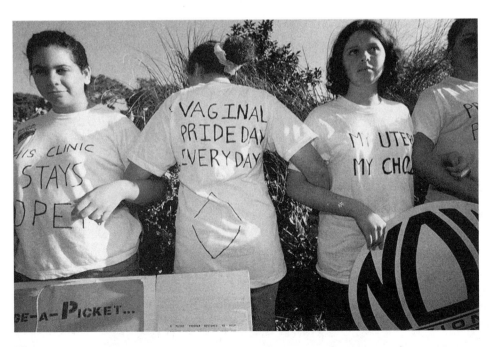

Moral entrepreneurs need not be wealthy or influential individuals. If they succeed in turning their interests into public policy, it is by virtue of their access to decision makers, skillful use of publicity, success in neutralizing any opposing viewpoints—and most of all, their initiative in making their desires known. For instance, the citizens of Northern Ireland were a key element in forcing the political compromise designed to stop decades of sectarian violence between Catholics and Protestants. Ordinary people like the men pictured here, whose voices had long been drowned out by strident and violent radicals on both sides of the conflict, helped to give political leaders the moral authority to move toward peace.

translated into law. Groups that seek to outlaw pornography, sexually explicit lyrics in rock music, abortion, gambling, and homosexuality, as well as groups that promote gun control, literacy, awareness of domestic violence, and support for AIDS research, are crusading for the creation of a new public conception of morality. These **moral entrepreneurs** (H. Becker, 1963) need not be wealthy or influential individuals. Instead, by virtue of their initiative, access to decision makers, skillful use of publicity, and success in neutralizing any opposing viewpoints, they are able to turn their interests into public policy (Hills, 1980). Just as a financial entrepreneur is in the business of selling a product to the public, a moral entrepreneur is in the business of selling a particular version of reality to the public.

Moral entrepreneurship is closely linked to certain social institutions. Religion, for example, provides many people with values that dictate what is right and wrong, proper and improper, good and bad (J. H. Turner, 1972). These values are sometimes formally written into a religious code (for example, the Ten Commandments or the Koran) that provides direct guidance for day-to-day life and the rationale that drives attempts to change the beliefs and behaviors of others.

If they have the political savvy to insinuate their belief systems into the legislative process, moral entrepreneurs can often exert significant influence over a society's definition of reality. In the early 20th century, for instance, the actions of a small group of women, the Women's Christian Temperance Union, led to the passage of the Eighteenth Amendment to the U.S. Constitution, which prohibited the use, possession, and sale of alcoholic beverages (Gusfield, 1963). These women used strong, religiously inspired arguments against the "evils" of alcohol to convince legislators it ought to be outlawed.

However, although religious codes of conduct provided the supportive ideology for the temperance movement in the United States, it was—on closer inspection—a political struggle among various interest groups. The struggle symbolized the conflict between the values of rural, middle-class Protestants and the values of immigrant, urban, working-class Catholics (Gusfield, 1963). Alcohol consumption was part of the everyday lives of these latter immigrants, and the temperance movement became a symbolic crusade for rural Protestants trying to maintain their position in a rapidly changing society. Arguably, the Eighteenth Amendment outlawing the sale and consumption of alcohol was eventually repealed because temperance advocates were more passionate about the passage of Prohibition laws than their enforcement.

Appreciating the Contributions of Sociological Research

Up to this point, I've been describing how individuals, groups, organizations, and various social institutions go about constructing reality. We've seen that these realities sometimes shift with time, place, and individual perception. Faced with this type of fluctuation, sociologists, as well as scholars in other disciplines, seek to identify a more "real" reality through systematic, controlled research. The rules sociologists abide by when conducting research give them confidence that they are identifying more than just a personal version of reality. They hope to determine a reality as it exists for some community of people at a particular point in time.

Moving beyond the level of individual conclusions about the nature of social reality is crucial if we are to escape the distortions of personal interests and biases. A danger of relying on individual perceptions is that we are likely to conclude that our experiences are what everyone experiences. For example, the famous psychiatrist Sigmund Freud used his own childhood as the ultimate "proof" of the controversial concept the Oedipus conflict (the belief that sons are secretly in love with their mothers and jealous of their fathers). He wrote to a friend in 1897, "I have found, in my own case too, being in love with the mother and jealous of the father, and I now consider it a universal event of early childhood" (quoted in Astbury, 1996, p. 73).

To avoid the risk of such distortions, sociologists try to determine what most people believe or how most people behave. But in doing so, sociologists run the risk of simply restating what people already know. Indeed, a criticism of sociology you hear sometimes is that it is just a fancy version of common sense. A lot of the things that we think are obvious based on our personal observations, however, turn out not to be so straightforward under the closer scrutiny of social research. Consider the following "commonsense facts":

♦ Rape, assault, and murder occur most often between total strangers.
♦ Because of the high divorce rate in the United States, people are reluctant to get married.
♦ American children today are more likely to live in a single-parent household than they were 100 years ago.

Most of us probably believe these statements are true. Given what you've read or seen on television, they probably make a lot of sense. But how accurate are they?

According to the U.S. Bureau of Justice Statistics (2004b), only 15.5% of homicides involving male victims and 8.9% of homicides involving female victims are perpetrated by strangers; the vast majority are committed by neighbors, colleagues, acquaintances, and family members. In addition, only 47% of assaults, 37% of rapes, and 30% of attempted rapes occur between strangers (U.S. Bureau of Justice Statistics, 2004a). On college campuses, about 90% of college age rape victims know their attackers (U.S. Bureau of Justice Statistics, 2001). Although people close to us provide a great deal of pleasure in our lives, they are also the ones who can frustrate and hurt us the most.

According to the U.S. Bureau of the Census (2004a), in 2003 only about 5% of people between the ages of 55 and 64 had never been married. In fact, about two thirds of divorced women and three fourths of divorced men eventually remarry (Cherlin, 1992). Although we have become increasingly willing to end a bad marriage, we still tend to place a high value on the institution of marriage itself.

The percentage of children who live with one parent is roughly the same as it was a century ago. At that time life expectancy was much lower than it is today, so it was highly likely that before reaching adulthood a child would lose at least one parent to death (Kain, 1990).

As you can see, sometimes commonsense "facts" don't hold up under the weight of evidence provided by social research.

The Empirical Nature of Sociological Research

Research is all around us. Throughout our lives we are flooded with statistics that are supposedly the result of scientific studies—which detergents make clothes brighter, which soft drinks most people prefer, which chewing gum is recommended by four out of five dentists. Many of the important decisions we make, from purchasing a car to voting for a presidential candidate, are supported by some sort of research.

In addition, a significant proportion of our own lives is spent doing casual research. Every time we seek out the opinions of others, gauge the attitude of a group, or draw conclusions about an event, we engage in a form of research. Say, for example, that you thought your exam scores would improve if you studied with others. You then formed a study group. After the exam you compared your grade with the grade you received on the previous exam to see if there was any significant improvement. If there was, you would likely attribute your better performance to the study group. This is the essence of research: You had an idea about some social process, and you went out and tested it to see if you were correct.

Although useful and common, such personal research is fraught with problems. We may make inaccurate or selective observations, overgeneralize on the basis of a limited number of observations, or draw conclusions that protect our own interests (Babbie, 1992). Maybe your exam score would have improved, even without the study group, because you had a better understanding of the material this time and had a better sense of what the instructor expected.

Sociological research, which is a more sophisticated and structured form of the sort of individual inquiry we use every day, can avoid some of these pitfalls. Of course, sociological researchers are human beings, and they too make errors in observation, generalization, and analysis. But they have a greater chance of avoiding these errors because, first and foremost, sociological research is an empirical endeavor. **Empirical research** operates on the assumption that answers to questions about human behavior can be ascertained through controlled, systematic observations in the real world. Individuals can reach naïve conclusions based on their personal impressions of what happens in society. Great scholars can spend years thinking about human life and developing logical explanations about particular social phenomena. But for most sociologists, the strength of an explanation depends on how much empirical support it has.

Another characteristic of sociological research that makes it a better reflection of social reality than individual inquiry is that it is **probabilistic**. Instead of making absolute predictions, claiming that X always causes Y, most sociologists prefer to state that under certain conditions X will probably cause Y in most people—in other words, that human behavior operates within the laws of probability. Whenever sociologists set out to find the reasons, for example, for why people hold prejudiced beliefs, why some religious groups are more opposed to abortion than others, or why some countries have a higher birth rate than others, they are searching for the factors that would explain these phenomena most but not all of the time. For instance, adults with less than a high school education are more likely than adults with college degrees to be prejudiced toward other ethnoracial groups. But that doesn't mean that every single high school dropout is a bigot or that every college graduate is accepting of people who are ethnically or racially different. By focusing on the probability of some phenomenon occurring while at the same time allowing for exceptions and variations, sociologists provide a view of reality that simultaneously reflects the way things are and the way they can be.

Qualitative and Quantitative Research

In contrast to the casual way we carry out our personal research, sociologists seek to define reality through a careful process of collecting information and answering questions. Some sociologists collect nonnumeric information (text, written words, phrases, symbols, observations) that describes people, actions, or events in social life (called **qualitative research**) (Neuman, 1994). Others collect numeric data and rely on precise statistical analysis (called **quantitative research**). And some use a combination of both.

Qualitative researchers often go out and observe people and events as they happen in society. For instance, qualitative researchers interested in how additional children affect parents' ability to balance the demands of work and home may spend an entire day with a family, listening, observing, and asking questions. Once they've collected enough information, they go about interpreting their observations, looking for identifiable patterns in people's everyday lives.

Quantitative sociological researchers methodically record observations across a variety of situations; they design and choose questions in advance and ask them in a consistent way of a large number of people; they use sophisticated techniques to ensure that the characteristics of the people in a study are similar to those of the population at large; and they use computers to generate statistics from which confident conclusions can be drawn.

Both kinds of sociological research are subjected to the scrutiny of peers who will point out any mistakes and shortcomings. Researchers are obligated to report not only their results but also the methods they used to record observations or collect data and the conditions surrounding the study. Such detailed explanation allows other researchers to replicate a study—that is, to perform it themselves to see if the same results are obtained. The more a particular research result is replicated, the greater its acceptance as fact in the sociological community.

Theories, Variables, and Hypotheses

Whether qualitative or quantitative, social research is purposeful. Unlike personal research, which may be motivated by a hunch, whim, or immediate need, most social research is guided by a particular theory. A **theory** is a set of statements or propositions that seek to explain or predict a particular aspect of social life (Chafetz, 1978). Theory does not, as is popularly thought, mean conjecture or speculation. Ideally, theories explain the way things are, not the way they ought to be.

Research and theory closely depend on each other. Research without any underlying theoretical reasoning is simply a string of meaningless bits of information (C. W. Mills, 1959); theory without research is abstract and speculative.

Some theories—such as structural functionalism, conflict theory, and symbolic interactionism—are quite broad, seeking to explain why social order exists or how societies work overall. Other theories are more modest, seeking to explain more narrowly certain behaviors among specific groups of people. For example, Travis Hirschi (1969) developed a theory of juvenile delinquency called "social control theory," in which he argued that delinquent acts occur when an individual's bond to society is weak or broken. These bonds are derived from a person's attachments to others who obey the law, the rewards a person gains by acting nondelinquently (commitments), the amount of time a person engages in nondelinquent activity (involvements), and the degree to which a person is tied to society's conventional belief system.

To test theories, sociologists must translate abstract propositions into testable hypotheses. A **hypothesis** is a researchable prediction that specifies the relationship between two or more variables. A **variable** is any characteristic, attitude, behavior, or event that can take on two or more values or attributes. For example, the variable "marital status" has several categories: never married, cohabiting, married, separated, divorced, widowed. The variable "attitudes toward capital punishment" has categories ranging from strongly in favor to strongly oppose. Hirschi was interested in why juveniles engage in delinquent behavior. Such a question is far too general to study, so he developed a clear, specific, empirically testable prediction, or hypothesis, specifying a relationship between two variables: Strong "social bonds" will be associated with low levels of "delinquency."

In developing their hypotheses, sociologists distinguish between independent and dependent variables. The **independent variable** is the factor presumed to influence or create changes in another variable. The **dependent variable** is the one assumed to depend on, be influenced by, or change as a result of the independent variable. If we believe that gender affects people's attitudes toward abortion (that is, women will hold more favorable attitudes than men), then "gender" would be the independent variable influencing "attitudes toward abortion," the dependent variable. For Hirschi's theory of juvenile delinquency, the strength of the social bond was the independent variable and level of delinquency was the dependent variable.

The problem for quantitative social researchers, like Hirschi, is that the concepts that form the basis of theories are often abstract and not easy to observe or measure empirically. We can't directly study concepts such as "social bonds." So these variables must be translated into **indicators**: events, characteristics, or behaviors that can be observed or quantified.

In his survey of 1,200 boys in grades 6 through 12, Hirschi derived a set of indicators for his independent variable, the strength of the social bond. To determine the degree to which young people are attached to law-abiding others, Hirschi measured their attraction to parents, peers, and school officials. To determine the degree to which they derived rewards from acting nondelinquently, he asked them to assess the importance of such things as getting good grades. To determine the proportion of their lives spent in conventional activities, he asked them how much time they spent in school-oriented activities. Finally, to determine their ties to a conventional belief system, he asked them questions about their respect for the law and the police.

Hirschi measured the dependent variable, delinquent activity, by asking the boys if they'd ever stolen things, taken cars for rides without the owners' permission, banged up something on purpose that belonged to somebody else, or beaten up or hurt someone on purpose. In addition, he used school records and police records to measure acts that had come to the attention of authorities.

The empirical data he collected supported his hypothesis and therefore strengthened the power of his original theory.

Modes of Research

Although the answers to important sociological questions are not always simple or clear, the techniques sociologists use to collect and examine data allow them to draw informed and reliable conclusions about human behavior and social life. The most common techniques are experiments, field research, surveys, and unobtrusive research.

Experiments

An **experiment** is typically a research situation designed to elicit some sort of behavior under closely controlled laboratory circumstances. In its ideal form, the experimenter randomly places participants into two groups, then deliberately manipulates or introduces changes into the environment of one group of participants (called the "experimental group") and not the other (called the "control group"). Care is taken to ensure that the groups are relatively alike except for the variable that the experimenter manipulates. Any observed or measured differences between the groups can then be attributed to the effects of the experimental manipulation (Singleton, Straits, & Straits, 1993).

Experiments have a significant advantage over other types of research because the researcher can directly control all the relevant variables. Thus conclusions about the independent variable causing changes in the dependent variable can be made more convincingly. The artificial nature of most laboratory experiments, however, may make subjects behave differently from the way they would in their natural settings, leading some people to argue that experimentation in sociology is practically impossible (Silverman, 1982).

To overcome this difficulty, some sociologists have created experimental situations outside the laboratory. Arthur Beaman and his colleagues (Beaman, Klentz, Diener, & Svanum, 1979) conducted an experiment to see whether self-awareness decreases the likelihood of engaging in socially undesirable behavior—in this case, stealing. The researchers set up situations in which children arriving at several homes on Halloween night were sent into the living room alone, to take candy from a bowl. The children were first asked their names and ages and then told, "You may take one of the candies." For the experimental group, a large mirror was placed right next to the candy bowl so that the children couldn't help but see themselves. For the control group, there was no mirror. In the control group, 37% of the children took more than one candy, but only 4% of the children in the experimental group took more than one candy. The researchers concluded from this experiment that self-awareness can have a significant effect on honesty.

Field Research

In **field research**, qualitative sociologists observe events as they actually occur, without selecting experimental and control groups or purposely introducing any changes into the subjects' environment. Field research can take several forms. In **nonparticipant observation**, the researcher observes people without directly interacting with them and without their knowledge that they are being observed. Sociologist

Lyn Lofland (1973), for example, studied how strangers relate to one another in public places by going to bus depots, airports, stores, restaurants, and parks and secretly recording everything she saw.

Participant observation requires that the researcher interact with subjects. In some cases the researcher openly identifies him- or herself. For instance, to gain insight into how people balance work and family, over a period of three years sociologist Arlie Russell Hochschild (1997) observed employees at a large public relations company she called Amerco. She was particularly interested in why employees tend not to take advantage of available family leave policies. At Amerco, only 53 of 21,000 employees—all of them women—chose to switch to part-time work in response to the arrival of a new baby. Less than 1% of the employees shared a job or worked at home, even though the company permits it. Most of the workers worked a lot of overtime, coming in early and staying late. So why were these workers so unwilling to change their work lives to spend more time with their families even when the company would have supported them in doing so? Through her long-term observations of Amerco, Hochschild came to the conclusion that work has become a form of "home" and home has become "work." For many people at Amerco, home had become a place of frenzied activity and busy schedules, whereas work had become a sort of nurturing refuge where they could relax and share stories with friends. So they actually preferred spending more time at work.

This type of qualitative field research can be quite time consuming. Researchers can conduct only a limited number of interviews and can observe only a limited number of people and events. Hochschild collected rich information about people's work-family tradeoffs, but she could only study one corporation. It's risky to generalize from the experiences of a small group of workers in one company in one society to all workers in all sorts of work environments.

In more delicate situations, the researcher may go "under cover" and attempt to become a member of the group being observed. In the mid-1950s a social psychologist named Leon Festinger set out to examine how groups protect their beliefs in the face of undeniable contradictory evidence (Festinger, Riecken, & Schacter, 1956). He chose to study a "doomsday" cult that had organized around the belief that a substantial chunk of the Western Hemisphere would be destroyed by a cataclysmic flood on December 21, 1955. He knew that group members were highly sensitive to the public's skepticism and would probably be unwilling to answer an interviewer's questions about their activities and beliefs. So Festinger and his assistants decided to pose as individuals interested in joining the group. Eventually they became full-fledged members, participating in all the group's activities. When the great flood didn't occur on December 21, their leader began to make importance out of seemingly irrelevant recent news events. For instance, the Associated Press had reported that over the prior few days earthquakes had occurred in Nevada, California, and Italy. The damage brought about by these disasters became "proof" to the group members that cataclysms were actually happening. By infiltrating the group and passing himself off as a member, Festinger could witness firsthand the way that members came to terms with their failed prophecy: claiming that because of the group's efforts, their area had been spared from these upheavals.

Surveys

When it is impossible or impractical to carry out field observations or to set up a controlled experimental situation, social researchers use the survey method. **Surveys** require that the researcher pose a series of questions to respondents either orally, electronically, or on paper. The questions should be sufficiently clear so they are understood by the respondent the way the researcher wants them to be understood and measure what the researcher wants them to measure. In addition, the respondent is expected to answer the questions honestly and thoughtfully. The answers are often recorded in numerical form, so they can be statistically analyzed.

All of us have experienced surveys of one form or another. Every 10 years people who live in the United States are required to fill out questionnaires for the U.S. Census Bureau. At the end of some college courses you've probably filled out a course evaluation. Or perhaps you've been interviewed in a shopping mall or answered questions during a telephone survey.

Surveys typically use standardized formats. All subjects are asked the same questions in the same way, and large samples of people are used as subjects. When sociologists Philip Blumstein and Pepper Schwartz (1983) undertook a massive study of intimate couples in the United States, they sent questionnaires to people from every income level, age group, religion, political ideology, and educational background. Some of their respondents were cohabiting, others were married. Some had children, others were childless. Some were heterosexual, others homosexual. All couples filled out a 38-page questionnaire that asked questions about their leisure activities, emotional support, housework, finances, sexual relations, satisfaction, relations with children, and so forth. More than 6,000 couples participated. From these surveys Blumstein and Schwartz were able to draw conclusions about the importance of money, work, sexuality, power, and gender in couple's lives.

Unobtrusive Research

All the methods I've discussed so far—whether quantitative or qualitative—require the researcher to have some contact with the people being studied: giving them tasks to do in an experiment, or watching them (with or without their knowing that they are participating in social research), or asking them questions. The problem with these techniques is that the very act of intruding into people's lives may influence the phenomena being studied. Asking people questions about their voting intentions prior to an election, for instance, may affect their eventual voting behavior. Simply observing people can make them self-conscious and dramatically alter their behavior.

In the late 1920s, an engineer and a time study analyst (Roethlisberger & Dickson, 1939) were hired to study working conditions and worker productivity at an electric company in Hawthorne, Illinois. They were interested in finding out whether changing certain physical conditions in the plant could improve workers' productivity and satisfaction. They quickly discovered that increasing the lighting in the workroom was linked with workers producing more. Increasing the brightness of the lights again increased productivity even further. To bolster their conclusion, they decided to dim the lights to see if productivity dropped. Much to their dismay, productivity *increased again* when they darkened the room. They soon realized that the workers were responding more to the attention they were receiving from the researchers than to changes in their working conditions. This phenomenon is known as the "Hawthorne effect."

To avoid such influence, sociologists sometimes use another research technique, unobtrusive research, which requires no contact with people at all. **Unobtrusive research** is an examination of the evidence of social behavior that people create or leave behind. Suppose you wanted to know which exhibits are most popular at a museum (Webb, Campbell, Schwartz, Sechrest, & Grove, 1981). You could poll people, but they might tell you things that make them appear more intellectual and sophisticated than they really are. You could stand there and watch people, but they might become aware that you're observing them. Perhaps a better way would be to wait until the museum is empty and check the wear and tear on the floor in front of the exhibits. Those exhibits where the carpeting is worn down are probably the most popular. This is an example of unobtrusive research.

There are several types of unobtrusive research:

Analysis of existing data (also known as secondary data) relies on data gathered earlier by someone else for some other purpose. Émile Durkheim used this technique when he examined different suicide rates for different groups to gain insight into the underlying causes of suicide (see Chapter 1). Analysis of existing data is still used extensively by sociologists today. One of the most popular and convenient sources of data is the U.S. Census. Studies that examine broad, nationwide trends (for instance, marriage, divorce, or premarital childbearing rates) typically use existing census data.

Content analysis is the study of recorded communications—books, speeches, poems, songs, television commercials, Web sites, and so forth. For example, sociologists Bernice Pescosolido, Elizabeth Grauerholz, and Melissa Milkie (1997) analyzed close to 2,000 children's picture books published from 1937 to 1993 to see if there were any changes in the way African Americans were portrayed. They believed that these depictions could tell a lot about the shifting nature of race relations in the larger society. The researchers looked not only at the number of black characters in these books but also at whether they were portrayed positively or negatively. They found, among other things, that in times of high uncertainty in race relations and substantial protest and conflict over existing societal norms, Blacks virtually disappeared from picture books. Furthermore, depictions of intimate, equal interracial interactions and portrayals of Blacks as primary characters remained rare.

Historical analysis relies on existing historical documents as a source of research information. Sociologist Kai Erikson (1966) was interested in how communities construct definitions of acceptable and unacceptable behavior. For his book *Wayward Puritans,* he studied several "crime waves" among the Puritans of the Massachusetts Bay Colony in the late 17th century. Erikson examined court cases, diaries, birth and death records, letters, and other written documents of the period. Piecing together fragments of information 300 years old was not easy, but Erikson was able to draw some conclusions. He found that each time the colony was threatened in some way—by opposing religious groups, betrayals by community leaders, or the king of England's revocation of its charter—the numbers of convicted criminals and the severity of punishments significantly increased. Erikson believed that these fluctuations occurred because the community needed to restate its moral boundaries and reaffirm its authority.

Visual sociology is a method of studying society through photographs, video, and film. Some visual sociologists use these media to gather sociological data—much like documentary photographers and filmmakers do. The visual images they create are meant to tell a sociological story. Other visual sociologists analyze the meaning and purpose of existing visual texts, such as sports photographs, TV advertisements, and the photographic archives of corporations. The visual essays that appear throughout this book use this methodology to examine important issues of sociological interest.

All these methods allow sociological researchers to collect information without intruding upon and possibly changing the behavior of the people and groups they're studying.

The Trustworthiness of Social Research

Most sociologists see research as not only personally valuable but central to improving human knowledge and understanding. However, as consumers of this research, we must always ask, How accurate is this information? We tend to believe what we read in print or see reported on television or posted on Web sites. Unfortunately, much of what we see is either inaccurate or misleading. To evaluate the results of social research, we must examine the researcher's samples, the indicators used to measure important variables, and the researcher's personal qualities—namely values, interests, and ethics.

Samples

Frequently, sociological researchers are interested in the attitudes, behaviors, or characteristics of large groups—college students, women, sports enthusiasts, Brazilians, and so on. It would be impossible to interview, survey, or observe all these people directly. Hence, researchers must select from the larger population a smaller **sample** of respondents for study. The characteristics of this subgroup are supposed to approximate the characteristics of the entire population of interest. A sample is said to be **representative** if the small group being studied is in fact typical of the population as a whole. For instance, a sample of 100 students from your university should include roughly the same proportion of first-year students, sophomores, juniors, and seniors that characterizes the entire school population. Sampling techniques have become highly sophisticated, as illustrated by the relative accuracy of polls conducted to predict election results.

In the physical sciences, sampling is not an issue. Certain physical or chemical elements are assumed to be identical. One need only study a small number of vials of liquid nitrogen, because one vial of nitrogen should be the same as any other. Human beings, however, vary widely on every imaginable characteristic. You couldn't make a general statement about all Americans on the basis of an interview with one person. For that matter, you couldn't draw conclusions about all people from observing a sample consisting only of Americans, men, or teenagers. Samples that are not representative can lead to inaccurate and misleading conclusions.

Note the sampling problems revealed in the following letter to the editor of a small-town newspaper in the rural Midwest:

> I went to a restaurant yesterday for lunch. I began to feel guilty, when I reached into my pocket for a cigarette. . . . I was thinking of the government figures which estimated cigarette smokers at 26% of the population of the United States. But everywhere I looked inside that room, people were smoking. I decided to count them. There were 22 people in the room. . . . I was surprised to discover that the government's figures were an outright fabrication. . . . Seventeen people out of the 22 were cigarette smokers . . . that accounts for over 77% of the people in that restaurant. . . . The government's figures are understated by 51% and just plain wrong! (*Greencastle Banner Graphic,* 1992)

This letter writer assumed that the 22 people who frequented a small restaurant in a small, relatively poor rural town on a single day were an adequate representation of the entire U.S. population. Such a conclusion overlooks some important factors. Government studies show that the lower a person's income, the greater the likelihood that person will be a smoker. Furthermore, people in blue-collar or service jobs are more likely to smoke than people in white-collar jobs. Finally, the prevalence of smoking tends to be higher in rural areas of the Midwest and South than in other parts of the country (U.S. Department of Health and Human Services, 2005).

Indicators

As you recall, one problem sociologists face when doing research is that the variables they are interested in studying are usually difficult to see. What does powerlessness look like? How can you "see" marital satisfaction? How would you recognize alienation or social class? Sociologists thus resign themselves to measuring indicators of things that cannot be measured directly. Researchers measure events and behaviors commonly thought to accompany a particular variable, hoping that what they are measuring is a valid indicator of the concept they are interested in.

Suppose you believe that people's attitudes toward abortion are influenced by the strength of their religious beliefs, or "religiosity." You might hypothesize that the more religious someone is, the less accepting she or he will be of abortion rights. To test this hypothesis you must first figure out what you mean by "religious." What might be an indicator of the strength of someone's religious beliefs? You could determine if the subjects of your study identify themselves as members of some organized religion. But would this indicator tell how religious your subjects are? Probably not, because many people identify themselves as, say, Catholic or Jewish but are not religious at all. Likewise, some people who consider themselves quite religious don't identify with any organized religion. So this measure would focus on group differences but would fail to capture the intensity of a person's beliefs or the degree of religious interest.

Perhaps a better indicator would be some quantifiable behavior, such as the frequency of attendance at formal religious services (Babbie, 1986). Arguably, the more someone attends church, synagogue, or mosque, the more religious that person is. But here, too, we run into problems. Church attendance, for instance, may reflect family pressure, habit, or the desire to visit with others rather than religious commitment.

Furthermore, many very religious people are unable to attend services, because they are sick or disabled.

Frequency of prayer might be a better indicator. Obviously people who pray a lot are more religious than people who don't pray at all. But some religious people don't pray much, and some nonreligious people pray for things all the time. As you can see, indicators seldom perfectly reflect the concepts they are intended to measure.

Surveys are particularly susceptible to inaccurate indicators. A loaded phrase or an unfamiliar word in a survey question can dramatically affect people's responses in ways unintended by the researcher. The National Opinion Research Center asked in an annual survey of public attitudes if the United States was spending too much, too little, or about the right amount of money on "assistance to the poor." Two thirds of the respondents said the country was spending too little. But in a different study the word "welfare" was substituted for "assistance to the poor" in the question. This time nearly half of the respondents said the country was spending too much money (Kagay & Elder, 1992).

Values, Interests, and Ethics in Sociological Research

Along with samples and indicators, the researcher's own qualities can influence social research. Ideally, research is objective and nonbiased and measures what is and not what should be. However, the questions researchers ask and the way they interpret observations always take place in a particular cultural, political, and ideological context (Ballard, 1987; Denzin, 1989).

Consider the impact of values and interests. If prevailing social values identify an intact nuclear family as the best environment for children, then most researchers will be prone to notice the disadvantages and perhaps ignore the advantages of other family arrangements. Furthermore, research is sometimes carried out to support a narrowly defined political or economic interest, as when tobacco companies fund studies that show no relationship between smoking and cancer. The researcher who has received such a grant is hard-pressed to report negative results that may preclude further funding. This problem has become so bad that an organization of 12 major medical journals has proposed that pharmaceutical companies be required to register clinical trials at the beginning of drug studies so that negative and not just positive results would be publicly available (Meier, 2004).

We must remember that sociologists are people too, with their own biases, preconceptions, and expectations. Sociologists' values determine the kinds of information they gather about a particular social phenomenon. If you were conducting research on whether the criminal justice system is fair, would you study criminals, politicians, law enforcement personnel, judges, or victims? Each group would likely provide a different perception of the system. The most accurate picture of reality is likely to be based on the views of all subgroups involved.

In fact, values can influence the questions that researchers find important enough to address in the first place (Reinharz, 1992). For instance, research on families has historically reflected the interests of men by viewing female-headed households as dysfunctional or deficient (Thorne & Yalom, 1982). Similarly, the male bias affects the questions researched in studying women's work (Acker, 1978). The term *labor force* has traditionally referred to those working for pay and has excluded those doing unpaid work such as housework and volunteer jobs—areas that are predominantly female. Thus, findings on labor force participation are more likely to reflect the significant elements of men's lives than of women's lives. You can see that a lack of data does not necessarily indicate that a phenomenon or a problem doesn't exist. Perhaps all it indicates is that no researcher has yet undertaken a systematic study of it.

Ethics is another personal quality that affects the trustworthiness of social research. Research, as I mentioned earlier, often represents an intrusion into people's lives—it may disrupt their ordinary activities and it often requires them to reveal personal information about themselves. Ethical researchers agree, therefore, that they should protect the rights of subjects and minimize the amount of harm or disruption subjects might experience as a result of being part of a study. Ethical researchers agree that no one should be forced to participate in research, that those who do participate ought to be fully informed of the possible risks involved, and that every precaution ought to be taken to protect the confidentiality and anonymity of participants. Sociologists almost always conduct their research under the scrutiny of university review committees for the protection of human participants.

At the same time, however, researchers must attempt to secure the most accurate information possible. Sometimes this requirement conflicts with ethical considerations. For instance, how does one go about gathering information about people who may be involved in dangerous behavior or who do not want or cannot have their identities revealed? Sociologist Patricia Adler (1985) was interested in studying the worlds of drug dealers and smugglers. The illegal nature of their work makes them, by necessity, secretive, deceitful, and mistrustful, not the sort of individuals who make ideal survey or interview respondents. So Adler had to establish a significant level of rapport and trust. Although she never became actively involved in drug trafficking, she did become a part of the dealers' and smugglers' social world and participated in their daily activities. Only by studying these criminals in their natural setting was she able to see the full complexity of the world of drug smuggling. Her research, however, raises important questions related to trustworthiness and ethics: Did her closeness to her subjects make it impossible to study them objectively? Did she have an obligation to report illegal activity to law enforcement officials?

Laud Humphreys
The Tearoom Trade

Most sociologists agree that the need to understand the depth and complexity of the drug world outweighed the ethical issues raised by Adler's research strategy. There is less agreement and more controversy, however, over situations in which researchers misrepresent their identities in order to gather information. Consider the 1970 study called *The Tearoom Trade,* by Laud Humphreys, a study many sociologists find ethically indefensible. Humphreys was interested in studying anonymous and casual homosexual encounters among strangers. He decided to focus on interactions in "tearooms," which are places, such as public restrooms, where male homosexuals go for anonymous sex. (This study was done well before the HIV/AIDS epidemic significantly curtailed such activity.)

Because of the potentially stigmatizing nature of this phenomenon, Humphreys couldn't just come right out and ask people about their actions. So he decided to engage in a secretive form of participant observation. He posed as a lookout, called a "watchqueen," whose job was to warn of intruders as the people he was studying engaged in sexual acts with one another in public restrooms. In this way he was able to conduct very detailed observations of these encounters.

Humphreys also wanted to know about the regular lives of these men. Whenever possible he wrote down the license numbers of the participants' cars and tracked down their names and addresses with the help of a friend in the local police department. About a year later he arranged for these individuals to be part of a simple medical survey being conducted by some of his colleagues. He then disguised himself and visited their homes, supposedly to conduct interviews for the medical survey. He found that most of the men were heterosexual, had families, and were rather respected members of their communities. In short, they led altogether conventional lives.

Although this information shed a great deal of light on the nature of anonymous homosexual acts, some critics argued that Humphreys had violated the ethics of research by deceiving his unsuspecting subjects and violating their privacy rights. Some critics also noted that Humphreys might have been sued for invasion of privacy if he had not been studying a group of people rendered powerless by their potential embarrassment. Others, however, supported Humphreys, arguing that he could have studied this topic in no other way. In fact, his book won a prestigious award. But 35 years later, the ethical controversy surrounding this study remains.

Conclusion

In this chapter, I have described some of the processes by which reality is constructed, communicated, manipulated, and accepted. Reality, whether in the form of everyday observations or formal research, is ultimately a human creation. Different people can create different conceptions of reality.

This issue can be raised from a personal level to a global one. People in every culture believe that their reality is the paramount one. Who is right? Can we truly believe that a reality in direct conflict with ours is equally valid? If we profess that everyone should have the right to believe what she or he wants, are we acknowledging the socially constructed nature of reality or merely being tolerant of those who are not "smart enough" to think as we do? Do we have the right to tell other people or other cultures that what they do or believe is wrong only because it conflicts with our definition of reality? Exasperating and complex, these questions lie at the core of international relations, global commerce—and everyday life.

YOUR TURN

The reality we take for granted is a social construction. This is particularly apparent when we look at the information presented to us as fact through published academic research, word of mouth, or the media. Reality is influenced by the individuals and organizations responsible for creating, assembling, and disseminating this information.

Choose an event that is currently making national headlines. It could be a story about the president or Congress, a major tragedy or disaster, or a highly publicized criminal trial. Over the course of a week, analyze how this story is being covered by the following:

- ◆ Your local newspaper
- ◆ The major national newspapers (*USA Today,* the *New York Times,* the *Washington Post,* the *Wall Street Journal*)
- ◆ Mainstream news magazines (*Time, Newsweek, U.S. News & World Report*)
- ◆ Alternative magazines (*Utne Reader, Mother Jones, In These Times,* and so on)
- ◆ A local radio station
- ◆ National Public Radio (NPR)
- ◆ A local TV station
- ◆ The major networks (NBC, CBS, ABC, Fox, CNN)
- ◆ The Internet (chat rooms, Web sites, blogs, and so on)
- ◆ Late-night talk shows featuring topical comedy (such as Jon Stewart's *The Daily Show, The Late Show With David Letterman,* or Jay Leno's *Tonight Show*).

Pay particular attention to the following:

- ◆ The amount of time or space devoted to the story
- ◆ The "tone" of the coverage (Supportive or critical? Purely factual or reflective of certain political opinions? Specific, objective language or biased, inflammatory language?)

Summarize your findings. What were the differences in how the story was covered (for example, local versus national media, print versus electronic media, one TV network versus another, mainstream versus alternative press)? What were the similarities?

Interpret your findings. What do these differences and similarities suggest about the people who run these organizations? Whose political or economic interests are being served or undermined by the manner in which the story is being presented to the public? Which medium do you think is providing the most accurate, objective coverage? Why?

CHAPTER HIGHLIGHTS

- ◆ The social construction of reality (truth, knowledge, and so on) is the process by which reality is discovered, made known, reinforced, and changed by members of society.

- ◆ Language is the medium through which reality construction takes place. It enables us to think,

interpret, and define. Linguistic categories reflect aspects of a culture that are relevant and meaningful to people's lives.

- ◆ Not all of us possess the same ability to define reality. Individuals and groups in positions of power have the ability to control information, define values, create myths, manipulate events, and ultimately influence what others take for granted.

♦ The purpose of a discipline such as sociology is to amass a body of knowledge that provides the public with useful information about

how society works. This is done, quantitatively and qualitatively, through systematic social research—experiments, field research, surveys, and unobtrusive research. It is important to keep in mind, however, that this form of reality is also a social construction, shaped by the people who fund, conduct, and report on social research.

KEY TERMS

analysis of existing data Type of unobtrusive research that relies on data gathered earlier by someone else for some other purpose

content analysis Form of unobtrusive research that studies the content of recorded messages, such as books, speeches, poems, songs, television shows, Web sites, and advertisements

dependent variable Experimental variable that is assumed to be caused by, or to change as a result of, the independent variable

empirical research Research that operates from the ideological position that questions about human behavior can be answered only through controlled, systematic observations in the real world

experiment Research method designed to elicit some sort of behavior, typically conducted under closely controlled laboratory circumstances

field research Type of social research in which the researcher observes events as they actually occur

historical analysis Form of social research that relies on existing historical documents as a source of data

hypothesis Researchable prediction that specifies the relationship between two or more variables

incorrigible proposition Unquestioned cultural belief that cannot be proved wrong no matter what happens to dispute it

independent variable Experimental variable presumed to cause or influence the dependent variable

indicator Measurable event, characteristic, or behavior commonly thought to reflect a particular concept

moral entrepreneurs Groups that work to have their moral concerns translated into law

nonparticipant observation Form of field research in which the researcher observes people without directly interacting with them and without letting them know that they are being observed

participant observation Form of field research in which the researcher interacts with subjects, sometimes hiding his or her identity

probabilistic Capable of identifying only those forces that have a high likelihood, but not a certainty, of influencing human action

qualitative research sociological research based on nonnumerical information (text, written words, phrases, symbols, observations) that describes people, actions, or events in social life

quantitative research sociological research based on the collection of numerical data that uses precise statistical analysis

representative Typical of the whole population being studied

sample Subgroup chosen for a study because its characteristics approximate those of the entire population

self-fulfilling prophecy Assumption or prediction that in itself causes the expected event to occur, thus seeming to confirm the prophecy's accuracy

social construction of reality Process through which the members of a society discover, make known, reaffirm, and alter a collective version of facts, knowledge, and "truth"

survey Form of social research in which the researcher asks subjects a series of questions, either verbally or on paper

theory Set of statements or propositions that seeks to explain or predict a particular aspect of social life

unobtrusive research Research technique in which the researcher, without direct contact with the subjects, examines the evidence of social behavior that people create or leave behind

variable Any characteristic, attitude, behavior, or event that can take on two or more values or attributes

visual sociology Method of studying society that uses photographs, video, and film either as means of gathering data or as sources of data about social life

---
◆

STUDY SITE ON THE WEB

Don't forget the interactive quizzes and other learning aids at www.pineforge.com/newman 6study. In the Resources File for this chapter, you'll also find more on building reality, including:

Sociologists at Work

◆ Harold Garfinkel: Putting Meaning Into Meaningless Situations

◆ Robert Rosenthal and Lenore Jacobson: Pygmalion in the Classroom

Micro-Macro Connection

◆ Constructing Reality in Stages

4 Building Order
Culture and History

Dimensions of Culture

Cultural Expectations and Social Order

Cultural Variation and Everyday Experience

In Madagascar, the harvest months of August and September mark the *famadihana*—the "turning of the bones." Families receive messages from *razana*—their dead loved ones—who may say they are uncomfortable or need new clothes. In an elaborate ceremony that can last for days, families feast, sing, and dig up the graves of the deceased. The bodies are wrapped in shrouds and seated at the dinner table. Family news is whispered to them, and toasts are drunk. Widows and widowers can often be seen dancing with the bones of their dead spouses. The exhumed bones are then oiled and perfumed and laid back onto their "beds" inside the family tomb (Perlez, 1991).

In the late 19th and early 20th centuries, dating and courtship in North America were based on a ritualized system known as "calling." Although the process varied by region and social class, the following general guidelines were involved:

> When a girl reached the proper age or had her first "season" (depending on her family's social level), she became eligible to receive male callers. At first her mother or guardian invited young men to call; in subsequent seasons the young lady . . . could bestow an invitation to call upon any unmarried man to whom she had been properly introduced at a private dance, dinner, or other "entertainment." . . . Other young men . . . could be brought to call by friends or relatives of the girl's family, subject to her prior permission. . . . The call itself was a complicated event. A myriad of rules governed everything: the proper amount of time between invitation and visit (two weeks or less); whether or not refreshments should be served . . . ; chaperonage (the first call must be made on mother and daughter . . .); appropriate topics of conversation (the man's interests, but never too personal); how leave should be taken (on no account should the woman accompany [her caller] to the door nor stand talking while he struggles with his coat). (B. L. Bailey, 1988, pp. 15–16)

How could anybody dig up the body of a dead relative? Why would young men and young women follow such elaborate rules just so they could go on a date? Such practices seem peculiar, silly, or backward to most of us, but to the people involved, they are or were simply the taken-for-granted, "right" ways of doing things.

Some of the things you do may seem equally incomprehensible to an outside observer. For instance, you may not think twice about eating a juicy T-bone steak, but someone from a culture that views cows as sacred would be horrified at the thought. You may routinely shave your face, legs, or armpits, but imagine what these practices would look like in a culture where such acts are considered blasphemous. You may think a Spaniard's fondness for bullfighting is "absurd," yet millions of people in the United States shell out a lot of money each year to watch large men in brightly colored helmets knock each other down while they chase, throw, carry, and kick an object made out of the hide of a dead pig. You may pity the turn-of-the-century woman who squeezed her body into an ultra-tight corset in order to achieve the wasp-waisted figure men considered attractive. Yet many women today (as well as some men) routinely coat their skin with flesh-colored makeup, use harsh chemicals to change the color of their hair, pay to have someone cut into their faces to decrease the size of their noses or tighten the skin around their chins, and even reduce their food intake to the point of starvation to become more slender.

The legitimacy of certain practices and ideas can be understood only within the unique context of the group or society in which they occur. What is considered abnormal in one case may be perfectly normal, even necessary, in another. It takes sociological imagination to see that time and place have a great influence on what people consider normal.

Ancestor worship in Madagascar is a custom that has been around for centuries, impervious to the arrival of Christian churches and Western ideals. To the people who practice it, the ritual of burial, disinterment, and reburial is more important than marriage. The physical body may die, but the *fanahy* or soul lives on. The Malagasy believe that spirits stay with the bones and have needs for earthly goods like food and clothing. It's up to the living to provide these things. In exchange, the dead take care of living relatives by determining their health, wealth, and fertility and by helping them communicate with God. In short, the custom is quite rational and beneficial: The individual's own earthly well-being and spiritual salvation depend on it.

Likewise, the practice of calling played an integral part in late 19th-century U.S. culture. It maintained the social class structure by serving as a test of suitability, breeding, and background (B. L. Bailey, 1988). Calling enabled the middle and upper classes to protect themselves from what many at the time considered the "intrusions" of urban life and to screen out the disruptive effects of social and geographic mobility that reached unprecedented levels at the turn of the century. It also allowed parents to control the relationships of their children, thereby increasing the likelihood that their pedigree would remain intact.

These phenomena illustrate the important role played by culture and history in creating social order. Whether we're talking about our own ordinary rituals or those practiced by some distant society, the normative patterns that mark the millions of seemingly trivial actions and social encounters of our everyday lives are what make society possible. They tell us what to expect from others and what others should expect from us. In this chapter, by looking at the various taken-for-granted aspects of culture that lend structure to our daily lives, I examine how order is created and maintained in society. In the process I compare specific aspects of our culture to others, past and present.

Dimensions of Culture

In Chapter 2 you saw that culture is one of the key elements that make up a society. In everyday conversation, however, the term *culture* is often used only when discussing something "foreign." We rarely feel the need to question why we do certain things in the course of our everyday lives—we just do them. It's other people in other lands whose rituals and beliefs need explaining. What we often fail to realize is that culture is "doing its job" most effectively when it is unnoticed. We're least likely to speak about what we take for granted; and it's those cultural silences that are most familiar to members and most important for the enduring stability of social order (Perin, 1988). Only in times of dramatic social change and moral uncertainty, or when circumstances force us to compare our society to another (for example, when traveling abroad), do we become aware that a distinct set of cultural rules and values influences us too.

We can know a lot about someone just by knowing something about his or her culture:

> Even those of us who pride ourselves on our individualism follow most of the time a pattern not of our own making. We brush our teeth on arising. We put on pants—not a loincloth or a grass skirt. . . . We sleep in a bed—not a hammock or on a sheep pelt. I do not have to know the individual and his [or her] life history to be able to predict these and countless other regularities. (Kluckholm, 2000, p. 83)

To a large degree, we are products of the culture and historical epoch in which we reside. From a very young age we learn, with a startling amount of accuracy, that certain types of shelter, food, tools, clothing, modes of transportation, music, sports, and art characterize our culture and make it different from others. Without much conscious effort, we also learn what to believe, what to value, and which actions are proper or improper in both public and private.

Material and Nonmaterial Culture

Culture consists of all the products of a society that are created over time and shared. These products may be tangible or intangible. The term **nonmaterial culture** refers to all the nonphysical products of society that are created over time and shared: knowledge, beliefs, customs, values, morals, symbols, and so on. Nonmaterial culture also includes common patterns of behavior and the forms of interaction appropriate in a particular society. It is a "design for living" that distinguishes one society from another. Like an owner's manual for social life, nonmaterial culture tells us how our society works, what we are to believe is possible, what we are to value, how we are to conduct our everyday lives, and what to do if something breaks down. Without an understanding of a society's nonmaterial culture, people's behaviors—not to mention the symbolic significance of their material world—would be thoroughly incomprehensible.

The values that reside in nonmaterial culture often support a given society's economic and political systems. For example, in 2002, the Pew Research Center conducted a worldwide poll of 38,000 people in 44 countries. One question asked respondents if they agreed with the statement, "Success in life is pretty much determined by forces outside our control." Over 60% of Americans and Canadians disagreed, reflecting the cultural attitude that our fate is determined by our own individual achievements. Such an attitude is an essential component of a political system based on individual rights and an economic system that is based on the principle of individual merit where, theoretically, everyone has control over their own fate. In contrast, over 60% of German, Italian, Turkish, Pakistani, Indian, and Bangladeshi respondents agreed that individuals have little control over their fate, suggesting a more fatalistic cultural attitude (cited in Leland, 2004b).

Material culture includes the physical artifacts that shape or reflect the lives of members of a particular society: distinctive clothing, buildings, inventions, food, artwork, literature, music, and so on. Some of the most important elements of material culture are technological achievements, which are the ways members of a society apply knowledge to adapt to changing social, economic, or environmental conditions. For instance, plastic products have provided people with cheaper and more convenient packaging of needed goods—and in the process forever altered shopping and consumption patterns.

Similarly, the advent of the automobile gives people greater mobility to take advantage of economic or residential opportunities elsewhere and thereby dramatically changes some of their values and the way they live. In advanced industrialized countries such as the United States and Canada, the automobile has been widely available since the early 20th century, so we have become accustomed to the cultural changes associated with it, such as suburban living, a massive national highway system, and unchaperoned teen dating. But the changes are more noticeable today in places such as Nepal and rural China, where the automobile is just beginning to have a dramatic impact on people's lives.

Changes in material culture often transform the physical environment, creating the need for additional alterations in material and nonmaterial culture. The enormous amount of nonbiodegradable plastic piling up in overflowing landfills, for example, has spawned a vast array of advances in recycling and other eco-friendly technologies. Likewise, heavy reliance on the automobile has created several serious problems in urban areas throughout the world: air pollution, depletion of fossil fuel reserves, traffic, and suburban sprawl. These problems, in turn, have created the need for changes in travel patterns and arrangements, as well as further material developments, such as pollution-reducing devices, hybrid automobiles, and alternative fuel sources.

❖
Micro-Macro Connection
The Chair

Even the simplest and most taken-for-granted material objects of our everyday lives carry enormous cultural weight. Take, for example, the common chair. We spend a huge chunk of our lives sitting in chairs—in dining rooms, kitchens, living rooms, classrooms, libraries, offices, patios, cars, buses, movie theaters, restaurants, and so on. You're probably sitting in one at this very moment.

Chairs supposedly make our lives comfortable. To be able to relax, kick off your shoes, and plop down on the old La-Z-Boy after a hard day's work is one of life's great pleasures. But such comfort has a steep cost. Ironically, lower back pain, often caused by bad sitting posture or poorly designed chairs, is second only to the common cold as the leading cause of absenteeism from work (Cranz, 1998). And our sedentary lifestyle has created a nation of people who are woefully out of shape.

Like all pieces of material culture, chairs are human creations. But once they're built, they start to shape us. The type of chair you use in your sociology class immediately places you in the role of student. And whether these chairs are arranged in rows or in a circle determines the degree of interaction expected of you in class. Children's first institutional lessons in controlling their bodies typically involve the chairs they are told to "sit still" in. Sitting quietly in rows of hard, straight chairs is not a natural state of being for young children. But it certainly helps teachers maintain authority and keep disruptive behaviors safely contained.

Chairs often take on important cultural significance beyond their functionality. For instance, the chair a person sits in may define that person's social status. In antiquity, only the most powerful and prestigious members of a society had access to chairs; the throne is one of the most enduring symbols of royalty worldwide. When the Pope issues an authoritative decree to Catholics around the world, he is said to be speaking *ex cathedra,* which literally means "from the chair." In some families children learn very quickly the consequences of sitting in or otherwise sullying "Dad's chair." The "chair" of an academic department can wield a great deal of power. On the other end of the spectrum, the "electric chair" is reserved for the lowest and most despicable of citizens, whose heinous crimes have led society to pronounce them unfit to live.

The right-angled posture required to sit in a chair, which we assume to be the universally proper way to sit, is used by only a third to half of the people worldwide (Cranz, 1998). In many parts of the world people sit on floors, mats, carpets, or platforms. A Chinese man will likely squat when waiting for a bus; a Japanese woman kneels when eating; an Arab might sit cross-legged on the floor when reading.

Regardless of whether we use a chair or what sort of chair we use, one thing is clear: this habit was created, modified, nurtured, and reformed in response to cultural—and not anatomical—forces. Our subjective experiences of comfort are socially constructed, and our bodies respond accordingly. For the American it *really is* more comfortable to sit in a chair; for the rural Arab it *really is* more comfortable to sit on the floor. That these choices are experienced subjectively as personally pleasant doesn't mean that culture isn't at work here.

Global Culture

Although culture gives each society its distinctive character, cultural "purity" is all but obsolete (Griswold, 1994). Transnational media, global communication and transportation systems, and centuries of international migration have contributed to a worldwide swapping of cultural elements. For instance, American retailers are a common fixture worldwide. Wal-Mart has nearly 5,000 stores in Asia, Latin America, and North America (Wal-Mart, 2003). Starbucks has over 1,500 coffeehouses in 31 countries (Starbucks, 2005). American pizza, too, which originally came to us from Naples, Italy, has migrated to every corner of the globe. Domino's Pizza now has over 7,500 stores in more than 50 countries (Domino's, 2005); Pizza Hut has stores in 84 countries (Pizza Hut, 2005). According to the Canadian Broadcasting Company (2003), only 30% of television shows, 18% of English-language magazines, 28% of books, 13% of music recordings, and 2% of feature films that Canadians consume are actually produced in Canada. What were once unique features of U.S. material culture—such as blue jeans and fast food—can now be found on nearly every continent. It wouldn't be particularly surprising to find people wearing faded Levis in a remote village in the Andes Mountains of Peru or munching on Big Macs in Bangkok.

In some societies, people see imported elements of culture as dangerous encroachments on long-held traditions and national unity. Of special concern is the increasing influence of U.S. culture on other countries. A few years ago, culture ministers from 20 different countries on four continents met to discuss how best to maintain their own cultures in a global environment dominated by U.S. media (Croteau & Hoynes, 2000). They were responding to examples like these:

♦ Approximately two thirds of French respondents to a survey felt that the United States exerted too much cultural influence on Europe (Daley, 2000). A French sheep farmer named José Bové became something of a national hero for vandalizing McDonald's restaurants, a symbol of what many French consider to be the unwanted intrusion of U.S. food culture.

♦ In Austria, an organization called the Pro-Christkind Association launched a campaign against Santa Claus, claiming that he is nothing more than an advertising symbol of American culture and consumption habits (Landler, 2002).

♦ Okinawa, Japan, has, historically, had the highest proportion of people over the age of 100 in the world and the greatest life expectancy of any region in Japan. But, increasingly, Okinawans are living and eating like Americans. They walk less, eat fewer vegetables, and eat more hamburgers than they used to. Okinawa now has the most American-style fast food restaurants of any city in Japan. As a result, average weight and rates of heart disease, cerebral hemorrhage, and lung cancer have all increased. Okinawans now rank 26th in life expectancy among Japanese administrative regions (Onishi, 2004a; Takayama, 2003).

Emotions can run especially high when the integrity of a culture's language is at stake. About 60% of all existing languages have fewer than 10,000 speakers. These languages are highly vulnerable to disappearance in a global culture. Indeed, each year about 30 languages around the world become extinct. Australia once had 250 different languages; today there are fewer than 20 (J. Raymond, 1998). One linguist predicted that at least half of the world's roughly 6,500 languages will die out during the 21st century. Taking their place will be a handful of dominant languages that, in a technologically connected world, are seen as "linguistic passports" to education and a successful economic future (P. H. Lewis, 1998).

Foremost among these major languages is English, which today shapes communication all over the world. The word for home run in Cuba is *jonrón*. In many Spanish-speaking countries, people type e-mails on their *computadoras*. The French commonly use words like *le week-end* and *le shopping*. People are recognizing that in a world of collapsing borders a common language is useful. And because of pervasive U.S. cultural influences and technologies, English is an understandable choice. For instance, even though the number of non-English users on the Internet grows each year, about 80% of the world's electronically stored information is in English (Crystal, 2003). It's estimated that by the middle of the 21st century, half the world's population will be able to speak English—compared to about 12% now (Rodriguez, 2002).

The growth of English—and especially U.S. English—as a sort of "world" language has had a profound effect on the way people in other countries go about their business. For example, the Swiss government decreed that all Swiss children above the age of 6 must learn English. In Chile, the government wants to make all its 15 million citizens fluent in English within a generation (Rohter, 2004).

But not everyone is happy about such developments. In 1994 France enacted a law—called the Toubon Law—that makes French the mandatory language in a variety of situations, ranging from advertising to the workplace documents employees need to do their jobs. In 2004, workers at a French branch of General Electric that manufactures health equipment sued the company for violating this law because all of its internal e-mails, instruction manuals, and software applications are printed only in English. Similarly, in an effort to limit the influence of American popular music, the Israeli Parliament approved a bill requiring that half of the songs on national radio stations must be in Hebrew. According to the sponsor of the bill, "We are putting up a protective wall against the flood of foreign culture" (quoted in Greenberg, 1998, p. 10).

In the United States many people are concerned with the encroaching influence not of English but of Spanish. Many Americans fret over the primacy of English when they see street signs, billboards, election ballots, and automated teller machines using Spanish. In 2002, the state of Texas held the first-ever gubernatorial debate entirely in Spanish (Rodriguez, 2002). To forestall the possibility that the United States might someday become a bilingual nation, over half of the states have passed legislation declaring English as their official language.

Subcultures

Sociologists and anthropologists usually speak of culture as a characteristic of an entire society. But culture can also exist in smaller, more narrowly defined units. A **subculture** consists of the values, behaviors, and physical artifacts of a group that distinguishes itself from the larger culture. Think of it as a culture within a culture. Racial and ethnic groups, religions, age groups, even geographic areas often develop their own distinct subcultures.

Consider life at your university. You are probably well aware of the material and nonmaterial culture that is unique to your campus. Perhaps some landmark—a bell tower or an ornate archway—is the defining symbol of the university, or maybe some area or piece of art occupies a hallowed place in campus life. I'm sure you know your school mascot and the school colors, which you can no doubt purchase in T-shirt form at the campus book store. In addition, when you first arrived at school, you probably had to learn a tremendous amount of new information about the nonmaterial culture just to survive—how to register for courses; how to address a professor; where to eat and study; what administrators, faculty, and fellow students expect of you. At my university, the student newspaper publishes a glossary of common words, phrases, and nicknames at the beginning of each academic year to aid first-year students in their adjustment to life on campus. Just as you have to learn how to be a member of your society, you have to learn how to be a member of your university subculture.

But placing a label on a subculture sometimes obscures its complexity and diversity. For instance, you often hear people talk about the U.S. "teen subculture" as if it were a single, self-contained entity that is the same everywhere in our society. But such a characterization overlooks the multitude of subgroups within that subculture:

> On any sustained wander through the world of American youth, one meets . . . an endless array of ardent skaters, skins, rockers, ravers, rebels, heshers, punks, Goths, jocks, Rude Boys, hippies, preps, rappers, neo-Nazis, cheerleaders, Satanists, and straight-edged anarchists. This is just an arbitrary, incomplete catalogue of a few high-profile formations—the kind that tend to have their own magazines, Web sites, fashion lines, and music playlists, not to mention "beliefs." There are thousands of smaller sects and splinters and tendencies, gangs and subgangs and cliques, rising and falling all the time, each with a party line on a range of cultural issues, large and small. (Finnegan, 1998, p. 349)

Although certain subcultures may appear to dramatically conflict with the beliefs and values of the dominant culture, they never exist completely independent of that culture. For instance, alienated youth may adorn themselves in the angry and rebellious fashion trappings of gangsta rappers or antiglobal anarchists, but they still must conform to many of the dictates of the larger culture by exchanging money for necessary goods and services, going to school, and eventually getting a job so they can support themselves.

History: The "Archives" for Everyday Living

Like culture, history is simultaneously everywhere and invisible. We rarely see the connection between our personal lives and the larger historical context in which we live. Just as culture tends to be equated with the foreign, history tends to be equated with the past. Yet it too has a pervasive influence on today's society.

It is all too easy to use contemporary criteria to try to understand the thoughts and actions of people who lived long ago. For example, in 1997 the New Orleans School Board voted unanimously to change the name of George Washington Elementary School. The board as a matter of policy opposes naming schools for former slave owners or for people who didn't believe in equal rights for all, no matter what their other accomplishments. When Washington died in 1799, he owned 316 slaves (Sack, 1997).

Abraham Lincoln, one of history's most influential proponents of liberty and equality, once said, "There is a physical difference between the white and black races which I believe will forever forbid the two races living together on terms of social and political equality" (quoted in Gould, 1981, p. 35). Similar views of racial separation were voiced by such important historical figures as Benjamin Franklin, Thomas Jefferson, and Charles Darwin. Such comments, if uttered today, would be taken as indications of a deeply held prejudice.

However, we must understand such beliefs and behaviors not merely as signs of personal bigotry but as reflections of the dominant cultural belief system of the times. In other words, they are social constructions. As repugnant as we might find these attitudes, they were taken as undeniable truths by the scientific communities of their era. Innate "racial inferiority" was as much an established "scientific fact" then as the expansion of the universe is today. (See Chapter 11 for more detail on the belief in innate racial inferiority.) The norms and values that govern everyday life in a given society are also likely to change over time. Some cultural practices that were wholly unacceptable in the past have now become commonplace. Premarital sex and house-husbands no longer incite the sort of moral outrage or suspicion among the middle and upper classes that they once did.

Other acts have become less acceptable, even criminal. In the United States, there was a time when people could smoke cigarettes anywhere and anytime they pleased—in supermarkets, restaurants, movie theaters, even hospitals. Now, with the increase in health awareness, smoking in public buildings (and even outdoor public facilities) has been severely restricted or outlawed in many locales.

Historical shifts in the cultural acceptance of certain behaviors involve more than just a societal realization of the danger of such behaviors. Actually, as the conflict perspective would point out, such designations are greatly influenced by social and economic concerns. Take, for instance, the criminalization of opium—the substance from which heroin is derived. During the 19th century, the use of opium was legal in many parts of the world; it was commonly used for therapeutic purposes as a pain reliever, a cold medicine, and a cough suppressant (Inciardi, 1992). The typical "heroin addict" at the time in the United States was a white middle-class housewife.

By the early 20th century, however, things had changed considerably. In the United States, there was a growing fear, particularly on the West Coast, of economic competition from Chinese laborers who had been "imported" to work on the railroads. Workers began to see Chinese immigrants as a direct threat to their material interests. At the same time, these immigrants became equated with opium use (Hagan, 1985). What followed must have made perfectly logical sense at the time: If a despised group characteristically engages in a particular behavior, there must be something wrong with that behavior. A moral consensus soon emerged that focused on the presumed link between the Chinese and narcotics (Bonnie & Whitebread, 1974). It wasn't long before opium use became the dreaded "Oriental dope problem." By 1914 tight legislative controls restricted the U.S. distribution of opium to authorized medical prescriptions only. By 1925 it was completely outlawed (Becker, 1963).

Cultural Expectations and Social Order

Despite periodic shifts in the acceptability of specific acts, culture and history provide people with a common bond, a sense of shared personal experiences. That we can live together at all depends on the fact that we share a tremendous amount of cultural knowledge. This knowledge allows us to predict, with a fair amount of certainty, what most people will do in a given situation. I can assume that when I say "Hi, how are you?" you will reply "Fine." You probably won't launch into some long-winded explanation of your mental, physical, and emotional condition at that precise moment, because doing so would violate the cultural rules governing casual greetings.

The actions of individuals are not simply functions of personality types or psychological predispositions; rather, they are also a reflection of shared cultural expectations. Culture provides us with information about which of these actions are preferred, accepted, or disapproved of at a given time (McCall & Simmons, 1978). Take, for example, sexuality. American culture is often characterized as a **heteronormative culture**—that is, a culture where heterosexuality is accepted as the normal, taken-for-granted mode of sexual expression. Social institutions and social policies reinforce the belief that sexual relationships ought to exist between males and females. Cultural representations of just about every aspect of intimate and family life—dating, sex, marriage, childbearing, retirement, and so on—presume a world in which men are sexually and affectionately attracted to women and women to men (Macgillivray, 2000). Think of the flurry of magazine and TV advertisements we're subjected to in the weeks prior to Valentine's Day that depict men and women embracing, gazing longingly into each other's eyes, and buying each other expensive jewelry. Adolescent women seeing a gynecologist for the first time can expect to be given information on birth control, highlighting the assumption that they will have sex with men, it's just a matter of when. Even some sports reflect heteronormativity. In competitive figure skating the "pairs" competition always consists of women partnered with men (Wildman & Davis, 2002).

In a heteronormative society, heterosexuals are socially privileged because their relationships and lifestyles are affirmed in every facet of the culture. Such privilege includes having positive media images of people with the same sexual orientation; not having to lie about who you are, what you do, and where you seek entertainment; not having to worry about losing a job because of your sexual orientation; receiving validation from your religious community; being able to marry and adopt children; and being able to join the Boy Scouts or serve openly in the military (Macgillivray, 2000, p. 304).

Recall from Chapter 2 that norms are the rules that govern the routine social encounters in which we all participate. Although everyday norms are sometimes difficult to identify and describe, they reflect commonly held assumptions about conventional behavior. Consider the unspoken norms in a situation we've all experienced, shopping at a supermarket:

> There is a customer role to be played in grocery stores. There generally is a standard of orderliness. Shoppers are not seen pushing each other out of the way, picking things out of each other's shopping carts, or sitting on the floor eating from a recently opened can. How does one "know" how the role of customer is to be played? Aside from the "No Shirt. No Bare Feet" sign on the door . . . there is no clear listing of shopping rules.

Evidence of the implied existence of such rules can be found in the way people react to a fellow shopper dressed in a gorilla suit or to someone who violates the norms for waiting in line at the checkout counter. One may feel that rules are being broken when one finds oneself standing in line with melting ice cream behind a grandmother who takes out her grandchildren's photographs to show the clerk. Such behavior violates the norms of universalism (all customers are to be treated equally) and efficiency; the grocery store is not a context in which one shares one's private self with others, particularly anonymous others (Kearl & Gordon, 1992, p. 274).

Norms can be generalized in similar situations within a culture. That is, we can be reasonably certain that grocery store behavior that is appropriate in Baton Rouge will be appropriate in Bakersfield or Butte as well. The grocery store experience itself would be chaotic if there weren't a certain degree of agreement over how we should act. Without such unspoken rules, every situation would have to be interpreted, analyzed, and responded to as if it were an entirely new occasion. Social life (not to mention preparing meals) would be utterly unmanageable.

Cultural norms are not static rules, however. They often change as the culture itself changes. A compelling reason for norms to change is to accommodate new technologies.

❖ ─────────────────────────────

Micro-Macro Connection
Can You Hear Me Now?

One of the most popular technological devices in contemporary society today is the cell phone. Cell phones were first mass-marketed to the public in 1984. Ten years later, 24 million Americans had them. Today, that figure has exceeded 182 million—over half of the U.S. population (see Exhibit 4.1). In 2004, the amount of time all these people spent on their cell phones surpassed one *trillion* minutes (Cellular Telecommunications and Internet Association, 2005). What was once the sole province of the powerful and the well-to-do is now a mass-market item that virtually everyone can obtain. As a result, cell phones have completely revolutionized the way we communicate, work, form relationships, and recreate in our everyday lives.

Telephone conversations were once activities that people took great pains to keep private, and they were by necessity stationary. Phones were either in people's own homes or their workplaces. On those occasions when people had to use a phone away from home or work, they turned to public telephone booths—relics of material culture that have gone the way of the dinosaur. In these enclosed boxes, people could shut out the rest of the world while talking privately on the phone.

Cell phones have changed all that. For one thing, these devices have completely altered our sense of place. When phones were anchored in a particular location you knew when you called someone where that person was. Now, the first question people typically ask when calling someone's cell phone is "Where are you?" The other day, I called a friend's cell phone. There was no answer and the recorded message started out with the common, "I'm not here right now . . ." I had to laugh. What does "here" actually mean when someone's phone is, by design, *not* here (or anywhere in particular, for that matter)?

Exhibit 4.1   Trends in Cell Phone Usage

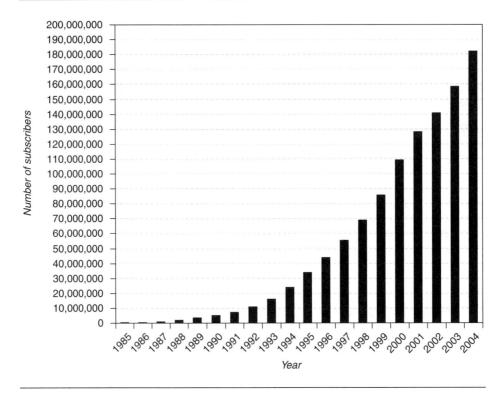

Source: Cellular and Telecommunications and Internet Association, 2005. Used with permission.

More importantly, people speaking on mobile cell phones today often seem more engaged in a public broadcast than an intimate conversation. Perhaps you've experienced a variation of this common scene:

> With just five minutes to takeoff, the young man across the aisle . . . whipped out his cell phone and began a hurried and boisterous conversation, explaining the fine points of marketing his new Christmas-gift web site to an unseen underling. With glazed eyes staring at the seat in front of him, the executive unconsciously pounded his foot in rhythm to his conversation, oblivious to the 15 surrounding passengers glaring at this human loudspeaker in seat 23B. (Taub, 2001, p. D1)

People's "need" to constantly talk to (or text message) others as they go about their daily lives has grown as a result of access to technology that makes phone conversations possible anywhere and anytime, and not the other way around. Cellular technology did not develop because people were clamoring for constant access. Today, though, it's common to see people talking on their phones while driving (although, out of concern for safety, New York, New Jersey, and other states have passed laws to control drivers' use of cell phones). People can be seen (and heard) talking on phones while riding stationary bikes in fitness centers or while sitting on toilets in public restrooms. Most of my students know to turn off their ringers before coming to class. But it's rare these days to get through a class period without hearing the telltale buzzing sound of a cell phone on "vibrate." And it's a common sight on campuses all across the country to see scores of students spilling from rooms into the hallway at the end of class already engaged in conversations on their cell phones (and I doubt it's to discuss the scintillating sociological insight they just learned!). Some airlines now allow passengers to use their phones until the plane pushes back from the gate and the instant the plane touches down. But that's not good enough for some cell phone users, and so the Federal Communications Commission has begun contemplating a change in federal aviation policy that would allow cell phone usage on planes in flight. Such conversational urgency was unknown a mere five years ago. Indeed, some experts liken this sort of cell phone usage to an addiction (Hubert, 2005). As one author put it, cell phones are the "cigarettes of this decade" (quoted in Leland, 2005, p. 2).

The rapid diffusion of such a visible technology caught us unawares. As one author put it, "We should recognize that we're on a technological roller coaster and things are changing fast and there are levels of rudeness that we are just discovering" (quoted in Belson, 2004, p. 14). But a social backlash has begun to impose limits on people's behavior. Huffs of disgust and resentful rolled eyes await the person whose cell phone rings to the tune of the *Star Wars* theme song while in line at the supermarket or who decides to answer a call in the middle of a face-to-face conversation with a dismissive, "Excuse me, I've got to take this. It's important." Movie theaters, concert halls, libraries, and business conferences now routinely post reminders to people to turn off their cell phones. Major golf tournaments now require fans to actually hand over their phones prior to entering the course. Trains in Britain, Japan, Switzerland, and the United States now have phone-free quiet cars.

Some go even further. At Bergen Airport in Norway, a system has been installed that automatically shuts off travelers' cell phones before they board the plane (Taub, 2001). In 2004, a passenger on a flight from Miami to Philadelphia refused repeated requests by flight attendants to turn off her cell phone so the plane could take off. The plane was forced to return to the terminal, but not before the caller slapped a federal air marshal (Belson, 2004). She was handcuffed, taken from the plane and arrested on assault charges, much to the delight, I would suspect, of the other passengers. As with other forms of technology, eventually people will come to some normative agreement about proper cell phone etiquette in different social situations and order will be restored.

❖ ❖

Social Institutions and Cultural Norms

Large social institutions are closely related to culture. For one thing, some institutions reflect deeply held cultural values. A free-market economy, for instance, reflects the cultural values of achievement, competition, material acquisition, and so on. A democratic government reflects the values of individual freedom and citizen participation. Other institutions—such as education, religion, and family—provide the mechanisms through which culture and subculture are transmitted across generations.

Institutions are also strongly supported by cultural norms. When a pattern of behavior becomes widely accepted within a particular social institution and taken for granted in society, sociologists say it has become an **institutionalized norm** (DiMaggio & Powell, 1991). For instance, the institutionalized (that is, culturally acceptable) way of becoming financially successful in many developed societies is to get a college degree (and perhaps an advanced degree after that), start out in an entry-level position somewhere, and eventually work your way to the top. Even things that most of us would condemn have, at times, been institutionalized and encouraged by society. Slavery, for example, was for several hundred years a culturally, politically, and economically acceptable practice in the United States. The buying and selling of slaves were strongly approved by the nation's most powerful forces as well as by many ordinary people (Birenbaum & Sagarin, 1976).

Institutionalized norms constrain people's behavior by making some lines of action unthinkable. But they don't just limit options, they also establish the setting in which people discover their preferences and begin to see the world in a particular way (DiMaggio & Powell, 1991). The orientation and training sessions people are expected to participate in when they start a job, for example, clearly indicate the organization's expectations and each person's new responsibilities. Other employees' acceptance of these expectations as legitimate reinforces the idea that organizational norms shouldn't be questioned. Similarly, the military ritualizes the process of becoming a full-fledged member through training, oaths of allegiance, and public recognition of the passage from one rank to another. In doing so it ensures conformity to military norms and an understanding of the "rules of engagement," the specific norms that govern fighting on the battlefield. Religious congregations reinforce "appropriate" lifestyles and downplay inappropriate ones through collective worship services.

When institutions change, so, too, do institutionalized norms. Changes in the institution of the U.S. family, for instance, have created some new expectations: Children are now expected to be more independent; fathers are expected to be more involved in the nurturing of children. In the political realm, shifting public opinion as well as political necessity eventually led to the abolition of slavery.

Shifts in one institution are often linked to shifts in another. The abolition of slavery in the United States, for instance, meant that the entire economic system of the South had to be restructured, from a plantation economy to one characterized by smaller landholdings and more industry. In Russia, the collapse of communism over a decade ago strengthened the role of religious organizations in providing people with normative guidelines. In the United States today, the fact that women are no longer expected to be the sole caretakers of children has meant an increase in the number of mothers who enter the paid labor force, which in turn has created higher demand for organized day care.

❖
Micro-Macro Connection
The "Right" Emotions

To illustrate the enormous power of institutionalized norms in our private experiences, I turn to a common element of everyday life—emotions. We all experience emotions as physical, sometimes instantaneous responses to life events. Thus we're inclined to see emotions as natural and universal. Yet emotional display comes under the strict control of cultural norms. In Greece, widows traditionally are expected to grieve over the loss of their husbands for periods of time that would be seen as excessive in the United States, where two months of such grieving might be considered a sign of major depression (Horwitz, 2002).

Every society has many unwritten rules about which emotions are appropriate to feel, which are appropriate to display, and how intense the emotional display should be under specific circumstances. For instance, in our culture, we're supposed to be sad at funerals, happy at weddings, and angry when we are insulted. We're supposed to feel joy when we receive good news but not show too much of it if our good fortune is at someone else's expense. We're supposed to be mildly upset if we get a *B–* in a course instead of a *B+*, but not to sink into severe depression. In extreme cases the violation of emotional display norms can lead to grave sanctions, such as being diagnosed as mentally ill (Pugliesi, 1987; Thoits, 1985).

When people hide or alter their emotions to fit the situation, they are playing a significant role in maintaining social order within broader social institutions. Take televised beauty pageants, for example. As the field of contestants is reduced to the final two, the camera zooms in on both of them. Usually they're standing on stage hugging each other in shaky anticipation of the final verdict. When the winner is announced, the runner-up is the picture of grace and charm, all smiles and congratulations. But we all know better. She has just lost the contest of her life on national television and has got to be sad, angry, or at the very least disappointed. Why does the runner-up suppress the urge to show her true emotions? Part of the reason is that she understands that there's more at stake than her feelings. Imagine what would happen to the multimillion-dollar beauty contest industry if the losers began to display their bitterness and discontent on stage—arguing with judges, shouting at the winners, and so forth.

Cultural norms about expressing emotions are often linked to institutional concerns and needs. In her book *The Managed Heart*, Arlie Russell Hochschild (1983) describes the feeling rules required by occupations in which employees have a great deal of contact with the public. Flight attendants, for example, must constantly be good-natured and calm under dangerous conditions. They must make their work appear effortless and handle other people's feelings as deftly as their own. This ability is not just a matter of living up to social expectations—it is part of their job description. A "smile" becomes an economic asset and a public relations tool.

Likewise, doctors and nurses are trained to show kind concern for their patients, not disgust or alarm. Furthermore, they cannot become too emotionally involved with patients, because they see pain, suffering, and death every day. It is difficult not to become attached to patients, but such emotional outlay would inevitably lead to burnout, making effective job performance impossible. Doctors and nurses are more successful in their jobs when they can keep their emotions under control.

Some companies now include explicit instructions on emotional control and display as part of their training programs for new employees. This is especially true in service sector jobs where contact with customers occurs over the phone:

> Remember, smiling can be heard as well as seen. . . . Have a smile in your voice and avoid sounding abrupt. . . . Try to make the caller feel you are there for them . . . [avoid] a disinterested, monotonous tone to voice. . . . Use language which conveys understanding of and empathy for the caller's individual situation, e.g., "are you OK?" "was anyone hurt?" "that must have been very distressing for you." (Telephone performance guidelines, insurance company) (Cameron, 1999)

> You must never sound bored on a call. Your telephone manner should convey the impression that you have been waiting for that individual call all day. . . . Our commitment is to give the caller an impression of excitement, friendliness, helpfulness, and courtesy. (Manual for directory assistance operators) (Cameron, 1999)

The ability to enact convincing performances has become even more important given the rise of management techniques that use customer or client input as a means of assessing employees. Many service sector companies now survey customers and use undercover "secret shoppers" or other forms of surveillance to gather information on workers, making appropriate emotional display even more important. Hochschild warns that this kind of "emotional labor" eventually takes a heavy psychological toll on the workers, who are required to adopt a display of emotions that reflects corporate needs and not their own. These people become increasingly estranged from their true feelings (Hochschild, 1983).

Although it is not surprising that organizations would have an interest in emotional displays by members, it is perhaps less obvious that particular emotions are linked to larger societal concerns such as politics and economics, often as a method of social control (Kearl & Gordon, 1992). For instance, the conflict perspective points out that some regimes may use fear to quell dissent and enforce obedience. Earlier in this century, in response to the increasing political and economic strength of African Americans, many white southerners used fear to control Blacks, through the threat of lynching and other forms of violence. Similarly, religious leaders often use the fear of eternal damnation to make sure their followers cooperate.

The effectiveness of invoking emotions such as guilt, anxiety, and shame waxes and wanes as social climates change. In the past, when communities were smaller and more interdependent, social behavior could be easily regulated by the threat of shame. If people broke a law or violated some norm of morality, they would bring humiliation on themselves, their families, and the community at large. But as societies became more complex, such close ties began to disappear. Today, the political control of behavior through emotion is more likely to be directed inward, in the form of guilt and anxiety. For instance, if working mothers are implicated by politicians as contributing to the "breakdown" of the traditional family by leaving the raising of their children to others,

more and more mothers will experience guilt when they seek employment outside the home (Berg, 1992).

Norms governing the expression of emotions give us a way to communicate and maintain social order. They perpetuate institutions by creating powerful cultural expectations that are difficult to violate.

❖ ❖

Norms and Sanctions

Most norms provide only a general framework of expectations; rarely do they tell us exactly how to act, and rarely are they obeyed by all people at all times. Furthermore, norms may be ambiguous or contradictory. It is no surprise, then, that behavior sometimes departs markedly from normative expectations. When it does, negative **sanctions** may be applied. A sanction is a direct social response to some behavior; a negative sanction is one that punishes or otherwise discourages violations of social norms and symbolically reinforces the culture's values and morals.

Different norms evoke different sanctions when violated. **Mores** (pronounced MORE-ayz) are norms, sometimes codified into laws, that are taken very seriously by society. Violation of some mores can elicit severe, state-sponsored sanctions, such as serving time in prison for armed robbery. Other mores may be equally serious but are much less formally stated. Sanctions for violating these norms may take the form of public ostracism or exclusion from the group, as when one is excommunicated for going against the moral doctrine of one's church.

The vast majority of everyday norms are relatively minor, however; violation of these norms, called **folkways**, carries much less serious punishment. For instance, if I chew with my mouth open and food dribbles down my chin, others may show outward signs of disapproval and consider me a "disgusting pig." I may receive fewer dinner invitations, but I won't be arrested or banished from my community.

According to the structural-functionalist perspective, each time a community moves to sanction an act, it strengthens the boundaries between normative and non-normative behavior (Erikson, 1966). In the process, the rest of us are warned of what is in store if we, too, violate the norms. In the 17th century, for example, criminals and religious heretics were executed at high noon in the public square for all to see. The spectacle was meant to be a vivid and symbolic reaffirmation of the community's norms. Today, such harsh sanctions are likely to be hidden from the public eye. However, the publicity surrounding executions, as well as the visibility of less severe sanctions, serves the same purpose—to declare to the community where the line between acceptable and unacceptable behavior lies. By sanctioning the person who violates a norm, society informs its members what type of person cannot live "normally" within its boundaries (Pfohl, 1994).

In-Groups and Ethnocentrism

As children, most of us were taught that we live in the greatest country on Earth. We may also have been taught to have pride in our religious, racial, or ethnic group.

But the belief that our group is the "best" means that other groups are "not the best." Distinguishing between our in-group and out-groups is not unusual; people tend to evaluate other cultures in comparison to their own. This tendency is called **ethnocentrism.**

Ethnocentrism results from the nature of human interaction itself. Much of our everyday lives is spent in groups and organizations. By their very character these collectivities consist of individuals with some, though not necessarily all, shared interests. The same is true for larger cultures. To the extent that we spend a majority of our time with others "like us," our interactions with others "not like us" will be limited, and they will remain "foreign" or "mysterious" to us. Similarity breeds comfort; difference breeds discomfort. For example, despite laws against the practice, many Japanese shopkeepers are so uncomfortable dealing with foreigners that they refuse to serve them (French, 1999a). In fact, when Japanese citizens who have lived abroad for a long time return to Japan, they find that they are no longer regarded as fully Japanese and are treated with the sort of cold disdain foreigners there often experience (French, 2000a).

Another reason for the existence of ethnocentrism is the loyalty we develop to our particular culture or subculture (Charon, 1992). Different values, beliefs, and actions come to be seen not merely as different ways of thinking and doing but as threats to our own beliefs and values. Such perceptions, for instance, underlie much of the resentment of and hostility toward recently arrived immigrants. Even groups whose position in society is strong and secure can find the encroachment of other ways of life threatening. For example, a school superintendent in Mustang, Oklahoma, got into trouble recently for including references to Kwanzaa and Chanukah as well as Christmas in an annual school play and for removing a live nativity scene from the end of it so as not to highlight one faith too much over others. Christian parents became outraged, suing the school for discrimination and voting down an $11 million school bond (Zernike, 2004). In 1996 the national convention of Southern Baptists—the largest Protestant denomination in the United States—adopted a resolution calling for a major campaign to convert Jews to Christianity. Many Southern Baptists believe that Christianity is the culmination of Jewish history (Garment, 1996). More recently some Southern Baptist congregations have targeted Hindus, Moslems, Mormons, and Jehovah's Witnesses for conversion as well ("Baptists Seek to Convert," 2000).

Cultural loyalty is encouraged by institutional ritual and symbolism. In this country, saying the Pledge of Allegiance at the beginning of the school day, playing the "Star-Spangled Banner" at sports events, and observing holidays such as Memorial Day, the Fourth of July, and Veterans' Day all reinforce loyalty to U.S. culture. The American flag is considered such an important national symbol that an entire code of etiquette with specific instructions on how to display it exists to ensure that it is treated with reverence. These are the "sacred objects" of U.S. culture (Durkheim, 1915/1954). The importance of these objects is especially pronounced when people in society feel threatened. You will recall the enormous number of American flags, patriotic songs, pins, T-shirts, and magnetic ribbons on cars that exploded onto the cultural landscape after the September 11, 2001 attacks and during the wars in Iraq and Afghanistan. Religious artifacts and symbols, uniforms and team colors, and distinctive ethnic clothing all foster a sense of pride and identity and hold a community of similar people together, often to the exclusion of others.

Sometimes, respect for these cultural objects must be enforced under the threat of punishment. For years, some members of the U.S. Congress have been trying to ensure loyalty to the American flag by proposing a Constitutional amendment banning its desecration. In Japan, 243 teachers were punished in 2004 for not standing and singing the national anthem at the beginning of the school day (Onishi, 2004b).

Cultural Variation and Everyday Experience

As populations grow more ethnically and racially diverse and as the people of the world become linked more closely by commerce, transportation, and communication, the likelihood of individuals from different cultures and subcultures living together increases. An awareness of cultural differences helps ease everyday interactions in a multicultural society and can be crucial in international relations.

Consider, for example, the way people look at each other. The meanings of certain gazes appear universal. For instance, in most societies people convey positive attitudes and emotions with longer gazes and convey negative attitudes and emotions with shorter ones. In all cultures, people notice when someone is gazing inappropriately. But just what is considered "inappropriate" varies from culture to culture. For instance, Japanese speakers tend to focus on the listener's neck, rather than the eyes, during conversations. Swedes, when conversing, are likely to look at one another for long periods of time. But in most of Latin America people consider it rude and disrespectful to gaze too long at a superior. When a Latino/a child in an American school is admonished by a teacher, the child will likely lower his or her eyes as a sign of respect. But what do American teachers demand of the child they are scolding? "Look at me! Pay attention!" (Argyle, 2000).

Many of the clashes we hear about can be traced to a lack of awareness of differences in cultural expectations. For example, in 1997 a Danish woman visiting New York City was arrested and charged with child neglect for leaving her infant child alone on the sidewalk outside a restaurant while she ate lunch inside. In Denmark such a practice is common and considered appropriate. To reduce potentially danger-ous cultural clashes, the U.S. Marine Corps distributes "Iraq Culture Smart Cards" to American military personnel upon their arrival in Iraq. The cards contain instructions on such matters as how to shake hands, what gestures are appropriate, and how to act when in Iraqi homes (Edidin, 2005).

Cultural variation reflects more than simply differences in people's habits and customs. It indicates that even the most taken-for-granted truths in our lives, the things we assume are universal and unambiguous, are subject to different interpreta-tions and definitions worldwide. Two important examples of such variation are beliefs about health and illness and definitions of sex.

Health and Illness

Medical beliefs and practices always reflect the cultural values of a society (Coe, 1978). We can't claim to have a disease that doesn't exist in our culture. In Malaysia a man may be diagnosed with *koro,* a sudden, intense anxiety that his sexual organs will recede into his body, causing death. In some Latin American countries, a person can suffer from *susto,* an illness tied to a frightening event that makes the soul leave the body, causing unhappiness and sickness (American Psychiatric Association, 2000). Neither of these conditions exists as a medical diagnosis in other parts of the world. But they are not simply anthropological curiosities. They show that culture shapes notions of health and illness.

What are even more compelling, though, are the dramatic cultural differences in medical treatment among societies that share many other values, beliefs, norms, and structural elements. In the United States, medical treatment tends to derive from an aggressive "can do" spirit. Doctors in the United States are much more likely than European doctors to prescribe drugs and resort to surgery (Payer, 1988). U.S. women are more likely than their European counterparts to undergo radical mastectomies, deliver their babies by cesarean section, and undergo routine hysterectomies while still in their 40s. People in the United States tend to see their bodies as machines that require annual checkups for routine maintenance. Diseases are enemies that need to be conquered (for example, people here try to "beat" cancer).

In contrast, British medicine is much more subdued. British physicians don't recommend routine examinations, seldom prescribe drugs, and order about half as many x-ray studies as U.S. doctors do. British patients are also much less likely to have surgery. These attitudes also influence the perceptions of patients. People who are quiet and withdrawn—which U.S. doctors may consider symptoms of clinical depression—tend to be seen by British psychiatrists as perfectly normal.

The French are keenly sensitive to bodily appearance, which is why French physicians are more likely to treat breast and other types of cancer with radiation rather than surgery. The French believe that a patient's "constitution," or physical makeup, is as important in the onset of disease as germs and bacteria. They are more likely to prescribe vitamins to bolster the body than antibiotics to fight germs.

In addition to determining the nature of illness, cultural attitudes also determine what it means to be sick and how sickness is experienced by individuals. Each society has a **sick role**, a widely understood set of rules about how people are supposed to behave when sick (Parsons, 1951). The sick role entails certain obligations (things sick people are expected to do) as well as certain privileges (things sick people are entitled to). Here are some common elements of the sick role in U.S. society:

♦ Because we tend to think of most illnesses as things that happen *to* people, individuals may be exempted from responsibility for the condition itself. At the same time, though, they're expected to recognize the condition as undesirable and something that should be overcome as soon as possible.

♦ Individuals who are allowed to occupy the sick role are excused from ordinary daily duties and expectations. This privilege, of course, varies with the severity of the illness. Compare someone with cancer to someone with the flu, for instance. National legislation—in the form of the Family & Medical Leave Act—and private workplace sick leave policies are the institutional manifestation of these expectations.

♦ Depending on the magnitude of the malady, sick people may be given relief from the ordinary norms of etiquette and propriety. Think of the nasty moods, actions, or insults you're able to "get away with" when you're sick that people wouldn't tolerate from you if you were well.

♦ Sick people are entitled to ask for and receive care and sympathy from others. But sympathy requests operate under their own set of cultural regulations. For instance, one should not claim too much sympathy, for too long, or for too many problems. In other words, sick people are expected to underplay their problems to avoid the appearance of self-pity. At the same time, though, they are expected to graciously accept some expressions of sympathy so as not to appear ungrateful (Clark, 1997).

♦ People occupying the sick role are required to take the culturally prescribed actions that will aid in the process of recovery, including, if the condition is serious enough, seeking help from a culturally appropriate health care professional (Parsons, 1951). Sometimes, to obtain the privilege of exemption from normal social obligations, people must be documented as officially ill from a culturally acceptable source. In the U.S., that means a "doctor's note" (Lorber, 2000). Without such validation your boss might not give you the day off or your instructor might not allow you to take a make-up exam.

Failure on the part of sick people either to exercise their rights or to fulfill the obligations of the sick role may elicit sanctions from the group (Coe, 1978). For instance, those who do not appear to want to recover or who seem to enjoy being sick quickly lose sympathy. A person may also give up legal rights by not seeking or following expert advice. Parents who, because of their religious beliefs, prevent culturally approved medical intervention for their sick children have been arrested and charged with child endangerment or worse. If you are hospitalized and your attending physician doesn't think you ought to be discharged, but you leave anyway, your records will indicate that you have left "A.M.A."—against medical advice. This designation protects the doctor and the hospital from any liability should your condition worsen.

Like illness itself, sick role expectations are culturally influenced. Anthropologists describe a practice found in parts of Japan, China, India, Estonia, and Spain called the *couvade,* from a French term meaning "cowardly inactivity." During childbirth, the father may lie down beside the mother and scream with pain. Following the birth of the child, the mother is expected to return to her normal duties right away, whereas the father goes to bed, sometimes for up to 40 days! It is the father, not the mother, who is relieved of ordinary social responsibilities and who is eligible for sympathy from the village.

While different cultures define the sick role differently, it can also vary considerably along social class lines within the same culture (Freund & McGuire, 1991). Someone might have a debilitating disease, but without health insurance she or he may not have the wherewithal to seek the care of health professionals (and receive an official diagnosis) or may not be able to take time off of work for fear of losing her or his job. In short, socioeconomic factors may preclude such people from claiming sick role status.

Sex

The culture we grow up in shapes our most fundamental beliefs, even about what most people would consider the basic, universal facts of life. For instance, we take for granted that humans can be divided into two clearly identifiable sexes—males and females—that are determined at the time of conception. If you asked someone

(Text continues on page 128)

Funeral Rituals in the Netherlands

Marrie Bot

Rituals for the dead are typically dominated by religious beliefs and norms. In the Netherlands, however, rapid secularization and massive immigration have had a great impact on death ceremonies.

The sudden death of my father in 1984 made me reflect on death, funerals, and mourning rituals. I realized then how little is known about the manner in which the dead are cared for, among either the native Dutch population or the ethnic minorities who have settled in the Netherlands over the past decades. I began my project in 1990 by setting up a network of informants and mediators of 10 population groups. From 1990 to 1998 I attended more than 100 funerals of Roman Catholic, Protestant, Jewish, and secular Dutch groups. I also photographed the death rituals of many ethnic groups living in the Netherlands, including Creoles and Hindus from Surinam; Pakistani, Iranian, and Surinam-Javanese Muslims; Cape Verdeans; and Chinese.

These photos are from my book *A Last Farewell: Funeral and Mourning Rituals in the Multi-cultural Society of the Netherlands*. It shows the rituals and death customs from the moment the dead person is washed to the last mourning rituals, which are sometimes repeated many years after the death of a person. I also conducted a comprehensive study into the origin and the meaning of the different rituals. This book was the first overview of death in a multi-cultural society.

❖ The deceased person, a young woman, is taken to the cemetery by a traditional Dutch funeral coach drawn by Friesian horses. In the past the entire cortege was made up of coaches, which have now been replaced by black funeral cars. For nostalgic reasons the horse-drawn funeral coach is now only used at the request of the relatives.

❖ At the end of the cremation ceremony of a 13-year-old boy, white balloons were sent up in the presence of his parents, brother, fellow pupils, and scouting friends.

❖ A man and a woman looked after a friend who suffered from Hodgkin's disease. After he died, they washed their friend themselves and dressed him in his favorite party suit. Because they did not want him to be laid out in an impersonal funeral parlor, they laid him in his own bed at home. From time to time during the days preceding the funeral ceremony, they sat with him and with other friends.

Although I was interested in the ethnic experience, I noticed that secularization has also changed funeral rituals in the Netherlands. Under the influence of the predominantly Protestant culture, Dutch death ceremonies were always very formal and sober. But by 1997, 60% of the Dutch population had become secular, 19% Roman Catholic, and only 21% Protestant. Traditionally the dead were buried, but nowadays more than half of the population prefers cremation. And by the end of the 1980s, AIDS and cancer patients were asking for personalized farewell rituals. The media reported on these new types of rituals, and planning one's own cremation or funeral became a generally accepted option.

The arrival of immigrants with their own diverse funeral and mourning rituals also caused many changes. The Dutch law regulating the disposal of the dead has been adjusted to meet the needs of these groups. Every population group in the Netherlands may now bury or cremate its dead as they see fit.

Jewish Funeral Rituals

From the 16th century, Jews from southern and eastern Europe have emigrated to the Netherlands. More than 140,000 mainly poor Jews lived in the Netherlands around 1940, but most of them died in the German concentration camps during World War II. At the moment around 30,000 Jews live in the Netherlands. Only 25% of them belong to an orthodox or liberal religious community. The other Jews have assimilated and consider their Jewishness as a cultural identity based on ancestry.

For those who do observe the religious rules, the dead are buried at a Jewish cemetery, where graves are left eternally. At most Dutch cemeteries, graves are sometimes removed after 30 years.

The traditional Jewish mourning period lasts seven days to a year, depending on the relationship of the next of kin. The relatives have to adhere to strict rules.

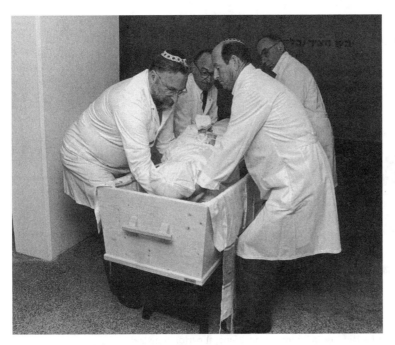

❖ Under traditional Jewish law, the dead are buried. The deceased person is immediately covered with a sheet. Nobody, not even a close relative, is allowed to see the dead person. Viewing the dead is common among other groups in the Netherlands. With the Jews, neither relatives nor the undertaker lay out the deceased; rather, a Jewish funeral association handles this task. Its members dress the deceased in white clothes, because after death everybody is the same to God, regardless of position in life.

Surinam-Creole Death Rituals

Creoles are the descendants of the African slaves in the former Dutch colony of Surinam. Many Surinam people emigrated to the Netherlands when Surinam became independent in 1975. Some 100,000 Creoles now live in the Netherlands, mainly in the large cities. They have assimilated into Dutch society but have kept many of their own cultural and religious traditions. Protestant-Christian and Winti beliefs play an important role in their funeral rituals.

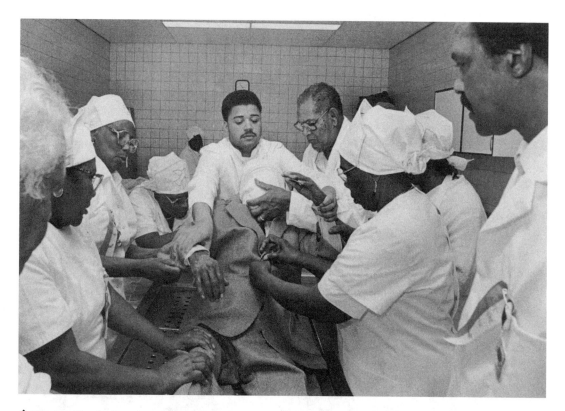

❖ When a Creole dies, the relatives hire a Creole brotherhood that specializes in laying out the dead. Their members, the *Dinari*, perform the washing and dressing rituals with great care in a funeral parlor. The deceased is asked for permission before each ritual is performed, while Creole and Christian songs are sung. The songs are alternated with the drinking of rum and brandy. The next of kin may not be present during these "secret" rituals.

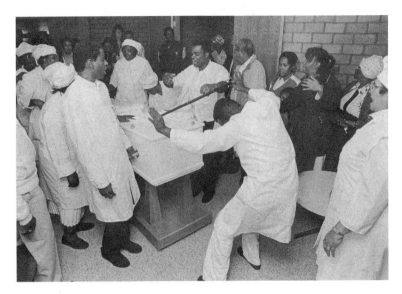

❖ At the wake, the deceased is carried into the room while the *Dinari* sing and dance. To the accompaniment of loud crying and lamenting, the relatives carry out the farewell rituals. However, no tears may fall on the dead person, because then his or her soul could not leave in peace, which would bring bad luck for the relatives.

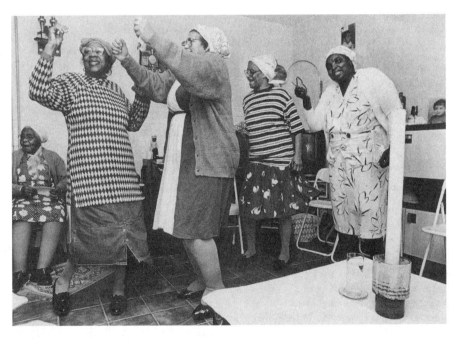

❖ After the burial, the relatives and friends gather on the eighth day *(aiti dey)* and during the sixth week *(siksi wiki)* at home. A meal for the deceased is put outside, and in the living-room a candle and a glass of water are put on a table laid with a white table cloth. According to Winti belief, this arrangement will maintain the contact between the living and the soul of the dead and the spirits of the ancestors. All those present read from the Bible and sing Christian and Creole songs from 8 o'clock in the evening until 5 o'clock in the morning. After midnight the atmosphere can become more cheerful, and people drink, dance, and reminisce about the deceased.

Islamic Funeral Rituals

There are some 600,000 Muslims in the Netherlands. They come from a great many different countries, such as Turkey, Morocco, Pakistan (migrant workers), Surinam, Indonesia (a former Dutch colony), Iran, and many African countries (asylum seekers). They are a heterogeneous population, who combine the general rules of the Koran with their own cultural and religious traditions, which are expressed during the burial ceremonies.

Muslims are allowed to bury their dead at cemeteries in the Netherlands according to their rules: They can bury their dead within 24 hours, without a coffin, and at graveyards that are only for Muslims. The largest group of Muslims, the Turks and Moroccans, still prefer taking their dead to their native country and burying them there.

Death is the will of Allah, and therefore deep mourning may last only three days. The condolence reception is at the home of the deceased person's family. Most Muslims continue the death rituals for 40 days, however. On certain days the men read the Koran for the salvation of the soul of the deceased. After they have finished reading, relatives show their gratitude by offering them a large meal on behalf of the deceased. Women keep themselves apart in the kitchen or bedroom.

❖ Relatives or volunteers of the same gender as the dead person wash him or her following standard Islamic rules. The Surinam-Javanese in the photo are liberal and sometimes allow the washing rituals to be performed by someone of the opposite sex. The dead person must be wrapped in a white shroud, because after death everyone is the same to Allah.

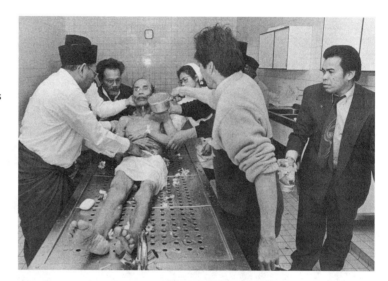

❖ After the ritual washing, Pakistani men recite the death prayers, led by an imam. Women are not allowed to be present because the sexes are routinely segregated and also because their loud wailing and sobbing would disturb the peace of the dead. At the end of the ceremony, the men bid farewell by walking past the coffin.

Chinese Ancestor Worship

At the beginning of the 20th century, the Chinese came to the Netherlands from China, Hong Kong, Surinam, Indonesia, and Vietnam. It is a diverse group consisting of some 60,000 people. Most Chinese keep themselves apart from mainstream Dutch society. They work mostly in restaurants owned by other Chinese and have relationships among themselves based on their country of origin and language.

The death cult plays an important role for all traditional Chinese. It is a combination of elements of the three Chinese religions: Taoism, Confucianism, and Buddhism. Faith teaches that the dead continue to live in the dangerous underworld while they are on their way to the Western Paradise. The dead continue to influence the lives of the relatives. The living have a lifelong obligation to help their ancestors on their journey to paradise by making sacrifices. They hope that their ancestors will show their gratitude by keeping them healthy, making them rich, and granting them sons.

❖ At the burial the relatives place a meal and incense at the grave, and they also burn paper clothes and large stacks of fake money called "hell bank notes." The son must conduct these rituals. Three times a year relatives visit the graves to honor all ancestors. The Surinam-Chinese family in the photo is making a threefold sacrifice at the Rotterdam cemetery—for the father in the grave, for their grandparents buried in Surinam, and for their great-grandfather in China.

Surinam-Hindu Death Rituals

The Surinam-Hindustani are descendants of the contract workers who were taken from north India (Hindustan) to Surinam around 1900. Since the independence of Surinam, some 100,000 Surinam Hindustani have emigrated to the Netherlands. About 80% of them are Hindus, 16% Muslims, and 4% Christians.

The Surinam Hindus live predominantly in the larger cities and have adopted the life style and work pattern of the Western world. At home they adhere to the Hindu faith and rules, which are mainly practiced during the obligatory ceremonies, the *sanskaars*, connected to rites of passage. The rituals for the dead are most important. The deceased is carefully washed and smartly dressed in the funeral parlor by the relatives.

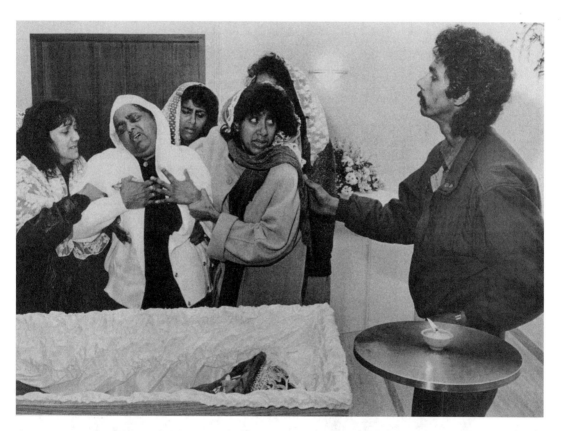

❖ Receptions for viewing the dead and making condolences are held every day in the funeral parlor until the day of the cremation. Just as at Creole funerals, the closest relatives participate in the ritual crying and wailing, and sometimes people faint. With orthodox Hindus, the son or husband carries out all the rituals for the deceased. On the day of the cremation his head is shaved, except for a small tuft of hair on the top, which is regarded as the seat of his wisdom. He is now clean and ready to perform his task.

❖ On the same day that the cremation takes place, the son, supervised by the Hindu priest called *Pundit*, carries out a sacrifice ritual lasting hours. Its purpose is to protect the deceased father until the moment of the cremation. One of the funeral parlors in Rotterdam has special facilities for Hindus and Chinese so that they can perform their fire offerings.

❖ The relatives, and often hundreds of friends of the deceased, bid a ritual farewell in the funeral parlor. These gatherings are often very emotional.

❖ During the year of mourning, the four offering rituals for the soul of the dead person are very important. On the 10th day and the 13th day, and in the 6th and 12th month, the entire extended family gathers at the home of the deceased. This photo shows the offering ritual on the 13th day. The ceremony begins at 10 o'clock in the morning and continues until 3 o'clock in the afternoon. The home bar has been covered, as alcohol is banned during the mourning rituals. In this special case the brother of the deceased woman, who is divorced, conducts the offering rituals because the woman's son is still too young. Nevertheless, the boy's head was also shaven, and he had to participate in the ritual with his uncle on the 10th and 13th day.

The person making the offerings has to carry out a number of complicated proceedings under the supervision of the *Pundit*. He takes care that the deceased will have a new cosmic body and hence will be able to complete the difficult journey to *Yama*, the realm of the dead. There the deceased will be united with his or her ancestors and await reincarnation. During every ceremony, a meal for the deceased is put outside, and gifts are offered to the *Pundit* to help the deceased during his or her journey.

After the rituals the guests will eat a special vegetarian meal and usually stay chatting for a long time.

how to distinguish between males and females, the response would probably focus on observable physical characteristics—body shape, hair, voice, facial features, and so on. When biologists distinguish between the sexes, they, too, refer to physical traits—chromosomes (XX for female, XY for male), sex glands (ovaries or testes), hormones (estrogen or testosterone), internal sex organs (uterus or prostate gland), external genitalia (vagina or penis), reproductive capacities (pregnancy or impregnation), germ cells produced (ova or sperm), and secondary sex characteristics (hips and breasts or facial hair and deep voice).

These characteristics, and hence the two biological sex categories, male and female, are usually assumed to be biologically determined, permanent (you are what you're born with), universal (males are males and females are females whether one lives in Bangladesh or Baltimore; in the 5th century or the 21st century), exhaustive (everyone can be placed into one of the two categories), and mutually exclusive (you can only be one or the other sex; you can't be both). This set of beliefs is called the **sexual dichotomy.**

If you think about it, our entire culture is built around the sexual dichotomy. We have separate clothing sections for men and women, separate hygienic products, separate sections in the shoe stores, separate dormitory floors, separate public restrooms, and so on. The sexual dichotomy is so obvious that we simply assume it to be in the nature of things.

But upon closer inspection, the natural reality of the sexual dichotomy begins to break down. **Transsexuals**—people who identify with a different sex and sometimes undergo hormone treatment and surgery to change their sex—challenge the idea that male and female are permanent biological characteristics. The impermanence of sex received official recognition of sorts when the International Olympic Committee's Executive Board approved a proposal to allow transsexuals to compete in the 2004 Athens Olympics. Athletes who had undergone sex reassignment surgery—either male-to-female or female-to-male—were eligible to compete as long as they had been legally recognized as a member of the "new" sex and it had been at least two years since their surgery. Shortly afterward, the Ladies European Golf Tour enacted a similar policy, allowing a 37-year old Danish male-to-female transsexual to play in one of their professional golf tournaments.

Other features of the sexual dichotomy—namely mutual exclusivity, exhaustiveness, and universality—are challenged when we examine sex categories cross-culturally. Throughout human history and across all societies, certain people have transcended the categories of male and female. They may be born with anatomical and/or genital configurations that are ambiguous. Or they may simply choose to live their lives in ways that don't conform to existing gender expectations associated with their sex (see Chapter 5 for more information about the distinction between sex and gender).

In Navajo culture, for instance, one could be identified as male, female, or *nadle*—a third sex assigned to those whose sex-typed anatomical characteristics were ambiguous at birth (Lang, 1998). Physically normal individuals also had the opportunity to choose to become *nadle* if they so desired. The gender status of *nadle* is simultaneously masculine and feminine. They are allowed to perform the tasks and take up the occupations of both men and women. For the Chuckchi of Eastern Siberia, a biological male child with feminine physical traits gradually transforms into a "soft man." Although he keeps his masculine name, he is expected to live as a woman (Williams, 1992). The *hijras* of India are born as men, but by choice they have their genitals surgically removed (Nanda, 2003). This operation transforms them not into women but into *hijras*, who live as women—dressing, standing, walking, and sitting as women. Many figures in Hindu mythology are neither male nor female. Hence Indian culture not only accommodates the *hijras* but views them as meaningful, even powerful beings.

Such cross-cultural examples illustrate that our taken-for-granted beliefs about sex and gender are not held worldwide. In other cultures, sex is not dichotomous, exhaustive, or permanent.

The sexual dichotomy is not challenge-free in the United States either. **Intersexuals**, for instance, are individuals in whom sexual differentiation is either incomplete or ambiguous. They may have the chromosomal pattern of a female but the external genitals of a male, or they may have both ovaries and testicles. Experts estimate that about 1.7% of all babies born have some form of intersexuality, meaning that they are born with sexual organs that don't completely fit into standard sex categories (Fausto-Sterling, 2000).

It is interesting to note that the medical response to intersexuals supports the cultural and historical belief that there are two and only two sexes. Intersexuality is usually defined by biologists as a defective combination of the two existing categories and not as a third, fourth, or fifth category unto itself. Furthermore, on the diagnosis of intersexuality, a decision is always made to define the individual as either male or female. In societies with advanced medical technology, surgical and chemical means may be used to establish consistency between anatomy and the social label. Every month dozens of sexually ambiguous newborns are "assigned" a sex and undergo surgery to confirm the designation (Cowley, 1997). About 90% are designated female, because creating a vagina is considered surgically easier than creating a penis (Angier, 1997b).

However, an increasingly vocal group of intersexuals protest that many of the surgical techniques used to "correct" the problem of visually ambiguous genitals are mutilating and potentially harmful. They cite cases of intersexuals being robbed of any sexual sensation in the attempt to surgically "normalize" them—that is, give them the physical appearance of either a male or a female. The founder of the Intersex Society of North America eloquently summed up her organization's frustration: "They can't conceive of leaving someone alone" (quoted in Angier, 1997a, p. A10).

The medical profession can't leave these individuals alone because to do so would undermine our cultural understanding of sex. Drastic surgical intervention is undertaken not because the infant's life is threatened but because our entire social structure is organized around having two and only two sexes (Lorber, 1989). The male-female dichotomy in our culture is so essential to our way of life that those who challenge it are often considered disloyal to the most fundamental of biological "facts." To suggest that the labels "male" and "female" are not sufficient to categorize everyone is to threaten a basic organizing principle of social life.

Conclusion

Over the span of a year or two, most cultures seem to have a stable set of norms about the acceptability of certain behaviors. This stability is illusory, however. From the perspective of a generation or even a decade later, that sense of order would give way to a sense of change (McCall & Simmons, 1978). Behaviors, values, beliefs, and morals fluctuate with startling frequency. Thus, comparisons across eras, in addition to comparisons across cultures, can provide rich insight into shifting definitions of acceptability, the nature of everyday life, and ultimately large-scale social change and stability.

The cultural and historical underpinnings of our private lives help us see the relationship among the individual, society, and social order. Cultural practices add continuity and order to social life.

To an individual, culture appears massive and unrelenting; but at the same time it cannot exist without people. Norms govern our lives, whether we live by them or rebel against them. But to fully understand the relationship between the individual and society we must look beyond the fact that culture and history shape our lives; we must see them as human constructions as well.

❖

YOUR TURN

Although everyday norms underlie all we do, they remain largely unnoticed and unquestioned. The best proof of the existence of these norms lies in our reactions when they are violated. The following suggestions for proving the existence of norms are based on an exercise used by Jodi O'Brien at Seattle University. If you like, choose a different unspoken norm that lends order and predictability to daily social interactions, and try breaking it.

- ❖ Make a purchase in a department store, and offer to pay more than the listed price. Try to convince the clerk that you think the merchandise is worth the price you are offering.
- ❖ Send a close family member a birthday card months away from his or her actual birthday.
- ❖ Talk to yourself in a public place.
- ❖ Stand or sit close to a stranger or stand far away from a good friend or lover during the course of an ordinary conversation.
- ❖ Select an occasion—going to class, going on a date, going to the library—and dress differently from the expected "uniform." Treat your attire as absolutely appropriate to the circumstances.
- ❖ Whenever someone says to you "See you later," ask him or her probing questions: "When?" "Do you have some plans to get together later?" "What do you mean by 'see'?" and so on. Or when someone says, "How's it going?" ask, "What do you mean by 'it'?" "What do you mean by 'going'?"
- ❖ In a restaurant offer to pay for your meal before you order it, or order dessert first, then the main course, then appetizers, then drinks.

It is particularly important that this behavior be neither flagrantly bizarre—such as going to class dressed as a chicken—nor a violation of the law. Such acts do not address the power of the subtle, unspoken norms that, symbolic interactionism argues, make social life orderly. Also, do not do anything that might seriously inconvenience or humiliate someone else or put you in danger. Finally, make sure the norm has something to do with keeping order in face-to-face interactions. For instance, coming to class 10 minutes late violates a social norm, but it doesn't disrupt interactional order. Above all, remember to treat your violation as perfectly normal. You must give the impression that what you are doing is perfectly acceptable and ordinary.

As you conduct your exercises, record your own feelings and reactions as well as those of the subjects. What were people's initial reactions? What did they do to try to "normalize" your behavior? How did you feel breaching this norm? Was it uncomfortable? If so, why?

If possible, try also to debrief your subjects afterward: Tell them what you were really doing, and then interview them regarding their interpretations of the experience. You are likely to collect additional information on how people attempt to "explain away" unusual and strange circumstances and how they attempt to restore order to the situation. What are the implications of these sorts of "experiments" for understanding human behavior and the nature of social order in this society?

◆

CHAPTER HIGHLIGHTS

◆ Culture provides members of a society with a common bond, a sense that we see certain facets of society in similar ways. That we can live together at all depends on the fact that members of a society share a certain amount of cultural knowledge.

◆ Norms—the rules and standards that govern all social encounters—provide order in our lives. They reflect commonly held assumptions about conventional behavior. Norm violations mark the boundaries of acceptable behavior and symbolically reaffirm what society defines as right and wrong.

◆ The more ethnically and culturally diverse a society is, the greater the likelihood of normative clashes between groups.

◆ Over the span of a few years, most cultures present an image of stability and agreement regarding normative boundaries. This agreement is illusory, however. Over a generation or even a decade, that sense of order is replaced by a sense of change.

◆

KEY TERMS

ethnocentrism Tendency to judge other cultures using one's own as a standard

folkway Informal norm that is mildly punished when violated

heteronormative culture Culture in which heterosexuality is accepted as the normal, taken-for-granted mode of sexual expression

institutionalized norm Pattern of behavior within existing social institutions that is widely accepted in a society

intersexuals Individuals in whom sexual differentiation is either incomplete or ambiguous

material culture Artifacts of a society, which represent adaptations to the social and physical environment

more Highly codified, formal, systematized norm that brings severe punishment when violated

nonmaterial culture Knowledge, beliefs, customs, values, morals, and symbols that are shared by members of a society and that distinguish the society from others

sanction Social response that punishes or otherwise discourages violations of a social norm

sexual dichotomy Belief that two biological sex categories, male and female, are permanent, universal, exhaustive, and mutually exclusive

sick role Set of norms governing how one is supposed to behave and what one is entitled to when sick

subculture Values, behaviors, and artifacts of a group that distinguish its members from the larger culture

transsexuals People who identify with a different sex and sometimes undergo hormone treatment and surgery to change their sex

————————————————————◆

STUDY SITE ON THE WEB

Don't forget the interactive quizzes and other learning aids at www.pineforge.com/newman6 study. In the Resources File for this chapter, you'll also find more on building order, including:

Micro-Macro Connections

♦ Childhood as a Social Construction

♦ Female Genital Mutilation

♦ Time as a Social Construction

♦ Transracial Adoption

Building Identity
Socialization

My family once lived in a suburb just outside New York City. One day, when I was 9 years old, my parents sat me down and told me that we were going to be moving. They had narrowed down our ultimate destination to two possibilities: Laredo, Texas, or Burbank, California. After some rather intense debate, they chose Burbank. And so we headed "out West," where from age 9 to age 18 I lived in the shadow of the entertainment industry and all its glamour, glitz, and movie stars. It wasn't long before I became a typical sun-worshiping, Frisbee-throwing, southern California kid.

I often wonder how differently I would have turned out if my parents had chosen Laredo and I had spent my formative years in Southern Texas instead of in the middle of Tinsel Town. Would I have a fondness for 10-gallon hats and snakeskin boots instead of tennis shoes and shorts? Would I have grown up with country music instead of the Beach Boys? Would my goals, beliefs, or sense of morality be different? In short, would I be a different person?

Try to imagine what your life would be like if you had grown up under different circumstances. What if your father had been a harpsichord enthusiast instead of a Cubs fan? What if your family had been Jewish instead of Episcopalian? What if you had had an older brother instead of a younger sister? What if you had lived on a farm instead of in a big city? What if you had been born in the 1940s instead of the 1980s? Your tastes, preferences, and hobbies, as well as your values, ambitions, and aspirations, would no doubt be different. But more profoundly, your self-concept, self-esteem, personality—the essence of who you are—would be altered too.

Consider the broader social and historical circumstances of your life. What kind of impact might they have had on the type of person you are? Talk to elderly people who were children back in the 1930s, and they will speak of the permanent impact that the Great Depression had on them (Elder & Liker, 1982). Imagine spending your childhood as a Jew in Nazi Germany. That couldn't help but shape your outlook on life. The same can be said for growing up black in the American South in the segregated 1950s or white in Colorado Springs during the George W. Bush presidency.

Becoming the person you are cannot be separated from the people, historical events, and social circumstances that surround you. In this chapter I examine the process of socialization—how we learn what's expected of us in our families, our communities, and our culture and how we learn to behave according to those expectations. The primary focus will be on the development of identity. **Identity** is our most essential and personal characteristic. It consists of our membership in various social groups (race, ethnicity, religion, gender, and so on), the traits we show, and the traits others ascribe to us. Our identity locates us in the social world, thoroughly affecting everything we do, feel, say, and think in our lives. Most people tend to believe that our self-concept, our sense of "maleness" or "femaleness," and our racial and ethnic identities are biologically or psychologically determined and therefore permanent and unchangeable. But as you will discover, these characteristics are social constructions: as much a product of our social surroundings and the significant people in our lives as a product of our physical traits and innate predispositions.

Social Structure and the Construction of Human Beings

The question of how we become who we are has for centuries grabbed the attention of biologists, psychologists, anthropologists, sociologists, philosophers, and novelists. The issue is usually framed as a debate between *nature* (we are who we are because we were born that way) and *nurture* (we are who we are because of the way we were treated while growing up). Are we simply the predetermined product of our genes and biochemistry, or are we "created" from scratch by the people and the social institutions that surround us?

The answer to this question swings back and forth depending on the dominant cultural mood. In the late 19th and early 20th centuries genetics became a popular explanation for human behavior, including a variety of social problems such as crime, poverty, and mental deficiency. Scientists, borrowing from the selective breeding practices used with racehorses and livestock, advocated programs of *eugenics*, or controlled mating to ensure that the "defective" genes of troublesome individuals would not be passed on to future generations. Theories of genetic inferiority became the cornerstone of Adolph Hitler's horrors in Nazi Germany during World War II. After the war, most people wanted to get as far away from such "nature" arguments as possible. So in the 1950s and 1960s people heavily emphasized environmental influences on behavior, especially the role of early family experiences in shaping children's future personalities (Gould, 1997).

Today, because of the growing cultural emphasis on scientific technology, genetic explanations have again become fashionable. In recent years researchers have claimed that such diverse social phenomena as shyness, impulsiveness, intelligence, aggression, obesity, risk taking, alcoholism, and addiction to gambling are at least partly due to heredity. Some political scientists even claim that people's emotional reactions to controversial issues like the death penalty, taxes, and abortion are strongly influenced by their genetic inheritance (Carey, 2005b). The success of the Human Genome Project—an undertaking meant to identify all the 20,000 to 25,000 genes in human DNA—will no doubt add fuel to "nature" arguments in the years to come.

Yet we are apparently not ready to say that nurture plays no role. Not too long ago, a psychologist named Judith Harris (1998) achieved notoriety for her rather stunning suggestion that the home environment has virtually no effect on children. She claims that the only thing parents contribute to their child's development is their genetic material; that nothing parents do or say makes much of a difference at all as to what sort of adult the child will eventually become. But even Harris acknowledges that nature alone isn't sufficient to predict a child's development. She points out that later in life, peer groups play a powerful role in shaping a child's personality. Although Harris's book has been roundly criticized, it does ultimately support the view that, when all is said and done, both nature and nurture are responsible for who we become. Both genetic inheritance and social environment matter.

Most sociologists would argue that human beings are much more than a collection of physical and psychological characteristics; they reflect society's influence as well. That's not to say that inborn traits are of absolutely no importance. Certainly our physical appearance and strength, genetic predisposition to sickness, and so on have some effect on our personal development. Furthermore, our every thought and action is the result of a complex series of neurological and electrochemical events in our brains and bodies. When we feel the need to eat we are reacting to a physiological sensation—stomach contractions—brought about by a lowering of blood sugar. Satisfying hunger is clearly a biological process. But the way we react to the sensation of hunger cannot be predicted by physiology alone. What, when, how, and how often we eat are all matters of cultural forces that we learn over time. When you say something like, "I'm starving but it's too early to eat dinner" you're signaling the power of cultural training in overriding physiological demands.

Likewise, society can magnify physical differences or cover them up. We've collectively decided that some differences are socially irrelevant (for example, eye color) and that some are important enough to be embedded in our most important social institutions (for example, gender and skin color), giving rise to different rights, duties, expectations, and access to educational, economic, and political opportunities.

Who we become is influenced by the behaviors and attitudes of significant people in our lives as well as by cultural and institutional forces. As these things change, so do we. This proposition is not altogether comforting. It implies that who we are may in some ways be "accidental," the result of a series of social coincidences, chance encounters, decisions made by others, and political, economic, and historical events that are in large measure beyond our control—such as growing up in California rather than Texas.

Socialization: Becoming Who We Are

The structural-functionalist perspective points out that the fundamental task of any society is to reproduce itself—to create members whose behaviors, desires, and goals correspond to those that the particular society deems appropriate and desirable. Through the powerful and ubiquitous process of **socialization,** the needs of society become the needs of the individual.

Socialization is a process of learning. To socialize someone is to train that person to behave appropriately. It is the means by which people acquire a vast array of social skills, such as driving a car, converting fractions into decimals, speaking the language correctly, or using a fork instead of a knife to eat peas. But socialization is also the way we learn how to perceive our world; how to interact with others; what it means to be male or female; how, when, why, and with whom to be sexual; what we should and shouldn't do to and for others under certain circumstances; what our society defines as moral and immoral; and so on. In short, it is the process by which we internalize all that cultural information I discussed in Chapter 4.

Although socialization occurs throughout our lives, the basic, formative instruction of life occurs early on. Young children must be taught the fundamental values, knowledge, and beliefs of their culture. Some of the socialization that occurs during childhood—often called **anticipatory socialization**—is the primary means by which young individuals acquire the values and orientations found in the statuses they will likely enter in the future (Merton, 1957). Household chores, a childhood job, sports, dance lessons, dating, and many other types of experiences give youngsters an opportunity to rehearse for the kinds of roles that await them in adulthood.

The Acquisition of Self

The most important outcome of the socialization process is the development of a sense of self. The term **self** refers to the unique set of traits, behaviors, and attitudes that distinguishes one person from the next.

The self is both the active source of behavior and its passive object (Mead, 1934). As an active source, the self can initiate action, which is frequently directed toward others. Imagine, for example, that Rob and Lisa are having dinner in a restaurant. Lisa has a self that can perceive Rob, talk to him, evaluate him, maybe even try to manipulate or persuade him to act in a way that is consistent with her interests. Lisa also has a self that is a potential object of others' behavior: She can be perceived, talked to, evaluated, manipulated, or persuaded by Rob.

Lisa can also direct these activities toward herself. She can perceive, evaluate, motivate, and even talk to herself. This is called **reflexive behavior**. To have a self is to have the ability to plan, observe, guide, and respond to one's own behavior (Mead, 1934). Think of all the times you have tried to motivate yourself to act by saying something such as "All right, if I read 20 more pages of this boring sociology textbook, I'll make myself a hot fudge sundae." To do this you must simultaneously be the motivator and the one being motivated—the seer and the seen.

At this very moment you are initiating an action: reading this book. But you also have the ability (now that I've mentioned it!) to be aware of your reading behavior, to reflexively observe yourself reading, and even to evaluate how well you are doing. This sounds like some sort of mystical out-of-body experience, but it isn't. Nothing is more fundamental to human thought and action than this capacity for self-awareness. It allows us to control our own behavior and interact smoothly with other self-aware individuals.

At birth, human babies have no sense of self. This is not to say that infants don't act on their own. Anyone who has been around babies knows that they have a tremendous ability to initiate action, ranging all the way from Kodak-moment cute to downright disgusting. They cry, eat, sleep, play with squeaky rubber toys, and eliminate waste, all with exquisite panache and regularity. From the very first days of life they respond to the sounds, sights, smells, and touches of others.

But this behavior is not characterized by the sort of self-consciousness that characterizes later behavior. Babies don't say to themselves, "I can't *believe* how loud I can cry" or "I wonder if Mom will feed me if I scream." As children grow older, though, they begin to exert greater control over their conduct. Part of this transformation is biological. As they mature, they become more adept at muscle control. But physical development is only part of the picture. Humans must acquire certain cognitive capacities through interactions with others, including the abilities to differentiate between self and others, to understand and use symbolic language, and to take the roles of others.

The Differentiation of Self

To distinguish between yourself and others, you must at minimum be able to recognize yourself as a distinct entity (Mead, 1934). The first step in the acquisition of self, then, is learning to distinguish our own faces and bodies from the rest of the physical environment. Surprisingly, we are not born with this ability. Not only are newborns incapable of recognizing themselves, they also cannot even discriminate the boundaries between their bodies and the bodies of others. Infants will pull their own hair to the point of excruciating pain but will not realize that the hair they're pulling and the hair that they feel being pulled is the same hair.

With cognitive growth and social experience, infants gradually recognize themselves as unique physical objects. Most studies in this area indicate that children usually develop this ability at about 18 months (Bertenthal & Fischer, 1978). If you make a large mark on a child's forehead with a washable marker, hold the youngster up to a mirror, and observe whether the child reaches up to wipe away the smudge, you can tell if the youngster recognizes that the image in the mirror is his or her own.

Language Acquisition and the Looking-Glass Self

The next important step in the acquisition of self is the development of speech (Hewitt, 1988). Symbolic interactionism points out that mastery of language is crucial in children's efforts to differentiate themselves as distinct social as well as physical objects (Denzin, 1977). Certainly language acquisition relies on neurological development. But the ability to grasp the nuances of one's own language requires input from others. Most parents talk to their children from the start. Gradually, children learn to make sounds, imitate sounds, and use sounds as symbols for particular physical sensations or objects. Children learn that the sounds "Mama" and "Dada" are the sounds associated with two important objects in their life. Soon children learn that other objects—toys, animals, foods, Aunt Donna, Uncle Marc—have unique sounds associated with them as well.

This learning process gives the child access into the preexisting linguistic world in which his or her parents and others live (Hewitt, 1988). The objects named are not only those recognized within the larger culture but also those recognized within the family's particular social group. The child learns the names of concrete objects (balls, buildings, furniture) as well as abstract ideas that cannot be directly perceived (for example, God, happiness, peace, and idea).

By learning that people and other objects have names, the child also begins to learn that these objects can be related to one another in a multitude of named ways. Depending on who is talking to whom, the same person can be called several different names. The object "Daddy" is called, by various other people, "David," "Dave,"

"Dr. Newman," "Professor Newman," "Honey," and "Bud." Furthermore, the child learns that different people can be referred to by the same name. All those other kids at the park have someone they also call "Mama."

Amid these monumental discoveries young children learn that they too are objects that have names. A child who learns that others are referring to her when they make the sound "Elena," and that she too can use "Elena" to refer to herself, has taken a significant leap forward in the acquisition of self. The child now can visualize herself as a part of the named world and the named relationships to which she belongs.

The self that initially emerges from this process is a rather simple one. "Elena" is just a name associated with a body, which explains why very young children just learning to form sentences may refer to themselves by their name instead of the first-person pronoun (for example, "Elena is hungry" instead of "I am hungry"). A more sophisticated sense of self is derived from the child's ability to learn the meaning of this named object.

Children learn the meaning of named objects in their environment by observing the way other people act toward those objects. By observing people sitting on a chair, they learn what "chair" means. Parental warnings allow them to learn that a "hot stove" is something to be avoided. Similarly, by observing how people act toward them they learn the meaning of themselves. People treat children in a variety of ways: care for them, punish them, love them, neglect them, teach them. If parents, relatives, and other significant people perceive a child as smart, they act toward him or her that way. Thus the child eventually comes to believe he or she is a smart person. One of the earliest symbolic interactionists, Charles Horton Cooley (1902), referred to this process as acquisition of the **looking-glass self**. He argued that we use the reactions of others toward us as mirrors in which we see ourselves and determine our self-worth. Through this process, we imagine how we might look to other people, we interpret their responses to us, and we form a self-concept. If we think people perceive us favorably, we're likely to develop a positive self-concept. Conversely, if we detect unfavorable reactions, our self-concept will likely be negative. Hence feelings of pride or shame are always the product of the reflected appraisals of others.

How the child-as-named-object is defined by others is linked to larger societal considerations as well. Every culture has its own way of defining individuals at various stages of the life cycle. Children are not always defined, and have not always been defined, as a special subpopulation whose innocence requires nurturing and protection (Ariès, 1962). In some societies they are expected to behave like adults and are held accountable for their actions just as adults would be. Under such cultural circumstances, a 5-year-old's self-concept may be derived from how well she or he contributes economically to the family, not from how cute or playful she or he is. Moreover, every society has its own standards of beauty and success. If thinness is a culturally desirable characteristic, a thin child is more likely to garner positive responses and develop a positive self-image than a child who violates this norm (that is, an obese child).

The Development of Role Taking

This process would be pretty simple if everyone in our lives saw us in exactly the same way. But different people expect or desire different things from us. Children eventually learn to modify their behavior to suit different people. Four-year-old Rafael learns, for instance, that his 3-year-old sister loves it when he sticks his finger up his nose, but he also knows that his father doesn't find this behavior at all amusing. So Rafael will avoid such conduct when his father is around but will proceed to amuse his sister with this trick when Papa is gone. The ability to use other people's perspectives and expectations in formulating one's own behavior is called **role taking** (Mead, 1934).

Role-taking ability develops gradually, paralleling the increasing maturation of linguistic abilities. Operating from the symbolic interactionist perspective, George Herbert Mead (1934) identified two major stages in the development of role-taking ability and, ultimately, in the socialization of the self: the play stage and the game stage. The **play stage** occurs when children are just beginning to hone their language skills. Role taking at the play stage is quite simple in form, limited to taking the perspective of one other person at a time. Very young children cannot see themselves from different perspectives simultaneously. They have no idea that certain behaviors may be unacceptable to a variety of people across a range of situations. They know only that this particular person who is in their immediate presence will approve or not approve of this conduct. Children cannot see that their father's disapproval of public nose picking reflects the attitudes of a larger group and is generally unacceptable. This more sophisticated form of self-control develops at the next stage of the socialization process: the game stage.

The **game stage** occurs about the time that children first begin to participate in organized activities such as school events and team sports. The difference between role taking at the play and game stages parallels the difference between childhood play behavior and game behavior. Play is not guided by a specific set of rules. Play has no ultimate object, no clearly organized competition, no winners and losers. Children playing baseball at the play stage have no sense of strategy and may not even be aware of the rules and object of the game. They may be able to hit, catch, and throw the ball but have no idea how their behavior is linked to that of their teammates. If a little girl is playing third base and the ball is hit to her, she may turn around and throw the ball to the left fielder, not because it will help her team win the game but because that's where her best friend happens to be.

At the game stage, in contrast, children develop a sense of the object of the game. They realize that each player on the team is part of an organized network of roles determined by the rules of the game. Children know they must continually adapt their behavior to the team's needs in order to achieve a goal. To do so, they must imagine the group's perspective and predict how both their teammates and the opponents will act under certain circumstances.

With regard to social behavior at the game stage, not only does the child learn to respond to the demands of several people, but he or she can also respond to the demands of the community or even society as a whole. Sociologists call the perspective of society and its constituent values and attitudes the **generalized other.** The generalized other becomes larger as a child matures, growing to include family, peer group, school, and finally the larger social community. "Mama doesn't like it when I take off my pants in a restaurant" (play stage) eventually becomes "It's never acceptable to take off one's pants in public" (game stage). Notice how such an understanding requires an ability to generalize behavior across a variety of situations. The child realizes that "public" consists of restaurants, shopping malls, school classrooms, neighbors' living rooms, and so forth.

This ability is crucial because it enables the individual to resist the influence of specific people who happen to be in his or her immediate presence. The boy who defies his peers by not joining them in an act of petty shoplifting is showing the power of the generalized other ("Stealing, no matter where or with whom, is bad"). During the game stage, the attitudes and expectations of the generalized other are incorporated into one's values and self-concept.

Real life is not always that simple, though. People from markedly different backgrounds are likely to internalize different sets of group attitudes and values. A devout Catholic contemplating divorce, for instance, is taking the role of a different generalized other than an atheist contemplating divorce. Likewise, the social worlds and social standards of men and women are different, as are those of children and adults, parents and nonparents, middle-class and working-class people, and people who grew up in different societies.

Nor is role-taking ability static. It changes in response to interactions with others. When people feel that they can understand another person's perspective, as say that of an intimate partner, they are likely to become concerned about or at least aware of how their behavior will affect that other person (Cast, 2004). Furthermore, as we move from one institutional context to another, we adopt the perspective of the appropriate group and can become, for all intents and purposes, a different person. At school we behave one way, at church another, at a family gathering still another. We are as many different people as there are groups and organizations of which we are members.

Common sense suggests that people who have a great deal of knowledge and experience should be the best role takers. For example, parents should be more sensitive to their children's views than vice versa, because they are older and wiser and were children once themselves. However, given the dynamics of power and dependence, people in superior positions tend to be less sensitive to subordinates and, as a result, may not be required to conform their behavior to—nor even to be aware of—the wishes and desires of others (Tsushima & Gecas, 2001). You can see this phenomenon in many areas of social life. First-year college students are typically more aware of the actions and interests of upper-class students than vice versa. Low-level employees must be sensitive to the behaviors and preferences of those above them if they want to achieve occupational success and mobility. On a broader scale, less powerful nations must have heightened sensitivity to the activities of their more powerful neighbors. I have heard some Canadians complain that they are expected to know virtually everything about the United States—its culture as well as its economic and political systems—whereas most people in the United States tend to be rather oblivious to even the most accessible elements of Canadian politics and culture.

In sum, the ability to imagine another person's attitudes and intentions and thereby to anticipate that person's behavior is essential for everyday social interaction. Through role taking we can envision how others perceive us and what their response may be to some action we're contemplating. Hence, we can select behaviors that are likely to meet with the approval of the person or persons with whom we are interacting and can avoid behaviors that might meet with their disapproval. Role taking is thus a crucial component of self-control and social order. It transforms a biological being into a social being who is capable of conforming his or her behavior to societal expectations. It is the means by which culture is incorporated into the self and makes group life possible (Cast, 2004).

Resocialization

Socialization does not end when childhood ends; it continues throughout our lives. Adults must be **resocialized** into a new set of norms, values, and expectations each time they leave behind old social contexts or roles and enter new ones (Ebaugh, 1988; Pescosolido, 1986; Simpson, 1979). For instance, we have to learn how to think and act like a spouse when we marry (P.L. Berger & Kellner, 1964), a parent when we have kids (A. Rossi, 1968), and a divorced person when a marriage ends (Vaughan, 1986). Every new group or organization we enter, every new friendship we form, every new life-changing experience we have, requires the formation of new identities and socialization into new sets of norms and beliefs.

Sometimes resocialization is forceful and intense. In prisons, mental hospitals, monasteries, military training camps, and other **total institutions** (Goffman, 1961), groups of individuals are separated from the broader society and forced to lead an enclosed, formally administered life. Previous socialization experiences are systematically destroyed and new ones developed to serve the interests of the group. In an army boot camp, for instance, the individual must learn to look, act, and think like a soldier and learn to see the world from the soldier's perspective. To aid in this transformation, recruits are stripped of old civilian identity markers (clothes, personal possessions, hairstyle) and forced to take on new ones that nullify individuality and also identify the newcomers' subordinate status (uniforms, identification numbers, similar haircuts). The newcomer is also subjected to constant scrutiny. Conformity is mandatory. Any misstep is met with punishment or humiliation.

Eventually the individual learns to identify with the ideology of the total institution. In the boot camp, the uniformity of values and appearance is intended to create a sense of solidarity among the soldiers and thereby make the military more effective in carrying out its tasks. Part of the reason for all the controversy over diversity in the military—first with the inclusion of African Americans, then with women, and now with homosexuals—is that it introduces diverse beliefs, values, appearances, and lifestyles into a context where, from an institutional perspective, similarity is essential.

The mechanisms of resocialization have been tragically exploited from time to time. Two noteworthy examples are the mass suicides of 911 members of Jim Jones's People's Temple in Jonestown, Guyana, in 1978 and the 1993 armed standoff and subsequent destruction of David Koresh's Branch Davidian compound in Waco, Texas. Jones and Koresh told their followers that to achieve better and more meaningful lives, they would have to isolate themselves, severing all ties to their previous lives—all previous values, relationships, emotional bonds, and so on. The members abandoned their past "disreputable" selves so totally and were resocialized and indoctrinated by their leaders so completely that their ability to make decisions on their own behalf was impaired (Coser & Coser, 1993). When people are physically and emotionally cut off from their friends and family, they can be influenced, cajoled, or threatened into doing virtually anything, even injuring others or taking their own lives.

Less drastically, but no less deliberately, certain occupations require the resocialization of new entrants. Often the purpose is simply to make sure people who work in the organization share the same professional values, methods, and vocabulary. Many large companies, for example, have orientation programs for new employees to teach them what will be expected of them as they begin their new jobs. Sometimes the purpose is to make new entrants abandon their original expectations and adopt a more realistic view of the occupation. Police recruits who believe their job is to protect people must learn that deadly force is appropriate and sometimes necessary in the line of duty (J. Hunt, 1985). Many medical students become less idealistic and more realistic as they learn about the exhausting demands of their profession (H. S. Becker & Geer, 1958; Hafferty, 1991). Such resocialization is especially important in occupations that deal with highly emotional matters, such as the funeral industry.

Spencer Cahill
The Professional Socialization of Funeral Directors

Funeral directors routinely deal with death and corpses. They are exposed to sights, smells, and sounds that most people would find frightening or repulsive. And they must discuss cold, practical matters, such as prices and methods of payment, with grief-stricken clients, without appearing callous. Thus the occupational socialization of funeral directors is as important as that in any other profession that deals with human tragedy (clergy, doctors, nurses, police detectives, and so on). But unlike these other professionals, for whom death is merely one aspect of the job, funeral directors exist solely for the purpose of dealing with death.

To study the process of becoming a funeral director, sociologist Spencer Cahill (1999) spent five months as a participant observer in a mortuary science program at a community college. In most states, funeral directors must complete an accredited program in mortuary science before getting their license to practice. Cahill regularly attended classes on such topics as health and sanitation science, psychology of grief, and embalming. He also talked informally with the other students and interviewed eight of them formally. What was especially unique about his research approach was that instead of taking the stance of the detached, objective researcher, Cahill incorporated his own feelings and emotional reactions into his analysis.

He found that the entire mortuary science education program serves to *normalize* the work, so that students become comfortable with death. Reminders of death are a constant presence. Nothing is hidden. For instance, all the classrooms contain some artifacts of death, such as refrigerated compartments that hold corpses, stainless steel embalming tables, and caskets. All the instructors Cahill observed spread their lecture notes on a body gurney, forgoing the traditional lectern and table. It was also common practice for instructors to leave the door open between the classroom and the embalming laboratory, allowing the lingering smell of decomposing bodies to drift into the classroom.

Because other students on campus tend to shun them, the mortuary science students often stick together, providing an almost constant network of support. From these casual interactions (as well as their conversations with instructors) these students learn an occupational language that communicates professional authority and calm composure toward things most of the public would find upsetting. For example, the students learn to see the corpse not as an individual person with a history and a family, but as a series of technical puzzles and problems posed by the cause of death (for example, ingested substances, chemical changes, injuries sustained before death).

However, Cahill points out that professional socialization is not enough to create funeral directors. He notes that students for whom death has always been a mystery or students who are predisposed to becoming queasy don't last very long in the program. In contrast, those who are familiar with death or who have somehow worked with the dead before (such as the sons or daughters of funeral directors) were the most likely to succeed.

Eventually the mortuary science students who complete the program adopt the identity of funeral director. They learn to normalize death and acquire the perceptions, judgments, and emotional management skills required of this occupation. As one well-socialized student put it, "What we do is far less depressing than what nurses and doctors do. We only get the body after the death and do not have to watch all the suffering" (quoted in Cahill, 1999, p. 109).

The Self in Cultural Context

When we imagine how others will respond to our actions, we choose from a limited set of lines of conduct that are part of the wider culture. In the United States, the self is likely to incorporate key virtues such as self-reliance and individualism. Hence personal goals tend to be favored over group goals (Bellah ct al., 1985). In the United States, people readily change their group membership as it suits them—switching churches or even religions, leaving one employer for another, moving from neighborhood to neighborhood (Goleman, 1990).

In most non-Western cultures, however, the self is more likely to be collectivist; that is, personal identity is less important than group identity in a **collectivist culture** (Gergen, 1991). In India, for instance, feelings of self-esteem and prestige derive more from the reputation and honor of one's family than from any individual achievements (Roland, 1988). In a collectivist setting, a high value is placed on preserving one's public image so as not to bring shame on one's family, tribe, or community (Triandis, McCusker, & Hui, 1990). Overcoming personal interests and temptations to show loyalty to one's group and other authorities is celebrated. During the 1998 Winter Olympics observers noted that most players on the Japanese hockey team didn't want to score too many goals, for fear of drawing attention to themselves and away from the team.

In contrast, in **individualist cultures** such as the United States, personal accomplishments are a key part of one's self-concept. The amount of respect we deserve is determined in large part by our level of expertise. For example, before a public speech a guest lecturer will likely be introduced to her audience as "a distinguished scholar, a leader in her field" along with a list of her academic credentials and scholarly achievements. In Asia, however, people would consider such pronouncements self-centered and egotistical. Asian lecturers usually begin their talks by telling the audience how *little* they know about the topic at hand (Goleman, 1990).

But even in an individualist society such as the United States, our personal identities are inseparable from the various groups and organizations to which we belong. Consider the network revealed in Exhibit 5.1, which shows the contents of a person's

What can you tell about the owner of the wallet whose contents are shown here? More important, what can you tell from the wallet's contents about the importance of groups, organizations, and institutions in our lives? To lose a wallet is to lose tangible evidence of personal identity and our connections to the social structure.

Depending on whom you talk to, money ❶ is either "the root of all evil" or "what makes the world go 'round." There's no denying that money is vitally important in the lives of most people. The entire structure of Western societies is built around it. But the money in our wallets has no intrinsic value. It is merely paper. It is valuable only because we, as a collective, agree to give it symbolic value. In fact, the dollar bill is one of the most internationally recognized symbols, readily accepted throughout the world.

We need identification cards to use the services of many of the organizations and groups to which we belong. Forget your membership card, and you can't work out in your local gym; forget your meal card, and you can't eat in your campus dining hall; forget your video store card, and you can't rent that movie you were dying to see. Some office buildings, in the interest of security, have issued identification cards that employees must use just to get into the building.

Most of us carry a variety of credit cards for department stores or other retail outlets ❷. But credit cards do more than simply enable us to make purchases without having to pay cash right away. They represent power, status, and prestige. Credit card companies have created a whole system of hierarchy and privilege. If you have a regular credit card,

Exhibit 5.1   A Sociological Portrait of Identity

you're just a regular citizen; own a gold card and you have access to more money and more privileges; a platinum or titanium card puts you at the top of the heap, giving you even more opportunities. Other organizations have tried to use this status system. The Preferred Reader ❸ card you see here is an example.

Your driver's license ❹ is the most frequently asked-for identification card. What does this say about the cultural importance of automobiles in our lives? What are some of the reasons people ask to see our driver's licenses? The necessity of having this identification card has caused many people who don't need or want to drive to take a driving test.

The library card ❺, like many identification and credit cards, encodes information about you into its bar code. Magnetic strips and bar codes connect you to huge data banks that keep track of your creditworthiness and your record of payments (not to mention whether you have any overdue books). Some of these data banks also sell your name to marketing organizations that provide information about your patterns of consumption—maybe not always accurately—for future marketing campaigns. The catalogs that multiply in your mailbox can probably be traced back to an identification strip on one of your cards.

The contents of a wallet reflect important sociological ideas. As you make your way through this book, notice how concepts such as social identity, deviance, socialization, power, organizations, institutions, race, gender, class, and family can be "seen" by taking a peek inside your wallet.

wallet. Thus to fully understand how we become who we are, we must know the norms and values of our society, family, peers, coworkers, and all the others who are a part of our lives. Beyond that, we must also understand our position in the social structure. We must know to what extent our race and ethnicity, social class, and religion set limits on the kinds of social relationships we can and will form. And we must know how institutions affect the way we're socialized. All of these things affect our identity, as well as our ability to take the roles of people who differ from us.

Socialization and Stratification: Growing Up With Inequality

Socialization does not take place in a vacuum. Your social class, your race and ethnicity, and your sex and gender all become significant features of your social identity. Were you born into a poor or a well-to-do family? Are you a member of a racial minority or a member of the dominant group? Are you male or female? These elements of identity shape your experiences with other people and the larger society and will direct you along a certain life path. In most societies, social class, race and ethnicity, and gender are the key determinants of people's opportunities throughout their lives.

Social Class

Social classes consist of people who occupy similar positions of power, privilege, and prestige. People's positions in the class system affect virtually every aspect of their lives, including political preferences, sexual behavior, religious affiliation, diet, and life expectancy. The conflict perspective points out that even in a relatively open society such as the United States, parents' social class determines children's access to certain educational, occupational, and residential opportunities. But the relationship between class and socialization is not simply about parents providing (or not providing) their children with the resources of a comfortable childhood (for instance, a nice house, plenty of toys, access to good schools). In addition, parents' class standing influences the values and orientations children learn and the identities they develop.

In Chapter 10 you will learn much more about how social class affects attitudes, behaviors, and opportunities. The important point here is that social class and socialization are linked. Sociologist Melvin L. Kohn (1979) interviewed 200 working-class and 200 middle-class American couples who had at least one child of fifth-grade age. He found that the middle-class parents were more likely to promote such values as self-direction, independence, and curiosity than were the working-class parents. A more recent study found that middle-class parents are more likely than working-class parents to foster their children's talents through organized leisure activities and experiences that require logical reasoning (Lareau, 2003). Other researchers have found this tendency especially strong among middle-class mothers (Xiao, 2000).

Conversely, working-class parents were more likely than middle-class parents to emphasize conformity to external authority, a common characteristic of the blue-collar jobs they're likely to have later on (Kohn, 1979). Principally, they want their children to be neat and clean and to follow the rules.

Of course, not all middle-class parents, or working-class parents, raise their children in these ways, and many factors other than social class influence parental values (Wright & Wright, 1976). Nevertheless, Kohn found that these general tendencies were consistent regardless of the sex of the child or the size and composition of the family. In a study of African American women, those from middle-class backgrounds reported that their parents had higher expectations for them and were more involved in their education than African American women from working-class backgrounds reported (Hill, 1997).

Moreover, others have found that despite cultural differences, social class standing influences child socialization in European (Poland, Germany) and non-Western (Japan, Taiwan) societies (Schooler, 1996; Williamson, 1984; Yi, Chang, & Chang, 2004).

Sudden shifts in social class standing—due, for instance, to an unexpected job loss—can also affect the way parents socialize their children. Parents who lose their jobs can become irritable, tense, and moody and their disciplinary style more arbitrary. They may come to rely less on reasoning and more on hostile comments and physical punishment. As a result, children's sense of self, their aspirations, and their school performance suffer (cited in Rothstein, 2001).

Class differences in socialization are also directly related to future goals. Working-class parents tend to believe that eventual occupational success and survival depend on their children's ability to conform to and obey authority (Kohn, 1979). Middle-class parents are likely to believe that their children's future success will result from assertiveness and initiative. Hence middle-class children's feelings of control over their own destiny are likely to be much stronger than those of working-class children.

❖
Annette Lareau
Unequal Childhoods

Class-based differences in parenting values and approaches to child rearing can also influence how children learn to interact with others. Sociologist Annette Lareau (2003) conducted intensive interviews with 12 families of different racial and class backgrounds with children between the ages of 8 and 10. She and her associates visited each family about 20 times over the span of a month. She found subtle, but important, class differences in the lessons children learned about dealing with others:

> There was quite a bit more talking in middle-class homes than in working-class and poor homes, leading to the development of greater verbal agility, larger vocabularies, more comfort with authority figures, and more familiarity with abstract concepts. Importantly, children also developed skill differences in interacting with authority figures in institutions and at home. Middle-class children . . . learn, [when young], to shake the hands of adults and look them in the eye. . . . Researchers stress the importance of eye contact, firm handshakes, and displaying comfort with bosses during [job interviews]. In poor families . . . however, family members usually do not look each other in the eye when conversing. . . . They [may] live in neighborhoods where it can be dangerous to look people in the eye too long (p. 5).

Children's evolving sense of entitlement also tends to be based on their class standing. Middle- and upper-class children often take for granted the right to be involved in activities like organized sports and music lessons, to attend summer enrichment programs, and to go on out-of-town class field trips. These activities are not simply recreational. Many of them replicate key aspects of the adult workplace, like meeting new people and learning to work effectively with them. Travel experiences give these children a level of comfort with unfamiliar surroundings that they can use in the future when called on to take a trip for business or interact with people from different regions (Lareau, 2003). The skills that are developed while involved in these experiences will provide a smooth fit with the behaviors and expectations of other social institutions these children will encounter when they become adults.

The importance that middle-class families place on their children's involvement in such activities is hard to miss. Many of these families routinely spend thousands of dollars a year promoting their children's extracurricular activities, which often determine the daily and weekly schedules for the entire family. The pace of life can be hectic as parents and children race from soccer games to tae kwon do practice to piano lessons. Middle-class adults' leisure time is often completely absorbed by their children's involvements, further illustrating the value they attach to such activities and the assumption that they will provide their children with interpersonal advantages in the future.

Lareau found that in working-class and poor families, the organization and rhythm of daily life is quite different:

> Although money was in short supply, children's lives were more relaxed and, more importantly, the pace of life was slower. Children played with other children outside the house. . . . Some children had organized activities, but they were far fewer than in middle-class families. Other times, children wanted to be in organized activities, but economic constraints, compounded by lack of transportation, made participation prohibitive. . . . In addition, since they were not riding around in cars with parents going to organized activities or being directed by adults in structured activities, children in working-class and poor families had more autonomy from adults . . . and long stretches of free time (Lareau, 2003, pp. 35–36).

Although children from working-class and poor families may not be so well socialized for future organizational and interpersonal demands of corporate America, one has to wonder if their upbringing doesn't give them an advantage or two over heavily scheduled middle-class children. For instance, they may be more likely to acquire "street smarts"—being aware of potential interpersonal and environmental threats and being able to deal with them—and to develop resourcefulness and creativity in organizing their own social networks and enterprises.

Race and Ethnicity

Several years ago, shortly after an unarmed West African immigrant was shot and killed by four white police officers in Bronx, New York, some of my students became embroiled in a heated discussion of the incident. One student, who was white, expressed concern that because of the terrible actions of these individual officers, young children of all races would now grow up mistrusting or even hating the police. As a child, she said, she had been taught that the role of the police is to help people and that if she were ever in trouble or lost she could approach an officer for assistance. She never questioned whether or not the police could be trusted.

Some of the African American students in class quickly pointed out that their socialization experiences had been quite different. Parents and others in their neighborhoods had taught them never to trust the police, because officers were just as likely to harass them as to help them. They were taught to seek out neighbors and relatives, not the police, if they ever needed help. To them the police were not knights in shining armor but bullies with badges. But now, in the wake of several other incidents around the country where police injured or killed people of color, some parents and civic leaders feel it is essential to teach black and Latino/a children how to respond safely when approached by the police. The NAACP, the Allstate Insurance Company, and the National Organization of Black Law Enforcement Executives have published brochures and held community forums on "guidelines for interacting with law enforcement officials." Among other things, children are being taught to speak when asked to speak, to stop when ordered to stop, to never make any sudden movements, and to always display their open hands to show they aren't armed (Barry, 2000).

Although these two perspectives of my students are not representative of every white or every black person in the United States, the interchange illustrates the stark impact race and ethnicity can have on socialization. For white children, learning about their racial identity is less about defining their race than it is about learning how to handle privileges and behaviors associated with being white in a predominantly white society (Van Ausdale & Feagin, 2001). Chances are good that schools and religious organizations will reinforce the socialization messages expressed to white children in their families—for example, that "hard work will pay off in the long run" or "you can be anything you want as long as you work hard."

For children who are members of ethnoracial minorities, however, learning about their race occurs within a different and much more complex social environment (Hughes & Chen, 1997). These children must live simultaneously in two different worlds: their ethnoracial community and the "mainstream" (that is, white) society. Hence, they're likely to be exposed to several different types of socialization experience while growing up: that which includes information about the mainstream culture, that which focuses on their minority status in society, and that which focuses on the history and cultural heritage of their ethnoracial group (Thornton, 1997). Parents often emphasize one type of orientation over others:

> Parents who possess a mainstream orientation are not likely to emphasize race but more so emphasize self-confidence, personal self-esteem, competence, and hard work to defend against societal insults and racial barriers. Those who possess a minority orientation are more likely to emphasize the significance of race in society and the institutional barriers their children will likely confront due to their racial and ethnic background. Parents who possess a . . . cultural orientation are more likely to emphasize the history and achievement of [their group]. Parents possessing this orientation attempt to instill a sense of racial pride in their children (Scott, 2003, p. 523).

In ethnoracial groups that have been able to overcome discrimination and achieve at high levels—such as some Asian-American groups—ethnic socialization can focus

149

simply on the values of their culture of origin. But among groups that by-and-large remain disadvantaged, such as African Americans, Native Americans, and Latino/as parents' discussion of race is more likely to focus on preparing their children for prejudice, ethnic hatred, and mistreatment in a society set up to ignore or actively exclude them (McLoyd, Cauce, Takeuchi, & Wilson, 2000; Staples, 1992). For instance, these children may be taught that "hard work" alone might not be enough to get ahead in this society. Even African American children from affluent homes in racially integrated neighborhoods need reassurances about the racial conflicts they will inevitably encounter (Comer & Poussaint, 1992). These are lessons that children in the dominant racial group seldom require, for reasons explored in greater depth in Chapter 11.

Gender

As you recall from Chapter 4, the sexual dichotomy—the belief that there are two and only two sexes—is not universal. Cultures are even more likely to differ in what is expected of people based on their sex and in how male and female children are to be socialized.

Before discussing this aspect of socialization, it's necessary to distinguish between two concepts: sex and gender. **Sex** is typically used to refer to a person's biological maleness or femaleness. **Gender** designates masculinity and femininity, the psychological, social, and cultural aspects of maleness and femaleness (Kessler & McKenna, 1978). This distinction is important because it reminds us that male-female differences in behaviors or experiences do not spring naturally from biological differences between the sexes (Lips, 1993).

The gender socialization process begins the moment a child is born. A physician, nurse, or midwife immediately starts that infant on a career as a male or female by authoritatively declaring whether it is a boy or girl. In most U.S. hospitals the infant boy is wrapped in a blue blanket, the infant girl in a pink one. From that point on, the developmental paths of American males and females diverge. The subsequent messages that individuals receive from families, books, television, and schools not only teach and reinforce gender-typed expectations but also influence the formation of their self-concepts.

If you were to ask parents whether they treated sons any differently from daughters, most would probably say no. Yet there is considerable evidence that what parents do and what they say they do are two different things (Lips, 1993; Lytton & Romney, 1991). In one study, 30 first-time parents were asked to describe their infants at less than 24 hours old. They frequently resorted to common gender stereotypes. Those with daughters described them as "tiny," "soft," "fine-featured," and "delicate." Sons were seen as "strong," "alert," "hardy," and "coordinated" (J. Z. Rubin, Provenzano, & Luria, 1974). A replication of this study two decades later found that U.S. parents continue to perceive their infants in gender-stereotyped ways, although less so than in the 1970s (Karraker, Vogel, & Lake, 1995). Parents also tend to engage in rougher physical play with infant sons than with infant daughters and use subtle differences in tone of voice and different pet names, such as "Sweetie" versus "Tiger" (MacDonald & Parke, 1986; Tauber, 1979).

New parents can be very sensitive about the correct identification of their child's sex. Even parents who claim to consider sex and gender irrelevant may spend a great deal of time ensuring that their child has the culturally appropriate gender appearance. Parents of a girl baby who has yet to grow hair (a visible sign of gender in many cultures) often tape pink ribbons to the bald baby's head to avoid potential misidentification. In many Latin American countries, families have baby girls' ears pierced and earrings placed in them to provide an unmistakable indicator of the child's sex and gender.

In a culture where sex and gender are centrally important and any ambiguity is distasteful, gender identification of babies helps in maintaining social order. When my elder son was an infant, I dressed him on several occasions in a pink, frilly snowsuit in order to observe the reactions of others. (Having a sociologist for a father can be rather difficult from time to time!) Invariably someone would approach us and start playing with the baby. Some variation of the following interchange inevitably ensued:

"Oh, she's so cute! What's your little girl's name?"

"Zachary."

"Isn't Zachary a boy's name?"

"He's a boy."

At this point the responses would range from stunned confusion and awkward laughter to dirty looks and outright anger. Clearly people felt that I had emotionally abused my son somehow. I had purposely breached a fundamental gender norm and thereby created, in their minds, unnecessary trauma (for him) and interactional confusion (for them).

Both boys and girls learn at a very young age to adopt gender as an organizing principle (Howard & Hollander, 1997). By the age of 3 or so most children can accurately answer the question "Are you a boy or a girl?" (see, for example, Kohlberg, 1966). To a young child, being a boy or a girl is simply another characteristic, like having brown hair or 10 fingers. The child at this age has no conception that gender is a category into which every human can be placed (Kessler & McKenna, 1978). But by the age of 5 or so, most children have developed a fair number of gender stereotypes (often incorrect) that they then use to guide their own perceptions and activities (Martin & Ruble, 2004). They also use these stereotypes to form impressions of others. A boy, for instance, may avoid approaching a new girl who's moved into the neighborhood because he assumes that she will be interested in "girl" things. Acting on this assumption reinforces the original belief that boys and girls are different. Indeed, to children at this age, gender is typically seen as a characteristic that is fixed and permanent. Statements like "Doctors are men" and "Nurses are women" are uttered as inflexible, objective "truths." A few years later, though, their attitudes toward gender become considerably more flexible, although such flexibility may not be reflected in their actual behaviors (Martin & Ruble, 2004).

It's important to note that gender socialization is not a passive process in which children simply absorb the information that bombards them. As part of the process of finding meaning in their social worlds, children actively construct gender as a social category. From an early age, they are like "gender detectives," searching for cues about gender, such as who should and shouldn't engage in certain activities, who can play with whom, and why girls and boys differ (Martin & Ruble, 2004, p. 67).

Parents and other family members may also provide their children with explicit instructions on proper gender behavior, such as "Big boys don't cry" or "Act like a young lady." For instance, one recent study of mothers' reactions to their children's misbehaviors found that they tend to be more concerned about injuries and safety issues with their daughters and tend to focus more on disciplinary issues with their sons (Morrongiello & Hogg, 2004).

Evidence suggests that such instructions are particularly rigid and restrictive for U.S. boys (Franklin, 1988). Indeed, the social costs for "gender-inappropriate" behavior are disproportionately severe for boys. Consider the different connotations and implications of the words *sissy* and *tomboy*. The girl who is a tomboy may fight, curse, compete in sports, and climb trees, but her entire gender identity is not called into question by the label. Girls, in general, are given license to do "boy things" (Kimmel, 2004). Indeed, tomboyness, if considered negative at all, is typically seen as transitory, a stage that a girl will eventually grow out of. But the chances for boys to play "girl games" without ridicule are rare and the risks for doing so are steep. The sissy is not simply a boy who enjoys female pursuits. He is suspiciously soft and effeminate. His sissyness is likely to be seen as reflective of his sexual essence, a sign to some of his impending homosexuality.

As children grow older, parents tend to encourage more gender-typed activities. For instance, American boys are more likely to mow the lawn, shovel snow, take out the garbage, and do the yard work, whereas girls tend to clean the house, wash dishes, cook, and babysit the younger children (L. White & Brinkerhoff, 1981). These discrepancies are clearly linked to the different social roles ascribed to men and women, which are discussed in more detail in Chapter 12.

Parents maintain their children's gender identity through the things they routinely provide for them: clothes, adornments, books, videos, and so forth. Clothes, for example, not only inform others about the sex of an individual, they also send messages about how that person ought to be treated and direct behavior along traditional gender lines (Shakin, Shakin, & Sternglanz, 1985). Frilly outfits do not lend themselves easily to rough and dirty play. Likewise, it is difficult to walk quickly or assertively in high heels and tight miniskirts. Clothes for boys and men rarely restrict physical movement in this way. Toys and games are an especially influential source of gender information parents provide their children.

❖ Micro-Macro Connection
Girls' Toys and Boys' Toys

Like most people over the age of 40, I can remember a time when toys played a very different role in American children's lives from the role they play today. When I was a child, my friends and I didn't have many toys and we usually ended up improvising playthings out of available materials, like tree branches, empty boxes, and old tennis rackets. When we did receive a new toy it was usually a special occasion, such as a birthday, a holiday, or a cavity-free dental checkup. Every once in a while we'd save up enough money, walk down to the local toy shop, and buy some toy for ourselves that we'd been coveting for months. The toys were simple and straightforward—wagons, fire engines, dolls, balls, trains, board games—and we'd use them and use them until they broke or wore out. When our parents detected a significant spurt in our maturity, they might get us a toy that required special caution: a chemistry set, an Easy Bake oven, an electric racing car set.

Today toys have changed. Toy making is now a multibillion-dollar business, part of a giant transnational, interconnected industry. It's virtually impossible to buy a toy these days that's not linked to some new film, television show, fast food restaurant, or other high-powered marketing campaign. Toy companies now commonly produce TV cartoons based on their own toy lines. Parents find it difficult to resist their children's wishes, which are likely to be formed by television advertisements. Try taking a child to McDonald's without having to purchase a toy there. The quaint toyshop of the past has been replaced by the massive toy mega-warehouse filled with endless aisles stocked floor to ceiling with boxes sporting eye-popping colors and screaming images. Even serious world events are now linked to toys. In 2003, the video game industry kept a close eye on the war in Iraq for battle weapons and tools that could be turned into toys ("Toymakers Study Troops," 2003). Toys, it seems, have lost their innocence.

But the current state of the toy industry is not simply a result of profit-hungry corporations trying to find new ways to exploit the child market (G. Cross, 1997). Toys have always played a significant role in teaching children about prevailing cultural conceptions of gender. In the 1950s—a time in U.S. history when most adults had endless faith in the goodness of technological progress—Erector sets and chemistry sets were supposed to encourage boys to be engineers and scientists. Dollhouses and baby dolls taught girls to be modern homemakers and mothers during a time when girls typically assumed they'd occupy those roles in adulthood.

A quick glance at Saturday morning television commercials, toy store shelves, or manufacturers' Web sites these days reveals that toys and games remain solidly segregated along gender lines. "Girls' toys" still revolve around themes of domesticity, fashion, and motherhood and "boys' toys" emphasize action and adventure (Renzetti & Curran, 2003). Gender-specific toys foster different traits and skills in children and thereby further segregate boys and girls into different patterns of social development. "Boys' toys" encourage invention, exploration, competition, and aggression. "Girls' toys" encourage creativity, nurturing, and physical attractiveness (C. L. Miller, 1987).

Dolls, makeup kits, and toy kitchens continue to be the most profitable items in the girls' market. The highly stereotypical "Barbie" doll has been one of the best-selling girls' toys for decades. Barbie takes in over $1 billion in annual sales. Ninety-five percent of girls aged 3 to 11 own at least one Barbie, the average number of Barbie dolls an American girl owns is eight (G. Cross, 1997).

Toy manufacturers also continue to make fortunes promoting war toys, competitive games of strategy, and sports paraphernalia for boys. In 1983 the popular action figure GI Joe got his own TV show; by 1988, two thirds of American boys between the ages of 5 and 11 owned Joes (G. Cross, 1997). Today, the boys' toy market is saturated with plastic descendants of Joe: high-tech soldiers, muscle-bound action figures from popular comic books and movies, and intergalactic warriors. In 2003, George W. Bush was immortalized with a Joe-like action figure depicting him in a naval flight suit.

Video games have become a particularly lucrative product in recent years. Most video games are designed by males for other males. Female characters in these games are often provocatively sexual, scantily clad, and voluptuous. The developers of one game, *BMX XXX*, were forced to add clothing to their topless female riders after major retailers refused to carry the game. Many games portray female characters as prostitutes and strippers, who are frequent targets of violence at the hands of psychopathic male characters. In *Duke Nukem 3D*, the player is awarded bonus points for shooting naked, bound prostitutes and strippers who plead "Kill me!" In *Grand Theft Auto 3*, players can beat prostitutes to death with baseball bats after having sex with them (Media Awareness Network, 2005). The gender messages in such games may have a detrimental effect on both boys' attitudes toward girls and women and their conceptions of appropriate male behavior.

From time to time toy manufacturers have attempted—usually only halfheartedly—to blur the lines between boys' and girls' toys. A few years ago, the Hasbro toy company tried to interest boys in troll dolls, which are traditionally popular among girls. What it came up with were old-fashioned action figures in the shape of a troll, with names like "Troll Warrior" and "Battle Troll" (Lawson, 1993). Other companies have tried to sell girls action figures and building blocks, which are typically the province of boys, but have drifted into traditional gender stereotypes. Mattel's "Wonder Woman" action figure fights not with swords or machine guns but with a wand that sprays bubbles. The popular Legos building blocks that many boys use to make towers and monsters still come in vivid primary colors. But they are now also available in pastel colors and come in kits that can be used to make jewelry and doll houses.

For the most part, toy manufacturers are still quick to exploit the gender-distinct roles children are encouraged to pursue when they become adults. For instance, Mattel makes a pregnant version of Barbie's friend Midge (called "Happy Family Midge"). She comes with a distended tummy that, when removed, reveals a 1¾-inch baby nestled in the doll's plastic uterus. The doll comes with everything a girl needs to play out the birth and care of the new baby, including diapers (pink if it's a girl; blue if it's a boy), a birth certificate, bottles, rattles, changing table, tub, and crib. This doll clearly teaches young girls the cultural value of motherhood, a role most girls are encouraged and expected to enter later in life. One would be hard-pressed to find a comparable toy, popular among boys, that prepares them for future roles as fathers.

Institutions and Socialization

It should be clear by now that becoming who we are is a complex process embedded in the larger social structure. We are much more than the sum of our anatomical and neurological parts. Not only can cultural attitudes toward race, class, and gender dramatically affect our personal identities, but various social institutions—in particular, the educational system, religious organizations, and the mass media—exert considerable influence on our self-concept, our values, and our perspectives as well.

Education

In contemporary industrial societies, the most powerful institutional agent of socialization, after the family, is education. In fact, according to the structural-functionalist perspective, the primary reason that schools exist is to socialize young people. Children formally enter the school system around age 5 when they begin kindergarten, although many enter earlier in preschool or nursery school. At this point, the "personalized" instruction of the family is replaced by the "impersonalized" instruction of the school, where children in most developed countries will remain for the next 13 years or longer. No other nonfamily institution has such extended and consistent control over a person's social growth.

Although schools are officially charged with equipping students with the knowledge and skills they need to fulfill various roles in society (for example, reading, writing, mathematics), they also teach students important social, political, and economic values. When students set up simulated grocery stores or banks, they are learning about the importance of free enterprise and finance in a capitalist society; when they hold mock elections, they are being introduced to a democratic political system; when they spend time tending a school garden, they are learning to nurture the earth.

More subtly, schools teach students what they can expect for themselves in the world. In many school districts, children are grouped into different programs, or tracks, based on an assessment of their academic abilities. In a typical high school, for example, some students will take a course of study designed to prepare them for college, whereas others will take more general or vocational courses designed to prepare them for work after they graduate. **Tracking** clearly determines future outcomes: Students in the higher tracks often go on to prestigious universities; those in the lower tracks may not go to college at all and, if they do go, might enroll in community colleges. Tracking can, therefore, ultimately affect employment opportunities, income levels, and overall quality of life.

Ironically, although individual accomplishment is stressed in U.S. schools, through grades and report cards, students learn that their future success in society may be determined as much by who they are as by what they achieve. Ample evidence shows that teachers react to students on the basis of race, religion, social class, and gender (Wilkinson & Marrett, 1985). It is in school that many children are first exposed to the fact that people and groups are ranked in society, and soon they get a sense of their own standing in the social hierarchy.

Some sociologists argue that schooling in most cultures is designed not so much to provide children with factual information and encourage creativity as to produce passive, nonproblematic conformists who will fit into the existing social order (Gracey, 1991). This training in conformity involves several different dimensions (Brint, 1998). First, there is *behavioral* conformity. Teachers in the early grades typically keep children in line by controlling their bodily movements, such as making them sit still or forcing them to raise their hands before speaking. Second, schools teach *moral* conformity. Teachers often instruct children about such virtues as honesty, courage, kindness, fairness, and respect. Finally, schools teach children to conform to *culturally* approved styles and outlooks. In some societies, teachers reward their students for showing a quick wit; in other societies children are rewarded for demonstrating thoughtfulness

(Text continues on page 162)

Becoming a Mariner

Liz Grauerholz and Rebecca Smith

The U.S. Merchant Marine is the country's fleet of commercial ships, which becomes an auxiliary to the Navy during wartime. In peacetime, merchant mariners are responsible for safely and efficiently transporting cargoes and passengers on the oceans and through inland waterways. Even in peacetime, it is a job fraught with physical and mental challenges.

The importance of the merchant seamen to the war effort was reflected in the establishment of the U.S. Merchant Marine Academy at King's Point on Long Island in New York in 1943. It is a four-year institution of higher learning that prepares young men and women to become naval reserve officers or merchant mariners. It is one of the five official U.S. service academies, in the same category as West Point and the U.S. Air Force Academy. Approximately 950 men and women are enrolled at any given time. Six state marine academies sanctioned by the U.S. Department of Transportation offer training for mariners as well.

❖ Transporting a full load of iron ore through the ice-choked waters of the Great Lakes in winter requires a high level of training and commitment.

All the merchant marine academies put students through an extensive resocialization process. Students not only take academic courses leading to a college degree but also acquire the professional skills of mariners and the norms and values of people who are required to work in harmony in close quarters in difficult circumstances.

At first, resocialization revolves around confidence- and community-building exercises.

Many non-military universities have similar exercises during first-year orientation.

The Merchant Marine has existed in this country since 1775. As a new country with no navy, the United States relied heavily on its merchant seamen for defense against the British during the War of 1812. After the outbreak of World War II, many ordinary seamen were recruited to staff supply ships running a gauntlet of German submarines.

Let's Finish the Job!

URGENT—
EXPERIENCED SEAMEN NEEDED!

WIRE COLLECT: Merchant Marine · Washington, D. C.
or inquire your Maritime Union or U. S. Employment Service

❖ First-year students at the Maine Maritime Academy begin their orientation with a challenge course that requires teams participate to solve problems and watch out for each other's safety.

As midshipmen at the Academy, students are required to take courses in the humanities, social sciences, math, and science. The curriculum is similar to that found in many engineering and business programs. However, Academy students spend almost a year on board a ship. They also learn a wide variety of practical skills, such as reading maps and radar screens, administering to sick shipmates, maintaining and repairing ship engines and other equipment, and deploying lifeboats.

❖ Learning to tie ship cables

❖ Reading maps on the bridge of a ship

Some aspects of indoctrination at the U.S. Merchant Marine Academy are more militaristic, as at the other service academies or in ROTC programs at non-military universities. Students at the academy are required to march in formation as they move from one activity to another, learning discipline and the subordination of personal preferences to the unit's needs and rhythms. Unique outward expressions of individuality conflict with the Academy's goal of transforming a motley group of cadets into like-minded mariners.

Much of the responsibility for indoctrination falls on fellow students. Below an upper-class student sanctions an infraction of the academy's norms. None of the other students in the mess hall question this form of discipline; in fact, they studiously concentrate on finishing their meal.

❖ Everyday life is also tightly controlled. Meticulous attention to outward appearance is considered a crucial element of personal discipline.

❖ At the Academy, as at other total institutions, the authorities frequently check the success of the resocialization process. Formal inspections are commonplace.

❖ And in order to graduate, students at the Academy have to take one or more licensing exams administered by the U.S. Coast Guard.

The solemnity of graduation is broken by a variety of celebratory rituals, including the tossing of caps into the air—much like the ritual at many college graduation ceremonies. Unique to the U.S. Merchant Marine Academy, though, is a fully dressed leap into the pool. It symbolizes release but is far from spontaneous. Note that the female graduates are wearing bathing suits under their uniforms, indicating that this ritual too is an artifact of the resocialization process.

❖ Unlike their non-military counterparts, the graduating midshipmen must take an oath, pledging their unwavering commitment to the service of their country.

and asking deep, probing questions. Such training socializes students to adopt traits that people consider culturally desirable within that society.

Sometimes these different dimensions overlap. Rules against arguing with the teacher, for instance, teach children the moral "goodness" of respecting authority. But they can also foster passivity and give students their first taste of control by authoritative adults other than their parents. Such classroom regulations, then, help impose discipline while at the same time they prepare children for what they will face in the larger culture. Obeying the kindergarten teacher today prepares the individual for obeying the high school teacher, college professor, and boss tomorrow.

Many of these lessons vary by gender. In an observational study of five preschool classrooms in the United States, sociologist Karin Martin (1998) found, among other things, that teachers tend to discourage girls from speaking loudly and place tighter restrictions on their movement than they do on boys. In addition, preschool teachers are more likely to physically restrain boys—for example, by holding them to stop them from running—than girls. Such actions go a long way in telling boys and girls, even at this early age, that they are being perceived differently and are held to different standards of behavior. Unequal treatment of female and male students persists throughout elementary school, high school, and beyond, creating inequalities in outcomes, as you will see in Chapter 12.

It may seem that the educational system is overwhelmingly dedicated to fitting every student into preordained roles. However, some teachers and alternative schools do instill values at odds with existing social arrangements. The point is that because formal education is so important in the everyday lives of most children, the agenda of a particular school system cannot help but influence the types of people they will eventually become.

Religion

As the structural-functionalist perspective tells us, religion is the social institution that tends to the spiritual needs of individuals and serves as a major source of cultural knowledge. It plays a key role in developing people's ideas about right and wrong. It also helps form people's identities by providing coherence and continuity to the episodes that make up each individual's life (Kearl, 1980). Religious rites of passage, such as baptisms, bar and bat mitzvahs, confirmations, and weddings, reaffirm an individual's religious identity while impressing on her or him the rights and obligations attached to each new status (J. H. Turner, 1972).

Religion occupies a complex and curious place in U.S. life. Structural changes in society have made religious affiliation somewhat unstable in recent years. For instance, as people move from one location to another, many of the ties that bind them to the same religion—most notably networks of family and friends—are broken. Only about 45% of adults attend religious services regularly (The Barna Group, 2005). Over the past couple of decades, many of the most powerful religious groups experienced a decline in membership. For instance, between 1990 and 2000, the Lutheran Church suffered a 3.2% drop in membership, the Episcopal Church 5.3%, the United Methodist Church 6.7%, the Presbyterian Church 11.6%, and the United Church of Christ 14.8% (American Religion Data Archive, 2002).

But membership decline does not necessarily mean that religion is losing its socializing influence in U.S. society. Indeed, at the same time that membership in some religions has shrunk, that of so-called conservative churches (Roman Catholic Church, Church of Jesus Christ of Latter-day Saints, Assemblies of God, Christian Churches, and Southern Baptists) has increased (American Religion Data Archive, 2002). And new religions are constantly emerging. Of the 1,600 or so recognized religions and denominations in the United States today, half were founded after 1965. Furthermore, immigration has helped fuel an increase in non-Christian religions. The number of Hindus in the United States has grown from 70,000 in 1977 to close to 800,000 today. Between 1990 and 2001, membership in a variety of non-Christian religious groups grew significantly, including Muslim, Buddhist, Hindu, Unitarian/Universalist, Scientologist, Baha'i, Taoist, New Age, Eckankar, Sikh, Wiccan, Druid, and Santerian.

Religion may not look the same as it did 50 years ago, but it still remains a fundamental socializing agent in most Americans' lives (see Exhibit 5.2). Indeed, compared to most other Western democracies, such as Canada, Australia, Germany, France, and Great Britain, people in the United States stand out for the depth of their religious beliefs (Zoll, 2005). Consider these facts:

- Eighty-four percent of U.S. adults say that religion plays a big role in their lives (cited in Zoll, 2005). In contrast, 52% of Norwegians and 55% of Swedes say that God doesn't matter to them at all (cited in Ferguson, 2004).
- Among U.S. residents, 62% have no doubts that God exists; only 2% express outright disbelief. A greater percentage of U.S. adults, no matter what their religious affiliation, believe in life after death today than in the 1970s (Greeley & Hout, 1999).
- Americans are three times as likely to say they believe in the virgin birth of Jesus (83%) as in evolution (28%) (Kristof, 2003).
- Nine out of every 10 homes contain at least one Bible. About one third of U.S. residents believe that the Bible is the actual word of God and that it was divinely inspired (Shorto, 1997).
- Among U.S. adults, 71% believe in heaven and 57% believe in the devil. Sixty percent say grace at family meals (Niebuhr, 1996).
- Two thirds of Americans feel that it is important that an American president have strong religious beliefs (Pew Forum on Religion and Public Life, 2004).
- Over half of U.S. adults feel that the lesson of September 11 attacks was that there is too little (not too much) religion in the world. Close to half say they believe that the United States has special protection from God (Pew Forum on Religion and Public Life, 2002).

In short, religion remains a significant part of U.S. life. We still consider ourselves "one nation under God," and our money still proclaims our trust in God. It's virtually impossible to watch a sporting event these days without seeing a baseball player cross himself before batting, a football player point skyward after scoring a touchdown, a basketball player in a postgame interview thank God for guiding the shot that led to his team's victory, or groups of opposing players kneeling together in prayer after a game. Sales of Christian books, computer games, videos, and toys are going up each year. The contemporary Christian music genre is a $1-billion-a-year business in itself. Enrollment in evangelical colleges has grown steadily over the past decade, as has the number of families choosing to homeschool their children for religious reasons (Talbot, 2000a).

Exhibit 5.2   How U.S. Adults Rate Their Religiosity

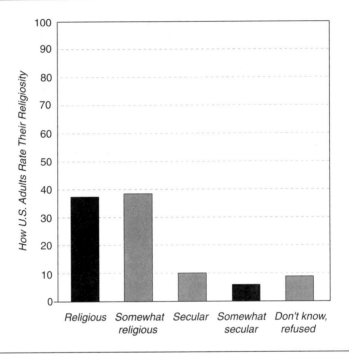

Source: Kosmin & Mayer, 2001.

In recent years, religion has become a key component of the American political system. Americans are far more likely than people in other industrialized countries to be willing to mix politics and religion. As one author put it, "America is the last country left whose citizens don't laugh out loud when their leader asks God to bless the country" (Ignatieff, 2005, p. 47). In one study, close to 40% of U.S. adults said religious leaders should try to influence policymakers (cited in Zoll, 2005). The Indiana State House of Representatives begins each session with a daily prayer containing phrases such as, "In the strong name of Jesus our savior," "We pray this in Christ's name," and "I appeal to our Lord and savior, Jesus Christ" (Ryckaert, 2005, p. 1).

Nationally, since the re-election of George W. Bush in 2004, conservative religious groups have grown in political influence, in part because of the electoral boost they gave the president. While John Kerry, his opponent in the election, received support from some moderate religious groups, evangelical Protestants and conservative Catholics turned out in higher numbers and voted overwhelmingly for Bush. Members of these groups were more likely than those of less conservative religious denominations to indicate that faith had a direct impact on their vote (Green, Smidt, Guth, & Kellstedt, 2005). Many people went even further, suggesting that Bush's re-election was divinely determined. According to the undersecretary of defense for intelligence, "George Bush was not elected by a majority of the voters in the United States, he was appointed by God" (quoted in Maharidge, 2004, p. 80). During Bush's administration, some of the most powerful members of Congress (Tom DeLay, Bill Frist, Rick Santorum, to name a few) made the infusion of religion into government their number one priority. The influence of religion in policy making is likely to guarantee that it remains a significant socializing force in American society for many years to come.

Mass Media

Another powerful institutional socializer is the media. Researchers estimate that by the time the average U.S. student graduates from high school, she or he will have spent more time watching television than sitting in classrooms (Croteau & Hoynes, 2000). Newspapers, magazines, television, radio, and film transmit persuasive messages on the nature of reality. They also tell us the type of person we "should" be, from how we should perform our jobs to how different social classes live to what our intimate relationships and families are supposed to look like. The media teach us about prevailing values, beliefs, myths, stereotypes, and trends (Gitlin, 1979) and provide an avenue through which we learn new attitudes and behavior (Bandura & Walters, 1963). Sociologists, psychologists, and, of course, politicians continue to debate the degree to which sex and violence in film, television, and video games influence behavior, particularly among young people.

These lessons begin early. Children's books, for instance, teach youngsters what other little boys or girls in their culture do and what is expected of them. In the early 1970s, Lenore Weitzman and her colleagues studied the portrayal of gender in popular U.S. preschool books (Weitzman, Eifler, Hodada, & Ross, 1972). They found that boys played a more significant role in the stories than girls by a ratio of 11 to 1. Boys were more likely to be portrayed in adventurous pursuits or activities that required independence and strength; girls were likely to be confined to indoor activities and portrayed as passive and dependent. These gender stereotypes in children's books decreased only slightly over the next several decades (S. B. Peterson & Lach, 1990). Recent attempts to publish more nonsexist children's books have had little impact on the overall market. For instance, elementary school reading textbooks still primarily portray males as aggressive, argumentative, and competitive (Evans & Davies, 2000). "Gender equality" in children's books usually involves female characters taking on characteristics and roles typically associated with males. These books rarely, if ever, portray male characters adopting female traits (Diekman & Murnen, 2004).

Television images of males and females also have a strong influence on children's perceptions and behaviors. Children who watch a lot of television are more likely to hold stereotypical attitudes toward gender, exhibit gender-related characteristics, and engage in gender-related activities than children who watch little television (M. Morgan, 1987; Signorielli, 1990). In one study, girls who did not have stereotypical conceptions of gender to begin with showed a significant increase in such attitudes after two years of heavy television watching (M. Morgan, 1982). In another study, 4- to 6-year-old children refused to play with a particular toy after watching two Muppets on TV who said the toy was OK only for the other sex (Cobb, Stevens-Long, & Goldstein, 1982).

These effects are not surprising given the programming that children encounter. Despite some notable exceptions (for example, *Sesame Street*), most children's television shows continue to portray males and females in stereotypical gender roles. A study of 41 Saturday morning cartoons found that male characters are more likely than female characters to occupy leadership roles, act aggressively, give guidance to or come to the rescue of others, express opinions, ask questions, and achieve their goals. In addition, males are more likely to be portrayed in some kind of recognizable occupation, whereas females are more likely to be cast in the role of caregiver (Thompson & Zerbinos, 1995). Even the media coverage of female sports events tends to focus on the physical appearance and sexual attractiveness of the athletes and not just their competitive accomplishments (Shugart, 2003).

Television commercials also perpetuate stereotypes. One study of 467 commercials shown between children's cartoons found that, as in the shows themselves, male characters are more likely than female characters to be in a major role, to be active rather than passive, and to be depicted in an occupational setting (S. Davis, 2003). Similarly, an analysis of over 500 U.S. and Australian commercials targeting children found that girls were much more likely than boys to be portrayed as shy, giggly, and passive (Browne, 1998). The differences were less pronounced in Australia, however, where activists have had more success in countering gender stereotypes in the media than in the United States. Such images are not trivial, given that U.S. children watch over 20,000 TV commercials a year.

The socializing influence of the media extends beyond stereotypical images of gender. Consider the role that televised sports play in teaching people in the United States certain cultural values (Gitlin, 1979). Television has reduced the sports experience to a sequence of individual achievements—a cultural value on which the entire U.S. social structure is based. We have grown used to hearing such descriptions as "world record holder," "superstar," and "greatest player of all time." Praise is heaped not only on individuals and the occasional "dynasty" team but also on more specific actions: "best 3-point shooter," "best backhand," "best at hitting with two outs and runners in scoring position," "best open field tackler," "best chip out of a sand trap." Such characterizations not only perpetuate the importance of individual achievement but also give the impression that it is always possible to find something, however narrowly defined, at which one can be "best" (Gitlin, 1979).

Nowhere is the media emphasis on individual achievement more obvious than in the most emblematic play in professional basketball today: the slam dunk. It's impossible to watch television highlights of a basketball game without seeing a thunderous, explosive, gravity-defying dunk:

> The dunk is a declaration of power and dominance, of machismo. In a team game, an ensemble of five players a side, it is an expression of self. In a sport devoted to selling sneakers, the dunk is a marketing tour de force, the money shot at the end of every worthy basketball sequence. (Sokolove, 2005, p. 42)

To some observers, though, fans' obsession with acrobatic dunks has made the fundamentals of success, namely teamwork and sacrifice, seem irrelevant (Sokolove, 2005). In a world where muscled-up athletes whose only reliable offensive skill is the ability to dunk the ball can earn millions and where ESPN nationally televises the games of high school phenoms, it's not surprising that individual athleticism has overshadowed the collaborative aspect of the game. Consequently, many young players today are more concerned with perfecting their individual moves than with developing other skills—passing, rebounding, shooting from various spots on the floor, playing defense, and other less glamorous but no less essential elements of a team effort.

Conclusion

Becoming the people we are is a complex social process. Those intimate characteristics we hold so dear—our self-concept, our gender, and our racial and ethnic identity—reflect larger cultural attitudes, values, and expectations. Yet we are not perfect reflections of society's values. Despite all the powerful socializing institutions that pull our developmental strings, we continue to be and will always be individuals.

Sometimes we ignore our generalized others and strike out on our own with complete disregard for community standards and attitudes. Sometimes we form self-concepts that contradict the information we receive from others about ourselves. Sometimes we willingly violate the expectations associated with our social class, gender, or race. Societal influence can go only so far in explaining how we become who we are. The rest—that which makes us truly unique—remains a fascinating mystery.

◆

YOUR TURN

Being a child or an adolescent is not simply a biological stage of development. It is a social identity. People's experiences with this identity emerge from a particular cultural and historical context as well as the process of socialization that takes place within their families. But many other social institutions assist in the process of raising children, often in ways that aren't immediately apparent.

To see firsthand how such socialization works, visit a large shopping mall. Most malls today have children's clothing stores (for example, Baby Gap). If yours doesn't, go to one of the large department stores and find the children's clothing section. Start with the infants' clothes. Is there a difference between "girls' clothes" and "boys' clothes"? Note the differences in the style, color, and texture of boys' versus girls' clothes. Collect the same information for clothes designed for toddlers, preschoolers, and elementary school age children.

Now find a store that specializes in clothes for preteens and teenagers. How do clothing styles differ along gender lines at this age level?

After collecting your data, try to interpret the differences you noticed. Why do they exist? What do these differences say about the kinds of social activities in which boys and girls are expected or encouraged to engage? For instance, which clothes are "rugged" and which are "dainty"? How do such differences reinforce our cultural conceptions of masculinity and femininity? Turning your attention to teenagers, how do popular clothing styles encourage sexuality?

The next stop on your sociological shopping trip is a toy store. Can you detect a boys' section and a girls' section? How do you know? How do the toys differ? What sorts of interactions with other children do the toys encourage? Competition? Cooperation? Which toys are designed for active play? Which seem to encourage passive play? For what sorts of adult roles do the toys prepare children? Provide specific examples.

Finally, find a bookstore that has a children's book section. Which books are more likely to interest boys? Which will interest girls? Are there different sections for "boy" and "girl" books? What are the differences in the sorts of characters and plots that are portrayed? Does the bookstore have a section that contains books designed to help adolescents through puberty? If so, do these books offer different advice to adolescent boys and girls?

Use your findings in all these areas—clothing, toys, and books—to analyze the role that consumer products play in socializing children into "appropriate" gender roles. Is there more or less gender segregation as children get older? Do you think manufacturers, publishers, retail outlets, and so on are simply responding to market demands (that is, do they make gender-specific products because that's what people want), or do they play a role in creating those demands?

CHAPTER HIGHLIGHTS

♦ Socialization is the process by which individuals learn their culture and learn to live according to the norms of a particular society. It is how we learn to perceive our world, gain a sense of our own identity, and interact appropriately with others. It also tells us what we should and should not do across a range of situations.

♦ One of the most important outcomes of socialization for an individual is the development of a sense of self. To acquire a self, children must learn to recognize themselves as unique physical objects, master language, learn to take the roles of others, and, in effect, see themselves from another's perspective.

♦ Socialization is not just a process that occurs during childhood. Adults must be resocialized into a new galaxy of norms, values, and expectations each time they leave or abandon old roles and enter new ones.

♦ Through socialization we learn the social expectations that go with our social class, racial or ethnic group, and gender.

♦ Socialization occurs within the context of several social institutions—family first, and then schools, religious institutions, and the mass media.

KEY TERMS

anticipatory socialization Process through which people acquire the values and orientations found in statuses they will likely enter in the future

collectivist culture Culture in which personal accomplishments are less important in the formation of identity than group membership

game stage Stage in the development of self during which a child acquires the ability to take the role of a group or community (the generalized other) and to conform his or her behavior to broad, societal expectations

gender Psychological, social, and cultural aspects of maleness and femaleness

generalized other Perspective of the larger society and its constituent values and attitudes

identity Essential aspect of who we are, consisting of our sense of self, gender, race, ethnicity, and religion

individualist culture Culture in which personal accomplishments are a more important component of one's self-concept than group membership

looking-glass self Sense of who we are that is defined by incorporating the reflected appraisals of others

play stage Stage in the development of self during which a child develops the ability to take a role, but only from the perspective of one person at a time

reflexive behavior Behavior in which the person initiating an action is the same as the person toward whom the action is directed

resocialization Process of learning new values, norms, and expectations when an adult leaves an old role and enters a new one

role taking Ability to see oneself from the perspective of others and to use that perspective in formulating one's own behavior

self Unique set of traits, behaviors, and attitudes that distinguishes one person from the next; the active source and passive object of behavior

sex Biological maleness or femaleness

socialization Process through which one learns how to act according to the rules and expectations of a particular culture

total institution Place where individuals are cut off from the wider society for an appreciable period and where together they lead an enclosed, formally administered life

tracking Grouping of students into different curricular programs, or tracks, based on an assessment of their academic abilities

---

◆

STUDY SITE ON THE WEB

Don't forget the interactive quizzes and other learning aids at www.pineforge.com/ newman6study. In the Resources File for this chapter, you'll also find more on building identity, including:

Sociologists at Work

♦ Wade Clark Roof: Abandoning Religion

Micro-Macro Connections

♦ Gender in Structural Context
♦ Language and Gender

Supporting Identity
The Presentation of Self

Forming Impressions of Others

Managing Impressions

Mismanaging Impressions: Spoiled Identities

On Christmas Day 1981, I met my soon-to-be wife's family for the first time. For this group of important strangers, I knew I had to be on my best behavior and say and do all the right things. I wanted to make sure the impression they formed of me was that of a likable fellow whom they'd be proud to call a member of the family someday.

As people busily opened their presents, I noticed the wide and gleeful eyes of my wife's 14-year-old sister as she unwrapped what was to her a special gift—her very own basketball. Being the youngest in a family of eight kids, she didn't have much she could call her own, so this was a significant moment for her. She had finally broken away from a life filled with hand-me-downs and communal equipment. She hugged that ball as if it were a puppy.

I saw my chance to make the perfect first impression. "I'm not a bad basketball player," I thought to myself. "I'll take her outside to the basketball hoop in the driveway, impress her with my shooting skills, become her idol, and win family approval."

"Hey, Mary," I said, "let's go out and shoot some hoops." After we stepped outside I grabbed the new ball from her. "Look at this," I said as I flung it toward the basket from about 40 feet away. We both watched as the ball arced gracefully toward its destination, and for a brief moment I actually thought it was going to go in. But that was not to be.

As if guided by the taunting hand of fate, the ball struck an exposed bolt that protruded from the base of the supporting pole of the hoop. There was a sickeningly loud pop, followed by a hissing sound as the ball fluttered to the ground like a deflated balloon. It sat there lifeless, never having experienced the joy of "swishing" through a net. For that matter, it had never even been bounced on the ground in its short-lived inflated state.

For a few seconds we both stood numb and motionless. Then I turned to apologize to the 14-year-old girl whose once cheerful eyes now harbored the kind of hate and resentment usually reserved for ax murderers and IRS auditors. In a flash, she burst into tears and ran into the house, shrieking, "*That guy* popped my ball!" It was hardly the heroic identity I was striving for. As the angry mob poured into the backyard to stare at the villainous and still somewhat unknown perpetrator, I became painfully aware of the fragile nature of the self-images we try to project to others.

We all have been in situations—a first date, a job interview, a first meeting with a girlfriend or boyfriend's family—in which we feel compelled to "make a good impression." We try to present a favorable image of ourselves so that others will make positive judgments of us. This phenomenon is not only an important and universal aspect of our personal lives but a key element of social structure as well.

In this chapter I examine the social creation of images. How do we form impressions of others? What do we do to control the impressions others form of us? I also discuss broader sociological applications of these actions. What are the institutional motivations behind individuals' attempts to control others' impressions of them? How do groups and organizations present and manage collective impressions? Finally, what happens when these attempts fail and images are spoiled, as mine was in the story I just told?

Forming Impressions of Others

When we first meet someone, we form an immediate impression based on observable cues such as age, ascribed status characteristics such as race and gender, individual attributes such as physical appearance, and verbal and nonverbal expressions. All these indicators help us form a quick picture of the other person's identity.

Keep in mind that the importance of this information—the value attached to a certain age, race, or gender; the particular physical or personality traits a society defines as desirable; the meaning of certain words and gestures—varies across time and place. Hence the impressions that people form of others—good, bad, or indifferent—must always be understood within the appropriate cultural and historical context. For instance, an emotionally expressive person in the United States may give the impression of being energetic and outgoing; in Thailand or Japan that person may be considered dangerous or crazy; and in the United Kingdom such a person may seem boorish and rude.

Social Group Membership

Age, sex, race, and to a certain degree ethnicity can often be determined merely by looking at a person; social class is less obvious but sometimes becomes known early in an encounter with another person, through the person's language, mannerisms, or dress. Our socialization experiences have taught us to expect that people displaying these signs of social group membership have certain characteristics, as Chapter 5 explained. For instance, if all you know about a person you've not yet met is that she's 85 years old, you might predict that she has low energy, poor memory, and a conservative approach to life. Think about your expectations when you learn that a new roommate is from a different country—or, for that matter, from a different region of this country. Of course, such expectations are rarely completely accurate. Nevertheless, we begin social interactions with these culturally defined conceptions of how people from certain social groups are likely to act, what their tastes and preferences might be, and what values and attitudes they are likely to hold.

This information is so pervasive and so quickly processed that we usually notice it only when it isn't there. If you spend a lot of time in Internet chat rooms, you may have noticed how awkward it can be to form a friendship or carry on a discussion when you don't know whether you are interacting with someone of the same sex or with someone of a different sex or whether the person is much older or much younger than you are. Social group membership provides the necessary backdrop to all encounters between people who have little if any prior knowledge of one another.

Physical Appearance

We confirm or modify early impressions based on social group membership by assessing other characteristics that are easily perceivable, such as a person's physical appearance (Berndt & Heller, 1986). The way people dress and decorate their bodies communicates their feelings, beliefs, and group identity to others. People's clothes, jewelry, hairstyles, and so on can also indicate their ethnicity, social class, age, cultural tastes, morality, and political attitudes.

But again, these impressions can be influenced by our cultural background. Physical appearance is enormously important in U.S. culture. Everywhere we turn, it seems, we are encouraged to believe that if our skin isn't free of blemishes, if we are too short or too tall, if we are over- or underweight, if our hair isn't stylish, if our clothes don't reflect the latest fashion trend, we have fallen short. Although we readily acknowledge that using a person's physical appearance to form an impression is shallow and unfair, we usually do it anyway.

Research confirms that physical appearance affects our perceptions and judgments of others. For instance, the impressions adults form of young children are heavily influenced by the child's attractiveness (Clifford & Walster, 1973; Dion, 1972). One recent study of people in supermarkets found that parents of attractive children take more precautions to ensure their safety—such as buckling them into the shopping cart—than parents of unattractive children (cited in Bakalar, 2005). Attractive men are perceived as more masculine and attractive women more feminine than their less attractive counterparts (Gillen, 1981). Research on jury deliberations in legal trials suggests that attractive defendants are treated better (for example, receive shorter jail sentences) than less attractive defendants (Stewart, 1980). In addition, we often assume that physically attractive people possess other desirable traits, such as sensitivity, kindness, strength, and sexual responsiveness (Dion, Berscheid, & Walster, 1972).

Physical attractiveness is still a more salient interpersonal and economic issue for women than for men, even though women have more money, political clout, and legal recognition today than ever. For instance, in 2003, a sales manager for L'Oreal cosmetics company was dismissed because she refused to fire a saleswoman in a Macy's department store who wasn't considered attractive enough (Greenhouse, 2003). An article on a talented, all-female chamber music trio called Eroica stated, "The Eroica Trio not only plays beautiful music, it has also created a marketing sensation for being 'easy on the eye'" (W. Smith, 2002, p. 4). The columnist George Will once described Secretary of Labor Elaine Chao as "slender as a stiletto" (Will, 2003, p. 68). It's hard to imagine physical attractiveness being the focus of attention for male salespeople, classical musicians, or cabinet members.

Women around the world cause themselves serious pain and injury as they alter their bodies to conform with cultural definitions of beauty. In China, for example, hundreds of women each year, convinced that being taller would improve their job and marriage prospects, subject themselves to a procedure in which their leg bones are broken, separated, and stretched. Metal pins and screws pull the bones apart a fraction of a millimeter a day, sometimes for close to two years. Many Chinese women have lost the ability to walk from this treatment; others have suffered permanent, disfiguring bone damage (C.S. Smith, 2002). In the United States, a growing number of affluent women undergo potentially dangerous cosmetic foot surgery each year to reduce the size of their toes so that they can fit into today's fashionable, narrow high-heeled shoes (G. Harris, 2003).

At the individual level, the emphasis on physical appearance devalues a person's other attributes and accomplishments; at the institutional level it plays an important role in the nation's economy by sustaining several multibillion-dollar enterprises, including the advertising, fashion, cosmetics, and weight loss industries (Schur, 1984).

Micro-Macro Connection
Obesity

In U.S. society and in most industrialized societies, the negative effects of being considered unattractive are perhaps felt most strongly by those whose body size does not meet cultural standards (Allon, 1982; English, 1991). Against a cultural backdrop that glorifies thinness, fat is seen as repulsive, ugly, and unclean (LeBesco, 2004). People are likely to judge an overweight person as lacking in willpower and as being self-indulgent, personally offensive, and even morally and socially unfit (Millman, 1980). A study of mental health caseworkers found that these individuals were more likely to assign negative psychological symptoms (for example, being too emotional or agitated, being unhygienic, engaging in inappropriate behavior) to obese patients than to thin patients (Young & Powell, 1985).

Negative perceptions of obesity clearly affect people's economic opportunities. Research has found significant discrimination against obese and overweight people at every stage of the employment cycle, including hiring, placement, compensation, promotion, discipline, and discharge (Roehling, 1999). One study of young people in Britain found that the heaviest 10% of their age group earned 7.4% less than their nonobese peers and that the heaviest 1% earned 11.4% less (cited in "Physical Traits," 1994).

In high-visibility occupations such as public relations and sales, overweight people are often regarded as unemployable because they might project a negative image of the company they are working for. In 2002, for instance, a 5-foot, 8-inch, 240-pound fitness instructor was rejected by Jazzercise because she didn't meet the company's requirement that instructors "look trim." She was told in a letter, "Jazzercise sells fitness. Consequently, a Jazzercise applicant must have a high muscle-to-fat ratio and look leaner than the public" (P. L. Brown, 2002, p. A20). A casino in Atlantic City recently warned its cocktail waitresses that if they gained more than 10% of their current weight, they'd be suspended without pay for 90 days while they tried to lose the extra pounds. If their weight loss efforts were unsuccessful, they'd be fired (I. Peterson, 2005).

Discrimination against obese people is not universal. In Mexico, for example, people are significantly less concerned than Americans are about their own weight and are more accepting of overweight people (Crandall & Martinez, 1996). In Niger, being overweight—ideally with rolls of fat, stretch marks, and a large behind—is considered an essential part of female beauty. Women who aren't sufficiently round are considered unfit for marriage (Popenoe, 2005). Among the Calabari people of southeastern Nigeria, soon-to-be brides are sent to farms where caretakers feed them huge amounts of food to fatten them up for the wedding day (Onishi, 2002).

In the U.S., the value attached to particular body types is linked to race, class, and gender. By official measures, approximately 57% of American Whites and 34% of Asian Americans are either overweight or obese. Among African Americans and Latino/as the figures are 69% and 65% respectively. Fifty-four percent of Americans with a college degree are either overweight or obese compared to 66% of people who have less than a high school diploma (U.S. Bureau of the Census, 2004a).

Being overweight is often equated with poverty, where sedentary lifestyles and high-fat diets can be commonplace (Gilman, 2004). Weight problems are compounded in poor communities by the fact that the key determinants of physical activity—safe playgrounds, access to high quality, low cost food, and transportation to play areas—are either inadequate or nonexistent. In addition, fast-food companies have grown more aggressive in targeting poor, inner-city neighborhoods. One out of every four McDonald's hamburgers sold today is purchased by consumers in the inner city (Critser, 2000).

The association of obesity, class, and race is often tinged with prejudice. The cultural devaluation of fat tends to combine with the devaluation of poverty and of "nonwhiteness":

> The fact that African, Native American, and Latin cultural traditions [define] large bodies as beautiful—and that, in general, poor people of all colors are heavier and eat fattier diets than the well-to-do—allows an ugly stew of hatreds to come together in the abhorrence with which we regard fleshy bodies, especially if they are dark-skinned, ineptly groomed, or cheaply dressed. (Weismantel, 2005, p. 51)

Many cases have been reported of fat children being removed from their homes because their obesity is taken as a sign that they are victims of abuse and neglect. These incidents almost always involve people of color and the poor or working class. Caseworkers tend to blame the parents for unacceptable cultural traditions and, allegedly, their ignorance of healthy lifestyles (LeBesco, 2004).

As with physical appearance in general, women feel the contemporary distaste for obesity particularly strongly. The consequences of girls' and women's weight dissatisfaction are widespread. According to statistics compiled by the National Eating Disorders Association (2004):

- Forty-two percent of first- to third-grade girls want to be thinner, 51% of 9- to10-year-old girls feel better about themselves when they're on a diet, and 81% of 10-year-olds are afraid of being fat.
- Ninety percent of college women attempt to control their weight through dieting.

◆ On any given day about half of American women are on a diet, even though within one to five years, 95% of them will likely regain the weight they've lost.

◆ About 90% of Americans diagnosed with eating disorders (anorexia, bulimia, binge eating) are girls or women.

Female weight concern has large-scale implications because of the role it plays in the growth and success of the diet "industry": low-calorie foods and beverages, diet books, prescription medicines, weight loss organizations, and so forth. The pharmaceutical industry spends billions of dollars each year on research designed to develop new obesity drugs. About 200 such drugs are currently being tested for eventual FDA approval (S. Saul, 2005). The Federal Trade Commission estimates that annual sales of diet foods and beverages alone is about $40 billion annually (cited in Kolata, 2004b).

But weight concerns are not shared equally by all U.S. women. About 78% of African American women and 72% of Latina women are overweight, compared to 57% of white women (National Center for Health Statistics, 2003). Yet white women are significantly more likely than women of ethnoracial minorities to be concerned about their weight and to exhibit disordered eating behaviors (Abrams, Allen, & Gray, 1993). In one study, 90% of white junior high and high school girls voiced dissatisfaction with their bodies compared to 30% of black teens (Parker, Nichter, Nichter, Vuckovic, Sims, & Ritenbaugh, 1995). Indeed, black adolescents tend to perceive themselves as thinner than they actually are, whereas white adolescents tend to perceive themselves as heavier than they actually are.

African American women, especially poor and working-class African American women, worry less than women of other races about dieting or about being thin (Molloy & Herzberger, 1998). One study found that although African American women are more likely than white women to weigh more than 120% of their recommended body weight, they are much less likely to perceive themselves as overweight or to suffer blows to their self-esteem as a result (Averett & Korenman, 1999). When black women do diet, their efforts to lose weight are more realistic and less extreme than white women's attempts. More affluent African American women, though, are likely to be exposed to dominant white preferences, attitudes, and ideals about beauty and weight. Indeed, the risk of disordered eating increases for African American women who have a strong desire to assimilate into the dominant white culture (Abrams et al., 1993).

Unnecessary concern over weight shows how powerful cultural beliefs are in the formation of self-concepts. At best, the failure to meet broad cultural standards of thinness can lower self-esteem and generate antagonism toward one's own body. At worst, it can lead to life-threatening eating disorders. Such drastic responses indicate the importance of body size—and physical appearance, in general—in forming impressions of other people.

Verbal and Nonverbal Expression

Another important piece of information we use in forming impressions of others is what people express to us verbally or nonverbally. Through speech, movement, posture, and gestures, people provide cues about their values, attitudes, sentiments, personality, and history (Stone, 1981). Sometimes these forms of communication are used purposely to convey meaning. However, some physical expressions, such as a shaky voice, a flushed face, and trembling hands, are difficult to control. They convey an impression whether we want to or not.

Most of us are quite proficient at "reading" even the subtlest nonverbal messages. We learn early that a raised eyebrow, a nod of the head, or a slight hand gesture can mean something important in a social encounter. So crucial is this ability in maintaining orderly interactions that some psychologists consider a deficiency in it to be a learning disability akin to severe reading problems (Goleman, 1989).

Managing Impressions

People form impressions of others and present impressions of themselves at the same time. This ability to create impressions is the defining feature of human interaction. Naturally, we try to create impressions of ourselves that give us advantages—by making us seem attractive or powerful or otherwise worthy of people's attention and esteem. Of course, that's what I was trying to do when I attempted the ill-fated jump shot with my future sister-in-law's new basketball.

The process by which people attempt to present a favorable public image of themselves is called **impression management.** Erving Goffman (1959), the sociologist most responsible for the scholarly examination of impression management, portrays everyday life as a series of social interactions in which a person is motivated to "sell" a particular image to others. The primary goal of impression management is to project a particular identity that will increase the likelihood of obtaining favorable outcomes from others in particular social situations (E. E. Jones & Pittman, 1982; Stryker, 1980). To do so, we can strategically furnish or conceal information. At times we may need to advertise, exaggerate, or even fabricate our positive qualities; at other times we conceal or camouflage behaviors or attributes that we believe others will find unappealing.

Obtaining favorable outcomes through impression management is usually associated with social approval—that is, with being respected and liked by others. However, different circumstances may require projecting different identities (E. E. Jones & Pittman, 1982). Perhaps you've been in situations where you tried to appear helpless in order to get someone else to do a task you really didn't want to do, or maybe you tried to appear as powerful and fearsome as you could to intimidate someone into doing something for you. Perhaps you "played dumb" to avoid challenging a superior (Gove, Hughes, & Geerkin, 1980). As social beings, we have the ability to tailor our images to fit the requirements of a particular situation.

Goffman argues that impression management is not used just to present false or inflated images of ourselves. Many real attributes we possess are not immediately apparent to others, or our actions may be misinterpreted. Imagine yourself taking the final exam in your sociology course. You look up from your paper and make brief eye contact with the instructor. You are not cheating, but you think the instructor may interpret your wandering eyes as an indication of cheating. Chances are you

(Text continues on page 185)

Looking Cool

Liz Grauerholz and Rebecca Smith

Physical appearance is an important projection of our self-image. From a rather early age, just like people everywhere, we seem to have an inherent understanding of how our dress and demeanor affect the way that other people judge us and react to us.

The concern with appearance is at its peak during the teen years. Looking cool has been a primary concern among young people for decades. Of course, what "hip" or "cool" means varies considerably over time. In these photos, note not only the style of clothing but also your reaction to each style. What image do you think these young people were trying to project? What are the obvious differences from era to era? Is there anything that seems to remain the same?

❖ 1920s

❖ 1940s

❖ 1950s

❖ 1960s

❖ 1980s

178

Today we can see some similarities with earlier teen styles, such as the ongoing trend toward casual attire. But these days, cutting-edge fashion is likely to reflect a hard-edged, urban "street" image associated with rap and hip hop, even among people who have the financial means to project an image of wealth and privilege.

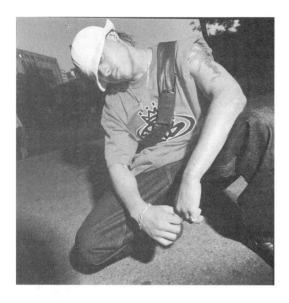

❖ In an era of globalization, we should not be surprised to see teens all over the world dressing in similar styles, like this young woman in Russia.

❖ "Street" style has even made it onto the modeling runways

Some teens react to the commercialization of "cool" by pushing the boundaries even further. What seems to characterize the most extreme versions of cool is an image that runs contrary to parental desires and, indeed, might be downright antagonistic toward adult values.

Ironically, while some of their peers are attempting to look cool by rejecting adults' values as much as possible, many other teens try to look cool by adopting the accoutrements of adult vices: alcohol, cigarettes, and sexually revealing clothing.

Traditionally, clothing has revealed much about a person's class status. Which of these young men appears to be upper class and which appears to be lower class? Would you be surprised to learn that they are equally well educated and come from equally wealthy families?

❖ This couple sends an interesting message about class: his heavy gold jewelry hints at wealth, while ripped jeans like hers have traditionally been a visual indicator of poverty.

Another interesting way to look cool these days is to adopt some form of permanent body adornment: tattooing, body piercing, tongue splitting, teeth sharpening, and so on. What are we to make of their recent popularity? Body adornment has been used historically throughout the world to communicate group status and membership—as is the case with this traditionally tattooed Tahitian man.

❖ In this country, tattoos originated with men—mostly in the military—who used them either to signify their masculinity and patriotism or to remind them of home (girlfriends, mother). Today "getting ink" is quite popular among young people—both men and women. But what is the message?

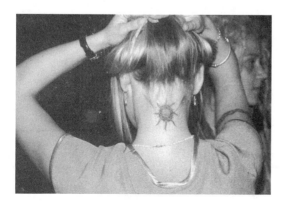

❖ Jewelry has also traditionally been a way to communicate identity and membership in groups. The elaborate nose ring shown here identifies this individual as a nomad from the Great Thar Desert in Rajasthan, India.

❖ But what about these individuals? What do piercings signify? To which group do their wearers belong?

will consciously overemphasize your noncheating behavior by acting as though you're in deep thought or by glancing up at the clock to highlight your "law-abiding" image.

Often people try to present a favorable image of themselves by altering their physical appearance. Clothing and body adornment can be used to manipulate and manage the impressions others form of us. People can dress to convey the impression that they are worthy of respect or, at the very least, attention (Lauer & Handel, 1977). Businesspeople are acutely aware of and usually conform to a corporate dress code; even if the code is "business casual," those who dress too casually are not taken seriously. Children often signal their entry into the world of adolescence by wearing the clothing of their peers and refusing to wear the clothing chosen by their parents (Stone, 1981). The purveyors of pop, hip-hop, crunk, heavy metal, lounge, rave, dance/house/techno, reggae-ska, and other musical subcultures use clothing and hairstyle as an expression of identity and social rebellion. And as you are well aware, fashion is a significant element of the student subculture on most college campuses (Moffatt, 1989). In short, by what they wear, people tell one another who they are, where they come from, and what they stand for.

Image Making

In our individualistic, competitive society, appearances can sometimes provide a critically important edge. A person's desire to maximize prestige, wealth, and power can be the driving force behind a thorough makeover. Two prominent examples are Americans' pursuit of never-ending youthfulness through the alteration of their bodies and politicians' pursuit of a popular identity through a carefully controlled public image. As you will see, these efforts are not something a person undertakes on her or his own. Whole industries have evolved that are devoted to making and remaking images for the public eye.

The Illusion of Youth

The desire to manage impressions by changing physical appearance motivates some people to do far more than try a new hairstyle, get a tattoo, or buy a new outfit or two. People in the United States are willing to spend huge sums of money to surgically alter their looks. According to the American Society of Plastic Surgeons (2005a), an estimated 1.7 million Americans underwent cosmetic surgery in 2004, spending over $8.4 billion in the process. Another 7.5 million underwent nonsurgical treatments such as botox injections, cellulite treatments, chemical peels, and collagen injections. These figures represent a 24% increase over 2000. Exhibit 6.1 shows the growing popularity of cosmetic surgery.

Although most cosmetic surgery is still performed on middle-aged women, more and more men and young people are opting for it. Between 2000 and 2004, the number of men having cosmetic surgery increased 16%, and the number having noninvasive treatments increased 43%. During that same period, there was a 20% increase in the number of cosmetic surgeries performed on people under age 18 (American Society of Plastic Surgeons, 2005a).

The desire to surgically alter one's appearance is not a uniquely American phenomenon. Brazil has more plastic surgeons per capita than anywhere else in the world.

Exhibit 6.1   The Popularity of Cosmetic Surgery in the United States

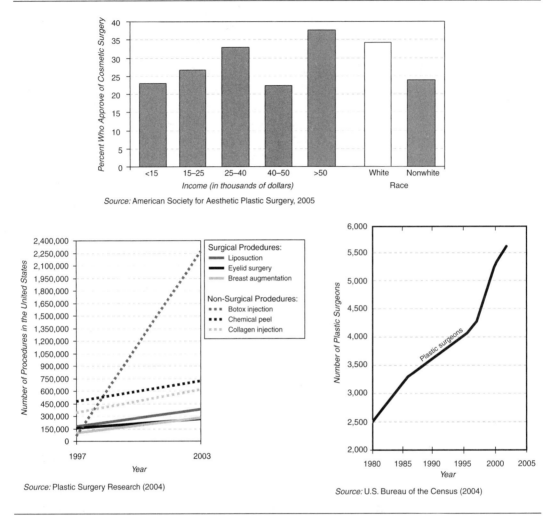

Source: American Society for Aesthetic Plastic Surgery, 2005

Source: Plastic Surgery Research (2004)

Source: U.S. Bureau of the Census (2004)

Source: American Society of Plastic Surgeons, 2005b; Plastic Surgery Research.info, 2004; U.S. Bureau of the Census, 2004a.

In 2001, the Brazilian contestant in the Miss Universe contest scandalized many non-Brazilians by speaking freely and publicly about her breast implants, cheekbone reconstruction, silicone remolding of her chin, pinned-back ears, and liposuction. She told reporters, "I have to work on my figure to get it where I want it. It's something I need for my profession. . . . I have a doctorate in body measurement" (Kulick & Machado-Borges, 2005, p. 128).

In China, the growing cosmetic surgery industry now takes in over $2.4 billion a year as people with newfound affluence rush to go under the knife to become *renzao meinu*—or "manmade beauties." In fact, China now hosts an "Artificial Beauty" contest, where people from all over the globe compete to become the world's most beautiful product of plastic surgery (Ang, 2004).

The growing popularity of cosmetic surgery reflects an alarming level of discontent among people over the way they look. Psychiatrists estimate that 1 to 2% of the U.S. population suffers from something called "body dysmorphic disorder," which has become more common over the last decade or so (Wartik, 2003). These individuals are so self-conscious about their looks that their lives are constricted in some significant way, from feeling inhibited during lovemaking to becoming homebound or even suicidal.

The television industry has taken advantage of this overall sense of bodily dissatisfaction. Popular reality shows like *The Swan, Extreme Makeover,* and *I Want a Famous Face* take people who are unhappy with the way they look and, with the help of extensive plastic surgery, transform them into what they hope are reborn beauties. But the standard of attractiveness to which the participants aspire remains narrow and stereotypical. And because they undergo many of the same cosmetic procedures, carried out by the same surgeons (C. Orenstein, 2004), the contestants on these shows tend to end up bearing an eerie resemblance to one another:

> The cheeks of the patients are all planed upward; lips are uniformly swollen to rubber-doll proportions; breasts stand at military attention. The men have new superhero chins. Mouths, to a person, are packed with teeth as big and white as Chiclets. (Kuczynski, 2004, p. 1)

But perhaps that conformity is the whole point. To give the impression of being youthful and fit, they need to present an image that is in keeping with our society's notions of what constitutes physical beauty.

Political Portraits

If you have ever seen a U.S. political party's national convention prior to a presidential election, you have witnessed a highly professional effort at image making. Music, balloons, lighting, logos, colors, even individual delegates in the audience are all transformed into stage props that are manipulated to project images of patriotism, unity, organization, and effectiveness. At the center is the candidate, who must personally present an image (also professionally crafted) that will appeal to the voting public. Campaign staffs are concerned as much with assuring that their candidate "appears presidential" as they are with his positions on key political issues.

Consider the image crafted for George W. Bush. He grew up in a wealthy family. He was educated at an elite prep school and a prestigious Ivy League university. His father was a lifelong politician and former U.S. president. His business interests and stint as governor of Texas made him a wealthy and powerful man in his own right. Yet during the presidential campaigns of 2000 and 2004, Bush, with the help of his advisers and handlers, decided that the best strategy for winning election was to present himself as an anti-intellectual, down-to-earth, "likable guy" who was more interested in slapping backs, telling jokes, and chopping wood than in discussing the nuances of foreign and domestic policy. In 2004, this strategy was specifically managed to highlight the contrasts between Bush and his opponent, John Kerry, a candidate who was portrayed a stiff East Coast snob with a condescending air, whose hobbies consisted of windsurfing and reading esoteric novels, and who spoke French to reporters.

Presidential impression management continues past Election Day. The president, with the help or hindrance of the media, must play simultaneously to international and domestic audiences (P. Hall, 1990). The international audience consists of foreign allies and adversaries, whom he must convince of his authority and his ability to fulfill commitments. The domestic audience is the voting public, whom he must impress through the portrayal of "presidential character": good health, decisiveness, control, a stable home and family life, and so forth. Like all politicians, a president must be prepared to use impression management throughout his tenure to get a favorable result in an opinion poll or a desired vote in Congress or some international body, like the United Nations or meetings of the G-8 economic powers.

To both Republican and Democratic observers, George W. Bush is an expert in the art of political impression management. In addition to having the usual media and public relations experts in the White House, the president has several former television producers on his staff of advisers (Bumiller, 2003). Through both of his terms in office, all public appearances have taken place in tightly staged and perfectly lighted settings. He gives virtually no unscripted, spontaneous news conferences. The White House communications director provided a glimpse into high-stakes impression management:

> We pay particular attention to not only what the president says but what the American people see. Americans are leading busy lives, and sometimes they don't have the opportunity to read a story or listen to an entire broadcast. But if they can have an instant understanding of what the president is talking about by seeing 60 seconds of television, you accomplish your goals as communicators. So we take it seriously. (quoted in Bumiller, 2003, p. A1)

Often a president's goals are accomplished through "gesture politics"—actions or initiatives that are largely symbolic and convey, whether purposefully or not, particular characteristics. National leaders frequently find themselves judged not so much by the effectiveness of their policies but by how the public responds to their gestures:

> At least one European newspaper described President Bush's effort to aid tsunami victims [in 2004] as a bid to show U.S. compassion. What was important was not the particulars of Bush's own aid plan, but whether the public would find it convincingly noble. . . . In the public mind [programs] are secondary to (and their success is dependent on) the personal gestures that accompany them. (Caldwell, 2005, p. 11)

Bush's media relations team has proved time and again to be masters of gesture politics. When he traveled the country in 2005 trying to create support for his plan to revamp Social Security, audiences were carefully selected so that they consisted only of enthusiastic backers. One Republican group in particular, FreedomWorks, works closely with the White House to provide lists of people to appear with the president at his frequent town hall meetings throughout the country (Bailey, Wolffe, & Lipper, 2005). Perhaps the most elaborate (and controversial) staged event was the president's 2003 speech aboard the USS *Abraham Lincoln* announcing the end of major combat operations in Iraq. Every aspect of that event—from the timing of his landing in a fighter plane on the deck of the carrier (when the sun was setting) to the crew's shirt colors—was tightly managed and choreographed. Not surprisingly, Bush's approval ratings were quite high following this successful instance of presidential image making.

Dramaturgy: Actors on a Social Stage

"All the world's a stage,/ And all the men and women merely players:/ They have their exits and their entrances;/ And one man in his time plays many parts," wrote William Shakespeare in *As You Like It*. Analyzing social interaction as a series of theatrical performances—what sociologists call **dramaturgy**—has been a staple of symbolic interactionism for decades. Like Shakespeare, sociologists like Goffman (1959) argue that people in everyday life are similar to actors on a stage. The "audience" consists of people who observe the behavior of others, the "roles" are the images people are trying to project, and the "script" consists of their communication with others. The goal is to enact a performance that is believable to a particular audience and that allows us to achieve the goals we desire. Every aspect of social life can be examined dramaturgically, from the ritualized greetings of strangers to the everyday dynamics of our family, school, and work lives.

Front Stage and Back Stage

A key structural element of dramaturgy is the distinction between front stage and back stage. In the theater, front stage is where the performance takes place. In contrast, back stage is where makeup is removed, lines are rehearsed, performances are rehashed, and people can fall "out of character."

In social interaction, **front stage** is where people maintain the appropriate appearance as they interact with others. For workers in a restaurant, front stage is the dining room where the customers (the audience) are present. Here the servers (the actors) are expected to present themselves as upbeat, happy, competent, and courteous. **Back stage**, however, is the region where people can knowingly violate their impression management performances. In the restaurant, back stage is the kitchen area where the once courteous servers now shout, shove dishes, and even complain about or make fun of the customers.

The barrier between front and back stage is crucial to successful impression management because it blocks the audience from seeing behavior that would ruin the performance. During a therapy session (front stage), psychiatrists usually appear extremely interested in everything their patients say and show considerable sympathy for their problems. At a dinner party with colleagues or at home with family (back stage), however, they may express total boredom with and disdain for the patients' disclosures. If patients were to see such back stage behavior, not only would the performance be disrupted, but the psychiatrist's professional credibility and reputation would suffer as well. One study found that beneath their mask of neutrality, many psychiatrists harbor strong and professionally inappropriate feelings—including hatred, fear, anger, and sexual arousal—toward their patients (cited in Goleman, 1993).

Peter Ubel
Elevator Talk Among Doctors and Nurses

We all take for granted, when visiting a doctor's office or a hospital, that the doctors and nurses will protect the confidentiality of their patients. Yet the temptation to talk about patients behind their backs ("back stage") is often hard to resist. Dr. Peter Ubel and his colleagues (Ubel, Zell, Miller, Fischer, Peters-Stefani, & Arnold, 1995) sent observers to five Pennsylvania hospitals to determine the frequency and nature of inappropriate talk about patients among hospital personnel. The researchers were particularly interested in conversations that could easily be overheard by people who shouldn't be privy to such information. They decided to focus on elevator talk.

Of the 259 elevator rides they observed during which passengers had a chance to converse, inappropriate comments were made 14% of the time. The observers found that the remarks fell into four distinct categories:

Comments violating patient confidentiality: The majority of back stage comments inappropriately disclosed factual information about a patient's condition. These remarks were usually simple declarations, such as "Mr. X was readmitted last night for more chemo." In other situations, the comments exposed professional disagreement over a particular course of action. For instance, in one case two physicians had a heated debate over the merits of removing parts of either one or two lungs from a patient.

Unprofessional remarks and motivation: Another category of comments consisted of remarks that raised questions about medical personnel's ability or desire to provide quality care. For instance, doctors or nurses sometimes complained that they were too tired or too sick to do their jobs well. On some occasions, physicians were heard talking about how they were just biding their time in the hospital until they could go elsewhere and make large amounts of money. Such comments clearly call into question their primary motivation.

Comments raising questions about quality of patient care: Some conversations consisted of personnel complaining about hospital resources and facilities, thereby raising doubts about whether the institution offered good patient care. Other times, nurses or doctors would question the qualifications of a colleague. Although the motivation behind such remarks is not always clear, people who come to visit their loved ones in a hospital and overhear these casual conversations are not always capable of weighing unsubstantiated information.

Derogatory comments about patients or their families: The last category of inappropriate back stage comments were direct insults about patients, focusing on such traits as weight or body odor. Such comments reflect poorly on the compassion of health care workers. In addition, visitors' anxiety about the quality of care may increase if visitors are led to believe that the staff doesn't like them or their loved ones.

This research points to the institutional importance of maintaining boundaries between front and back stage. Health care workers will always talk about patients behind their backs. But in a field such as medicine, which deals with extremely delicate personal information and life and death decisions, the credibility of the profession depends on workers' ability to correctly determine when a location is, in fact, private back stage. Public awareness of these sorts of remarks can have serious economic, political, and perhaps even legal consequences. The problem has become so bad that elevators in some California hospitals now carry posted warnings reminding medical personnel to refrain from talking about patients.

Props

Successful impression management also depends on the control of objects called *props* that convey identity. In the theater props must be handled deftly for an effective performance. A gun that doesn't go off when it's supposed to or a chair that unexpectedly collapses can destroy an entire play. The same is true in social interaction. For instance, college students may make sure their school books are in clear view and beer bottles disposed of as they prepare for an upcoming visit from their parents. Similarly, someone may spend a great deal of time setting a romantic mood for a dinner date at home—the right music, the right lighting, pictures of former lovers hidden from view, and so on.

Sometimes people use props to create an environment that reinforces some individuals' authority over others. Note the way props were used to intimidate this professor as he testified before Congress:

> And then I was called to the witness stand. Now, the chair is something nobody talks about. It is low and extremely puffy. When you sit in it your butt just keeps sinking, and suddenly the tabletop is up to your chest. The senators peer down at you from above, and the power dynamic is terrifying. (Jenkins, 1999, p. 21)

Viewing impression management from a dramaturgical perspective reminds us that our everyday actions rarely occur in a social vacuum. Indeed, our behaviors are often structured with an eye toward how they might be perceived by particular "audiences."

Social Influences on Impression Management

Up to this point, I've described impression management and dramaturgy from the viewpoint of individual people driven by a personal desire to present themselves in the most advantageous light possible. But social group membership may also influence the sorts of images a person tries to present in social interaction. The elements of a person's identity—age, gender, race and ethnicity, religion, social class, occupational status—influence others' immediate expectations, which can be self-fulfilling. In other words, members of certain social groups may manage impressions somewhat differently from nonmembers because of society's preconceived notions about them. Race or ethnicity and social status are among the most notable influences on impression management.

Race and Ethnicity

People of racial or ethnic minorities are often forced to present self-images that are consistent with the expectations or stereotypes of others. In a society in which race is a primary source of inequality, living up (or down) to such expectations may be one of the few ways people can participate actively in public life while retaining their own cultural identity. Individuals from disadvantaged groups may appear to fit common racial or ethnic stereotypes in public (front stage), but an analysis of private (back stage) behavior often indicates that they are keenly aware of the identities they've been forced to present. Impression management is obviously an important survival tactic.

Elijah Anderson
Streetwise

Throughout the 1980s, sociologist Elijah Anderson carried out observational research in a racially, ethnically, and economically diverse area of Philadelphia he called Village-Northton. The area was home to two communities: one black and very poor, the other middle to upper income and predominantly white. Anderson was particularly interested in how young black men—the overwhelming majority of whom were civil and law abiding—managed public impressions to deal with the assumption of Village residents that all young black men are dangerous.

Anderson discovered that a central theme for most area residents was maintaining safety on the streets and avoiding violent and drug-related crime. Incapable of making distinctions between law-abiding black males and others, people relied for protection on broad stereotypes: Whites are law abiding and trustworthy; young black men are crime prone and dangerous.

Residents of the area, including black men themselves, were likely to defer to unknown black males on the street. Women—particularly white women—clutched their purses and edged up closer to their companions as they walked down the street. Many pedestrians crossed the street or averted their eyes from young black men, who were seen as unpredictable and menacing.

Some of the young black men in the Village developed certain interactional strategies to overcome the immediate assumption that they were dangerous. For instance, many came to believe that if they presented a certain appearance or carried certain props with them in public that represented law-abiding behavior (for instance, a briefcase, a shirt and tie, a college identification card), they would be treated better in contacts with the police or others in the neighborhood. In addition, they often used friendly or deferential greetings as a kind of pre-emptive peace offering, designed to advise others of their civil intentions. Or they went to great lengths to behave in ways contrary to the presumed expectations of Whites:

> I find myself being extra nice to whites. A lot of times I be walking down the streets . . . and I see somebody white. . . . I know they are afraid of me. They don't know me, but they intimidated. . . . So I might smile, just to reassure them. . . . At other times I find myself opening doors, you know. Holding the elevator. Putting myself in a certain light, you know, to change whatever doubts they may have. (E. Anderson, 1990, pp. 185–186)

Such impression management requires an enormous amount of effort and places responsibility for ensuring social order on this man. He feels compelled to put strangers at ease so he can go about his own business. He understands that his mere presence makes others nervous and uncomfortable. He recognizes that trustworthiness—an ascribed characteristic of Whites—is something Blacks must work hard to achieve.

Other young black men, less willing to bear the burden of social order, capitalized on the fear they knew they could evoke. Some purposely "put on a swagger" or adopted a menacing stance to intimidate other pedestrians. Some purposely created discomfort in those they considered "ignorant" enough to be unnecessarily afraid of them.

According to Anderson, law-abiding youths have an interest in giving the impression that they are dangerous: It is a way to keep others at bay. The right looks and moves ensure safe passage on the street. Notice how this young man used such a strategy as a protective device:

> When I walk the streets, I put this expression on my face that tells the next person I'm not to be messed with. That "You messing with the wrong fellow. You just try it. Try it.". . . I'll put my hand in my pocket, even if I ain't got no gun. Nobody wants to get shot. . . . Some guys go to singing. They try to let people know they crazy. 'Cause if you crazy [capable of anything], they'll leave you alone. And I have looked right in they face [muggers] and said, "Yo, I'm not the one." Give 'em that crazy look, then walk away. . . . They catch your drift quick. (E. Anderson, 1990, p. 177)

The irony of such survival tactics is that they make it even more difficult for others to distinguish between those who are law abiding and those who are crime prone. By exhibiting an air of danger and toughness, the young black man may avoid being ridiculed or even victimized by his own peers, but he risks further alienating law-abiding Whites and Blacks. Members of racial or ethnic minorities face many such special dilemmas in impression management, whether they attempt to contradict stereotypes or embrace them.

Social Status

A person's relative position in society can also influence impression management. Like the young black men in Anderson's study, some working-class youths, frustrated by their lack of access to the middle-class world and their inability to meet the requirements of "respectability" as defined by the dominant culture, may present themselves as malicious or dangerous. A tough image helps them gain attention or achieve status and respect within their group (Campbell, 1987; A. K. Cohen, 1955).

Conversely, those who occupy the dominant classes of society can get the attention and respect we all want with very little effort (Derber, 1979). They get special consideration in restaurants, shops, and other public settings. They monopolize the starring roles in politics and economics and also claim more than their share of attention in ordinary interactions. By displaying the symbolic props of material success—large homes, tasteful furnishings, luxury cars, expensive clothes and jewelry—social strivers know that they can impress others and thereby reinforce their own sense of worth and status.

The visual trappings of social class have become harder to spot in recent years. Easily available credit, for instance, has given more Americans access to the traditional high-end props of the well-to-do. A middle-class family can now own a flat-screen television or a fancy sports car. Eighty-one percent of Americans in a recent study indicated that they had felt some pressure to buy high-priced goods (cited in Steinhauer, 2005). So the truly wealthy have ratcheted up the visual display of social class, buying even more expensive products like $130,000 cars and $400 bottles of wine and using posh services like personal chefs and private jets.

Status differences in impression management permeate the world of work as well. Those at the very top of an organization need not advertise their high status because it is already known to people with whom they interact regularly. Their occupational status is a permanently recognized "badge of ability" (Derber, 1979, p. 83). Other people, however, must consciously solicit the attention to which they feel they are entitled. For example, physicians in hospitals may wear stethoscopes and hospital garb to communicate their high-status identity to others from outside the hospital; female doctors often wear white coats so they will not be mistaken for nurses. Those who have no way of exhibiting an occupational badge or whose occupation is seen as inferior must resort to alternative strategies, particularly in interactions with high-status others. They may find themselves subtly or blatantly disclosing their status, talking constantly, or shifting the conversation to a topic about which they have some expertise (Trudgill, 1972).

Impression management plays a prominent role in the socialization process within many professions (Hochschild, 1983). Managers and CEOs in large companies, for instance, become acutely aware through their rise up the corporate ladder of the image they must exude through their dress and demeanor. Salespeople are trained in presenting themselves as knowledgeable, trustworthy, and above all honest. Medical school students learn how to manage their emotions in front of patients and to present the image of "competent physicians." New teachers learn what images are most effective in getting students to comply. One teacher described the importance of impression management this way:

> You can't ever let them get the upper hand on you or you're through. So I start out tough. The first day I get a new class in, I let them know who's boss. . . . You've got to start off tough, then you can ease up as you go along. If you start out easygoing, when you try to be tough, they'll just look at you and laugh. (Goffman, 1959, p. 12)

In any given interaction, one person is likely to have more power than others (Wrong, 1988). When we first hear the word *power,* we think of it in terms of orders, threats, and coercion. But noncoercive forms of power—the signs and symbols of dominance, the subtle messages of threat, the gestures of submission—are much more common to impression management in social encounters (Henley, 1977). The humiliation of being powerless is felt by people who are ignored or interrupted, are intimidated by another's presence, are afraid to approach or touch a superior, or have their privacy freely invaded by another.

The norms that govern the way people address each other also reflect underlying power differences. For instance, the conversations that take place between friends or siblings are commonly marked by the mutual use of such informal terms as first names or nicknames. When status is unequal, though, the lower-status person is often required to use terms of respect such as *Sir* or *Ma'am* or *Doctor*. In the South in years past, every white person had the privilege of addressing any black person by first name and receiving the respectful form of address in return. President George W. Bush's fondness for making up funny nicknames for people on his staff or members of Congress may appear amiable and friendly, but it also reinforces power differences. These people are still required to address him as "Mr. President."

Another example of the symbolic power of forms of address is the way that child actors often change their names when they reach adulthood—for instance, from Ricky to Rick—to convey a desired sense of maturity. Similarly, an uncle's habit of calling me "Davey" when I first became a professor was irritating not because I didn't like the name but because it didn't fit with the professional image I was trying to present.

Status differences are even more clearly institutionalized in some languages. In Spanish, *tu* is the familiar word for "you," which is used when one is talking to a subordinate or to a person of equal status. *Usted* also means "you," but it is the formal version, used when one is addressing a person of superior status. The terms we use to address others may on the surface appear simply to be forms of etiquette. However, forms of address convey a great deal of information about who we think we are in relation to the others we encounter.

Collective Impression Management

We often find ourselves in situations that require a "couple" image, a "group" image, or an "organizational" image of some sort. These impressions are more complex than individual ones, and their management often requires the help and cooperation of others. For example, business partners often present a united front and a joint image of trustworthiness to their clients. Goffman (1959) uses the term **performance team** to describe those individuals who intimately cooperate in staging a performance that leads an audience to form an impression of one or all of the team members.

Team members are highly dependent on one another and must show a fair amount of trust and loyalty, because each member has the power to disrupt or "give away" the performance at any moment. Individuals who cannot be trusted—such as political advisers who have worked for another party or people who are emotionally unstable and unpredictable—thus make poor teammates.

One of the most obvious performance teams is the married couple. Couples are socially obligated to present a believable and cooperative image, particularly if the audience does not know them very well. Few things are as uncomfortable as being audience to a couple that is fighting, bickering, or putting each other down. The cultural value of marriage—and, by extension, the institution of family—is publicly reinforced by the ability of couples to collectively project contented images of a loving relationship.

Like individual impression management, successful teamwork depends on maintaining the boundary between front and back stage. If a couple's teamwork is cohesive and the performance believable, the partners can give the impression that they are happy and content even if they have had a bitter fight moments before going out in public. But the boundary between front and back stage is fragile, and third parties may undermine the best efforts at impression management. Imagine a dinner guest being informed by a precocious 4-year-old that "Mommy and Daddy stopped yelling and screaming those bad words at each other when you showed up." Young children who can speak but are not yet schooled in the social conventions of everyday interaction are not, from the dramaturgical perspective, trustworthy performance teammates. They are often too honest to maintain a front. They are naturally inclined to let audiences back stage, thereby disrupting both the order of the situation and the identities the actors have attempted to claim.

The ability to go back stage periodically is crucial to maintaining a sound team relationship. Not only does it give the team a place to rehearse public performances, but it also provides a refuge from outside scrutiny. For married couples, tensions can rise if they must constantly be "on" for an audience. This is precisely why out-of-town house guests become a burden after a long visit or why living with one or the other partner's parents becomes so difficult. The couple has no back stage, no chance for privacy, no place to go to escape the demands of audience expectations.

Organizations must carefully manage their impressions, too, as a way of establishing their legitimacy (Ginzel, Kramer, & Sutton, 2004). Those that depend on public approval for their survival have to develop effective team performances to manage public perceptions (S. J. Taylor & Bogdan, 1980). Take, for instance, the way U.S. law enforcement organizations present high-profile crime suspects to the public. The suspect being transported from one place to another is usually in shackles with armed officers on either side. Occasionally the officers try to hide the alleged perpetrator's face with a coat or a hat, even though we are likely to know who he or she is. The "perp walk," as it is known, is a decades-long tradition designed not only to satisfy the press but to give police an opportunity to gloat over their latest capture and, in the process, humiliate the suspect (Labaton, 1996). Moreover, if staged well, the perp walk makes the suspect look dangerous, the kind of person who would mail letter bombs, blow up federal office buildings, or commit serial murder. If prisoners are left unshaven, unkempt, and presented in orange prison jumpsuits, the public gets the impression that they've already been convicted.

Individual impression management and organizational impression management are governed by the same principles (Hochschild, 1983). Take, for instance, the management of props and physical space. Hospitals usually line their walls with soothing paintings designed to calm, not agitate; children's wards are often filled with colorful images of familiar cartoon characters. Other types of physical structures may be managed to convey images of power and dominance. For instance, the White House is symbolically the center of world politics. Some of the most important international decisions are made within its walls. But at the same time,

> The building itself—with its white walls, serene proportions, classical Greek tympanum and colonnade—has become the symbol of a power that radiates not only strength but also peace, freedom, and harmony. The rich and positive symbolism has been daily reinforced by the media broadcasting throughout the world pictures of this resplendent mansion, the opulent elegance of the Oval Room, the . . . professionalism and impeccable white shirts of the president's men, the beautiful green lawns with a cheerful and self-confident president and his playful dog nimbly stepping out of the helicopter as if he were a Greek God alighting from Olympus. (Hankiss, 2001, p. 1)

In any society, people often find themselves in situations where they must depend on others for the successful performance of the roles they play as individuals. Without teamwork, many individual and organizational performances would fail, interactions would fall apart, and ultimately social order would be threatened (Henslin, 1991).

Mismanaging Impressions: Spoiled Identities

We sometimes fail miserably in our attempts to project favorable images of ourselves to others. We may mishandle props, blow our lines, mistakenly allow the audience back stage, or otherwise destroy the credibility of our performances. Some of us manage to recover from ineffective impression management quite quickly; others suffer an extended devaluation of their identities. What happens when impression management is unsuccessful? What do we do to regain identities and restore social order?

Embarrassment

A common emotional reaction to impression mismanagement is **embarrassment**, the spontaneous feeling we experience when the identity we are presenting is suddenly and unexpectedly discredited in front of others (E. Gross & Stone, 1964). An adolescent boy trying to look "cool" in front of his friends may have his tough image shattered by the unexpected arrival of his mother in the family minivan. We can see his embarrassment in the fixed smile, the nervous hollow laugh, the busy hands, and the downward glance that conceals his eyes from the gaze of others (Goffman, 1967). Embarrassment can come from a multitude of sources: lack of poise (for example, stumbling, spilling a drink, inappropriately exposing body parts), intrusion into the private settings of others (a man walking into a women's restroom), improper dress for a particular social occasion, and so on.

Embarrassment is sociologically important because it has the potential to destroy the orderliness of a social situation. Imagine being at your graduation ceremony. As the class valedictorian is giving the commencement address, a gust of wind blows her note cards off the podium. As she reaches down to collect them, she knocks over the microphone and tears her gown. In front of hundreds of people she stands there, flustered, not knowing what to say or do. The situation would be uncomfortable and embarrassing not only for her but for you and the rest of the audience as well.

Because embarrassment is disruptive for all concerned, it is in everyone's best interest to cooperate in reducing or eliminating it. To call attention to such an act may be as embarrassing as the original episode itself, so we may pretend not to notice the faux pas (Lindesmith et al., 1991). By suppressing signs of recognition, we make it easier for the person to regain composure (Goffman, 1967). A mutual commitment to supporting others' social identities, even when those identities are in danger, is a fundamental norm of social interaction.

At times, however, embarrassment is used strategically to disrupt another person's impression management. Practical jokes, for instance, are intentional attempts to cause someone else to lose identity. More seriously, groups and organizations may use embarrassment or the threat of embarrassment (for example, hazing) to encourage a preferred activity or discourage behavior that may be damaging to the group. Such embarrassment reasserts the power structure of the group, because only certain people can legitimately embarrass others. A low-status employee, for instance, has much less freedom to embarrass a superior or make him or her the target of a joke than vice versa (R. Coser, 1960).

Groups and organizations, as entities, may also be embarrassed. A few years ago, the entire health care industry in New Zealand suffered an embarrassing blow to its image when it was discovered that a con artist professing to be a psychiatrist and Harvard graduate had been practicing medicine there for more than a year. In 2005, the state government of New Jersey was embarrassed by disclosures that it had been subsidizing the purchase of Viagra for convicted sex offenders in its prisons. That same year, the online information service LexisNexis was embarrassed by the revelation that computer hackers had gained access to the personal information (social security numbers, drivers' license numbers, addresses) of over 300,000 customers.

When events challenge an organization's public image, leaders are often compelled to engage in activities that protect, repair, and enhance that image (Ginzel et al., 2004). For example, every year *U.S. News & World Report* publishes its rankings of the top American universities. Schools that receive high rankings boast of that fact in their recruitment materials and on their Web sites. When a university falls in its ranking from one year to the next though, officials face the unenviable task of scrambling to mend the school's reputation so that alums continue to donate money and prospective students still consider applying. Typically, schools that have dropped in the rankings opt to downplay the rankings' relevance and criticize the magazine's methodology and ranking criteria that only a year earlier (when they were ranked higher) were considered sound and trustworthy.

Most government agencies and large corporations now have public relations departments that carefully manage the corporate image by controlling negative publicity (E. Gross, 1984). In 1999, the International Olympic Committee hired a public relations firm to repair an image tarnished by reports that members of the organizing committee for the 2002 Winter Olympics in Salt Lake City had bribed international officials. One insurance company offers a corporate liability policy that pays policyholders up to $50,000 for the emergency hiring of an image consultant to help manage embarrassing public relations disasters (Landler, 1996).

Sometimes a single false rumor causes massive corporate embarrassment. In 1993, for example, a rash of reports surfaced around the United States from people who claimed to have found hypodermic needles and syringes in cans of Diet Pepsi. Investigators eventually found the claims to be unsubstantiated. Nevertheless, stores in many parts of the country began to pull the product off their shelves or offer refunds to worried customers. The Food and Drug Administration even advised consumers to buy Pepsi in glass or plastic bottles rather than cans. The phenomenon was a public relations nightmare for Pepsi. Facing severe financial losses, the company mounted a massive and expensive media campaign—which included TV commercials, talk show appearances, full-page newspaper ads, and a toll-free consumer hotline—to counteract the embarrassment and costly fallout of a spoiled public image.

Remedies for Spoiled Identities

Organizations and governments can enlist the aid of experts to overcome the debilitating effects of negative images, but individuals are left to their own devices. Fixing a spoiled identity is not easy. The mere knowledge that we are being evaluated negatively can impede our thought, speech, and action. Nevertheless, the major responsibility for restoring order lies with the person or group whose actions disrupted things in the first place.

To restore social order and overcome a spoiled identity, the transgressor will use an **aligning action** (Stokes & Hewitt, 1976). Sometimes aligning can be done easily and quickly. If you step on a person's foot while standing in line at a cafeteria, a simple apology may be all that's needed to avoid the impression that you're a clumsy oaf. By apologizing, you acknowledge that such an act is wrong and send the message that you are not ordinarily a breaker of such social norms. Other situations, however, call for more detailed repairs:

♦ An **account** is a verbal statement designed to explain unanticipated, embarrassing, or unacceptable behavior (C. W. Mills, 1940; M. Scott & Lyman, 1968). For example, an individual may cite events beyond her or his control ("I was late for the wedding because there was a lot of traffic on the highway") or blame others ("I spilled my milk because somebody pushed me"). An alternative is to define the offending behavior as appropriate under the circumstances, perhaps by denying that anyone was hurt by the act ("Yeah, I stole the car, but no one got hurt"), claiming that the victim deserved to be victimized ("I beat him up, but he had it coming"), or claiming higher, unselfish motives ("I stole food, but I did it to feed my family").

♦ A **disclaimer** is a verbal assertion given before the fact to forestall any complaints or negative implications (Hewitt & Stokes, 1975). If we think something we are about to do or say will threaten our identity or be used by others to judge us negatively, we may use a disclaimer. Phrases such as "This may sound crazy to you, but . . ." or "I probably don't know what I'm talking about, but . . ." or "I'm not a racist, but . . ." introduce acts or expressions that ordinarily might be considered undesirable. As long as a disclaimer is provided, a person claiming to be nonracist feels he or she can go ahead and make a racist statement, and a self-proclaimed nonexpert can pretend to be an expert.

Accounts and disclaimers are important links between the individual and society. We use them to explicitly define the relationship between our questionable conduct and prevailing cultural norms. That is, by using aligning actions we publicly reaffirm our commitment to the social order that our conduct has violated and thereby defend the sanctity of our social identities and the "goodness" of society.

In some cases, the provision of accounts has become a lucrative business. Cell phone-based alibi clubs have sprung up in the United States, Europe, and Asia to serve the needs of people who need to lie to spouses or bosses about why they are late or where they are. Club members can send out a text message request to other members who then help to provide an excuse. Cell phones can also be equipped to play background sounds—like car traffic, thunderstorms, or ambulance sirens—to help add credibility to the caller's falsification of her or his whereabouts (Richtel, 2004).

Other people may also try to deal with a transgressor's spoiled identity through a process called **cooling out** (Goffman, 1952), gently persuading someone who has lost face to accept a less desirable but still reasonable alternative identity. People engaged in cooling out seek to persuade rather than force offenders to change. It's an attempt to minimize distress. The challenge is to keep the offender from realizing that he or she is being persuaded.

Cooling out is a common element of social life; it is one of the major functions of consumer complaint personnel, coaches, doctors, and priests. Cooling out also plays a major part in informal relationships. A partner who terminates a dating or courting relationship might persuade the other person to remain a "good friend," gently pushing the person into a lesser role without completely destroying his or her self-worth.

Cooling out is often motivated by institutional pressures. Consider the environment of higher education. The aspirations of many people in U.S. society are encouraged by open-door admissions policies in some universities and most community colleges (Karabel, 1972). There is a widely held cultural belief that higher education is linked to better employment opportunities and that anyone can go to college. Discrepancies, however, inevitably arise between people's aspirations and their ability to succeed. If educational institutions simply kicked unqualified students out of school, the result would likely be widespread public pressure and anxiety over the system itself. Hence, most community colleges opt for a "soft response" of cooling out the unqualified student (B. Clark, 1960). A counselor may direct a poor student toward an alternative major that would be easier but still "not that different" from the student's original goal—for example, nurse's aide instead of registered nurse. Or the counselor might encourage the student to seek employment after graduation from a two-year program rather than transfer to a four-year university. That is, the student is gently persuaded to redefine him- or herself.

Institutional cooling-out processes such as these are inherent in an educational system that doesn't have clear selection criteria. In the United States, admission into college is based on some combination of achievement (tests, grades), aptitude (standardized test scores), and personality traits (interviews, letters of recommendation). In contrast, educational selection in Japan is based on a single criterion: achievement as measured by exams and grades. National universities do not allow any exceptions. Because career paths are clearly and quickly defined, Japanese higher education has no need for an institutionalized cooling-out process (Kariya & Rosenbaum, 1987).

Stigma

The permanent spoiling of someone's identity is called **stigma**. A stigma is a deeply discrediting characteristic, widely viewed as an insurmountable obstacle preventing competent or morally trustworthy behavior (Goffman, 1963). Stigmas spoil the identities of individuals regardless of other attributes those individuals might have. According to Goffman, the three types of stigma are defects of the body (for example, severe scars, blindness, paralyzed or missing limbs); defects of character (for example, dishonesty, weak will, unorthodox beliefs inferred from a known record of mental illness, imprisonment, substance abuse); and membership in devalued social groups, such as certain races, religions, or ethnicities. The impression management task when faced with stigma is not so much to recapture a tarnished identity as to minimize the social damage.

Some stigmas are worse than others. For instance, the use of eyeglasses to compensate for a sensory deficiency (poor vision) is usually considered far less stigmatizing than the use of hearing aids to compensate for a different sensory deficiency (poor hearing). Contemporary hearing aids are designed to be as small and unnoticeable as possible. Eyeglasses, on the other hand, have become a common fashion accessory, often sold in their own trendy boutiques.

Stigma varies across time and culture as well. Being a Christian in the 21st century is very different from being one in A.D. 100, and being a Christian in the United States is different from being one in the Arab Middle East (Ainlay, Becker, & Coleman, 1986). As you saw earlier in this chapter, obesity is stigmatized in contemporary Western societies but was seen as desirable, attractive, and symbolic of status and wealth in the past (Clinard & Meier, 1979) and is still seen that way in some other cultures today.

Interactions between the stigmatized and the nonstigmatized—called "mixed contacts"—can sometimes be uneasy. We have all felt uncomfortable with people who are "different" in appearance or behavior. Stigma initiates a judgment process that colors impressions and sets up barriers to interaction (E. E. Jones, Farina, Hastorf, Markus, Miller, & Scott, 1984).

Whether intentionally or not, nonstigmatized individuals often pressure stigmatized people to conform to "inferior" identities. A person in a wheelchair who is discouraged from going camping or a blind person who is discouraged from venturing out of the house alone is not given the chance to develop important skills and is thus kept dependent.

Nonstigmatized people often avoid mixed contacts because they anticipate discomfort and are unsure how to act (Goffman, 1963). Research shows that when interacting with a person who is physically disabled, an able-bodied person is likely to be more inhibited, be more rigid, and end the interaction sooner than if the other person were also able-bodied (Kleck, 1968; Kleck, Ono, & Hastorf, 1966). On the one hand, the able-bodied person may fear that showing direct sympathy or interest in a disabled person's condition could be regarded as rude or intrusive. On the other hand, ignoring it may make the interaction artificial and awkward or create impossible demands (Michener, DeLamater, & Schwartz, 1986).

As for people with stigmatizing conditions, they often sense that others are evaluating them negatively. One study of people diagnosed with a mental disorder found that they had all at one time or another been shunned, avoided, patronized, or discriminated against when others found out about their condition (Wahl, 1999). Consider also the case of Mark Breimhorst, a Stanford University graduate. Mr. Breimhorst has no hands. When he was applying to business schools in 1998, he received permission to take the Graduate Management Admissions Test on a computer and was given 25% more time to accommodate his disability. His results were mailed out to prospective graduate schools with the notation "*Scores obtained under special circumstances.*" Mr. Breimhorst was not admitted to any of the business schools to which he applied. He filed a federal lawsuit against the testing service, challenging the way they flag the scores of students who need accommodations. Such notations, he argued, are stigmatizing because they create suspicion that the scores are less valid than others (Lewin, 2000). In 2003, the testing service stopped flagging the results of students who receive special accommodations.

Faced with the strong possibility of discrimination, people with stigmatizing conditions often use coping strategies to establish the most favorable identity possible. One strategy is to try to hide the stigma. People who are hard of hearing, for instance, may learn to read lips or otherwise interact with people as if they could hear perfectly; those with bodily stigmas may opt for surgery to permanently conceal their condition.

Michael Petrunik and Clifford Shearing (1983) studied the coping strategies used by people who stutter. Common public reactions to stutterers include pity, condescension, ridicule, and impatience. The researchers observed and took part in weekly therapy groups for stutterers over a period of 13 years. In addition they conducted in-depth interviews with stutterers, their families and friends, speech therapists, and other medical practitioners. They found that some stutterers hide their stigma by avoiding speaking situations or by not using particularly troublesome words. Others structure situations so that someone else does the talking. For example, in a restaurant stutterers may encourage others to order first. As soon as an acceptable item is mentioned, they simply duplicate the order by saying, "Me, too" or "Same here."

Some stigmatized individuals, particularly those whose conditions are not immediately observable, use a policy of selective disclosure. Sociologist Charlene E. Miall (1989) interviewed and surveyed 70 infertile women, nearly all of whom characterized infertility as something negative, an indication of failure, or an inability to function "normally." Most of the women were concerned that others' knowledge of their infertility would be stigmatizing. So they engaged in some form of information control. Many simply concealed the information from everyone except medical personnel and infertility counselors. Others used medical accounts, saying, "It's beyond my control." Some disclosed the information only to people they felt would not think ill of them. Some even used the disclosure of their infertility to gain control of a situation by deliberately shocking their "normal" audience (Miall, 1989).

Of course, not all stigmas can be hidden. Some individuals can only minimize the degree to which their stigmas intrude on and disrupt the interaction. One tactic is to use self-deprecating humor—telling little jokes about their shortcomings—to relieve the tension felt by the nonstigmatized. Others may try to focus attention on attributes unrelated to the stigma. For instance, a person in a wheelchair may carry around esoteric books in a conspicuous manner to show others that she or he still has a brain that works well.

Still others with stigmas boldly call attention to their condition by mastering areas thought to be closed to them (such as mountain climbing for an amputee). And some organize a movement to counter social oppression. For instance, the National Association to Advance Fat Acceptance helps fat people ("fat" is the preferred adjective, by the way) cope with a society that hates their size and lobbies state legislatures to combat "size discrimination." They have organized civil rights protests in Washington, D.C., lobbied health care professionals for tolerance and acceptance, and organized campaigns against insurance discrimination and the dubious "science" of weight loss programs (LeBesco, 2004). Similarly, a disabled singing group routinely performs a song titled "Let the Children Stare," to convey the message that no good comes from ignoring disabilities (D. Martin, 1997). Many of these individuals embrace their disabilities as a vital part of their identity and say they would reject being cured, even if it were possible. Rather, they want the world to adapt to their needs. As one disabled person put it, "We will not change to fit the mold. Instead, we will destroy the mold and change the world to make sure there is room for everyone" (quoted in D. Martin, 1997, p. E1).

But overcoming the problems created by stigma cannot be accomplished solely through individual impression management or collective demonstrations. Long-lasting improvements can be accomplished only by changing cultural beliefs about the nature of stigma (Link, Mirotznik, & Cullen, 1991). As long as we hold stigmatized individuals solely responsible for dealing with the stigma, only some of them will be able to overcome the social limitations of their condition.

Conclusion

After reading this chapter, you may have an image of human beings as cunning, manipulative, and cynical play actors whose lives are merely a string of phony performances carefully designed to fit the selfish needs of the moment. The impression manager comes across as someone who consciously and fraudulently presents an inaccurate image in order to take advantage of a particular situation. Even the person who seems not to care about his or her appearance may be consciously cultivating the image of "not caring."

There's no denying that people consciously manufacture images of themselves that allow them to achieve some desired goal. Most of us go through life trying to create the impression that we're attractive, honest, competent, and sincere. To that end we carefully manage our appearance, present qualities we think others will admire, and hide qualities we think they won't. When caught in an act that may threaten the impression we're trying to foster, we strategically use statements that disclaim, excuse, or justify it.

So who is the real you? If people freely change their images to suit the expectations of a given audience, is there something more stable that characterizes them across all situations?

If you are aware that the impression you are managing is not the real you, then you must have some knowledge of what *is* the real you. And what you are may, in fact, transcend the demands of particular situations. Some basic, pervasive part of your being may allow you to choose from a repertoire of identities the one that best suits the immediate needs of the situation. As you ponder this possibility, realize that your feelings about impression management reflect your beliefs about the nature of individuals and the role society and others play in our everyday lives.

YOUR TURN

Impression management is a tool most of us use to present ourselves as likable people. Occasionally, however, our attempts fail. Survey several friends or classmates and have them describe their most embarrassing moment. What were the circumstances surrounding the incident? What identities were they trying to present? How did the attempt to claim these identities fail? How did these people immediately react, physically and behaviorally, to the embarrassment? How did they try to overcome the embarrassment and return order? Did they offer some sort of account? Were the consequences of the failed impression management temporary or permanent? What did the witnesses to the embarrassing incident do? Did their reactions alleviate or intensify the embarrassment?

Once you've gathered a substantial number of stories (about 12 or 15), see if you can find some common themes. What are the most frequent types of embarrassing situations? What are the most frequent reactions? If your class is large, your instructor can have you report your results to a small group of fellow students or to the entire class. What kinds of patterns can you identify in the embarrassing stories people tell? Are there gender, ethnic, or age differences in what people find embarrassing?

Sociologists Edward Gross and Gregory Stone have written, "In the wreckage left by embarrassment lie the broken foundations of social transactions" (1964, p. 2). What do you suppose they meant by that? Discuss the sociological importance of embarrassment (and, more important, the reactions to embarrassment) in terms of the maintenance of interactional and social order.

CHAPTER HIGHLIGHTS

- ◆ A significant portion of social life is influenced by the images we form of others and the images others form of us.

- ◆ Impression formation is based initially on our assessment of ascribed social group membership (race, age, gender, and so on), individual physical appearance, and verbal and nonverbal messages.

- ◆ While we are gathering information about others to form impressions of them, we are fully aware that they are doing the same thing. Impression management is the process by which we attempt to control and manipulate information about ourselves to influence the impressions others form of us. Impression management can be both individual and collective.

- ◆ Impression mismanagement can lead to the creation of damaged identities, which must be repaired in order to sustain social interaction.

KEY TERMS

account Statement designed to explain unanticipated, embarrassing, or unacceptable behavior after the behavior has occurred

aligning action Action taken to restore an identity that has been damaged

back stage Area of social interaction away from the view of an audience, where people can rehearse and rehash their behavior

cooling out Gently persuading someone who has lost face to accept a less desirable but still reasonable alternative identity

disclaimer Assertion designed to forestall any complaints or negative reactions to a behavior or statement that is about to occur

dramaturgy Study of social interaction as theater, in which people ("actors") project images ("play roles") in front of others ("audience")

embarrassment Spontaneous feeling that is experienced when the identity someone is presenting is suddenly and unexpectedly discredited in front of others

front stage Area of social interaction where people perform and work to maintain appropriate impressions

impression management Act of presenting a favorable public image of oneself so that others will form positive judgments

performance team Set of individuals who cooperate in staging a performance that leads an audience to form an impression of one or all team members

stigma Deeply discrediting characteristic that is viewed as an obstacle to competent or morally trustworthy behavior

---

STUDY SITE ON THE WEB

Don't forget the interactive quizzes and other learning aids at www.pineforge.com/newman6 study. In the Resource Files for this chapter, you will also find more on building image, including:

Sociologists at Work

♦ Ronny Turner and Charles Edgley: Mortuary Performances
♦ Philip Blumstein: "Altercasting" Your Date

Micro-Macro Connections

♦ Accounting for a Spoiled Identity
♦ Managing Impressions on the Internet

7

Building Social Relationships
Intimacy and Families

So far, the 21st century has been a strange and challenging time for the type of relationships that we're used to thinking about as the foundation of social life:

♦ Over half of young adults between the ages of 18 and 24 (more than 13 million individuals) live with their parents (Fields & Casper, 2001); over 29 million American adults live by themselves (U.S. Bureau of the Census, 2004a).

♦ Some of the most popular "reality" television shows in the 2000s—*Joe Millionaire, Married by America, The Bachelor, The Bachelorette, Mr. Personality, The 5th Wheel, Change of Heart, Temptation Island, Beauty and the Geek, Hooking Up, Who Wants to Marry a Multimillionaire?*—have given new meaning to the terms *dating, intimacy,* and *relationship.*

♦ For busy professionals who don't have the time to go on television shows to find their true loves, "speed dating" has become popular. At organized speed dating events, an individual will meet a new prospect every few minutes, engage in some small talk, and move on to another prospect when a bell rings. People can meet and rate up to 30 potential "dates" in a single night (Barker, 2002).

♦ The term *friends with benefits* (or *privileges*) has become a common part of the vocabulary of young people today, describing relationships with close friends that include sex but don't involve emotional commitment or expectations of exclusivity.

♦ The overall birth rate in the United States is the lowest it's been since national data have been available (B.E. Hamilton, Martin, & Sutton, 2003).

♦ Of all births in the United States, 34% are to unmarried mothers (U.S. Bureau of the Census, 2004a); and 61% of women and 55% of men in a national survey said they'd be willing to raise a child on their own without a spouse or partner (cited in Edwards, 2000).

♦ A growing number of American parents and children rely on text messaging to communicate with each other, in place of face-to-face conversation (Schwartz, 2004).

♦ Public opposition toward gay parenting in the U.S. remains high despite official statements from the American Academy of Pediatrics, the Child Welfare League, and the American Psychological Association that children with same-sex parents do as well as children raised in "traditional" families (DuLong, 2002; Kelly, 2002).

Some people might see these events as "proof" that society is going downhill fast; others may see them simply as neutral signs that society is changing.

Like every other aspect of our individual lives, intimate relationships must be understood within the broader contours of our society. This chapter takes a sociological peek into their private and public aspects and explores the role that these relationships, especially family bonds, play in our sense of self. Why are these relationships so important to us? How do societal factors such as social institutions, gender, race, and social class affect our perceptions of intimacy and belonging? How do they affect family life? And why are the desirable aspects of these relationships so often outweighed by the negative aspects, such as family violence?

Life With Others

The quality and quantity of our social relationships are the standards against which many of us judge the quality and happiness of our lives (Campbell, Converse, & Rodgers, 1976). We spend a tremendous amount of time worrying about our friendships, families, and romantic relationships, contemplating new ones, obsessing over past ones, trying to make them work, or fretting over how to get into or get out of one.

Although we hunger for intimacy and sometimes spend a lot of time and money attempting to get it, our social relationships are fraught with difficulty. For over a century, sociologists have been writing that people who live in complex, urban, industrial or postindustrial societies gradually become less integrated and connected to others (Durkheim, 1893/1947; Riesman, 1950; Tönnies, 1887/1957). We're more mobile in our careers, more willing to relocate, and thus more likely to break social ties than people were, say, a century ago. In the United States, the proportion of people who socialize with neighbors more than once a year has steadily declined over the last two decades. Membership in church-related groups, civic organizations (such as the Red Cross, Boy Scouts, and PTA), and fraternal organizations (such as the Lions, Elks, and Shriners) has likewise decreased. Between 1980 and 1993, the total number of bowlers in the United States increased by 10%, but team bowling in organized leagues decreased by 40% (Putnam, 1995). During the same period, the number of U.S. adults living alone almost doubled; single people who have never married now make up about one fourth of the adult population in this country (U.S. Bureau of the Census, 2004a).

Some sociologists attribute these trends to U.S. culture's emphasis on individualism. It takes away a sense of community, diminishing the ability to establish ties with others and making it easier for people to walk away from groups that they see as unfulfilling (Bellah et al., 1985; Sidel, 1986). In a national poll a while back, 25%

of Americans said that for $10 million they'd abandon their entire family (J. Peterson & Kim, 1991). The high value that contemporary society places on individual achievement and success can make social relationships, even family relationships, seem expendable.

By contrast, in collectivist societies such as India and Japan, group ties play a more substantial role in people's everyday lives. There, people consider duty, sacrifice, and compromise more desirable traits than personal success and individual achievement. They assume group connections are the best guarantee for an individual's well-being. Hence feelings of group loyalty and responsibility for other members tend to be strong.

Even in most individualist cultures, however, social relationships play an important societal role: They help control the actions of individuals by socializing group members to a particular set of norms and values (see Chapter 5). If you've ever done something that met with disapproval from your friends or family or expressed an unpopular opinion to them, you certainly know the discomfort of standing out and violating a group's standards. Whenever a member says or does something that is out of line with group norms, other members may increase their communication with that person in an effort to change her or his mind (Rodin, 1985). Or they may simply reject him or her, either blatantly or subtly, to keep the group and its values and perceptions intact (Schacter, 1951).

Despite the inevitable conflicts in close relationships and the difficulties of maintaining ties in an individualistic, mobile, high-tech society, people still place a high value on belonging and intimacy and take great pains to achieve them. For instance, a growing number of older women who are single, widowed, or divorced are looking for support not through marriage but through long-term friendships with other women who are at a similar stage in their lives (Gross, 2004a). Similarly, we may be spending more time than ever at work (Schor, 1991) to the detriment of relationships with our families, but for many people forming ties with coworkers can be just as emotionally fulfilling (Wuthnow, 1994). And many of us spend a great deal of our time in local hangouts (such as bars and coffee shops) where we can find comfort and good company (Oldenburg & Brissett, 1982). Many people find the sense of belonging they crave in these small groups of friends and like-minded neighbors and coworkers.

Social Diversity and Intimate Choices

Our bonds with coworkers, neighbors, and friends are certainly an important part of our social lives, but the sense of belonging and closeness that comes from intimate, romantic relationships has become one of the prime obsessions of the 21st century. Popular magazines, self-help books, supermarket tabloids, Web sites, Internet chat rooms, and television talk shows overflow with advice, warnings, and pseudoscientific analyses of every conceivable aspect of these relationships.

Most people in the United States assume that love is all they need to establish a fulfilling, long-lasting relationship. But their intimate choices are far from free and private. The choices they make regarding whom to date, live with, or marry are governed by two important social rules that limit the field of eligible partners: exogamy and endogamy.

Exogamy rules specify that individuals must form intimate relationships outside certain social groups to which they belong, most particularly their immediate family. In almost all societies, exogamy rules prohibit marrying siblings, parents, and children. You could look at the opposition to homosexual marriages as, in part, an exogamy rule: that a person should only be allowed to marry someone outside his or her sex. Rules of exogamy often extend to certain people outside the nuclear family too, such as cousins, grandparents, aunts, uncles, and, in some societies, stepsiblings. The logic behind these restrictions is that children of such unions face a greater risk of birth defects. In 2002, however, scientists at the University of Washington published a study indicating that the health risks of children born to first cousins were no greater than those faced by other children (Grady, 2002). Still, 24 states completely prohibit first cousins to marry.

The rules of exogamy are applied differently in different cultures. In 2003, a young Indian couple was beaten to death by members of their own families for being lovers. In their community, it was considered incest for two people from the same village to fall in love. A resident of the village said, "In our society all the families living in a village are all sons and daughters of the whole village. We are like brothers and sisters. The marriage of brothers and sisters is not accepted" (quoted in Waldman, 2003, p. A4).

The rules of **endogamy**, which is marriage *within* certain social groups of which one is a member (such as race, class, and religion), also affect intimate choices. In some countries, such as Pakistan, most marriages are arranged by families or respected community elders to preserve group identities, with little thought for the compatibility or shared affection of the partners. According to one historian, arranged marriages turn strangers into relatives, keep peace within villages, and establish permanent trading connections (Coontz, 2005).

In contrast, the choice of marital partners in the United States and most other Western countries is supposedly more open, a matter of personal preference. But the vast majority of intimate relationships in the United States—and, indeed, throughout the world—occur between people from the same religion, racial or ethnic group, and social class. To be sure, similar backgrounds—and thus similar beliefs, values, and experiences—increase the likelihood that two individuals will be attracted to each other. However, the rules of endogamy also reflect a cultural distaste for relationships that cross group boundaries.

An interesting question for sociologists today is whether the increasing diversity of the population in the United States is likely to alter intimate choices and thus conceptions of the "typical" family in years to come. Whether families become more similar or more diverse in the future depends on the continuing power of endogamy rules and whether the formation of relationships across religious, racial, or social class lines becomes more common than it is today.

Religious Background in Intimate Choices

Throughout history, many societies have had endogamy rules relating to religion: Only people with the same religious background were allowed to marry. Marrying outside one's religion is more common than it once was in industrialized countries, however, because greater mobility and freer communication bring people from diverse religious backgrounds into contact. In the United States, it's estimated that between one quarter and one half of all marriages occur between people of different religions ("Breaking the rules," 2002; Robinson, 1999).

Nevertheless, most religious leaders still actively discourage interfaith marriages. They worry about maintaining their religion's influence and its related ethnic identity within a diverse and complex society (M. M. Gordon, 1964). In 2004, the Vatican issued an official church document discouraging marriage between Catholics and all non-Christians, especially Muslims (Feuer, 2004). The concern is that such marriages may further weaken people's religious beliefs and values, lead to the raising of children in a different faith, or encourage family members to abandon religion entirely.

The situation facing American Jews provides a good example of the consequences of interfaith marriage. The percentage of Jews in the U.S. population has declined from 4% to a little over 2% in the past 50 years (Safire, 1995; U.S. Bureau of the Census, 2004a). Although only 1 Jew in 10 married a non-Jew in 1945, close to 1 in 2 does so today. A lower birth rate among Jews compared to other groups, coupled with the like-lihood that interfaith families will not raise children as Jews, explains, in part, why the Jewish population has been dropping steadily (Goodstein, 2003b).

A statement issued in 1973 by Reform Judaism's Central Conference of American Rabbis (the most liberal, and therefore the most tolerant, branch of U.S. Judaism) defined interfaith marriages as "contrary to Jewish tradition" and discouraged rabbis from officiating at them (Niebuhr, 1996). Indeed, most rabbis today refuse to perform interfaith weddings, even though there is some evidence that interfaith couples who have been married by rabbis are likely to raise their children as Jews.

Many Jewish leaders fear that the outcome of this trend will be not only the shrinking of the Jewish population but also the erosion and perhaps extinction of an entire way of life. They believe that the survival of U.S. Jewry depends on maintaining the integrity of traditional Jewish values and institutions. Young people who decide to marry outside the faith "are threatening to transform Judaism into a religion of half-remembered rituals, forgotten ancestors and buried beliefs" (Rosen, 1997, p. 7).

Race and Ethnicity in Intimate Choices

Relationships that cross racial or ethnic lines have become more common in U.S. society. In 1970, there were 300,000 interracial married couples (or about 0.7% of all marriages). Today there are 3.1 million interracial couples, constituting 5.4% of all U.S. marriages (Lee & Edmonston, 2005). The typical interracial couple is a white person with a spouse of a different race; marriage between two people of different racial minority groups is relatively infrequent. In addition, marriages between a Latino/a and a non-Latino/a (regardless of race) increased from 1.3% of all married couples in 1970 to 3.2% today. About 25% of Latino/as marry someone of a different ethnic group, a rate that has been fairly stable since the 1980s (Lee & Edmonston, 2005).

Racial and ethnic endogamy is a global phenomenon, forming the basis of social structure in most societies worldwide (Murdock, 1949). The issue is an especially emo-tional one in U.S. society, however. The first law against interracial marriage was enacted in Maryland in 1661, prohibiting whites from marrying Native Americans or African Americans. Over the next 300 years or so, 38 more states put such laws on the books, expanding their coverage to include Chinese, Japanese, and Filipino Americans. It was believed that a mixing of the races (then referred to as "mongrelization") would destroy the racial purity (and superiority) of whites. The irony, of course, is that racial mixing had been taking place since the very beginning, much of it through white slave owners forcing sexual activity on black slaves.

Legal sanctions against interracial marriage persisted well into the 20th century. In 1958, for example, when Richard Loving (who was white) and his new wife, Mildred Jeter Loving (who was black), moved to their new home in Virginia, a sheriff arrived to arrest them for violating a state law that prohibited interracial marriages. The Lovings were sentenced to 1 year in jail but then learned that the judge would suspend the sentence if they left the state and promised not to return for 25 years. They agreed, but, after leaving town, sued the state of Virginia. In 1967 the U.S. Supreme Court ruled in their favor, concluding that using racial classifications to restrict freedom to marry was unconstitutional. Sixteen states had their interracial marriage prohibition laws struck down with this ruling.

Almost 50 years later, people are no longer banished for marrying someone of a different race. Nevertheless, even though attitudes are becoming more tolerant, discomfort with interracial relationships still lingers. Two states—South Carolina and Alabama—had laws against interracial marriage on the books until the mid-1990s. Even today, rural judges can sometimes make it difficult for interracial couples to marry (B. Staples, 1999).

People involved in interracial relationships state that the most difficult problem they face, both before and after marriage, is racism (Rosenblatt, Karis, & Powell, 1995). About half of the black-white couples in one study felt that biracial marriage makes things harder for them, and about two thirds reported that their parents had a problem with the relationship, at least initially (Fears & Deane, 2001).

Social Class in Intimate Choices

If we were to base our ideas about the formation of romantic relationships on what we see in movies, we might be tempted to conclude that divisions based on social class don't matter in U.S. society or perhaps don't exist at all. Films such as *Titanic, The Wedding Planner, Maid in Manhattan, Good Will Hunting, Fools Rush In, Sweet Home Alabama,* and *Pretty Woman* send the message that the power of love is strong enough to blow away differences in education, pedigree, resources, and tastes. When it comes to love, Hollywood's United States is a classless society.

In reality, however, social class is a powerful factor in whom we choose to marry. Around the world, people face strong pressures to choose marital partners from the same social standing (Carter & Glick, 1976; Kalmijn, 1994). Even if two individuals from different races, ethnic groups, or religions marry, chances are they will have similar socioeconomic backgrounds. Certainly some people do marry a person from a different social class, but the class tends to be an adjacent one—for instance, an upper-middle-class woman who marries a middle-class man. Marriages between people of vastly different class rankings are quite rare. The reason is that individuals from similar social classes are more likely to come into contact and to share values, tastes, goals, expectations, and educational background.

The U.S. education system plays a particularly important role in bringing people from similar class backgrounds together. Neighborhoods—and thus neighborhood schools—tend to be homogeneous with regard to social class. College continues class segregation. People from upper-class backgrounds are considerably more likely to attend costly private schools, whereas those from the middle class are most likely to enroll in state universities and those from the working class are most likely to enroll in community colleges. These structural conditions increase the odds that the people whom college students meet and form intimate relationships with will come from a similar class background.

Family Life

To most people's way of thinking, intimate relationships form the cornerstone of families. Of all the groups we belong to, family is usually the most significant. Our family of origin provides us with a personal history, and it, along with the families we build later in life, provides much of our identity. Perhaps no facet of human existence occupies more time, effort, and emotion. Because of its importance in everyday life, sociologists consider family one of the main social institutions, a social structure that addresses not only our personal needs but also the fundamental needs of society (see Chapter 2).

Historical Trends in Family Life

Many functionalist sociologists have voiced concern over the current state of family as a social institution. Over time, they argue, the family has been losing many, if not all, of its traditional purposes (Lasch, 1977). Historically, the family was where children received most of their education and religious training. It was where both children and adults could expect to receive emotional nurturing and support. It was the institution that regulated sexual activity and reproduction. And it was also the economic center of society, where family members worked together to earn a living and support one another financially.

But as the economy shifted from a system based on small, privately owned agricultural enterprises to one based on massive industrial manufacturing, the role of the family changed. Economic production moved from the home to the factory, and families became more dependent on the money that members earned outside the home. Schools began to take over the teaching of skills and values that were once a part of everyday home life. Even the family's role as a source of emotional security and nurturing began to diminish as it became less able to shield its members from the harsh realities of modern life (Lasch, 1977).

For all these reasons many people, from research scholars to politicians to everyday people on the street, are concerned about the survival of the contemporary family. Anxiety over the future of families has generated some strident calls for a return to the "good ol' days" of family life. The belief in a lost "golden age" of family has led some to depict the present as a period of rapid decline and inevitable family breakdown (Coontz, 2005; Hareven, 1992; Skolnick, 1991). Critics often pessimistically cite high divorce rates, large numbers of out-of-wedlock births, changing gender roles (most notably, the increase in working mothers), and a de-emphasis on heterosexual marriage as troublesome characteristics of contemporary families. However, families have always been diverse in structure and have always faced difficulties protecting members from economic hardship, internal violence, political upheaval, and social change. Calls for a return to the "good ol' days" are, in the end, calls for a return to something that has never truly existed. By glorifying a mythical and idealized past, we artificially limit ourselves to an inaccurate image of what we think a "normal" family ought to look like.

Trends in Family Structure

The reality of American family life has never quite fit its nostalgic image. According to sociologist William J. Goode (1971), the traditional family of the past that people in the United States speak so fondly of and want to recreate is somewhat of a myth. He calls the idealized image of the past "the classical family of Western nostalgia":

> It is a pretty picture of life down on grandma's farm. There are lots of happy children, and many kinfolk live together in a large rambling house. Everyone works hard. Most of the food to be eaten during the winter is grown, preserved, and stored on the farm. . . . Father is stern and reserved and has the final decision in all important matters. . . . All boys and girls marry, and marry young. . . . After marriage, the couple lives harmoniously, either near the boy's parents or with them. . . . No one divorces. (p. 624)

Like most stereotypes, this one is not altogether accurate. In the 19th century American adults had a shorter life expectancy than adults today, so due to the death of a parent, children were actually *more* likely then than they are today to live in a single-parent home (Kain, 1990). Even children fortunate enough to come from intact families usually left home to work as servants or apprentices in other people's homes. Furthermore, although close to 18% of U.S. children live in poverty today (DeNavas-Walt, Proctor, & Lee, 2005), a larger proportion lived in orphanages at the beginning of the 20th century—and not just because their parents had died. Many were there because their parents simply couldn't afford to raise them. Rates of alcohol and drug abuse, dropping out of school, and domestic violence were also higher a century ago than they are today (Coontz, 1992).

Also contrary to popular beliefs, father-breadwinner/mother-homemaker households were not the universal family form in the 19th and early 20th centuries. For instance, by 1900 one fifth of American women worked outside the home (Staggenborg, 1998). But the experiences of employed women varied along class and race lines. For middle- and upper-class white women, few professions other than teaching and nursing were available. Because their income was probably not essential for the survival of the household, most could enter and exit the labor force in response to family demands or take on volunteer work to fill up their free time when they weren't employed. In contrast, poor women were likely to work long hours, mostly in unskilled jobs in clothing factories, canning plants, or other industries.

Family life for women of color was even more affected by economic necessity. Black domestic servants, for instance, were often forced to leave their own families and live in their employer's home, where they were expected to work around the clock.

But most of them had little choice. Throughout U.S. history, black women have rarely had the luxury of being stay-at-home spouses and parents. In 1880, 73% of black single women and 35% of black married women reported holding paid jobs. Only 23% of white single women and 7% of white married women reported being in the paid labor force at that time (cited in Kessler-Harris, 1982).

Trends in Household Size

Perhaps the most pervasive myth regarding American families of the past is that of the primacy of the **extended family**—several generations living under the same roof. Today's more isolated **nuclear family**, consisting at most of only mother, father, and children, is often compared unfavorably to the image of these large, close-knit support networks. Research shows that U.S. families have always been fairly small and primarily nuclear (Blumstein & Schwartz, 1983; W. J. Goode, 1971; Hareven, 1992). This country has no strong tradition of large, extended multigenerational families living together. In fact, the highest proportion of extended family households ever recorded existed between 1850 and 1885 and was only around 20% of all households (Hareven, 1978). Because people didn't live as long then as they do today, most died before ever seeing their grandchildren. Even in the 1700s the typical family consisted of a husband, a wife, and approximately three children.

When households of the past were large, it was probably due to the presence of nonfamily members: servants, apprentices, boarders, and visitors. The reduction in average household size we've seen over the last several centuries was caused not by a decline in the number of extended relatives but by a decrease in nonfamily members living in a household, a reduction in the number of children in a family, and an increase in young adults living alone (Kobrin, 1976).

As people migrated to the United States from countries that did have a tradition of extended families, such as China, Greece, and Italy, often their first order of business was to surrender their extended families so they could create their own households. Reducing the size of their families was seen as a clear sign that they had become Americans. Large, multigenerational families simply didn't make economic sense anymore. Being able to move to a different state to pursue a job would be next to impossible with a bunch of grandparents, aunts, uncles, and cousins in tow.

In addition, it's not at all clear that families today are as isolated as some people make them out to be. More U.S. residents than ever have grandparents alive, and the ties between grandparents and grandchildren may be stronger than ever. Today, most adults see or talk to a parent on the phone at least once a week (Coontz, 1992). Extended family members may not live under the same roof, but they do stay in contact and provide advice, emotional support, and financial help when needed (K. Newman, 2005).

Trends in Divorce

Another oft-cited indicator of the demise of the U.S. family that is based on faulty conceptions of the past is the current high divorce rate. Many observers fear that the intact middle-class family depicted in 1950s television shows such as *Ozzie and*

Harriet, Father Knows Best, and *Leave It to Beaver* has crumbled away forever. The rise in the divorce rate has been attributed to the cultural movement toward "swinging singles, open marriages, alternative lifestyles, and women's liberation" in the 1960s and 1970s (Skolnick, 1991). True, this was a revolutionary period in U.S. history. Norms governing all aspects of social life were certainly changing.

What these conclusions overlook, however, is the longer historical trend in divorce in this country. Until World War II, it had been increasing steadily for over 100 years (see Exhibit 7.1). It rose sharply right after the war, most likely because of short courtships before the young men shipped out and the subsequent stress of separation. In the 1950s, the rate dropped just as sharply. The high divorce rates of the 1960s and 1970s, then, represented a return to a national trend that had been developing since the beginning of the 20th century. Indeed, since the mid-1980s the rate has actually been declining a bit.

Furthermore, the rate of "hidden" marital separation 100 years ago was probably not that much less than the rate of "visible" separation today (Sennett, 1984). For financial or religious reasons, divorce was not an option for many people in the past. For instance, divorce rates actually fell during the Great Depression of the 1930s. Did this mean that economic hardships were bringing more couples closer together so that spouses could provide one another with love and support that would get them through tough times? Hardly. With jobs and housing scarce, many couples simply couldn't

Exhibit 7.1   Historical Trends in American Divorce

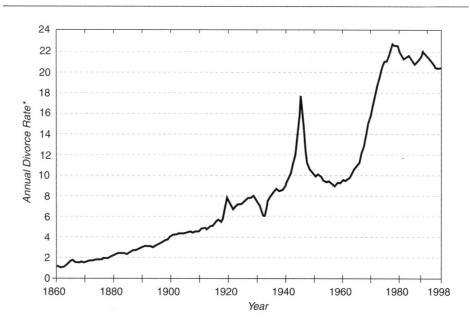

Source: Cherlin, 1992; U.S. Bureau of the Census, 1998, 2000.

*Per 1,000 married women 15 years old and over

afford to divorce. Rates of marital unhappiness and domestic violence increased. A significant number of people turned to the functional equivalents of divorce—desertion and abandonment—which have been around for centuries. So you can see that the divorce rate may have been lower in the past, but families found other ways to break up. The image of a warm, secure, stable family life in past times is at odds with the actual history of U.S. families (Skolnick, 1991).

The Culture of Intimacy and Family

Families can be found in every human society, and from a structural-functionalist perspective, they all address similar societal needs. However, the way families go about meeting these needs—their structure, customs, patterns of authority, and so on—differ widely across cultures. Thus ideas about what a family is and how people should behave within it are culturally determined.

Cultural Variation in Family Practices

Most of us take for granted that **monogamy**, the marriage of two people, is the fundamental building block of the family. Some families do exist without a married couple, and some people may have several spouses over their lifetimes. But monogamous marriage is the core component of our image of family (Sudarkasa, 2001).

In the United States, monogamous marriage between one man and one woman continues to be the only adult intimate relationship that is legally recognized, culturally approved, and endorsed by the Internal Revenue Service. It is still the one relationship in which sexual activity is not only acceptable but expected. No other relationship has achieved such status. Despite the growing number of couples choosing cohabitation over marriage, and overall public concern with the disintegration of marriage, monogamous heterosexual marriage remains the cultural standard against which all other types of intimate relationships are judged. Even the campaign to legally recognize permanent homosexual relationships is, in essence, a campaign to elevate those unions to the status of monogamous heterosexual marriage.

It may be hard to imagine a society that is not structured around the practice of monogamy, but many societies allow an individual to have several husbands or wives at the same time. This type of marriage is called **polygamy**. Some anthropologists estimate that about 75% of the world's societies prefer some type of polygamy, although few members within those societies actually have the resources to afford more than one spouse (Murdock, 1957; Nanda, 1994). Even in the United States, certain groups practice polygamy. Between 20,000 and 60,000 members of a dissident Mormon sect in Utah live in households that contain one husband and two or more wives (T. McCarthy, 2001). Although these marriages are technically illegal—as a condition of statehood Utah outlawed polygamy in 1896—few polygamists are ever prosecuted. In fact, 2001 marked the first time in 50 years that a person was convicted on polygamy charges. However, this case shouldn't be taken as an indicator that Utah is cracking down on polygamy. It involved a man—with five wives and 25 children—who decided to discuss his polygamous marriage openly on national talk shows, violating an unwritten rule that such arrangements would be quietly tolerated if the participants didn't speak publicly about them.

Societies differ in other taken-for-granted facets of family life. Take living arrangements, for example. In U.S. society, families tend to follow rules of **neolocal residence**—that is, young married couples are expected to establish their own households and separate from their respective families, when financially possible. However, only about 5% of the world's societies are neolocal (Murdock, 1957; Nanda, 1994). In most places married couples are expected to live with or near either the husband's relatives (called "patrilocal" residence) or the wife's relatives (called "matrilocal" residence).

Even the belief that members of a particular nuclear family ought to live together is not found everywhere. Among the Kipsigis of Kenya, for instance, the mother and children live in one house and the father lives in another. The Kipsigis are polygamous, so a man might have several homes for his several wives at one time (W. N. Stephens, 1963). Among the Thonga of southern Africa, children live with their grandmothers once they stop breastfeeding. They remain there for several years and are then returned to their parents. On the traditional Israeli kibbutz, or commune, children are raised not by their parents but in an "infants' house," where they are cared for by a trained nurse (Nanda, 1994).

Child-rearing philosophies vary cross-culturally too. Most people in the United States believe that young children are inherently helpless and dependent. They feel that if parents attend to the child's drives and desires with consistency, warmth, and affection, that child will learn to trust the parents, adopt their values, develop a sturdy self-concept, and turn out to be a well-rounded, normal individual. In contrast, in the highlands of Guatemala, parents believe that their child's personality is determined by the date of birth. The parents are almost entirely uninvolved in the child's life, standing aside so he or she can grow as nature intended. In many societies—Nigeria, Russia, Haiti, the Dominican Republic, and Mexico, to name a few—most parents think that the best way to teach children to be respectful and studious is to beat them. In contrast, most American child development experts believe that physical punishment can deaden the child's spirit and lead to violence later in life (Dugger, 1996). Despite these dramatic differences in child-rearing practices, most children in all these cultures grow up equally well adapted to their societies.

The U.S. Definition of Family

In its official statistics, the U.S. Bureau of the Census distinguishes between households and families. A **household** is composed of one or more people who occupy the same housing unit. A **family** consists of "two or more persons, including the householder, who are related by birth, marriage, or adoption, and who live together as one household" (U.S. Bureau of the Census, 2005a). Not all households contain families. If we accept this narrow definition of family, then other arrangements—homosexual relationships, nonmarital cohabitation, and various forms of group living—cannot be considered families in the strict sense of the word. By that standard, over a third of U.S. households are not families (see Exhibit 7.2).

Having one's living arrangements legally recognized as family has many practical implications. Benefits such as inheritance rights, insurance coverage, eligibility to live in certain apartment complexes, spousal immigration benefits, savings from joint tax returns, the ability to make medical decisions for another person, and visitation rights

Exhibit 7.2 The Diversity of U.S. Households

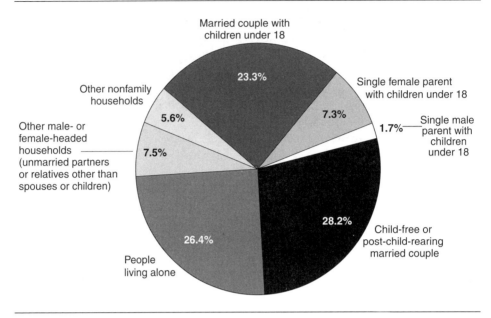

Sources: Fields, 2004; U.S. Bureau of the Census, 2004a.

in prisons and hospital intensive care units are determined by marital or family status. Members of relationships not defined as family relationships, no matter how committed, economically interdependent, or emotionally fulfilling, are not eligible. For instance, homosexual partners of victims of the September 11th attack on the Pentagon were not eligible for the same survivor benefits in the state of Virginia that heterosexual spouses were entitled to (Farmer, 2002).

Family has taken on enormous symbolic importance in American social life as well and has become a highly emotional political buzzword. Over the past two decades many politicians have defined as one of their primary goals the restoration of "traditional family values." Unfortunately, what exactly "traditional" or "family" means in the context of political debates is never made clear.

Strictly speaking, *traditional family* refers to people living together who are related by blood, marriage, or adoption. Politically, however, the term usually has more to do with family authority, parenting and marital commitment, and sexual expression (Hunter, 1991). Conservative critics deplore not only the greater visibility of cohabiting and homosexual couples but also the increasing numbers of single and working mothers, declining birth rates, and high rates of divorce. Despite all the political rhetoric, however, some women will continue to raise children alone, some couples will not have children, wives and mothers will continue to work outside the home, sex will never be confined to marriage, and gay men and lesbians will not all return to the closet.

(Text continues on page 227)

"Family Friendly"

Liz Grauerholz and Rebecca Smith

You'd be hard-pressed to find a topic that is so emotionally compelling and personally interesting to Americans as family. To politicians, espousing family's importance is an easy way to generate applause on the campaign trail, not to mention votes on Election Day. To social critics, fretting over its "breakdown" is an easy way to get the public riled up over relationships considered non-traditional. To advertisers, a reference to family is convenient shorthand for certain product features. To sociologists, it's an endless source of research topics. And to the rest of us, it has been, is now, and always will be both a valued cultural symbol and a vital lived experience. Few words carry as much cultural weight in the English language as "family." For all its political, cultural, economic, academic, and personal importance, however, "family" is a term that is not easily and quickly defined.

When most people think of the word "family," the image they have is bound to be a rather traditional one: two parents and their offspring.

Of course, as you know, the predominant cultural image of family is a bit of an illusion. Not all families look like the one on the previous page.

Many households consist of childless couples, single people (with or without children), or cohabitors (homosexual and heterosexual).

Yet the interface between society and family still seems to presuppose a traditional definition. Consider, for instance, the accommodations that social institutions make to families, often referred to collectively as "family friendly" products, services, or policies. What does it mean to call something "family friendly"?

Wholesomeness is an important part of the definition. A web site called "Family Friendly Sites" awards other web sites a "family friendly" emblem if the site

- Contains no adult-themed or sexually explicit text, images, or photographs
- Does not accept advertising for alcohol, tobacco, gambling, or pornography
- Does not promote hate, violence or discrimination in any way
- Does not promote any illegal substances or activities

❖ At a "family theme park" like Disneyland, for instance, you'll find no bars, strip clubs, or gambling halls.

"Family friendly" also implies something about size: large enough to accommodate children. You can bet that a vehicle advertised as a "family car" is one that has at least four doors, perhaps built-in child safety seats, and maybe even a mobile entertainment system. These features are obviously designed to appeal to drivers with children. "Family-size" food packaging indicates quantities for more than two people. Houses with "family rooms" are especially appealing to families with children.

"Family friendly" often means that special accommodations have been made for children's needs or capabilities. Family-friendly workplace policies, for instance, are meant to cater to the needs of parents, not the needs of non-parents or single people. In 2002, an assemblyman in the New Jersey State Legislature introduced a bill that would require all state park and forest facilities to provide a "family" bathroom for parents and children to use simultaneously. No such bathrooms were mandated for wives and husbands to use simultaneously, though they too are members of a family.

Some may argue that "family friendly" should not automatically be equated with "kid friendly"—that people without children also have the need to nurture intimate relationships. Few would argue, however, with the marketability of products and services designed specifically to accommodate children's capabilities.

Likewise, "family restaurants" cater to children's tastes. They're likely to feature simple, sturdy, easy-to-clean furnishings and standard, non-threatening food like hamburgers and macaroni and cheese.

❖ Parks and attractions designed to appeal to children allow plenty of hands-on activity and don't mind a little mess.

Interestingly, even though our culture likes to think of itself as "family-friendly"—that is, child friendly—in many ways it is not.

❖ In some cities, mothers who breastfeed in public have been arrested for indecent exposure.

❖ And in an effort to keep education costs and property taxes down, some cities are discouraging families with children from moving there. One New Jersey suburb enacted an ordinance limiting the size of new housing units to two bedrooms. In Illinois, a town imposed rules on new developments that prohibit sales to people under the age of 55 (Mansnerus, 2003).

Few people in this society want to ban children from public spaces altogether. But are there places where children really shouldn't be welcomed, such as elegant restaurants, workplaces, construction sites, hospital emergency rooms, college parties and classrooms?

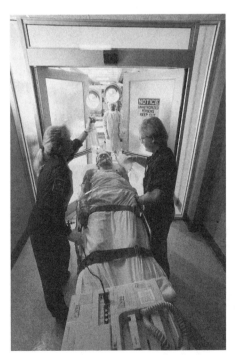

Family and Social Structure

All of us have experience with families of one form or another, so it's very tempting to look at this topic in individualistic, personal terms. However, the sociological imagination encourages us to think about how social forces affect this aspect of our private lives. As you will see, a focus on the influence of social structure—social institutions and sources of social inequality, such as gender, race, and class—can help us understand some of the dilemmas facing contemporary families.

How Other Institutions Influence Family

As a social institution, family is connected to other institutions in important ways. Consider, for instance, the effect that the wars in Iraq and Afghanistan have had on families. For as long as there have been wars, military families have been disrupted when one parent, almost always the father, either shipped out to sea or was deployed in another part of the world. But the structure of American families had changed in many ways by the time the current war began. According to the Pentagon, the number of single mothers and fathers in the military nearly doubled between the Gulf War in 1991 (47,685 single parents) and the Iraq War that began in 2003 (almost 90,000 single parents) (cited in Piore, 2003). However, the military as an institution has no special programs in place to assist single parents when they are deployed. Raising a child in the military has always been hard, but being a single parent raises special challenges and difficult choices, not the least of which is what to do with the children while the parent is gone.

The legal, political, religious, and economic forces that shape society are perhaps the institutions that most influence the identities and actions of individuals within family relationships. Keep in mind that individuals within families can act to influence society as well.

The Influence of Law and Politics

The relationship between the family and the law is obvious. Marriage, for instance, is a legal contract that determines legal rights and responsibilities. In the United States, each state legislature determines the age at which two people can marry, the health requirements, the length of the waiting period required before marriage, rules determining inheritance, and the division of property in case of divorce (Baca-Zinn & Eitzen, 1996).

In the case of homosexual unions, the law's power to either forbid or grant family rights and privileges is especially obvious. In some countries, gays and lesbians can have their relationships legally ratified. Belgium, Spain, and the Netherlands allow gay couples to legally marry, as do several provinces in Canada. France, Denmark, Portugal, and Germany allow same-sex couples to enter "civil unions" or "registered partnerships," which grant them many of the legal and economic benefits and responsibilities of heterosexual marriage (Lyall, 2004).

The matter is far from resolved in the United States, however. In 2004, Massachusetts became the only state to allow same-sex couples who are state residents to legally marry, though that decision continues to be challenged. A court ruling in Washington state that same year affirmed the constitutional rights of gay couples to marry. Vermont legalized civil unions (but not marriage) for same-sex couples in 2000 and Connecticut followed suit in 2005. Similar statutes have been on the books for years in numerous cities around the country, often extending full medical, dental, and life insurance benefits to the "domestic partners" of city employees. In addition, according to the Human Rights Campaign, a national advocacy group, over 8,000 employers—and 215 Fortune 500 companies—provide domestic partner benefits for their gay and lesbian workers (cited in Joyce, 2005).

But most states—42 at last count—have moved in the opposite direction, making their refusal to recognize such marriages explicit either by enacting statutes that define marriage as a union of a man and a woman or by including bans against same-sex marriage in their state constitutions (National Conference of State Legislatures, 2005). Courts in California, New York, New Mexico, and Oregon have nullified same-sex marriages that had been permitted by some cities (Mehren, 2005). Some states have gone even further. In 2005, the Michigan state legislature ruled that its law defining marriage as a relationship between one man and one woman meant that gay and lesbian state workers are not entitled to health benefits for their partners (Lyman, 2005). At the federal level, the 1996 Defense of Marriage Act formally reaffirms the definition of marriage as the union of one man and one woman; authorizes all states to refuse to accept same-sex marriages from other states if they ever become legal; and denies federal pension, health, and other benefits to same-sex couples.

State and federal laws usually reflect public opinion, and public opinion on legalizing same-sex marriage is indeed mixed. While acceptance of gays and lesbians in the military, in the workplace, as elementary school teachers, and as politicians has grown over the past several decades, support of laws allowing gay marriage is tepid at best. A nationwide survey found that the majority of Americans (about 61%) were opposed to a law that would allow homosexuals to marry (Grossman, 2003). Even people who consider themselves supportive of gay rights in general are ambivalent about legalizing gay marriage (Seelye & Elder, 2003).

Incidentally, heterosexual cohabitors have also faced difficulty achieving cultural recognition. Between 1990 and 2003, the number of heterosexual cohabiting couples increased from 3.2 million to 4.6 million, comprising about 5% of all U.S. households (Fields, 2004). But although public attitudes have grown more tolerant of unmarried adults living together, the law sometimes has been slower to adjust. Massachusetts did repeal a 1784 law banning "lewdly and lasciviously associating and cohabiting without the benefit of marriage"—but not until 1987 (Yardley, 2000). New Mexico and Arizona didn't repeal their "unlawful cohabitation" laws until 2001.

Politics and family are interconnected in other ways, too. Many of today's most pressing political issues—health insurance, Social Security, quality education, guaranteed parental leave in the workplace, teen pregnancy, the aging population, abortion, homelessness, poverty—are fundamentally family problems. For example, abortion didn't become a significant political issue until the late 1960s, when it became part of the larger movement for women's rights and reproductive freedom. Later the right-to-life movement framed the abortion debate not only as a moral and political issue but also as a symbolic crusade to define (or redefine) the role of motherhood and family within the larger society (Luker, 1984).

The Influence of Religion

You saw in Chapter 5 that religion is an important feature of everyday American life and a powerful agent of socialization. Religion can also play a role in virtually every stage of family life: dating, marriage, sexuality, childbearing decisions, parenthood, child discipline, responses to illness and death, household division of labor, and so on. One of the key aspects of religion is that it constrains people's behavior or at the very least encourages them to act in certain ways. This normative aspect of religion has important consequences for people's family experiences. For instance, all the major religions in the United States are strong supporters of marriage and childbearing. In recent years, more churches have begun requiring engaged couples to participate in premarital counseling and education programs before the wedding. In addition, religions almost universally prohibit sexual relations outside marriage. Some religions prohibit divorce or don't permit remarriage after divorce. Some oppose the use of contraceptives and encourage large families. In 2003, the Roman Catholic Pope publicly urged women worldwide to pay heed to what he called their "lofty vocation" as wives and mothers ("Pope Exalts Women," 2003). In highly religious families, a sacred text such as the Bible, the Koran, or the Talmud may serve not only as a source of faith but as a literal guidebook for every aspect of family life.

Religion's influence on family life needn't be so direct, however. For example, among Muslims and members of certain Christian denominations, families are expected to tithe, or donate, a certain amount of their income (10%, in most cases) to support their religious establishment. Although it is a charitable thing to do, tithing can create problems for families that are already financially strapped.

Most evidence suggests that religious involvement has a positive effect, especially for families raising children, such as higher levels of marital commitment (Larson & Goltz, 1989) and more positive parent-child relationships (Pearce & Axinn, 1998). "Spiritual wellness" is often cited as one of the most important qualities of family well-being (Stinnett & DeFrain, 1985).

However, in some situations the link between religious beliefs and actual family behavior may not be as strong as we might think. Even in highly religious families, the practical demands of modern life make it difficult to always subscribe to religious teachings. For instance, although fundamentalist Christians believe wives should stay at home and submit to the authority of their husbands, many fundamentalist women do work outside the home and exert powerful influence over family decisions (Ammerman, 1987). Moreover, although many religions stress the value of keeping families intact, increased religious involvement does not do much to strengthen troubled marriages (Booth, Johnson, Branaman, & Sica, 1995). Increased religious involvement may slightly decrease thoughts about divorce, but it doesn't necessarily enhance marital happiness or stop spouses from fighting.

The Influence of Economics

The world of economics affects virtually every aspect of family life, from the amount of money coming into the household to the day-to-day management of finances and major purchasing decisions. Money matters are closely tied to feelings of satisfaction within family relationships. When couples are disappointed with how much money they have or how it is spent, they find all aspects of their relationships less satisfying (Blumstein & Schwartz, 1983).

Such financial problems are not just private troubles. Rather, they are directly linked to larger economic patterns. Major alterations in an economy almost always have a profound impact on the family. For instance, per capita income in the United States improved a bit throughout the 1990s, but stagnated in the early and mid-2000s (U.S. Bureau of the Census, 2004a). As a consequence, many adults in the United States are having difficulty supporting a family. It now costs two-parent, middle-class families over $165,000 to raise a child to the age of 17, up from $25,230 in 1970 (U.S. Department of Agriculture, 2001).

At the global level, the competitive pressures of the international marketplace have forced many businesses and industries to make greater use of so-called disposable workers—those who work part time or on temporary contract. These jobs offer no benefits and no security and therefore make family life less stable. Other companies have reduced their costs by cutting salaries, laying off workers, or encouraging early retirement. Some businesses are relocating either to other countries or to other parts of the United States where they can pay lower wages (see Chapter 10 for a more detailed discussion). Relaxed rules on foreign investment and export duties have made it easy for American companies to open low-wage assembly plants abroad. For instance, over 11,500 U.S.-owned and -operated factories are located in Mexico along the 2,100-mile border with the United States (Vogeler, 2003). The companies obviously benefit, the impoverished workers in Mexico may benefit, but displaced U.S. workers and their families do not.

Financial uncertainty makes a stable family life very difficult. Sustaining a supportive, nurturing family environment is nearly impossible without adequate income or health care. When economic foundations are weak, the emotional bonds that tie a family together can be stretched to the breaking point.

❖ Micro-Macro Connection
Dual-Earner Parents

The financial strains of living in the 21st century have made it difficult for young couples to survive on only one income. Today, in 78% of married-couple families with children, both parents work outside the home for pay (National Partnership for Women & Families, 2005). That figure is up from 32% in 1976. By 2002, the percentage of households that consisted of a married couple dependent on a sole male breadwinner had dropped to about 20%, from a high of almost 60% in 1950 (Gerson, 1993; U.S. Bureau of the Census, 2003). Yet the workplace still tends to be built around the outdated belief that only one parent (typically the father) should be working. Such beliefs have created serious burdens for working parents.

Some experts feel that the single most important step society could take to help dual-earner families would be to help them deal with child care demands. The Family and Medical Leave Act (FMLA), signed into law by President Clinton in 1993, was a step in that direction: It guarantees some workers up to 12 weeks of unpaid sick leave per year for the birth or adoption of a child or to care for a sick child, parent, or spouse. However, it has some important qualifications that seriously limit its usefulness to the working population:

♦ The law covers only workers who have been employed continuously for at least one year and who have worked a total of at least 1,250 hours (or about 25 hours a week). As a result, temporary and part-time workers are not eligible.

♦ The law exempts companies with fewer than 50 workers.

♦ The law allows an employer to deny leave to a "key" employee—that is, one who is in the highest-paid 10% of its workforce—if allowing that person to take the leave would create "substantial and grievous injury" to the business's operations.

According to one survey, 88% of working women and 85% of working men indicated that expanding family and medical leave to make it more useful is an important legislative priority (AFL-CIO, 2002).

Currently, only 58% of American workers are covered by FMLA. In 2000, 16.5% of eligible and covered employees actually took leave (U.S. Department of Labor, 2001). Many of the eligible employees who don't take leave are parents who need the time off but don't take it because they can't afford to go without a paycheck. According to one survey, of those eligible workers who needed leave but didn't take it, 78% cited the inability to afford unpaid leave as the reason. In fact, 9% of employees who take unpaid leave under FMLA end up going on public assistance to make up for the lost wages (National Partnership for Women and Families, 2005).

In addition, relatively few employers go beyond the minimum unpaid leave policies mandated by FMLA. For instance, just 12% of American companies offer *paid* maternity leave to their employees. And only one state, California, guarantees workers paid family leave (although for no more than six weeks) for private sector employees (National Partnership for Women and Families, 2005).

Although FMLA represents an improvement over past conditions, the United States still lags behind other countries in terms of its support for dual-earner families. According to a Harvard University study of 168 countries, 163 guarantee paid leave to women in connection to childbirth and 45 guarantee paid paternity leave. Only Lesotho, Papua New Guinea, Swaziland, Australia, and the United States offer no paid family leave (cited in National Partnership for Women and Families, 2005). Consider the policies of a few other industrialized nations (Bell-Rowbotham & Lero, 2001):

♦ In France, mothers are provided 16 weeks off work at 84% pay for the first and second children, and 24 weeks off at the same rate of pay for the third and subsequent children. They also receive up to 3 years of unpaid leave with job protection.

♦ In Norway, parents can take 42 weeks of leave at 100% pay or 52 weeks at 80%. Fathers are entitled to 4 weeks of this leave. Parents can also combine part-time work and partial parental benefits. For example, one parent could take full leave at 100% pay for 42 weeks and the other could combine 80% work and 20% leave for nearly 2 years.

♦ In the United Kingdom, parents receive 18 weeks of maternity leave at 90% of their salary and 12 weeks at a flat rate. They can also take up to 40 weeks of unpaid family leave.

If we are truly concerned about preserving families, we need to improve the FMLA to reduce the conflict between work life and family life.

How Social Diversity Influences Family

We cannot talk about structural influences on family life without discussing the role of gender, class, and race. Gender is especially influential, explaining a variety of phenomena in intimate relationships, such as the way people talk to one another, how they express themselves sexually, how they communicate and deal with conflict, and what they feel their responsibilities are. Culturally defined gender expectations in families are certainly changing. But men and women are still likely to enter relationships with vastly different prospects, desires, and goals.

As you learned in Chapter 5, traditional gender role socialization encourages women to be sensitive, express affection, and reveal weakness, whereas men are taught to be competitive, strong, and emotionally inexpressive. These stereotypes have some basis in fact. Research has consistently shown that women have more close friends than men and are more romantic in their intimate relationships (Perlman & Fehr, 1987). Furthermore, women have been shown to be more concerned about, attentive to, and aware of the dynamics of their relationships than men are (see, for example, Fincham & Bradbury, 1987; Rusbult, Zembrodt, & Iwaniszek, 1986). Women even think more and talk more about their relationships than men do (Acitelli, 1988; Holtzworth-Munroe & Jacobson, 1985).

Ironically, such attentiveness and concern do not necessarily mean that women get more satisfaction out of family relationships than men do. In fact, the opposite may be true. According to one sociologist, every marriage actually contains two marriages: "his" and "hers"—and "his" seems to be the better deal (Bernard, 1972). Both married men and married women live longer and healthier lives than their single counterparts, but husbands typically enjoy greater health benefits—they get sick less often and have fewer emotional problems (Gove, Style, & Hughes, 1990; Ross, Mirowsky, & Goldstein, 1990; Waite & Gallagher, 2000). In contrast, three times as many married women as single women show signs of anxiety, depression, and emotional distress (Carr, 1988).

The reason for these differences lies in the relationship between cultural gender expectations and family demands. Because of the continued pressures of gender-typed family responsibilities, married women are more likely than married men to experience the stresses associated with parenthood and homemaking. Men have historically been able to feel they are fulfilling their family obligations by simply being financial providers. Most people still interpret a man's long hours on the job as an understandable sacrifice for his family's sake. Fathers rarely spend as much time worrying about the effect their work will have on their children as mothers do.

In contrast, even in the relatively "liberated" United States, women's employment outside the home is usually perceived as optional or, more seriously, as potentially damaging to the family. Some people think that women with children simply shouldn't work, even at part-time jobs, if they can afford to stay at home. In 1998 Deborah Eappen, a doctor whose baby son died while under the care of a British nanny, was severely criticized in the newspapers and on radio talk shows because she allegedly put her career before her family (she worked three days a week). Stories such as these force many working women to agonize over whether their financial well-being and personal independence are being purchased at the cost of their families.

Social class also has a substantial influence on family life. You saw in Chapter 5 that social class can determine the lessons that parents instill in their children. Social class affects families in other ways as well. All families, no matter what their class standing, must face the same issues: work, leisure, child rearing, and interpersonal relations (L. Rubin, 1994). But beneath the similarities we see dramatic differences in how these issues are handled. Because of heightened concern over class boundaries, ancestry, and maintenance of prestige, upper-class parents exert much more control over the dating behaviors of their children than lower-class parents do (Domhoff, 1983; M. K. Whyte, 1990). Upper-class families are also better able to use their wealth and resources in coping with some of the demands of family life. Finding adequate child care arrangements will probably not pose much of a dilemma to parents who can afford a full-time, live-in nanny. The picture for middle-class families, though, can be quite different, especially when it intersects with race.

❖
Mary Pattillo-McCoy
Privilege and Peril in Middle-Class Black Families

Concerned about how the combination of race and social class affects family life, sociologist Mary Pattillo-McCoy (1999) spent three and a half years in a middle-class black Chicago neighborhood she called "Groveland." She interviewed residents of all ages, including children. The only people she wasn't able to interview were young adults who had gone off to college. As a black, middle-class woman herself, Pattillo-McCoy quickly developed an affinity with the people she studied. She even had friends in common with some of her interviewees.

In many respects, the Groveland families were just like families in any other middle-class neighborhood. Parents saw their children's development into self-sufficient adults as their primary family goal. And they had the financial and social resources to help achieve this goal. Most of them had the wherewithal to pay for private schools, sports equipment, dance lessons, and other enriching activities for their children. Groveland children had access to technology and other resources that their counterparts in poor black neighborhoods did not.

Pattillo-McCoy also found that the Groveland middle-class families had to deal with markedly different problems than their white counterparts. For one thing, she found that the neighborhoods where many urban, middle-class African Americans live are likely to be close to poor neighborhoods. In contrast, white middle-class neighborhoods are typically geographically separated from poor areas. In Chicago, for example, 79% of Blacks are likely to live within a few blocks of a neighborhood where at least one third of the residents are poor; only 36% of white, middle-class Chicago dwellers live so close to a poor neighborhood (Pattillo-McCoy, 1999).

Thus Groveland parents had to spend a lot of time trying to protect their children from the negative influences found in the adjacent poor, inner-city areas. In doing so, they faced some challenges other middle-class parents were unlikely to face:

> Groveland parents . . . set limits on where their children can travel. They choose activities—church youth groups, magnet schools or accelerated programs in the local school, and the Boy Scouts and Girl Scouts—to increase the likelihood that their children will learn positive values and associate with youth from similar families. Still, many parents are working long hours to maintain their middle-class incomes. They cannot be with their children at all times. On their way to the grocery store or to school or to music lessons, Groveland's youth pass other young people whose parents are not as strict, who stay outside later, who have joined the local gang, or who earn enough money being a lookout at a drug house to buy new gym shoes. They also meet these peers in school and at the park. . . . For some teenagers, the fast life looks much more exciting than what their parents have to offer them, and they are drawn to it. The simple fact of living in a neighborhood where not all families have sufficient resources to direct their children away from deviance makes it difficult for parents to ensure positive outcomes for their children and their neighborhood. (Pattillo-McCoy, 1999, pp. 211–212)

Pattillo-McCoy found that, in many other respects as well, black middle-class families face social realities that are quite different from those faced by white middle-class families. Still, her research also shows that most families within a particular social class face many of the same opportunities and barriers.

Family Dilemmas

Given all the pressures on families from the society around them, it should be no surprise that some families experience serious problems. Those problems include divorce and its aftereffects and family violence.

Divorce

Although divorce is more common and more acceptable in some places than in others, virtually all societies have provisions—legal, communal, or religious—for dissolving marriages (McKenry & Price, 1995). In Chile, for example, divorce wasn't legal until 2005. Up to that point, many unhappy couples had opted for civil annulments, which required that they persuade a court that the marriage had not met legal requirements. Often they'd leave themselves legal loopholes on their wedding days so that if the relationship soured some time in the future they could end it. For instance, witnesses to a wedding would sometimes deliberately misspell their names or give an incorrect address. Or a couple might "illegally" marry in a town in which neither lived (Rohter, 2005).

Worldwide, divorce rates tend to be associated with socioeconomic development. The developing countries of Latin America (for example, Ecuador, Nicaragua, and Panama) and Asia (for example, Malaysia, Mongolia, and Sri Lanka) have substantially lower divorce rates than the developed countries of Western Europe and North America (Nugman, 2002). Furthermore, practically every industrialized country in the world experienced an increase in divorces between 1950 and 1990 (W. J. Goode, 1993), although their divorce rates vary quite a bit, as Exhibit 7.3 shows. In the last decade, for example, South Korea's divorce rate has grown by 250% (Onishi, 2003).

Even in societies that we would consider modern and developed, powerful religious forces can suppress divorce rates. For instance, in 1995 the Irish government began a campaign against the Catholic Church over the country's constitutional ban on divorce. The government estimated that at least 80,000 people were locked in

Exhibit 7.3   Divorce Rates in Selected Developed Countries

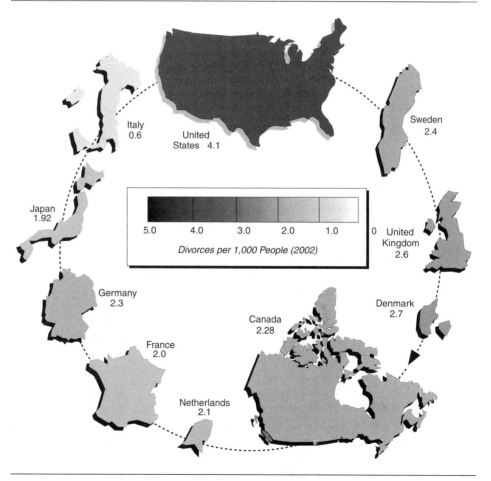

Source: Nugman, 2002.

broken marriages and that they deserved the right to end them and remarry. The Catholic bishops launched a massive advertising counterattack, arguing that even unhappily married people have an obligation to keep their marriages intact to provide a good example for society. The referendum passed by a minuscule margin, and in 1997, for the first time, people in Ireland had the right to legally divorce.

Although the dissolution of marriage is virtually universal, no society places a positive value on divorce. In fact, in most societies people who divorce are somehow penalized, either through formal controls such as fines, prohibitions against remarriage, excommunication, and forced alimony and child support or through informal means such as censure, gossip, and stigmatization.

The Normalization of Divorce

Fifty years ago, divorce was a topic people talked about in whispers if they talked about it at all. Today, of course, things are quite different. You'd be hard-pressed to find an 8-year-old who doesn't know what the word *divorce* means or who hasn't witnessed the end of a marriage, either that of her or his parents or of someone close. Divorce has become a part of everyday life. It's in our movies, television shows, and novels. The children's sections of bookstores stock picture books showing divorcing dinosaurs or Muppet babies worrying about the possibility of their parents divorcing. Hallmark has an entire line of greeting cards for parents whose children live elsewhere.

In an average year, there are over 1.2 million divorces in the United States, a rate of almost 20 divorces per 1,000 existing marriages (U.S. Bureau of the Census, 2004a). Roughly one in five American adults has ever divorced (Kreider, 2005). This rate has stabilized and even gone down a bit over the past few years, but it is still quite high, considering that the rate was about 14 divorces per 1,000 marriages in 1970 and 4 per 1,000 in 1900 (refer back to Exhibit 7.1). Experts project that close to one out of every two marriages that begins in a given year will eventually end in divorce (T. C. Martin & Bumpass, 1989). Such figures terrify people who are about to enter a "lifetime" relationship and distress those already married who want some sense of permanence (Blumstein & Schwartz, 1983).

Despite the traditional "family values" rhetoric we hear so much about these days, divorce tends to be unaffected by religiosity or political conservatism. For instance, several studies have found that born-again Christians are just as likely as anyone else to divorce (cited in Belluck, 2004). In addition, divorce rates are lowest in the so-called liberal states of the Northeast and upper Midwest and are highest in the conservative, heavily religious states of the South, such as Mississippi, Arkansas, Alabama, and Kentucky. Some sociologists argue that other factors more commonly found in these states—namely a younger age at marriage, less education, and lower socioeconomic status—render religiosity irrelevant. No matter how religious they are, young people who drop out of school and marry quickly not only lack emotional maturity but are highly susceptible to the economic strains that can create insurmountable problems in marriage.

At a cultural level, the causes of high divorce rates in Western societies include such things as the weakening of the family's traditional economic bonds, and the stress of shifting gender roles (Popenoe, 1993). One particularly influential factor has been a cultural change in the perception of marriage. Marriage has become a voluntary contract system that can be ended at the discretion of either spouse. In the past, when economic needs—not to mention such constraints as parental expectations or religious norms—held couples together, people "made do" with loveless, unsatisfying marriages because they had to. But when these constraints do not exist, people are less willing to make do (Coontz, 2005). Women's increasing earning power and decreasing economic dependence on men have made it easier to end an unsatisfying marriage.

In addition, people's overall attitudes toward divorce have become more accepting over the past several decades (Thornton, 1989). In the 1960s, a divorced politician didn't stand a chance of being elected in the United States. Today many of our most influential lawmakers are divorced. In the 1980s, Ronald Reagan's divorce and remarriage didn't prevent him from being elected—twice. In the 2004 national election, people barely mentioned presidential candidate John Kerry's divorce and remarriage. Most people now recognize that a divorce may be preferable to an unhappy marriage. In short, divorce is as much a part of U.S. family life as, well, marriage.

Changing perceptions of marriage and changing cultural attitudes toward divorce are typically accompanied by other structural changes. In the United States, modifications of existing divorce laws in the past two decades have made it easier for people to end an unsatisfying marriage. In the past, evidence of wrongdoing—adultery, desertion, abuse, and so forth—was required for courts to grant a divorce. But in the past 25 years every state has adopted a form of no-fault divorce. No-fault laws have eliminated the requirement that one partner be found guilty of some transgression. Instead, marriages are simply declared unworkable and are terminated. Today, for fees ranging from $50 to $300—a small fraction of what most lawyers would charge—couples can download the appropriate forms and get online help filling them out. As one divorcing man put it, "I filled out the forms in the course of a night—it took three hours—and saved $2,000" (quoted in Crary, 2003, p. A6).

Many critics argue that these laws and innovations have made divorce too easy and too quick. Indeed, there seems to a growing desire in some areas of the country to return to more restrictive divorce laws. One survey found that 55% of U.S. citizens favor making it harder to leave a marriage when one partner wants to maintain it (cited in Leland, 1996). Some states—Indiana, New Hampshire, Colorado, and Georgia, to name a few—have passed laws that impose mandatory waiting periods for couples contemplating divorce. Other states have toyed with the idea of providing financial incentives—in the form of discounted marriage licenses—for couples who participate in premarital counseling. In 1997, the Louisiana State Legislature passed a measure forcing engaged couples to choose between a standard marriage contract, which permits no-fault divorce, and a "covenant marriage," which could be dissolved only by a mutually agreed-on two-year separation or proof of fault, chiefly adultery, abandonment, or abuse (Loe, 1997). Arizona followed suit in 1998 as did Arkansas in 2001. Critics of such measures note that instead of having a positive impact on family life, the result might be an increase in contentious, expensive, potentially child-harming divorces and in unhappy, perhaps even dangerous marriages.

Children, Divorce, and Single Parenting

Over a million U.S. children each year see their parents divorce (U.S. Bureau of the Census, 2000). In 1960, 9% of children under 18 lived with a single parent; by 2002, the figure had increased to 28% (Fields, 2003). If the divorce rate remains high and out-of-wedlock birth continues its upward trend—34% of all births in the United States are to unmarried women (U.S. Bureau of the Census, 2004a)—perhaps as many as 60% of U.S. children born in the early 2000s will live in a single-parent family before the age of 16 (Furstenberg & Cherlin, 1991). Moreover, the odds of growing up in a single-parent family are higher for some racial groups than others (see Exhibit 7.4).

Although divorce can be traumatic for adults, most recover after a period of years. Children, however, have a more difficult time adjusting. For them, divorce may set a series of potentially disruptive changes in motion. They may have to move to a new home in a new neighborhood, make new friends, and go to a new school. Because the

Exhibit 7.4   Family Composition and Race

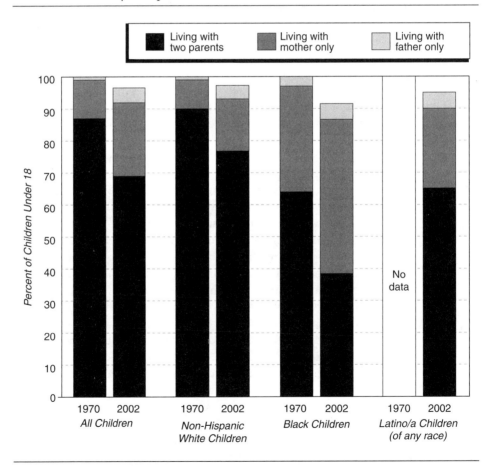

Source: U.S. Bureau of the Census, 2003, Table 3C.

overwhelming majority of children of divorce live with their mothers, they may also experience a decline in their standard of living. The earning capacity of women is lower than that of men to begin with. Furthermore, noncustodial fathers do not always pay child support. In about 63% of divorces where mothers have physical custody, fathers are required to pay child support. Of these, 45% pay the full amount, 29% pay a partial amount, and 25% pay nothing (U.S. Bureau of the Census, 2004a). About half of divorced mothers with custody of children therefore don't receive any financial assistance at all. Award rates are especially low for African American and Latina women, who suffer from higher rates of poverty to begin with (Klawitter, 1994).

The relationship that children have with their noncustodial parent also tends to deteriorate over time. One national study found that half of U.S. children whose parents were divorced and who were living with their mothers hadn't seen their fathers in the last year, and only one out of six had regular, weekly contact with their noncustodial father. Children were most likely to see their fathers immediately after the separation. But after several years, contact dropped off sharply (Furstenberg & Nord, 1985). Another study found that 75% of noncustodial fathers never attend their child's school events, 85% never help them with their homework, and 65% never take their children on vacations (Teachman, 1991). Fewer than one in five noncustodial fathers have significant influence over their children's health care, education, religion, or other matters important to their welfare (Arendell, 1995).

What are the long-term effects of divorce on children? A substantial body of research shows that regardless of race or education of parents, children raised in single-parent homes have more problems at every stage of life than children from two-parent families. An extensive review of studies published during the 1990s found that children from divorced families fare worse in terms of academic success, psychological adjustment, self-concept, social competence, and long-term health than children from intact, two-parent families (Amato, 2000). In adulthood, they are at greater risk of low socioeconomic attainment, increased marital difficulties, and divorce (Diekmann & Engelhardt, 1999).

These differences are typically attributed to factors such as the absence of a father, increased strain on the custodial parent to keep the household running, and emotional stress and anger associated with the separation. However, the causes of these problems are more likely to be factors that can also be found in two-parent families: low income, poor living conditions, lack of parental supervision, and marital discord (Amato & Sobolewski, 2001; Cherlin, 1992).

Some critics argue that the standard research design in studies on the impact of divorce on children—comparing children whose parents have divorced to children in happy, intact families—is flawed. Indeed, if we compare kids from divorced families to kids from intact families whose parents are unhappily married or whose families experience a great deal of conflict, we find that the type and frequency of emotional and interpersonal problems are similar for both sets of children (Cherlin et al., 1991). In fact, children who grow up in intact families marked by frequent conflict may actually have the most problems. This research suggests that behavioral problems are caused not by the divorce itself but by exposure to conflict between the parents both before and after the divorce (Stewart, Copeland, Chester, Malley, & Barenbaum, 1997). In short, the simple fact of growing up in a single-parent family may not be as important in the development of a child as the way parents relate to each other and to the child.

Remarriage and the Reconstructed Family

About one-third of existing marriages in the United States today involve at least one partner who was previously married (Kreider, 2005). This statistic suggests that although people are quite willing to escape a bad marriage, they have not necessarily given up on the concept of marriage entirely.

Although they are fairly common, remarriages are not without their difficulties. The divorce rate for remarriages is actually slightly higher than the rate for first marriages. In the United States, 39% of remarriages end within the first 10 years, compared to 33% of first marriages (Bramlett & Mosher, 2001).

Remarriage may be more unstable than first marriages because the traditional roles, relationships, and norms of family don't apply. We have no set of institutional expectations for relationships between former and current spouses, between stepparents and stepchildren, between step- and half-siblings, and with extended kin (Ahrons & Rodgers, 1987). Laws and customs have been slow to catch up. For instance, do stepchildren have legal claims to their stepparents' property? Do incest rules apply to stepsiblings?

Remarriage is particularly difficult when children are involved. Although most stepparents build strong, durable, loving relationships with their partner's children, others face difficulties. When a new stepparent enters the former single-parent family, the entire system may be thrown out of balance. He or she may be seen as an outsider, or worse, an intruder. Stepsiblings may be asked to share bedrooms or other possessions. They may see their connection to their biological parent as giving them greater claim on that parent's affection and resources. Rules and habits change and, for a time, confusion, resentment, and hostility may be the norm. Conflict is common in all types of families, but conflict over such issues as favoritism, divided loyalties, the right to discipline, and financial responsibility is particularly likely in reconstructed families.

The high divorce rate of remarriages and the high levels of conflict within some reconstituted families are not simply an outgrowth of people's psychological inability to sustain intimate relationships, as some analysts have claimed. The fact that remarriages are not fully institutionalized is what makes them susceptible to failure. The lack of clear role definitions, the absence of established societal norms, and the increased complexity of the family structure itself increase the likelihood of tension and turmoil. Perhaps, though, as we develop standard ways of defining and coping with reconstructed families, remarriage may become more institutionalized and less problematic. Until then, remarriage will continue to create a great deal of tension and confusion.

Family Violence

Ironically, the home—that loving place that nourishes us when the outside world has sucked away our life energy—can also be one of the most violent places in a society. Worldwide, wife beating occurs in about 85% of societies. A recent study of intimate violence in developing countries found that about one third of women in Egypt and Nicaragua and close to one half of women in Peru, Colombia, and Zambia have been beaten by their spouses or partners (Kishor & Johnson, 2004). Husband beating occurs less frequently—in about 27% of societies—and occurs less often than wife beating in those societies where both are present (Levinson, 1989). In the United States, the likelihood that a man will be assaulted by someone in his own family is 20 times higher than the odds that he will be assaulted by a stranger; however, women are 200 times more likely to be assaulted by a family member than by an outsider (Straus, 1991).

Exact statistics about the prevalence of violence among intimates are difficult to collect. In the United States, domestic violence is usually concealed and private, typically occurring in seclusion, beyond the watchful eyes of relatives, neighbors, and strangers. Even with the more stringent rules for police reporting that have been instituted in the past decade or two, most incidents of domestic violence are never reported; others are dismissed as accidents. It's been estimated that only about half the cases of non lethal violence against women are reported to the police (Rennison & Welchans, 2000). Furthermore, definitions of abuse and reporting practices vary from agency to agency.

For instance, according to the U.S. Bureau of Justice Statistics (Rennison, 2003), there were close to 700,000 non-lethal violent acts committed by current spouses, former spouses, boyfriends, or girlfriends in 2001 (the last year for which such figures are available). Women accounted for 85% of the victims of these incidents. Interestingly, although the number of non-lethal acts of intimate violence dropped by over 40% between 1993 and 2001, the number of homicides has remained fairly constant (Rennison, 2003). Of all homicides involving female victims, 40% to 50% are committed by an intimate partner (Campbell, 2003).

Other studies place the prevalence rate for intimate partner violence higher. For instance, the National Violence Against Women Survey of 16,000 women and men across the country found that nearly 25% of surveyed women and 7.6% of men said they'd been raped or physically assaulted by a spouse, partner, or date at some point in their lifetimes (Tjaden & Thoennes, 2000). Within the previous 12 months, 1.5% of women and 0.9% of men reported being raped or physically assaulted. According to these estimates, about 1.5 million women and over 800,000 men are assaulted by an intimate partner annually in the United States, well above the official Bureau of Justice Statistics figures.

Although the number of cases of domestic violence in heterosexual relationships has been dropping steadily, it's been increasing in gay couples. Between 2000 and 2001, there was a 25% increase in reported incidents of intimate violence among homosexual couples (National Coalition of Anti-Violence Programs, 2002). Some experts feel this increase doesn't necessarily reflect an increase in violence but, rather, reflects increased attention to the heretofore hidden problem of gay and lesbian intimate violence.

Children are even more likely to be victims of intimate violence than adult family members. In some poverty-stricken countries, children may be consigned to unpleasant and dangerous labor, sold to buy food for the rest of the family, or even murdered in infancy. In the United States, one in seven adults claims to have been sexually abused as a child, and one in six claims to have been physically abused (cited in Coontz, 1992). There were about 900,000 substantiated cases of child maltreatment in 2002, up from 690,000 in 1990 (U.S. Bureau of the Census, 2004a). Some researchers think this figure should be closer to "several million" (D.J. English, 1998). Indeed, if we include slapping and spanking a child in our definition of child abuse, then approximately 9 out of every 10 children under the age of three in the United States have been the object of some sort of physical violence at the hands of their parents or caretakers

(Straus & Gelles, 1990). According to the U.S. Department of Health and Human Services (2004), 1,400 children died of abuse or neglect in 2002. Over three quarters of the victims were three years old or younger.

Although it would be comforting to believe that domestic violence is rare and occurs only in families that harbor a "sick" parent or spouse, it actually happens with alarming frequency and is likely to be committed by people we would otherwise consider normal. Spouse or partner abuse and child abuse—not to mention elder abuse and violence between siblings—occur in every culture, class, race, and religion. Domestic violence is not an aberration; it is a fundamental characteristic of the way we relate to one another in private, intimate settings.

Family Violence in Cultural Context

Individual-level factors such as frustration over money, stress, and alcohol and drug use are frequently cited as major causes of domestic violence. To some analysts, batterers are either psychopaths or people who are just plain prone to violence. But to fully understand domestic violence, we must take a look at some important characteristics of the society in which it occurs.

The United States is fundamentally committed to the use of violence to achieve desirable ends (Straus, 1977). For many people violence is considered the appropriate means by which to resolve certain problems. Furthermore, violence pervades the culture. It is in our streets, our schools, our movies, our television shows, our toy stores, our spectator sports, and our government. It's even in our everyday language: We *assault* problems, *conquer* fears, *beat* others to the punch, *pound* home ideas, and *shoot down* opinions (Ewing, 1992). How many times have you heard a parent "playfully" warn a misbehaving child that he or she is "cruising for a bruising?"

In addition to the pervasiveness of violence in the culture, families have several characteristics that increase the probability of conflict. For instance, we spend a lot of time with family members and interact with them across a wide range of situations. The intimacy of these interactions is intense. Emotions run deep. The anger we may feel toward a stranger or an acquaintance never approaches the intensity of the anger we feel toward a spouse—or for that matter toward a sibling or a child.

Moreover, we also know more about family members than we know about other people in our lives. We know their likes and dislikes, their fears, and their desires. And they know these things about us too. If someone in your family insults you, you know immediately what you can say to get even. Spouses usually know the "buttons" they can push to hurt or infuriate each other. Arguments can escalate into violence when one partner focuses on the other's vulnerabilities and insecurities.

Finally, family life contains endless sources of stress. For one thing, we expect a lot from our families: emotional and financial support, warmth, comfort, and intimacy. When these expectations aren't fulfilled, stress levels escalate. Stressful life circumstances also contribute (Gelles & Straus, 1988). The birth and raising of a child, financial problems, employment transitions (voluntary or involuntary), illness, old age, death, and so on are all events that potentially increase stress. Indeed, a pregnant or recently pregnant woman is more likely to be the victim of a homicide than to die of any other cause (Horon & Cheng, 2001).

We must also look at the broader conceptions of gender that exist within a society. Male dominance in human societies has a long and rather infamous history. Roman law, for instance, justified a husband's killing his wife for reasons such as adultery, wine drinking, and other so-called inappropriate behaviors (Steinmetz, Clavan, & Stein, 1990). Most societies in the world remain dominated by and built around the interests of men. Men occupy the high-status positions, make important decisions and exercise political power, tend to dominate interpersonal relationships, and occupy the roles society defines as most valuable (Frieze, Parsons, Johnson, Ruble, & Zellman, 1978).

Male dominance has sometimes led to a double standard of acceptable violence. In 1994, a Maryland man who killed his wife with a hunting rifle four hours after finding her in bed with another man pleaded guilty to voluntary manslaughter and was sentenced to 18 months in prison. The sentence was half as long as the prosecution recommended. The judge in the case said afterward that he wished he didn't have to send the man to prison at all. A day after this case, another judge handed down a three-year sentence to a woman who pleaded guilty to voluntary manslaughter for killing her husband after 11 years of abuse. Her sentence was three times longer than what the prosecutors in that case had sought (Lewin, 1994).

Men who beat their partners are not necessarily psychotic, deranged, "sick" individuals. Rather, they are often men who believe that male dominance is their birthright. Such men are actually living up to cultural prescriptions that are cherished in many societies—aggressiveness, male dominance, and female subordination (Dobash & Dobash, 1979). We have a deeply entrenched tendency to perceive domestic violence as "normal" violence, as something that, though not necessarily desirable, is not surprising or unexpected either. Consequently, much of the research in this area has focused on the victims rather than on the perpetrators.

Personal and Institutional Responses to Abuse

One question that has captured the attention of many marriage and family researchers is, Why do women stay in abusive relationships in societies that have made divorce relatively simple? During the 1960s, the *masochism thesis*—that is, that women like being humiliated and hurt—was the predominant reason offered by psychiatrists (see, for example, Saul, 1972). Even today, many psychiatrists believe masochism—or "self-defeating personality disorder," as it is now called—should be a "legitimate" medical explanation for women who stay in abusive relationships. Other contemporary explanations focus on the woman's character flaws, such as a weak will or pathological emotional attachment.

All these explanations focus on the victim while paying little attention to her social situation. From a conflict perspective, we can see that in a society reluctant to punish abusers, many women may perceive that they have no alternatives and may feel physically, economically, and emotionally trapped in their relationships. Many of them leave, sometimes on several occasions, but find that the opportunities outside the relationship are not sufficient, and end up returning (D. J. Anderson, 2003). Indeed, the broader economic structure conspires to keep women in abusive relationships. Women who are unemployed and cannot support themselves financially are significantly less likely to leave an abusive marriage than women who are employed and who therefore have their own source of income (Strube & Barbour, 1983).

The perception that battered women simply sit back and take the abuse, thinking they somehow deserve it, is inaccurate. One study of 1,000 battered and formerly battered women nationwide found that they tried a number of active strategies to end the violence directed against them (Bowker, 1993). They tried to talk men out of beating them, extracted promises that the men wouldn't batter them anymore, avoided their abuser physically or avoided certain volatile topics, hid or ran away, and even fought back physically. Many of these individual strategies had limited effectiveness, however, and so most of these battered women eventually turned to people outside the relationship for informal support, advice, and sheltering. From these informal sources, the women generally progressed to organizations in the community, such as police, social service and counseling agencies, women's groups, and battered women's shelters. Some of these women were able, eventually, to end the violence; others weren't. In any case, as the study points out, most women actively try to end their victimization.

It's also important to keep in mind that leaving the relationship doesn't always end the violence. In fact, it may escalate it. One study found that victims who temporarily leave an abusive relationship suffer increased violence compared to those who never leave. Moreover, almost three quarters of visits battered women make to hospital emergency rooms occur after a separation; of abused women who are killed, 75% of them are victimized after separation (Anderson, 2003).

In some cases, the social organizations and institutions that are designed to help battered women are to blame. As recently as 15 years ago, for instance, emergency room workers routinely interviewed battered women about their injuries with their husbands present. The courts, too, have historically treated spousal violence less seriously than other crimes, making it even more difficult for women to seek help. For instance, an Indiana prosecutor once refused to prosecute for murder a man who beat and kicked his ex-wife to death in the presence of a witness and raped her as she lay dying. Filing a manslaughter charge instead, the prosecutor said, "He didn't mean to kill her. He just meant to give her a good thumping" (quoted in A. Jones, 1980, p. 308).

Sometimes the resources in place to assist battered women are simply inadequate. In rural areas with no public transportation, shelters exist but may be inaccessible to women who live miles away and don't own a car. In small towns, confidentiality is virtually impossible. The fact that people tend to know one another can dissuade a woman from calling a local sheriff's office for help, because the person answering might be a friend or relative of her abusive partner.

The problem of inadequate resources is not limited to scarcely populated rural areas, however. Several years ago in New York City, for instance, the mayor launched a massive campaign against domestic violence. Most buses and subways began displaying posters encouraging battered women to come forward and seek help from city-supported shelters and other services. But there weren't nearly enough beds available in the shelters to serve all the women who called the Victim Services hotline. Such women can be so desperate that they agree to be bused hundreds of miles away to a place where shelter is available. This remedy may get them out of harm's way, but it may also wreck their work lives, endanger welfare checks, and disrupt their children's schooling.

In sum, the decision to stay in an abusive relationship is the result not of irrationality or mental dysfunction but of rational choices women make in response to an array of conditions, including fear of and harassment by the abuser, the everyday realities of dependence, and the lack of institutional support (Baker, 1997). Broader societal circumstances may also play a role. In the months after the September 11 attacks, for instance, many battered women made the decision not to leave their relationship, clinging to familiar surroundings and coming to believe that a bad home was better than none in such unstable times. As a consequence, shelters reported dwindling demand for beds in their facilities in the immediate aftermath of the attacks (Lewin, 2001). In their need to acknowledge such realities, battered women are no different from any other individuals seeking to negotiate the complexities of social life.

Conclusion

Social relationships form the center of our personal universes. Life with intimates provides us with the sense of belonging that most of us need. However, although these relationships are the principal source of identity, community, happiness, and satisfaction for many, they can be the source of tremendous anguish and suffering for others.

Family, the most structured and culturally valued intimate relationship, is simultaneously a public and a private institution. True, most intimate and family behavior occurs away from the watchful eyes of others; we alone have access to our thoughts, desires, and feelings regarding those with whom we are intimately involved. But people around us, the government, even society as a whole, have a vested interest in what happens in our intimate lives.

The social institutions and culture that make up our society also shape the very nature and definition of "family." Today the boundaries of that definition are being pushed by rapidly increasing numbers of "nontraditional" families—dual-earner couples, single-parent households, cohabitors, the voluntarily single, same-sex couples, and so on.

Every family relationship, whether it violates or conforms to current social norms, reflects the dominant ideals and beliefs about what a marriage or a family ought to look like. Although each relationship is unique, this uniqueness will always be bounded by the broader constraints of our cultural, group, and institutional values.

◆

YOUR TURN

There is no universal definition of "family." Our ideas about what a family is depend on the culture we grew up in. Within a particular culture, people may also debate what a family is and which groups get to be defined as a family.

With so much disagreement, it would be interesting to find out how people actually define a family. Go to a spot on campus with a lot of foot traffic, and ask passersby for their definition of the word *family*. See if you can find any patterns in people's responses. Do you see a tendency to focus on blood relations, or is the emotional component of family more important? Is the presence of children necessary to definitions of family?

To delve deeper into the diversity of family definitions and experiences, pose the following questions to several friends or classmates. Try to acquire as diverse a sample of respondents as possible by talking to people from different cultural, racial, ethnic, religious, gender, and age groups:

- How many brothers and sisters do you have?
- If they are younger, did your parents expect you to help take care of them?
- Did you share a room with any of them while you were growing up?
- How many different houses and/or apartments did you live in while growing up?
- How often do you see your grandparents?
- Did you ever have grandparents or other relatives living in your house?
- Do you address your relatives by family terms ("Uncle Bob," "Aunt Beth," "Grandpa," "Grandma") or by first name?
- Do you expect to help support your parents when you are older?

Did you notice any interesting trends in people's responses? What do their answers say about the structure of their families? Did you find any consistent differences across cultural, gender, class, race, or age lines? For instance, does the likelihood of sharing a room with a sibling differ for people who grew up in different eras? Do members of different ethnic groups maintain different degrees of contact with grandparents or other relatives? Do they have different expectations about supporting their parents in the future? What do these different responses tell us about the broader structural context within which we live our family lives?

A variation on this exercise would be to examine the content of the personal Web pages that more and more families are now posting on the Internet. (If you are using a search engine such as Yahoo, narrow your search by going to the following subcategories: society and culture → people → personal home pages → families.) When I last checked, there were several thousand such sites listed alphabetically. Randomly select 50 or so (or more if you have time or are able to work in groups), and try to document the different categories of information families include about themselves—factual information (for example, size and location of family), likes and dislikes, opinions on political or social issues, links to other Web sites, and so on. Do these pages tend to focus on nuclear families, or do they include information about extended family members? Are certain racial, ethnic, or religious groups over- or underrepresented? Did you notice any differences in the Web pages of U.S. families versus families from other societies? What do the content and design of these home pages tell us about the nature and importance of family in people's lives? How can you explain the willingness of these families to expose such private aspects of their lives to the vast, public domain of the Internet?

CHAPTER HIGHLIGHTS

- In this culture, close relationships are the standard against which we judge the quality and happiness of our everyday lives. Yet in complex, individualistic societies they are becoming more difficult to establish and sustain.

- Many people in the United States long for a return to the "golden age" of the family. But the image of the U.S. family of the past is largely a myth.

- Although monogamous marriage is the only sexual relationship that has achieved widespread cultural legitimacy in the United States, other forms of intimacy (for example, extra- and premarital sex, polygamy) are considered legitimate in other societies.

- Although we like to think that the things we do in our family relationships are completely private experiences, they are continually influenced by large-scale political interests and economic pressures. Furthermore, our choices of romantic partners are governed to some degree by cultural rules that encourage us to form relationships within certain social groups and outside others.

♦ Divorce is not a solely private experience. It occurs within a cultural, historical, and community context. The high rate of remarriage after divorce indicates that people still view the institution of marriage as desirable.

♦ Instead of viewing domestic violence (spouse abuse and child abuse) as a product of "sick" individuals, sociologists are likely to view it as the product of a culture that tolerates violence in a variety of situations, traditionally grants men authority over women in family roles, and values family privacy and autonomy over the well-being of individual members.

KEY TERMS

endogamy Marriage within one's social group

exogamy Marriage outside one's social group

extended family Family unit consisting of the parent-child nuclear family and other relatives, such as grandparents, aunts, uncles, and cousins

family Two or more persons, including the householder, who are related by birth, marriage, or adoption, and who live together as one household

household Living arrangement composed of one or more people who occupy a housing unit

monogamy Marriage of one man and one woman

neolocal residence Living arrangement in which a married couple sets up residence separate from either spouse's family

nuclear family Family unit consisting of at least one parent and one child

polygamy Marriage of one person to more than one spouse at the same time

STUDY SITE ON THE WEB

Don't forget the interactive quizzes and other learning aids at www.pineforge.com/newman6 study. In the Resources File for this chapter, you'll also find more on building social relationships, including:

Sociologists at Work

♦ Robert Wuthnow: The Quest for Community

♦ Lillian Rubin: Working-Class Families

Micro-Macro Connections

♦ Divorce as a Personal Experience

♦ Virtual Communities in the Global Village

♦ Public Tolerance of Domestic Violence

8

Constructing Difference
Social Deviance

Defining Deviance

Explaining Deviant Behavior

Linking Power, Deviance, and Social Control

In 1984, 22-year-old Kelly Michaels moved to New York to pursue her dream of becoming an actress. She was a mild-mannered, devout Catholic who loved children. To support herself she began working at the Wee Care Preschool in a New Jersey suburb. By all accounts the kids there loved her (Hass, 1995).

Two weeks after Michaels left Wee Care for a better-paying job at another nursery school, a 4-year-old boy who was enrolled at Wee Care was taken to a doctor. A nurse rubbed his back and explained that she was going to take his temperature rectally. He said something like "That's what teacher [Michaels] does to me at nap time." Although it was unclear exactly what he meant by this—Michaels sometimes rubbed children's backs to get them to sleep and did take their temperature with a plastic forehead strip—the boy's alarmed mother, who happened to be the daughter of a local judge, called the school and the police (Michaels, 1993). The police questioned the child, as well as other children at Wee Care, searching for evidence that Michaels had sexually abused them. As word spread of the investigation, worried parents phoned other parents to share stories about the latest allegations. The police encouraged parents to seek state-funded psychological help for themselves as well as their children. In turn, the therapists encouraged the parents to cooperate with authorities in prosecuting Michaels.

That casual comment made by one little boy in a doctor's office touched off a 16-month investigation by the Division of Youth and Family Services that eventually ended in a 235-count indictment against Michaels. During the investigation, scores of parents became convinced that Michaels had raped their children with silverware, wooden spoons, LEGOs, and light bulbs; that she had played "Jingle Bells" on the piano while naked; that she had licked peanut butter off children's genitals, made them drink her urine, and forced them to eat excrement off the floor (Hass, 1995).

By the time the trial began, Kelly was being called the most hated woman in all New Jersey. The 10-month trial was filled with a host of inconsistencies and question-able legal tactics. Prosecutors never provided any substantiated evidence of abuse, yet they portrayed Michaels as "actressy" and "deviously charming." Everything she did was interpreted from the assumption that she was a "monster." For instance, if she was kind and patient with the children, that meant she was trying to seduce them. None of the other teachers at the day care center had heard or seen anything, even though most of the alleged abuse took place during children's nap time in a room set off only by a plastic curtain. The judge in the trial allowed the children to testify on closed-circuit TV while sitting on his lap and denied the defense experts the opportunity to cross-examine the children. One of the prosecution's witnesses—a child therapist—testified that the children who denied being molested by Ms. Michaels suffered from something called "child sexual abuse accommodation syndrome," a psychological condition that made them deny the abuse. In fact, the more the children denied it, the more certain the child therapist was that the abuse had actually happened.

Michaels was found guilty of 115 counts of assault, sexual abuse, and terrorist threats and sentenced to 47 years in prison. In 1993, after she had spent five years in prison—including an 18-month stint in solitary confinement—a state appellate court overturned the conviction. Later, the New Jersey State Supreme Court upheld the appellate court's decision, decrying the original conviction with outrage. The court wrote that all 20 children who testified against Michaels had been led, bribed, or threatened (Hass, 1995).

You might think that a formal declaration of innocence from such a powerful body as a state supreme court would change people's feelings about Kelly Michaels. Yet she remained a target of hate. Several civil suits were filed against Michaels by parents who still believed their children—aged three to five at the time—were sexually abused. One mother said she might try to kill Michaels with her bare hands if she had the chance. Even after Michaels's conviction on sexual abuse charges had been overturned, the media continued to identify her as a criminal. For instance, an Associated Press news release about her thwarted attempt to sue the county and the state was titled "Sex Offender's Case Denied in Court" (2001).

Why was it so hard for people to admit that Michaels was innocent? For one thing, at a time when child molestation was becoming a national obsession, the case reflected our darkest collective fears. The terrifying message was that our children could be hurt not only by creepy, middle-aged men but also by seemingly safe, 22-year-old college women. In the frenzy over children's safety, no one seemed willing to defend the principle of reasonable doubt.

Even more striking about this case is what it says about the way individuals think. Once people in the community concluded Kelly Michaels had committed these horrible acts, no amount of conflicting evidence was going to sway them to believe otherwise. Deviant labels and what they imply in people's minds can overshadow everything else about that person. When at the conclusion of her trial Michaels was formally tagged a criminal, the public degradation acquired its legal legitimacy. From that point on, she would never again be able to reclaim a normal life and in many people's minds would forever be a "child molester."

Few of us have spent five years in prison as a wrongly convicted child molester. But people are judged on the basis of deviant stereotypes all the time. Perhaps there have been times in your life when you acquired some sort of inaccurate reputation that you couldn't shed. In this chapter, I examine several questions related to this phenomenon: What is deviance? How does society attempt to control deviant behavior? Who gets to define what is and is not deviant? And what are the consequences of being identified by others as deviant?

Defining Deviance

In its broadest sense, the term *deviance* refers to socially disapproved behavior—the violation of some agreed-on norm that prevails in a community or in society at large. Staring at a stranger in an elevator, talking to oneself in public, wearing outlandish clothes, robbing a bank, and sending deadly anthrax spores through the mail can all be considered deviant acts. If we define deviance simply as any norm violation, then most deviance is rather trivial—even "normal"—such as driving over the speed limit or walking across the street when the light is red. Most of us, at some point in our lives, occupy statuses or engage in behaviors that others could regard as deviant. But most sociologists focus on deviant acts that are assaults on mores, the most serious of a society's norms. It's this type of deviance to which I will devote most of my attention in this chapter.

The determination of which behaviors or characteristics are deviant and which are normal is complex. We usually assume that people agree about what and who is deviant. For instance, no one would challenge the notion that child abuse is bad and that child abusers ought to be punished. But the level of agreement within a given society over what is deviant—what specific acts constitute child abuse—can vary tremendously. Spanking may be a perfectly acceptable method of discipline to one person but be considered a cruel form of abuse to another.

To make the issue more complicated, some sociologists identified with structural-functionalism (for example, Durkheim, 1958; Erikson, 1966) argue that deviance, as a class of behaviors, is not always bad for society and may actually serve a useful purpose. As you may recall from Chapter 4, norm violations help define the cultural and moral boundaries that distinguish right from wrong, increase feelings of in-group togetherness for those who unite in opposition to deviance from group norms, and encourage society to revise itself and respond to new concerns. At the surface level, individual acts of deviance are disruptive and generate varying degrees of social disapproval, but at a deeper level they can contribute to the maintenance and continuity of every society.

As you may have guessed, sociologists usually don't judge whether a given behavior should or shouldn't be considered deviant. Instead, they examine how deviance comes about and what it means to society. One of their primary concerns is whether people respond to deviance from the perspective that all human behavior can be classified as essentially good or bad (absolutists) or from the perspective that definitions of deviance are socially created (relativists).

Absolutist Definitions of Deviance

According to **absolutism**, there are two fundamental types of human behavior: (1) that which is inherently proper and good and (2) that which is obviously improper, immoral, evil, and bad. The distinction is clear and identifiable. The quality of deviance can be found in the very nature of the act. Right and wrong exist prior to socially created rules, norms, and customs and independently of people's subjective judgments (E. Goode, 1994).

Absolutist definitions of deviance are often accompanied by strong emotional reactions. For instance, speaking about homosexual marriage, the televangelist Jimmy Swaggart expressed these sentiments:

I'm trying to find the correct name for it . . . this utter absolute, asinine, idiotic stupidity of men marrying men. . . . I've never seen a man in my life I wanted to marry. And I'm gonna be blunt and plain; if one ever looks at me like that, I'm gonna kill him and tell God he died ("Jimmy Swaggart," 2004, p. 1).

Such extreme sentiments might seem at odds with what appears to be growing cultural acknowledgment and tolerance of homosexuality. Some of the most popular American television shows these days, such as *Will and Grace*, *Queer Eye for the Straight Guy*, *Queer as Folk*, *The L Word*, and *Boy Meets Boy*, feature gay characters and gay themes. Gay and lesbian consumers are openly courted by the entertainment and tourism industries. In 2003, the U.S. Supreme Court ruled that state laws banning sex between homosexuals were unconstitutional.

However, a large number of people still believe in the absolute deviance of homosexuality. A nationwide study found that although Americans seem to be showing increasing tolerance for and acceptance of people of different religions and different racial and ethnic groups, large numbers of people still commonly describe homosexuality as absoutely absolutely "sick," "immoral," "sinful," "perverted," and "abnormal" (A. Wolfe, 1998). In 2004, county commissioners in Rhea County Tennessee voted 8–0 to ask state lawmakers to amend the criminal code so that the county could charge homosexuals with "crimes against nature," thereby banning them from living in the county ("Rhea county officials," 2004). According to the U.S. Defense Department's "Don't Ask, Don't Tell" policy, military personnel are not to be asked about their sexual orientation and cannot be discharged simply for being gay. However, engaging in sexual conduct with a member of the same sex is grounds for discharge. Gay soldiers in Iraq and Afghanistan reported that the official policy impedes their access to support services (Frank, 2004). The Boy Scouts of America prohibits openly gay men from being troop leaders, claiming that they do not provide the sort of role model they want young scouts exposed to, and in 2000 the United States Supreme Court upheld this policy.

An absolutist definition of deviance implies something about society's relationship with the person who is considered deviant. Many people consider "deviants" to be psychologically, and perhaps even anatomically, different from ordinary, conforming people. The attribute or behavior that serves as the basic reason for defining a person as deviant in the first place is considered pervasive and essential to his or her entire character (Hills, 1980). People automatically assume that the bearer of one deviant trait has other undesirable traits (H. Becker, 1963). Respectable, conventional qualities become insignificant. It doesn't matter, for instance, that the "sexual deviant" has an otherwise ordinary life, that the "schizophrenic" has recovered, or that the violent act of the "batterer" was completely atypical of the rest of his or her life. In short, the deviant act or trait becomes a sort of moral identity, signifying a judgment about the overall worth of the individual (J. Katz, 1975). Being defined as deviant means being identified as someone who cannot and should not be treated as an ordinary human being.

There's another element of unfairness involved in the absolutist approach. People routinely make judgments of deviance and deviants on the basis of stereotypes. If you ask someone to imagine what a typical drug addict looks like, for instance, chances are the response will describe a dirty, poor, strung-out young man living on the streets and resorting to theft to support his habit. The image probably wouldn't be one of a middle-class alcoholic stay-at-home mother or a clean-shaven, hard-working physician hooked on prescription drugs, even though these groups constitute a higher percentage of drug addicts than any other in U.S. society (Pfohl, 1994). When sociologists William Chambliss and Richard H. Nagasawa (1969) compared the arrest rates of white, African American, and Japanese American youths in Seattle, they found that ethnic stereotypes led police to overestimate the involvement of African Americans in criminal activities and to underestimate the involvement of Japanese Americans.

As this study indicates, in U.S. society the consequences of stereotypes regarding deviance fall heavily on members of racial and ethnic minorities. Latinos and African Americans make up about 53% of the male population in state and federal prisons and local jails even though they comprise only about 27% of the general male population (U.S. Bureau of the Census, 2004a). The Bureau of Justice Statistics estimates that 12% of black men, close to 4% of Latino men, but only 1.6% of white men in their 20s are currently in prison or jail (Harrison & Karberg, 2004). According to the Justice Policy Institute (2002), the number of black men in jail or prison has grown so much in the past two decades that there are now more black men behind bars than are enrolled in colleges and universities. Race and ethnicity also affect the amount of time a convict spends in prison. The average federal prison sentence for Blacks is about six years, compared to four years for Whites (United States Sentencing Commission, 2004).

Although some people may see such figures as clear evidence of higher rates of minority involvement in crime, other statistics seem to suggest something different. For instance, African Americans make up about 12% of the nation's population and constitute roughly the same percentage (13%) of all illegal drug users; yet they account for 28% of defendants charged with a drug offense and 40% of drug offenders in federal prisons (Butterfield, 1995; Scalia, 2001). In 75% of cases in which a federal prosecutor sought the death penalty between 1995 and 2000, the defendant was a member of an ethnoracial minority group; and in half the cases, the defendant was black (cited in Bonner & Lacey, 2000). Exhibit 8.1 shows the black-white disparity in arrests, convictions, and length of sentence for certain types of crime.

Oversimplified images of deviants always fall short of accounting for every individual. The vast majority of African Americans do not commit crimes, just as the vast majority of gay men are not sexual predators, the vast majority of Italians are not involved in the Mafia, and the vast majority of Arab Americans are not terrorists. Nevertheless, the degree to which such images are thought to characterize an entire group is important, because it determines individual and societal responses. If affluent housewives and businesspeople who abuse drugs are not considered typical drug addicts, they will never be the focus of law enforcement attention, collective moral outrage, political rhetoric, or public policy.

Relativist Definitions of Deviance

Reliance on a strict absolutist definition of deviance can lead to narrow and often inaccurate perceptions of many important social problems. This shortcoming can be avoided by employing a second approach to defining deviance, **relativism**, which draws from symbolic interactionism and the conflict perspective. This approach states that deviance is not inherent in any particular act, belief, or condition; instead, it is socially

Exhibit 8.1   Racial Differences in Arrests, Convictions, and Sentencing

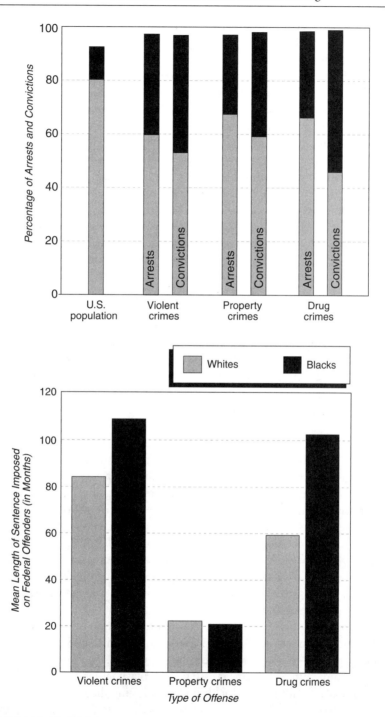

constructed, a creation of collective human judgments and ideas. Like beauty, it is in the eye of the beholder. The relativist approach is useful when the focus of study is the process by which some group of people or some type of behavior is defined as deviant.

For the relativist, complex societies consist of different groups with different values and interests. Sometimes these groups agree and cooperate to achieve a common goal, as when different segments of society join together to fight a foreign enemy. But more often than not there is conflict and struggle among groups to realize their own interests and goals.

Different people can thus have dramatically different interpretations of the same event. In 1995, a 35-year-old white man named William Masters was taking his usual armed, late-night walk through a barren neighborhood in Los Angeles. He came on two young Latino men spray-painting graffiti beneath a freeway overpass. Masters wrote down the license number of their car on a small piece of paper. When the men saw him and demanded the paper, Masters pulled out his 9-millimeter pistol and shot them—wounding one and killing the other. He told police that the men threatened him with a screwdriver and that he acted in self-defense, even though both were shot in the back. He was not charged with murder. Eventually he was found guilty of one count of carrying a concealed gun in public and one count of carrying a loaded gun in public—charges that carried a maximum of 18 months in jail and a $2,000 fine.

Shortly after his arrest, Masters claimed that his actions shouldn't be defined as deviant. He told one interviewer he was sure people were glad that as an intended victim he had gotten away and that no jury would ever convict him (Mydans, 1995). Many people agreed. Callers to talk radio shows and letters to newspapers applauded him for his vigilant antigraffiti efforts and for his foresight in carrying a weapon for self-protection. A few suggested that society would be better off with more people like William around (Mydans, 1995). But others expressed dismay at the verdict and argued that Masters was simply a racist out looking for trouble. They felt he was a deviant who literally got away with murder.

All those who expressed opinions on this case would likely agree on one thing: "Murder" is a deviant act at the far end of the spectrum of social acceptability. However, their perceptions of whether William Masters was a murderer were quite different. Was he a "hero" or a "killer"? An "avenging angel" or a "dangerous deviant"? The answers to these questions lie not in the objective act of taking another's life but in the way others defined and responded to such an act.

To fully understand the societal and personal implications of deviance designations, we must look at how these definitions are created and perpetuated. One key factor is who is doing the defining. One person's crime is another person's act of moral conscience; one group's evil is another group's virtue; one culture's terrorist is another culture's freedom fighter.

Definitions of deviance are also always relative to particular cultural standards. In Singapore a young vandal is a serious deviant (punishable by caning), as is a person who leaves chewed gum where it can be stepped on. The fine for simply bringing one stick of gum into Singapore is $10,000. A blasphemer in a fundamentalist Islamic society may be put to death for simply questioning the existence of God, an "offense" most Westerners would probably consider trivial. In Bulgaria, the punishment for a second drunk driving conviction is execution. In El Salvador, a drunk driver could face a firing squad for his or her first offense.

Deviance definitions undergo changes over time as well. For instance, several states at one time had laws that were designed specifically to protect women's virtue. Florida had a law that prohibited women from parachuting on Sundays. Michigan law made it a crime for men to use profanity in front of women. In Texas, it was a crime for women to adjust their stockings in public. The state of Washington still has a law on the books that makes it illegal to call a woman a "hussy" or "strumpet" in public (Kershaw, 2005).

Social conflict often reflects differing cultural conceptions of deviance. In 2005, for instance, an appeals court in Florida upheld a judge's earlier ruling that a Muslim woman could not wear a burka—a traditional veil that covers all but a woman's eyes—in her driver's license photo. In 2005, the U.S. Supreme Court ruled that the federal government could prohibit the medicinal use of marijuana even in the 11 states that explicitly permit it (Greenhouse, 2005a). Even though people in the United States who wear burkas or smoke marijuana for medical purposes don't consider themselves deviant, these court rulings meant they could be defined and treated that way by the dominant culture.

The absolutist approach assumes that certain individual characteristics are typical of all deviants, but the relativist approach acknowledges that there is no typical deviant. In fact, the same act committed by two different people may be defined very differently. For example, the police regularly harass, arrest, and jail street prostitutes. But in the 1980s, Sydney Biddle Barrows, a wealthy descendant of an original Plymouth colonist, established a high-class brothel as a business enterprise and became known as the "Mayflower Madam." Instead of spending time in prison for breaking the law, she made the talk show circuit and wrote a best-selling book. Clearly, her socioeconomic status and pedigree influenced public definitions regarding the deviant nature of her activities. When *she* did it, somehow it wasn't so bad.

Immediate situational circumstances, such as the time and location of an act, can influence definitions of deviance too. Drinking alcohol on the weekend is more acceptable than drinking during the week; drinking in the evening is more acceptable than drinking in the morning; drinking in a bar is more acceptable than drinking in a college classroom; and so on. In 2005, the state of Florida expanded its self-defense law so that people could use concealed guns or other deadly force to defend themselves in public places without first trying to escape (Goodnough, 2005). Had William Masters lived in Miami instead of Los Angeles, he would have simply been defined as a citizen exercising his legal right.

If deviance is relative, then even acts of extreme violence may be defined as acceptable under certain circumstances. Killings committed under the auspices of the government—shooting looters during a riot, killing enemy soldiers during wartime, or executing convicted murderers—fall outside the category of behaviors deemed deviant and problematic in society. However, a relativist approach to defining deviance doesn't mean that we can't be upset by activities that some people consider acceptable:

> Relativity does not require moral indifference, and it does not mean that one can never be . . . horrified by what one experiences in another group or culture. . . . [It] just reminds us that our personal beliefs or our cultural understandings are not necessarily found everywhere. (Curra, 2000, p. 13)

Relativists, like absolutists, acknowledge that every society identifies certain individuals and certain behaviors as bothersome and disruptive and therefore as justifiable

(Text continues on page 261)

A Culture of Tramps

Douglas Harper

People typically see their own culture as normal and may be startled to learn that other people around them have a different culture. That may especially be the case for subcultures that are defined by mainstream society as "deviant," such as the "tramp" culture pictured here.

Like any other culture, however, even the tramp culture has a clear set of norms. For example, after a tramp has worked for weeks or months, within the tramp culture it is appropriate to drink up one's wages in a drunken binge that may last for days or even weeks. Excessive drinking causes problems for tramps, but they define it as a normal part of their culture, like a football player who regards his injuries as inevitable.

❖ I met this tramp, Carl, in Minneapolis. Suffering through a hangover after a three-week drunk, he was heading 2,000 miles to the apple harvest in Washington State. He accepted my company because I had a sack of food. We "buddied up," which is a tramp expression noting a relationship of limited but specific commitment.

❖ Carl's gear for a 2,000-mile migration to the apple harvest included a razor and a mirror. He was finished with his drunk, and he knew he needed to shave and clean up to get a job. After he shaved, he handed me the razor and told me that either I shaved or I'd be heading the rest of the way by myself. The tramp understood that his life consisted of several identities and that the shift from a skid row drunk to a worker required specific attention to his appearance.

Freight trains are a particularly important and challenging part of tramp culture. They are complicated and dangerous. Tramps watch others ride trains and are quick to point out amateurs who don't know the cultural ropes or failures in the culture who may be smart but remain incompetent in the ways of tramps.

❖ Tramps know where and how to ride freights. Here we rode on an exposed auto carrier, which is one of the least desirable places on a freight train. Riders are exposed to the elements, but worse than that, they are visible to yard police. Tramps prefer to ride inside empty boxcars or under the truck trailers bolted onto flatcars, called "piggybacks." There are at least 20 different places a tramp may ride a freight, and tramps spend a great deal of time arguing their comparative advantages.

❖ There were eventually 38 men in this boxcar, as it approached the towns where the apple orchards were situated. During the hot afternoon a tramp entered the car with a bottle of wine, but most tramps shied away. It is a strong tramp norm not to get drunk on a freight train, because to do so places the rider in great danger. Most tramps remembered the norms and passed on a tempting cold drink.

The culture of tramps is connected to what has been called the "macro" or structural aspect of society. We look at homeless people and see only a social problem or evidence of individual failure. But the tramps I met on trains and during apple harvests are homeless only some of the year, and then they ride a freight perhaps thousands of miles to become workers somewhere else. In the Pacific Northwest tramps pick fruit. They usually leave their wages in the harvest towns, where they either spend it getting drunk or have it stolen by "jack-rollers" or the police. Tramps define this way of spending money as normal, and their behavior services an agricultural economy that needs intensive but intermittent labor. We take for granted that our fruits and vegetables await us in clean and orderly stores, but these products have come to us because a culture of probably homeless workers have labored for paltry wages in circumstances where they have little if any social power. In the case of tramps, their own cultural definition of their lives and fate justifies what is, in fact, an exploitative labor situation.

❖ While waiting to be hired for the apple harvest, tramps assembled at one of many "jungles" in the area. In the jungles, tramps lived by norms: food was shared, the camp was kept clean, and firewood was replaced. But when we were hired to work in an orchard, we were given a one-room cabin in which to live. Suddenly we had transformed from tramps to workers. We got an advance on our wages, bought cans of beans and Spaghetti-O's, and began living under a roof. The change in Carl was remarkable. Suddenly he was master of a different world.

Note that I refer to these men as "tramps" because that is how they define themselves. The existence of a distinctive culture is often signaled by words that have meaning only within the framework of that culture. When tramps see another man in a freight car, they see a *bindle-stiff*, an *Airedale*, a *mission-stiff*, a *rubber tramp*, a *jack-roller*, or one of many other categories of tramps. Each of these labels defines a certain set of actions, possessions, behaviors, and beliefs. In other words, they are not casual definitions but definitions that indicate an individual's identity. They are no less important or socially powerful than our own cultural definitions.

❖ Tramps define themselves by how they travel and what they do. This man is a "bindle-stiff" because he carries his gear in an old-fashioned manner, tied into what are called bindles. A bindle-stiff usually spends his time in the less-threatening environments of smaller cities or freight yards in the American West. His identity is made complete by his dog on a hand-made leash. Here he enters the relatively hostile environment of Seattle, where many will prey on an elderly tramp. He may be visiting family, for many tramps keep family connections. Or he may be on his way to the freight yard to catch a train to a jungle, an orchard, or another city.

❖ When a tramp can no longer take care of himself on the open road, he retires to a mission. He then becomes a "mission stiff," like the tramp in this photograph. Since tramps value independence, the admission that one must leave the road to retire to a mission is a radical redefinition of one's self. Tramps talk of retiring to a small cabin in the woods but seldom accumulate enough money to do it. Rather, they end their days in a homemade shack by a freight yard or in a mission when the weather turns too cold to live outside. It is at the ends of their lives that the inconsistencies in their self-definitions and their actual situations become most apparent.

❖ The tramps pictured here live in Boston. On the surface they appear to be the same as the tramps pictured earlier. Yet their culture is profoundly different. In the East single homeless men are not an agricultural labor force, and it is more difficult for them to ride freights. Without work and mobility, the tramp becomes a stationary homeless man, reduced to begging and scavenging. Still, the homeless man lives in a culture. These two men are in a "bottle gang," furtively sharing a pint of cheap wine they have purchased from a day's work panhandling and scavenging for spare change.

To study culture one must participate as well as observe. To study tramps I rode freight trains, lived in hobo jungles and skid row missions, and picked apples in orchards where all the workers were tramps. I became something of an expert in tramp culture, which eventually made these arcane cultural situations part of my own understanding of the world and the nature of deviance.

targets of social control, whether through treatment, punishment, spiritual healing, or correction. However, to a relativist the main concerns in defining deviance are not so much what is committed but rather who commits the act, who labels it, and where and when it occurs. Some people have the wherewithal to avoid having their acts defined as deviant; others may fit a certain profile and be defined as deviant even if they've done nothing wrong. Definitions of deviant behavior change over time, and certain acts are acceptable to some groups and not others. The definitions most likely to persevere over time are those that have the support of influential segments of the population or have widespread agreement among the members of that society.

The Elements of Deviance

The two perspectives on defining deviance raise some complex and controversial issues. Nevertheless, the most applicable definition of deviance we're left with goes something like this: **Deviance** is behavior (how people act), ideas (how people think), or attributes (how people appear) that some people in society—though not necessarily all people—find offensive, wrong, immoral, sinful, evil, strange, or disgusting.

This definition consists of three elements (Aday, 1990):

♦ *Expectation:* Some sort of behavioral expectation must exist, a norm that defines appropriate, acceptable behavior, ideas, or characteristics. The expectations may be implicit or explicit, formal or informal, and more or less widely shared.

♦ *Violation:* Deviance implies some violation of normative expectations. The violation may be real or alleged; that is, an accusation of wrongdoing may be enough to give someone the reputation of deviance.

♦ *Reaction:* An individual, group, or society must react to the deviance. The reaction is likely to lead to some sort of response: avoidance, criticism, warnings, punishment, or treatment. The reaction may accurately reflect the facts, or it may bear little relation to what really happened, as when people are punished or ostracized for acts they did not commit.

Deviance, then, cannot exist if people don't have some idea of what's appropriate, if someone hasn't been perceived as violating some social norm, and if others haven't reacted.

❖
Micro-Macro Connection
Sexual Abuse and the Clergy

Some waves of deviance are considered so horrible that they fundamentally change people's perceptions of the individuals involved, no matter how respectable they might have been previously. In 2002, *The Boston Globe* published a story about a Catholic priest who had sexually molested children in six Boston parishes between 1962 and 1993 (cited in Jost, 2002). It wasn't the first time such behavior had received media or Church attention. For decades, isolated stories about sexual abuse by clergy had periodically popped up in the press. In 1993, a conference of Catholic bishops appointed a committee to study sexual abuse and even the Pope acknowledged the gravity of the issue.

What gave the 2002 *Boston Globe* story unusual impact was that it focused attention on the institutional handling of sexual abuse allegations over the years. In the past, priests had routinely been allowed to remain in their posts despite repeated accusations and even admissions of sexual misconduct. In other cases, the Church quietly reassigned abusive priests to different parishes. The 2002 story pointed out that Church officials had known of this particular priest's behavior since 1984, nine years before he was finally removed from his last parish. Further investigation revealed that the archdiocese of Boston had quietly settled suits against 70 priests over the preceding decade, often stipulating that in exchange for financial settlement, victims were not to discuss the cases publicly (Jost, 2002).

Under mounting public pressure, Boston's Cardinal Bernard Law agreed to give prosecutors the names of 100 other priests who had been accused of sexual molestation over the years. In 2003, the Boston Archdiocese agreed to pay $85 million to settle over 500 lawsuits brought by people who claimed they were sexually abused by priests. Eventually similar stories of sexual abuse began appearing in Catholic dioceses in New York, Los Angeles, Cleveland, Philadelphia, St. Louis, and many other areas of the country. In Louisville, for instance, plaintiffs accused 34 out of 115 active priests of sexual molestation (Goodstein, 2003a).

It soon became clear that although the problem was most severe in the Catholic Church, it wasn't unique to Catholics. Charges of clergy sexual abuse involving Orthodox Jewish rabbis, Protestant ministers, and Hare Krishna gurus were disclosed. What many had hoped was an isolated problem of a few individual bad priests became a full-scale, national scandal that crossed geographic and denominational boundaries.

One sociologically interesting element of this scandal is that it clearly shows the limitations of relying on stereotypical beliefs about what "deviants" look like. If there is any profession that fails to fit the image of "deviance," it's got to be the clergy. Priests, ministers, rabbis, and imams are often the most respected individuals in their communities. Most of them are able to confidently preach against sin and extol a virtuous life. Certainly, like Kelly Michaels, they don't fit the stereotype of the sleazy, drooling "child molester."

So it's no surprise that there wasn't much of an institutional response or even much public outrage when allegations of abuse were reported in the past. Even when such charges were substantiated, the collective response was that these were "sick" priests, glaring exceptions to the stereotype of the clergy as benevolent shepherds. They were problematic individuals who, with enough compassion and psychiatric treatment, could change their ways.

But the current scandal drew widespread public outrage as more and more charges of deception and cover-ups emerged. Devout Catholics found their everyday lives shattered and their faith in their Church crushed. As one theologian put it,

> This is the greatest crisis in the modern history of the Catholic Church. It raises serious questions about the integrity of its priesthood, and the Catholic Church just can't function without a priesthood that has the support and trust of its people. (quoted in Jost, 2002, p. 395)

According to a 2002 Gallup poll, nearly one third of American Catholics withheld weekly monetary offerings to the Church in the wake of the scandal (cited in Mulrine, 2003). With shrinking financial support, several dioceses around the country were forced to close churches. The Boston Archdiocese, for instance, closed 65 of its 357 parishes in 2004 ("Boston Archdiocese," 2004). One Catholic reform group estimates that the clergy sexual abuse scandal will eventually cost U.S. dioceses between $2 and $3 billion in settlements to victims (cited in Kusmer, 2005). Victims' advocacy groups continue to put pressure on the Church to adopt a "zero tolerance" policy.

When there are only a few cases of deviance, they're easy to dismiss as anomalies. However, when they occur by the hundreds, all across the country and in a variety of religions, they come to represent a glaring problem at the institutional level and thus become more likely to provoke serious societal reaction.

Explaining Deviant Behavior

This question of how certain acts and certain people come to be defined as deviant is different from the question of why people do or don't commit acts that are considered deviant. Most sociological theories addressing the question of deviant behavior focus on people's personal characteristics, the environmental forces on them, and the effectiveness of various methods to control them.

The structural-functionalist perspective, for instance, tells us that it is in society's interest to socialize everyone to strive for success so that the most able and talented people will come to occupy the most important positions. Sociologist Robert Merton's "strain theory" (1957) argues that the probability of committing deviant acts increases when people experience a strain or contradiction between these culturally defined success goals and access to the legitimate means by which they can achieve those goals. Those who believe that being wealthy and achieving the "American Dream" are important goals but who have no money, no employment opportunities, and no access to higher education, Merton argues, are more inclined than others to try to achieve the goal of success through illegitimate means. One of the most consistent findings in criminal research is the correlation between unemployment (a factor closely associated with economic disadvantage) and property crime (Hagan, 2000). In this sense, people who sell, say, illegal drugs or stolen video game consoles to get rich are motivated by the same desires as people who sell real estate to get rich. People who lack access to legitimate means may also reject the culturally defined goal of success and retreat from society altogether. According to Merton, such deviants as vagrants, chronic drunks, drug addicts, and the mentally ill fall into this category.

Another sociologist, Edwin Sutherland, bases his theory of deviance (Sutherland & Cressey, 1955) on the symbolic-interactionist principle that we all interpret life through the symbols and meanings we learn in our interactions with others. Sutherland argues that individuals learn deviant patterns of behavior from the people with whom they associate on a regular basis: friends, family members, peers. Through our associations with these influential individuals, we learn not only the techniques for committing deviant acts (for example, how to pick a lock or how to snort cocaine) but also a set of beliefs and attitudes that justify or rationalize the behavior (Sykes & Matza, 1957). To commit deviant acts, on a regular basis, we must learn how to perceive those acts as normal.

Deterring Deviance

Some sociologists have turned away from the issue of why some people violate norms to the issue of why more people don't (see, for example, Hirschi, 1969). Their concern is with the mechanisms society has in place to control or constrain people's behavior. **Deterrence theory** assumes that people are rational decision makers who calculate the potential costs and benefits of behavior before they act. If the benefits of a deviant act (for instance, money or psychological satisfaction) outweigh the costs (for instance, getting caught and punished), we will be inclined to do it. Conversely, if the costs exceed the benefits, the theory predicts that we'll decide it's not worth the risk (van den Haag, 1975).

The controversy surrounding capital punishment is, essentially, a debate over its true capacity to deter potentially violent criminals. According to deterrence theory, a punishment, to be effective, must be swift as well as certain and severe. However, capital punishment is anything but swift. Currently, more than 3,300 inmates are on death row in the United States, but only about 950 prisoners have been executed since 1976, when the death penalty was reinstated (U.S. Bureau of Justice Statistics, 2004c). Death row inmates typically spend over a decade awaiting execution, and some have been there for over 20 years (Death Penalty Information Center, 2005).

In addition, opponents of the death penalty argue that violent offenders are often under the influence of drugs or alcohol or are consumed by passion when they commit an act of violence; their violence is more or less spontaneous. Hence they may not be thinking rationally (weighing the potential benefits of the act against the costs of punishment) at the time of the crime. The threat of being condemned to death may not deter such people when they are committing the act. Researchers have, indeed, found little empirical support for the argument that the publicized threat of capital punishment reduces murders (W. C. Bailey, 1990; Galliher & Galliher, 2002). Nor have they found that well-publicized executions deter homicides (R. D. Peterson & Bailey, 1991). In fact, over the last two decades, the homicide rate in the 38 states with the death penalty has been 48% to 100% higher than in the 12 states without the death penalty (Bonner & Fessenden, 2000).

Most societies around the world have abandoned the use of capital punishment for both moral and practical reasons: It isn't humane, and it doesn't deter crime. Nevertheless, the majority of U.S. citizens continue to favor the death penalty and believe it is a useful tool in fighting crime (Galliher & Galliher, 2002). Recent legislative efforts to increase the number of offenses punishable by the death penalty and to reduce the number of "death row" appeals an offender can file reflect this popular attitude.

Labeling Deviants

These theories help us to explain why some people engage in deviant acts whereas others don't, but they bypass the question of why certain acts committed by certain people are considered deviant in the first place. **Labeling theory** attempts to answer this question by characterizing a deviant person as someone—such as preschool teacher Kelly Michaels—to whom the label "deviant" has been successfully applied (Becker, 1963; Lemert, 1972). According to this theory, the process of being singled out, defined, and reacted to as deviant changes a person in the eyes of others and has important life consequences for the individual. Once the label sticks, others may react toward the labeled deviant with rejection, suspicion, withdrawal, fear, mistrust, and hatred (A. K. Cohen, 1966). A deviant label suggests that the person holding it is habitually given to the types of undesirable motives and behavior thought to be typical of others so labeled. The "ex-convict" is seen as a cold-blooded and ruthless character without hope of reform, the "mental patient" as dangerous and unpredictable, the "alcoholic" as weak willed, the "prostitute" as dirty and immoral.

The problem, of course, is that such labels overgeneralize and can be misleading. For instance, a study by two marketing professors found that convicted felons showed just as much integrity as MBA students on a test of ethics related to difficult business situations. In fact, the convicts were less likely than the students to indicate that they'd steal employees from competitors or scrimp on customer service to increase profits ("MBA vs. Prison," 1999).

The type of deviant who receives the harshest expressions of public outrage changes with some regularity. At various points in time, child molesters, crack addicts, and drug dealers have claimed the title of society's worst deviant. Currently foreign terrorists fit the bill. Often collective hostility is directed toward deviants who don't seem to pose the gravest societal threat. People who smoke in public or who talk on cell phones while driving have also taken their turns recently as targets of public ire. Although SUVs were the most popular vehicles on the market a couple of years ago, SUV owners became the new deviants when the economy and fuel supplies became more uncertain, the cost of gasoline skyrocketed, and environmental change became a bigger concern. In 2003, a group calling itself the Earth Liberation Front claimed to have set fire to SUVs at a Pennsylvania dealership. Posters at a San Francisco peace rally prior to the war with Iraq said "Draft SUV drivers first." The Evangelical Environmental Network, a coalition of Christian groups, ran TV ads asking, "What would Jesus drive?" The answer was, Not an SUV. One columnist even linked SUV ownership to support of terrorism (P. L. Brown, 2003).

Judges around the country have started to use deviant labels, in the form of public humiliation, as an alternative to incarceration. For example, an Illinois man convicted of assault was required to place a large sign at the end of his driveway that reads "Warning: A Violent Felon Lives Here. Travel at Your Own Risk." In some states, convicted drunk drivers have to put special license plates on their cars; convicted shoplifters must take out ads in local newspapers, use their photograph, and announce their crimes. The Chicago police department posts photographs and partial addresses of men arrested for soliciting prostitution on its Web site, even though they haven't yet been convicted. Other cities, like Denver, Akron, and Durham, post this information on local television stations. Oakland and Omaha display photographs of such offenders on prominent billboards (Ruethling, 2005). Such penalties are designed to shame the labeled individuals into behaving properly and to deter others from committing such crimes. They also satisfy the public's need for dramatic moral condemnation of deviants (Hoffman, 1997).

Deviant labels can impair an individual's eligibility to enter a broad range of socially acceptable roles. Consider the impact on convicted sex offenders of the 1994 Federal Crime Bill. This law requires states to register and track convicted sex offenders for 10 years after their release from prison and to privately notify police departments when the sex offenders move into a new community. In 1996, the U.S. Senate approved a measure requiring all states to make public the whereabouts of paroled sex offenders. In Louisiana, homeowners can sign up to be notified by e-mail when registered sex offenders move to within a mile of their homes; the service provides maps showing where the sex offenders live ("Site Warns of New Neighbors," 2001). Many states and localities publicize information about particular sex offenders on their official Web sites. Sixteen states have "sexually violent predator" statutes that give officials the power to commit violent sex offenders to mental hospitals involuntarily or to retain them in prison indefinitely *after* their prison terms are up (C. Goldberg, 2001). These are convicts who have "paid their debt" to society by serving their mandated prison sentences. Under these laws convicted sex offenders can never fully shed their deviant identity. Finding a decent place to live or a decent job may be a problem for the rest of their lives.

All ex-convicts experience the "stickiness" of labels to some degree. Potential employers often refuse to hire ex-convicts, even when the crime has nothing to do with the job requirements. Like the public at large, many employers believe that prisons do not rehabilitate but actually make convicts more deviant by teaching them better ways to commit crime and by providing social networks for criminal activity on the outside (R. Johnson, 1987). These suspicions can vary by race. A study of ex-offenders in New York found that white men with prison records receive far more job offers than black men with identical records (cited in von Zielbauer, 2005). In fact, other research has found that white ex-offenders are more likely to be hired than black men who have led law-abiding lives (Pager, 2003).

In addition, being labeled as deviant may actually increase the probability that the behavior itself will stay the same or become worse (Archer, 1985). Thus a great many ex-convicts in the United States do return to prison. According to the U.S. Department of Justice, a little over two thirds of all ex-convicts released in 1994 were arrested for a new offense within three years, and 47% were convicted again (see Exhibit 8.2).

Deviant labels are so powerful that a mere charge of criminal activity can conjure up suspicions of tainted character (R. D. Schwartz & J. H. Skolnick, 1962). You may recall the case of Richard Jewell, the security guard originally suspected of setting off the bomb that killed two people and injured more than a hundred during the 1996 Summer Olympics in Atlanta. Newspapers and television news shows "convicted" him even though no criminal charges were ever filed. Operating on unsubstantiated tips and hearsay, the FBI launched a full investigation of Jewell's life and character. Three months later the Justice Department sent him a letter stating that he was no longer a suspect. Jewell sued a newspaper, a radio station, and a television network for the stigmatizing effect their stories had on his life. He eventually settled out of court and built a satisfactory life for himself. But it took years.

Exhibit 8.2   Recidivism Rates of Prisoners Released in 1994

Source: Langan & Levin, 2002, Table 2.

❖
Nancy Herman
Becoming an Ex-Crazy

Sociologist Nancy Herman (1993) was interested in how labeling can weaken a person's self-image, create "deviant" patterns of behavior, and lead to social rejection. She was especially concerned with how former mental patients are reintegrated into society after their release from a psychiatric hospital. She decided to study ex-mental patients because her father had been an occupational therapist at a large psychiatric institute in Ontario, Canada. She spent most of her childhood and adolescence roaming the halls talking to patients. From time to time patients would spend Thanksgiving and Christmas with her family.

For this study, she conducted in-depth interviews with 146 former nonchronic mental patients (hospitalized in short intervals for less than two years) and 139 former chronic mental patients (hospitalized continuously for two or more years). She interviewed them in a variety of settings, such as coffee shops, malls, and their own homes. Many subjects invited her to their self-help group meetings, therapy sessions, even protest marches.

Herman found that these ex-patients, on release, noticed right away that friends, neighbors, coworkers, and family members were responding to them on the basis of their "mental illness" label and not on the basis of their identity prior to hospitalization. Although their treatment was complete (that is, they were "cured" of their "illness"), others still saw them as defective. They were often made to feel like failures for not measuring up to the rest of "normal" society. As one woman put it,

When I was released, I presumed that I could resume with the "good times" once again. I was treated—I paid my dues. But I was wrong. From the first moment I set foot back onto the streets of "Wilsonville" and I tried to return to my kids . . . I learned the hard way that my kids didn't want nothing to do with me. They were scared to let me near the grand-kids—that I might do something to them. They told me this right to my face. . . . Having mental illness is like having any other illness like heart troubles, but people sure do treat you different. If you have heart troubles, you get treated, and then you come out good as new and your family still loves you. But that's not so with mental illness . . . you come out and people treat you worse than a dog! (quoted in Herman, 1993, p. 303)

On release, some of the former patients Herman interviewed were quite open about their illness and attempted to present themselves in as "normal" a way as they could. Others became political activists who used their "ex–mental patient" label to try to dispel common myths about mental illness or to advocate for patients' rights. But most of the former patients spent a great deal of time selectively concealing and disclosing information regarding their illness and treatment. Strategies of concealment included avoiding certain individuals, redirecting conversations so that the topic was less likely to come up, lying about their absence, and withdrawing from social interaction. Constant concern with people "finding out" created a great deal of anxiety, fear, and frustration, as described by this 56-year-old woman:

It's a very difficult thing. It's not easy to distinguish the good ones from the bad ones. . . . You've gotta figure out who you can tell about your illness and who you better not tell. It is a tremendous stress and strain that you have to live with 24 hours a day! (quoted in Herman, 1993, p. 306)

The stickiness of the "crazy" label is difficult for former mental patients. However, Herman's research also shows that ex-patients are not powerless victims of negative societal reactions, passively accepting the deviant identity others attribute to them. Rather, they are strategists and impression managers who play active roles in transforming themselves from "abnormal" to "normal."

Linking Power, Deviance, and Social Control

Because deviance is socially defined, the behaviors and conditions that come to be called "deviant" can at times appear somewhat arbitrary. Sociologists working from the conflict perspective would say that the definition of and response to deviance is often a form of social control exerted by more powerful people and groups over less powerful people and groups. In U.S. society, the predominant means of controlling those whose behavior does not conform to the norms established by the powerful are criminalization and medicalization. Labeling people either as criminals or as sick people gives socially powerful individuals, groups, and organizations a way to marginalize and discount certain people who challenge the status quo. Criminalization and medicalization also have economic and other benefits for certain powerful groups.

The Criminalization of Deviance

Presumably, certain acts are defined as crimes because they offend the majority of people in a given society. Many of us trust our legal institutions—legislators, courts, and police—to regulate social behavior in the interest of the common good. But according to the conflict perspective, most societies ensure that those offenders who are processed through the criminal justice system are members of the lowest socioeconomic class (Reiman, 2004). Poor people are more likely to get arrested, be formally charged with a crime, have their cases go to trial, get convicted, and receive harsher sentences than more affluent citizens (Parenti, 1995; Reiman, 2004). In 2002, 69 poor people in Atlanta who had been arrested on petty charges—shoplifting, trespassing, public drunkenness—and who couldn't afford bail remained in jail for weeks and, in some cases months, awaiting a lawyer and a court date, despite a law that requires anyone arrested for a misdemeanor to go before a judge or lawyer within 48 hours. All of them had spent more time behind bars than they would have had they been convicted (Rimer, 2002).

The quality of legal representation for defendants in criminal cases is also severely skewed along socioeconomic lines. When wealthy individuals are tried for capital crimes (an occurrence that, in and of itself, is rare) they are usually able to afford effective legal representation. In contrast, poor defendants in such cases are often represented by public defenders, who have fewer resources available for investigative work and who may have little, if any, experience in such matters. For instance, in one Alabama case, the public defender for a poor man facing the death penalty had never tried a capital case and had no money to hire an investigator before the case went to trial. The defendant was sentenced to death. Similarly, a poor man in Texas, sentenced to death in 1996, was appointed an attorney for his appeal who had never handled such cases and who had been sanctioned several times for neglecting his clients. The man's appeal was denied and he was executed in 2002.

Cases like these have intensified the national debate over race and class disparities in the quality of legal representation. In response, some states have taken steps to address such biases, especially in the way that capital cases are handled:

- In 1998, Kentucky became the first state to pass a "Racial Justice Act," a law that allows defendants in capital cases to use statistical evidence of racial bias to show that their race influenced the decision to seek the death penalty.
- In 2001, the governor of Illinois called for a moratorium on executions in his state after 13 men on death row—most of whom were either Latino or African American and all of whom were poor and were represented in their trials by public defenders—were proven innocent. Two years later, he commuted all death sentences in the state to prison terms of life or less after declaring the system fundamentally flawed and unfair (Wilgoren, 2003).
- In 2001, the American Bar Association passed a resolution calling for a nationwide moratorium on executions (Fleischaker, 2004).
- In 2002, the governor of Maryland imposed a moratorium on executions in his state because of concerns over racial bias. In Maryland, 81% of homicide victims are African American, yet 84% of death sentences were cases involving white victims. Two thirds of the people on death row there are African American (Amnesty International, 2004a).

Persistent imbalances in the justice system go beyond the way poor people are treated by police, judges, attorneys, and juries. If they were simply a matter of discrimination against the poor, the situation would be relatively easy to deal with. Instead, they occur because the actions of poor individuals are more likely to be **criminalized**—that is, officially defined as crimes in the first place. When poor people do commit certain crimes—car theft, burglary, assault, illegal drug use, and so on— they become "typical criminals" in the public eye (Reiman, 2004).

The Social Reality of Crime

Followers of the conflict perspective point out that powerful groups often try to foster a belief that society's rules are under attack by deviants and that official action against them is needed. The strategy has worked well. In polls taken in the United States in the 1980s and 1990s, an average of 83% of respondents felt that the justice system was not harsh enough in dealing with criminals (Gaubatz, 1995). Governments at the state and federal level responded to the popular sentiment by "getting tough on crime"—cracking down on drug users and dealers, reviving the death penalty, scaling back parole eligibility, lengthening prison sentences, and building more prisons. By 1999, 15 states had abolished parole boards and early release programs, resulting in more prisoners serving their full sentences (Butterfield, 1999).

Not surprisingly, the inmate population in this country has swelled. According to the Justice Department, the number of inmates in U.S. prisons has grown exponentially over the past several decades. In 1970 there were fewer than 200,000 people in state and federal prisons; by 2004 that figure had grown to 2.1 million (U.S. Bureau of Justice Statistics, 2005). At any given point in time, over 3% of the adult American population is either on probation, in jail or prison, or on parole (U.S. Bureau of the Census, 2004a). In 2002, the U.S. incarceration rate was 476 prisoners per 100,000 people, a figure no other industrialized country comes close to. For instance, the rate in Canada is 105 per 100,000; in Germany it's 95 (cited in Uggen & Manza, 2002).

There's some evidence that these "get tough" actions may be working. The FBI reports that rates of violent crime and property crime have been dropping steadily since the early 1990s (U.S. Bureau of the Census, 2004a). Exhibit 8.3 shows the statistical relationship between incarceration rates and crime rates.

But other problems have popped up. Newly released inmates—who are likely to be poor and members of ethnoracial minorities—are significantly less likely than their counterparts of two decades ago to find jobs and stay out of the kind of trouble that leads to further imprisonment (Butterfield, 2000). Many states have sharply curtailed education, job training, and other rehabilitation programs inside prison. In addition, parole officers are quicker to rescind a newly released inmate's parole for relatively minor infractions, such as failing a drug test. In California, for instance, four out of five former inmates who return to prison do so *not* for committing new crimes but for violating the conditions of their parole.

The question you might ask is, Who benefits when it becomes so hard for ex-convicts to stay out of prison? According to advocates of the conflict perspective, the law is not a mechanism that merely protects good people from bad people; it is a political instrument used by specific groups to further their own interests, often at the expense

Exhibit 8.3   Rising Incarceration Rates, Decreasing Crime Rates

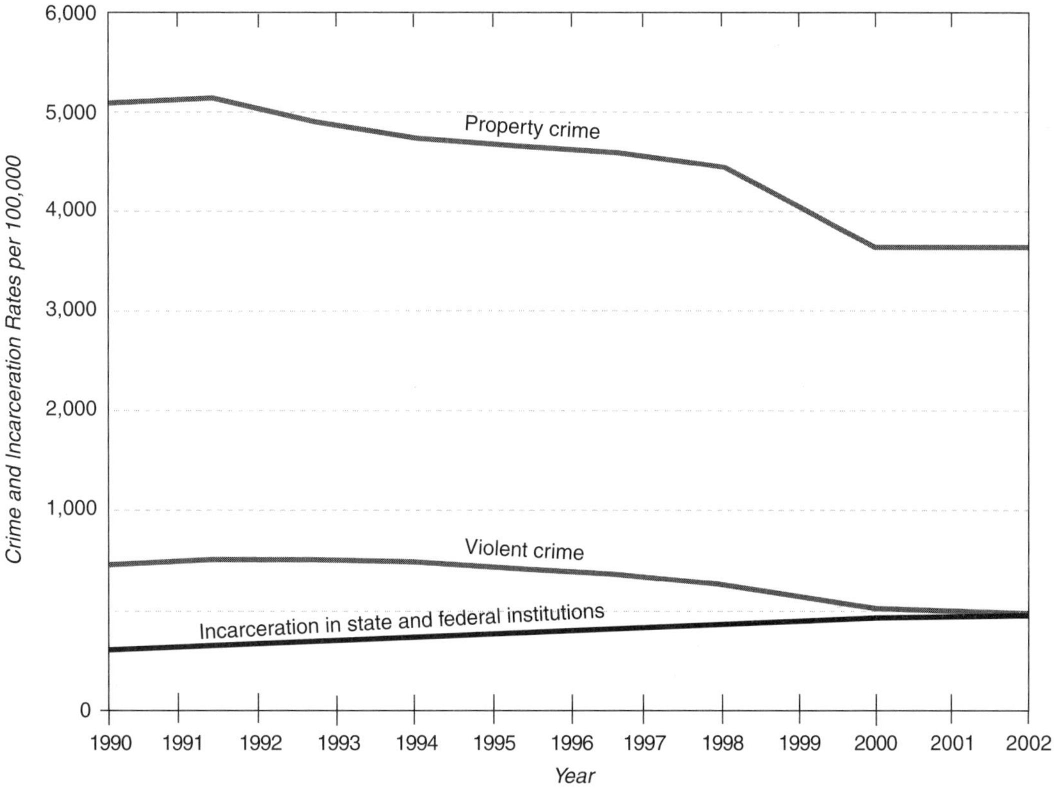

Source: U.S. Bureau of the Census, 2004a.

of others (Chambliss, 1964; Quinney, 1970). Law is, of course, determined by legislative action. But legislatures are greatly influenced by powerful segments of society, such as lobbying groups, political action committees, individual campaign contributors, and so on. Tellingly, the acts that conflict with the economic or political interests of the groups that have the power to influence public policy are more likely to be criminalized (and more likely to be punished) than are the deviant acts of the powerful. For instance, it's against the law to fail to report income on one's annual tax return. But poor working people are far more likely to be audited by the Internal Revenue Service than wealthy people (Johnston, 2002a). That's not surprising, given that the IRS looks for tax cheating by wage earners much more closely than it does by corporations or by people whose money comes from their own businesses, investments, partnerships, and trusts.

Through the mass media, dominant groups influence the public to look at crime in ways that are favorable to them. The selective portrayal of crime plays an important role in shaping public perceptions of the "crime problem" and therefore its "official" definition. When politicians talk about fighting the U.S. crime problem, or when news shows report fluctuations in crime rates, they are almost always referring to street crimes (illegal drug use, robbery, burglary, murder, assault, and so on) rather than corporate crimes, governmental crimes, or crimes more likely to be committed by people in influential positions:

> Press coverage focuses public attention on crime in the streets with scarcely a mention of "crime in the suites," downplaying such ... crimes as briberies, embezzlements, kickbacks, monopolistic restraints of trade, illegal uses of public funds by private interests, occupational safety violations, unsafe consumer goods, and environmental poisonings. (Parenti, 1986, p. 12)

Such coverage creates a way of perceiving crime that becomes social reality. We accept the "fact" that certain people or actions are a threat to the well-being of the entire society and therefore a threat to our own personal interests. Consequently, many of us are willing to tolerate the violation of others' civil rights in the interests of controlling crime. In the months following the attacks of September 11, 2001, the federal government eased restrictions on the surveillance, apprehension, interrogation, and detention of suspected terrorists. To many people, this is the price we must pay to ensure public safety and national security. Others, however, worry that such abuses are disproportionately directed toward people of color or people at the lower end of the socioeconomic spectrum.

Corporate Crime

People in the United States take for granted that street crime is our worst social problem and that corporate crime is not as dangerous or as costly (Reiman, 2004). U.S. citizens shake their heads over the exploitative practices of corporations or wealthy despots in such places as the rain forests of Brazil and Indonesia and the sweatshops of Southeast Asia. However, unsafe work conditions; dangerous chemicals in the air, water, and food; faulty products; unnecessary surgery; and shoddy emergency medical services actually put people who live in the United States into more constant and imminent physical danger than do ordinary street crimes. Approximately 17,000 Americans were murdered in 2002 (U.S. Bureau of the Census, 2004a). At the same time, it's estimated that 56,000 Americans die each year on the job or from occupational diseases such as black lung and asbestos. Hundreds of thousands more die from pollution, contaminated foods, hazardous consumer products, and hospital malpractice (Mokhiber, 1999). The Centers for Disease Control estimates that 90,000 people die each year from infections they contract during hospital stays (cited in Connolly, 2005).

Corporate crime also poses greater economic threats to Americans than street crime does. The FBI estimates that burglary and robbery cost the United States $3.8 billion a year. In contrast, the cost of "white collar" crimes like corporate fraud, bribery, embezzlement, insurance fraud, securities fraud, and so on amounts to over $400 billion a year (Reiman, 2004).

Some people actually do view certain types of corporate crime (such as knowingly manufacturing defective products) as more serious than street crimes (Mokhiber, 2000). And in a few high profile cases, executives convicted of corporate malfeasance have received prison sentences of 15 to 25 years (though in the majority of such cases, the punishments are far less severe). Politicians have been quick to jump on the anti-corporate-crime bandwagon in recent years, passing legislation ensuring the accuracy and reliability of corporate disclosures and increasing the penalties for corporate fraud. In 2002, President Bush appointed a Corporate Fraud Task Force that he said would operate like a "financial crimes SWAT team" (quoted in Johnston, 2002b, p. 6). Unfortunately, the group had no direct authority to investigate or prosecute cases and no money or additional staffing for the effort.

Not surprisingly, even when their dangerous actions violate the law, corporations themselves rarely receive heavy criminal punishment (Reiman, 2004). For example, in 2004, the pharmaceutical company GlaxoSmithKline agreed to settle a $2.5 million lawsuit brought by the state of New York alleging that the company had hidden results of drug trials showing that its antidepressant Paxil might have dangerous side effects, like increasing suicidal thoughts in children. At Congressional hearings lawmakers berated executives from GlaxoSmithKline and other drug companies for hiding study results that challenged the effectiveness of their drugs. The companies promised to do better. But according to studies financed by the National Institutes of Health, crucial facts about many clinical trials continue to be withheld from the Food and Drug Administration (cited in Berenson, 2005).

To ease the inconvenience of prosecution for corporate wrongdoers, the U.S. Justice Department has instituted a form of corporate probation. Several major companies that have been charged with billions of dollars worth of accounting fraud, bid rigging, and other illegal financial schemes—including American International Group, PNC Financial Services Group, Merrill Lynch, and AOL-Time Warner—have agreed to *deferred prosecutions,* in which they accept responsibility for wrongdoing, agree not to fight the charges, agree to cooperate, pay a fine, and implement changes in corporate structure to prevent future criminal wrongdoing. If the company abides by the agreement for a period of time—usually 12 months—prosecutors will drop all charges (Mokhiber & Weissman, 2004). Such arrangements are meant to avoid more drastic punishment, which could destroy these companies and cost thousands of innocent employees their jobs. As the Attorney General of New York said, "You don't want to be swinging a meat ax when a scalpel is appropriate" (quoted in Lohr, 2005b, p. B1).

But the imbalance in the legal response to these crimes versus street crimes is glaring. If you were an individual who had stolen millions of dollars from a bank, a shop owner who had defrauded your customers of billions of dollars, or a small businessperson who had knowingly manufactured a potentially lethal product, it's highly unlikely that you would be allowed to carry on with life as usual. Our massive law enforcement and criminal justice machinery would no doubt mobilize its vast resources to see that you were prosecuted to the full extent of the law. Yet large corporations engage in such activities every day largely without much public outcry or moral panic. Most aren't even prosecuted under criminal statutes. Between 1982 and 2002, about 170,000 American workers died on the job. During that same period, federal and state workplace safety agencies investigated 1,798 fatality cases in which companies *willfully* violated workplace safety laws—for instance, by removing safety devices to speed up production, by denying workers proper safety gear, or by simply ignoring explicit safety warnings. But only 104 of these cases were ever prosecuted. And of those cases, only 16 resulted in criminal convictions (Barstow, 2003).

Why aren't these dangerous and costly corporate acts considered as deviant as face-to-face street crime? According to sociologist Jeffrey Reiman (2004), the answer resides in the perceived circumstances surrounding these acts. People typically see the injuries caused by corporate crime as unintentional, indirect, and a consequence of an endeavor defined in this culture as legitimate or socially productive: making a profit. In most people's minds, someone who tries to harm someone else is usually considered more evil than someone who harms without intending to. Moreover, harming someone directly seems more deviant than harming someone indirectly. Finally, harm that results from illegitimate activities is usually considered more serious than harm that is a by-product of standard business activities.

The Menace of "Illegal" Drugs

Different cultures show varying levels of tolerance when it comes to drug use. For instance, throughout the South Pacific people commonly chew betel nuts for their stimulant effects; in the Bolivian and Peruvian Andes people chew coca leaves during their ordinary workday. The Huichol of central Mexico ingest peyote—a small cactus that produces hallucinations—as part of their religious rituals. And in the United States we wink at the use of many substances that alter people's states of mind, such as coffee, chocolate, and alcohol.

But when it comes to illegal drugs, American attitudes change dramatically. Like the term *terrorist,* the term *drugs* is an easy and popular scapegoat on which to heap our collective hatred. The United States has been described as a *temperance culture* (H.G. Levine, 1992)—one in which self-control and industriousness are perceived as desirable characteristics of productive citizens. In such an environment, drug-induced states of altered consciousness are likely to be perceived as a loss of control and thus feared as a threat to the economic and physical well-being of the population.

The United States has been in an ill-defined, undeclared, but highly publicized "war" against illegal drugs for many years. The Drug Enforcement Administration, the FBI, and the U.S. Customs Service seized almost 3 million pounds of illegal drugs in 2003, over four times as much as was seized in 1990 (U.S. Bureau of the Census, 2004a). During that same period, the drug arrest rate increased from 435 people per 100,000 to 505 per 100,000. More people are behind bars in the United States for drug offenses than are in prison for all crimes in England, France, Germany, and Japan combined (Egan, 1999).

With so much attention and resources now focused on the "War on Terror," it would seem that the fight against drug dealers and users could no longer be a national priority. Indeed, cuts in the federal budget have reduced the availability of resources devoted to drug enforcement, and some antidrug programs and agencies have been folded into antiterrorism efforts. Nevertheless, there remains a widespread belief that although terrorists pose an external danger, drug users and drug dealers are slowly destroying the country from within and therefore need to be stopped.

Many conflict sociologists, though, argue that antidrug campaigns and legislative activities are driven chiefly by political interests (see, for example, E. Goode, 1989). The war on drugs in the United States has permitted greater social control over groups perceived to be threatening, such as young minority men, and has mobilized voter support for candidates who profess to be "tough" on drugs. Capitalizing on the "drug menace" as a personal and societal threat is a common and effective political tactic (Ben-Yehuda, 1990).

The very definition of which substances are "illegal drugs" is influenced by powerful interests. Behind the phrase "war on drugs" is the assumption that illegal drugs (marijuana, ecstasy, cocaine, methamphetamines, heroin, and so forth) are the most dangerous substances and the ones that must be eradicated. However, the difference between legal and illegal drugs is not necessarily a function of their relative danger. The National Commission on Marijuana and Drug Abuse defines a drug as any chemical that affects the structure and function of a living organism (cited in Fine, 1990). Such a definition includes alcohol, nicotine, caffeine, all types of prescription and over-the-counter medication, herbal remedies, and perhaps even salt and sugar. These substances, even though they can sometimes be harmful and addictive, are either completely legal or legal under certain restrictions.

Tobacco, for example, is a clearer health risk than alcohol, marijuana, or even heroin (Reiman, 2004) but has only recently been discussed in terms of drug abuse. Tobacco is estimated to kill 440,000 U.S. residents annually. In fact, one in every five deaths in the United States is smoking related. More people die from tobacco use in this country than from HIV/AIDS, illegal drug use, alcohol use, motor vehicle injuries, suicides, and murders combined (Centers for Disease Control, 2004).

In 2003, the U.S. Justice Department took the unprecedented step of demanding that the nation's biggest cigarette makers forfeit $289 billion in profits derived from over 50 years of dangerous and "fraudulent" marketing practices, such as manipulating nicotine levels, lying to customers about the health effects of smoking, and directing advertising campaigns at children (Lichtblau, 2003). But knowing the hazards of selling and smoking cigarettes has not prompted our society to outlaw it entirely, as we have outlawed marijuana smoking and cocaine use. Criminalizing tobacco would have a disastrous impact on many large corporations and on several states whose economies depend on this crop. The tobacco industry has one of the most powerful lobbies in Washington. In fact, in 2005, the Justice Department decided to reduce the amount it sought in its case from $289 billion to a mere $10 billion, out of concern over the financial impact that the original amount would have on the tobacco companies (Leonnig, 2005).

The response to drug users also shows how conceptions of deviance are socially constructed. Society does not stigmatize and scorn "respectable" people addicted to legal substances. Police don't harass abusers of prescription drugs, ransack their homes, or develop creative ways of apprehending and arresting them. Yet such tactics—not to mention illegal searches and seizures, wiretapping, surveillance of the U.S. mail, and other invasions of privacy (Wisotsky, 1998)—may be used against "typical" addicts or suspected drug sellers, even if such measures cross the line of ethics and individual, constitutional rights.

The "drug courier profile" is another reflection of how the war on drugs targets some people but not others. The profile is a set of characteristics law enforcement agencies use to identify drug smugglers in public facilities such as airports, train stations, bus depots, and interstate highways. Officers look for people who are obviously in a hurry, have bought a one-way ticket or paid for the ticket with cash, have changed travel plans at the last minute, are the first to get off the plane, or fly to or from Miami or Detroit or any other city known for having heavy drug traffic. The U.S. Supreme Court ruled in 1989 that such factors, as well as a person's physical appearance, can amount to a "reasonable suspicion." In addition, law enforcement agencies commonly recruit hotel managers and employees to act as confidential informers about people who fit the profile. Front desk clerks, bellhops, and porters are trained to be suspicious of people who ask for corner rooms, who haul trailers behind their cars, or who frequently move from room to room (Kocieniewski, 1999). Hotel managers routinely allow state troopers, without warrants, to look at the credit card receipts and registration information of all the guests. In return, the managers are assured that any searches or arrests will occur off hotel premises.

For all the reliance on the profiles, they have proved relatively ineffective. Statistics on airport searches in Denver, Pittsburgh, and Buffalo show that only about 3% of these searches result in an arrest (cited in Duke, 1994). Critics also argue that damaging stereotypes, particularly racial ones, are a key element of the drug courier profile. For instance, hotel informants are trained to pay particular attention to guests who speak Spanish. In 1991 the *Pittsburgh Press* examined 121 cases in which travelers were searched and no drugs were found. Of these people, 77% were black, Latino, or Asian. In Memphis about 75% of the air travelers stopped by Drug Enforcement Administration agents were black, yet only 4% of the flying public is black. A Rutgers University statistician found that on a stretch of the New Jersey Turnpike, only 4.7% of all traffic consisted of late-model cars with out-of-state license plates driven by African American men. However, more than 80% of the cars that were stopped and drivers who were interrogated on the highway fit that description (cited in Duke, 1994).

Meanwhile, little has been accomplished in the way of stopping the illegal activities of the rich and powerful interests that participate in the drug industry. Established financial institutions often launder drug money, despite laws against it (Parenti, 1995). Massive international crime organizations that ensure the flow of illicit drugs into the country have grown bigger and richer, despite a decades-long attempt to stop them (Bullington, 1993). Unlike low-status users and small-time dealers of illegal drugs, these organizations wield tremendous economic power and political influence (Godson & Olson, 1995).

The Medicalization of Deviance

One of the most powerful forces in defining deviance in the United States today is the medical establishment. The field of medicine has been extremely successful in equating deviance with individual illness. Each time we automatically refer to bizarre or troublesome behavior as "sick," we help to perpetuate the perception that deviance is like a disease. **Medicalization** is the definition of behavior as a medical problem or illness and the mandating or licensing of the medical profession to provide some type of treatment for it (Conrad, 1975). Many physicians, psychologists, psychiatrists, therapists, insurance agents, and the entire pharmaceutical industry in the United States benefit from a medicalized view of certain deviant acts.

Conduct once categorized simply as misbehavior often gets redefined as a psychiatric disease, disorder, or syndrome. Between 1952 and 2000, the number of mental disorders officially recognized by the American Psychiatric Association increased from

110 to close to 400 (Caplan, 1995; Horwitz, 2002). Many of these designations seem to have nothing to do with illness. Take for instance a malady called "Conduct Disorder," a diagnosis restricted to children and adolescents. According to the American Psychiatric Association (2000), the "symptoms" of this disorder include bullying or threatening behavior toward others, physical cruelty, destruction of property, theft, and violations of other rules like staying out late despite parental prohibitions. In another era, this sort of misbehavior was called "juvenile delinquency."

To accommodate the growing number of "illnesses," the number of psychiatric professionals has almost tripled over the last two decades—as has the number of people seeking psychiatric help. The combined indirect and related costs of mental "illness" in this society, including lost productivity, lost earnings due to illness, and social costs, are estimated to be at least $113 billion annually (National Mental Health Association, 2005). The World Health Organization estimates that at any given point in time close to 8% of the American population—or approximately 24 million people—have a serious mental disorder (cited in McNeil, 2004a). A study sponsored by the National Institute of Mental Health estimates 55% of Americans will suffer from a diagnosable mental disorder sometime during their lifetime (cited in Carey, 2005a). Along with alcoholism, drug addiction, and serious mental illness, these disorders now include overeating, undereating, shyness, school stress, distress over failed romance, poor performance in school, addiction to using the Internet, and excessive gambling, shopping, and sex. Some scientists even argue that men's marital infidelity is a neurological disorder that can be controlled with drugs (Kirn, 2004).

Why has the medical view of deviance become so dominant? One reason is that medical explanations of troublesome social problems and deviant behaviors are appealing to a society that wants simple explanations for complex social problems. If violent behavior is the result of a dysfunction in a person's brain, it then becomes a problem of defective, violent individuals, not of the larger societal context within which violent acts take place. Likewise, when our doctor or therapist tells us our anxiety, depression, crabbiness, and insecurity will vanish if we simply take a drug, we are spared the difficult task of looking at the social complexities of our lives or the structure of our society.

The medicalization of deviance also appeals to humanitarian values. The designation of a problem as an illness removes legal and moral scrutiny or punishment in favor of therapeutic treatment (Zola, 1986). The alcoholic is no longer a sinner or a criminal but a victim, someone whose behavior is an "illness," beyond his or her control. Children who have trouble learning in school aren't disobedient and disruptive, they are "sick." If people are violating norms because of a disease that has invaded their bodies, they should not be held morally responsible. Medicalization creates less social stigma and condemnation of people labeled deviant.

Despite its enormous public appeal, though, the tendency to medicalize deviance has serious social consequences (Conrad & Schneider, 1992). These include the individualization of complex social issues and the depoliticization of deviance.

Individualizing Complex Social Issues

U.S. culture often emphasizes the individual over the social structure. Instead of seeing certain deviant behaviors as symptoms of a faulty social system—blocked economic opportunities, neighborhood decay, repressive social institutions, or unattainable cultural standards—people in the United States tend to see such behaviors as expressions of individual traits or shortcomings. Depression, alcoholism, eating disorders, and so on are "diseases" that lie within the person and hence can be remedied only through actions aimed at the individual (Kovel, 1980).

Individualistic medical explanations of deviance are not necessarily wrong. Some violent people do have brain diseases, and some people diagnosed with clinical depression do have imbalances of chemicals in their brains. But when we focus exclusively on these explanations for everyone whose behavior diverges from social expectations, the solutions we seek focus on the perpetrator alone, to the exclusion of everything else.

Consider the problem of attention deficit hyperactivity disorder (ADHD), one of the most commonly diagnosed maladies among U.S. children today. A child diagnosed with ADHD is difficult to deal with at home and in the classroom. He or she fidgets and squirms, has difficulty remaining seated, can't sustain attention in tasks or play activities, can't follow rules, talks excessively, and is easily distracted (American Psychiatric Association, 2000).

Fifty years ago, such children were considered bad or troublesome and would have been subjected to punishment or even expulsion from school. Today, however, most hyperactive behavior is diagnosed as a symptom of a mental disorder, and drugs are prescribed to treat it. An estimated four million children in the United States are taking drugs to curb their overactivity or inattentiveness (President's Council on Bioethics, 2003). In one school district in the southeastern United States, 18% to 20% of fifth-grade boys were taking such drugs (cited in Koch, 1999). Between 2000 and 2003, spending for drugs used to treat ADHD increased 183% for all children and 369% for children under the age of five (AIS Health, 2004). This growth is part of an alarming trend toward the increased use of drugs for children in general (Safer, Zito, & dosReis, 2003). Critics worry not only about the drugs' safety but also about the mixed messages children receive when they are handed a daily pill to medicate away their troublesome behavior, while at the same time they're being told to say no to drugs (Koch, 1999).

Despite occasional adverse side effects, the drugs used to treat ADHD are generally successful in quieting unruly and annoying behavior (Whalen & Henker, 1977). But are we ignoring the possibility that hyperactive behavior may be a child's adaptation to his or her social environment? In some cases, it may be a response to an educational system that discourages individual expression (Conrad, 1975). Narrowly defined norms of acceptable behavior make it difficult if not impossible for children to pursue their own desires and needs. Some pediatricians argue that the symptoms of ADHD may just be children's natural reaction to living in a fast-paced, stressful world (Diller, 1998).

I'm not suggesting that all children who are diagnosed with ADHD are disruptive simply because they are bored in school or because their individual creativity and vitality have been squashed by unsympathetic teachers. Some children do have debilitating problems that require treatment. The point is that from an institutional perspective, the tendency to label disruptiveness as an individual disorder protects the school system's legitimacy and authority. The institution could not function if disruptiveness were tolerated (Tobin, Wu, & Davidson, 1989). But imagine if our educational system promoted and encouraged free individual expression rather than obedience and discipline. In such an environment, overactivity wouldn't be considered disruptive and wouldn't be a problem in need of a medical solution.

When inconvenient behavior is translated into an individual sickness, medical remedies (that is, drugs) become a convenient tool for enforcing conformity and upholding the values of society. When parents say they want "better children," they typically mean they want children who are in line with our culture's values: "well-adjusted, well-behaved, sociable, attentive, high-performing, and academically adept" (President's Council on Bioethics, 2003, p. 73). Parents who *don't* want their children to have these characteristics become objects of suspicion.

We have come to rely on drugs not just to cure infections or fight pain but to help us through many of our common problems in living, such as anxiety, sleep problems, overeating, sadness, fears, and so on. Antidepressant drugs, in particular, have become so popular that they are now a prominent feature of the culture.

❖ _____

Micro-Macro Connection
The Pharmaceutical Personality

Prozac arrived on the scene in 1987 as a treatment for depression, and almost as soon as it hit the market, it was being hailed as a miracle drug. Not only was it effective and easy to prescribe, it was relatively free of the weight gain, low blood pressure, irregular heart rhythms, and other side effects common with other antidepressant drugs. By 1990, Prozac had become the top-selling antidepressant in the world, a position it held until 2000. At its peak, Prozac brought in $3 billion in annual revenues (Zuckoff, 2000). Sales have slipped recently as cheaper, generic versions have entered the market. Nevertheless, antidepressant drugs such as Prozac, Zoloft, Paxil, Celexa, and Wellbutrin have become a $12-billion-a-year industry (E. Goode, 2002). GlaxoSmithKline spent more money—$91 million—advertising Paxil in 2001 than Nike spent advertising its top shoes (Elliot, 2003). In 2002, 8.5% of the U.S. civilian, noninstitutionalized population had a prescription for an antidepressant (Stagnitti, 2005).

Antidepressants quickly grew to be more than just treatments for depression, however. They are now regularly prescribed for people with eating disorders, obsessive-compulsive disorders, anxiety disorders, social phobias, obesity, gambling addiction, and family problems. A version of Prozac called Sarafem is prescribed for women complaining of premenstrual difficulties. Some people use drugs like Prozac to enhance job performance, improve their alertness and concentration, overcome boredom, think more clearly, become more assertive, or get along better with their mates.

Clearly, the therapeutic realm of antidepressants has expanded beyond clinical depression to include more of what were once thought of as ordinary life stresses. In his book *Listening to Prozac* (1997), psychiatrist Peter Kramer—an avid proponent and energetic prescriber of the drug—argues that Prozac can (and perhaps should) also be used to remove aspects of personality we find objectionable. He likens the use of Prozac in overcoming undesirable psychological traits to the use of cosmetic surgery in overcoming undesirable physical ones.

Many people who have benefited from Prozac describe it in adoring, almost worshipful terms. They weren't healed, they were transformed. Shy introverts report turning into social butterflies, mediocre workers turn into on-the-job dynamos, the bored become interested and alert, even the unattractive begin to feel more beautiful. Some people see Prozac as nothing short of a divine creation:

> As my husband and I watched the results of Prozac, we knew that the medication was God's gift to us. Breakthroughs . . . like Prozac are evidence of His grace. I now *feel* God's love for me as I never have before. . . . I believe that it is helping me be more true to the person God created me to be. (emphasis in original; quoted in "Christian Faith," 1995, p. 17)

According to Kramer, his patients feel "better than well" shortly after they begin taking the drug. They report improvement in their popularity, business sense, self-image, energy, and sexual appeal (Kramer, 1997). One patient was having trouble at work and had recently broken up with her boyfriend. Kramer prescribed Prozac. Within weeks she was dating several men and handling her job demands smoothly. She even received a substantial pay raise. Convinced that the drug created these improvements in her life, she happily referred to herself as "Ms. Prozac."

Antidepressants are appealing for economic reasons as well. Because traditional psychotherapy (patients talking to therapists about their problems) is time consuming and expensive, efforts to cut health care costs work against its use. A psychiatrist or psychologist may charge 10 times more for a single, hour-long session than it costs for one week's worth of antidepressants. Many prepaid health care plans have begun to limit or exclude extensive talk therapy in their coverage, thereby indirectly encouraging greater use of such drugs as Prozac (M. H. Cooper, 1994).

In light of these benefits, we should perhaps not be surprised that Prozac has become a cultural icon. The drug pops up in magazine cartoons and David Letterman and Jay Leno jokes. As one writer noted, "Prozac has attained the familiarity of Kleenex" (Crowley, 1994, p. 41). Even the word *Prozac* is now an entry in *Webster's New World Dictionary,* defined as a quick-relief cure-all.

Antidepressants certainly have helped tens of millions of people in serious need. However, their popularity raises fundamental sociological questions about the role drugs ought to play in everyday life. Critics fear that antidepressants—as well as other drugs that can modify character—are aimed not just at "sick patients" but at people who already function at a high level and want enriched memory, enhanced intelligence, heightened concentration, and a transformation of bad moods into good ones. In a fast-paced, achievement-oriented society such as the United States, the motivations for gaining a competitive edge—whether in school, on the job, or in interpersonal relations—are obvious. Those who earn higher grades, sell more cars, or come across as more charming and attractive can reap enormous financial and social benefits.

But once people begin to use a drug to chemically enhance performance, those who do not use the drug—whether for reasons of principle or because they can't afford it—risk losing out and becoming the less rewarded and less valuable members of the community (President's Council on Bioethics, 2003). Would we, as a society, have to resort to legal regulation—much like the ban on athletic performance enhancers such as anabolic steroids—to prevent a desperate race to keep up?

On a more profound level, if we can use existing pharmaceutical technology to chemically eradicate sadness and despair—to create a world in which pain can be "erased as easily and fully as dirty words on a school blackboard" (Mauro, 1994, p. 46)— why would anyone ever put up with emotional discomfort? In the past, people simply assumed that despair was part of the human condition. Suffering made us stronger. Just as physical pain prevents us from burning ourselves if we get too close to a fire, per- haps mental pain, too, serves a purpose, such as motivating us to change life situations that are getting us into trouble. There's the spiritual element as well: "One reconceives sadness as sickness only by emptying it of psychic or spiritual significance and turning it into a mere thing of the body" (President's Council on Bioethics, 2003, p. 261).

But people today are more inclined to believe they have a right not to be unhappy. Sadness is inconvenient and prevents us from reaching our potential. And if there's a pill to get rid of it quickly and cheaply, then why not use it?

Antidepressants have not yet completely redefined society. Quite possibly depres- sion, unlike polio or smallpox, will never be essentially wiped out. But the technologi- cal possibilities not only of antidepressants but of brain scanning techniques, genetic modification, and drugs as yet unknown raise important issues about the role of medicine in defining deviance, controlling behavior, constructing personality, and ultimately determining social life and the culture that guides it.

❖ ❖

Depoliticizing Deviance

The process of individualizing and medicalizing social problems robs deviant behavior of its power to send a message about malfunctioning elements of society. Disruptive behaviors or statements automatically lose their power to prompt social change when they are seen as symptoms of individual defects or illnesses. We need not pay attention to the critical remarks of an opponent if that opponent is labeled as mentally ill. Totalitarian regimes often declare political dissidents insane and confine them to hospitals in an attempt to quiet dangerous political criticism. The Chinese gov- ernment, for instance, has forcibly hospitalized and medicated hundreds of followers of the outlawed spiritual movement Falun Gong, which it has condemned as a dangerous cult (Eckholm, 2001).

Such practices are not found only in foreign countries. In 1945, the famous U.S. poet Ezra Pound, who was living in Italy, was brought back to the United States to stand trial for treason. He was accused of making anti–United States radio broadcasts from Rome during World War II. But the court, prosecution, and defense, together with several psychiatrists, agreed that he was mentally unfit to stand trial. He was committed to St. Elizabeth's Mental Hospital in Washington, D.C., where he remained for the next 13 years. Although some have argued that confining Pound in a mental hospital helped him avoid an almost certain prison sentence, others suggest that declaring him "men- tally ill" not only punished him for subversive conduct but also allowed the government to discount statements he had made that attempted to undermine the U.S. war effort.

The political use of medicalization is not restricted to our distant past. A *Dallas Morning News* investigation discovered that high-ranking U.S. military commanders have tried to discredit and intimidate subordinates who report security and safety violations or military overpricing by ordering them to undergo psychiatric evaluations or by sending them to a mental ward (Timms & McGonigle, 1992). One West Point cadet spent a month in a psychiatric ward for reporting widespread illegal drug use at the academy. He met officer patients in the ward who had objected to army policy and who were involuntarily receiving electric shock treatments. And a chief petty officer in the air force contends that his forced hospitalization was part of a retaliation for reporting payroll abuses at Dallas Naval Air Station. He insightfully describes the power of medical labels to discredit his political criticism: "What happened was nobody would speak to me. Let's face it. After someone has gone to a mental ward, you kind of question what's going on. It was a nice ploy, and it worked. What they did was totally neutralize me" (quoted in Timms & McGonigle, 1992).

Creating the image of deviants as sick people who must be dealt with through medical therapies is a powerful way for dominant groups in society to maintain conformity and protect themselves from those whom they fear or who challenge the way "normal" social life is organized (Pfohl, 1994). The seemingly merciful medical labels not only reduce individual responsibility but also reduce the likelihood that such potentially contagious political criticism will be taken seriously (Hills, 1980).

Conclusion

When we talk about deviance, we usually speak of extreme forms: crime, mental illness, substance abuse, and so on. These activities are indeed troublesome, but for most people they remain comfortably distant phenomena. I think most of us would like to cling to the belief that deviants are "them" and normal people are "us."

The lesson I hope you take away from this chapter, however, is that the issue of deviance is, essentially, an issue of social definition. As a group, community, or society, we decide which differences are benign and which are dangerous. Standards and expectations change. Norms come and go. The consequence is that each of us could be considered deviant to some degree by some audience. We have all broken unspoken interactional norms; many of us have even broken the law. To a lesser degree, we are all potentially like Kelly Michaels, subject to being erroneously labeled deviant and unfairly treated as a result. Given the right—or wrong—circumstances, all of us risk being negatively labeled or acquiring a bad reputation.

This chapter has examined deviance as both a micro- and a macro-level sociological phenomenon, as something that plays a profound role in individual lives and in society as a whole. Although sociologists are interested in the broad social and political processes that create cultural definitions of deviance, they are also interested in the ways these definitions are applied in everyday life. Societal definitions have their most potent effect when expressed face-to-face. We can talk about such powerful institutions as medicine creating definitions of deviance that are consistent with broader political or economic interests, but if these definitions aren't accepted as appropriate to some degree by a majority, they will be ineffectual. Again, we see the value of developing the sociological imagination, which helps us understand the complex interplay between individuals and the culture and community within which they live.

YOUR TURN

People's perceptions of deviant acts and individuals are a crucial element of our understanding of deviance. From a conflict perspective, these perceptions are usually consistent with the goals and interests of those in power. But what exactly are people's perceptions of deviance?

Make copies of the following list, and find 20 to 30 people who would be willing to read it and answer a few questions. Try to get an equal proportion of males and females and younger and older people. Have each person rank the following "deviant" acts in order from 1 to 15, with 15 being the most serious and 1 the least serious. Do not define for them what is meant by "serious."

♦ Catching your spouse with a lover and killing them both
♦ Embezzling your employer's funds
♦ Robbing a supermarket with a gun
♦ Forcibly raping a stranger in a park
♦ Selling liquor to minors
♦ Killing a suspected burglar in your home
♦ Practicing medicine without a license
♦ Soliciting for prostitution
♦ Blowing up a building with people in it
♦ Hitting your child
♦ Selling cocaine
♦ Manufacturing and selling cars known to have dangerous defects
♦ Forcibly raping a former romantic partner or spouse
♦ Being drunk in public
♦ Killing a person for a fee
♦ Conspiring to fix the prices of machines sold to businesses

After the volunteers are finished, ask them how they decided on their rankings. What criteria did they use for judging the seriousness of each act? Where did their perceptions come from? Why do they think the "less serious" acts on the list are against the law?

After collecting all your data, compute the average ranking for each of the 15 items. (For each item, add all the ranking scores and divide by the number of responses.) The larger the average score, the more the perceived seriousness of that act. Which acts were considered the most serious and which the least serious? Was there a fair amount of agreement among the people in your sample? Were there any differences between the ratings of men and women? Between older and younger people? Between people of different racial or ethnic groups? Use the conflict perspective to discuss the role these perceptions play in the nature and control of deviance.*

CHAPTER HIGHLIGHTS

♦ According to an absolutist definition of deviance, there are two fundamental types of behavior: that which is inherently acceptable and that which is inherently unacceptable. In contrast, a relativist definition of deviance suggests that it is not a property inherent in any particular act, belief, or condition. Instead, deviance is a definition of behavior that is socially created by collective human judgments. Hence, like beauty, deviance is in the eye of the beholder.

---

*Most of the 15 items in this exercise are adapted from Rossi, Waite, Bose, & Berk, 1974.

- The labeling theory of deviance argues that deviance is a consequence of the application of rules and sanctions to an offender. Deviant labels can impede individuals' everyday social life by forming expectations of them in the minds of others.

- According to conflict theory, the definition of deviance is a form of social control exerted by more powerful people and groups over less powerful ones.

- The criminal justice system and the medical profession have had a great deal of influence in defining, explaining, and controlling deviant behavior. Criminalization is the process by which certain behaviors come to be defined as crimes. Medicalization is the depiction of deviance as a medical problem or illness.

KEY TERMS

absolutism Approach to defining deviance that rests on the assumption that all human behavior can be considered either inherently good or inherently bad

criminalization Official definition of an act of deviance as a crime

deterrence theory Theory of deviance positing that people will be prevented from engaging in deviant acts if they judge the costs of such an act to outweigh its benefits

deviance Behavior, ideas, or attributes of an individual or group that some people in society find offensive

labeling theory Theory stating that deviance is the consequence of the application of rules and sanctions to an offender; a deviant is an individual to whom the identity "deviant" has been successfully applied

medicalization Definition of behavior as a medical problem and mandating the medical profession to provide some kind of treatment for it

relativism Approach to defining deviance that rests on the assumption that deviance is socially created by collective human judgments and ideas

STUDY SITE ON THE WEB

Don't forget the interactive quizzes and other learning aids at www.pineforge.com/newman6 study. In the Resources File for this chapter, you'll also find more on constructing difference, including:

Sociologists at Work

- David Rosenhan: Being Sane in Insane Places
- Richard Schwartz and Jerome Skolnick: The Criminal Applicant
- Frank Tannenbaum: The Dramatization of Evil
- Christopher Uggen and Jeff Manza: Prisoners and Presidents

Micro-Macro Connections

- Drug Trade and Global Deviance
- Power, Deviance, and Insanity
- Social Control Through Medicine

PART III

Social Structure, Institutions, and Everyday Life

Up to this point, I have been discussing how our everyday lives are constructed and ordered. But this is only part of the picture. What does social life look like from the top down? Once the architecture is constructed and in place, what influence does it exert on our everyday lives? To answer these questions, the remaining chapters investigate the organizational and institutional pressures on everyday life and the various sources of structural inequality in society: social class and wealth, race and ethnicity, and gender. Global institutions and population trends are other structural influences on everyday life. These facets of society may seem ominous and impenetrable. However, you will see that our lives don't completely fall under the control of the social structure. As the concept of the sociological imagination suggests, the collective actions of individuals often bring about fundamental changes in society.

The Structure of Society
Organizations, Social Institutions, and Globalization

History will no doubt mark the 2000 presidential election as one of the most bizarre political events of all time. The chaos began on election night. Early in the evening, Al Gore, the Democratic candidate, was projected as the winner of Florida's 25 electoral votes, giving him the inside track to the presidency; a few hours later that projection was rescinded and Florida was labeled "too close to call." In the early morning hours of the following day, George W. Bush, the Republican candidate, was projected as the winner of Florida, and therefore the election, only to have that projection withdrawn when Florida, again, was declared "too close to call." The ensuing month brought a daily dose of street protests; charges of voter fraud; machine and manual recounts; debates over absentee votes, scrutiny of dimpled chads and butterfly ballots; lawsuits and countersuits; controversial political decisions and legal rulings. On December 13, the U.S. Supreme Court finally made its definitive ruling, on a 5–4 vote. The Court essentially declared George W. Bush the next president, even though he had received several hundred thousand fewer votes nationwide than his challenger.

To listen to the domestic and foreign news media tell it at the time, the most powerful country in the world was in a state of utter political confusion. The situation was described in either mocking or apocalyptic terms. U.S. citizens were losing their moral authority to lecture other countries about the virtues of democracy. We were about to face a "constitutional crisis." We were going to be a country without a leader. We were on the brink of anarchy.

Of course, none of that happened. As one journalist put it, "[T]he apparatus of government is still in place, skilled politicians and career civil servants still keep things running, and ultimately nothing apocalyptic is likely to happen. . . . The system will work and life will go on" (Belluck, 2001, p. A9). Perhaps the most shocking thing of all was that to the average U.S. citizen, nothing really changed during the electoral confusion in Florida. Buses, trains, and planes still ran on time. Food was still being delivered to grocery shelves. People were still shopping for holiday gifts. Government services were still being provided. Even the stock market remained solid. We all simply went about our business, pausing now and then to witness the political spectacle or to debate with friends and family at the dinner table or with coworkers at the water cooler.

Why didn't the country collapse during this electoral epic? Why didn't violence erupt in the streets and some well-armed faction attempt to forcefully resolve the impasse? To answer that question, we must turn to one of the key concepts of this book: social structure. Despite strong emotions, dire predictions, and sometimes confrontational behavior of the more partisan individuals, the political system remained intact. Whether we agreed with the ultimate outcome or not, our legal and political institutions functioned as they were designed to. From local precincts and campaign organizations to state legislatures and courts to the highest court in the land, the system continued to function. To be sure, the motives of some of the individual players were highly partisan. But the structure itself rose above the actions of these individuals and prevented the sort of large-scale catastrophe that media pundits predicted. Indeed, fears that similar problems would occur during the 2004 presidential election never materialized. Though there were some reports of electoral improprieties during that election, there were no major crises.

One of the great sociological paradoxes of human existence is that we are capable of producing a social structure that we then experience as something other than a human product. It is ironic that we spend most of our lives either within or responding to the influence of larger structural entities—particularly in a society such as the United States that so fiercely extols the virtues of rugged individualism and personal accomplishment.

This chapter focuses on our relationship with the social structure we construct and maintain, both locally and globally. This focus requires us to examine the structure not only from the individual's perspective but also from the macrosociological perspective of the organizations and institutions themselves. Many important social issues look quite different depending on the perspective we use to understand them.

Social Structure and Everyday Life

As you may recall from Chapter 2, **social structure** is the framework of society that exists above the level of individuals and provides the social setting in which individuals interact with one another to form relationships. It includes the social institutions, organizations, groups, statuses and roles, cultural beliefs, and institutionalized norms that add order and predictability to our private lives The concept of structure is important because it implies a patterned regularity to the way we live our individual lives and in the way societies work. We could not draw any meaningful conclusions about human behavior if we started with the notion that society is haphazard and that things happen by chance alone.

If you know what to look for, you can see social structure everywhere. Consider, for instance, the components of social structure that affect the experience of going to school. Within the broad U.S. educational institution, there are examples of every component of social structure:

- ◆ *Organizations:* National Education Association, National Teachers' Association, state teachers' associations, accrediting agencies, local school boards, local administrative boards, and so on
- ◆ *Groups:* faculty, administrators, student body, classes, clubs, cafeteria staff, and so on
- ◆ *Statuses:* dean, teacher, student, principal, custodian, coach, librarian, and so on
- ◆ *Role expectations:* teaching, learning, disciplining, making and taking tests, coaching, and so on
- ◆ *Cultural beliefs:* for example, the belief that education is the principal means of achieving financial success, that it makes possible a complex division of labor, and that it makes a technologically advanced society possible
- ◆ *Institutionalized norms:* the expectation that everyone attend school until the age of 16, school rules that determine acceptable behavior (such as not running in the halls, not screaming in class, staying on the school grounds until classes are over), and so on (Saunders, 1991).

The massive structure of the educational system is a reality that determines life chances and choices. You may choose which science class to take in high school, whether to go on to college, and what to major in once you get there, but the admissions policies of potential colleges and the availability of jobs to people with and without a college education are factors beyond your control. You're reading this book right now not because of your fondness for fine literature but because of the structural requirements of being a college student. You know you must graduate to increase your chances of getting a good job. To graduate, you must get good grades in your classes. To get good grades in your classes, you must keep up with the material so you're prepared for exams. You might rather be doing a number of other things right now—reading a better book, swimming, making love, watching TV, sleeping, doing absolutely nothing—but these personal preferences must take a back seat for the time being to the more immediate structural demands of college life.

Structural demands of the educational system have a broader impact as well. Course grades, standardized test scores, and class rankings are emphasized so much institutionwide and create such personal anxiety for students that they may actually overshadow learning and intellectual growth:

> Throughout our school years, we are taught to believe from society that grades display intelligence. Because of this, our motivation, learning, and personal growth are placed second to attaining the ultimate goal—the grade. . . . We are programmed to imitate what the teacher wants. If we don't, we get a bad grade. . . . Imitation, competition, and fear of grades hinders our discovery. (Bell & McGrane, 1999, p. 2)

A competitive educational atmosphere can sometimes create incompatibility between the needs of the individual student and the needs of the system. Suppose your instructor told you that she was going to give everyone in the class an *A* as long as they showed up every day. Your immediate reaction might be joy, because such a grade would no doubt improve your personal grade point average. But what if all instructors in all courses at your school decided to do the same thing? Everybody who simply showed up for class would graduate with a perfect GPA. How would you feel then? Certainly your joy might be tempered by the knowledge that the reputation of your school would suffer. As long as the institution of education is structured on the "survival of the fittest" assumption that only the smartest or hardest-working students earn the top grades, such changes—personally beneficial though they may be—will be perceived by others as a sign that your school is academically inferior. Hence your long-term interests may actually be best served by a highly competitive system that ensures that some of your fellow students will get lower grades than you.

Structural factors can also sometimes overwhelm individuals' best efforts to exercise their will. Take, for example, the tsunami disaster of 2004, which killed over 200,000 people in South Asia and Eastern Africa and left millions homeless. Millions of ordinary people around the world pledged to help the victims, alongside promises of billions of dollars in aid and military assistance made by 19 nations. Close to 30% of Americans donated money to the cause, and another 37% indicated that they intended to do so (Lester, 2005). Two weeks after the disaster, the charitable organization "Save the Children" had received more than $10 million in donations over the Internet alone. In a typical month, the organization receives between $30,000 and $50,000 (Strom, 2005).

But such dramatic individual benevolence was hobbled and almost crushed at the organizational level. When two dozen government and aid organizations arrived in the hardest hit regions of Indonesia a week or two after the tsunami hit, they found that looters and black market traders had already descended on the wreckage. And some devastated areas had yet to see any relief workers while others were swarming with doctors and nurses. Moreover, the presence of foreign military and relief workers soon created resentment in the Indonesian government. In response, it imposed travel restrictions on foreign aid workers, citing security concerns, and demanded that all foreign military personnel be out of the country in three months. In one of the hardest hit areas, Banda Aceh, relief organizations found themselves in the middle of a civil war, operating alongside paramilitary rebels (officially regarded as terrorists by the U.S. government) and an Indonesian military known for its corruption and rights abuses (Wehrfritz & Cochrane, 2005). Despite the presence of thousands of caring and generous individuals who came to help, these structural factors conspired to slow down the relief process.

Even when it's operating as it's designed to, social structure can cause problems. Mistakes are sometimes the end result of a chain of events set in motion by a system that either induces errors or makes them difficult to detect and correct. For instance, it's estimated that 98,000 Americans die unnecessarily each year in hospitals as a result of medical mistakes—drug mix-ups, surgical errors, misdiagnoses, and so forth (Health Grades, 2004). More Americans die from these errors every six months than died during the 14 years of the Vietnam War. The tendency to sue individual doctors or nurses for malpractice in such cases demonstrates an overwhelming cultural perception that these errors are caused by individual incompetence.

But what appear to be obvious errors in human judgment are often, on closer inspection, linked to broader system failures. Up to a quarter of unanticipated injuries and deaths to hospital patients occur because of a systemwide shortage of nurses (Stolberg, 2002). Nationwide, about 12% of all nursing positions are vacant, and only about one in eight nurses is under age 30. In addition, an analysis of 334 drug errors in hospitals found that system failure was responsible for most of them—for example, poor dissemination of drug knowledge to doctors, inadequate availability of patient information, faulty systems for checking correct dosage, and inefficient hospital procedure (Leape & Bates, 1995).

A report by the Institute of Medicine (1999a) recognizes that the problem of unnecessary hospital deaths lies beyond individual health care workers. It recommends that the health care system build safety concerns into its operations at all levels. It suggests creating a national center for patient safety, establishing a mandatory nationwide reporting system, placing greater emphasis on safety and training in licensing and accreditation evaluations, and developing a "culture of safety" that would help make the reduction of medical errors a top professional priority. Safety procedures in other industries—the commercial airline industry, for example, where copilots are required to make sure pilots are performing at a top level—have already proved that structural solutions can reduce problems for individuals, not just create them.

Social Dilemmas: Individual Interests and Structural Needs

Although social structure can clearly affect the lives of individuals, individual actions can also have an enormous effect on social structure and stability. Sometimes those actions are coordinated to benefit a collection of individuals, and sometimes they're undertaken independently and for personal gain. Let's say a group of residents wants to make sure that their neighborhood is free of crime. Each individual could go on a personal crusade to stop crime, but it seems more logical and efficient for everyone to volunteer at some point to "patrol" at night or to chip in money to improve street lighting.

In actuality, though, people seldom voluntarily act to achieve a common objective unless coerced to do so. Instead, they usually act to ensure their own personal interests (Cross & Guyer, 1980; Messick & Brewer, 1983; Olsen, 1965). Say that the neighbors decide to fight crime by improving street lighting. Some may decide that the rational thing to do is to not voluntarily donate money for a new streetlight because they figure others will do so. That way, they could enjoy the benefits of safer streets without spending their own money. If every person individually decides not to donate, they may save some cash in the short run, but the new streetlight will never be purchased, and everyone will suffer in the long run. The experience of each person in a group pursuing his or her self-interest, regardless of the potential ruin for everyone, is known as a **social dilemma** (Messick & Brewer, 1983).

Major social problems such as environmental pollution can be understood as stemming, at least in part, from the decisions made by people acting in their own interest as opposed to the collective interest. My flinging one bag of trash onto the highway may not seem so significant or destructive. But large numbers of people doing the same thing would be very destructive. If we think of nations as individual actors and the planet as the community to which they belong, many problems that have global significance—including inadequate recycling, failure to conserve energy, and species extinction—can also be understood from this perspective. Two important types of social dilemmas, at both the local level and broader levels, are the tragedy of the commons and the free-rider problem.

The Tragedy of the Commons

The term *commons* was originally used to describe the public pasture ground, often located in the center of medieval towns, where all the local herders could bring their animals to graze. When everyone used the commons in moderation, the grass could regenerate, resulting in a perpetual supply of food for the herds (Hardin & Baden, 1977).

However, each herder could boost his or her profits by letting the animals eat as much as they wanted, thereby increasing their size and the price they could fetch at market. But when many of the herders came to this same conclusion and allowed their growing herds to eat as much of the grass as they wanted for as long as they wanted, the grass in the commons could not regenerate fast enough to feed them all. The tragic result was that the commons collapsed and the herds that grazed on it died or were sold off. Tragedy ensued, because the short-term needs of the individual overshadowed the long-term collective needs of the group.

In this illustration, the common resource was grazing land, and the group was relatively small. However, the **tragedy of the commons** model can be applied to any situation in which common (but limited) resources are available to everyone. For example, consider a behavior on computer networks called "selfish routing" ("Is Selfish Routing," 2003). When you send a message or download information on the Internet, the routing system is programmed to seek the fastest route possible. When many "routers" simultaneously try to send data via the fastest route, that route becomes overly congested and, as I'm sure you've experienced at certain times of the day, connection speeds slow down to a frustrating crawl.

The impulse to seek individual gain over the collective good becomes particularly troublesome when personal well-being is at stake. In the flood-prone summer of 1993 a river overflowed its banks in Des Moines, Iowa, wiping out a filtration system and making the municipal water supply unsafe. To restore full water service, the system had to be refilled with clean water. The situation was urgent. Without full water pressure in the city's water pipes, not only were residents without regular water service, but fire engines couldn't use hydrants. Local officials asked everyone to voluntarily refrain from using tap water in their homes and businesses for a few days. If all the city's residents had limited their water use as asked, everyone in the community would have had water within a couple of days. For some individuals, however, the temptation to use water secretly in the privacy of their own homes was too hard to resist. So many residents violated the city's request that the resumption of full water service was delayed for many more days (Bradsher, 1993). As a result of individuals seeking their own short-term benefits, the entire community suffered.

Why do such dilemmas occur? Part of the problem is a lack of communication and a lack of trust among individual members of a community. I may want to conserve water by using it sparingly, but if I think my neighbors are hoarding, I too will hoard to make sure I don't go without. Hence I may follow a line of action that results in a positive outcome for me but that may eventually have a negative outcome for the community. A "sensible" strategy for the common good—that is, one of moderation and conservation—is quite easy to abandon at the first sign of someone else achieving short-term gains for him- or herself.

The problem is made worse when individuals think that meeting their individual needs will not affect the community. "Is my using an extra gallon of water during a drought *really* going to harm the community?" The dilemma arises when everyone, or at least a substantial number of people, concludes that it will not. As we collectively ignore or downplay the consequences of our actions, we collectively overuse the resource and pave the way for disasters that none of us has caused individually (Edney, 1979).

The Free-Rider Problem

Social dilemmas can also occur when people refrain from contributing something to a common resource because the resource is available regardless of their contribution. Why pay for something that's available for free? For example, it is irrational, from an individual's point of view, to donate money to public television. I can enjoy *Sesame Street, Nova,* and *Masterpiece Theater* without paying a penny. My small personal donation wouldn't be more than a tiny drop in public television's budgetary bucket. From my point of view, I have no incentive to incur any costs when I don't have to. If everyone acted this way, however, we would all eventually lose the resource. If public television depended solely on voluntary donations—corporate grants and sponsorships actually keep it going—it would have disappeared a long time ago.

Sociologists sometimes refer to this situation as the **free-rider problem** (Olsen, 1965). As the term implies, a free rider is an individual who acquires a good or service without risking any personal costs or contributing anything in return. Free-rider behavior can be seen in a variety of everyday activities, from reading a magazine at a newsstand without buying it to downloading music files for free from other people's collections. We all enjoy the benefits our tax dollars provide—police, firefighters, smooth roads, and other municipal services. But if taxes were voluntary, would anyone willingly pay for these services?

We can see evidence of the free-rider problem at the institutional level. People often talk about children as a vital resource on whom the future of the country and the planet depend. The care and education of these children can be seen as a public resource. All society benefits when children are well-educated and in good physical and psychological health. Yet taxpayers—especially those without children—often don't see that increasing taxes to improve schools, raise teachers' salaries, or hire more youth social workers will benefit them in the long run.

Solutions to Social Dilemmas

Social dilemmas can be solved or at least reduced in several ways. Some sociologists and economists argue that privatization is the best solution. When people own a particular resource, the argument goes, they'll be motivated to preserve it. But privatization creates other problems. For one thing, it's difficult to divide up and sell off resources like air or water. In addition, parties that own a large chunk of a resource may have little interest in seeing that it is shared equitably. For example, several years ago city leaders in Cochabamba, Bolivia, decided that the best way to save a decrepit water supply system was to sell it to a private corporation that would be motivated to keep it in good repair. But the sale led to exorbitant water bills for city residents and eventually to riots by poor people who could no longer afford drinkable water (Gardner, 2005).

Establishing communication among individuals is another way that the negative effects of social dilemmas can be reduced. When everybody knows what everybody else is up to, they may be less likely to hoard a resource or more likely to pay their fair share. In addition, when individual actions are identifiable, feelings of personal responsibility are likely to increase (Edney & Harper, 1978). However, this solution is not very practical when the group or community is quite large, such as an entire country, for instance.

Another solution is centralized, usually government, control of resources. The United States, for example, has a system of national forests that allows the government to regulate its use for recreation and commerce (Gardner, 2005). Often centralized control of a resource involves coercion—through restrictive rules or laws—to prevent people from seeking their self-interested goals. Requiring people to pay taxes is one example. Another example is setting up union "closed shops," meaning that to work at a company an employee must join the union and pay union dues. Without this requirement, individual employees would be able to enjoy the benefits provided by the union—higher wages, shorter hours, better working conditions—without having to pay anything for them. To reduce overfishing and radical depletion of fish species, many nations with commercial fishing industries have joined international oversight organizations that enforce limits on the harvest of certain species. And the city government of Des Moines set up an emergency hot line that people could call to anonymously turn in violators of the water rules I described earlier. If a city crew found the water meter running, the valve at the curb would be turned off for a week. No appeals were allowed, and water users were never told who turned them in. In addition, the offenders' names and addresses were immediately made known to reporters under Iowa's open records rules and spread across the state by newspapers, radio, and television (Bradsher, 1993). It was a drastic step, but the long-term welfare of the entire community was at stake.

The Structure of Organizations

Social life has far more complex functions than simply trying to balance individual and collective interests. Those of us who live in a complex society are all, to varying degrees, organizational creatures. We're born in organizations, educated in them, spend most of our adult lives working for them, and will most likely die in them (E. Gross & Etzioni, 1985). Organizations help meet our most basic needs.

Think about the food you eat every day. The farm where the food is produced is probably a huge organization, as are the unions that protect the workers who produce the food and the transportation companies that bring it to your local stores. And all this is controlled by a vast network of financial organizations that set prices and by governmental agencies that ensure the food's safety.

To prepare the food that is produced, delivered, and sold, you have to use products made by other organizations—a sink, a refrigerator, a microwave, a stove. To use those appliances, you have to make arrangements with other organizations, such as the water and power departments, the gas company, and the electric company. And to pay these bills, you must use still other organizations—the postal service, your bank, and credit companies.

Where does the money to pay the bills come from? Most likely from a job someone in your household has. If you are employed, you probably work for yet another organization. And when you receive a paycheck, the Internal Revenue Service steps in to take its share.

What about the car you use to get to that job? No doubt a huge multinational corporation manufactured it. Such corporations also produced and delivered the fuel on which the car runs. The roads you travel on to get to your destinations are built and maintained by massive organizations within the state and federal governments. You aren't even allowed to drive unless you are covered by insurance, which is available only through an authorized organization.

What if things aren't going well? Say you become sick, or you have an accident, or you have a dispute with someone. Here, too, organizations come into play. You have to use hospitals, police departments, and courts.

You get the picture? Life in a complex society is a life touched by public and private organizations at every turn. In such a society things must be done in a formal, planned, and unified way. For instance, the people responsible for producing our food can't informally and spontaneously make decisions about what to grow and when to grow it. The people responsible for selling it to us can't make its availability random and unpredictable. Imagine what a mess your life would be if you didn't know when your local supermarket would be open or what sorts of food would be available for purchase. What if one day it sold nothing but unsalted peanuts, the next day only plums, and the day after that just frozen chicken wings?

In a small-scale community where people grow their own food and the local mom-and-pop store provides everything else, the lack of structure might not be a problem. But this type of informal arrangement can't work in a massive society. There must be a relatively efficient and predictable system of providing goods and services to large numbers of people. The tasks that need to be carried out just to keep that system going are too complex for a single person—accounting, sales, marketing, research and development, public relations, insurance, maintenance, shipping and receiving, and so on. This complexity makes bureaucracy necessary.

Bureaucracies: Playing by the Rules

The famous 19th-century sociologist Max Weber (VAY-ber) was vitally interested in understanding the complexities of modern society. He noted that human beings could not accomplish such feats as building cities, running huge enterprises, and governing large and diverse populations without bureaucracies. Bureaucracies were certainly an efficient and rational means of managing large groups of people, although Weber acknowledged that these qualities could easily dehumanize those who work in and are served by these organizations.

Today we tend to see bureaucracies primarily as impersonal, rigid machines that trespass into our personal lives. Bureaucracies conjure up images of rows of desks occupied by faceless workers, endless lines and forms to fill out, and frustration over "red tape" and senseless policies. Indeed, the word *bureaucrat* has taken on such a negative connotation that to be called one is an insult. Keep in mind, however, that in a sociological sense **bureaucracy** is simply a large hierarchical organization that is governed by formal rules and regulations and that has a clear specification of work tasks.

This specific type of organization has three important characteristics:

Division of labor: The bureaucracy has a clear-cut **division of labor**, which is carefully specified by written job descriptions for each position. The bureaucracy theoretically becomes more efficient because it employs only specialized experts, with every one of them responsible only for the effective performance of her or his narrowly defined duties (Blau & Meyer, 1987). The division of labor enables large organizations to accomplish more ambitious goals than would be possible if everyone acted independently. Tasks become highly specific, sometimes to the point that it is illegal to perform someone else's task. In hospitals, for instance, orderlies don't prescribe drugs, nurses don't perform surgery, and doctors don't help patients fill out their insurance forms.

Hierarchy of authority: Not only are tasks divided in a bureaucracy, but they are also ranked in a **hierarchy of authority** (Weber, 1946). Most U.S. bureaucracies are organized in a pyramid shape with a few people at the top who have a lot of power and many at the bottom who have virtually none. In such a chain of command, people at one level are responsible to those above them and can exert authority over those below. Authority tends to be attached to the position and not to the person occupying the position, so that the bureaucracy will not stop functioning in the event of a retirement or a death. The hierarchy of authority in bureaucracies not only allows some people to control others, it also justifies paying some people higher salaries than others.

Impersonality: Bureaucracies are governed by an elaborate system of rules and regulations that ensure a particular task will be done the same way by each person occupying a position. With a system of rules, people don't have to "reinvent the wheel" each time a problem arises. Furthermore, rules help ensure that bureaucrats perform their tasks impartially and impersonally. Ironically, the very factors that make the typical bureaucrat unpopular with the public—an aloof attitude, lack of genuine concern—actually allow the organization to run more efficiently. We may want the person administering our driver's license examination to care about us, but think of how you'd feel if the road-test examiner had decided to stop for a cup of coffee with the person who was taking the driver's test before you.

Your university is a clear example of a bureaucratic organization. It has a definite division of labor that involves janitors, secretaries, librarians, coaches, professors, administrators, trustees, and students. The tasks that people are responsible for are highly specialized. Professors in the Spanish department don't teach courses in biology. In large universities the specialization of tasks is even more narrowly defined. Sociology professors who teach criminology probably don't teach demography.

Although the power afforded different positions varies from school to school, all universities have some sort of hierarchy of authority. Usually this hierarchy consists of janitors, groundskeepers, and food service workers at the bottom, followed by students, staff employees, teaching assistants, part-time instructors, professors, and department chairs. At the administrative level are associate deans, deans, vice presidents, and ultimately the president of the university and the board of trustees.

In addition, universities are governed by strict and sometimes exasperating sets of rules. There are rules regarding when and how students can register for classes, rules about when grades must be turned in by professors, graduation requirements, and behavioral policies. Strict adherence by university employees to these rules and policies—sometimes to the chagrin of the frustrated student who can't register for the one political science class he or she needs to graduate—is likely to give universities their final bureaucratic characteristic: impersonality.

As people are fitted into roles within bureaucracies that completely determine their duties, responsibilities, and rights, they often become rigid and inflexible and are less concerned with the quality of their work than with whether they and others are playing by the rules. Hence, people become oriented more toward conformity and getting through the day than toward problem solving and critical thinking. They are the source of frustrating procedures and practices that often seem designed not to permit but to prevent things from happening (G. Morgan, 1986).

Although he stressed the functional necessity of bureaucracies in complex Western societies, Weber warned that they could take on a life of their own, becoming impersonal "iron cages" for those within them. He feared that bureaucracies might one day dominate every part of society, locking people in a system that allows movement only from one dehumanizing bureaucracy to another. Weber's fears have been largely realized. The bureaucratic model pervades every corner of modern society. The most successful bureaucracies not only dominate the business landscape, but they have also come to influence our entire way of life.

George Ritzer
The McDonaldization of Society

Sociologist George Ritzer (2000) uses the McDonald's restaurant chain as a metaphor for bureaucratization. Each day about 50 million people eat at a McDonald's restaurant. In 2003 alone, McDonald's cash registers rang up more than $40 billion in sales (McDonald's Corporation, 2003). The more than 31,000 McDonald's restaurants in the United States and in 119 other countries can be found in every corner of life—in airports, shopping malls, movie theaters, and college campuses—in nearly every significant town and city across the United States and on the main thoroughfares in major foreign cities.

For Ritzer, **McDonaldization** is "the process by which the principles of the fast-food restaurant are coming to dominate more and more sectors of American society as well as of the rest of the world" (Ritzer, 2000, p. 1). Indeed, McDonald's phenomenal success has spawned countless other fast-food chains that emulate its model: Kentucky Fried Chicken, Taco Bell, Domino's Pizza, Long John Silver's, and many others. Its formula has also influenced countless other types of businesses, among them Toys "R" Us, Starbucks, Econo-Lodge motels, Pearle Vision Centers, Jiffy Lube, Barnes & Noble bookstores, and Blockbuster Video. The model is so powerful that some businesses have gotten nicknames reflecting McDonald's influence: Newly constructed houses in expensive subdivisions are called "McMansions," drive-in medical facilities are called "McDoctors," a national chain of child care centers is "McChild," the newspaper *USA Today* is called "McPaper" (Ritzer, 2000, p. 10).

The success of McDonald's is more than just McDonaldization. McDonald's has become a sacred institution, occupying a central place in popular culture. The "golden arches" of McDonald's are among the most identifiable symbols in society today. When we're not driving past them, we see them on television.

McDonald's appeals to us in a variety of ways:

> The restaurants themselves are depicted as spick-and-span, the food is said to be fresh and nutritious, the employees are shown to be young and eager, the managers appear gentle and caring, and the dining experience itself seems to be fun-filled. We are even led to believe that we contribute, at least indirectly, to charities by supporting the company that supports Ronald McDonald Houses for sick children. (Ritzer, 2000, pp. 7–8)

According to Ritzer, McDonald's (and every company that imitates it) has been so successful primarily because it fits Weber's model of the classic bureaucracy. It has a clear division of labor and a uniform system of rules that make it highly efficient and predictable. No matter where you are, you know what to expect when you go into a McDonald's. Even without looking at the overhead menu, you know what your choices will be; and once you've ordered your hamburger, you know that the ketchup will be in the same place on the sandwich it always is. French fries cook in precisely 3 minutes and 10 seconds; hamburger patties in 108 seconds. The appeal of such predictability is unmistakable. As one observer put it, McDonald's customers "are not in search of 'the best burger I've ever had' but rather 'the same burger I've always had'" (Drucker, 1996, p. 47).

In addition, if you've ever watched the workers behind the counter, you know that each has specialized tasks that are narrowly defined:

> By combining twentieth-century computer technology with nineteenth-century time-and-motion studies, the McDonald's corporation has broken the jobs of griddleman, waitress, cashier and even manager down into small, simple steps. . . . The corporation has systematically extracted the decision-making elements from filling french fry boxes or scheduling staff. . . . They relentlessly weed out all variables that might make it necessary to make a decision at the store level, whether on pickles or on cleaning procedures. (Garson, 1988, p. 37)

McDonaldization is likely to continue, and even spread, for several reasons:

- *It is impelled by economic interests:* Profit-making enterprises will go on emulating the McDonald's bureaucratic model because the increased use of nonhuman technology and the uniformity of its product reap greater efficiency and therefore higher profits.

* *It has become a culturally desirable process:* Our desire for efficiency, speed, predictability, and control often blinds us to the fact that fast foods (as well as their household equivalent, microwavable prepared foods) actually cost us more financially and nutritionally than meals we prepare ourselves from scratch. Moreover, most of us have soothing emotional memories of McDonald's: It's where we went after Little League games, it's where we hung out as teenagers, it's where we stopped on the way to the hospital for the birth of a first child, and so on.

* *It parallels other changes occurring in society:* With the increasing number of dual-earner couples, families are less likely to have someone with the time or the desire to buy the ingredients, prepare the meal, bring everyone together to eat it, and clean up afterward. Furthermore, a society that emphasizes mobility is one in which the fast-food mentality will thrive.

But McDonaldization does have a downside. Although the efficiency, speed, and predictability of this model may be appealing and comforting to some, the system as a whole has made social life more homogeneous, more rigid, and less personal. The smile on the face of the employee taking your order is a requirement of the position, not a sign of sincere delight in serving you. The fast-food model has robbed us of our spontaneity, creativity, and desire for uniqueness, trapping us in Weber's "iron cage"— a bureaucratic culture that requires little thought about anything and leaves virtually nothing to chance.

The Hierarchical Makeup of Organizations

Given the previous descriptions, you might think that everyone within a bureaucracy feels alienated, depersonalized, or perhaps even exploited. But a person's experience in a large bureaucracy depends in part on where she or he fits in the overall hierarchy of the organization. As the conflict perspective points out, although some people are dehumanized by their place in the hierarchy, others may actually benefit from theirs.

The Upper Echelons

People at the top of large organizations have come the furthest within the bureaucracy, are the fewest in number, and get the most out of their position. One interesting and disturbing characteristic of bureaucracies is that, despite the recent influx of women and people of color into executive positions around the world, executives still tend to be homogeneous: predominantly male, members of the dominant ethnic group, and middle or upper class (DiMaggio & Powell, 1983; Kanter, 1977; W. H. Whyte, 1956; Zweigenhaft, 1987). According to the U.S. Bureau of the Census (2004a), 90% of chief executives in the United States are white and 77% are men. All but six of the chief executive officers in the 500 largest American companies are men (Catalyst, 2002). In addition, executives' educational, social, and familial experiences are remarkably similar (Kanter, 1977; C. W. Mills, 1956). This homogeneity is caused not only by historical prejudices in hiring and promotion practices but also by the nature of top-level jobs.

Upper-level executives don't have clearly bounded jobs with neatly defined responsibilities. The executive must be prepared to use his or her discretion and be flexible enough to deal with a variety of different problems at all times. However, the bulk of the executive's time is spent not in making major decisions, creating, and planning but in attending meetings, writing memos, responding to phone messages and faxes, and participating in company-related social gatherings.

Because the role of the executive is, by nature, vague, no clear-cut criteria exist by which to evaluate whether a person is performing the job effectively. Such things as sales and production records or profit margins can provide only indirect indicators of an executive's competence. Asked what makes an executive effective, top-level employees indicated, as the most important criteria, such vague factors as the ability to communicate and to win acceptance (Kanter, 1977). In such an environment, rapid responses, common language, and common understanding are important. From the perspective of the organization, the best way to ensure efficiency, then, is to limit top-level jobs to people who are similar to one another, who have had similar experiences, and who come from similar backgrounds. The result is a closed circle of executives who resemble one another but who are insulated from the rest of the organization. Because of the structure of their occupational roles, white male executives are sometimes uncomfortable with people they see as different, such as racial and ethnic minorities and women.

A self-fulfilling prophecy is embedded in this structure as well. The more closed and exclusive the network of executives, the more difficult it is for "outsiders" to break in. The insiders then perceive the difficulty of outsiders to gain access to the top level of the organization as a sign of their incompetence and an indicator that the insiders were right to close their ranks in the first place.

The Middle Ground

The middle is in some ways the most depressing segment of a bureaucracy (Kanter & Stein, 1979). The people in the middle are caught between those below, whose cooperation they need, and those above, who selectively grant them the authority to implement organizational policy. Hence, middle-level employees are sometimes trapped in a world of conflicting role expectations.

Often the morale of people in the middle is sustained by their belief that they have a shot at the top. If I believe I have a chance to be promoted at some point in the future, my boring and unfulfilling job as a middle-level manager will hold different meaning for me than it would if I expect to remain in the same position forever (McHugh, 1968). Unpleasant tasks may be minor inconveniences, but they are the price I have to pay. This hope of future promotion may drive people in the middle to concentrate on accumulating bits of status and privilege so they can make enough of an impact to gain recognition from those above.

For most middle-level employees, however, the hope of upward mobility is just that—hope. Because of the pyramid-shaped structure of most bureaucracies, the vast majority of middle-level employees will not move up. Many simply fail in the increasingly competitive push for advancement into the upper echelons of the organization. Others are stuck in jobs that provide little or no opportunity for advancement. Some people are able to develop a comfortable niche in the middle (Kanter & Stein, 1979), but others are likely to harbor a bitterness that creates feelings of alienation and anger and may manifest itself in attempts to retaliate and punish the company.

The structure of most large organizations often forces middle-level managers to become cautious in their approach to their jobs. Unwilling to jeopardize the limited privileges they have attained, middle-level managers may become controlling, coercive, and demanding in their relationships with the people they supervise, ruling their narrow domain with an iron hand (Kanter & Stein, 1979).

For some people in the middle, membership in the organization becomes their life, often to the detriment of other roles and relationships. Almost 50 years ago sociologist William H. Whyte (1956) described how the personal lives of rising young executives were often overshadowed by their desire to succeed in the corporate world. Large organizations instilled in their employees a corporate social ethic, a belief that "belongingness" to the group was the ultimate need of the individual. Such beliefs encouraged total commitment to the organization, making a person's private life irrelevant for smooth organizational functioning.

Whyte's depiction of the private costs of organizational life rings true today. Organizations still value team players, middle-level employees who place organizational interests above their own (Jackall, 1988). To be a good team player, one must avoid expressing strong political or moral opinions, sacrifice one's home life by putting in long hours, and be forever obedient to one's superiors. Being seen as a loyal and effective group member and sticking to one's assigned position are also important. Distinctive characteristics, such as being abrasive or pushy or not knowing when to back off, are dangerous in the bureaucratic world. According to one study, one of the most damaging things that can be said about a middle-level manager is that she or he is brilliant. This judgment usually signals that the individual has publicly asserted her or his intelligence and is perceived as a threat to others (Jackall, 1988).

Interestingly, although organizations still value the ideal of team play, some individuals today seem to be less willing to sacrifice their personal lives and beliefs for the organization. Two sociologists, Paul Leinberger and Bruce Tucker (1991), interviewed the sons and daughters of the original "organization men" whom Whyte had interviewed back in the 1950s. Leinberger and Tucker found that these individuals were very different from their parents in values and attitudes. They tended to be individualists, more inclined to pursue self-fulfillment than a feeling of belongingness to the organization. Given recent social trends, this finding is not surprising. In an era when corporate mergers, relocations, and downsizing are commonplace, organizational loyalty makes less sense for the individual.

Although few people want to go back to a past when middle-level employees sacrificed everything for their career aspirations, Leinberger and Tucker (1991) point out that today's cultural emphasis on individualism has also created other problems, such as feelings of isolation, the inability to commit to others, and the absence of a sense of community.

The Lower Echelons

Those who stand lowest in the organization's hierarchy are paid the least, valued the least, and considered the most expendable (Kanter & Stein, 1979). The real sign that one is at the bottom is the degree to which he or she is controlled by others. People at the bottom typically don't have the right to define their occupational tasks themselves. They have little discretion, little autonomy, little freedom, and little influence. In the university bureaucracy, for example, students usually don't have much say over the content of their courses, the curriculum of their major, or the requirements necessary for graduation.

Most corporations are still organized in terms of ideas developed in the early 1900s. The fundamental principle is that a highly specific division of labor increases productivity and lowers costs. Hence managers usually subdivide the low-level work tasks in a bureaucratic organization into small parts that unskilled workers can perform repetitively. This structure provides management with the maximum control over workers' jobs, and the workers themselves become "an indistinguishable swarm" (Kanter & Stein, 1979, p. 178).

Technological advancements often coincide with the subdivision of low-level jobs and a decline in the level of skills required to do them (Hartmann, Kraut, & Tilly, 1989). For example, in the insurance industry the skilled work of assigning risks and assessing people's claims has been increasingly incorporated into computer software programs. What once required a great deal of human judgment and discretion is now almost completely routinized. Less-skilled, less-experienced, lower-paid clerks can now perform the work once performed by skilled workers and professionals (Hartmann et al., 1989).

This process, called **de-skilling**, creates jobs that require obedience and passivity rather than talent and experience. De-skilling provides organizations and even entire industries with clear financial benefits, but it also creates low levels of job satisfaction among the employees. Dull and repetitive tasks that offer little challenge, such as assembly line work, account for a substantial amount of the discontent experienced by workers at the bottom of large bureaucracies.

Not surprisingly, lower-level workers are often subjected to a different set of rules and expectations than their managerial counterparts. Some observers characterize the situation as a two-tier system of morality (Ehrenreich, 2002). Low-paid employees are required to work hard, abide by laws, and respect rules. Their personalities are psychologically scrutinized during the application process, and they're subjected to random drug tests once they're hired. Sometimes they're even expected to donate their time to the organization free of charge, even though federal and state laws require that hourly employees be paid for every minute they work. In 2004, the U.S. Department of Labor brought enforcement actions against scores of companies, including T-Mobile, Wal-Mart, Starbucks, and Radio Shack, that routinely required their employees to work off-the-clock (S. Greenhouse, 2004a). Ironically, these cases emerged at the same time that wealthy corporate executives at several large corporations were being accused of concealing debts, lying about profits, and engaging in insider trading.

When workers can take an active role in their jobs—such as making decisions and providing input to superiors on a regular basis—they are much less alienated and find their jobs more rewarding and satisfying than do workers who lack such autonomy (Hodson, 1996). For instance, over the past 15 years or so, some U.S. hospitals have experimented with redesigning their low-wage, low-skill occupations, such as food service workers, housekeepers, and nursing assistants. These hospitals seek to stabilize the workforce and improve patients' experiences by increasing skill training, diversifying the sorts of tasks workers are responsible for, and creating more autonomy and flexibility. These measures have been shown to reduce turnover and increase job satisfaction (Appelbaum, Berg, Frost, & Preuss, 2003).

Without such workplace innovations, the task facing many workers at the bottom is to make their occupational lives tolerable and more dignified by exerting some kind of control over the work they do (Hodson, 2001). Lower-level employees are rarely completely powerless and can at times be autonomous, even creative, in their positions. The sheer size of large corporations makes it next to impossible for middle- and upper-level managers to supervise lower-level workers directly and continuously. Thus substantial opportunities exist, even in the most highly structured and repetitive jobs, for workers either to redefine the immediate nature of their tasks or to willingly and secretly violate the expectations and orders of superiors. For instance, one study found that clerical, service, and manual workers often figure out ways to do required chores in less than the time allotted by management. They can then spend the rest of their time doing what they want (Hodson, 1991). In those workplaces with a union presence and a history of conflict between workers and supervisors, collective worker resistance (such as organized strikes) and individual resistance (such as absenteeism and work avoidance) can give lower-level workers a sense of control (Roscigno & Hodson, 2004).

In sum, lower-level workers are not necessarily powerless automatons whose lives are totally structured from above. In fact, the authority of middle-level managers thoroughly depends on their subordinates' willingness to cooperate and abide by management's directives. People who don't care about the organization because they feel it doesn't care about them can allow mistakes to go through, put in the minimum amount of time possible, or engage in deliberate sabotage. Such worker resistance can be disastrous for the manager and for the organization as a whole (Armstrong, Goodman, & Hyman, 1981). When they are organized, lower-level workers can even exert tremendous influence over the policies of a company, through strikes, slowdowns, and collective bargaining arrangements.

The Construction of Organizational Reality

According to the symbolic interactionist perspective, organizations are created, maintained, and changed through the everyday actions of their members (G. Morgan, 1986). The language of an organization is one of the ways it creates its own reality. At one level, new members must learn the jargon of the organization to survive within it. To function within the military system, for example, a recruit must learn the meaning of a dizzying array of words, phrases, acronyms, abbreviations, slang, sounds, and symbols that are unintelligible to outsiders (Evered, 1983). More important, language helps generate and maintain the organization by marking boundaries between insiders and outsiders.

For an organization to work well, everyone must also internalize the same rules, values, and beliefs. Corporate slogans—such as "When you're here, you're family" (Olive Garden), "Just do it" (Nike), "You're in good hands" (Allstate Insurance), "We try harder" (Avis), and "Think different" (Apple)—communicate the values around which organizations build and symbolize important aspects of the corporate philosophy

(G. Morgan, 1986). In some organizations, new members are told stories about the founding of the organization, its charismatic leaders, or some other significant event that becomes a metaphor for the culture of that organization.

Whatever the official rules, beliefs, and values of the organization, people have their own ideas and may develop their own informal structure within the larger formal structure of the organization (Meyer & Rowan, 1977). For example, many college instructors tell their students that class discussion is important and that they may use it as a criterion for assigning a final grade. Yet rarely does every student in a class, or even a majority of students, participate. Most college students know that a small group of people—perhaps 3 or 4 in a class of 40—can be counted on to respond to questions asked by the professor or to comment on any issue raised in class. These students relieve the remainder of the class from the burden of having to talk at all (Karp & Yoels, 1976). But although these talkative students are carrying the discussion for the entire class, they tend to be disliked by others. A strong norm among many students says that people shouldn't talk too much in class (Karp & Yoels, 1976). Students who speak up all the time upset the normative arrangement of the classroom and, in the students' eyes, may increase the instructor's expectations, hurting everyone in the long run. Other students indicate their annoyance by audibly sighing, rolling their eyes, rattling their notebooks, or openly snickering when a classmate talks too much.

One of the fascinating ironies of large organizations is that if everyone followed every rule exactly and literally, the organization would eventually self-destruct. For example, the goal of the highly bureaucratized criminal court system is to ensure justice by punishing those who have violated society's laws. The U.S. Constitution guarantees each person accused of committing a serious crime a timely trial by a jury of peers. However, public defenders, district attorneys, private attorneys, and judges actually work closely together to bypass the courtroom and move offenders through the system in an orderly fashion (Sudnow, 1965). Only a small percentage of criminal cases—between 10% and 20%—ever go to trial (Gibbons, 1992). The rest are either dismissed or, more commonly, settled through plea bargaining, an arrangement whereby, in exchange for a less severe punishment, the accused pleads guilty to a less serious crime than the original charge. Over 93% of criminal convictions in federal cases result from guilty pleas rather than trials (U.S. Sentencing Commission, 1998).

If judges and attorneys followed the procedural rules to the letter and provided all their clients with the jury trial that is their constitutional right, the system would break down. The courts, already overtaxed, would be incapable of handling the volume of cases. Thus the informal system of plea bargaining has taken root, allowing the courts to continue functioning. Those individuals who play exclusively by the rules, such as a young, idealistic public defender who wants to take all her or his cases to trial, are subject to informal sanctions by judges and superiors, such as inconvenient trial dates or heavier caseloads.

In sum, organizational life is a combination of formal structural rules and informal patterns of behavior. Codified rules are sometimes violated and new, unspoken ones created instead. Stated organizational goals often conflict with the real ones. Despite what may appear to be a clear chain of command, the informal structure—friendships, coalitions, and so on—often has more of an impact on how things are done.

Organizations and Institutions

Understanding the influence of organizations on our everyday lives tells only part of the story. Organizations themselves exist within a larger structural context, acting as a sort of liaison between people and major social institutions such as the economic system, government, religion, health care, and education. As we saw in Chapter 2, institutions are stable sets of statuses, roles, groups, and organizations that provide the foundation for behavior in certain major areas of social life. They are patterned ways of solving the problems and meeting the needs of a particular society.

Organizational Networks Within Institutions

Like individual people, organizations are born, grow, become overweight, slim down, migrate, form relationships with others, and die. They interact with one another, too, cooperating on some occasions and competing on others, depending on the prevailing economic and political winds. They even lie, cheat, and steal from time to time. As with people, some organizations are extremely powerful and can dictate the manner in which other organizations go about their business.

The state of Texas accounts for about 15% of the entire national textbook market (Stille, 2002). A provision in the Texas Education Code states that textbooks should promote decency, democracy, patriotism, and the free-enterprise system. A coalition of various watchdog organizations in Texas scours textbooks each year in search of material they consider inappropriate or offensive. For instance, in 2004, the Texas Board of Education approved new high school health textbooks that emphasized abstinence and contained no mention of condoms. It approved these books only after the publishers agreed to replace the term "married partners" with "husband and wife," and the term "when two people marry" with "when a man and a woman marry" (Gott, 2004). The economic importance of Texas forces many publishers to write their books with that state's rules in mind.

Similarly, when giant corporations such as General Electric, Microsoft, Coca-Cola, and IBM change their operations or come up with an innovative new product, they immediately influence the practices of other organizations throughout their respective industries. If one of these titans decides to downsize or expand its operations, the effects are felt throughout the entire financial community.

But even powerful organizations like these cannot stand alone. Massive networks of organizations are linked by common goals and needs. The networks are often so complex that organizations from very different fields find themselves dependent on one another for survival.

❖❖
Micro-Macro Connection
The U.S. Health Care System

Consider the U.S. health care system, one of our most important social institutions. Think about the vast network of organizations that are necessary for a single patient in a single hospital to receive treatment. First of all, the hospital is tightly linked to all the other hospitals in the area. A change in one, such as a reduction in the number of patients treated in the emergency room or the opening of a new state-of-the-art trauma center, would quickly have consequences for all the others. The linkage among hospitals enables the transfer of equipment, staff, and patients from one hospital to another when necessary.

To be accredited and staffed, the hospital must also connect to formal training organizations such as medical schools, nursing schools, and teaching hospitals. These organizations usually affiliate with larger universities, thus expanding the links in the network. And, of course, the American Medical Association and various licensing agencies oversee the establishment of training policies and credentials.

To survive financially, the hospital must also make connections to funding organizations. Hospitals have traditionally been owned and operated by a variety of governmental, religious, nonprofit, and for-profit organizations. They must operate under a set of strict regulations, which means they must also link to the city, state, and federal governmental agencies responsible for certification, such as the Joint Commission on Accreditation of Hospitals (Perrow, 1986). Add to these relationships the links to the medical equipment industry, the drug industry, insurance companies, food service providers, the legal profession, charities, political action committees working on health care reform, and patients' rights groups, and the system becomes even more complex.

The vast network of organizations within the health care system must also work together in response to broader societal demands and crises. For instance, in the wake of the 1995 Oklahoma City bombing, the attacks of September 11, 2001, and the anthrax attacks in the fall of 2001, the Institute of Medicine (2003) published a report warning that the nation's current mental health, public health, medical, and emergency systems were not equipped to respond to terrorism. At the organizational level, gaps exist in the coordination of agencies and services, the training and supervision of professionals, and the dissemination of information to the general public. The report concluded that only a multilayered approach—involving the federal departments of Health and Human Services and Homeland Security, state and local disaster planners, and relevant professionals in all areas of health care—could stave off potential disaster.

Despite the health care system's complexity, size, and importance, when patients go to a hospital they don't see it as a node in a vast network. Patients are obviously much less interested in the hospital's organizational links than they are in whether their nurse is kind or whether their doctor treats them effectively and compassionately. Yet in a 2003 study, one out of three doctors reported that they had purposely withheld information from patients about potentially helpful treatments because they knew those treatments weren't covered by the patients' health insurance (Wynia, VanGeest, Cummins, & Wilson, 2003). The needs of the larger system can sometimes clash with an individual's health care needs, making even face-to-face interactions problematic, maybe even detrimental to the patient's health.

❖ ❖

Institutional Pressures Toward Similarity

If you think about how many varieties of organizations exist in the world, you might be tempted to focus on their obvious differences. Some are large, others small. Some are formal and complex, others informal and simple. Some have a pyramid-shaped chain of command, others are more egalitarian (E. Gross & Etzioni, 1985). Sociologists have long been interested in the unique ways different organizations adapt to changing political, economic, cultural, or environmental circumstances. However, organizations seem to be more similar than different and even tend to imitate one another's actions as they become established in a particular institution (DiMaggio & Powell, 1983).

Organizational similarity is not really that surprising. Because of the nature of the problems that organizations in the same industry have to address, they come to adopt similar methods of dealing with them. For instance, the major U.S. commercial television networks—NBC, ABC, CBS, and Fox—see the success one network has with a particular type of program and try to attract viewers in much the same way. As you well know, the perceived popularity of a certain type of television show creates an irritating avalanche of similar shows on other networks—such as romance-based "reality" shows (*The Bachelor* and its successors), shows where people compete with one another to see who will perform the grossest or most fearsome feats (*Survivor, Fear Factor,* and the like), shows where people secretly redecorate their friends' houses (*While You Were Out* and *Trading Spaces*), shows where families exchange a member (*Trading Spouses* and *Wife Swap*), and glorified talent contests (*American Idol, Rock Star,* and *So You Think You Can Dance*). In 2005, several networks hastily developed pilot shows that were similar to ABC's new hit shows *Desperate Housewives* and *Lost.* In short, instead of adjusting directly to changes in the social environment, such as the shifting tastes of the television-viewing public, organizations end up adjusting to what other organizations are doing (DiMaggio & Powell, 1983).

The surprising fact is that the imitated practices are not necessarily more effective or successful. After once-novel strategies have spread throughout an industry, they no longer improve the organization's performance. Viewers eventually get sick of home redecorating shows, shows where people are romantically humiliated for a national audience, or shows where ordinary people are plopped down in some exotic locale and are filmed getting on each other's nerves and betraying one another for a lot of money. The net effect of the imitations is to reduce innovation within the industry.

In times of institutional uncertainty, the tendency for organizations to emulate one another is heightened (DiMaggio & Powell, 1983). When new technologies are poorly understood, when the physical environment is undergoing dramatic changes, or when local, state, and federal governments are creating new regulations or setting new agendas, organizations are likely to be somewhat confused about how things ought to be done. Just as individuals look to one another to help define ambiguous situations and determine an appropriate course of action (as described in Chapter 2), so do organizations.

Take changes in the field of higher education, for instance. Many colleges and universities across the country are being forced to address the problem of how to attract more students. Such was the case several years ago at the university where I teach. An outside consultant was called in to design a new marketing program for the school. He had some clear strategies for "packaging" the school's image to make it more attractive to prospective students: redesigned brochures, a new recruitment video, a flashy Web site, state-of-the-art direct mailing techniques, and so on. But he was doing the same thing for several other schools competing for the same shrinking pool of students. He admitted that many of the "novel" strategies he advised us to use were things other universities were already using. We were addressing a new and uncertain dilemma by replicating the practices of other organizations in the network.

Organizations also resemble one another because those who run them, particularly professionals, tend to come from similar training backgrounds. In many institutions, the professional career track is so closely guarded that the individuals who make it to the top are practically indistinguishable from one another (DiMaggio & Powell, 1983). For example, medical schools are important centers for the development of organizational norms among doctors. The fact that most doctors belong to the American Medical Association creates a pool of individuals with similar attitudes and approaches across a range of organizations. When these doctors become administrators, they will likely bring this common approach to running a hospital.

Certain organizational forms dominate not necessarily because they are the most effective means of achieving goals but because social forces such as institutional uncertainty and the power of professions to provide individuals with a single normative standard create pressures toward similarity. Such similarity makes it easier for organizations to interact with one another and to be acknowledged as legitimate and reputable within the field (DiMaggio & Powell, 1983). But this homogeneity is not without its costs. When organizations replicate one another, institutional change becomes difficult, and the iron cage of bureaucracy becomes harder to escape.

Globalization and Social Institutions

You've seen throughout this book so far the enormous effect that globalization is having on everyday life. Many of our important social institutions have become international in scope—notably communications, economics, education, and religion. How do such global institutions meet the needs of human beings around the world?

Communication Media

Electronics and telecommunications give people worldwide, immediate access to other cultures, making it practically impossible for societies to exist in complete isolation. Certainly the Internet has done more to bring people from disparate cultures together than any other communications device. American films are popular in every corner of the globe, but even they have an international twist. Many of the male stars in those films come from elsewhere: Russell Crowe and Heath Ledger (Australia), Jackie Chan (Hong Kong), Antonio Banderas (Spain), Jude Law (England), Colin Farrell (Ireland), and Ewan MacGregor (Scotland), to name a few. At the same time, films from other parts of the world have become popular here too.

No other medium can match television though for the size of its audiences and its access to people's homes. Between 1980 and 1997, the number of households with television sets worldwide increased by over 100 million, with the most dramatic growth occurring in Africa, Asia, and Latin America (see Exhibit 9.1). Television is

Exhibit 9.1 Global Growth in Television Ownership

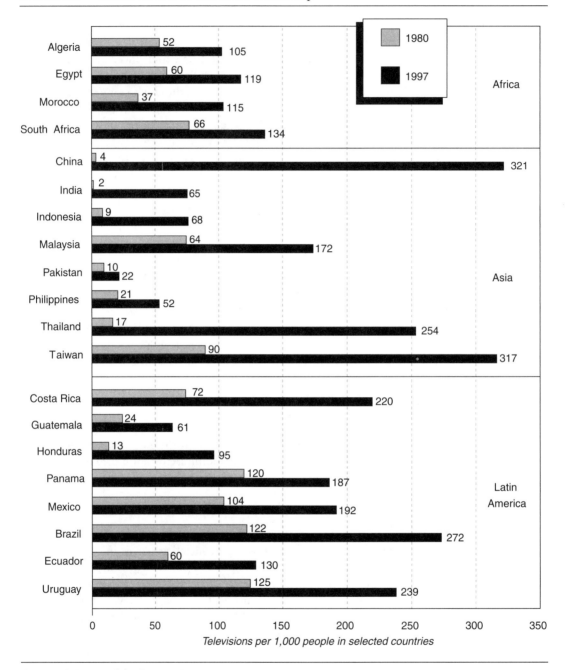

Source: U.S. Bureau of the Census, 2002.

watched by over 3 billion people a day (C. Barker, 1997). Televised coverage of soccer's 2002 World Cup reached 213 countries with over 41,000 hours of dedicated programming (FIFA, 2003).

The global impact of television is not just a matter of numbers, though. For instance, in the late 1980s Soviet and East European governments were unable to prevent the reception of Western television broadcasts. Street protests taking place in one country were watched by millions of people in others, many of whom took to the streets themselves. The 1989 revolutions that marked the fall of the Soviet Union and other regimes in the Soviet bloc have been called the first "television revolutions" (Giddens, 2000). Al-Jazeera, the Arabic news channel, is based in Qatar, but its broadcasts about events in the Middle East are available worldwide.

Television doesn't simply provide people around the world with useful, practical information. It provides a commercial outlet for an ever-expanding international market. You can find U.S.-made sitcoms, dramas, reality shows, music videos—and, above all, commercials—all over the world today. U.S. media corporations control 60% of the film distribution networks in Europe, and over half the movies shown on European television are made in the United States. MTV reaches over 400 million households and over 1 billion people worldwide (J.L. Roberts, 2005); CNN broadcasts to over 800 million people in 210 nations and territories around the world (Croteau & Hoynes, 2000).

That's not to say that people elsewhere watch only U.S. television shows. The top-rated shows in almost any country are, by and large, local products. But even locally produced television shows may be influenced by U.S. television. *America's Funniest Home Videos* is copied as *Smile, Please* in Germany and *Beadle's About* in England (Croteau & Hoynes, 2000). *Sesame Street* airs in over 120 countries worldwide. While some countries simply show a dubbed version of the American show, other countries have actually created their own, completely unique *Sesame Street* shows, with characters and segments representing their own cultures (Nationmaster.com, 2005).

In Mexico, a New York–based advocacy group joined with sociologists and television producers a few years back to create a U.S.-style soap opera called *Acompañame* (*Come Along With Me*). The show depicts the effects of family planning on three women's lives. In one episode, a husband accompanies his wife to a birth control clinic. In the six months following this episode, registration at Mexico's family planning clinics jumped by 33% (cited in Steiner, 1998).

Economics

Looking around my office at this moment, I notice that my telephone, radio, and computer were made in Japan; my desk and chair in the United States; my watch in Switzerland; my stapler in Great Britain; my calculator in Taiwan; my shoes in Korea; my pants in Hong Kong; my bottle of water in France; the frame holding my kids' picture in Thailand; and my briefcase, paper clips, scissors, and tea kettle in China. Because of the rapid increase in recent years in the economic links among producing nations, your life is probably similarly filled with products made in other countries. Global trade grew from $380 billion in 1950 to $5.86 trillion by the end of the 20th century, a 1500% increase (L. R. Brown & Flavin, 1999), although a global recession in the 2000s slowed the rate of growth somewhat (World Bank, 2004).

Economic globalization is more than just a matter of more goods being shipped from one place to another. For instance, there's a pretty good chance that if you contact someone online or by phone to prepare your taxes, provide legal advice, track your lost luggage, solve your software problem, or review your long-distance phone bill, you'll be dealing with someone working at a call center in Bangalore, India (Friedman, 2005). The large pool of English-speaking, technologically savvy Indian workers willing to work for low wages has attracted the phone service operations of such companies as American Express, Sprint, Citibank, General Electric, Ford, Hewlett Packard, and IBM (Lakshmi, 2005).

If a product wasn't entirely manufactured in another country, it's a good bet that some of its component parts were. For instance, the Boeing 777 wide-body airplane is a shining example of U.S. dominance in advanced aeronautical technologies, but sections of the aircraft are actually manufactured in 12 different countries (Greider, 1997).

Even ordinary, everyday products can have a complex global pedigree. Several years ago, economist Pietra Rivoli (2005) bought a $5 souvenir T-shirt in Fort Lauderdale, Florida. The colorful beach motif on the shirt was printed at a manufacturing company in Miami. The fabric for the shirt, though, was knit into cloth and sewn into shirts at a textile factory in Shanghai, China. The material for the shirt originally came from West Texas, part of the millions of bales of cotton that are exported from the United States to China each year.

The economic processes involved in globalization have made national boundaries all but irrelevant. **Multinational corporations**, businesses that have extended their markets and production facilities globally, have become increasingly powerful over the past several decades. They control a significant portion of the world's wealth, heavily influence the tastes of people everywhere, and don't owe their allegiance to any one country's political authority or culture. At the same time, international financial organizations such as the World Bank, the World Trade Organization, and the International Monetary Fund loan money to countries all over the world to finance development and reconstruction projects. (For more on the global economic impact of international financial organizations and multinational corporations, see Chapter 10.) With the costs of communication and computing falling rapidly, barriers of time and space that traditionally separated national markets have also been falling. Even the most remote rural villagers are linked to the world economy as they carry out transactions over the Internet and send and receive goods around the world.

A global economy has its everyday advantages. Goods and services manufactured in a country where wages are lower are less expensive for consumers in other countries. Universally accepted credit cards such as Visa and MasterCard make international travel more convenient. Snack bars in overseas airports accept American money, as do foreign establishments around the world that are near U.S. borders or military facilities. Global economic influence has also enabled a significant portion of the world's population to be healthier, eat better, and live longer than the royalty of past civilizations (Kurtz, 1995).

We may barely be aware of how the taken-for-granted elements of our daily lives connect to the lives of people in faraway places. For instance, most of today's popular electronic gadgets could not work without a little-known gritty, superheavy mud called coltan. Once it is refined in U.S. and European factories, coltan becomes tantalum, a remarkable heat-resistant conductor of electricity. Capacitors made of tantalum can be found inside practically every laptop, pager, personal digital assistant, and cell phone in the world (Harden, 2001). But coltan does not exist in the United States or Japan. Its largest quantities lie in the rain forests of eastern Congo. It is mined there in much the same way that gold was mined in California in the 1800s. Miners spend days in the muck, digging up mud and sloshing it around in plastic tubs until the coltan settles to the bottom. On a good day, a miner can produce about a kilogram of the stuff. Miners earn up to $50 a week, quite a high figure considering that most people in this region live on the equivalent of $10 a month ("What Is Coltan?" 2002).

But global trade has also created some interesting everyday dilemmas. For instance, for centuries Spanish workers—as well as workers in many Latin American countries— have enjoyed the workday *siesta,* a long afternoon nap or an extended lunch, sometimes lasting until 5 p.m. But the owners of some Spanish factories and retail stores are beginning to realize that shutting down operations every afternoon so workers can take their *siestas* is incompatible with Spain's growing integration into the global economy. As the president of a Spanish research group that advocates doing away with the *siesta* put it, "In a globalized world, we have to have schedules that are more similar to those in the rest of the world so we can be better connected" (quoted in McLean, 2005, p. 4).

Global financial institutions must also keep close track of holidays around the world to avoid trying to do business on nonbusiness days. In some countries, holidays are determined by the lunar calendar, which not only varies from year to year but may vary from area to area within a country based on local customs. In other countries, such as France, the dates of some bank holidays are a matter of negotiations between the banks and the unions that represent their employees. Even weekends are defined differently in different countries. In Taiwan, the weekend consists of every Sunday and the second and fourth Saturday of each month. In Malaysia, it is every Sunday and only the first Saturday of every month. And in Lithuania, one-day weekends are occasionally followed by four-day weekends (Henriques, 1999).

Globalization has fostered some more serious social problems as well, including higher levels of unemployment in countries that maintain labor and environmental protections and the exploitation of people in poor, developing countries. The result is a worldwide system of inequality whose problems are often invisible to consumers. For instance, many of the best and most beautiful roses Americans buy for their loved ones each year come from the rich volcanic soil of Ecuador. These flowers help generate about $240 million a year and tens of thousands of jobs for this once-impoverished region. But the Ecuadorian workers who harvest roses are exposed each day to a toxic mix of pesticides and fungicides (Thompson, 2003). They work with severe headaches and rashes for the benefit of wealthier customers of the world who are largely unaware of the conditions under which these fragrant symbols of love and romance are produced. We may wish to do our part to make life better for the rose harvesters of Ecuador, as well as other poor workers around the world, but it's hard to take any effective action. For instance, boycotts of exploitative manufacturers are a double-edged sword. The origin of products is seldom clear-cut, and local workers are typically glad to have jobs they wouldn't have had otherwise. Pressure to compete in the global

(*Text continues on page 320*)

The Trail of the Tomato

Deborah Barndt

The life cycle of a tomato reveals how globalization touches us daily. In a collaborative cross-border research project, we followed the trail of a tomato from a Mexican field to a Canadian fast-food restaurant. The key characteristic of this process is the many steps between production and consumption. Most of us are unaware of who has planted, picked, sorted, packed, processed, transported, prepared, and sold the food we eat. The trail of the tomato also reflects power relationships between the North and the South (in this case, between Mexico in the South and the United States and Canada in the North), as well as inequalities based on gender, race, and class.

As a northern "gringa" researcher documenting Mexican women, I too reflected and reinforced power differences. When I photographed women picking and packing tomatoes, my camera was a symbol of my privilege.

Although it was an awkward reminder of the differences in our social power, some women workers befriended me and invited me to visit them later in their rural community.

Returning to Mexico four months later (the picking season abruptly ended by a premature freeze), I found these women in their homes, no longer salaried workers in a multinational operation. With camera and tape recorder, I followed Teresa through her day as she prepared food for her family. Teresa is a salaried worker for an agro-export company based on monocultural (one-crop) production, which has an impact on the health of both the land and the people who work it. Her story reflects the shifting role of women in the new global economy. It also illustrates how subsistence and market economies coexist and how family economies remain the economic and social base for Mexican peasants.

❖ When I first met Teresa in December, she was picking tomatoes and supervising workers in an agribusiness tomato plantation outside of Sayula, in the state of Jalisco, Mexico.

With 40 pails to fill for the 28-peso ($5–6) daily wage, she couldn't talk much then, so she invited me to visit her sometime in her village, half an hour away.

When I returned to Mexico four months later, the tomato harvest had prematurely ended due to a freeze. I found Teresa, her family, and many coworkers at home in Gomez Farias.

❖ *Teresa:* I was born in 1930 in a family of five kids. My papa died when I was two, so my mama had to raise us on her own. I never went to school. They brought books into the rancho, and my brothers taught themselves to read. But not me, I didn't learn; I'm like a *burrito* (little donkey).

❖ *Teresa:* We got married when I was 17, and I kept doing the same work. Now I'm 67, and Pedro's 72, five years older than me.

We had 16 children—imagine! The oldest is 47 and the youngest is 21. Nine of them are still alive; seven died of illness, of bronchitis (from the cold).

Our two oldest daughters are married and live in Tlapapa; three married sons and two daughters live here. They visit often and help; we share what we have. While we are alive, as long as God offers us the gift of life, we help each other.

We get eggs from our chickens. From time to time, we eat beef, chicken, squash, carrots, lettuce.

When the day dawns, with God's blessing, we find things to eat, even if it's just beans.

❖ *Teresa:* Our grandchildren are studying, but when they're not in school, they come to work in the fields on the weekends and during vacations; they get the same pay as others.

❖ *Teresa:* Everyone has their job. My husband and I are the *cabos* (foremen) for our *tabla* (field). Some are *piscadores* (pickers), others are *vaciadoras* (who empty the pails), others are *aquadores* (they bring us water) and *apuntadoras* (who record the number of pails).

❖ *Pedro:* Before, we worked harder, we worked with animals. We cultivated three crops together—corn, squash, and beans—in the same field. We rotated from one lot to another.

Before, the tomatoes and corn grew well without chemicals. We used the waste of animals as fertilizer; we put it on the plants; it was very good and would last for two to three years.

The fertilizer we use now only lasts for one season. It's expensive and very strong. It kills the squash, and the *milpa* (field) becomes very sad. The corn grows well, it grows tall, but the fertilizer damages the squash and the beans.

❖ *Teresa:* The chemicals bother us, if they get into our lungs. Those who don't cover themselves suffer more. We put one handkerchief in the back, one in the front, just leaving a slot open for the eyes. This protects us from the pesticides, the insects, the sun.

❖ *Teresa:* We all feel the economic crisis. The work in Sayula stopped in February because of the freeze. There is no *chamba* (work) now. We can't keep working, so we don't earn any money. It's very depressing; we're sad when we're not working.

When we find work, we're happy.

In a broader sense, this visual essay exposes only one piece of a globalized food system: Teresa doesn't know where the tomatoes she picks end up, and she can contribute only a small part of the story about where they come from. This has been one of the most powerful and recurring themes in our efforts to trace the trail of the tomato: No one has the whole picture, and most actors in the system understand only their small piece of the long and complex process. Nonetheless, Teresa's story begins to fill a void in our distanced, northern understanding of where our food comes from and what impact its production has on other people and lands.

❖ *Teresa:* I've seen big trailer trucks on the highway; I've wondered where they're going. They come from far away and they go far away; we don't know where.

The tomatoes don't stay here.

❖ When I showed these photos to Teresa, she wasn't aware of the work of 500 women in the packing plant just five minutes from where she picks tomatoes.

At the other end of the food chain, Teresa's photo story became a catalyst for conversations with Susan, one of hundreds of supermarket cashiers in Canada who eventually sell these tomatoes to consumers. Susan's responses reflect her curiosity about and empathy with the women working at the other end of the food chain:

> We live in different cultures, with different climates and different life experiences, and yet we're going through the same things. [For example,] Teresa used to make her own tortillas but now she has to go and work. And she's feeling that pull just like the North American women are: Should I stay at home with the kids? Should I go to work? She's feeling the economic thing, obviously because everybody has to survive, everybody has to eat. She's taking care of the family, that's a priority in her life; I'd like to think that in my life that's a priority.

Teresa had mentioned the freeze that cut short their harvest season and left them unemployed; Susan remembers the impact the freeze in the South had on prices in her store. Signs were posted in the produce department explaining why the vegetables were suddenly so expensive.

The Mexican pickers, when hearing about the Canadians who receive and sell the fruits of their labor, raised this question: "I often wonder what happens to our tomatoes. I wonder if they realize the work we have done so they can eat tomatoes." This, at least, is a connection between women workers nurtured by a red fruit that makes a long journey, passing from one hand to another.

marketplace also erodes the ability of governments to set their own economic policies, protect national interests, or adequately protect workers and the environment.

Finally, many critics deplore the way that economic globalization is homogenizing cultures and values around the world:

> A few decades ago, it was still possible to leave home and go somewhere else: the architecture was different, the . . . language, lifestyles, dress, and values were different. That was a time when we could speak of cultural diversity. But with economic globalization, diversity is fast disappearing. . . . When global hotel chains advertise to tourists that all their rooms in every city of the world are identical, they don't mention that the cities are becoming identical too: cars, noise, smog, corporate highrises, violence, fast food . . . Nikes, Levi's, Barbie Dolls, American TV. . . . What's the point of leaving home? (Turning Point Project, 1999, p. A7)

In the 21st-century consumer culture, Wal-Mart, Nike, Coca-Cola, McDonald's, Starbucks, and other corporate icons have truly become universal symbols. The global economy is not simply a worldwide system of finance and production. It is a way of life that affects peoples and cultures in every corner of the globe in sometimes obvious and sometimes hidden ways.

Education

The prospect of international competition in a global economy can foster changes in a country's educational system. For instance, American students attend school an average of 180 days a year, compared to 190 days in Germany and 208 days in eastern Asian nations. Moreover, during four years of high school, the average American student devotes approximately 1,462 hours to math, science, language and social studies. The average Japanese student will spend 3,190 hours studying these subjects. In Germany, the figure is 3,628 hours (cited in Bainbridge, 2005).

Not surprisingly, students in other industrialized countries consistently outperform U.S. students in such fields as math and science, causing alarm among many educational experts and political leaders. One cross-national study found that even though American students are improving, the United States' global ranking based on math and science scores of fourth- and eighth-graders has not changed much over the past decade (National Center for Education Statistics, 2004). Another study of the math performance of 15-year-olds in 40 countries found that the United States had the poorest outcome per dollar spent on education of any country in the study (cited in Norris, 2004).

This international disadvantage extends to higher education. For example, the Scholastic Aptitude Test (SAT)—the standardized test students take before entering college—is not offered in China. So Chinese high school students who want to attend American universities must take the Graduate Record Exam, or GRE, a standardized test usually taken by people applying to graduate school. Even though the Chinese high school students are competing against American college graduates, they always score in the top percentiles worldwide (Kristof, 2002).

Concern over our ability to compete in the global marketplace has led to nationwide calls for such educational reforms as heavier emphasis on math and science, more time spent on foundational skills such as reading and writing, increased computer literacy, and training in political geography and international relations. Many school districts around the country have adopted longer school days and a year-round schedule to improve student performance. In one Houston school district, for instance, students attend classes every day from 7:25 a.m. to 5 p.m., two or three Saturdays a month, and several weeks during the summer (Wilgoren, 2001). Several years ago, the Atlanta public school system eliminated recess in its elementary schools, calling it a waste of time that would be better spent on academics.

Improving educational competitiveness is often difficult in the face of economic pressures. School districts in about 15 states have been forced to go to a four-day school week because of budgetary shortfalls (Wilgoren, 2002).

But some critics feel that we already place far too much emphasis on performance and achievement in this society and that children end up suffering as a result (Mannon, 1997). They often point to Japan, not as a model but as a cautionary tale. Many Japanese children attend classes all day, then go to one of the many private "cram" schools where they study for college entrance exams until 10 or 11 p.m. Even three-year-olds may spend hours a day memorizing stories, learning vocabulary, making calendars, and taking achievement tests (WuDunn, 1996). But their educational accomplishments often come at a steep price. Some Japanese sociologists blame the intense competitive pressures children face for the dramatic rise in youth crime over the past few years. Historically, passing grueling exams and getting into the top high schools and elite colleges was a virtual guarantee of a prestigious job. But Japan's recent economic stagnation and record unemployment have begun to shatter the implicit social contract that, in the past, justified all the hard work and sacrifice. Many Japanese youth rebel when they discover that not only do they not have much of a social life, they have no job prospects either (French, 1999b). About one in three Japanese elementary school teachers have experienced at least one disruptive classroom incident, such as students mocking their authority, walking out of class, or even physically attacking them (cited in French, 2002).

Few people in the United States would argue that we should emulate the pressurized Japanese educational model. At the same time, though, the demands of global economy and concerns over Americans' ability to compete internationally will continue to exert influence on legislators and education reformers.

Religion

Another institution influenced by globalization is religion. Despite the enormous variety of cultures and ethnicities that exist today, nearly two thirds of the world's population belongs to just three major religions—Christianity, Hinduism, and Islam—which have successfully crossed national boundaries for centuries. Exhibit 9.2 shows how dominant these world religions are.

Some denominations are globalizing to deal with shrinking memberships in the countries where they originated:

♦ Outside the United States and Canada, the Mormon Church has grown by over 500%—to more than six million members—since 1980. Nearly 10% of that growth has come in the past five years (cited in Kress, 2005).

♦ Ten times as many members of the Assemblies of God, a Pentecostal denomination, live overseas as live in the United States, its birthplace.

Exhibit 9.2 Dominance of World Religions

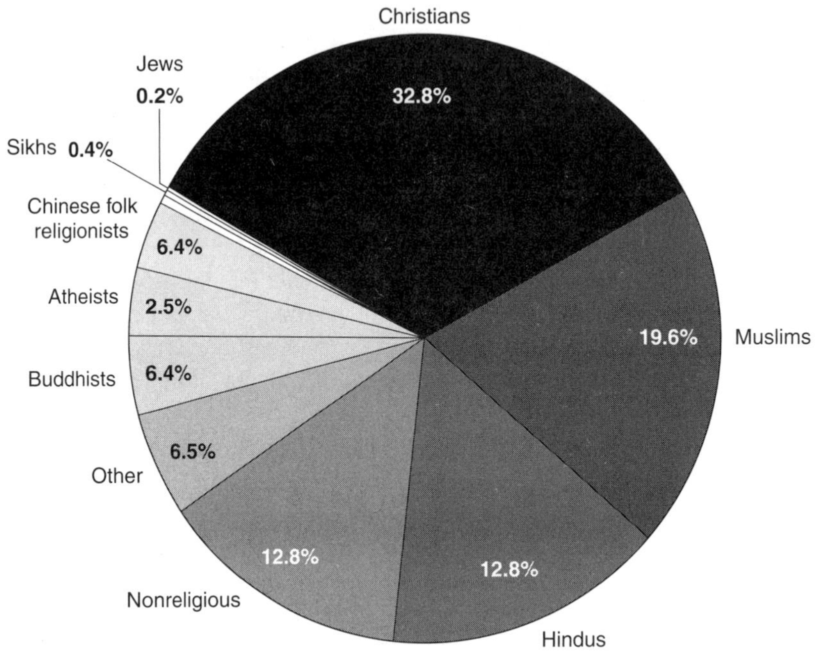

Source: U.S. Bureau of the Census, 1999.

♦ The Methodist Church lost one million U.S. members between 1980 and 1995 but gained about 500,000 elsewhere, mostly in Africa (Niebuhr, 1998b).
♦ The Anglican Church is growing faster in Africa than in its traditional bases, Great Britain and North America (Niebuhr, 1998a).

This globalization of religion is ironically creating crises for religious communities. Exposure to competing worldviews challenges traditional beliefs. In some cases, religions have reacted with a forceful revitalization of ancient, fundamentalist traditions (Kurtz, 1995). Witness the growing trend toward governments defining themselves in narrowly religious terms. The ascension of fundamentalist Islamic government in Iran, the growing influence of Orthodox Jews in Israeli politics, and the continuing conflict between Hindus and Muslims in India attest to the fact that many people today believe religion cannot be separated from a nation's social and political destiny.

The rise of religious nationalism around the world has created an obvious threat to global security. The attacks of September 11, 2001 are the most glaring illustration. Radical elements sometimes use religious texts—in this case, the Koran—as a justification for violence against societies that they blame for moral decline and economic exploitation. Elsewhere, the possibility of violence by supporters of religious nationalist movements has brought down political regimes, changed the outcomes of elections, strained international relations, and made some parts of the world dangerous places for travelers (Juergensmeyer, 1996).

But religion has also played a positive role in world affairs and has created dramatic social changes. According to Max Weber, the spread of Protestant beliefs throughout Europe made the growth of modern capitalism possible. Protestantism maintained that worldly achievements, such as the accumulation of wealth through hard work, are a sign of God's favor. But early Protestants also believed that God frowns on vulgar displays of wealth, such as big houses, fancy clothes, and so forth. So people were motivated to save and reinvest their wealth rather than spend it frivolously. You can see how such beliefs made large-scale and long-term economic growth possible (Weber, 1904/1977). A recent study of 59 Christian, Buddhist, Muslim, and Hindu countries found that strong religious beliefs tend to stimulate economic growth because of their association with individual traits like honesty, work ethic, thrift, and openness to strangers (Barro & McCleary, 2003).

The influence of religious movements on social life continues. In the 1960s television pictures of Buddhist monks setting themselves on fire in Vietnam to protest the war fed the growing antiwar movement in the United States. In the 1970s and 1980s, images of Catholic priests and nuns challenging government policies in Central and South America provoked a heightened awareness worldwide of the plight of indigenous people there. Today, followers of the Dalai Lama are raising global awareness of the plight of Tibetans who seek independence from China. Their actions have led to the establishment of organizations such as the International Campaign for Tibet, which has growing support worldwide.

Conclusion

More than three centuries ago, John Donne wrote, "No man is an island, entire of itself; every man is a piece of the continent, a part of the main." The same can be said of contemporary social life. We are not isolated individuals whose lives are simply functions of personal characteristics and predispositions. We are social beings. We are part of aggregations of other social beings. We have a powerful need to belong to something larger than ourselves. As a result, we constantly affect and are affected by our associations with others, whether face to face or in well-structured groups, massive bureaucratic organizations, or all-encompassing social institutions.

Throughout Part II of this book, I discussed how society and culture affect everyday experiences and how those experiences help to construct and maintain social order. The development of self and self-controlled behavior, the influence of cultural norms, responses to deviance, and so on are all topics that provide insight into how we are able to live together in a relatively orderly and predictable way. In this chapter, however, you can see that the social structure, though created and maintained by the actions of individuals, is more than just the sum of those actions. Organizations interact at a level well above the individual; institutions are organized in a massive, global system.

Social structure is bigger than any of us, exerts enormous control over our lives, and is an objectified reality that appears to exist independently of us. But it cannot exist without us. I'm reminded of a skit from the old British comedy show *Monty*

Python's Flying Circus, in which a high-rise apartment building stood erect only because its inhabitants believed in it. When they doubted its existence, it began to crumble. Like that building, social structure requires constant human support. Once we as a society are no longer able to sustain our organizations or believe in our institutions, they fall apart.

YOUR TURN

One of the major criticisms of complex contemporary society is its sometimes dehumanizing way of life. To see this consequence of bureaucratization firsthand, visit several fast-food restaurants close to your home (McDonald's, Taco Bell, Kentucky Fried Chicken, Long John Silver's, and the like). Observe the overall structure of the establishment. How is the work area situated in regard to the customer area? Are the cooking facilities hidden from public view? Note the number of employees and the gender and age configuration of the staff. Observe the way the customers are processed. Can you detect a "script" that the employees follow? How do they address customers? How are orders filled? Is there any room for "ad-libbing"? Does each worker seem responsible for a single task (grilling burgers, bagging fries, operating the cash register, cleaning tables)? Do male employees seem to work in different areas from female employees? Is there an apparent hierarchy among the workers? What is the manager's role? Are you able to detect the ways in which ordinary workers might "resist" on a daily basis (breaking the group's norms, sabotage, labor-management conflicts)?

Compare your findings across the different restaurants you observed. How much similarity in routine is there? Is some common procedure characteristic of all fast-food restaurants, or does each restaurant have a unique way of running? How do such things as diversity and creativity fit into the procedure?

Once you've observed several fast-food restaurants, go to some other retail businesses in your area. See if you can find any similarities between the way these stores operate and the way the fast-food restaurants function.

Drawing from this chapter's discussion of the features of bureaucracies and the notion of McDonaldization, discuss how the systems employed in these businesses maximize efficiency at the cost of dehumanizing the people involved, both workers and customers.

CHAPTER HIGHLIGHTS

♦ Social structure is both a source of predictability and a source of problems in everyday life. Sometimes individual interests coincide with structural needs; other times they conflict.

♦ By virtue of living in society, we are all organizational creatures. We are born in organizations, educated in them, spend most of our adult lives working in them, and will probably die in them.

♦ A common form of organization in a complex society is the bureaucracy. A bureaucracy is a large hierarchical organization that is governed by a system of rules and regulations, has a clear specification of work tasks, and has a well-defined division of labor.

♦ The everyday experience of bureaucratic organizations is determined by where one fits into the hierarchical structure. Bureaucracies look very different depending on whether one is situated at the top, middle, or bottom.

♦ Organizations are more than structures, rules, policies, goals, job descriptions, and standard operating procedures. Each organization, and each division within an organization, develops its own norms, values, and language.

♦ Organizations exist within highly interconnected networks. In times of institutional or environmental uncertainty, organizations tend to imitate one another, adopting similar activities, policies, and goals.

♦ As national borders become increasingly permeable, cultures and social institutions become more global in nature.

KEY TERMS

bureaucracy Large hierarchical organization governed by formal rules and regulations and having clearly specified work tasks

de-skilling Subdivision of low-level jobs into small, highly specific tasks requiring less skilled employees

division of labor Specialization of different people or groups in different tasks, characteristic of most bureaucracies

free-rider problem Tendency for people to refrain from contributing to the common good when a resource is available without requiring any personal cost or contribution

hierarchy of authority Ranking of people or tasks in a bureaucracy from those at the top, where there is a great deal of power and authority, to those at the bottom, where there is very little power and authority

McDonaldization Process by which the characteristics and principles of the fast-food restaurant come to dominate other areas of social life

multinational corporation Company that has manufacturing, production, and marketing divisions in multiple countries

social dilemma Potential for a society's long-term ruin because of individuals' tendency to pursue their own short-term interests

social structure Framework of society—social institutions, organizations, groups, statuses and roles, cultural beliefs, and institutionalized norms—which adds order and predictability to our private lives

tragedy of the commons Situation in which people acting individually and in their own interest use up commonly available (but limited) resources, creating disaster for the entire community

STUDY SITE ON THE WEB

Don't forget the interactive quizzes and other learning aids at www.pineforge.com/newman 6study. In the Resource Files for this chapter, you will also find more on the structure of society, including:

Sociologists at Work

♦ Barbara Garson: Money Makes the World Go 'Round

Micro-Macro Connection

♦ AIDS Epidemic

The Architecture of Stratification
Social Class and Inequality

If you've seen the 1997 Hollywood film *Titanic,* you know that the famous ship had every amenity and comfort: Turkish baths, the finest orchestras, intricately tiled walls, the best cuisine. What it didn't have when it hit an iceberg and began to sink were enough lifeboats. There was room for only 1,178 of the 2,207 passengers and crew members on board. Over the span of two hours on that cold April night in 1912, as the "unsinkable" ocean liner was engulfed by the frigid waters of the North Atlantic, more than 1,500 people lost their lives.

This part of the story is well known. What is less well known is that some of the passengers actually had much better survival chances than others. More than 60% of the people from the wealthy first-class deck were saved; 36% of the people from the second-class deck were saved; and 24% of the people from the lowest, or "steerage," class were saved. The figures were even more striking for women and children, who, by virtue of chivalrous tradition, were entitled to be spared first. In first class, 97% of the women and children survived; in second class, 89% survived. However, only 42% of the women and children in steerage were saved (W. Hall, 1986).

One reason why so many wealthier passengers survived was that the lifeboats were accessed from the higher first- and second-class decks. The locked doors and other barriers erected to keep third-class passengers from venturing to upper decks during the cruise were not removed when disaster struck. In addition, little effort was made to save the people in steerage. Some were forcibly kept down by sailors standing guard.

For passengers on the *Titanic,* social inequality meant more than just differences in the comfort of accommodations or the quality of the food they ate. It literally meant life or death. This situation can serve as a metaphor for what many people face in today's society. Those at the top have easy access to various "lifeboats" in times of social or economic disaster; others face locked gates, segregated decks, and policies that make even survival exceedingly difficult (Sidel, 1986).

Let's turn the clock ahead to the summer of 2005, when Hurricane Katrina killed over 1,000 people in the Gulf Coast region of the U.S. South. Most of these people died not because of the torrential rains and high winds that accompanied the hurricane, but because of the flooding that occurred when the levees that ordinarily protect the low-lying areas of New Orleans (which were in need of repair to begin with) were breached. In addition to the fatalities, hundreds of thousands of people lost everything they owned.

The storm and its aftermath did not affect all residents equally. The neighborhoods with significant flooding had a lower median income, a higher poverty rate, and a higher percentage of households without a vehicle than areas that experienced little or no flooding (Schwartz, Revkin, & Wald, 2005). Those of us watching the tragedy unfold on television could not help but notice the obvious fact that the vast majority of the evacuees who were forced to live like animals for days in the sweltering darkness of the New Orleans Superdome and convention center were poor people of color who came from the most vulnerable parts of the city. These were individuals who either didn't have the necessary transportation to evacuate the city prior to the hurricane or who stayed behind to tend to sick and elderly relatives who couldn't be moved. Again we see how the lack of economic resources can have direct, physical consequences for people's lives.

In this chapter, I look at the basic issues of class inequality and stratification. In subsequent chapters, I explore two other facets of inequality: race and/or ethnicity and gender. It's important to note, however, that although class, race and ethnicity, and gender are covered in separate chapters, these components of our identities are not experienced separately. They are all interrelated, and they combine to determine individuals' positions in society. For instance, a person doesn't live his life just as a working-class person, just as a man, or just as an Asian American. He is all these things—and more—simultaneously (Newman, 2007).

Stratification Systems

Inequality is woven into the fabric of all societies through a structured system of **stratification**, the ranking of entire groups of people that perpetuates unequal rewards and life chances in a society. Just as geologists talk about strata of rock, which are layered one on top of another, the "social strata" of people are arranged from low to high. All societies, past and present, have had some form of stratification, although societies may vary in the degree of inequality between strata. The four main forms of stratification that sociologists have identified—all of which continue to exist in contemporary societies—are slavery, caste systems, estate systems, and social class systems.

Slavery

One of the most persistent forms of stratification in the world is slavery. **Slavery** is an economic form of inequality in which some people are the property of others. Their lives are owned, controlled, coerced, and restricted. One can become a slave in a variety of ways: through birth, military defeat, debt, or, as in the United States up until the mid-19th century, capture and commercial trade (Kerbo, 1991). Because slaves are considered possessions, they are denied the rights and life chances other people take for granted.

Slavery has occurred in some form or another almost everywhere in the world at some time:

> It was common in ancient Babylon, Persia, Egypt and the Roman Empire. It was found in Asia and Africa. It did not disappear in Western Europe until late in the Middle Ages, and was still present in the Western Hemisphere when the early Spanish explorers arrived. Press-gangs rowing ancient Mediterranean war boats, captive victims in pre-Columbian sacrificial rites, Africans brought to the Americas in chains—all are recognizable, indisputable examples of enslavement. (Crossette, 1997b, p. D4)

❖
Micro-Macro Connection
Buying and Selling Humans

It's tempting to see slavery as an economic system that is simply a horrible vestige of a distant past. But the United Nations estimates that there are 12.3 million people—mostly women and children—bought, sold, transported, or kept against their will in the world today (U.S. Department of State, 2005). Some are forced to labor in sweatshops or become domestic servants. Others are sold into prostitution, sex tourism, or even forced marriage. Children in Togo and Benin (in West Africa) are sometimes seized from their villages and sold into servitude in Nigeria, Gabon, and elsewhere. Debt bondage is still practiced in certain parts of South Asia. In India, children are sometimes enslaved, mutilated, and transported to Saudi Arabia to plead for money outside mosques (Crossette, 1997b). In Bangladesh, boys as young as four are sold and put to work as camel jockeys in the Persian Gulf; girls are sent to India and forced to work as prostitutes and maids (Sengupta, 2002).

Human trafficking is not simply a foreign problem either. The CIA estimates that as many as 50,000 women and children from Asia, Eastern Europe, and Latin America are brought to the United States each year and forced to work as prostitutes, laborers, or servants (Brinkley, 2000). In 1997 federal agents in North Carolina and New York found more than 70 illegal Mexican immigrants—most of whom were deaf—being held in bondage and forced to peddle trinkets at local shopping centers and in subway stations. They were crowded into apartments, monitored while working, forced to turn over all their earnings, and prevented from leaving. In 2002, police in Plainfield, New Jersey, raided a house expecting to find a brothel of illegal aliens. Instead they found a group of teenage girls from Mexico who were being held captive as sex-slaves in squalid conditions (Landesman, 2004).

Traffickers find victims in several ways. Frequently, they take out ads in local newspapers offering good jobs at high pay in exciting cities. In politically unstable countries with high rates of poverty and unemployment, destitute women see these offers as opportunities to help their families financially. Traffickers often use fraudulent modeling, matchmaking, or travel agencies to lure unsuspecting victims. They may even visit families in local villages, assuring them that their daughters will be taught a useful trade or skill or even promising parents that they themselves will marry the daughters. Traffickers deftly target the weakest and most vulnerable populations to victimize. Seventy percent of the world's poor are girls and women (Clark, 2003). Their low cultural status in many countries makes their victimization all that much easier.

What makes human trafficking especially pernicious is that people are at risk in precisely those environments that are usually considered safe: their villages and their families. Impoverished parents, guardians, and husbands—who have nothing else of exchange value—often help to abduct and sell family members, seeing it not as an act of betrayal but as a way of earning money or paying off a debt. A study of Yemeni children sold into slavery in Saudi Arabia found that the vast majority of cases involved some level of parental agreement and support (cited in Al-Attab, 2005). In China, where males significantly outnumber females, young women and girls may be sold by their impoverished families to potential bridegrooms. Between 1991 and 1996, Chinese police freed about 88,000 women and girls who were being held for this purpose (Goodwin, 2003). Such familial cooperation makes the detection and prosecution of human trafficking even more difficult than it already is.

Caste Systems

Some societies today retain a second form of stratification: a **caste system.** Traditionally, one's caste, which determines one's lifestyle, prestige, and occupational choices, was fixed at birth and couldn't be changed. Ancient Hindu scriptures, for instance, identified the strict hierarchy of elite, warrior, merchant, servant, and untouchable castes. The rights and duties associated with membership in each caste were clear. In India, "untouchables"—members of the lowest caste—were once required by law to hide from, or, if that wasn't possible, to bow in the presence of anyone from a higher caste. They were routinely denied the right to enter Hindu temples or to draw water from wells reserved for members of the higher castes, who feared they would suffer ritual pollution if they touched or otherwise came in contact with an untouchable.

According to Human Rights Watch (2001), over 250 million people worldwide—in India, Pakistan, Nepal, Bangladesh, Sri Lanka, Japan, Nigeria Senegal, Mauritania, and elsewhere—continue to suffer severe caste discrimination. They are victims of exploitation and violence and face massive obstacles to their full attainment of civil, political, economic, and cultural rights.

Things are beginning to change, however. In India, for instance, laws have been passed that prohibit caste-based discrimination. The poorest Indians are now voting and joining political parties in record numbers. In fact, more "untouchables" (or Dalits, as they prefer to be called) vote than members of the upper caste (Dugger, 1999a). But the caste system still serves as a powerful source of stratification and oppression. Cultural norms still encourage people to take the occupation of their parents and marry within their caste (Weber, 1970). Even Indians living in the United States find that caste sometimes colors their experiences with friends and business associates (J. Berger, 2004).

Estate Systems

A third form of stratification is the **estate system**, or **feudal system**, which develops when high-status groups own land and have power based on their noble birth (Kerbo, 1991). Estate systems were most commonly found in preindustrial societies. In medieval Europe, the highest "estate" in society was occupied by the aristocracy, who derived their wealth and power from large-scale landholdings. The clergy formed the next estate. Although they had lower status than the aristocracy, they still claimed considerable status because the Catholic Church itself owned a great deal of land and exerted influence over people's lives. The last, or "third," estate was reserved for commoners: serfs, peasants, artisans, and merchants. Movement between estates was possible though infrequent. Occasionally a commoner might be knighted or a wealthy merchant might become an aristocrat.

Some reminders of the estate system can still be seen today. In Great Britain, for instance, Parliament's House of Lords is still occupied primarily by people of "noble birth," and a small group of aristocratic families still sits at the top of the social ladder, where they enjoy tremendous inherited wealth and exercise significant political power.

Social Class Systems

Stratification systems in contemporary industrialized societies are most likely to be based on social class. A **social class** is a group of people who share a similar economic position in society based on their wealth and income. Class is essentially, therefore, an economic stratification system. It is a means of ranking people or groups that determines access to important resources and life chances. Less obviously perhaps, social class standing provides people with an understanding of the world and where they fit into it compared to others.

Closely related to the concept of class is **socioeconomic status**—the prestige, honor, respect, and power associated with different class positions in society (Weber, 1970). Socioeconomic status is obviously influenced by wealth and income, but it can also be derived from *achieved* characteristics, such as educational attainment and occupational prestige, and from *ascribed* characteristics, such as race, ethnicity, gender, and family pedigree. For instance, the occupational prestige of high school teachers is far higher than that of carpenters, plumbers, and mechanics (J. A. Davis & Smith, 1986), even though teachers usually earn substantially less. Organized criminals and leaders of illegal drug cartels may be millionaires and live in luxurious homes, but they lack prestige and honor in mainstream society.

Class systems differ from other systems of stratification in that they raise no legal barriers to **social mobility**, the movement of people or groups from one level to another. Theoretically, all members of a class system, no matter how destitute they are, can rise to the top. In practice, however, mobility between classes may be difficult for some people. Recent economic studies have found that it takes five or six generations to erase the advantages or disadvantages of a person's economic origins (Krueger, 2002). Within the span of a single generation there isn't much social mobility—wealthy parents tend to have wealthy children; poor parents tend to have poor children. Likewise, race and gender have historically determined a person's access to educational, social, and employment opportunities. Women of color are especially likely to face barriers to upward mobility, in terms of both economic disadvantage and lack of emotional support from their families (Higginbotham & Weber, 1992).

To determine a person's class standing, contemporary sociologists usually compile information on measurable factors such as annual income, accumulated wealth, occupation, and educational attainment. But the boundaries between classes tend to be fuzzy and subjective. Some have argued that there aren't any discrete classes with clearly defined boundaries at all but, rather, that what exists is a socioeconomic continuum on which to rank individuals (Blau & Duncan, 1967). Nevertheless, distinct class designations remain a part of everyday thinking, political initiatives, and social research. The **upper class** (which some sociologists define as the highest-earning 5% of the U.S. population) is usually thought to include owners of vast amounts of property and other forms of wealth, major shareholders and owners of large corporations, top financiers, rich celebrities and politicians, and members of prestigious families. The **middle class** (roughly 45% of the population) is likely to include college-educated managers, supervisors, executives, owners of small businesses, and professionals (for example, lawyers, doctors, teachers, and engineers). The **working class** (about 35% of the population) typically includes industrial and factory workers, office workers, clerks, and farm and manual laborers. Most working-class people don't own their own homes and don't attend college. Finally, the "poor" (about 15% of the population) consists of people who work for minimum wages or are chronically unemployed. They are sometimes referred to as the **lower class** or **underclass** (Walton, 1990; E. O. Wright, Costello, Hachen, & Sprague, 1982).

As we'll see throughout this chapter, class standing can determine a whole host of life chances, including access to higher education, high-paying jobs, and premium health care. For example, for an annual fee of upwards of $20,000, wealthy individuals can buy special access to their physician via 24/7 cell phone, fax, and e-mail; same-day appointments with a guaranteed waiting time of no more than 15 minutes; nutrition and exercise physiology exams at the patients' homes; nurses to accompany them when they go to see specialists; and routine physicals that are so thorough they can last up to three days (Belluck, 2002; Garfinkel, 2003). Physical comfort is also linked to social class. For instance, Virgin Atlantic Airlines now offers its first class passengers leather armchairs with matching ottomans that turn into double beds. Emirates Airlines offers first class passengers their own enclosed suites complete with minibar, 19-inch television, bed, and "dine on demand" room service (Rosato, 2004). Space for such amenities comes at the expense of ordinary passengers in coach sections where leg room and elbow room are typically minimal. First class sections usually contain more flight attendants per person than coach sections, and the first class attendants respond more quickly to call buttons. In addition, first class passengers have access to shorter check-in lines at airports and, since September 11, 2001, some of the nation's airlines have set up special express security lines for them so as to avoid unnecessary delays (Squadron, 2005). Such exclusive personal attention reinforces feelings of power and privilege.

The media help to support these feelings by focusing much of their favorable attention on the concerns of the wealthy. Television air time is filled with advertisements for luxury cars, cruise vacations, diamond jewelry, and other things that only the well-to-do can hope to afford. If you take a peek at the "style" section of a major metropolitan newspaper, you'll likely find a focus on high-priced fashion, designer home décor, costly vacation spots, investment opportunities in foreign real estate, expensive restaurants, and etiquette for lavish, formal dinner parties. And, of course, we receive regular reports about the glamorous lifestyles of wealthy professional athletes, film stars, TV personalities, and other celebrities.

Conversely, people in the lower classes routinely face barriers in their daily lives. Poor people must often make use of public facilities (health clinics, laundromats, public transportation, and so on) to carry out the day-to-day tasks that wealthier people can carry out privately. As you may recall from Chapter 8, working-class and poor people are more likely to get arrested, get convicted, go to prison, and receive the death penalty than are upper-class people (Reiman, 2004). Research also shows that those at lower levels of the stratification system are more likely to die prematurely from homicide, accidents, or inadequate health care than are people at higher levels. People whose families earn less than $5,000 a year can expect to live about 25% fewer years than people from families that earn over $50,000 (Deaton & Paxson, 1999). Even after controlling for age, sex, race, family size, and education, the risk of death steadily decreases as income goes up (Marmot, 2004).

People's perceptions of where they are in the stratification system affect their beliefs about its nature. For instance, a recent nationwide poll found that lower-income individuals are more likely than wealthy individuals to believe that the rich have too much power and that there is significant class tension in society today (cited in J. Scott & Leonhardt, 2005). In contrast, upper-class people are likely to see stratification as a hierarchy of positions in which opportunities for success and advancement are fairly distributed on the basis of individual merit. They are more likely than their lower-income counterparts to cite "natural ability," "a good education," and "hard work" as factors that are essential to get ahead in life. Poorer people tend to cite such reasons as "coming from a wealthy family" or "knowing the right people" (cited in J. Scott & Leonhardt, 2005). As you will see later in this chapter, however, the lack of success may be caused as much by external, societal factors as by personal failings.

At the institutional level, people in the upper reaches of the American class system control the government, large corporations, the majority of privately held corporate stock, the media, universities, councils for national and international affairs, and so on (Domhoff, 1998). Hence members of this class enjoy political and economic power to a degree not available to members of other classes. These power differentials extend down to the local level. For example, the town of Wilson, North Carolina, voted a few years ago to prohibit people from keeping old sofas on their front porches (Bragg, 1998). For generations, poor people in the area—unable to purchase expensive outdoor furniture—have kept their worn-out sofas and chairs on the porch, where they can still be used. But more affluent residents saw the practice as "low class" and approved the ban to make neighborhoods more presentable.

The existence of an upper class doesn't necessarily imply that other classes are totally powerless, however (Domhoff, 1998). Under certain circumstances, people at the lower end of the class system can help determine the shape of society. Consider, for instance, the 2004 presidential election. The Democratic candidate, John Kerry, received his strongest support from people with college educations in cities with populations over 500,000 (Connelly, 2004). Although wealthier people tended to vote Republican, George W. Bush's victory was fueled by the votes of a very different constituency: religious, rural, working-class, blue-collar Americans without college degrees, the very people who are likely to view the "upper class" with disdain and suspicion. The fact that both candidates were extremely affluent and came from families of privilege didn't seem to matter.

(Text continues on page 341)

Images of Social Class

Douglas Harper

Social classes exist in the United States, notwithstanding our egalitarian ideals. Just consider how people in the three different social locations depicted here experience some of the same features of everyday life.

❖ Housing density and conditions

❖ Interior spaces

As you look at these photographs, examine the clothes that people wear and the possessions that surround them. Try to infer from the photographs what their typical activities are. Then study the body language of the people in the three class settings. How do they face the camera and one another? Do posture, expression, and emotion seem to be functions of social class?

❖ Working conditions

❖ Gathering spots

Consider particularly the lives of children. What have these children already learned about their social roles? What would happen if the children from one setting were placed into a different class location?

❖ Children's postures and possessions

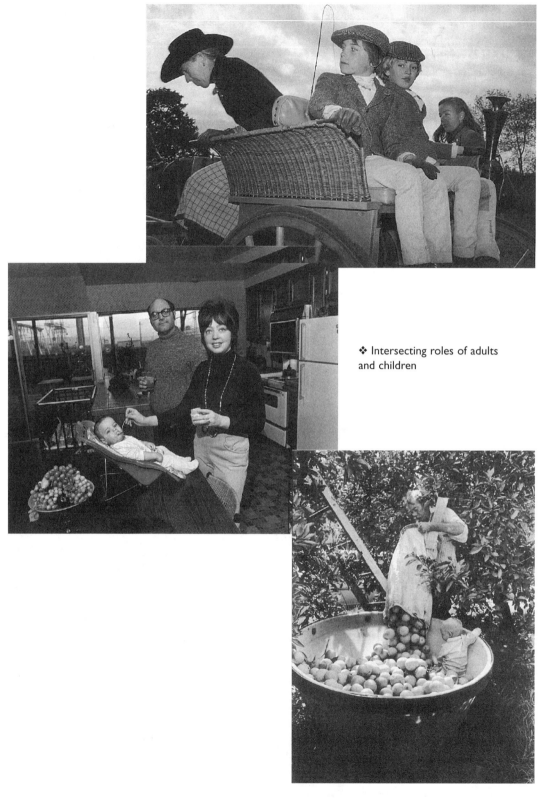

❖ Intersecting roles of adults and children

❖ Pets

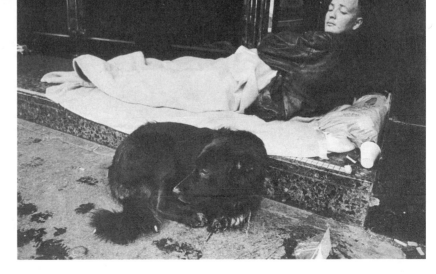

❖ Water recreation

The United States is often billed as a society in which all who apply themselves are socially mobile. As you consider these photographs, ask yourself whether effort alone would be sufficient to move people from one of these class locations to another. Finally, as you look at these photographs, think about the structural and historical forces in society that have created the context for class-based experiences.

Sociological Perspectives on Stratification

Sociologists have long been interested in figuring out why societies are stratified. Two perspectives—the structural-functionalist perspective and the conflict perspective—offer insights into the sources and purposes of social inequality. They are often presumed to be competing views, but we can actually use them together to deepen our understanding of why social inequality exists, how it develops, and why it is so persistent.

The Structural-Functionalist View of Stratification

From a structural-functionalist perspective, the answers to these questions lie in a society's inevitable need for order. Because social inequality is found in some form in all societies and thus is apparently unavoidable, inequality must somehow be necessary for societies to run smoothly.

As with bureaucracies, the efficient functioning of society requires that various tasks be allocated through a strictly defined division of labor. If the tasks associated with all social positions in a society were equally pleasant, were equally important, and required the same talents, who got into which position would make no difference. But structural-functionalists argue that it does make a difference. Some occupations, such as teaching and medicine, are more important for the well-being of society than others and require greater talent and training. Society's dilemma is to make sure that the most talented people perform the most important tasks. One way to ensure this distribution of tasks is to assign higher rewards—better pay, greater prestige, more social privileges—to some positions in society so that they will be attractive to people with the necessary talents and abilities (K. Davis & Moore, 1945). Presumably, if these talented people were not offered sufficiently high rewards, they would have no reason to take on the difficult and demanding tasks associated with important positions. Why would people go through the agony and costs of many years of medical school without some promise of compensation and high prestige?

If an important position is easily filled, however, it needn't be heavily rewarded (K. Davis & Moore, 1945). Imagine what our society would be like without people who remove our trash. Not only would our streets be unsightly, but our collective health would suffer, too. Therefore, garbage collectors serve a vital social function. But they don't get paid very much, and trash removal certainly isn't a highly respected occupation. Why aren't garbage collectors higher up in the hierarchy of occupations? According to the structural-functionalist perspective, it is because we have no shortage of people with the skills needed to collect garbage. Physicians also serve the collective health needs of a society. But because of the skills and training needed to be a doctor, society must offer rewards high enough to ensure that qualified people will want to enter the medical profession.

When we examine the pay scales of actual occupations, however, the structural-functionalist explanation comes up short. One look at the salary structure in our society reveals obvious instances of highly rewarded positions that are not as functionally important as positions that receive smaller rewards. Entertainers and professional athletes are among the highest-paid people in Western societies. The golfer Tiger Woods and the German Formula I race car driver Michael Schumacher each make about $80 million a year. Entertainers such as Mel Gibson, Oprah Winfrey, Tom Cruise, Jim Carrey, and Bruce Springsteen are among the wealthiest of Americans, earning from $45 million to $210 million a year. You might say that golfers, race car drivers, talk show hosts, actors, comedians, and singers serve important social functions by providing the rest of us with a recreational release from the demands of ordinary life; and the best entertainers and athletes do have rare skills indeed. However, society probably can do without another music album, TV show, or golf tournament more easily than it can do without competent physicians, scientists, computer programmers, teachers, or even trash collectors.

Furthermore, the structural-functionalist argument that only a limited number of talented people are around to occupy important social positions is probably overstated. Many people have the talent to become doctors. What they lack is access to training. And why are some people—women and racial and ethnic minorities—paid less for or excluded entirely from certain jobs? The debates over equal employment opportunity and equal pay for equal work are essentially debates over how the functional importance of certain positions is determined.

Finally, when functionalists claim that stratification serves the needs of society, we must ask, Whose needs? A system of slavery obviously meets the economic needs of one group at the expense of another, but that doesn't make it acceptable. In a class-stratified society, those individuals who receive the greatest rewards have the resources to make sure they continue receiving such rewards. Over time, the competition for the most desirable positions will become less open and less competitive. The offspring of "talented"—that is, high-status—parents will inevitably have an advantage over equally talented people who are born into less successful families. Hence, social background and not personal aptitude may become the primary criterion for filling important social positions (Tumin, 1953).

The structural-functionalist perspective gives us important insight into how societies ensure that all positions in the division of labor are filled. Every society, no matter how simple or complex, differentiates people in terms of prestige and esteem and possesses a certain amount of institutional inequality. But this perspective doesn't address the fact that stratification can be unjust and divisive, a source of social *disorder* (Tumin, 1953).

The Conflict View of Stratification

Conflict theorists are among those who argue that social inequality is neither a societal necessity nor a source of social order. They see it as a primary source of conflict, coercion, and unhappiness. Stratification ultimately rests on the unequal distribution of resources—some people have them, others don't. Important resources include money, land, information, education, health care, safety, and adequate housing. Those people high in the stratification system can control these resources because they are the ones who set the rules. The conflict perspective takes it as a fundamental truth that stratification systems serve the interests of those at the top and not the survival needs of the entire society.

Resources are an especially important source of power when they are scarce. Sometimes their scarcity is natural, such as the amount of land available to control. Other times, however, the scarcity of a resource is artificially created. For instance, in 1890 the founder of DeBeers, the South African company that currently controls two thirds of the international diamond market, realized that the sheer abundance of diamonds in southern Africa would make them virtually worthless on the international market. So he decided to carefully limit the number of diamonds released for sale each year. This artificially created rarity, coupled with a carefully cultivated image of romance, is what made diamonds so expensive and what continues to make companies such as DeBeers so powerful today (Harden, 2000).

Rich and politically powerful individuals frequently work together to create or maintain privilege, often at the expense of the middle and lower classes (K. Phillips, 2002). The U.S. Senate, for example, is dominated by people—both Republicans and Democrats—who are far wealthier than the citizens they represent. Thus from the conflict perspective, it's not at all surprising that politicians would make decisions that benefit the wealthy. For instance, on the same day in 2005 that the U.S. House of Representatives voted for a full gradual repeal of the estate tax—a tax that affects only the wealthiest Americans—it also passed a bill that made it more difficult for debt-ridden lower-income individuals and families to file for bankruptcy protection (Labaton, 2005; Rosenbaum, 2005). To provide financial aid to the victims of Hurricane Katrina, many members of Congress favored cutting the budgets of existing social programs that helped other needy citizens rather than repealing tax cuts for upper-class Americans.

What the conflict perspective gives us that the structural-functionalist perspective doesn't is an acknowledgment of the interconnected roles that economic and political institutions play in creating and maintaining a stratified society.

The Marxian Class Model

Karl Marx and Friedrich Engels (1848/1982) are the original proponents of the view that societies are divided into conflicting classes. They felt that in modern societies, two major classes emerge: *capitalists* (or the bourgeoisie), who own the **means of production**—land, commercial enterprises, factories and wealth—and are able to purchase the labor of others; and *workers* (or the proletariat), who neither own the means of production nor have the ability to purchase the labor of others. Workers, instead, must sell their own labor power to others in order to survive. Some workers, including store managers and factory supervisors, may control other workers, but their power is minimal compared to that exerted over them by those in the capitalist class. Marx and Engels supplemented this two-tiered conception of class by adding a third tier, the *petite bourgeoisie,* which is a transitional class of people who own the means of production but don't purchase the labor power of others. This class consists of self-employed skilled laborers and businesspeople who are economically self-sufficient but don't have a staff of subordinate workers (R.V. Robinson & Kelley, 1979). Exhibit 10.1 diagrams the positions of the three classes.

Capitalists have considerable sway over what will be produced, how much will be produced, who will get it, how much money people will be paid to produce it, and so forth. Such influence allows them to control other people's livelihoods, the communities in which people live, and the economic decisions that affect the entire society. In such a structure, the rich inevitably tend to get richer, to use their wealth to create more wealth for themselves, and to act in ways that will protect their interests and positions in society.

Exhibit 10.1   Marx's Model of Class

	Control labor of others	Do not control labor of others
Own means of production (land, factories, etc.)	*Capitalists*	*Petite bourgeoisie*
Do not own means of production	*Workers*	*Workers*

Ultimately the wealthy gain the ability to influence important social institutions such as the government, the media, the schools, and the courts. Those in power have access to the means necessary to create and promote a reality that justifies their exploitative actions. Their version of reality is so influential that even those who are harmed by it come to accept it. Marx and Engels called this phenomenon **false consciousness**. False consciousness is crucial because it is the primary means by which the powerful classes in society prevent protest and revolution. As long as large numbers of poor people continue to believe that wealth and success are solely the products of individual hard work and effort rather than structured inequalities in society—that is, believe what in the United States has been called the American Dream—resentment and animosity toward the rich will be minimized and people will perceive the inequalities as fair and deserved (R.V. Robinson & Bell, 1978).

A Neo-Marxian Model of Stratification

In Marx's time, the heyday of industrial development in the mid-19th century, ownership of property and control of labor in a capitalist system were synonymous. Most jobs were either on farms or in factories. Lumping all those who didn't own productive resources into one class and all those who did into another made sense. However, the nature of capitalism has changed a lot since then. Today a person with a novel idea for a product or service, a computer with Internet access, and a telephone can go into business and make a lot of money. Corporations have become much larger and more bureaucratic, with a long, multilevel chain of command. Ownership of corporations lies in the hands of stockholders (foreign as well as domestic), who often have no connections at all to the everyday workings of the business. Thus ownership and management are separated. The powerful people who run large businesses and control workers on a day-to-day basis are frequently not the same people who own the businesses.

In light of changing realities, conflict sociologists such as Ralf Dahrendorf (1959) began arguing for an explanation of class stratification that focuses primarily on differing levels of authority among the members of society. What's important is not just who owns the means of production but who can exercise influence over others. **Authority** is the possession of some status or quality that compels others to obey (Starr, 1982). A person with authority has the power to order or forbid behavior in others (Wrong, 1988). Such commands don't require the use of force or persuasion, nor do they need to be explained or justified. Rulers have authority over the ruled, as do teachers over students, employers over employees, and parents over children. These authority relationships are not fixed, of course: Children fight with their parents, students disagree with their teachers, and workers protest against their bosses. But though the legitimacy of the authority may sometimes be called into question, the ongoing dependence of the subordinates maintains it. The worker may disagree with the boss, and the student may disagree with the teacher—but the boss still signs the paycheck and the teacher still assigns final grades.

Like Marx and Engels, Dahrendorf believed that relations between classes inherently involve conflicts of interest. Rulers often maintain their position in society by ordering or forcing people with less authority to do things that benefit the rulers. But by emphasizing authority, Dahrendorf argued that stratification is not exclusively an economic phenomenon. Instead, it comes from the social relations between people who possess different degrees of power.

Dahrendorf's ideas on the motivating force behind social stratification have since been expanded. Sociologist Erik Olin Wright and his colleagues (E. O. Wright, 1976; E. O. Wright et al., 1982; E. O. Wright & Perrone, 1977) have developed a model that incorporates both the ownership of means of production and the exercise of authority over others. The capitalist and petite bourgeoisie classes in this scheme are identical to those of Marx and Engels. What is different is that the classes of people who do not own society's productive resources (Marx and Engels's worker class) are divided into two classes: managers and workers (see Exhibit 10.2).

Wright's approach gives us a sense that social class is not simply a reflection of income or the extent to which one group exercises authority over another. A lawyer,

Exhibit 10.2   Wright's Model of Class

	Exercise authority	Do not exercise authority
Own means of production	*Capitalists*	*Petite bourgeoisie*
Do not own means of production	*Managers*	*Workers*

plumber, or cook, for instance, could conceivably fall into any of the four class categories. They may own their own businesses and hire assistants (which would place them in the capitalist class), work for a large company and have subordinates (placing them in the manager class), work for a large company without any subordinates (placing them in the worker class), or be self-employed (placing them in the petite bourgeoisie) (R. V. Robinson & Kelley, 1979).

Wright's approach also emphasizes that class conflict is more than just a clash between rich and poor. Societies have, in fact, multiple lines of conflict—economic, political, administrative, and social. Some positions, or what Wright calls *contradictory class locations,* fall between two major classes. Individuals in these positions have trouble identifying with one side or the other. Middle managers and supervisors, for instance, can align with workers because both are subordinates of capitalist owners. Yet because middle managers and supervisors can exercise authority over some people, they also share the interests and concerns of owners.

Class Inequality in the United States

One of the ideological cornerstones of U.S. society is the belief that all people are created equal and that only personal shortcomings can impede a person's progress up the social ladder. After all, the United States is billed as the "land of opportunity." Our cultural folklore is filled with stories of disadvantaged individuals who use their courage and resolve to overcome all adversity. We don't like to acknowledge that class inequality exists. But sociologists tell us that our place in the stratification system determines the course of our lives, in sometimes obvious and sometimes subtle ways.

Consider, for instance, admission to college. We usually assume that admissions decisions are based solely on a student's merit. To get into a top college, you generally need to show high academic achievement (reflected in high school grades) and intellectual potential (reflected in scores on standardized aptitude tests like the SAT). What could be fairer than to use these sorts of objective measures as the primary criteria for determining who gets an elite education that will open doors for a lifetime?

Would it disturb you to know that your SAT score may depend as much on your parents' financial status as on your own intellectual aptitude? Obviously, simply coming from a well-to-do family doesn't guarantee a high score on the SAT, but it can help. If you were fortunate enough to attend high school in an affluent, upper-class neighborhood, chances are your school offered SAT preparation courses. In some of these schools, students take practice SAT exams every year until they take the real one in their senior year. Even if a school doesn't provide such opportunities, private lessons from test preparation coaches are available to those who can afford them. Wealthy high schools are also significantly more likely than mid-level or poor high schools to offer advanced placement courses, another important tool that college admissions officers use to measure applicants (Berthelsen, 1999).

Access to these opportunities pays off. In 2004, the average combined SAT score for students whose families earned less than $10,000 a year was 872. The average score for students whose families earned more than $100,000 a year was 1115 (National Center for Fair and Open Testing, 2004).

The advantages that such resources provide would require some sacrifice from the families of many middle-class students and are obviously out of the reach of working-class and lower-class students in poorer school districts—all of whom may be just as intelligent and just as motivated as their wealthier counterparts.

How U.S. Society Is Stratified

Some sociologists have concluded that Americans aren't particularly class conscious: They don't recognize the class system, they don't think of themselves in terms of class membership, and they don't define their lives in class-related ways (see, for example, Hurst, 1979). A newspaper article on upper-class families in the United States began by stating, "They have become the most discussed social group in the United States. Yet few people acknowledge being a member" (Leonhardt, 2003a, p. 1). Research suggests, however, that Americans are in fact acutely aware of class distinctions and are quite willing to identify their position within the class system. The National Opinion Research Center found that 44.9% of respondents identified themselves as working class and 45.3% as middle class (cited in S.M. Miller & Ferroggiaro, 1995). (Compare these numbers with the estimates that about 35% of Americans are working class and 45% are middle class.) The point is that although the lines between class levels aren't all that clear, people in the United States implicitly acknowledge the existence of social classes in society.

Class distinctions go beyond differences in income and wealth, however. Lumping people into broad class categories based on how much they make tells us little about what they buy, what they watch, or whom they vote for. Such information, which is more likely to be found by examining the lives of people in the same profession who do the same kind of work (F.R. Lee, 2003), is what distinguishes one socioeconomic class from another. Indeed, people create and maintain class boundaries through their perceptions of moral, cultural, and lifestyle distinctions (Lamont, 1992). In the end, class is a statement about self-worth and the quality of one's life:

> It's composed of ideas, behavior, attitudes, values, and language; class is how you think, feel, act, look, dress, talk, move, walk; class is what stores you shop at, restaurants you eat in; class is the schools you attend, the education you attain; class is the very jobs you will work at throughout your adult life. Class even determines when we marry and become mothers. . . . We experience class at every level of our lives; class is who our friends are, where we live . . . even what kind of car we drive, if we own one. . . . In other words, class is socially constructed and all-encompassing. (Langston, 1992, p. 112)

The Upper Class

The upper class in the United States is a small, exclusive group that occupies the highest levels of status and prestige. For some, membership in the upper class is relatively recent, acquired through personal financial achievement. These families are usually headed by high-level executives in large corporations and highly compensated lawyers, doctors, scientists, entertainers, and professional athletes. Such individuals may have been born into poor, working-class, or middle-class families, but they have been able to climb the social ladder and create a comfortable life. They are sometimes called "the new rich."

Others, however, are born into wealth gained by earlier generations in their families (Langman, 1988). The formidable pedigree of "old wealth," not to mention the wealth itself, provides them with insulation from the rest of society. And their position in society is perpetuated through a set of exclusive clubs, resorts, charitable and cultural organizations, and social activities that provide members with a distinctive lifestyle and a perspective on the world that distinguishes them from the rest of society.

Sociologists G. William Domhoff (1983, 1998) and C. Wright Mills (1956) have made the case that members of the upper class can structure other social institutions to ensure that their personal interests are met and that the class itself endures. For example, the educational system plays not only a key socializing role (see Chapter 5) but also an important role in perpetuating or reproducing the U.S. class structure. In poor and working-class public schools, kids are subtly taught their place through authority relationships with teachers and principals so that they will be prepared for the subordinate work positions they will probably occupy in the future (Bowles & Gintis, 1976). Members of the highest reaches of the upper class, in contrast, often spend their childhoods in private schools, their adolescence in boarding schools, and their college years in well-endowed private universities (Domhoff, 1998). In addition to the standard curriculum, these schools teach vocabulary, inflection, styles of dress, aesthetic tastes, values, and manners (R. Collins, 1971). Required attendance at school functions; participation in esoteric sports such as lacrosse, squash, and crew; the wearing of school blazers or ties; and other "character-building" activities are designed to teach young people the unique lifestyle of the ruling class. In many ways, boarding schools function like such "total institutions" as prisons and convents (Goffman, 1961), isolating members from the outside world and providing them with routines and traditions that are highly effective agents of socialization.

In a study of more than 60 elite boarding schools in the United States and Great Britain, Peter Cookson and Caroline Persell (1985) showed how the philosophies and programs of boarding schools help transmit power and privilege. This school experience forms an everlasting social, political, and economic bond among all graduates, and the schools act as gatekeepers into prestigious universities. After graduates leave these universities, they connect with one another at the highest levels in the world of business, finance, and government. The director of development at Choate, an elite prep school in Connecticut, said:

> There is no door in this entire country that cannot be opened by a Choate graduate. I can go anywhere in this country and anywhere there's a man I want to see . . . I can find a Choate man to open that door for me. (quoted in Cookson & Persell, 1985, p. 200)

The privileged social status that is produced and maintained through the elite educational system practically guarantees that the people who occupy key political and economic positions will form a like-minded, cohesive group with little resemblance to the majority whose lives depend on their decisions.

The Middle Class

In discussing the U.S. class system, it is tempting to focus attention on the very top or the very bottom, overlooking the chunk of the population that falls somewhere in the ill-defined center of the U.S. class structure: the middle class. Ironically, the middle class has always been important in defining U.S. culture. Today every other class is measured and judged against the values and norms of the middle class. It is a universal class, a class that supposedly represents everyone (Ehrenreich, 1990). Not surprisingly, the middle class is a coveted political constituency. Liberal and conservative politicians alike court it. Policies are proclaimed on its behalf.

But the lofty cultural status of the middle class in U.S. society belies the difficulties it experiences. According to a national survey conducted by the Pew Research Center, only about a third of U.S. adults say they earn enough money to lead the kind of life they want, and about two thirds worry that good jobs will move overseas and that workers here will be left with jobs that don't pay enough (Kohut, 1999). According to some experts, many families with healthy incomes live close to the financial edge, one layoff or medical emergency away from financial crisis (Meckler, 1999). The rising cost of health care is making it increasingly difficult even for middle-class families to afford insurance coverage (Strom, 2003).

Median household incomes rose steadily throughout the 1980s and 1990s but leveled off and even fell a bit in the early 2000s (as depicted in Exhibit 10.3). The median wage actually dropped by about 2.2% between 2000 and 2002 (Mishel et al., 2004).

Not only do middle-class jobs pay less than they used to, but there are fewer of them to go around. Corporate downsizing and outsourcing have nibbled into stable, white-collar, middle-class occupations. Even solid high-tech companies eliminated thousands of middle-income jobs from their payrolls in the early 2000s because of slowdowns in the personal computer market and the bursting of the Internet bubble. Indeed, the number of Americans with college degrees who are unemployed for over six months tripled between 2001 and 2004 (cited in S. Greenhouse, 2004b).

Some economists and politicians argue that unemployment is not a serious problem and that jobs in the future will be plentiful. However, the types of jobs that will be available may not be the sort that will strengthen people's middle-class status. According to the U.S. Bureau of Labor Statistics, 7 out of 10 occupations that are forecasted to show the greatest growth between now and 2012 are in low-wage service fields that require little, if any, education or training: retail sales, customer service, food service, cashier, janitor, waitperson, nursing aide, and hospital orderly (cited in S. Greenhouse, 2004b). Most of these jobs pay less than $18,000 a year. By most accounts, high-paying jobs will continue to be in short supply, meaning that many college-educated people will be thwarted in their attempts to earn a comfortable living. It's no wonder that many middle-class Americans feel like they're on a treadmill that constantly threatens to throw them into a less desirable social class.

The Working Class

Members of the working class—people who work in factory, clerical, or low-paying sales jobs—are even more susceptible than the middle class to downturns in the economy. Most working-class people have only a high school education and earn an hourly wage rather than a salary. Although they may earn enough money to survive, they typically don't earn enough to accumulate significant savings or other assets. Under the best circumstances, they usually have difficulty buying a home or paying for

Exhibit 10.3   Growth in Median Household Income

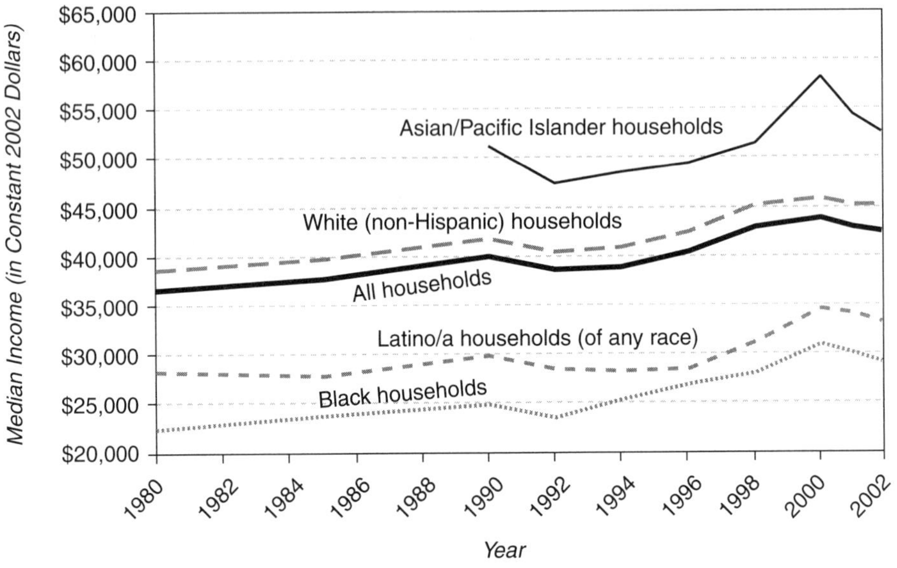

Source: U.S. Bureau of the Census, 2004a.

a child's education. When times are bad, they live their lives under the constant threat of layoffs, factory closings, and unemployment.

The working class has suffered disproportionately from the "structural adjustment" of the U.S. economy. In 2004, the U.S. Bureau of Labor Statistics reported that the hourly earnings of nonmanagement workers—ranging from nurses and teachers to assembly line workers—showed the steepest decline since 1991. As you might expect, race and ethnicity are also a factor. Decreases are much less significant for Asian Americans and Whites than for other ethnoracial groups. Across the board, though, the average production worker took home about $525.84 a week in 2003, the lowest level of weekly pay since 2001 (cited in Porter, 2004). Many people haven't had raises in years but have seen the cost of living (in particular, food, energy, and health care) rise steadily.

Many large companies have reduced their low-wage workforce. For instance, in 2005 because of its declining share of the American car market, General Motors announced plans to lay off 25,000 of its blue-collar hourly wage workers. That reduction was in addition to the 30,000 such jobs it cut over the previous five years (Hakim, 2005). Others have shut down their factories and shifted production either to other parts of the country or to overseas facilities.

To survive psychologically in an economically unstable world, many working-class people begin to define their jobs as irrelevant to their core identity. Instead of focusing on the dreariness or the insignificance of their work, they may come to view it as a noble act of sacrifice. A bricklayer put it simply: "My job is to work for my family"

(Sennett & Cobb, 1972, p. 135). Framing their work as sacrifice allows them to slip the bonds of the disappointing present and orient their lives toward their children's and grandchildren's future, something that gives them a sense of control they can't get through their jobs.

But it is especially difficult for working-class parents to sacrifice "successfully." Upper-class and middle-class parents make sacrifices so their children will have a life *like* theirs. Working-class parents sacrifice so their children will *not* have a life like theirs. Their lives are not a "model" but a "warning." The danger of this type of sacrifice is that if the children do fulfill the parents' wishes and rise above their quality of life, the parents may eventually become a burden or an embarrassment to them. Thus people who struggle to make ends meet are sometimes caught in a vicious trap. In addition, they must deal with public perceptions of them and their work that are decidedly negative.

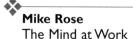

Mike Rose
The Mind at Work

Author Mike Rose (2004) grew up in a modest home, the son of working-class immigrants. Most of the adults in his family and in his neighborhood never graduated from high school, and all of them worked in blue-collar or service jobs their whole lives. He was fully aware, early on, that these manual laborers did not occupy a particularly valued place in American society. Low-paying jobs are often labeled "unskilled." Such workers are consistently marginalized either by more affluent people, who treat them as if they are invisible, or by widely held cultural stereotypes that they are unintelligent and unrefined. Because their work doesn't usually require advanced educational credentials, there's a belief that those who do it aren't that bright.

Rose set out to examine these stereotypes. He observed working-class workers on the job—waitresses, hair stylists, plumbers, welders, and so on—and took detailed notes of their activities. Once he became aware of the rhythms of their work, he began asking them questions, casual ones to start and then more and more specific ones as he got to know them better.

What he found was that apparently "mindless" working-class occupations require high levels of skill, judgment, and intelligence. Hair stylists, for example, must show an astonishing amount of aesthetic and mental agility when they turn vague requests ("I want something light and summery") into an actual hairstyle pleasing to the client. They must also have command of a remarkable range of knowledge—nutrition, hair growth patterns, the biology of skin, hair treatment chemicals, and popular images of beauty—in order to provide their clients not only with a look they want but with advice on how to maintain a stylish appearance. As one stylist described it:

> You've got to add up all these pieces of the puzzle, and then at the end you've got to come up with a thought, OK, it's gotta be this length, it's gotta be layered here, it's gotta be textured there. . . . It's not like we just start cutting. By the time I take my client to the shampoo bowl, after the consultation, I already have a little road map as to how I'm going to cut this haircut. (quoted in Rose, 2004, p. 33)

Similarly, working-class women who wait on tables in inexpensive diners and coffee shops must have advanced information processing skills, including an acute memory and the ability to make lightning-fast mathematical calculations. On the surface, restaurant work seems highly structured and determined—from the physical layout that guides people's movements to the norms of dining that are well known to customers and wait staff. Once seated, customers expect a series of events to unfold along a familiar time line. Indeed, their satisfaction (and the size of the tip they leave) is based on the manner in which the service meets these expectations.

Upon closer inspection, however, the restaurant environment is exceedingly complex and unpredictable. For instance, customers enter at different times and make requests at different stages of their meals, so each table proceeds at a different pace. This staggering of schedules maximizes the restaurant's flow of trade, but it increases the physical and cognitive demands on waitresses, especially during peak hours or when customers are particularly demanding. The meals themselves develop under their own different timetables. Some items cook quickly; others take a long time. And some have only a limited amount of time in which they can be served. So servers must also be aware of the temporal rhythm of the kitchen. And since the restaurant's profit depends on the constant turnover of customers, all this occurs under the pressure to move people along quickly:

> The work calls for strength and stamina; for memory capacity and strategy; for heightened attention, both to the overall layout and to specific areas and items; for the ability to take stock, prioritize tasks, cluster them, and make decisions on the fly. (Rose, 2004, p. 8)

Our collective failure to acknowledge the qualities and skills that even lower-status jobs require has helped to undermine a large chunk of the American working-class population. Rose's research is less of an objective assessment of these occupations than it is a plea to broaden our definitions of intelligence and to see dignity in the jobs that keep American society running.

The Poor

In an affluent society such as the United States, the people at the very bottom of the social class structure face constant humiliation in their everyday lives. You've heard the old saying "Money can't buy happiness." The implication is that true satisfaction in life is more than just a matter of being wealthy. Yet such a saying provides little comfort to people who can't pay their bills, don't know where their next meal is coming from or whether their job will even exist tomorrow, suffer from ill health, or have no home. Poverty pervades every aspect of a person's life. The entertainer Pearl Bailey perhaps summed it up best: "I've been rich and I've been poor. Rich is better."

The most publicly visible consequence of poverty is homelessness. No one knows for sure exactly how many homeless people live in the United States. The National Alliance to End Homelessness (2005) estimates that between 2.3 and 3.5 million people experience homelessness over the course of a year. According to a 2004 survey of 27 major American cities, 41% of homeless people are single men, 14% are single women, 40% are families with children, and 5% are children on their own. Of the homeless, 17% are employed, and fewer than a third are substance abusers (United States Conference of Mayors, 2004). Families with small children are the fastest-growing segment of the homeless population.

The reasons for homelessness in the United States are institutional ones: stagnating wages, changes in welfare programs, and perhaps most important, the lack of affordable housing. As rising wealth at the top end of society drives up housing prices, the poor have been left unable to afford decent housing and without federal and state programs to help (Shipler, 2004). In 2004, the George W. Bush administration cut the amount of federal rent subsidies in most large cities, forcing poor families to pay hundreds of extra dollars a month in rent (Chen, 2004).

According to the government, housing is considered "affordable" if it costs 30% of a family's income. The typical family hovering at the borders of poverty spends twice that on housing—about 60% of its after-tax income. By comparison, the average middle-class homeowner spends only 23% of his or her after-tax income on house payments. In 2003, the nationwide median housing wage—the minimum amount of money a person would have to make to afford rental housing—was $15.21 an hour, close to three times the federal minimum wage and a 37% increase over the 1999 amount. At the state level, between 36% and 60% of renters are unable to afford fair market rent for a two-bedroom apartment. Nowhere in the United States does a full-time, minimum-wage job provide enough income to afford adequate housing (National Low Income Housing Coalition, 2003).

Physical well-being is also related to poverty. Economic instability can influence health in obvious and not so obvious ways. For instance, social class can influence people's susceptibility to certain diseases. With each step down the income ladder comes an increased risk of headaches, varicose veins, respiratory infection, childhood asthma, hypertension, emotional distress, low-birth-weight babies, stroke, diabetes, and heart disease (Perez-Peña, 2003; Shweder, 1997). In addition, their neighborhoods are often unsafe and their homes insecure, increasing the likelihood of stress-related illness (L.D. Scott, 2005).

Poverty influences the type of health care people receive, their relationships with doctors, the support they can expect to get from their families, their access to health information, and the sorts of lifestyle changes (diet, exercise, and so on) they're told to make by doctors. According to the U.S. Bureau of the Census (cited in DeNavas-Walt et al., 2005), close to 46 million Americans (and over 8 million children) currently have no health insurance. Because of rapidly escalating health care costs and job losses, this number is increasing. Uninsured people are less likely than people who have health insurance to see a doctor when needed and are more likely to report being in poor health (Robert Wood Johnson Foundation, 2005). Uninsured parents also face decisions that more affluent parents never do, such as choosing between buying a child a birthday gift and paying to have the child's cavity filled. Without this safety net, one sickness or one accident can destroy a family financially.

In addition, approximately 11% of American households are "food insecure"—meaning that some members don't have enough to eat or the family uses strategies like eating less varied diets, participating in food assistance programs, or getting emergency food from community food pantries (Zeller 2004). That means that about 35 million poor Americans—including almost 13 million children—now live in households that experience hunger or the risk of hunger, an increase of 1.3 million since 2001 (Nord, Andrews, & Carlson, 2003).

The educational deck is likewise stacked against poor people. A report by the Education Trust (2002) showed that in most states those school districts with the neediest students receive far less state and local tax money—on average, just under $1,000 less per student—than those districts with the fewest poor students. Without adequate resources, teachers become frustrated and do not teach; children become cynical and do not learn. For many people, poor schools can produce feelings of powerlessness that continue throughout their lives (Bowles & Gintis, 1976).

Discipline and hierarchy, two crucial characteristics of a free-market economy, are taught early in the education system. The "successful" students are the ones who learn to submit to authority. But poor children's prior socialization—their manner of speech, dress, and action—does not fit that of the teachers and the school administration at large, so the children are subtly made to feel inadequate. Instead of developing as competent, hopeful members of society, many poor young people become resigned to their fate. Some become openly hostile to the educational system; others turn to crime (for instance, selling illegal drugs) as an alternative means of earning money.

Even if they graduate from high school, most poor children can't afford to attend college. Those who do are more likely to attend community colleges or state universities, which are less expensive but lack the quality and prestige of their more expensive counterparts. To make matters worse, the proportion of their income that poor families must spend for children to attend public universities—about 25% of their total annual income—has almost doubled since 1980. For wealthy families, who only spend an average of about 2% of their annual income on their children's education, there was no increase (Steinberg, 2002).

Thus, despite nationwide efforts to increase access to higher education, a greater proportion of college students today come from wealthy families than was the case two decades ago. Of course, students without family wealth do sometimes attend top universities with the help of need-based scholarships. But these schools, by and large, have no systematic plans for identifying, recruiting, or admitting low-income students. Only 3% of students in elite U.S. universities come from the poorest quarter of the population, and only 10% from the poorest half (Carnevale & Rose, 2003). Furthermore, poor college students don't fair as well as their more affluent counterparts. According to the U.S. Department of Education, only 41% of low-income students entering a four-year college graduate within five years. The graduation rate among high-income students is 66% (cited in Leonhardt, 2005). Such a gap is especially significant nowadays because a bachelor's degree is essential in today's global economy. According to the U.S. Bureau of the Census (2004a), people with some college experience but no degree earn, on average, a little less than $30,000 a year. College graduates on average earn over $50,000 a year. Numbers like these demonstrate that the educational system often serves to seal the fate of the poor instead of helping them succeed within the U.S. class system.

What Poverty Means in the United States

We hear the word *poverty* all the time. In common usage, poverty is usually conceived in economic terms, as the lack of sufficient money to ensure an adequate lifestyle. Sociologists, though, often distinguish between absolute and relative poverty. The term **absolute poverty** refers to the minimal requirements a human being needs to sustain a reasonably healthy life. The term **relative poverty** refers to one's economic position compared to the living standards of the majority in a given society. Absolute poverty means not having enough money for minimal food, clothing, and shelter, but relative poverty is more difficult to define. It reflects culturally defined aspirations and expectations. Poor people "generally feel better if they know that their position in life does not compare too badly with others in society" (quoted in Altman, 2003, p. 21). An annual family income of $5,000, which constitutes abject poverty in the United States, is perhaps five times higher than the *average* income in many developing countries. Life in a U.S. slum might be considered luxurious compared to the plight of tens of millions of starving people in other parts of the world.

The Poverty Line

The U.S. government uses an absolute definition of poverty to identify those people who can't afford what they need to survive. The official U.S. **poverty line** identifies the amount of yearly income a family requires to meet its basic needs. Those who fall below the line are considered officially poor. The poverty line is based on pretax money income only, which does not include food stamps, Medicaid, public housing, and other noncash benefits. The figure does vary according to family size, and it is adjusted each year to account for inflation. But it doesn't take into account regional differences in cost of living. In 2005, the official poverty line for a family of four—two parents and two children—was an annual income of $19,157.

That dollar amount is established by the U.S. Department of Agriculture and for decades has been computed from something called the Thrifty Food Plan. This plan, developed in the early 1960s, is used to calculate the cost of a subsistence diet, which is the bare minimum a family needs to survive. This cost is then multiplied by 3 because research at the time showed that the average family spent one third of its income on food each year. The resulting amount was adopted in 1969 as the government's official poverty line. Even though the plan is modified periodically to account for changes in dietary recommendations, the formula itself and the basic definition of poverty have remained the same for about four decades.

Many policymakers, sociologists, and concerned citizens question whether the current poverty line provides an accurate picture of basic needs in the United States. Several things have changed since the early 1960s. For instance, today food costs account for only about 13% of the average family's budget because the price of other things, such as housing and medical care, has inflated at much higher rates (U.S. Bureau of Labor Statistics, 2004a). In addition, there were fewer dual-earner or single-parent families in the past, meaning that fewer families had to pay for child care at that time. In short, today's family has many more expenses and therefore probably spends a greater proportion of its total income on nonfood items. The consequence is that the official poverty line is probably set too low today and therefore underestimates the extent of poverty in this country.

Deciding who is and isn't officially poor is not just a matter of words and labels. When the poverty line is too low, we fail to recognize the problems of the many families who have difficulty making ends meet but who are not officially defined as poor. A needy family making slightly more than the poverty line may not qualify for a variety of public assistance programs, such as housing benefits, Head Start, Medicaid, or Temporary Assistance for Needy Families. As a result, their standard of living may not be as good as that of a family that earns slightly less and therefore qualifies for these programs.

The U.S. Bureau of the Census is now experimenting with a new formula for determining the poverty line that would more accurately reflect contemporary spending patterns. Instead of simply using a subsistence food budget as the basis for the definition of poverty, this new formula would also consider expenses for housing, health care, transportation, utilities, child care, and personal expenses. It's estimated that this revised poverty line would be about $2,000 higher for a family of four than the current one, or roughly $21,200. Raising the official poverty line by $2,000 would have a dramatic effect on the number of people defined as officially poor. But don't expect the poverty line to be redefined anytime soon. The resulting increase in the number of officially poor families not only would bring obvious political costs to whatever administration happens to be in office but would certainly cause a demand for increased spending on social welfare programs—something few people in government these days are willing to consider.

Some economists also suggest that the exclusive focus on income in setting the poverty line underestimates the harmful long-term effects of poverty. Obviously, when families don't have enough income, they can't buy adequate food, clothing, and shelter. But when families don't have any assets, such as savings and home equity, they lose economic security and their ability to plan, dream, and pass on opportunities to their children (Boshara, 2002, p. 13).

The Near-Poor

Interestingly, the government seems to agree implicitly that the poverty line is too low. The U.S. Bureau of the Census defines individuals or families who earn between 100% and 125% of the poverty line as the **near-poor** or **working poor**. It estimates that about 39 million people who work full time and are not officially poor earn such low income that they are struggling financially (Lalasz, 2005). Their existence is fraught with irony. Because they fall above the poverty line, they escape academic attention and tend not to be the focal point of large-scale governmental assistance programs. At the same time, they are everywhere, doing the tasks with which others come into contact and depend on a daily basis:

> They serve you Big Macs and help you find merchandise at Wal-Mart. They harvest your food, clean your offices, and sew your clothes. In a California factory, they package lights for your kids' bikes. In a New Hampshire plant, they assemble books of wallpaper samples to help you redecorate. (Shipler, 2004, p. 3)

Beyond the financial difficulties and their relative invisibility, hovering on the margins of poverty has psychological consequences as well. The near-poor who receive public assistance often find that they are treated with disdain when they come into contact with the various bureaucrats who act as gatekeepers to government programs (Gilliom, 2001). For instance, every three months, people on food stamps must take time off of work and endure a humiliating meeting with their caseworkers to see if their food stamp allotment needs to be adjusted. A woman on food stamps once failed to include a utilities bill in the papers she provided to her caseworker. The caseworker punished her by withholding her food stamp benefits for two weeks. These types of interactions, coupled with the difficulties of managing relations with a boss, finding reliable day care, and coping with mountains of bills, can psychologically wither even the hardiest individual (Shipler, 2004).

When nothing out of the ordinary happens, the near-poor can manage. But an unexpected event—a sickness, an injury, the breakdown of a major appliance or automobile—can send them into poverty. It has been estimated that about one quarter of Americans hovering just above the poverty line will fall below it at some point in their lives, and then they have some difficult decisions to make. One study of 34,000 people nationwide found that during the cold winter months, families spend less on food and reduce their caloric intake by an average of 10% in order to pay their fuel bills (Bhattacharya, DeLeire, Haider, & Currie, 2003). Or imagine being a poor single mother with a sick child. One trip to the doctor might cost an entire week's food budget or a month of rent. Dental work or an eye examination is easily sacrificed when other pressing bills need to be paid. If she depends on a car to get to work and it breaks down, a few hundred dollars to fix it might mean not paying the electric bill that month and having less money for other necessities. When gasoline prices skyrocket to over $3 a gallon—as they did in 2005—many near-poor families find that they have to cut down on food purchases so they can afford to drive to work. These are choices that wealthier families never face.

The Poverty Rate

The **poverty rate,** the percentage of residents whose income falls below the official poverty line, is the measure that the U.S. government uses to track the success of its efforts to reduce poverty. Exhibit 10.4 shows how the poverty rate has fluctuated over the past few decades. In 2004 (the most recent year for which data are available), 12.7% of the population—or 37 million Americans—fell below the poverty line, up from 11.7% in 2001 (DeNavas-Walt et al., 2005). If we add the near-poor—people whose income is up to 25% higher than the poverty line—the number increases to over 47 million (U.S. Bureau of the Census, 2004a).

When used to describe national trends in poverty, the overall poverty rate can obscure important differences among subgroups of the population. For example, although two out of every three poor people in the United States are white, the poverty rate for non-Hispanic Whites (8.6%) is somewhat lower than that for Asian Americans (9.8%) and considerably lower than that for nonwhite Latino/as (21.9%) and African Americans (24.7%). The poverty rate in the South (14.1%) and West (12.6%) is higher than the rate in the Midwest (11.6%) and Northeast (11.6%) (DeNavas-Walt et al., 2005).

Exhibit 10.4   Historical Trends in the U.S. Poverty Rate

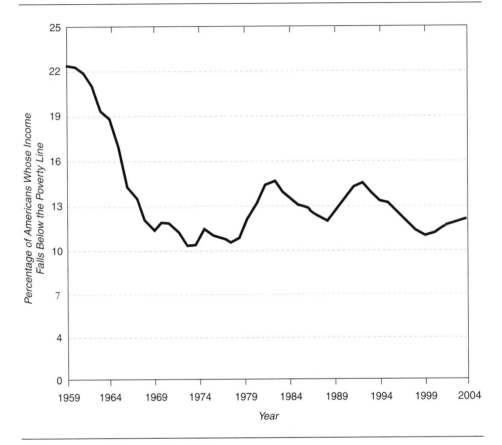

Source: DeNavas-Walt, Proctor, & Lee, 2005.

Although racial and ethnic minorities have consistently been rated among the poorest Americans, other groups have seen their status change over time. Before Social Security was instituted in 1935, many of the most destitute were those over age 65. As recently as 1970, 25% of U.S. residents over age 65 fell below the poverty line. Today, only 9.8% of the people in this age group are poor (DeNavas-Walt et al., 2005). Exhibit 10.5 shows how the poverty rate of older Americans has declined.

Taking their place among the poor, however, are women and children. The poverty rate for families headed by a single mother is 28.4%, compared to 13.5% for families headed by a single father, and 5.5% for married couple families (DeNavas-Walt et al., 2005). Over half of poor families are headed by single women. The risk of poverty increases dramatically when these women lack education. For example, 70% of young single mothers without a high school diploma are poor (Mishel, Bernstein, & Schmitt, 1997).

Although the rate of child poverty has declined a bit since the mid-1990s, 17.8% of U.S. residents under the age of 18 are poor and children under 6 are the poorest age group in the nation (19.9%) (DeNavas-Walt et al., 2005). Children under 18 represent 25% of the U.S. population but constitute 35.9% of all Americans living in poverty. The figures are especially bad for children of color: 28.2% of Latino/a children and 32.1% of African American children live in poor households (U.S. Bureau of the Census, 2004a).

The 17.8% poverty rate among U.S. children is the highest of any industrialized country. In Sweden, Norway, and Finland, for example, around 3% of all children live in poverty (Economic Policy Institute, 2004).

One of the key reasons why so many U.S. children are poor is their family structure. Over half of all children under the age of six who live in a female-headed household are poor, about five times the rate of children in married-couple families (DeNavas-Walt et al., 2005).

Why Poverty Persists

Even in the best of times, a prosperous country such as the United States has a sizable population of poor people. Why, in such an affluent society, is poverty a permanent fixture? To explain the persistence of poverty, we must look at enduring imbalances in income and wealth, the structural role poverty plays in larger social institutions, and the dominant cultural beliefs and attitudes that help support it.

Enduring Disparities in Income and Wealth

One reason why poverty is so persistent in the United States is the way that income and wealth are distributed. Although the strong economy of the late 1990s did lift many

Exhibit 10.5   Historical Trends in Poverty by Age

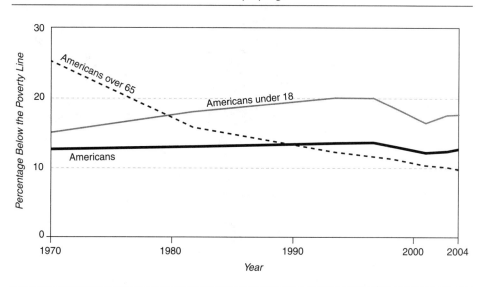

Sources: 1970–1999 data from U.S. Bureau of the Census, 2000b; 2001 data from Proctor & Dalaker, 2002; 2003 data from DeNavas-Walt, Proctor, & Lee, 2005.

U.S. residents out of poverty, the wide income gap between the richest and poorest segments of the population actually grew substantially (see Exhibit 10.6). In 2002 the annual income of the top 5% of U.S. families averaged $164,323; the annual income of the bottom 20% of families averaged $24,000 (U.S. Bureau of the Census, 2004a). The share of the nation's income earned by the richest 0.1% of Americans has more than doubled since the 1970s, reaching levels that were last seen in the 1920s. At the same time, the share of the bottom 90% has actually declined (cited in Johnston, 2005).

Between 1947 and 1979, incomes for all American families, rich and poor, grew at fairly similar rates. But things changed dramatically between the 1980s and 2000s (K. Phillips, 2002). In 1979, the average income for the top 1% of American earners was 33 times larger than the income of the lowest 20%. By 2000, the average income of the top 1% was 88.5 times larger than that of the bottom 20% (Economic Policy Institute, 2004).

Compensation for U.S. corporate executives is especially inflated and may contribute to this gap. In 1980, executives made 42 times more than factory workers; in 1998, they made 419 times more (Wolfe, 1999). To put it another way, in 1981 the 10 highest-paid American corporate executives were paid, on average, $3.5 million a year; in 2000 the 10 highest-paid executives made, on average, $154 million a year, a 4,300%

Exhibit 10.6   The Increasing Gap in Household Incomes

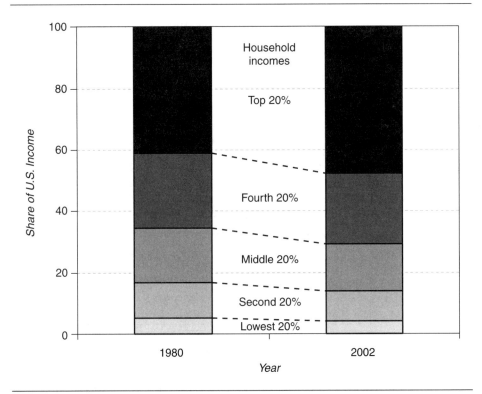

Source: U.S. Bureau of the Census, 2004a.

increase (K. Phillips, 2002). In fact, the average corporate chief executive now makes more in a single day than the average American worker makes in a typical *year* (Leonhardt, 2000). Krispy Kreme's chief executive is paid $760 *an hour* (Sloan, 2005). We may want to believe that personal effort and hard work solely determine our success, but it's hard to imagine that a CEO of, say, a TV manufacturing company works 400 times harder than a person who is making the TVs.

Although most U.S. residents paid more taxes as a percentage of income during the late 1990s and early 2000s than in previous decades, many of the wealthiest citizens paid less. According to the Internal Revenue Service, the only taxpayers whose share of income taxes actually declined in the early 2000s were those earning in the top 0.1% (cited in Johnston, 2005).

The United States has the greatest income inequality between poor and wealthy citizens of any industrialized nation. The wealthiest fifth of American families earns 10 times more than the poorest fifth (U.S. Bureau of the Census, 2004a). In France, the richest fifth earns seven times more than the poorest fifth; in Japan, four times more (K. Phillips, 2002). But to be fair, the income gap between rich and poor is worse in developing countries. For example, the richest 20% of Brazilians earn 64% of the income, whereas the poorest 20% earn 2.5% (Romero, 1999). Similar disparities exist in other Latin American countries and in most of sub-Saharan Africa.

Inequalities in income lead to even more striking inequalities in wealth. A lifetime of high earnings and inheritance from privileged parents creates a lasting advantage in ownership of property; of durable consumer goods such as cars, houses, and furniture; and of financial assets such as stocks, bonds, savings, and life insurance. The most prosperous 20% of U.S. households holds about 80% of the nation's wealth (up from 76% in 1984). And the wealthiest 1% of U.S. households, who have enjoyed two thirds of all increases in wealth over the past two decades, now owns close to 40% of the wealth. At the same time, the bottom 40% of households controls a mere 0.2% of the nation's wealth (Henwood, 2001; Keister & Moller, 2000). There are five times as many households with a net worth of over $10 million today than there were two decades ago (Johnston, 2005).

As a result, the United States is one of the most stratified of all industrial nations in regard to wealth as well as income. In Great Britain, for example, the wealthiest 1% of the population owns only 18% of the wealth—compared to 40% in the United States—despite Great Britain's long tradition of an elite aristocracy (Bradsher, 1995).

We will never live in a society with a perfectly equal distribution of income and wealth. Some people will always earn more, have more, and maybe even deserve more than others. But the magnitude of the gap between rich and poor in the United States challenges the notion that we live in a society where everyone is valued equally. As disparities in income and wealth grow, so too, does the gap in quality of life and access to opportunity between those at the top of society and those at the bottom.

The Social "Benefits" of Poverty

Recall the structural-functionalist assertion that stratification and inequality are necessary because they ensure that the most qualified and valuable people in society will occupy the most important positions. Social conditions exist and persist only if they are functional to society in some way. But functional for whom? If you were to survey people on the street and ask them if poverty is a good or bad thing, they would all, I'm sure, say, "Bad." Yet according to sociologist Herbert Gans (1971, 1996), within a free-market economy and competitive society such as the United States, poverty plays a necessary institutional role. Although structural-functionalism has often been criticized for its propensity to justify the status quo, Gans combines it with conflict thinking to identify several economic and social "functions" served by poverty that benefit all other classes in society:

♦ Poverty provides a ready pool of low-wage laborers who are available to do society's "dirty work." Poor people work at low wages primarily because they have little choice. When large numbers of poor people compete for scarce jobs, business owners can pay lower wages.

♦ Poverty ensures that there will be enough individuals, especially during times of high unemployment, to populate an all-volunteer military. To people with limited educational and occupational opportunities, military service holds out the promise of stable employment, comprehensive insurance coverage, a living wage, free schooling, and the development of marketable skills. In Iraq, U.S. military personnel have been disproportionately ethnoracial minorities from poor and working-class families (Halbfinger & Holmes, 2003). As you might guess, American casualties have also overwhelmingly been from families of modest means who live in sparsely populated rural counties (Cushing & Bishop, 2005; Golway, 2004). Military service is especially attractive to working-class immigrants. In 2004, the U.S. Congress enacted a law that shortens the waiting period for immigrants seeking citizenship if they volunteer to serve in the military. Many immigrants have enlisted—and dozens have died—simply because they needed the opportunity to improve their lives (Davey, 2004).

♦ Poverty supports occupations that either serve the poor or protect the rest of society from them: police officers, penologists, social workers, lawyers, pawnshop owners, and so on. Even drug dealers and loan sharks depend on the presence of a large population of poor people willing to pay for their illegal services.

♦ Poverty is the reason for the existence of the federal welfare system, which supports a network of private-sector businesses that make enormous profits by providing a wide range of goods and services. For instance, everyone who works in the system needs an office or clinic space in which to work, as well as supplies, equipment, and furnishings. Bankers, real estate developers, office system suppliers, computer manufacturers, and the construction and building industries profit each time a new welfare office, mental hospital, jail, unemployment office, or public housing project for the poor is needed (Bedard, 1991).

♦ Poverty is the reason why some people purchase goods and services that would otherwise go unused: secondhand appliances; day-old bread, fruits, and vegetables; deteriorated housing; dilapidated cars; incompetent physicians; and so forth. In 2002, dozens of Coca-Cola employees in Texas revealed that, for years, they were required to sell expired Coke to stores in poor neighborhoods. They were instructed to strip cans from their boxes, stuff them into fresh boxes with new dates stamped on the side, and stock them on store shelves in poor neighborhoods as if they were new (Winter, 2002). Clearly, this merchandise had little or no monetary value outside the poverty market; it was believed that the beverages couldn't be sold to wealthier Coke drinkers because they'd have noticed the difference.

♦ Poverty is a visible reminder to the rest of society of the "legitimacy" of the conventional values of hard work, thrift, and honesty. By violating, or seeming to violate, these mainstream values, the poor reaffirm these virtues. If poor people are thought to be lazy, their presence reinforces the ethic of hard work; if the poor single mother is condemned, the two-parent family is legitimated as the ideal.

♦ Poverty provides scapegoats for society's institutional problems. The alleged laziness of the jobless poor and the anger aimed at street people and beggars distract us from the failure of the economic system to adequately deal with the needs of all citizens. Likewise, the alleged personal shortcomings of slum dwellers and the homeless deflect attention from shoddy practices within the housing industry.

♦ Poverty provides a reference point against which others can compare themselves. Charity events allow upper- and middle-class people to symbolically demonstrate their concern and philanthropy and reinforce their feelings of moral superiority.

♦ Poverty provides the manual laborers that enable societies to produce many impressive achievements, from railroads to wilderness parks, in which all take national pride.

This explanation of poverty can easily be dismissed as cold and heartless. We certainly don't want to admit that poor people allow the rest of us to have comfortable and pleasant lifestyles. Yet this explanation is quite compelling. Just as society needs talented people to fill its important occupational positions, it also needs a stable population of poor people to fill its "less important" positions. If society fostered full equality, who would do the dirty work?

If we are truly serious about reducing poverty, then, we must find alternative ways of performing the societal functions it currently fulfills. But such a change will assuredly come at a cost to those who can now take advantage of poverty's presence. In short, poverty will be eliminated only when it becomes dysfunctional for people who *aren't* poor.

The Ideology of Competitive Individualism

Poverty also persists because of cultural beliefs and values that support the economic status quo. An important component of this value system in U.S. society is the belief in **competitive individualism** (Feagin, 1975; M. Lewis, 1978; Neubeck, 1986). As children, most of us are taught that nobody deserves a free ride. The way to be successful is to work hard, strive toward goals, and compete well against others. We are taught that we are fully responsible for our own economic fates. Stories of such people as Abraham Lincoln and Henry Ford, who rose above terrible conditions to make it to the top, reinforce the notion that anybody can be successful if he or she simply has the desire and puts in the necessary effort. All one needs to do is take the initiative.

The dark side of the U.S. belief in competitive individualism is that it all too easily justifies the unequal distribution of rewards and the existence of poverty. If people who are financially successful are thought to deserve the advantages they enjoy, allegedly because of individual hard work and desire, then the people who are suffering financially must likewise deserve their plight—because of their *lack of hard work and desire*. People in the United States have an intense desire to believe that good things happen to good people and bad things happen to bad people (J. Huber & Form, 1973; Lerner, 1970). In short, if a poor person is suffering, she or he "must have" done something to deserve it. The people who succeed, in contrast, must have been born smarter, stayed in school longer, or worked harder. The belief in competitive individualism gives people the sense that they can control their own fate.

People often justify poverty and inequality by emphasizing equal chances. Notice how this economist blames poverty on the willful actions of poor people who "choose" not to take advantage of available economic opportunities:

> Some poor people may choose not to work as hard as investment bankers working 70 hours a week. . . . One of the most amazing phenomena of recent years is why so many people . . . have not responded to the opportunities out there. (quoted in Stille, 2001, p. 19)

The belief system that such a comment reflects doesn't take into consideration the possibility that the competition itself may not be fair. Competitive individualism assumes that opportunities to learn a high-level trade or skill, or enter a profession, are available to everyone. Every person is supposed to have the chance to "be all that he or she can be." But the system may be rigged to favor those who already have power and privilege.

The Culture of Poverty

A variation of the belief in competitive individualism is the argument that poor people as a group possess beliefs, norms, values, and goals that are significantly different from those of the rest of society and that perpetuate a particular lifestyle that keeps them poor. Oscar Lewis (1968), the chief proponent of this **culture-of-poverty thesis**, maintained that poor people, resigned to their position in society, develop a unique value structure to deal with the improbability that they will become successful by the standards of the larger society. This culture is at odds with the dominant culture: in the United States, the middle-class belief in self-discipline and hard work.

Although the culture of poverty may keep people trapped in what appears (to the outside observer) to be an intolerable life, it nevertheless provides its own pleasures. Street life in the ghetto is exhilarating compared to a world where jobs are dull, arduous, and difficult to obtain and hold (P. Peterson, 1991). It is more fun to hang out, tell exaggerated stories, and exhibit one's latest purchases and conquests than to work and struggle in the "conventional" world. This extreme "present-orientedness"—the inability to live for the future (Banfield, 1970)—and not the lack of income or wealth is the principal cause of poverty, according to this view.

Once the culture of poverty comes into existence, Lewis argued, it is remarkably persistent: You can take the child out of the ghetto, but you can't take the ghetto out of the child. Furthermore, it is passed down from generation to generation. By age six or seven most children have absorbed the basic values and attitudes of their subculture, rendering them unable to take advantage of any opportunities that may present themselves later in life. Others have argued that a poor family with a history of welfare dependence tends to raise children who lack ambition, a solid work ethic, and self-reliance (Auletta, 1982).

Critics of the culture-of-poverty thesis point out that to generate such a persistent culture of poverty, a society must have a large group of the permanently poor. However, government statistics show that only a little over half of U.S. residents living in poverty in a given year are found to be poor the next, and considerably fewer than half remain poor over many years (Corcoran, 2001; Duncan, 1984; Sherraden, 1988). In a given two-year period, only 4.8% of all poor people are poor for the entire 24 months. Moreover, the average duration of poverty is less than 5 months (U.S. Bureau of the Census, 1999). In short, people tend to move in and out of poverty, undermining any single, long-standing, poverty-based lifestyle and value system that might exist.

Contrary to popular belief, not all poor people receive public assistance, either. In 2002 only about 28% of poor people received food stamps, 46% participated in Medicaid, 23% participated in school lunch programs, and 19% received some kind of housing assistance (U.S. Bureau of the Census, 2004a). As with poverty in general, people receiving government assistance move in and out of the system, making it difficult to sustain a tradition of dependence across generations.

Critics of the culture-of-poverty approach also contend that the behavior of poor people is largely caused by institutional impediments, such as a tradition of racial or ethnic prejudice and discrimination, residential segregation, limited economic opportunities, and occupational obstacles against advancement (Wilson, 1980). Poor African Americans, for example, still struggle to overcome the disadvantages of the slavery and Jim Crow laws that subjugated their ancestors. Other root causes of poverty include skyrocketing health care costs, a growing lack of affordable housing, and a changing economy that has all but eliminated entire classes of well-paying, low-skilled jobs.

Despite the lack of supportive evidence, the culture-of-poverty explanation remains popular. Many people strongly believe that poor people live by a different set of moral standards and therefore will remain in poverty unless forced to change their values. If poverty is a "way of life," then giving poor people enough money to raise them out of poverty is not the answer; changing their troublesome culture is.

The contemporary American welfare system reflects the belief that the best way to reduce poverty is to change poor people's lifestyles. In 1994, about five million U.S. citizens were on government assistance. By 2002, that figure had dropped to a little over two million (U.S. Bureau of the Census, 2004a). You might think that a booming economy is what helped to reduce U.S. citizens' dependence on government aid, but much of the reduction was actually due to a new welfare system that began in 1996. This system includes a mandatory work requirement (or enrollment in vocational training or community service) after two years of receiving assistance and a five-year lifetime limit to benefits for any family. In 2003, the U.S. House of Representatives passed a bill that imposed even stricter work conditions on people receiving federal cash assistance, such as working more hours per week (Pear, 2003). Ironically, the amount of money the government spends on welfare programs is less than half the amount it spends on assistance programs that serve predominantly middle-class recipients, such as Social Security, disability insurance, unemployment insurance, and Medicare (U.S. Bureau of the Census, 1998).

The assumptions behind such an approach to government assistance are clear: Making work mandatory will teach welfare recipients important work values and habits, make poor single mothers models of these values for their children, and cut the nation's welfare rolls. The underlying idea is that hard work will lead to the moral and financial rewards of family self-reliance. It will cure poverty and welfare dependence and ensure that new generations of children from single-parent families will be able to enter the American mainstream. Like competitive individualism, however, this ideology protects the nonpoor, the larger social structure, and the economic system from blame.

Global Development and Inequality

As you've seen elsewhere in this book, it is becoming increasingly difficult to understand life in any one society without understanding that society's place in the larger global context. The trend toward globalization (see Chapter 9) may have brought the world's inhabitants closer together, but they are not all benefiting equally. Nations have differing amounts of power to ensure that their interests are met. The more developed and less developed countries of the world experience serious inequalities in wealth that have immediate consequences for their citizens.

The Global Economic Gap

Just as an economic gap exists between rich and poor citizens within a single country, so too do economic gaps exist between rich and poor countries. The average per capita yearly income in Western Europe, the United States, Canada, and Japan is well over $29,000; in the less developed countries of the world it is just over $4,000 (Population Reference Bureau, 2005b). More than 2.7 billion people in less developed countries live on the equivalent of less than $2 a day. Close to half of all people living in sub-Saharan Africa survive on $1 a day (World Bank, 2003). Altogether, the wealthy developed countries of the world constitute roughly 20% of the world's population but account for 65% of the world's income. In contrast, less affluent, developing countries account for 67% of the world's population but only 18% of its income (McMichael, 1996). People who live in developed nations consume 86% of the world's goods and use 85% of the world's water (Shah, 2004).

The global gap in the quality of everyday life is especially striking. Only about 20% of school-aged children in poor countries are enrolled in secondary school, compared to 90% in affluent countries. In wealthy countries, 40% of college-age people go to college; in poor countries only 3% do (Bradshaw & Wallace, 1996). Particularly alarming are the dramatic differences between poor and rich countries in health and well-being.

❖
Micro-Macro Connection
The Global Health Divide

People around the world are living longer and healthier lives than ever before because of changes in public health policies over the last century—disease control, safe drinking water, effective medicine, and the like. But these improvements have not been shared equally by all the planet's inhabitants. For the over one billion people worldwide who live on less than one U.S. dollar per day, basic health services and medicines remain virtually nonexistent (D. Carr, 2004). People living in extreme poverty lack safe drinking water, decent housing, adequate sanitation, sufficient food, health education, professional health care, transportation, and secure employment.

According to the United Nations, hunger plagues an estimated 852 million people around the world and kills 5 million children each year (cited in Becker, 2004). In some developing countries, starving people resort to eating the leather off furniture or strapping flat stones to their stomachs to lessen the hunger pangs. In the slums of Haiti, people eat sun-baked biscuits made of butter, salt, water, and dirt (McNeil, 2004b).

Not surprisingly, poor countries lag behind wealthier countries on the most important measures of health: infant and child mortality, stunted growth, malnutrition, childhood vaccinations, prenatal and postnatal care, and life expectancy (Population Reference Bureau, 2004c). Millions of people die prematurely each year from diseases that, in more prosperous countries, are preventable, curable, or nonexistent. In Africa, for instance, infectious and parasitic diseases accounted for more than half of all deaths in 2001; in Europe such diseases accounted for only 2% of all deaths (D. Carr, 2004).

HIV/AIDS presents the most troubling global imbalance. The vast majority of HIV-infected people around the world are poor and don't have access to the effective, but extremely expensive, drug treatments that are readily available in the West. Consequently, though the number of AIDS cases and AIDS deaths is dropping in Western industrialized countries, it continues to increase in less developed countries (UN/AIDS, 2004). Poor countries in sub-Saharan Africa alone account for 62% of the world's victims of HIV/AIDS between the ages of 15 and 24, though not all countries in the region have the same rate of infection. Close to 9% of the adult population in these countries is infected with the disease (UN/AIDS, 2004). In 2003 alone, 2.2 million Africans died of AIDS. By contrast, the number of AIDS deaths in all high income countries *combined* (the United States, Western Europe, Australia, New Zealand, and Japan) was around 20,000 (UN/AIDS, 2004).

The effect that this disease has had on overall life expectancy is staggering. In the developed regions of North America and Europe, people born today can expect to live until they are close to 80. In the poorest, least developed countries in the world, life expectancy is well below 50. In African countries with high rates of HIV infection (Zimbabwe, Swaziland, Lesotho, Zambia, Malawi, Central African Republic, and Mozambique) life expectancy has now dropped below 40 (Dugger, 2004a). Such startling figures will have severe long-term consequences as millions of the world's poorest children become orphaned and face a lifetime of despair.

Even susceptibility to natural disasters is stratified globally. The poorest regions of the world are at the greatest risk for drought, tropical storms, earthquakes, tsunamis, and floods (Marsh, 2005). Four out of five poor people in Latin America and over half of poor people in Asia and Africa live on land that is highly vulnerable to natural degradation and disaster. These people often have no choice but to occupy the least valuable and most disaster-prone areas, such as riverbanks, unstable hills, and deforested lands. Developing countries contain 90% of the victims of natural disasters and bear 75% of the economic damage they cause (DeSouza, 2004).

It's important to note that the serious health problems faced by people in poor countries don't emerge solely from harmful environmental conditions or poverty. They are frequently influenced by the globalization of trade. For instance, in recent years, tobacco use has been declining in many countries of North America and Western Europe. The United States in particular has witnessed a fervent antismoking movement leading to a 20-year decline in cigarette consumption. Worldwide, though, 1.1 billion people smoke—about one third of the global population aged 15 and older (World Health Organization, 1999). And most of these smokers live in poor, developing countries. This figure is projected to reach 1.6 billion by 2025. Not surprisingly, tobacco companies have turned their attention to these foreign markets. Exports account for 33% of total U.S. cigarette production, up from 8% in 1984 (McGinn, 1997). If current trends continue, about 800 million of the world's 2 billion children will become smokers, and according to the World Health Organization, tobacco will eventually kill one third of them. Within 20 years, tobacco-induced illness is expected to replace infectious disease as the leading threat to human health worldwide (McGinn, 1997).

Politics may also get in the way of improving the health of people in developing countries. Wealthy countries could easily afford to provide regular vaccines, mosquito nets, soil nutrients, sufficient food, and clean water supplies to poor countries to address treatable problems like malaria and malnutrition. In fact, in 2005 the United Nations declared that ending world hunger and disease was "utterly affordable" and would only require that wealthy countries commit one half of one percent of their total incomes to aid poor countries. However, many of these nations have been notoriously reluctant to provide such assistance. The United States., for example, currently provides less than two tenths of one percent of its total income, the smallest percentage among major donor countries (Dugger, 2005). As long as expenditures for health care in poor countries remain a politically unpopular budget item in wealthy countries, the global health divide will persist.

Explanations for Global Stratification

How has global stratification come about? The conflict perspective explains not only stratification within a society but also stratification between societies. One way a country can use its power to control another is through **colonization**— invading and establishing control over a weaker country and its people in order to expand the colonizer's markets. Typically, the native people of the colony are forced to give up their culture. The colony serves as a source of labor and raw materials for the colonizer's industries and a market for their high-priced goods. Much of North and South America, Africa, and Asia were at one time or another under the colonial control of European countries such as Great Britain, France, Spain, Holland, and Portugal. The United States once controlled territories in Central and South America.

Although the direct conquest and subjugation of weak countries are rare today, wealthy countries are still able to exploit them for commercial gain. Powerful countries can use weaker countries as a source of cheap raw materials and cheap labor. Because of their access to better technology, wealthy nations are able to produce higher-quality, higher-priced goods at lower prices than are poor nations (D. A. Smith, 1993). They can also exert financial pressure on poorer nations by setting world prices on certain goods (Chase-Dunn & Rubinson, 1977). Because their economic base is weak, poor countries often have to borrow money or buy manufactured goods on credit from wealthy countries. The huge debt they build up locks them into a downward spiral of exploitation and poverty. They cannot develop an independent economy of their own and thus remain dependent on wealthy countries for their very survival (Frank, 1969).

But we must note that wealthy countries aren't always exploitative. In 2005, the wealthiest nations—the so-called Group of Eight—agreed to cancel more than $40 billion in debts owed by some of the poorest countries in the world in hopes of giving these countries a chance to escape the trap of poverty (Blustein, 2005).

Global Financial Organizations

It's not just powerful nations that have the ability to hold poor nations in their grip. Several international financial organizations play a significant role in determining the economic and social policies of developing countries. For instance, the World Bank funds reconstruction and development in these countries through investments and loans. It spends about $55 billion annually to better the lives of poor people worldwide (Dugger, 2004c). Similarly, the International Monetary Fund (IMF) tries to foster economic growth and international monetary cooperation through financial and technical assistance. The World Trade Organization (WTO) oversees the rules of trade between nations.

Although these organizations spend a lot of money to improve the standard of living in many poor countries by funding such projects as new roads or water treatment plants, there isn't much evidence that these projects have actually made much of a difference in people's lives (Dugger, 2004c). In fact, the countries that receive the aid of these organizations sometimes end up even more bankrupt and impoverished than before. When the World Bank and the IMF provide development credit, they do so with certain conditions attached. The conditions, often referred to as "structural adjustments," typically reflect a Western-style, free-market approach: reducing government spending, eliminating barriers to foreign ownership, privatizing public services, and paying high interest rates (Brutus, 1999).

Conditions such as these have at times threatened the welfare of citizens in recipient nations (Brutus, 1999; U.S. Network for Global Economic Justice, 2000):

◆ In Haiti, the IMF and World Bank blocked the government from raising the minimum wage and insisted that government services, such as sanitation and education, be cut in half. The desperate Haitian government complied, despite the fact that the life expectancy is 49 years for Haitian men and 53 years for women, that 45% of Haitians are illiterate, and that infant mortality is about 10%.

♦ In Mexico, the World Bank advised the government to abolish constitutionally guaranteed free education at the national university, making it virtually impossible for poor Mexicans to go to college.

♦ In Zimbabwe, the World Bank persuaded the government to shift production supports from food crops such as corn to export crops such as tobacco. As a result, malnutrition increased and infant mortality doubled.

You can see that global financial relationships between international lending institutions and poor countries are a double-edged sword. The countries certainly receive much-needed financial assistance. But in the process they sometimes become even more dependent and less able to improve conditions for their citizens.

Multinational Corporations

Global stratification has been made even more complex by the growth of massive multinational corporations, which can go outside their country's borders to pursue their financial interests if domestic opportunities aren't promising. They can invest their money in more lucrative foreign corporations or establish their businesses or factories abroad. U.S.-owned multinational corporations employ over 24 million people worldwide and have total assets of close to $14 trillion (U.S. Bureau of the Census, 2004a).

Often such success comes at a price. The largest U.S. multinational corporations achieved record earnings at the end of the 20th century, while hiring fewer Americans than ever. Between 1980 and 1999 the 500 largest corporations tripled their assets. At the same time, though, they eliminated almost five million U.S. jobs (K. Phillips, 2002). In 2005, I.B.M. laid off 13,000 American and European workers at the same time it was adding 14,000 workers in India to its payroll (Lohr, 2005a).

With their ability to quickly shift operations to friendly countries, multinational corporations find it easy to evade the governance of any one country. Their decisions reflect corporate goals and not necessarily the well-being or interests of any particular country. In fact, the largest multinational corporations have accumulated more wealth than most countries in the world, as Exhibit 10.7 shows.

From a structural-functionalist perspective, a U.S. company locating a production facility in a poor country would seem to benefit everyone involved. The host country benefits from the creation of new jobs and a higher standard of living. The corporation, of course, benefits from increased profits. And consumers in the country in which the corporation is based benefit from paying lower prices for the products that would cost more if manufactured at home. Furthermore, the entire planet benefits because these firms form allegiances to many different countries and therefore might help pressure them into settling their political disputes peacefully.

Multinational corporations are indeed a valuable part of the international economy. However, the conflict perspective argues that in the long run multinationals can actually perpetuate or even worsen global stratification. One common criticism

Exhibit 10.7   The Economic Power of Multinational Corporations

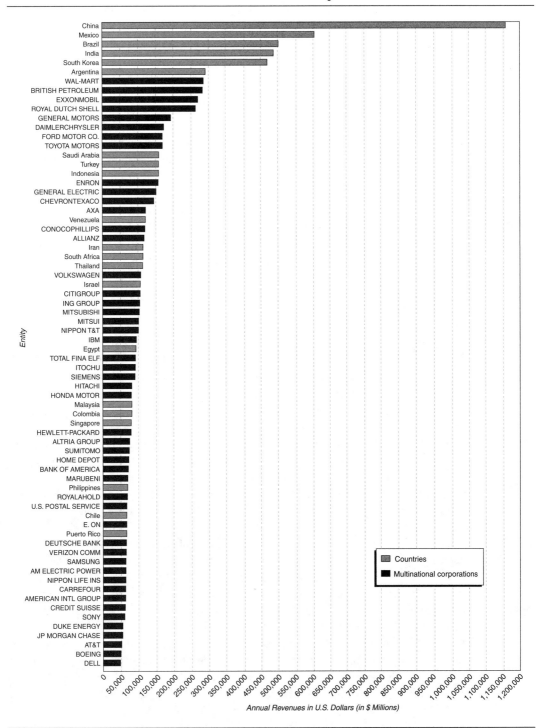

Source: Multinational sales data from *Fortune*, 2005; GDP data from World Bank, 2003.

of multinationals is that they exploit local workers and communities. Employees in foreign plants or factories often work under conditions that wouldn't be tolerated in wealthier countries. The most obvious inequity is the wage people earn. For example, according to the National Labor Committee for Worker and Human Rights (2001), senior seamstresses with six years experience at a Bangladesh factory that makes Disney clothing earn 17 cents an hour. Most work over 15 hours a day, seven days a week.

In addition, environmental regulations and occupational safety requirements that tend to drive up the cost of finished products, such as protection against dangerous conditions or substances, sometimes don't exist in other countries. Hence local workers may become sicker and the environment more polluted when foreign manufacturers set up facilities. For instance, U.S., Canadian, Australian, and European mining companies are digging mines of unprecedented size and destructiveness around the world. Many of these projects have caused not only significant deforestation but also the release of cyanide, arsenic, lead, and copper into nearby water supplies ("Tarnished Gold," 1999). Conditions in foreign factories were so bad and criticisms from human rights organizations so strong that a 1997 presidential task force created a code of conduct on wages, working conditions, and child labor for apparel factories that U.S. companies own and operate around the world.

The host countries themselves are equally likely to be exploited. The money that multinational corporations earn is rarely reinvested in the host country. In fact, 85% of the profit from exported products ends up in the hands of the multinational corporations, bankers, traders, and distributors (Braun, 1997). For example, in Brazil, one of the world's largest agricultural exporters, shipments abroad of fruits, vegetables, and soybeans have grown considerably over the past several decades. During the same period, however, the number of Brazilians who were undernourished grew from one third to two thirds of the population (Braun, 1997).

Local economies can suffer as well. For instance, supermarket chains owned by large multinational corporations have revolutionized food distribution worldwide. They are popular with consumers all over the world because of their lower prices and greater variety and convenience (Dugger, 2004b). But these stores tend to get their produce from large conglomerates that have more money and marketing know-how than small, local suppliers and can therefore provide cheaper fruits and vegetables. Hence the livelihoods of millions of struggling small farmers have been destroyed, widening the gap between the haves and the have-nots in developing countries.

Multinational corporations can also perpetuate global inequality by their decisions on when to develop certain products and where to market them. A case in point is the global pharmaceutical industry. North America, Japan, and Western Europe account for 80% of world drug sales, whereas Africa accounts for about 1% (cited in McNeil, 2000). A significant proportion of medical research today is devoted to drugs that are likely to sell in the lucrative markets of developed countries. These drugs are usually either "blockbuster" drugs (those that can earn upward of $1.5 billion a year) or "lifestyle" drugs (those that enhance the lives of generally healthy people). The astounding popularity—and profit-making capacity—of anti-impotence drugs like Viagra and Cialis and baldness drugs like Propecia and Rogaine are recent examples.

Impotence and baldness can be characterized as lifestyle troubles or embarrassing inconveniences but certainly not life-threatening illnesses.

This trend has global significance. Of the drugs introduced between 1975 and 1999 by the world's largest pharmaceutical companies, only 1% were created to combat diseases such as the tuberculosis, malaria, sleeping sickness, and acute lower-respiratory infections that kill or cripple millions each year in Africa, Asia, and South America (Silverstein, 1999). Cancer kills 76 million people a year. Between 1975 and 1999, 111 new cancer drugs became available. In contrast, tropical diseases kill 128 million people a year. However, only 13 new drugs to fight these diseases were developed between 1975 and 1999 (Cowley, 2005). The last truly new drug to treat tuberculosis—a disease that kills two million people a year, mostly in poor, developing countries—was invented over 30 years ago (McNeil, 2000).

But not all multinationals are hard-hearted organizations that ignore the well-being of their workers abroad, the well-being of the workforce at home whose jobs are being exported to other countries, or the health and welfare of poor people in developing nations. For many multinationals, relocating manufacturing facilities to another country where labor is less expensive is a necessary response to global economic pressures as well as the demands of domestic consumers for inexpensive products. But those processes that drive corporate decisions do sometimes drive individuals out of work, contribute to environmental and health problems, and reinforce global inequality.

Conclusion

In Chapter 1, I pondered the question of how free we really are to act as we wish. I described some of the personal, interpersonal, and structural considerations that limit or constrain our choices. In this chapter you have seen that this fundamental issue is affected by social stratification and inequality. Certain groups of people have a greater capacity to control their own lives than others. Our position in the stratification system can determine not only our ability to influence people and exert authority but a whole host of life chances as well, from financial stability to housing, education, and health care. The unequal distribution of economic resources, whether between wealthy and poor individuals in the same society or between wealthy and poor countries worldwide, has created a seemingly indestructible system of haves and have-nots.

The profound imbalances in wealth, power, and prestige that exist in the United States are especially ironic given how loudly and frequently U.S. citizens sing of their cultural commitment to the values of equality and justice. Nevertheless, the U.S. system is set up, like most others in the world, to promote, enhance, and protect the interests of those who reside at or near the top of the stratification system. Authority, wealth, and influence grant rights that are unknown to the vast majority of people.

It's rather shocking that in a country as wealthy as the United States, a comfortable, healthy, and stable life is well beyond the reach of tens of millions of people. Constant media images of wealth remind poor and working-class people that they are outsiders who can only watch and long to be part of that affluent world. And when disaster strikes, like Hurricane Katrina, poor people receive the message once again that their marginal status in society can have deadly consequences.

We speak of the poor as if they were an unchanging and faceless group to be pitied, despised, or feared. To talk of the "poverty problem" is to talk about some depersonalized, permanent fixture on the U.S. landscape. But poverty is people. It's people standing in soup kitchen lines and welfare lines. It's people living in rat-infested projects. It's people sleeping on sidewalks. It's people struggling to acquire things the rest of society takes for granted. It's people coming up short in their quest for the American Dream.

When we look at the institutional causes of poverty, we see that the personality or "cultural" traits often associated with poverty—low ambition, rejection of the work ethic, inability to plan for the future—might be better understood as consequences of poverty rather than causes of it. As long as the structural obstacles to stable employment, adequate wages, and a decent education continue to exist, so will the characteristic hopelessness associated with poverty.

---◆---

YOUR TURN

Even people whose income is well above the poverty line can sometimes find it difficult to make ends meet. Imagine a family of four living in your hometown. Suppose that both parents work, that one child is seven years old and in elementary school, and that the other is three and must be cared for during the day.

Make a list of all the goods and services this family needs to function at a minimum subsistence level—that is, at the poverty line. Be as complete as possible. Consider food, clothing, housing, transportation, medical care, child care, entertainment, and so on.

Estimate the minimum monthly cost of each item. If you currently live on your own and must pay these expenses yourself, use those figures as a starting point (but remember that you must estimate for a family of four). If you live in a dorm or at home, ask one of your parents (or anyone else who pays bills) what the expenses are for such goods and services. Call a local day care center to see what it charges for child care. Go to the local supermarket and compute the family food budget. For those expenses that aren't divided on a monthly basis (for example, the purchase of clothing and household appliances), estimate the yearly cost and divide by 12.

Once you have estimated the total monthly expenses, multiply by 12 to get the subsistence budget for the family of four. If your estimate is higher than the government's official poverty line (around $19,157), what sorts of items could you cut out of the budget for the family to be defined as officially poor and therefore eligible for certain government programs? By looking for ways to cut expenses from your minimal subsistence budget, you will get a good sense of what everyday life in poverty is like.

Describe the quality of life of this hypothetical family that makes too much to be officially poor and too little to sustain a comfortable life. What sorts of things are they forced to do without that a more affluent family might simply take for granted (for example, annual vacations, pocket money, a second car, eating out once a week)? What would be the impact of poverty on the lives of the children? How will the family's difficulty in meeting its basic subsistence needs translate into access to opportunities (education, jobs, health care) for the children later in life?

Source: Adapted from M. V. Miller, 1985.

CHAPTER HIGHLIGHTS

♦ Stratification is a ranking of entire groups of people, based on race, gender, or social class, that perpetuates unequal rewards and life chances in society.

♦ Social class is the primary means of stratification in many societies, including the United States. Contemporary sociologists are likely to define one's class standing as a combination of income, wealth, occupational prestige, and educational attainment. Social class is more than an economic position; it is a way of life that affects how we experience every facet of our lives.

♦ The structural-functionalist explanation of stratification is that higher rewards, such as prestige and large salaries, are afforded to the most important positions in society, thereby ensuring that the most qualified individuals will occupy the highest positions. Conflict theory argues that stratification reflects an unequal distribution of power in society and is a primary source of conflict and tension.

♦ The official U.S. poverty line, the dollar cutoff point that defines the amount of income necessary for subsistence living, may actually be set too low, thereby underestimating the proportion of the population that is suffering financially.

♦ Poverty persists because it serves economic and social functions. The ideology of competitive individualism—that to succeed in life all one has to do is work hard and win in competition with others—creates a belief that poor people are to blame for their own suffering. In addition, poverty receives institutional "support" from a distribution of wealth and income that is growing increasingly unequal.

♦ Stratification exists not only among different groups within the same society but also among different societies within a global community. Wealthy nations are better able to control the world's financial resources than poor nations are.

KEY TERMS

absolute poverty Inability to afford the minimal requirements for sustaining a reasonably healthy existence

authority Possession of some status or quality that compels others to obey one's directives or commands

caste system Stratification system based on heredity, with little movement allowed across strata

colonization Process of expanding economic markets by invading and establishing control over a weaker country and its people

competitive individualism Cultural belief that those who succeed in society are those who work the hardest and have the best abilities and that those who suffer don't work hard enough or lack necessary traits or abilities

culture-of-poverty thesis Belief that poor people, resigned to their position in society, develop a unique value structure to deal with their lack of success

estate system (feudal system) Stratification system in which high-status groups own land and have power based on birth

false consciousness Situation in which people in the lower classes come to accept a belief system that harms them; the primary means by which powerful classes in society prevent protest and revolution

lower class (underclass) In a society stratified by social class, a group of people who work for minimum wage or are chronically unemployed; the "poor"

means of production Land, commercial enterprises, factories, and wealth that form the economic basis of class societies

middle class In a society stratified by social class, a group of people who have an intermediate level of wealth, income, and prestige, such as managers, supervisors, executives, small business owners, and professionals

near-poor Individuals or families whose earnings are between 100% and 125% of the poverty line (see also **working poor)**

poverty line Amount of yearly income a family requires to meet its basic needs, according to the federal government

poverty rate Percentage of people whose income falls below the poverty line

relative poverty Individual's economic position compared to the living standards of the majority in the society

slavery Economic form of inequality in which some people are legally the property of others

social class Group of people who share a similar economic position in a society, based on their wealth and income

social mobility Movement of people or groups from one class to another

socioeconomic status Prestige, honor, respect, and lifestyle associated with different positions or groups in society

stratification Ranking system for groups of people that perpetuates unequal rewards and life chances in society

upper class In a society stratified by social class, a group of people who have high income and prestige and who own vast amounts of property and other forms of wealth, such as owners of large corporations, top financiers, rich celebrities and politicians, and members of prestigious families

working class In a society stratified by social class, a group of people who have a low level of wealth, income, and prestige, such as industrial and factory workers, office workers, clerks, and farm and manual laborers

working poor Employed people who consistently earn wages but do not make enough to survive (see also **near-poor)**

♦

STUDY SITE ON THE WEB

Don't forget the interactive quizzes and other learning aids at www.pineforge.com/newman6 study. In the Resource Files for this chapter, you will also find more on social class and inequality, including:

Sociologists at Work

- Ralf Dahrendorf: Explaining Class Conflict
- Susan Ostrander: Upper-Class Consciousness
- Joan Huber and William Form: Why the Rich Are Rich and the Poor Are Poor
- Scott Cummings and Del Taebel: Learning About the American Economic System

Micro-Macro Connections

- Corporate Interlocks
- Falling Through the Net
- Mass Media and Images of Social Class
- Welfare Reform
- The Global Tobacco Epidemic

The Architecture of Inequality
Race and Ethnicity

An interesting thing started happening when the U.S. government began to make its case in February, 2003, for an invasion of Iraq. Watching television, I was struck by the presence of members of historically underrepresented ethnoracial groups at the highest levels of international decision making and national security. There was Colin Powell, secretary of state at the time, presenting the case for war at the United Nations. There was Condoleezza Rice, then the national security adviser and visible spokesperson for the administration, offering support for the war effort on all the Sunday morning political talk shows. There was Gen. Vincent Brooks providing official daily military briefings for the international press during the war. After the suspension of military operations, Lt. Gen. Ricardo Sanchez served as commander of coalition forces in Iraq.

It wasn't just people associated with the war either. A quick look at President George W. Bush's present cabinet during his second term reveals an unprecedented number of people of color: Secretary of State Condoleezza Rice (African American), Secretary of Transportation Norman Mineta (Asian American), Secretary of Labor Elaine Chao (Asian American), Secretary of Commerce Carlos Gutierrez (Latino), Attorney General Alberto Gonzales (Latino), Secretary of Housing and Urban Development Alphonso Jackson (African American). Their lofty positions made me think about the tremendous gains that ethnoracial minorities have made in the last few years.

Nationwide, advances have been made not just politically but educationally, economically, and culturally. The percentage of African American and Latino/a college graduates has risen steadily over the past 10 years, as has the proportion of ethnoracial minority families that could be considered middle or upper class. More black and Latino/a families are headed by married couples than ever before (U.S. Bureau of the Census, 2004a). Once desolate inner-city neighborhoods have come to life. More Latino/as, Asian Americans, and Native Americans are in elected offices at the national, state, and local levels than ever.

The African American influence in pop culture is global—it's not uncommon to see fashion-conscious teenagers in Japan who tan themselves deep brown, dye and weave their hair into cornrows, and listen to Lil' Kim, Run-DMC, Mary J. Blige, and the Big Tymers (Genocchio, 2004). In this country, the trappings of hip-hop culture have become advertising mainstays in the fashion industry. In the 2000s, Latino/a musicians such as Ricky Martin, Marc Anthony, and Jennifer Lopez and African American artists like Jay-Z, Nelly, Snoop Dogg, and 50 Cent have achieved remarkable cross-over success. The most successful athletes in what were once exclusively white sports—tennis and golf—are people of color: Serena and Venus Williams and Tiger Woods. Close to one third of all major league baseball players are Latino (Lapchick, 2003). One popular book even proclaimed that racism in the United States is, for all intents and purposes, over (D'Souza, 1995).

Yet as I think of the significant strides ethnoracial minorities have made, my mind keeps pulling me toward a more troubling reality. Despite undeniable progress, African Americans, Latino/as, and Native Americans still remain, on average, the poorest and most disadvantaged of all groups in the United States; their average annual income is still substantially lower than that of Whites and Asian Americans (U.S. Bureau of the Census, 2004a). Of 18- and 19-year-olds, 23% of African Americans, 20% of Latino/ as, but only 10% of Whites are neither in school nor working (Dervarics, 2004b). More young black men have been to prison than have served in the military or earned a college degree (Pettit & Western, 2004). Of all ethnoracial groups in this society, African Americans have the lowest life expectancy; highest rate of infant mortality; highest rate of most cancers, diabetes, heart disease, high blood pressure, HIV/AIDS, and kidney failure; and highest rate of death from treatable illness, gunshot wound, and drug- or alcohol-induced causes (Center for the Advancement of Health, 2003; Institute of Medicine, 1999b; Stolberg, 1998b; U.S. Bureau of the Census, 2002; Zaldivar, 1998).

I also thought of specific events over the past few years that belie the image of racial progress and harmony:

♦ The white supremacist whose shooting spree in Illinois and Indiana left a black man and a Korean college student dead and nine others injured.
♦ The black man and white woman who, while walking down a street in Fayetteville, North Carolina, were shot and killed by white supremacists looking for "niggers" to torment.
♦ The Asian American man in California who was stabbed to death while roller blading. Police say the two young men arrested had Nazi paraphernalia and white supremacist posters in their apartment.
♦ The black man in Texas who was dragged behind a car driven by two white men until his body was torn apart.
♦ The destruction of mosques and the verbal harassment, physical assault, and even, in a few cases, murder of "Arab-looking" people in the days and weeks following the attacks on September 11, 2001.
♦ The Sikh man punched and kicked into unconsciousness by several men who were ridiculing him for wearing a turban they referred to as "dirty curtains."
♦ The black family in Indianapolis whose home was set on fire by gang members with ties to a white supremacist group who were trying to force the family to move away.

According to the FBI (2003), in 2002, there were close to 6,000 racially or ethnically motivated crimes of violence, a number that increases each year.

So how far have we really come? Which is the real United States? Is it the one that Martin Luther King, Jr. dreamed about in 1963, a place where race and ethnicity are losing their status as major criteria for judging the content of a person's character? Or is it the one perpetually plagued by economic inequality, prejudice, and hatred?

In the previous chapter, I examined the class stratification system. But social class doesn't influence social status and life chances on its own. This chapter focuses on another important determinant of social inequality: race and ethnicity.

Race and Ethnicity: More Than Just Biology

To most people, **race** is a category of individuals labeled and treated as similar because of common inborn biological traits, such as skin color; color and texture of hair; and shape of eyes, nose, or head. It is widely assumed that people who are placed in the same racial category share behavioral, psychological, and personality traits that are linked to their physical similarities. But sociologists typically use the term **ethnicity** to refer to the nonbiological traits—such as shared ancestry, culture, history, language, patterns of behavior, and beliefs—that provide members of a group with a sense of common identity. Whereas ethnicity is thought to be something that we learn from other people, race is commonly portrayed as an inherited and permanent biological characteristic that can easily be used to divide people into mutually exclusive groups.

But the concept of race isn't nearly so straightforward. For instance, people who consider themselves "white" may actually have darker skin and curlier hair than some people who consider themselves "black." In addition, some groups have features that do not neatly place them in one race or another. Australian Aboriginals have black skin and "Negroid" facial features but have blond, wavy hair. The black-skinned !Kung of Africa have epicanthic eye folds, a characteristic typical of Asian peoples.

Not surprisingly, there are no universal racial categories. South Africa has four legally defined races—black, white, colored, and Indian—but in England and Ireland the term *black* is used to refer to all people who are not white. In one small Irish town that is experiencing an unprecedented influx of refugees, anyone who is not Irish is considered black. As one resident puts it, "Either Romanians or Nigerians, we don't know the difference. They're all the same. They're all black" (quoted in Lyall, 2000, p. A6). Conversely, some African Americans visiting Africa for the first time are often stunned to learn that African Blacks consider them white. Brazilians have three primary races—*branco* (white), *prêto* (black), and *pardo* (mulatto)—but use dozens of more precise terms to categorize people based on minute differences in skin color, hair texture and length, and facial features. As Brazilians climb the class ladder through educational and economic achievement, their racial classification changes, as illustrated by popular Brazilian expressions such as "Money whitens" or "A rich Negro is a white man, and a poor white man is a Negro" (Marger, 1994, p. 441). In Puerto Rico, a U.S. territory, conceptions of race are markedly more fluid than they are in the states. Race is seen as a continuum of categories, with different shades of color as the norm and classifications that can change as one's socioeconomic circumstances change (Rodriguez & Cordero-Guzman, 2004).

The complex issue of defining race points up a complicated biological reality. Since the earliest humans appeared, they have consistently tended to migrate and interbreed.

Some surveys estimate that at least 75% of U.S. Blacks have some white ancestry (cited in L. Mathews, 1996). Indeed, there is no race gene—no gene that is 100% of one form in one race and 100% of a different form in another race (P. Brown, 1998).

That is not to say that race has absolutely *no* connection to biology. Geneticists have known for quite a while that some diseases are not evenly distributed across racial groups. The overwhelming majority of cases of sickle cell anemia, for instance, are among people of African descent; it is rare among non-Hispanic Whites (Black Health Care.com, 2003). Hemochromatosis, a disorder that causes the body to absorb too much iron, is virtually absent among people from India and China, but occurs in 7.5% of Scandinavians (Wade, 2002). But no disease is found *exclusively* in one racial group. Furthermore, it's unclear whether these differences are solely due to some inherited biological trait or to the life experiences and historical, geographical, and/or environmental location of certain groups.

For most sociologists, then, race is more meaningful as a social category than as a biological one. That is, the characteristics a society selects to distinguish one ethnoracial group from another shape social rankings and determine access to important resources. But they have less to do with innate physical or genetic differences than with what the prevailing culture defines as socially significant (American Sociological Association, 2002). For instance, Jews, Irish, and Italians were once defined as members of inferior races. They came to be seen as "white" only when they entered the mainstream culture and gained economic and political power (Bronner, 1998a). Sociologists have noted that more and more Americans feel comfortable simply changing out of the ethnic identities they were born into and taking on new ones (Hitt, 2005).

Historical changes in the categories used by the U.S. government in its decennial population censuses further illustrate shifting conceptions of race (Lee, 1993):

- In 1790, the first U.S. census used the following classifications: Free White Males, Free White Females, All Other Free Persons, and Slaves.
- In 1870, there were five races: White, Colored (Black), Mulatto (people with some black blood), Chinese, and Indian.
- Race categories in the 1890 census reflected white people's concern with race mixing and racial purity. Eight races were listed, half of them applying to black or partly black populations: White, Colored (Black), Mulatto (people with three eighths to five eighths black blood), Quadroon (people with one fourth black blood), Octoroon (people with one eighth black blood), Chinese, Japanese, and Indian.
- In 1900, Mulatto, Quadroon, and Octoroon were dropped, so that any amount of "black blood" meant a person had to be classified as "Black."
- In 1910 and 1920, Mulatto returned to the census form, only to disappear for good in 1930.
- Between 1930 and 2000, some racial classifications (such as Hindu, Eskimo, part-Hawaiian, and Mexican) appeared and disappeared. Others (Filipino, Korean, Hawaiian) made an appearance and have stayed ever since.
- Individuals filling out the 2000 census form had a wide array of racial categories from which to choose: White, Black, American Indian or Alaska Native, Asian Indian, Chinese, Filipino, Japanese, Korean, Vietnamese, Native Hawaiian, Guamanian or Chamorro, or Samoan.

You might have noticed that Latino/a is not included in the list of races on the latest census form. With the exception of the inclusion of "Mexican" in 1930, Spanish-speaking people have routinely been classified as "white." But because Latino/as can be members of any race, "Hispanic origin" is now considered by the Census Bureau, although it is defined not as a race but as an ethnicity. However, because so many Latino/a respondents to the 2000 census refused to identify themselves by any of the racial categories on the census form, "some other race" is now the fastest-growing category in the United States (Swarns, 2004).

In short, racial categories are not natural, biological groupings. They are created, inhabited, transformed, applied, and destroyed by people (Omi & Winant, 1992). What ties individuals together in a particular racial group is not a set of shared physical characteristics—because there aren't any physical characteristics shared by all members of a particular racial group—but the shared experience of being identified by others as members of that group (Piper, 1992).

❖
Micro-Macro Connection
Politics and Multiracial Identity

Definitions of race and the way those definitions are incorporated into people's individual identities are particularly difficult for people with mixed racial backgrounds. Since the era of slavery the United States has adhered to the "one-drop rule" regarding racial identity (F. J. Davis, 1991). The term dates back to a common law in the South that a "single drop of black blood" made a person black. Sociologists call this a *hypodescent* rule, meaning that racially mixed people are always assigned the status of the subordinate group (F. J. Davis, 1991). Conversely, other groups must meet a hereditary threshold in order to claim a particular ethnoracial identity. For instance, some Native Americans carry a card known as the C.D.I.B. (Certificate of Degree of Indian Blood) that indicates whether they have enough Indian blood to be considered Indian (Hitt, 2005).

People in the United States still tend to see race in categorical terms: black or white, red or yellow, brown or black. Even when faced with ambiguities, U.S. residents still try to put people into specific categories. Most multiracial people have experienced being arbitrarily assigned a racial identity by a school principal or an employer that may differ from the identity of other members of their families or may differ from their identity in other settings. Indeed, as recently as 1990, mixed-race people who identified themselves on the census form as "black-white" were counted as black; those who wrote "white-black" were counted as white (Lee, 1993).

But the dramatic growth in the number of multiracial children being born has upset traditional views of racial identity. Between 1970 and 2000, the number of children whose parents are of different races grew from 900,000 to over 3 million (Lee & Edmonston, 2005). More and more people of mixed racial heritage are fighting against traditional "one-drop" thinking and refusing to identify themselves as one race or another.

In the mid- to late-1990s, these individuals began lobbying Congress and the Bureau of the Census to add a multiracial category to the 2000 census. They argued that such a change would add visibility and legitimacy to a racial identity that has heretofore been ignored. Some argued that a multiracial category might soften the racial lines that divide the country (Stephan & Stephan, 1989). When people blend several races and ethnicities within their own bodies, race becomes a less potent social divider, thereby presenting a biological solution to the problem of racial injustice (White, 1997).

Not everyone thought such a change would be a good idea. Many civil rights organizations objected to the inclusion of a multiracial category (Farley, 2002). They worried that it would reduce the number of U.S. citizens claiming to belong to long-recognized ethnoracial minority groups, dilute the culture and political power of those groups, and make it more difficult to enforce civil rights laws (Mathews, 1996). Job discrimination lawsuits, affirmative action policies, and federal programs that assist minority businesses or that protect minority communities from environmental hazards all depend on official racial population data from the census. Furthermore, people who identify themselves as biracial or multiracial are sometimes perceived by members of established racial groups as sellouts who avoid discrimination by taking advantage of the confusion their mixed identity creates.

In the end, the civil rights organizations won. For the 2000 census, the government decided not to add a multiracial category to official forms. Instead it adopted a policy allowing people, for the first time, to identify themselves on the census form as members of more than one race. The new guidelines specify that those who check "white" and another category will be counted as a member of the minority (Holmes, 2000). Data from the 2000 census show that 2.4% of the population—or close to 7 million people—identify themselves as belonging to two or more races (U.S. Bureau of the Census, 2004a). As you might expect, people under the age of 17 were four times as likely as people over 50 to identify themselves as belonging to more than one race (cited in Schmitt, 2001b).

Some sociologists caution, however, that the Census Bureau's method of measuring multiracial identity—checking two or more race categories—does not adequately reflect the way people personally experience race. Sociologists David Harris and Jeremiah Sim (2002) examined data from the National Longitudinal Study of Adolescent Health, a survey containing information on the racial identity of a nation-wide sample of over 11,000 adolescents. They found that the way people racially classify themselves can be fluid, changing from context to context. For instance, almost twice as many adolescents identify themselves as multiracial when they're interviewed at school as when they're interviewed at home. Furthermore, only 87.6% expressed the same racial identities across different settings. This research is important because it shows that census data on multiracial identity don't necessarily account for people who self-identify as multiracial in everyday situations. When it comes to determining racial identity, political and social considerations, not biological ones, are the determining factors.

Histories of Oppression and Inequality

A quick glance at the history of the United States reveals a record of not just freedom, justice, and equality but also of conquest, discrimination, and exclusion. Racial and ethnic inequalities have manifested themselves in such phenomena as slavery and fraud;

widespread economic, educational, and political deprivation; the violent and nonviolent protests of the civil rights movement; and racially motivated hate crimes. Along the way such injustices have constricted people's access to the basic necessities of life, including housing, health care, a stable family life, and a means of making a decent living.

Every racial or ethnic minority has its own story of persecution. European immigrants—Irish, Italians, Poles, Jews, Greeks—were objects of hatred, suspicion, and discrimination when they first arrived in significant numbers in the United States. For instance, 19th-century newspaper want ads routinely noted, "No Irish need apply." Jews were refused admission to many U.S. universities until the mid-20th century. The National Origins Act of 1924 restricted immigration from southern Europe (mainly Greece and Italy) until the 1960s. Because these groups had the same skin color as the dominant white Protestants, however, they eventually overcame most of these obstacles and gained entry into mainstream society. Most recently, Arab Americans have become popular targets of hostility. According to the Council on American-Islamic Relations, incidents of harassment and violence against Muslims increased 70% between 2002 and 2003 ("Anti-Muslim Incidents Increase," 2004). For people of color who've been in this country the longest—namely, Native Americans, Latino/as, African Americans, and Asian Americans—racial equality has always been elusive.

Native Americans

The story of Native Americans includes racially inspired massacres, the takeover of their ancestral lands, their confinement on reservations, and unending governmental manipulation. Successive waves of white settlers seeking westward expansion in the 18th and 19th centuries pushed Native Americans off any land that the settlers considered desirable (U.S. Commission on Human Rights, 1992). A commonly held European belief that Native Americans were "savages" who should be displaced to make way for civilized Whites provided the ideological justification for conquering them.

According to the Fourteenth Amendment to the U.S. Constitution, "All persons born or naturalized in the United States, and subject to the jurisdiction thereof, are citizens of the United States and of the state wherein they reside." But despite the broad wording of this amendment, Native Americans were excluded from citizenship. In 1884 the U.S. Supreme Court ruled that Native Americans owed their allegiance to their tribe and so did not acquire citizenship on birth. Not until 1940 were all Native Americans born in the United States considered U.S. citizens (Haney López, 1996).

Despite their history of severe oppression, Native Americans have shown a remarkable ability to endure and in some cases to shrewdly promote their own economic interests. In the Pacific Northwest, for instance, some Indian tribes have successfully protected their rights to lucrative fishing waters (F. G. Cohen, 1986). Casinos and resorts have made some tribes wealthy. The Connecticut Sun, a professional women's basketball franchise, plays its home games on the grounds of a casino owned by the Mohegan tribe. Elsewhere, organizations have been formed to advance the financial concerns of Native Americans in industries such as gas, oil, and coal, where substantial reserves exist on Indian land (Snipp, 1986). However, intense struggles between large multinational corporations and Native American tribes continue today over control of these reserves.

(Text continues on page 390)

"Civilizing" the Indians

Eric Margolis

In 1879 an ex-Indian fighter named Captain Richard Pratt established the Indian Boarding School at Carlisle, Pennsylvania. Like other white Americans at the time, Pratt viewed Native Americans as "dirty," "ignorant," and "lazy." He devised a program of boarding schools that he believed would, in one or two generations, eliminate tribal culture by resocializing Indian children. He argued, "The Indian must die as an Indian and live as a man."

The Pratt plan took young children away from their families and tribes in the West and brought them to Pennsylvania and other locations. They had their hair cut and were given military uniforms. Their days were marked by rigid schedules enforced with bells and whistles to teach a sense of time. Half of the day they attended classes and half the time they worked on school farms and in factories intended to socialize young Indians to the dominant White culture. Pratt's Indian Schools functioned as "total institutions," in Erving Goffman's terms.

To demonstrate the "success" of his socialization program for Indian children, Pratt made "before" pictures of them when they arrived at the school and "after" pictures when they had been in cloudy Pennsylvania long enough to lose their tans.

The goal was to visibly portray a "whitening" (that is, "civilizing") process. Note that, in the "after" shot, the students were dressed in school uniforms that resembled the uniforms of the cavalry that defeated them in the Indian wars.

At the Indian schools, most of the children were trained for menial work: domestic servants, farmers, and factory workers. Thus the schools reinforced social class differences in addition to altering the racial identities of Native American children.

❖ Training as domestics, Seneca Training School, 1905

❖ Making tin utensils, Carlisle Indian School, circa 1900 to 1903

The schools reinforced gender distinctions too. Boys and girls were commonly separated for classes in shop and home economics. Although Native American cultures had diverse family structures, the Indian schools sought to replace that diversity with the 19th-century white American version: the male-dominated nuclear family. Thus girls were prepared for domesticity and boys as breadwinners.

Most important, however, was the curriculum of resocialization. Students were punished if they spoke in their native language or practiced their tribal religion; they were taught to obey Western clock time, work for wages, and cultivate a desire for money and consumer goods. The end product would be an assimilated Indian, one whose traditional way of thinking and tribal life style had been completely obliterated in favor of the individualism and the Protestant work ethic of American life.

Curiously, however, photographs of the school and classroom activities show that what was being taught was not a sense of individualism but regimentation and discipline, illustrated by military uniforms that suppressed individual personality.

❖ Albuquerque Indian School, which was established in 1881 and continued operating until 1982, when its program was transferred to the Santa Fe Indian School

Indian children did not always take this enforced ethnoracial resocialization quietly. There were many instances of resistance, ranging from stubborn refusal to participate to running away to vandalism and arson. Indian schools became notorious for constant surveillance and for discipline and punishment of resisting students.

Indian schools were the only federally financed education system—except for the military—that the United States ever developed. In 1900, nearly 18,000 Indian children were enrolled not just in Carlisle, Pennsylvania, but in places like Albuquerque, New Mexico; Flandreau, South Dakota; Chemawa, Oregon; Lawrence, Kansas; Mt. Pleasant, Michigan; Riverside, California; and Phoenix, Arizona. Government funding was used to build these imposing institutions and to make a detailed photographic record of the schools.

❖ Most of the schools had jails, like this one at the Sacaton, Arizona Indian school, where the most intransigent students were imprisoned.

❖ Mt. Pleasant Indian Industrial School, circa 1910

Perhaps we should not be surprised that the Indian schools failed to smoothly assimilate Native Americans into white American culture. Segregated boarding schools were clearly more effective at promoting social exclusion than guiding students into the mainstream of American life. After the schools were through with the children, they were doubly stigmatized: marked by their color in a racist society and miseducated for their tribal culture, whose traditions they lost and whose language they could sometimes no longer speak. Hence Native Americans thus remained second-class citizens well into the second half of the 20th century.

Today remedies are being sought for injustices against Native Americans. In 2003, a class action lawsuit was filed on behalf of some 100,000 Native Americans who, from 1890 to 1978, were forced to attend boarding schools run by the U.S. government. Alleging sexual, physical, and emotional abuse, the suit seeks damages in the amount of $25 billion.

Indian tribes have also opened a number of their own schools. These schools teach reverence for Indian ways along with the typical school curriculum of English and mathematics. Today's Indian students are thus better prepared to live in either their own culture or the dominant American culture while preserving their own ethnic heritage.

❖ In 1966 the Rough Rock Demonstration School opened in Chinle, Arizona, on the Navajo Reservation. It became a model for many other tribally run schools.

Latino/as

The history of Latino/as in this country has been diverse. Some groups have had a relatively positive experience. For instance, Cuban immigrants who flooded into this country in the late 1950s, fleeing Fidel Castro's Communist political regime, received an enthusiastic welcome (Suarez, 1998). Many of these early immigrants were wealthy business owners who set up lucrative businesses, particularly in south Florida. Today, Cuban American families are the most financially successful of any Latino/a group.

But other groups have experienced extreme resentment and oppression. For instance, when the United States expanded into the Southwest, white Americans moved into areas that were already inhabited by Mexicans. After a war that lasted from 1846 to 1848, Mexico lost half its national territory, including what are now Arizona, California, Colorado, New Mexico, Texas, Nevada, and Utah, as well as parts of Kansas, Oklahoma, and Wyoming.

In theory, Mexicans living on the U.S. side of the new border were to be given all the rights of U.S. citizens. In practice, however, their property rights were frequently violated, and they lost control of their mining, ranching, and farming industries. The exploitation of Mexican workers coincided with a developing economic system built around mining and large-scale agriculture, activities that demanded a large pool of cheap labor (J. Farley, 1982). Workers often had to house their families in primitive shacks with no electricity or plumbing for months on end while they performed seasonal labor.

Today the status of Latino/as is mixed. They now make up roughly the same proportion of the U.S. population as Blacks (U.S. Bureau of the Census, 2004b) and will soon outnumber them (see Exhibit 11.1). Larger numbers mean not only greater influence on the culture but more political clout. In 2004, a record 8 million Latino/as voted, electing the first Latino senators in over 25 years. That same year both major political parties spent a total of $13 million on Spanish-language television ads (Campo-Flores & Fineman, 2005). In 2005, Los Angeles elected its first Latino mayor.

Economically and educationally, though, the situation is less rosy. The average annual income for Latino/a individuals and families is still substantially lower than that of other groups (U.S. Bureau of the Census, 2004a). Latino/as are significantly more likely to drop out of school and less likely to go to college than are white, Asian American, or African American children.

African Americans

The experience of African Americans has been unique among ethnic groups in this country, because of the direct and indirect influences of slavery. From 1619, when the first black slaves were sold in Jamestown, Virginia, to 1865, when the Thirteenth Amendment was passed outlawing slavery, several million Blacks in this country endured the brutal reality of forced servitude. Slave owners controlled every aspect of a slave's life. They determined which slaves could marry and which marriages could be dissolved. The economic value of children (that is, future slaves) meant that slave owners had an interest in keeping slave marriages intact. But even the possibility of stable family life was an illusion. When economic troubles forced the sale of slaves to raise

Exhibit 11.1   Projected Changes in Ethnoracial Composition of the U.S. Population

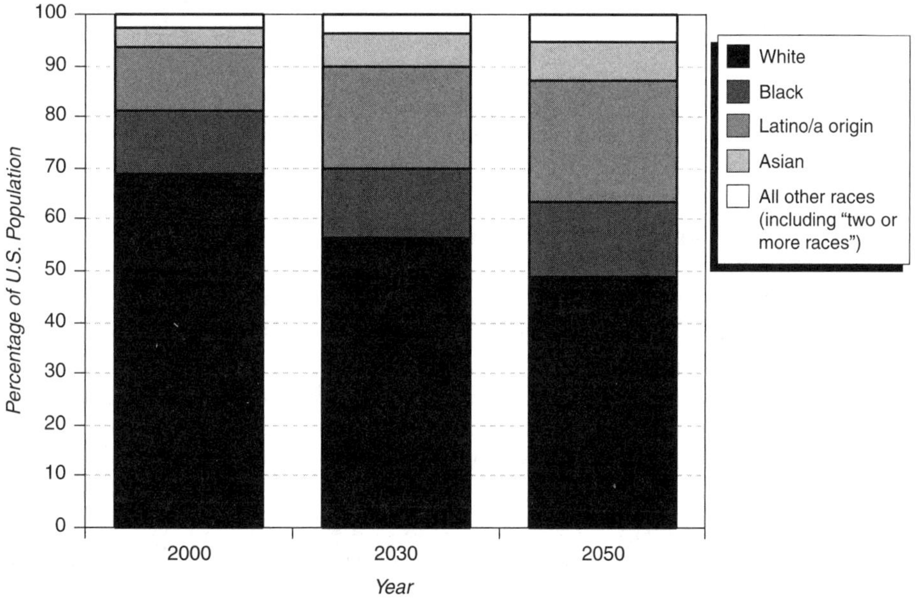

Source: U.S. Bureau of the Census, 2004b.

money, slave owners didn't hesitate to separate the very slave families they had once advocated. The threat of separation hung over every slave family.

Even after slavery was abolished, the conditions of life for U.S. Blacks showed little improvement. "Jim Crow" laws established rigid lines between the races. In 1896 the U.S. Supreme Court ruled that racial segregation in public facilities was constitutional. Unequal access to public transportation, schools, hotels, theaters, restaurants, campgrounds, drinking fountains, the military, and practically every other aspect of social life continued until the middle of the 20th century.

The quality of life for most African Americans remains below that of Whites. The median annual income for black households is $29,026, compared to $45,086 for Whites (U.S. Bureau of the Census, 2004a). Black unemployment is twice as high as that of Whites. Fewer than half of African American families own their own homes, compared to over 70% of white families (National Urban League, 2004). Nevertheless, blatant discrimination has declined in the last four decades, and some economic, educational, and political advances have been made. For instance, between 1992 and 1997 the number of black-owned businesses grew 26% and generated over $71 billion in revenues (U.S. Bureau of the Census, 2004a). The average annual income of $29,026 represents a significant increase over the average income of black households in 1990 ($23,979). And the median income of black women is about equal to that of white women (U.S. Bureau of the Census, 2004a). One author summed up the mixture of good news and bad news this way: "It's the best time ever to be black in America. . . . But not everyone's celebrating" (Cose, 1999, p. 29).

Asian Americans

When Chinese men came to this country in the second half of the 19th century to work in the mines and on the expanding railroad system, they were treated with hostility. The image of the "yellow peril" was fostered by rampant fears that hordes of Chinese workers would take scarce jobs and eventually overrun native-born Whites. U.S. law prevented Chinese laborers from becoming permanent citizens, from bringing their wives with them, and from marrying Whites when they got here. Eventually, laws were passed that put limits on and even prohibited Chinese immigration.

Early Japanese Americans faced similar circumstances. Like the Chinese, Japanese families created tight-knit, insulated communities where they were able to pool money and resources and achieve relative success. But their perceived success motivated lawmakers to enact the National Origins Act of 1924, which barred all further Japanese immigration. Hostility toward the Japanese reached a peak in 1941, following Japan's attack on Pearl Harbor. President Franklin Roosevelt signed an executive order authorizing the relocation and internment of Japanese immigrants and U.S. citizens of Japanese descent in camps surrounded by barbed wire, watch towers, and armed guards.

The irony of race for Chinese, Japanese, Koreans, Vietnamese, Cambodians, Laotians, Indians, and other Asian groups is that they are often perceived as "model minorities," or "America's greatest success story." Almost twice as many Asian Americans as Whites complete college, and their average household income is actually higher than that of the population as a whole (U.S. Bureau of the Census, 2004a).

But the expectations and resentment associated with being the "model minority" can be just as confining and oppressive as those created by more negative labels:

> While superficially complimentary to Asian Americans, the real purpose and effect of this portrayal is to celebrate the status quo in race relations. First, by over-emphasizing Asian American success, it de-emphasizes the problems Asian Americans continue to face from racial discrimination in all areas of public and private life. Second, by misrepresenting Asian American success as proof that America provides equal opportunities for those who conform and work hard, it excuses American society from careful scrutiny on issues of race in general, and on the persistence of racism against Asian Americans in particular. (ModelMinority.com, 2003, p. 1)

The examples of discrimination against Asian Americans are more common than you might think. Consider, for instance, the 2000 U.S. Department of Energy investigation of Wen Ho Lee, a Taiwan-born scientist at a nuclear weapons lab who was dismissed for security violations and suspected espionage. With little factual or legal evidence to support the charge that Lee was a spy, he was indicted on 59 counts and held in detention for nine months as a national security threat. In making their case against Lee, the government emphasized his Chinese ethnicity, promoting the perception that he had "divided loyalties" that prevented him from being a "real" American (Gee, 2004). Asian American employees at other nuclear labs nationwide faced systematic harassment and denial of advancement because they too were suspected of spying. All the news stories about successful Asian Americans can't hide lingering suspicion and resentment.

Racial and Ethnic Relations

U.S. society's long history of racial tension is unlikely to fade away entirely any time soon. Increasing numbers of ethnoracial minorities and an influx of non-English-speaking immigrants are heightening competition and conflict with the majority over society's resources, including various forms of wealth, prestige, and power. The unequal distribution of resources is often motivated by **racism,** the belief that humans are subdivided into distinct groups so different in their social behavior and mental and physical capacities that they can be ranked as superior or inferior (Marger, 1994). Racism can be expressed at the personal level through individual attitudes and behavior, at the cultural level in language and collective ideologies, and at the macrostructural level in the everyday workings of social institutions.

Personal Racism

Personal racism is the expression of racist attitudes or behaviors by individual people. This form of racism takes many obvious forms, such as individuals who use derogatory names when they refer to other ethnoracial groups or those who show clear disdain for and hostility toward members of other groups during face-to-face contacts. However, subtle forms of personal racism, such as the high school guidance counselor who steers minority students away from "hard" subjects toward those that do not prepare them for higher-paying jobs, are much more common. Whether blatant or subtle, personal racism rests on two important psychological constructs—stereotypes and prejudice.

Stereotypes

The word **stereotype** was first used by the political commentator Walter Lippmann in 1922. He defined it as an oversimplified picture of the world, one that satisfies our need to see our social environment as a more understandable and manageable place than it really is (Lippmann, 1922). It is the overgeneralized belief that a certain trait, behavior, or attitude characterizes all members of some identifiable group.

Casual observations easily refute the accuracy of common racial or ethnic stereotypes. Most African Americans aren't on welfare, most Jews aren't greedy, few Italians belong to the Mafia, not all Asian Americans excel in math, the vast majority of Muslims aren't terrorists, and so on. Overgeneralizations can never be true for every member of a group. Yet despite their obvious inaccuracy, stereotypes remain a common part of our everyday thinking. We all know what the stereotypes are, even if most of us choose not to express them or act on them.

The contemporary view is that stereotyping is a universal aspect of human thought (Hamilton, 1981). Our brains tend to divide the world into distinct categories: good and bad, strong and weak, them and us (Rothenberg, 1992). By allowing us to group information into easily identifiable categories, stereotypes make the processing of information and the formation of impressions more efficient. As you saw in Chapter 6, our lives would be utterly chaotic if we weren't able to quickly categorize and form expectations about people in terms of gender, race, age, ethnicity, and so on. What's important to remember, though, is that the actual content of stereotypes is by no means natural; it must be learned.

Television, films, books, magazines, and the Internet provide large audiences with both real and fantasized images of racial, religious, and ethnic groups: the savage Indian, the Jewish American princess, the fanatical Arab terrorist, and so on. Asians are frequently depicted as camera-wielding tourists, scholastic overachievers, or sinister warlords. Latino/as have historically been cast as "Latin lovers," "banditos," "greasers," or "lazy good-for-nothings" (Reyes & Rubie, 1994). An analysis of a random sample of television news shows aired in Los Angeles and Orange Counties in California revealed that Whites are more likely than African Americans and Latino/as to be portrayed on television news as victims of crime. Conversely, African Americans and Latino/as are more likely to be portrayed on news shows as lawbreakers than as crime victims (Dixon & Linz, 2000). Another study found that although people of color appear regularly in prime-time TV commercials, they usually appear as secondary characters. Furthermore, Whites are more likely to appear in ads for upscale products, beauty products, and home products. People of color, in contrast, are more likely to appear in ads for low-cost, low-nutrition products (like fast foods and soft drinks) and in athletic or sports equipment ads (Henderson & Baldasty, 2003).

Most of the scholarly focus on stereotypical media images concerns the portrayal of African Americans. Early television shows of the 1950s, including *Amos 'n Andy* and *The Beulah Show,* depicted Blacks as lazy clowns, opportunistic crooks, or happy, docile servants. But by the 1970s, *Sanford and Son, Good Times, What's Happening,* and the other so-called ghetto sitcoms were trying to represent African Americans more positively. They showed slums and housing projects as places where people could lead happy, loving, even humorous lives. When U.S. society itself could not achieve social reform through civil rights, television solved the problem by inventing symbols of black success and racial harmony (Gates, 1992).

Some shows seemingly overcame harmful racial stereotypes by depicting Blacks as strong, smart, and successful: *Julia* and *I Spy* in the 1960s; *Roots* and *The Jeffersons* in the 1970s; *Benson, A Different World,* and *The Cosby Show* in the 1980s; *The Fresh Prince of Bel-Air, Family Matters,* and *Moesha* in the 1990s; and *Gideon's Crossing, Jamie Foxx, Bernie Mac, The Parkers, My Wife and Kids, Malcolm & Eddie,* and *Kevin Hill* in the 2000s. In addition, popular shows with predominantly white casts, such as *CSI: Crime Scene Investigation, ER, Boston Public,* and *Law & Order,* show that Blacks and Whites often share the core values of U.S. culture.

But critics charge that many of the recent portrayals of African Americans continue to reflect some of the negative stereotypes of the 1950s. Working-class and poor African Americans—especially men—still may be depicted as a menace involved in such activities as crime, gang violence, drug use, and general aimlessness (Gray, 1995). Aggressive images of black men remain common fare in hip-hop music videos and popular video games as well.

In addition, opportunities for actors of color are limited. According to the Screen Actors Guild (2004), in 2003, only 23.5% of all television and movie roles went to African American, Latino/a, Asian, or Native American performers, although these groups make up more than 30% of the U.S. population. This figure represented a 3% decrease for African American actors, a 31% decrease for Latino/as, and a 35% decrease for Asian Americans from 2002. Furthermore, while the number of television series with multiracial casts has increased (Freeman, 2002), the number of prime-time television shows that are predominantly black, or Latino/a, or Asian has decreased. For instance, the number of predominantly black television shows reached its peak in 1997, when there were 15 such series. In 2001, there were only six. And all of these were comedies. No predominantly black dramatic series has ever succeeded on network television (Moss, 2001). Compounding the problem is the fact that the viewing audience remains largely segregated along racial lines (see Exhibit 11.2)

Among young people, this racial divide is narrowing. Offered both black and white shows, teenage viewers are willing to watch predominantly black shows (Hass, 1998). Hence we can hope that when today's teens grow into adults, they will bring with them a greater appreciation of racial and ethnic diversity, thus ensuring that certain aspects

Exhibit 11.2 Top Twenty Prime-Time TV Shows

Top 15 Prime Time TV Programs

Program	Black Rank	White Rank	Top 15 Programs Among Whites
Bernie Mac*	1	94	Friends
The Parkers*	2	131	E.R.
One on One*	3	134	Everybody Loves Raymond
Girlfriends*	4	131	CSI
My Wife & Kids*	5	54	Law and Order
NFL Monday Night Football	6	14	The West Wing
The Hughleys*	7	130	Becker
Titus	8	130	Survivor
CSI	9	4	JAG
Law and Order	10	5	Judging Amy
E.R.	11	2	Will and Grace
WWF Smackdown!	12	101	Frasier
The Steve Harvey Show*	13	131	Inside Schwartz
Law and Order: SVU	14	131	NFL Monday Night Football
The Practice	15	23	60 Minutes

Source: Initiative Media North America, 2002.

* Predominantly black casts.

of minority cultures—language patterns, values, sense of humor, and tastes in fashion, music, and theater—will continue to be a vital aspect of the larger U.S. culture.

Prejudice and Discrimination

When stereotypes are the basis for a set of rigidly held, unfavorable attitudes, beliefs, and feelings about members of a racial or ethnic group, they constitute **prejudice** (Allport, 1954). A good example of how prejudice affects social interaction is one study in which a group of Whites was shown a photograph of a white person holding a razor blade while arguing with a black person on a New York subway. Subjects were shown the picture for a split second and then asked to write down what they saw. More than half said they saw the black man holding the razor against the white man's throat (cited in Helmreich, 1992). The belief that all Blacks are violent was so powerful that it distorted people's perceptions. Similarly, a day after Hurricane Katrina hit, several Internet news outlets posted two similar photographs—one of a white victim wading in chest-high water, the other of a black victim. The caption that accompanied the photo of the white person said that she had "found" bread and water from a local grocery store. The caption for the photo of the black man said that he had just "looted" a local grocery store.

Prejudices can change as social conditions change. When people feel their cultural integrity or their economic livelihood is being threatened—by either the real or perceived infiltration of other ethnoracial groups—prejudicial attitudes can become more open and hostile. For instance, widespread anti-Catholic sentiment became especially virulent in the late 19th and early 20th centuries as waves of Catholic immigrants entered the country looking for a better life (Gusfield, 1963).

Specific historical events can shape prejudices too. The equation of Arab Muslims with violent terrorism has been a common prejudice for decades, dating back to the murder of eleven Israeli athletes during the 1972 Summer Olympics in Munich. But the September 11, 2001 attacks bolstered anti-Muslim prejudice. In one study of teachers' attitudes, relatively few of the respondents knew much about Islam. Nonetheless, one third of them associated the word *Islam* with terms like *terrorists, enemy, trouble,* and *war* (Mastrilli & Sardo-Brown, 2002). Another study found that a high level of anti-Islamic imagery in the media supported the negative portrayal of Muslims and helped to fuel the belief that all Muslims are terrorists (Khalema & Wannas-Jones, 2003).

Prejudiced beliefs would be of little significance if they didn't lead sometimes to discrimination. **Discrimination** is the unfair treatment of people based on some social characteristic. The 1964 Civil Rights Act prohibits discrimination or segregation on the grounds of race, color, religion, or national origin. This act has produced tremendous progress in U.S. race relations. Nevertheless, discrimination still exists.

When we think of discrimination we usually think of its most blatant forms—racial epithets, racially inspired hate crimes, blatant barriers to employment, and so on. Most of the time, though, discrimination is much more subtle, expressed as suspicion or avoidance; in fact, the person engaging in it may not even realize he or she is doing so. Psychologists Carl O. Word, Mark P. Zanna, and Joel Cooper (1974) created an experimental situation in which white subjects were led to believe they were interviewing applicants for a team position in a group decision-making experiment. The applicants, who were really confederates of the researchers, were both black and white. The results showed that the "interviewers" treated black applicants very differently from white ones. For instance, they placed their chairs at a significantly greater distance from the black interviewees. They leaned forward less and made less eye contact with the black applicants. In addition, they ended the interview sooner and tended to trip over their words.

In a second experiment, Word, Zanna, and Cooper sought to determine the effect such behavior would have on the applicants. In this experiment, the interviewers were the confederates of the experimenters. These new interviewers were trained to mimic the behaviors found among interviewers in the first experiment. This time, applicants who encountered the "less friendly" behavior—that is, reduced eye contact, greater physical distance, and so on—performed less adequately and showed less composure during the interview than the others.

These experiments illustrate the subtle process by which discrimination sometimes operates, even in people who are not self-consciously prejudiced. We are generally so unaware of our own nonverbal behavior that if we unwittingly give off signs of our dislike, we don't interpret others' subsequent behavior as a reaction to our nonverbal cues. Rather, we attribute it to some inherent trait in them. We may unknowingly prompt the very actions that we then use as evidence of some flaw or deficiency in that group.

From the point of view of those discriminated against, these subtle forms of discrimination are often harder to fight than overt bigotry. If you are excluded from a job because you're Asian or denied membership in a club because you're Jewish, you can fight to open those doors. Today, quite a few people have made it in (Blauner, 1992). But once inside, they still have many interpersonal barriers to overcome.

When such subtle behavior becomes common among large numbers of people, prejudice and discrimination become mutually reinforcing. Defining one group as inferior and thus denying them access to a decent education and jobs becomes a self-fulfilling prophecy, producing the very inferiority that the group was believed to possess in the first place.

Prejudice and discrimination may also occur within ethnoracial groups. For instance, some see **colorism**—prejudice between light-skinned and dark-skinned Blacks—as just as bad a problem as racial hatred expressed by Whites. Skin tone has been associated with social advantage among Blacks since the days of slavery, when light-skinned slaves were often allowed to work in the main house, but dark-skinned slaves were relegated to the fields (L. O. Graham, 1999). During the early to mid-20th century, many African American churches, social clubs, fraternities, and other organizations still used skin color to determine the suitability of candidates for membership. The so-called brown bag test restricted membership to those whose skin was lighter than the color of a brown paper bag (L.O. Graham, 1999). Contemporary studies have found that lighter-skinned Blacks have higher educational attainment, more prestigious occupations, and higher annual incomes than darker-skinned Blacks, regardless of their parents' socioeconomic status, sex, region of residence, age, or marital status (Hill, 2000; Keith & Herring, 1991). As a result, darker-skinned Blacks sometimes resent light-skinned Blacks, accusing them of "selling out" in an attempt to conform to white standards of beauty and behavior (F. J. Davis, 1991).

Colorism is not limited to African Americans. For instance, among Latino/as, the degree of "Indianness," or the darkness of one's skin, has long determined a person's status. After controlling for all other relevant factors, researchers have found that dark-skinned Mexican Americans who have a Native American physical appearance have fewer years of education than light-skinned Mexican Americans who appear more European (Murguia & Telles, 1996); they are more likely to live in segregated, low income neighborhoods (Relethford, Stern, Caskill, & Hazuda, 1983); and they consistently earn lower wages (Telles & Murguia, 1990).

Prejudice that exists within certain ethnoracial groups can sometimes arise from factors besides skin tone. Many black immigrants from the West Indies, for example, try to distance themselves as much as possible from U.S. Blacks, whom they feel are socially, culturally, and financially inferior. They refuse to call themselves "black" when they come to this country. Indeed, West Indian immigrants generally make substantially more money than U.S. Blacks, live in better neighborhoods, and have more stable families (Gladwell, 1996).

The Privilege of Having No Color

People who are members of a racial majority often have trouble appreciating the humiliating effects of everyday encounters with discrimination. They don't have to experience the petty indignities of racism, such as repeatedly being watched with suspicion in stores and on streets. Consequently, many Whites in the United States pay little attention to their own race, think people of color are obsessed with race and ethnicity, and find it difficult to understand the emotional and intellectual energy people of color devote to the subject (Haney López, 1996).

In a society in which they are the statistical and cultural majority, U.S. Whites rarely define their identity in terms of race. Whiteness is so obvious and normative that white people's racial identity is, for all intents and purposes, invisible. Whites enjoy the luxury of **racial transparency,** or "having no color" (Haney López, 1996). People in the United States are far more likely to hear "black" or "Asian" or "Latino" used as an adjective (for example, the black lawyer, the Latino teacher) than "white" (the white lawyer, the white teacher). Many Whites become conscious of their racial identity only when they find themselves in the company of large numbers of people of a different race. In short, Whites for the most part enjoy the privilege of not having to think about race, even though they have one:

> Each thing with which "they" have to contend as they navigate the waters of American life is one less thing Whites have to sweat: and that makes everything easier, from finding jobs, to getting loans, to attending college. . . . The virtual invisibility that whiteness affords those of us who have it is like psychological money in the bank, the proceeds of which we cash in every day while others are in a perpetual state of overdraft. (Wise, 2002, pp. 107–108)

Such a luxury provides advantages to Whites whether or not they approve of the way dominance has been conferred on them. One white author (McIntosh, 2001) catalogued all the everyday privileges she enjoyed (and often didn't notice) simply because she was white. They included such advantages as the ability to shop alone in a department store without being followed by suspicious salespeople, to buy greeting cards or children's picture books featuring people of her race, and to find bandages that match her skin color. In other words, Whites need not be bigots nor feel racially superior or more deserving than others to enjoy the privileges that their skin color brings.

Class, Race, and Discrimination

Some sociologists have argued that discriminatory treatment, as well as the unequal social and political status of some racial groups, is more a function of social class than of race. If this belief were accurate, the lives of middle- and upper-class people of color should be relatively free of discrimination. Yet they are not. For many highly successful minority professionals, lack of respect, faint praise, low expectations, shattered hopes, and even outright harassment and exclusion are common features of their lives. An African American woman who happens to be a Georgetown University law professor recounts an interaction with a colleague, a middle-aged white man, who explained to her that she should not be offended at being called a "jungle bunny" because "you are cute and so are bunnies" (quoted in Cose, 1993, p. 23). The result of such treatment is often utter frustration and despair:

> I have done everything I was supposed to do. I have stayed out of trouble with the law, gone to the right schools, and worked myself nearly to death. *What more do they want?* Why in God's name won't they accept me as a full human being? Why am I pigeonholed in a "black job"? Why am I constantly treated as if I were a drug addict, a thief, or a thug? Why am I still not allowed to aspire to the same things every white person in America takes as a birthright? Why, when I most want to be seen, am I suddenly invisible? (Cose, 1993, p. 1)

Sociologist Joe R. Feagin (1991) conducted in-depth interviews with 37 middle-class U.S. Blacks to determine the extent of discrimination directed against them in public situations. These 37 people, who were all college educated and held professional or managerial jobs, reported a variety of discriminatory incidents in such public places as hotels, jewelry stores, and restaurants. The incidents consisted of avoidance, poor service, closer scrutiny, verbal epithets, "hate stares," and police threats and harassment. Indeed, wealthy black residents of affluent neighborhoods all over the country complain that the police view them with suspicion simply because their skin color doesn't match the neighborhood. A 28-year-old New York lawyer said that when he walks into a store, the salespeople don't see his Ivy League university degrees, his status as an associate in his law firm—they see him only as a black man (L. Williams, 1991). Events like these are disturbing not only because of the racist attitudes that lay behind them but also because the people who experience them had come to believe that their upward social mobility protected them from such treatment. Feagin concludes that the stigma of color is still very important in the lives of African Americans, including affluent ones.

What some Whites may see as "minority paranoia" is a response to humiliation that has accumulated over the years and has become part of everyday life. One middle-class black woman interviewed by Feagin pointed out that whenever she leaves her home she must put on her "shield" and be prepared for the insults and discrimination she expects to receive in public places. The days of "No Negroes" and "No Indians" signs on public facilities may be gone, but less blatant contemporary expressions of personal racism serve as a constant reminder that in the 21st century, members of ethnoracial minorities—no matter what their class standing—are still stereotyped, prejudged, and discriminated against every day.

Quiet Racism

The nature of public attitudes in the United States toward racial and ethnic groups has changed over the past few decades, prompting many sociologists to rethink their ideas of what constitutes personal racism. One nationwide poll found that the proportion of U.S. residents who feel that race relations are improving and that progress has been made in reducing racial discrimination is the highest it's been since the early 1990s (Sack & Elder, 2000). Likewise, attitudes about integration in schools, housing, and jobs have improved markedly (Citrin, 1996; Schuman, Steeh, Bobo, & Krysan, 1997). However, Whites are three times more likely than Blacks to feel that too much is made out of problems facing Blacks today, and Blacks are twice as likely as Whites to feel that Whites still have a better chance of getting ahead (Sack & Elder, 2000). Although most U.S. Whites feel that schools should be integrated and that people of all races should have equal opportunities to enter any occupation, overwhelming majorities in national surveys oppose special government economic assistance to minorities and government efforts to desegregate schools, such as court-ordered busing. National polls show that 9 out of 10 Whites oppose preferential hiring and promotion of Blacks (Citrin, 1996) to offset ways in which Blacks have been disadvantaged.

These paradoxes have led some to argue that a subtle form of racism has emerged (Ansell, 2000; Sniderman & Tetlock, 1986). **Quiet racism** is linked to the traditional forms of personal racism by negative feelings toward certain groups. However, the feelings common to quiet racism are not hate or hostility but discomfort, uneasiness, and sometimes fear, which tend to motivate quiet avoidance rather than outright negative acts. Quiet racists are people who maintain that discrimination against a person because of his or her race or ethnicity is wrong but who nonetheless cannot entirely escape the cultural forces that give rise to racist beliefs in the first place.

The quiet racist might disagree strongly with a statement like "Mexicans have jobs that white people should have" but at the same time agree with a statement like "Mexicans living here should not push themselves where they are not wanted" (adapted from Meertens & Pettigrew, 1997). She or he might support ethnoracial equality in principle but justify opposition to government programs for ethnoracial minorities on the seemingly nonprejudiced grounds that one's rewards should be based exclusively on personal achievements and not race. What complicates the situation is that this type of racism is often expressed by people who consider themselves liberal, unbiased, and nonprejudiced. You can see why quiet racism can be more insidious than overt personal racism.

Community and legal pressures can have a significant impact on traditional expressions of bigotry. However, such techniques do little to change the values of people who are acutely aware of the social undesirability and the unfairness of their feelings but who hold them anyway.

The changing face of racism has serious institutional consequences as well. When racism remains quiet, people are tempted to assume that it has disappeared and thus to forget about helping groups that have traditionally been the objects of discrimination (Bonilla-Silva, 2003). Recent efforts to eliminate programs designed to help ethnoracial minorities exemplify this trend. Many Whites now believe that the only reason so many Blacks are unsuccessful is that they lack motivation and aren't committed to the "white" values of hard work, individualism, delayed gratification, and so on (Schuman & Krysan, 1999). Although these beliefs are more subtle than overt acts of bigotry, they have the same effect: On the basis of stereotypes they promote prejudice toward individuals.

Joe Feagin and Eileen O'Brien
White Men on Race

The racial views and perspectives of wealthy white men have received virtually no academic attention even though their attitudes have the potential to influence many people's lives. To overcome this deficit, sociologists Joe Feagin and Eileen O'Brien (2003) interviewed about 100 wealthy white male executives, managers, administrators, and professionals about a range of racial issues. Understanding the perceptions of these men is important because many of them have the power to shape policies, laws, and actions involving ethnoracial minorities and majorities.

Because of their socioeconomic status, these men have lived most of their lives in segregated well-to-do neighborhoods. As children and teenagers, they tended to go to schools that had few, if any, people of color. Only a handful of the interviewees reported long-term friendships with people of other races.

So their first and sometimes most significant encounters with ethnoracial minorities were often with domestic and other service workers, usually female maids or male servants:

> Although I don't remember my first experience of meeting a black person, I would assume it was . . . my grandfather's chauffeur when I was five years old. So to me, Blacks at that point were people that waited on you.

> My very first contact with a black person was with a black maid who essentially raised my sister and [me].

> Honestly, the first black person I ever met was probably a household employee at my parents' house a long time ago. (all quoted in Feagin & O'Brien, 2003, pp. 34–35)

Memories of these initial contacts are usually quite fond. Many men spoke lovingly of household servants because they were people who played an important role in raising them (some respondents even referred to their black maids and nannies as "second mothers").

However, they also were taught, early on, that the social distance between their families and "the help" had to be maintained. Furthermore, it's clear that the men didn't see these individuals as real people with real lives. Most of them were unaware that their maids and chauffeurs had spouses and children of their own and that their jobs made it difficult to sustain those relationships.

Feagin and O'Brien also found that in many ways wealthy white executives are not that different from "ordinary" white Americans when it comes to their stereotypes and prejudices. Some harbor deeply negative attitudes toward Americans of color that seem reminiscent of a bygone age:

> Well, let's look at the statistics. The Negro is about ten percent of the population and eighty percent of the crimes are committed by Negroes, so what does that tell you? . . . What does that tell us? Absolutely, of course, much more crime is committed by them. And anywhere they are, they're criminals. They're criminals here, they're criminals in Africa. (quoted in Feagin & O'Brien, 2003, p. 100)

Furthermore, they often see the advancement of Americans of color as a threat to the racial privileges they've come to take for granted and to their control over major social institutions. But since they are generally highly educated, most of them are well aware that they should not be too obviously negative in expressing their racial attitudes. Hence some couch their prejudices in sympathetic sounding language:

> There are many, many fine black families around. . . . Unfortunately, a large part of the black population has this family problem. . . . It's very, very difficult to generalize why some blacks work out fine while others don't, and the fact that some could work out exactly the same as anyone else leads me to believe that it's not because of the color; it's because of the environment they're brought up in. (quoted in Feagin & O'Brien, 2003, p. 104)

This is a classic example of quiet racism. Notice how this individual distances himself from the prejudices of the past while at the same time embracing the reality of racial inequality.

Not all the men interviewed by Feagin and O'Brien expressed prejudice. A minority of them held very positive attitudes about race relations. These individuals often voiced dismay over racial and class inequality and spoke of the need for a significant shift in the balance of economic and political power in the United States. The factor that seemed to separate these men from the others who held more traditional (and negative) attitudes toward race is the nature of the relationships they've had with Americans of color. Those who had long-term friendships or extended contact with members of other races were the ones who showed a willingness to consider dismantling the structures that perpetuate prejudice and racial inequality. Such a finding supports the idea that regular interpersonal interactions that cross ethnoracial boundaries can diminish stereotypes and prejudice.

The Cultural Ideology of Racism

If I stopped here in my discussion of racism, you might be inclined to consider it a phenomenon of individuals that could best be stopped by changing the way people think or by individual acts of kindness and respect. But the sociologically important thing about racism is that it exists not just in individuals' minds and actions but in a cultural ideology that both justifies the domination of some groups over others and provides a set of social norms that encourages differential treatment for these groups (O'Sullivan, See, & Wilson, 1988). From a conflict perspective, the cultural ideology of racism that exists in our language and in our prevailing collective beliefs helps to maintain racial and ethnic inequality.

Racism in Language

Certainly racial slurs and derogatory words reflect underlying racism. But racism in language is often less obvious. Consider the use of **panethnic labels**—general terms applied to diverse subgroups that are assumed to have something in common (Newman, 2007). Today, we use the general terms *Native American* or *American Indian* to refer to all of the 560 or so native peoples living in the U.S., despite their different languages and cultures. *Asian American* refers to a variety of peoples whose ethnic heritages and lifestyles are quite different from one another. Similarly, *Hispanic* or *Latino* refers to people whose backgrounds include such culturally diverse areas as Mexico, the Caribbean, Central America, and South America. To some, even the term *African American,* which is widely considered to be a positive racial label, glosses over the thousands of ethnic groups, class interests, and indigenous religions that exist on the continent of Africa. Reliance on panethnic labels allows users to overlook and ignore differences within a particular labeled group, thereby reinforcing stereotypes.

Racial identifiers often become equated with negative meanings. Consider, for instance, connotations for the words *black* and *white.* Among the definitions of *black* in *Webster's New Universal Unabridged Dictionary* are soiled and dirty, thoroughly evil, wicked, gloomy, marked by disaster, hostile, and disgraceful. The definition of *white,* in contrast, includes fairness of complexion, innocent, favorable, fortunate, pure, and spotless. The pervasive "goodness" of white and "badness" of black affects children at a very young age and provides white children with a false sense of superiority (Moore, 1992). Young children know the difference between a black lie, which is harmful and inexcusable, and a white lie, which is small, insignificant, and harmless.

Also important are the political implications of racially tinged terminology. Terms such as *economically disadvantaged, underclass, inner city,* and *underdeveloped* sound unprejudiced, but they are often used as stand-ins for overtly racial terms. For instance, a study of the 1995 Louisiana gubernatorial election revealed that the white candidate's stated opposition to affirmative action and his discussion of the crime problems in *inner city* neighborhoods (which everyone knew were black and Latino/a neighborhoods) subtly symbolized his racial attitudes, appealed to many white voters, and thereby contributed to his victory over a black candidate (Knuckey & Orey, 2000).

Language is just a small part of the overall problem of racist ideology in U.S. society. It seemingly pales in comparison to more visible issues such as racial violence and economic discrimination. We must remember, however, that language filters our perceptions. It affects the way people think from the time they first learn to speak. Fortunately, efforts are being made today to address the issue of language and its crucial role in maintaining racism and oppression. People are becoming more aware of the capacity of words to both glorify and degrade (Moore, 1992).

The Myth of Innate Racial Inferiority

Scientific-sounding theories of the innate inferiority of certain ethnoracial groups have long been used to explain why some groups lag behind others in such areas as educational achievement and financial success. These theories combine with the belief in competitive individualism (see Chapter 10) to justify all forms of prejudice and discrimination.

Appeals to biology and nature have been used throughout history to define the existing stratification system as proper and inevitable (Gould, 1981). What would you think of a person who harbored the following beliefs about Blacks?

> [Blacks] have less hair on the face and body. They secrete less by the kidneys, and more by the glands of the skin, which gives them a very strong and disagreeable odour. . . . They are at least as brave, and more adventuresome. But this may perhaps proceed from a want of forethought, which prevents their seeing a danger till it be present. . . . In imagination, they are dull, tasteless, and anomalous. . . . The improvement of the blacks in body and mind, in the first instance of their mixture with the whites, has been observed by every one, and proves that their inferiority is not the effect merely of their condition of life. . . . I advance it therefore . . . that the blacks . . . are inferior to the whites in the endowments both of body and mind.

A white supremacist? A raving bigot? An ignorant fanatic? How would your assessment of this person change if you found out that this passage was written by none other than Thomas Jefferson (1781/1955, pp. 138–143)? In the 18th and 19th centuries, no white person—not even one apparently committed to protecting people's right to "life, liberty and the pursuit of happiness"—doubted the correctness of natural racial rankings: Indians below Whites, and Blacks below everyone else. Other idols of Western culture—George Washington, Abraham Lincoln, Charles Darwin—held similar beliefs about the "natural inferiority" of some races, beliefs that were commonly accepted knowledge at the time but would at the very least be considered racially insensitive today.

The approval given by white scientists to conventional racial rankings arose not from objective data and careful research but from a cultural belief in the "goodness" and inevitability of racial stratification. Such beliefs were then twisted into independent, "scientific" support. Scientists, like everybody else, have attitudes and values that shape what they see. Such thinking is not the result of outright dishonesty or hypocrisy; rather, it is the combination of the way human minds work and the generally accepted knowledge of the day.

The belief in innate racial inferiority is not just a historical curiosity. Several years ago, the idea re-emerged in a book called *The Bell Curve: Intelligence and Class Structure in American Life* (Herrnstein & Murray, 1994). The authors argued that racial and ethnic differences in intelligence—as measured by IQ scores—must be due, at least in part, to heredity. The book set off a firestorm of debate that continues to this day.

From a conflict perspective, beliefs about racial inferiority provide advantages for the dominant group. These beliefs discourage subordinate groups from questioning their disadvantaged status. In addition, they provide moral justification for maintaining a society in which some groups are routinely deprived of their rights and privileges.

Whites could justify the enslavement of Blacks, and Nazis could justify the extermination of Jews and other "undesirables," by promoting the belief that those groups were biologically subhuman.

Despite energetic searches over the centuries, a link between "inferior" race-based genes and certain traits and abilities has not been found (Hacker, 1992). For one thing, comparing racial groups on, say, intelligence overlooks the range of differences within and between groups. Many African Americans are more intelligent than the average white person; many Whites are less intelligent than the average Native American. Variations such as these are difficult to explain in terms of genetic superiority of one race. Moreover, treating the over 200 million "white" people as a single (and intellectually superior) group is problematic at best and misleading at worst. It can't account for the wide variation in academic achievement among Whites of different national backgrounds. For instance, at the time *The Bell Curve* was written, 21% of white Americans of Irish descent completed college, whereas 22% of Italian Americans, 33% of Scottish Americans, and 51% of Russian Americans did so (Hacker, 1994). Finally, such comparisons also ignore a problem I described earlier in this chapter: that race itself is a meaningless biological category. How can we attribute racial differences in intelligence to genes when race itself is not traceable to a single gene?

Nevertheless, the idea that racial inferiority is innate remains appealing. If observable, physical differences among races are inherited, the argument goes, then why not differences in social behavior, intelligence, and leadership ability? Like the belief in competitive individualism we examined in the previous chapter, the belief in innate racial inferiority places the blame for suffering and economic failure on the individual rather than on the society in which that individual exists.

Micro-Macro Connection
Racial Superiority and the Dominant Black Athlete

The flip side of the belief in innate racial inferiority is the notion that some racial groups have a biologically rooted superiority in some areas of life. Take, for instance, the widely held belief that some racial groups are athletically superior to others. Today, black athletes dominate the highest levels of such sports as football, basketball, and track. In the United States, African Americans make up about 13% of the population but constitute 65% of players in the NFL and 78% of players in the NBA (Lapchick, 2003). Not surprisingly, many people see numbers like these and simply assume that Blacks must be "naturally" stronger, swifter, and more coordinated than Whites.

In the late 19th century, African Americans were allowed to play professional baseball alongside Whites; boxing, too, was racially integrated. But by the turn of the century, white athletes threatened to quit rather than share the field or the ring with black athletes. Early American heavyweight boxing champions such as John L. Sullivan and Jack Dempsey refused to fight black opponents. In 1888, baseball team owners tacitly agreed not to sign any more African American players. Their formal exclusion lasted until 1947, when Jackie Robinson became the first African American in the 20th century to play baseball in the major leagues (Sage, 2001).

The rationale behind excluding African Americans was not based on their inability to compete. On the contrary, it was based on the common belief that Blacks are athletically superior to Whites. Many 18th- and 19th-century scholars believed that black slaves were bred by their owners to be physically strong. In recent decades such ideas have taken on a scientific cast (Entine, 2000). For instance, some biologists argue that black athletes' muscles are better adapted to hot climates and therefore are better at providing energy quickly. Others have cited better power-to-weight ratios and longer Achilles tendons.

Black athletic superiority has become an almost taken-for-granted truth. Many black athletes, such as star baseball player Barry Bonds, have publicly expressed their belief that black success in sports is caused by Blacks' physical superiority to Whites. Hall of Fame basketball star Larry Bird (who is white) recently voiced his support for the contention that white players don't stack up to black players: "[Basketball] is a black man's game and it will be forever. I mean, the greatest athletes in the world are African-American" (Bird, 2004, p. 1).

The problem with the belief in black athletic superiority is that physical strength (a seemingly positive characteristic) is all too often associated with alleged social, moral, or intellectual deficiency. A nationally known sportscaster once commonly referred to powerful black athletes as "thoroughbreds," a term that simultaneously acknowledged their physical prowess and likened them to horses. Such comments strengthen the notion that black athletes are athletically superior but deficient in most other ways.

Extending this logic, physically outclassed white athletes are thought to rely on self-discipline, mental acuity, "a tireless work ethic," "fiery determination," and an unwavering attention to discipline and "fundamentals" in order to compete. In this way, successful white athletes become especially praiseworthy because they're able to overcome their "natural" limitations. Consider this self-assessment from a white collegiate basketball player:

> I know I'm not going to beat them with my quickness so I need to see exactly how they're playing me. . . . You have to study the game and watch every little thing to look for some kind of advantage. (quoted in Hutchens, 2002, p. D8)

Notice how his self-deprecating comment about his own lack of "quickness" becomes a virtue as it opens the way to his superior intellect and work ethic. Such ideas are reminiscent of 19th-century beliefs about the frailty of white women being a sign of their moral superiority and the hardiness of women of color being a sign of their moral inferiority.

Because of these pervasive stereotypes, the white public often tempers its admiration of black athletic superiority with contempt for what some consider an arrogant, undisciplined style. A few years ago, the National Football League decided to penalize players who wore uniforms that didn't conform to tight league regulations, who "trash talked" (taunted opponents), and who choreographed post-touchdown celebrations. These players were almost exclusively black.

Still the undeniable fact is that Blacks do dominate certain professional sports in the United States. One sociological explanation is that such domination results not from innate physical superiority alone but from a complex set of social conditions that channels a disproportionate number of physically talented Blacks into athletic careers (Edwards, 1971). Sport has long been perceived as one of the few avenues of social mobility open to members of certain ethnoracial minorities: baseball for Latinos; football and basketball for African Americans. A national survey found that by a margin of 3 to 1 over Whites, Blacks said that one of the most important reasons to play sports is "If I am successful at sports, I can make a lot of money" (cited in Price, 1997). Where children from other racial groups are being taught that a good education will pay off, many black children are being taught that a good education may not be enough to overcome the prejudice and discrimination that exist in society. Hence they are more likely to be encouraged to hone their physical skills and to spend more time perfecting this resource. A high school basketball coach put it this way: "Suburban [white] kids tend to play for the fun of it. Inner-city [black] kids look at basketball as a matter of life or death" (quoted in Price, 1997, p. 35).

Sport has always served as a source of tremendous pride in black and Latino/a communities. But highlighting the rags-to-riches stories of a tiny number of successful athletes is a double-edged sword. These high-profile athletes disguise the reality of how little social mobility actually results from sports participation. For African Americans, the odds of becoming a professional athlete (let alone an elite star) are about 5,000 to 1. As one sociologist once remarked, "you have a better chance of getting hit with a meteorite in the next 10 years than getting work as a professional athlete" (quoted in Sage, 2001, p. 283).

An overemphasis on athletic accomplishments can also discourage academic and occupational achievement in favor of physical self-expression, thereby harming ethnoracial minority communities in the long run. The vast majority of African Americans who participate in Division I football, basketball, and track and field never graduate from college. It might be more useful in the long run to focus on the fact that there are 12 times more black lawyers and 15 times more black physicians than there are black professional athletes (Sage, 2001).

Whether or not the emphasis on sports is a good thing and whether or not black athletes do have some anatomical advantage, we must always remember that so-called black athletic superiority is as much a social product as a biological one. Innate talent is never sufficient in itself to explain athletic excellence (D. F. Chambliss, 1989). If we rely simply on innate superiority to explain black success in sports, we overlook the broader social structural context in which everyday life is embedded.

Institutional Racism: Injustice Built Into the System

Anyone can be personally or quietly racist, and any ethnoracial group can develop a set of beliefs or a vocabulary that denigrates outsiders. But one form of racism, less obvious and more dangerous perhaps, can work only to the advantage of those who wield power in society: institutional racism. **Institutional racism** consists of established laws, customs, and practices that systematically reflect and produce racial inequalities in society, whether or not the individuals maintaining these practices have racist intentions (J. M. Jones, 1986). Thus a society can be racist even if only a small proportion of its members harbor racist beliefs. Because African Americans, Latino/as, Asian Americans, Native Americans, and other groups have historically been excluded from key positions of authority in social institutions, they often find themselves victimized by the routine workings of such structures.

Sometimes institutional discrimination is obvious and codified into the law. Until the early 1990s, for example, South Africa operated under an official system of *apartheid:* nonwhite groups were legally segregated and subjected to sanctioned forms of political and economic discrimination. In the United States, the forceful relocation of Native Americans in the 19th century, repressive Jim Crow laws in the 20th-century South, and the internment of Japanese Americans during World War II are all examples of legislated policies that purposely worked to the disadvantage of already disadvantaged groups.

Understanding less obvious forms of institutional racism is a great test of the sociological imagination. Because it is a built-in feature of social arrangements, institutional racism is often much more difficult to detect than acts of personal racism. Consider one well-established practice for granting home mortgage or home improvement loans. Many banks use zip codes to mark off the neighborhoods they consider high risk—that is, where property values are low and liable to drop even further. These practices make it virtually impossible for individuals in such areas to borrow money to buy or improve a home. Unfortunately, these are precisely the areas where minorities, with lower average incomes, are most likely to find an affordable home to purchase. Thus although individual bank officers are not denying loans to people because of their race—they are merely following their employers' policy—the resulting discrimination is the same.

Sometimes institutional racism is camouflaged behind claims that seem quite reasonable on their face. For instance, taxi companies protect the safety of their drivers by refusing service to what they consider dangerous neighborhoods. Similarly, home delivery businesses, such as pizza parlors, often refuse to deliver to some neighborhoods. A few years ago, Domino's Pizza was criticized in the media when it was revealed that the company was distributing software to its outlets to let them mark addresses on computers as green (deliver), yellow (curbside only), or red (no delivery). Businesses defend such policies as a rational response to the threat of sending easy-to-spot delivery personnel with cash into unsafe areas ("Pizza Must Go," 1996). Although such practices may be considered "good" business policy and are not intentionally racist, their consequences are racist because high-risk neighborhoods tend to be inhabited predominantly by people of color. Institutional racism is difficult to address in these cases because no individual "bad guy," no identifiable bigot, is the source of the discrimination.

Racism in one institution is often accompanied by racism in another. For instance, the traditional underrepresentation of certain ethnoracial groups in the best universities and the best graduate and professional programs affects their economic opportunities, which in turn affects their access to quality health care and housing (Wilson, 1987).

Residential segregation based on class and race is so prevalent in U.S. society that one sociologist refers to the situation as "American apartheid" (Massey, 1990). For instance, over 83% of Detroit-area Blacks live in the central city (Russell Sage Foundation, 2000), 30 years after laws were passed to prevent housing discrimination. White attitudes toward neighborhood integration have improved over the years, as

Exhibit 11.3 indicates. Yet overall levels of segregation—especially of Blacks and Whites—have remained quite high (R. Farley & Frey, 1994). Latino/as are slightly less residentially segregated than Blacks, and Asians are substantially less segregated than Blacks—but they all are still likely to live in racial or ethnic enclaves (Massey & Fischer, 1999). Residential segregation is not just about people living near others of the same race. Research indicates that it is associated with a variety of negative effects, such as a reduced likelihood of people running successful businesses (Fischer & Massey, 2000) and an increased likelihood of contracting certain deadly diseases (Collins & Williams, 1999).

The National Fair Housing Alliance (2004) estimates that 3.7 million incidents of housing discrimination based on race or ethnicity alone occurred in 2003. (This figure doesn't include unfair housing practices based on religion, gender, family status, or disability.) On occasion, such housing discrimination is personal, the result of individuals' blatant "we don't want you people here" attitudes. More commonly, though, it is institutional, politely and subtly driven by company policies (Pearce, 1979). Discriminatory policies include making fewer houses or rental units available to minorities, limiting their access to financial assistance, and steering them toward particular neighborhoods. One study found that African Americans were twice as likely as Whites, and Latino/as one-and-a-half times as likely as Whites, to be denied a conventional 30-year home loan (cited in Kilborn, 1999). When they do receive home loans, African Americans

Exhibit 11.3 Improving Attitudes Toward Ethnoracial Integration

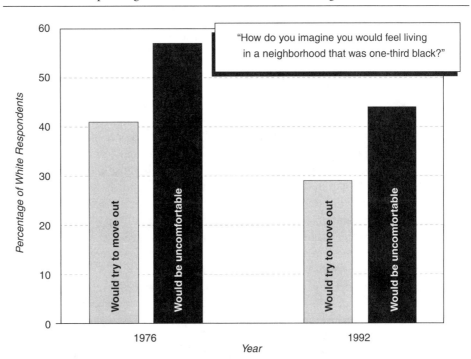

Source: Farley & Frey, 1994.

and Latino/as pay higher interest rates than Whites; the discrepancy is particularly noticeable for people of color with above-average incomes (cited in Leonhardt, 2002). Concern over such discrepancies led the National Association of Realtors and the U.S. Department of Housing and Urban Development to enact a cultural awareness program for real estate agents, to make them more aware of "racial steering" and help to increase minority opportunities in housing (Tahan, 1997).

Racial Inequality in the Economic System

Institutional racism is readily apparent throughout the U.S. economy. Consider participation in the labor force. Nineteen percent of American workers who earn minimum wage are African American and 17% are Latino/a (U.S. Department of Labor, 2004b). African Americans make up 10.7% of the entire civilian U.S. workforce but only 3.6% of lawyers, 5.0% of physicians, and 4.4% of architects and engineers. Similarly, Latino/as make up 12.6% of the labor force, but they are underrepresented in the fields of law (4.0%), medicine (4.7%), and engineering (5.2%) (U.S. Bureau of the Census, 2004a). At the same time, workers of color tend to be concentrated in lower-paying jobs (see Exhibit 11.4).

Because ethnoracial minorities are occupationally concentrated in low-paying jobs and geographically concentrated in poor inner-city neighborhoods, they are particularly vulnerable to economically motivated business changes, such as plant shutdowns, the automation of lower-level production jobs, and corporate relocations. For example, when a factory in a predominantly black or Latino/a section of a city moves to an all-white suburb, minority employees tend to face greater problems than white employees in securing housing in the new location or experience higher transportation costs in commuting to it (Squires, 1980). Perhaps it's no coincidence that, with the exception of Asian Americans, the rate of unemployment for people of color is twice as high as that of Whites (U.S. Bureau of the Census, 2004a).

People of color also remain marginal participants in the economy as owners of their own small businesses. Loan companies usually demand a credit history, some form of collateral, and evidence of potential success before they will lend money to prospective businesses. These are standard practices—and not in and of themselves racist—but they perpetuate racial inequalities because members of groups that have been exploited in the past tend to be poorer and thus have poor credit ratings and no collateral. Admittedly, poor people are greater credit risks than those with economic resources, and businesses in poorer communities must pay more for insurance because of the greater likelihood of theft or property damage. But of course, the higher costs of doing business in a poor community usually make small business loans to minority members even more necessary.

Financial concerns, not some deep-seated racial hatred, can also work to the disadvantage of retail customers who happen to be members of particular ethnoracial groups. For instance, in 2004, the Cracker Barrel restaurant chain agreed to overhaul its training and management practices after the U.S. Department of Justice accused it of widespread discrimination against African American diners in 50 locations. As a matter of policy, black customers were routinely given tables apart from Whites, seated after white customers who had arrived later, and given inferior service (Lichtblau,

Exhibit 11.4   Occupational Concentration by Race, Ethnicity, and Sex

	Men	*Women*
White	Marketing, advertising, and public relations managers; engineers, architects, and surveyors; dentists; firefighters; construction supervisors; tool and die makers	Physical therapists; dental hygienists; secretaries; bookkeepers; accounting and auditing clerks
Black	Vehicle washers and equipment cleaners; bus drivers; concrete workers; guards; sheriffs; bailiffs; and other law enforcement personnel	Social workers; postal clerks; dietitians; child-care workers and teacher's aides; private household cooks and cleaners; nursing aides and orderlies
Latina/o	Janitors and cleaners; construction trades; machine operators; cooks; drivers; laborers and helpers; roofers; groundskeepers, gardeners, farm and agricultural workers	Private household cleaners and servants; child-care workers; janitors and cleaners; health service occupations; sewing machine operators
Asian	Physicians; engineers; professors; technicians; cooks; launderers; longshore equipment operators	Marine-life workers; electrical assemblers; dressmakers; launderers
Native American	Marine-life workers; hunters; forestry (except logging); fishers	Welfare aides; child-care workers and teacher's aides; forestry (except logging)

Source: National Committee on Pay Equity, 1995.

2004). In this case and others like it, senior executives were convinced that customers of color were costing their companies money (H. Kohn, 1994). Hence the policies were not a matter of personal racism but a function of the competitive, profit-driven nature of the marketplace.

Interestingly, many *anti*racist actions may also be motivated by economic forces and not necessarily by personal desires to overcome racism. Network television in the 1990s and early 2000s had more series than ever featuring black characters. On the surface, the entertainment industry appears to be finally eradicating a long tradition of racial inequality. However, a Nielsen study shows that people in black households watch television about eight hours more per week than people in all other households (Nielson Media Research, 2002). The networks' decision to represent more Blacks on television appears to be financially motivated. The same could be said for other ethnoracial groups. For instance, Sí TV, an English-language cable network that targets young Latino/as, reaches over 10 million households (Ordoñez, 2005). In the San Francisco Bay area, which has a large concentration of Asian Americans and Asian immigrants, KTSF-TV broadcasts in 14 different Asian languages (Roy, 2003).

As long as companies are motivated to maximize their own interests (and profits), they are likely to adapt to market tastes. To the extent that those tastes reflect underlying prejudice, discrimination will continue. This structural-functionalist explanation of institutional racism is important because it enables us to see why discrimination is so difficult to end. The problem is not individual bigotry; it is the mistreatment that has been built into the system so effectively that it is sometimes difficult to see, let alone remove.

Racial Inequality in the Health Care System

As I pointed out at the beginning of this chapter, the economic and educational advances of minority groups over the past decade or so have been tempered by continuing disadvantages in health and health care. For example, black women are twice as likely as white women to suffer from heart disease, yet they are less likely to be prescribed standard preventive drugs (Jha et al., 2003). And members of ethnoracial minorities are routinely underrepresented as subjects in research on medical and psychiatric drug treatments (Vedantam, 2005).

Ethnoracial imbalances in health care are glaring when it comes to the most serious diseases. African Americans make up about 12% of the female population in this country, but account for 64% of female HIV infections (cited in Cowley & Murr, 2004). Almost twice as many African Americans with HIV/AIDS die compared to Whites, and the gap has increased over the last decade (Villarosa, 2004); HIV/AIDS is now the leading cause of death among African Americans between the ages of 25 and 44—ahead of heart disease, cancer, accidents, and homicides (Andriote, 2005).

As you can see in Exhibit 11.5, life expectancy and chronic sickness clearly vary along racial/ethnic lines. A white woman at the age of 20 can expect to live 60 or so more years and will experience chronic health problems for about 10 of those years. The average 20-year-old Native American woman can expect to live in poor health for 17 of her remaining 63 years. To make matters worse, members of ethnoracial minorities are also less likely than Whites to have access to health insurance. Almost 33% of Latino/as (especially those from Mexico and Central America) and 19.4% of African Americans lack any kind of health insurance, compared to 11.3% of non-Hispanic Whites (DeNavas-Walt et al., 2005).

Exhibit 11.5   Total Life Expectancy by Race/Ethnicity at Age 20

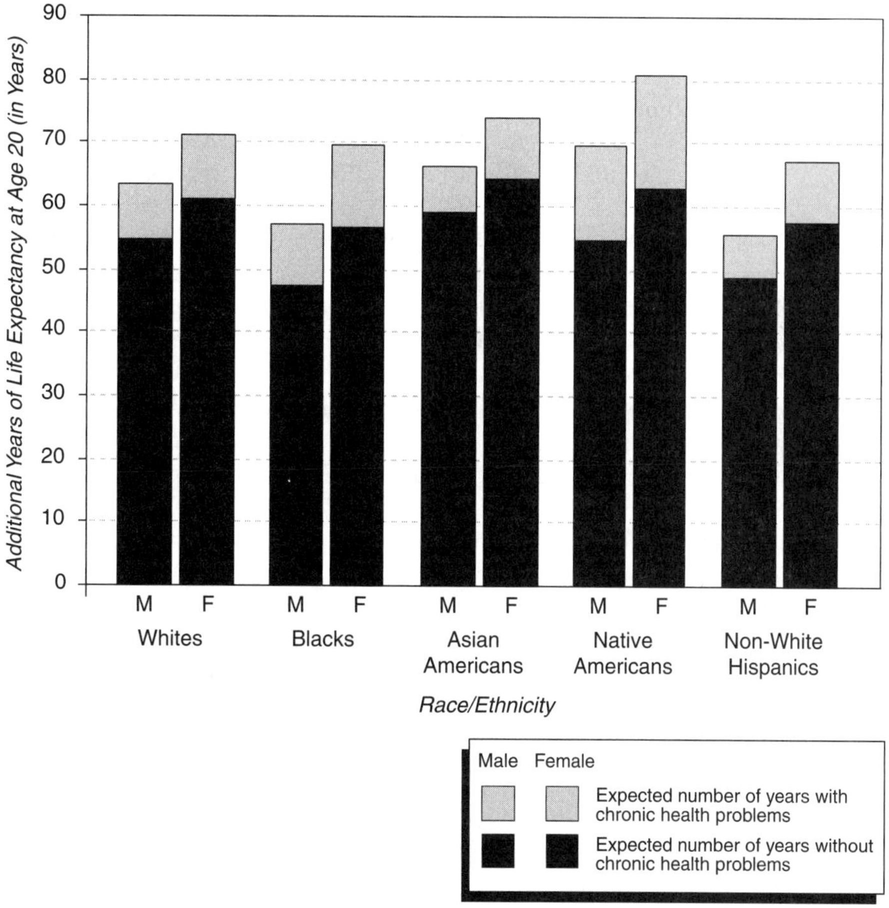

Source: Hayward & Heron, 1999.

We can't simply blame ruthless and bigoted doctors, nurses, medical researchers, or insurance agents for these differences. Instead, the financial considerations that drive the health care system create a context ripe for institutional racism. Consider racial differences in organ transplants. According to the Organ Procurement and Transplant Network (2004), in 2003 the national kidney transplant waiting list consisted of 39% Whites and 35% African Americans. (This figure in and of itself is telling: African Americans make up only about 12% of the population yet account for over one third of people in need of kidney transplants.) However, that same year, Whites received 57% of all kidney transplants while African Americans received only 23%. Such a discrepancy is likely linked to a policy transplant centers in some hospitals use called the "green screen." A liver transplant, for example, can cost anywhere from

$100,000 to $400,000, so most hospitals screen potential recipients for some kind of evidence up front that their insurance will cover the procedure. Because ethnoracial minorities are less likely than Whites to have medical insurance, they are less likely to receive a referral for transplant surgery (Stolberg, 1998a). Financial concerns and not outright racial prejudice lie at the heart of these policies.

Sometimes the institutional racism underlying threats to people's health is less obvious. For instance, people in neighborhoods where hazardous waste treatment plants or other sources of industrial pollution exist are disproportionately exposed to the unhealthful effects of air pollution, water pollution, and pesticides. The decisions on where to place such facilities are usually based not on the ethnoracial makeup of an area but on such factors as the cost of land, population density, and geological conditions. However, because the less desirable residential areas (and hence more desirable industrial areas) are disproportionately inhabited by poor people of color, these decisions have the effect of discriminating against them. For instance, Native American reservations, which have less stringent environmental regulations than other areas, have been targeted by the U.S. military for stockpiles of nuclear, chemical, and biological weapons and by private companies for solid waste landfills, hazardous waste incinerators, and nuclear waste storage facilities (Hooks & Smith, 2004). When it comes to the federal government cleaning up polluted areas, predominantly white communities see faster action, better results, and stiffer penalties for polluters than do communities where ethnoracial minorities predominate (Bullard, 2001).

Poor African American communities often have the worst conditions. Seven oil refineries and several hundred heavy industrial plants are situated along a stretch of the Mississippi River between Baton Rouge and New Orleans known as "cancer alley" (Koeppel, 1999). A study of toxic emissions in this area by the Environmental Protection Agency showed that 9 of the 10 major sources of industrial pollution are in predominantly black neighborhoods (Cushman, 1993). Overall, the greater the proportion of black residents in a community, the more likely it is that there will be industrial sources of air pollution within a two-mile radius of people's homes (Perlin, Sexton, & Wong, 1999).

Racist ideologies that inform health care and medical research understandably lead to mistrust of the system among some groups. Indeed, African Americans were once routinely used as subjects, frequently without their consent, for new medical treatments, experimental procedures, and medical demonstrations. The most infamous example was the Tuskegee syphilis study. In 1932, the U.S. Public Health Service initiated a study in Tuskegee, Alabama, to determine the natural course of untreated syphilis in black men. In exchange for their participation, the 400 men—all poor and most illiterate—received free meals, free medical exams, and burial insurance. The men were never told they had syphilis. Instead, they were told that they had "bad blood" and would receive treatment. In reality, they received no treatment. When penicillin became available in the early 1950s—the most effective treatment for syphilis—the men were not treated. In fact, the Public Health Service actively sought to prevent treatment. Even as the men began to die or to go blind or insane, penicillin was withheld. As soon as the experiment was publicized in 1972, it was stopped. Since then, the federal government has paid out more than $9 million in damages to victims and their families and heirs.

The Tuskegee study was driven not by the outright prejudice of individual medical researchers but by scientific rationale and dominant, taken-for-granted medical "facts" of the time. Prevailing medical opinion in the 1930s was that Blacks were born with strong sexual appetites and a lack of morality that made them particularly susceptible to sexually transmitted disease. This belief, coupled with the equally dominant belief that Blacks wouldn't seek treatment even if it were available, led the researchers to conclude that this segment of the population would provide the best subjects for their study.

The legacy of the Tuskegee study has been a pervasive distrust of the health care system among many people of color today that put them at even greater disadvantage. Today, many African Americans—as well as Latino/as and Native Americans—avoid participating in medical research because of their fear of being used as guinea pigs (cited in Alvidrez & Areán, 2002). Furthermore, members of ethnoracial minorities are often skeptical that their participation in clinical studies would be a benefit either to them personally or to their communities. Overall mistrust of the medical field has been cited as one of the reasons why African Americans have been slow to come for HIV testing and medical care (Dervarics, 2004a), are less likely than Whites to donate organs (Srikameswaran, 2002), and are less likely than Whites to agree to surgery for early stages of lung cancer (Bach, Cramer, Warren, & Begg, 1999).

Racial Inequality in the Educational System

In 1954, the U.S. Supreme Court ruled, in *Brown* v. *Board of Education of Topeka,* that racially segregated schools were unconstitutional because they were inherently unequal. School districts around the country were placed under court order to desegregate. But within the past 10 years, courts have lifted desegregation orders in at least three dozen school districts around the country. Not surprisingly, African American and Latino/a students are more isolated from white students today than they were 30 years ago (Frankenberg, Lee, & Orfield, 2003). A study by researchers at the Harvard Graduate School of Education found that 66% of all African American public school students and 70% of Latino/a students still attend predominantly minority schools, defined as those schools with more than 50% of their enrollment made up of either African American or Latino/a students. And about a third of black students attend schools in which at least 90% of the students are not white (Orfield & Yun, 1999). At the same time, most white students go to schools that are nearly all white, even in cities that have large minority populations. These figures represent the highest rates of school segregation reported in the last 25 years.

Schools where the majority of students are not white are likely to be schools where poverty is concentrated. This is not the case with majority-white schools, which almost always enroll high proportions of middle-class students (Orfield & Yun, 1999).

The racial mix of the classroom thus has important implications for the quality of the education that students receive. Concentrated poverty tends to be linked to lower educational achievement. Schools in poor communities lack the financial and therefore educational resources that schools in more affluent communities have (see Chapter 10). Poor schools offer fewer advanced courses than wealthier schools, hire fewer teachers with credentials in the subjects they're teaching, and have more unstable enrollments, higher dropout rates, and more students with untreated health problems. Furthermore, poor school districts face increasing financial pressures because of recent reductions in federal assistance programs. Regardless of the quality of the school at the elementary and secondary levels, the rising cost of higher education reduces the number of students of color who are able to attend college. Consequently, Blacks and Latino/as continue to have lower levels of educational attainment than Whites and Asian Americans (see Exhibit 11.6).

Lack of money isn't the only problem, though. Common institutional practices within the educational system may perpetuate inequality. Consider the widespread use of standardized tests, which are often used as the basis for "tracking" students—that is, as Chapter 5 explains, assigning them to different educational programs based on their intellectual abilities. Standardized tests supposedly measure innate intelligence. Many

Exhibit 11.6   Race, Ethnicity, and Educational Achievement

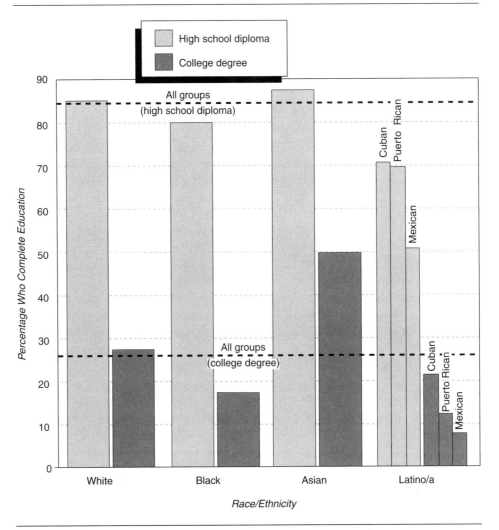

Source: U.S. Bureau of the Census, 2004a.

educational experts agree, however, that these tests are culture bound, tapping an individual's familiarity with a specific range of white, middle-class experiences rather than indicating innate intelligence (Hout & Lucas, 2001). Hence members of ethnoracial minorities consistently score lower on these tests than Whites (Jencks & Phillips, 1998).

Despite the potential for bias, more and more states across the country are requiring high school students to pass a standardized test to graduate. At the same time, though, many universities and other educational organizations have begun seeking alternative ways to determine eligibility for admission. For instance, some universities now use a "strivers" approach, whereby college applicants whose SAT scores fall in the borderline range for many selective colleges but who manage to exceed the historical average for students from similar backgrounds by at least 200 points would be deemed "strivers" and given special consideration (K. J. Cooper, 1999). The Texas legislature went a step further, ordering the University of Texas system to accept all students who graduate in the top 10% of their class, regardless of their SAT scores. In 1999 a U.S. district court judge ruled that the NCAA could no longer use SAT scores to determine athletic eligibility. The court concluded that the test is culturally biased and therefore discriminates against underprivileged students. And in 2001 the president of the University of California proposed that the massive state university system he oversees end its use of all standardized aptitude tests as a requirement of admission (Schemo, 2001).

These changes indicate a significant effort to undermine institutional racism in the educational system, which is, according to some sociologists, the largest barrier to racial equality that exists in this country today (Jencks & Phillips, 1998).

Racial Inequality in the Legal System

As we saw in Chapter 8, race and ethnicity determine people's experiences in the criminal justice system. For instance, law enforcement agencies around the country—such as police departments, state patrols, the Drug Enforcement Administration, the U.S. Customs Service, the Justice Department, the Department of Homeland Security—have come under attack in recent years for their long-standing policies of **racial profiling**: the use of ethnoracial stereotypes in making investigative stops and arrests.

With such biases distorting arrest rates, ethnoracial imbalances are sure to exist in incarceration rates as well. Latinos and African Americans make up about 53% of the male population in state and federal prisons and local jails even though they comprise only about 27% of the general male population (U.S. Bureau of the Census, 2004a). As you recall from Chapter 8, the Bureau of Justice Statistics estimates that 12% of black males, close to 4% of Latino males, but only 1.6% of white males in their 20s are currently in prison or jail (Harrison & Karberg, 2004). Race and ethnicity also affect the amount of time a convict spends locked up. With convictions for similar crimes, the average federal prison sentence for Whites is 33% shorter than it is for Blacks (United States Sentencing Commission, 2004).

Similar discrepancies exist among youthful offenders. A 2000 U.S. Department of Justice report found that at every step of the juvenile justice system black and Latino/a youths are treated more severely than Whites charged with similar crimes. They are more likely to be arrested, held in jail, sent to juvenile or adult court for trial, convicted, and given longer prison sentences. For those charged with violent crimes, Blacks were nine times as likely as Whites to be sent to prison. The average length of incarceration for similar offenses was 254 days for Blacks, 305 days for Latinos, and 193 days for Whites. For those youths charged with drug offenses, Blacks were 48 times more likely than Whites to be sentenced to prison (cited in Butterfield, 2000).

Certainly one reason for this imbalance is the personal biases of some individual police officers, attorneys, and judges. For instance, in 2005, the U.S. Supreme Court overturned the murder conviction of an African American death row inmate because jury selection in the case had been tainted by personal racism. The prosecuting attorney used peremptory challenges to exclude 10 of 11 potential black jurors. As one justice put it, the evidence was "too powerful to conclude anything but discrimination" (quoted in L. Greenhouse, 2005b, p. A1).

But in the face of such consistent imbalances, we must also examine the possibility that racial discrimination in the law exists at the institutional level. Consider, for instance, discrepancies in prison sentences for the possession and use of cocaine. Although the two types of cocaine—powdered and crack—cause similar physical reactions, the sentences for those convicted of selling them are vastly different. The average length of a sentence for selling less than 25 grams of crack cocaine is 65 months; for powdered cocaine it is 14 months. According to federal law, it would take 500 grams of powdered cocaine (or 5,000 doses) to draw the same mandatory minimum sentence of five years in prison that a person convicted of possessing 5 grams (or 10 doses) of crack cocaine would get (Coyle, 2003).

Many law enforcement officials argue that the different levels of punishment are justified because crack cocaine is more closely associated with violence than powdered cocaine, it is more dangerous to the user, and it is more likely to cause birth defects in babies whose mothers use it while pregnant. However, a study of the physiological and psychoactive effects of different forms of cocaine found they are so similar as to make the existing discrepancy in punishment "excessive." In addition, other research has found that the effects of maternal crack use on fetuses are no different from those of tobacco or alcohol use (cited in Coyle, 2003).

Some sociologists argue that the problems associated with crack usage have as much to do with poverty, unemployment, and homelessness as with the drug itself (Duster, 1997). And others point to the skewed racial distribution of the users of crack versus the users of powdered cocaine. In 2000, 93% of those convicted of crack possession were black and Latino/a; only 6% were white. By contrast, 30.3% of those convicted of powdered cocaine possession were black, 18% were white, and 51% were Latino/a (though most of these individuals are white) (Coyle, 2003).

In this federal drug policy, we see a clear example of institutional racism. Regardless of intent, the consequences of this law are discriminatory. Blacks are serving longer prison sentences for drug offenses not because of bigoted judges and juries but because they are more likely to use a drug that is punished more severely than others.

Remedies for Institutional Racism: Affirmative Action

If tomorrow all people in the United States were to wake up with absolutely no hatred, prejudice, or animosity toward other groups, institutional racism would still exist. It is part of the structure of society. Thus it requires a structural solution.

You have already seen how the educational system and the legal system are undertaking limited measures to overcome certain types of institutional racism. However, the most far-reaching structural solution to the problem of institutional racism has been **affirmative action.** Affirmative action is a governmental policy, developed in the 1960s, that requires organizations to seek out members of minority groups and women for educational or occupational positions from which they had previously been excluded. One assumption is that past discrimination has left certain people ill equipped to compete with others as equals today. Another assumption is that organizations will not change discriminatory policies unless they are forced to do so.

Contrary to popular belief, employers and university admissions officers are not compelled to institute hiring or admissions quotas or to compromise standards to meet affirmative action goals. They are simply required to gather all relevant information on all qualified applicants, to interview minority candidates, and to make sure minorities have access to needed information. Government agencies and private firms doing business with the government, for instance, are required to publicly announce job openings at least 45 days prior to the cutoff day for applications (Cherry, 1989).

Quotas have been only a last resort, reserved for situations in which organizations are not making good-faith efforts to seek out qualified minority candidates. If an organization announces a job opening in newspapers that reach only the white community, encourages college applicants only in white-dominated schools, or uses discriminatory procedures to eliminate minorities from consideration, the government can then impose quotas.

Affirmative action policies have been used successfully in several areas of social life. Cities have been ordered to bus children to schools outside their neighborhoods to eliminate school segregation. Businesses, unions, universities, and local governments accused of discrimination in hiring or admissions have been sued under the 1964 Civil Rights Act. In part because of such actions, more than 40% of U.S. colleges and universities reported enrollment gains among African Americans and Latino/as during the mid-1990s (cited in Worsnop, 1996). People of color now hold a greater percentage of management, white-collar, and upper-level blue-collar jobs than ever before. Even young black men—historically the most economically disadvantaged and alienated group in the United States—are working in record numbers (Nasar & Mitchell, 1999). Wages and salaries, relative to those of Whites, have also improved somewhat.

Despite its successes, affirmative action remains highly controversial, coming under attack from all directions. Some politically liberal critics, for example, argue that the lives of people for whom affirmative action policies were originally designed—the poorest and most disadvantaged—remain largely unchanged. Although the percentages of Blacks and Whites earning mid-range incomes are roughly the same now, there continues to be a large discrepancy at the top and bottom income levels (U.S. Bureau of the Census, 2004a). Top U.S. colleges are accepting more students of color today than ever before. But these students tend to come from middle-class or upper-class backgrounds. For example, of the 8% of Harvard's undergraduates who are black, only a handful are from poor families in which all four grandparents were born in this country and were descendents of slaves (Rimer & Arenson, 2004). In addition, many schools don't provide enough support to ensure that those students from historically disadvantaged groups actually graduate. The six-year graduation rate for Native American, Latino/a, and African American students is well below 50%, compared to 60% for white students and 65% for Asian students (Carey, 2005). Because a college degree is associated with success later in life (bachelor's degree holders earn about twice as much a year as those with high school diplomas), such educational disappointment can have far-reaching social and personal effects.

Conservative critics argue that preferential treatment of any group, even one whose rights have been historically unrecognized, is demeaning to the people it's supposed to help and unfair to everyone else, amounting to a form of "reverse" discrimination. After four decades of such criticisms, many Whites have come to believe that affirmative action should be abolished (Citrin, 1996). More than three fourths of Whites now feel that qualified Blacks should not receive preference over equally qualified Whites in such matters as getting into college or getting jobs (Citrin, 1996).

Ironically, however, other forms of preferential treatment continue to operate without much criticism. For instance, those people who are most likely to receive favored treatment when it comes to college admissions are white, affluent "legacies," or children of alumni. Playing favorites with alumni children is a common practice at almost every private college and many public institutions as well. At some highly selective universities, legacies are twice as likely to be accepted as unconnected applicants with similar or better credentials (Larew, 2003). Some schools reserve a certain number of spaces for legacies. In one recent year at Harvard, marginally qualified legacies outnumbered all African American, Mexican American, Puerto Rican, and Native American students combined.

Nevertheless, the threats to affirmative action are increasing. In 1996, California voters approved Proposition 209, a referendum that bans the consideration of race, ethnicity, and sex in the public sector, including college admissions. Prior to the ban, African Americans, Latino/as, and Native Americans made up 23.1% of first-year students in the University of California system. The first year after the ban went into effect, that figure fell to 10.4% (Bronner, 1998b). Similarly, in 1996 a federal court barred the University of Texas from using race as a factor in admissions. Since this ruling, there has been a significant decrease in black and Latino/a admissions at the University of Texas. During that same period, the number of white students admitted to the university has stayed the same and the number of Asian American students has risen (Steinberg, 2003).

The legality of affirmative action was upheld, however, in a landmark 2003 case involving admissions policies at the University of Michigan. The U.S. Supreme Court ruled that race may be considered in a limited capacity by universities in their admissions decisions. Immediately after this ruling, the University of Texas announced it would resume the practice of using race as a factor in admissions decisions (Winter, 2003). Although the Supreme Court decision addressed only policies in public, tax-supported institutions, it will no doubt have implications for private schools and businesses around the country.

Despite these trends in the federal courts, affirmative action remains a divisive issue. In a society with a tradition of racial stratification, what is the best way to overcome institutional and personal inequality? Does it take discriminating in the opposite direction to "make things equal," or is it enough simply to treat people equally from this point on?

Here's one way to think about these questions: Imagine a fictitious final game of a basketball tournament between University A and University B. The rules of the game clearly favor University A. Its team is allowed five players on the court, but team B is allowed only four. Team A gets 4 points for every basket made; team B gets 2. Team A is given 2 points for each free throw made; team B gets 1. Team A is allowed to physically impede the progress of the opposing players without being called for a foul, and so on. At halftime team A leads team B by a score of 70 to 15. During halftime, tournament officials decide that the current rules have made the game completely unfair and have harmed the interests of team B. They declare that from now on each team will have the same number of players on the court and receive the same number of points per basket. But there's a slight problem—when the game resumes after halftime, the score is still 70 to 15!

In other words, just because opportunities have been equalized doesn't mean that the accumulated disadvantages of the past have been entirely erased. Such is the problem we face today. We can legislate hiring and admission polices that do away with unfair advantages to any group, but is that action enough to address a long history of exclusion? For a long time to come, members of certain groups will continue to be underrepresented in traditionally white positions. Can U.S. citizens achieve complete equality without forcing those who have benefited historically to give up some of their advantages? The answer to this question is complex, controversial, and emotionally charged and will have a great impact on the nature of ethnoracial relations in the United States in the 21st century.

Global Perspectives on Racism

Given the focus of this chapter so far, you might be tempted to conclude that racism and racial inequality are purely U.S. phenomena. Certainly these problems are very obvious in a society such as the United States, which is so ethnically and racially diverse and which has had such a long history of bitter conflict. But ethnoracial tension is the worldwide rule, not the exception.

Like disadvantaged ethnoracial groups in the United States, minority groups in other countries suffer discrimination that ruins their opportunities for success. For example, even though legal racial discrimination in the form of apartheid ended in South Africa in the early 1990s, many biracial people (known as "coloreds") still live as second-class citizens, despised as the offspring of forbidden racial mixing (Polgreen, 2003). During soccer matches all across Europe, black players are routinely subject to racist taunts, monkey noises, and hurled bananas from White fans. In Eastern European countries such as Slovakia, Romania, Hungary, and the Czech Republic, discrimination against the Roma—or Gypsies—is the norm. They have been despised for centuries as thieving subhumans with no allegiance to the law. They are stereotyped as loud, dirty, indecent, and sloppy. According to a poll of Czech attitudes, 39% of the population feel that "only force is effective" in dealing with Gypsies (cited in Erlanger, 2000). As a result of such attitudes, Gypsies suffer disproportionately from poverty, interethnic violence, discrimination, illiteracy, and disease. In Sofia, the capital of Bulgaria, the unemployment rate among Romas is 94%. In some Roma neighborhoods, 80% of residents have only an elementary school education (Wood, 2005).

Mexico offers another example. All Mexican citizens are considered legally equal under the country's constitution. Yet it is a society deeply divided along racial lines, particularly between dark-skinned people of Indian descent and light-skinned people of Spanish descent. Ironically, most Mexicans are of mixed lineage, so that nearly all of them could be considered at least part Indian. But Mexicans who are considered Indians are the object of severe discrimination. Although 1 in 10 Mexicans is purely Indian, no Indians serve in the presidential cabinet and only a handful are in the congress. More than 80% of Mexico's Indian communities suffer high levels of poverty. Nearly half of all Indians are illiterate and only 14% complete sixth grade. The Indians refer to themselves as "Mexico's most forgotten people" (DePalma, 1996).

The racism in Eastern Europe and Mexico—as in most other areas—has deep historical roots. Sociologists once believed that the global forces of industrialization and modernization would create ethnoracially diverse societies where people's loyalty would be directed to the national society rather than their racial or ethnic community (Deutsch, 1966). But the opposite has happened. At a time when people from every corner of the globe are linked technologically, economically, and ecologically and when mass migrations mix people from different races, religions, and cultures in unprecedented numbers, racial and ethnic hostilities are at an all-time high (Barber, 1992).

Ethnic conflict today typically has little to do with material or economic interests. It tends to center on less tangible resources such as power, security, respect, or social status. Ethnic groups fight about such abstractions as identity and cultural recognition. Conflicts usually arise as a result of the distorted images groups have of one other, which create deep emotions, extreme opinions, and ultimately explosions of violence (Forbes, 1997).

Judging by what we see going on in the world today, we might conclude that hostility between groups is among the most universal of human feelings (Schlesinger, 1992). Look at any major newspaper and you will see stories of ethnic conflict and violence: Jews and Palestinians in Israel, Chechens and Russians in the former Soviet Union, Janjaweed and Darfurians in Sudan, Hindus and Muslims in India, Lendus and Hemas in Congo, Georgians and Ossetians in the Georgian Republic, Tajiks and Pashtun in Afghanistan, Sunnis and Shi'ites in Iraq, and the Ijaw and Itsekiri in Nigeria. In Great Britain, France, and Germany, loud and sometimes violent resentment occurs between the native-born and immigrants from Africa, Eastern Europe, and the Middle East. In the United States, such animosity is likely to be directed toward immigrants from Latin America and Asia (see Chapter 13 for more detail). When people feel that their survival is threatened, they often blame others for their problems, particularly newly arrived others who look and act differently. Racial and ethnic hatred costs the lives of millions of people each year.

But global forces don't just increase ethnoracial tension and inequality; sometimes they help to resolve it. In South Africa, for example, the end of apartheid in the early 1990s was the result of an international boycott. In the 1980s, the global media brought the world pictures and stories of the brutal treatment of South African Blacks. When consumers in the United States and other industrial nations stopped buying products from companies that held investments in South Africa, the companies began to withdraw their money. The minority white government felt the sting as domestic economic problems mounted. As a result of these pressures, the white population of South Africa voted to abolish apartheid. Shortly thereafter, the first black president, Nelson Mandela, was elected. In 1996 a new constitution was adopted that officially and peacefully completed South Africa's transition from white supremacy to nonracial democracy. The document renounces the racism of the past and guarantees all South Africans broad freedoms of speech, movement, and political activity (Daley, 1996). Although serious inequalities and animosities remain, the country is well on its way toward unity and stability.

Conclusion

On April 16, 1963, the Reverend Martin Luther King, Jr. was arrested and jailed for leading a civil rights demonstration in Birmingham, Alabama. At that time, not only were Blacks subjected to daily doses of fear, violence, and humiliation, but they also had to constantly fight what Dr. King called "a degenerating sense of nobodiness." Torn between the brutal reality of a racist society and a fierce optimism for the future, he wrote from his jail cell,

> Let us all hope that the dark clouds of racial prejudice will soon pass away and the deep fog of misunderstanding will be lifted from our fear-drenched communities and in some not too distant tomorrow the radiant stars of love and brotherhood will shine over our great nation with all of their scintillating beauty. (King, 1991, p. 158)

More than 40 years later, our society—like most societies around the globe—still struggles with the debilitating effects of personal and institutional discrimination based on race, religion, and ethnicity. In the United States, lynchings and state-supported segregation have given way to a form of racism that resides not in bloodshed and flagrant exclusion but in the day-to-day workings of our major social institutions. Despite recent gains, people of color still suffer noticeable disadvantages in economics, education, politics, employment, health care, vulnerability to crime, and many other areas. When opportunities to learn, legislate, and make a living are unequally distributed according to race, all facets of life remain unequal.

Five decades after racial segregation was ruled unconstitutional in the United States, the complete integration of such fundamental social institutions as public schools, government, and business has only partially been achieved. And some are questioning the very value of integration. One reason why race relations are so problematic today is that public debate over the issue confuses personal racism and institutional racism. Different types of racism require different solutions. We cannot put an end to economic deprivation or massive residential segregation by trying to convince people not to stereotype other groups.

I realize that this chapter has been rather depressing. After reading it, you may have a hard time imagining a society without racial or ethnic stratification, one where skin color is about as relevant in determining people's life chances as eye color. We must remember, however, that differences do not have to imply inequality. The transformation from difference to disadvantage is a social construction. The people of every society decide which differences should be irrelevant and which should be the primary criteria for making social and legal distinctions between groups of people. The good news is that because we construct these differences, we can tear them down.

YOUR TURN

A curious and disturbing feature of prejudice is that many of our beliefs and attitudes about other racial or ethnic groups are formed without any direct contact with members of those groups. The media—most notably television—play a significant role in providing the public with often inaccurate and oversimplified ethnoracial information that indirectly shapes public attitudes.

For one week, observe several prime-time television shows that feature prominent African American, Latino/a, and Asian characters. The shows can be either comedies or dramas. Note the number of characters on each show who are people of color. Pay particular attention to the way the characters are portrayed. What is their apparent social class standing? How does their behavior conform to common stereotypes associated with members of these groups? How frequently do their words or actions refer to their own race or ethnicity? Do the plots of the shows revolve around what you might consider "racial" themes? That is, how often does the issue of race or ethnicity come up during the course of the show?

Expand your analysis to examine the role of race and ethnicity in stand-up comedy. What proportion of comedians of color use race as part of their act compared to white comedians? What are the consequences of such comedians as Chris Rock, Dave Chappelle, Margaret Cho, George Lopez, and Carlos Mencia playing on racial stereotypes in their acts?

Interpret your observations sociologically. What are the implicit messages communicated by the portrayal of ethnoracial minorities in American media? What role does humor play in reinforcing or fighting prejudice? Are characters who do not act in stereotypical ways conforming instead to a white, middle-class standard? If so, how will this portrayal ultimately affect public perceptions of race?

CHAPTER HIGHLIGHTS

◆ The history of race and ethnicity in U.S. society is an ambivalent one. Famous sayings about equality conflict with the experiences of most ethnoracial minorities—experiences of oppression, violence, and exploitation. Opportunities for life, liberty, and the pursuit of happiness have always been distributed along racial and ethnic lines.

◆ Personal racism is manifested in the form of bigotry, prejudice, and individual acts of discrimination. Quiet racism is expressed not directly but rather indirectly, through anxiety about or avoidance of minorities.

◆ Racism can also be found in a language and cultural ideology that justifies a set of social norms prescribing differential treatment of certain groups.

◆ Institutional racism exists in established institutional practices and customs that reflect, produce, and maintain ethnoracial inequality. Institutional racism is more difficult to detect than personal racism and hence is more difficult to stop. Because such racism exists at a level above personal attitudes, it will not disappear simply by reducing people's prejudices.

◆ Ethnoracial conflict is not just an American phenomenon. It is a global reality.

KEY TERMS

affirmative action Program designed to seek out members of minority groups for positions from which they had previously been excluded, thereby seeking to overcome institutional racism

colorism Prejudice within an ethnoracial group, most notably between light-skinned and dark-skinned Blacks

discrimination Unfair treatment of people based on some social characteristic, such as race, ethnicity, or sex

ethnicity Sense of community that derives from the cultural heritage shared by a category of people with common ancestry

institutional racism Laws, customs, and practices that systematically reflect and produce racial and ethnic inequalities in a society, whether or not the individuals maintaining these laws, customs, and practices have racist intentions

panethnic labels General terms applied to diverse subgroups that are assumed to have something in common

personal racism Individual expression of racist attitudes or behaviors

prejudice Rigidly held, unfavorable attitudes, beliefs, and feelings about members of a different group, based on a social characteristic such as race, ethnicity, or gender

quiet racism Form of racism expressed subtly and indirectly through feelings of discomfort, uneasiness, and fear, which motivate avoidance rather than blatant discrimination

race Category of people labeled and treated as similar because of some common biological traits, such as skin color, texture of hair, and shape of eyes

racial profiling Law enforcement agencies' use of ethnoracial stereotypes in making investigative stops

racial transparency Tendency for the race of a society's majority to be so obvious, normative, and unremarkable that it becomes, for all intents and purposes, invisible

racism Belief that humans are subdivided into distinct groups that are different in their social behavior and innate capacities and that can be ranked as superior or inferior

stereotype Overgeneralized belief that a certain trait, behavior, or attitude characterizes all members of some identifiable group

STUDY SITE ON THE WEB

Don't forget the interactive quizzes and other learning aids at www.pineforge.com/newman6 study. In the Resource Files for this chapter, you will also find more on ethnoracial inequality, including:

Sociologists at Work

♦ Diana Pearce: Institutional Racism and Real Estate

♦ Claude Steele: Racial Stereotypes and Educational Performance

Micro-Macro Connections

♦ Assimilation Versus Multiculturalism

♦ IQ Tests and Ethnic Bias

♦ Racial Profiling

12
The Architecture of Inequality
Sex and Gender

Sexism at the Personal Level

The Ideology of Sexism: Biology as Destiny

Institutions and Sexual Inequality

The Global Devaluation of Women

At a women's rights convention held in Seneca Falls, New York, participants created a modified version of the Declaration of Independence. They called it the Declaration of Sentiments and Resolutions. Here are some excerpts from that document:

> We hold these truths to be self-evident: that all men and women are created equal. . . . The history of mankind is a history of repeated injuries . . . on the part of man toward woman, having in direct object the establishment of an absolute tyranny over her:
>
> > He has compelled her to submit to laws, in the formation of which she had no voice.
> >
> > He has monopolized nearly all profitable [occupations], and from those she is permitted to follow, she receives but a scanty remuneration. He closes against her all the avenues to wealth and distinction which he considers most honorable to himself.
> >
> > He has endeavored, in every way that he could, to destroy her confidence in her own powers, to lessen her self-respect, and to make her willing to lead a dependent and abject life.
>
> In view of their social degradation and in view of the unjust laws above mentioned, and because women do feel themselves aggrieved, oppressed, and fraudulently deprived of the most sacred rights, we insist that they have immediate admission to all the rights and privileges which belong to them as citizens of the United States.

The women who wrote this declaration were not the women's liberationists of the 1960s and 1970s or the radical feminists of the 1990s and 2000s. They were participants in the first convention in support of women's rights ever held in the United States—in 1848 (Declaration of Sentiments, 1848/2001, pp. 449–450). We tend to think that women of the past were either content with their second-class status or unaware that it could be otherwise. As you can see from the preceding declaration, though, 150 years ago U.S. women were anything but passive, ignorant victims of discrimination.

Many people are also inclined to believe that the battle against gender inequality has finally been won. Beginning with the civil rights movement of the 1960s and the so-called sexual revolution of the 1970s, a process of liberation has given contemporary American women opportunities that equal men's. After all, almost as many American women as men work in the paid labor force, the majority of college students these days are women, and women play a prominent role in business, politics, and entertainment. Perhaps you will be surprised to learn in this chapter, then, that women's struggle to overcome economic, legal, and social inequality is no less relevant in the 21st century than it was in 1848.

In Chapter 5, I discussed the difference between sex and gender and how we learn to become boys and girls, men and women, within the appropriate social and cultural context. Being placed in a gender category affects everything we do in life. But gender is more than just a source of personal identity that sets societal expectations; it is a location in the stratification system and a major criterion for the distribution of important resources in most societies. Sex and gender are perhaps the most important determinants of stratification worldwide.

In this chapter, I explore the lives and experiences of women living in societies constructed, for the most part, by and for men. Several important questions are addressed: What are sexism and gender discrimination? How are they expressed and felt at the personal level? How is inequality based on sex and gender supported by cultural beliefs and symbols? At the institutional level, how is inequality related to family and work roles? What are its legal and economic consequences? And finally, how pervasive is gender inequality around the world?

Sexism at the Personal Level

What do you think of when you hear the word *sexism?* The husband who won't let his wife work outside the home? The construction worker who whistles and shouts vulgar comments at female passersby? The office worker who tells lewd jokes about women at the watercooler? Perhaps you think of the woman who mocks men's interpersonal skills or their ham-fisted attempts at romance? Sexism is all those things, to be sure. But sociologically speaking, **sexism** refers to a system of beliefs that assert the inferiority of one sex and that justify discrimination based on gender—that is, on feminine or masculine roles and behaviors. At the personal level, sexism refers to attitudes and behaviors communicated in everyday interaction.

In male-dominated societies, or **patriarchies**, which exist in every quadrant of the globe, cultural beliefs and values typically give higher prestige and importance to men than to women. Throughout such a society, inequality affects girls and women in everything from the perceptions, thoughts, and social interactions of individuals to the organization of social institutions. Above all, gender inequality in a patriarchy provides men with privileged access to socially valued resources and furnishes them with the ability to influence the political, economic, and personal decisions of others. **Matriarchies**, which are societies that give preference to women, are rare in the contemporary world.

Even the most democratic societies tend to be patriarchal to some degree. Research on U.S. gender stereotypes, for instance, has shown that they have changed little over the years (D. L. Berger & Williams, 1991). Some researchers have shown that women are consistently perceived as more passive, emotional, easily influenced, and dependent than men (Broverman, Vogel, Broverman, Clarkson, & Rosenkrantz, 1972; Deaux & Kite, 1987; Tavris & Offir, 1984). Others have noted the myriad ways personal sexism is expressed in U.S. society, both overtly and subtly, through physical domination, condescending comments, sabotage, and exploitation (Benokraitis & Feagin, 1993). One study found that although some forms of personal sexism are motivated by hostility, others are motivated by benevolence, as when men assume women are helpless and thus feel compelled to offer assistance (Glick & Fiske, 1996). Such attitudes and behaviors not only place women in a lower-status position compared to men but also channel them into less advantageous social opportunities.

Men, of course, aren't the only ones who can be personally sexist. Certainly many women dislike men, judge them on the basis of stereotypes, hold prejudiced attitudes toward them, objectify them sexually, consider them inferior, and even discriminate against them socially or professionally. We must keep in mind, though, that male sexism occupies a very different place in society from female sexism. The historical balance of power in patriarchal societies has allowed men as a group to subordinate women socially and sometimes legally to protect male interests and privileges. Because men dominate society, their sexism has more cultural legitimacy, is more likely to be reflected in social institutions, and has more serious consequences than women's sexism.

Sexism and Social Interaction

Everyday social interaction is fraught with reminders that women play a subordinate role in our society. The average woman is reminded frequently of this role, through subtle (and sometimes not so subtle) social arrangements and gender references. Men often have a hard time understanding women's reactions to personal encounters between the sexes. Just as white people enjoy racial transparency (see Chapter 11), members of the dominant sex take for granted the social arrangements that serve their interests.

For example, consider the following tongue-in-cheek quote from a female newspaper columnist:

> By whistling and yelling at attractive but insecure young men, we women may actually help them feel better about themselves, and give them new appreciation of their bodies. Some might say women were descending to the level of male street-corner oafs, but I'm willing to take that risk. If, with so little effort, I can bring joy to my fellow man, then I am willing to whistle at cute guys going down the street. (Viets, 1992, p. 5)

If you're a man, you may wonder why the columnist is bothering to make fun of "wolf whistles." The answer simply is that this behavior means different things when directed at men versus women. Unsolicited sexual attention may be an enjoyable, esteem-enhancing experience for men, but it doesn't have the weight of a long tradition of subordination attached to it, nor is it linked in any way to the threat of violence. Men aren't **objectified**—that is, treated like objects rather than people—in the same way that women are. Their entire worth is not being condensed into a quick and crude assessment of their physical appearance. For women, who must often fight to be taken seriously in their social, private, and professional lives, whistles and lewd comments serve as a reminder that their social value continues to be based primarily on their looks.

Communication patterns also show the effects of unconscious personal sexism. Research in the symbolic interactionist tradition suggests that women and men converse in different ways (Parlee, 1989; Tannen, 1990). For instance, women are more likely than men to use a tag question at the end of a statement: "She's a good professor, *don't you think?*" They are also more likely to use such modifiers and hedges as *sort of* and *kind of* and to be more polite and deferential in their speech (Lakoff, 1975). But such techniques may make the speaker sound less powerful and therefore call into question her credibility and qualifications. Imagine if your math professor always said things like "The answer to the problem is $3x + y$, *isn't it?*" Or if your boss said, "We're going to pursue the Johnson account, *is that OK?*"

The implicit, nonverbal messages of social interaction—body movements, facial expressions, posture—also have more serious implications and consequences for women than for men. For example, femininity is typically gauged by how little space women take up; masculinity is judged by men's expansiveness and the strength of their gestures. Women's bodily demeanor tends to be restrained and restricted (Henley, 1977). What is typically considered "ladylike"—crossed legs, folded arms—is also an expression of submission. Men's freedom of movement—feet on the desk, legs spread, straddling a chair—conveys power and dominance. Such interactional norms place women who are in authoritative positions in a no-win situation. If, on the one hand, they meet cultural definitions of femininity by being passive, polite, submissive, and vulnerable, they fail to meet the requirements of authority. If, on the other hand, they exercise their authority by being assertive, confident, dominant, and tough, their femininity may be called into question (J.L. Mills, 1985).

Nonverbal cues can also play an important role in providing people with information about their social worth. Thus they sometimes serve to keep women "in their place." In India, for instance, crowded buses and trains are frequently the site of "Eve-teasing"—a euphemism for the common practice of men fondling and groping women they happen to be pressed up against in the crowd. In Japan, such actions have gotten so bad on crowded trains that rail companies have introduced "women only" cars to protect women from unwanted fondling. The fact that men can more freely touch women than vice versa serves as a reminder that women's bodies are not considered entirely their own.

American women are also routinely exposed to unwelcome leers, comments, requests for sexual favors, and unwanted physical contact in a variety of institutional settings, from schools to workplaces. According to the American Association of University Women (2001), about 83% of girls have been subjected to sexual harassment in school, ranging from the spread of sexual rumors about them to coerced sexual activity. The Equal Employment Opportunity Commission (2005) resolved close to 14,000 cases of workplace sexual harassment in 2004, but these figures obviously don't include episodes that are never reported. Some estimate that as many as 70% of women experience some kind of harassment in the workplace ("Sexual Harassment Statistics," 2004). From a conflict perspective, cases of sexual harassment are expressions of and attempts to reinforce positions of dominance and power (Uggen & Blackstone, 2004).

The vast majority of harassment cases involve male assertions of power over women. But women aren't the only victims. An overbearing, sexually aggressive female boss or a gay superior may come on to a male subordinate. But more commonly, it's heterosexual men who create a hostile environment for other heterosexual men. According to the Equal Employment Opportunity Commission (2005), sexual harassment charges filed by men increased from 9.1% of all cases in 1992 to 15.1% of all cases in 2004. These claims often involve "bullying," "hazing," "goosing," a variety of sexual insults, and other boorish behaviors. In 1998, the U.S. Supreme Court ruled that in cases of men harassing other men, a plaintiff could win a suit if the alleged harasser was homosexual and therefore motivated by sexual desire, if the harasser was motivated by a general hostility toward men, or if men were systematically treated differently from women in the workplace (Talbot, 2002).

In an odd twist, by the logic of this final criterion, an alleged harasser could be innocent if he could show that he had equal contempt for men and women. Indeed, this defense was used successfully in 2000 in a case involving a bisexual male supervisor who had punished a female employee for not sleeping with him and threw away a male employee's belongings when he didn't succumb to the boss's advances. The court ruled that "conduct occurring equally to members of both genders cannot be discrimination 'because of sex'" (quoted in Talbot, 2002).

❖
Laura Miller
Gender, Power, and Harassment in the Military

Abuses of power based on sex and gender are especially dramatic in the masculine culture of the military. When a woman fought a legal battle in the mid-1990s to be admitted into the Citadel—at that point, an all-male military academy of over 1,900 students—she became a target of harassment and ridicule. Alumni sold T-shirts that read "1,952 Bulldogs and One Bitch" (Vojdik, 2002, p. 68). In 2000, the only female three-star general in the army at the time filed a sexual harassment complaint against another general. She retired a few months later. In 2003, several dozen female cadets at the Air Force Academy accused officials there not only of failing to investigate their sexual assault complaints but of discouraging women from reporting these incidents and retaliating against the women when they did complain (Thomas & Healy, 2003). In 2004, the Pentagon revealed that in the preceding year and a half there had been 112 reports of serious sexual misconduct—including rape and sexual assault—committed by male American military personnel against female American military personnel in Iraq, Afghanistan, and Kuwait (Schmitt, 2004).

Misconduct against women has become pervasive in the entire military system. A survey conducted by the General Accounting Office found that 59% of female students at the Air Force Academy, 50% at the Naval Academy, and 76% at West Point reported experiencing one or more forms of sexual harassment (cited in N. Katz, 2003). The problem goes beyond individually violent military personnel. In 2004, a Pentagon report concluded that the root cause of the problem is a decade's worth of failure on the part of commanding officers to acknowledge its severity (cited in Shanker, 2004).

The U.S. military has been almost exclusively male for most of its history, except for female medical, clerical, and logistics personnel. Men still make up the vast majority of the armed forces and hold all the highest positions of authority. Even today, depending on the branch of service, women make up only about 15% of active duty personnel (Segal & Segal, 2004).

Some women have been able to climb the military ladder and achieve the rank of lieutenant, captain, major, or even general. These women create a special dilemma for male soldiers because female officers simultaneously occupy a subordinate position (because they are women) and a superior position (because they are commanding officers in a highly stratified military hierarchy). So how do lower-level male soldiers—whose gender grants them power but whose military rank makes them inferior—respond?

Sociologist Laura Miller (1997) set out to answer this question by doing field research at eight U.S. Army posts and two national training centers. She also lived with U.S. Army personnel overseas, in Somalia and Haiti. In addition, she collected survey data from over 4,000 American soldiers, both enlisted personnel and officers. On the basis of her research, Miller draws a distinction between *sexual* harassment (unwanted sexual comments or advances) and the more common *gender* harassment (harassment that is used to enforce traditional gender roles or is used in response to the violation of those roles). She considered such statements as "Women can't drive trucks" or "Women can't fire heavy artillery" to be gender harassment. Gender harassment is also often used against men, as when they fail to live up to the masculine ideal and are called "ladies" or "girls" by their comrades or commanding officers.

Many of the men Miller studied strongly believed that they are the disadvantaged sex in the military. They were convinced that women's physical training requirements are easier than men's, that women can "get away with more," and that women receive special breaks, such as avoiding demanding physical duty because of menstrual cramps. As one enlisted man stated, "They want equal rights, but don't want to do what it takes to become equal" (quoted in L. Miller, 1997, p. 48). In short, many male soldiers had come to believe that any woman's power in the military is gained illegitimately.

Often men resorted to subtle forms of gender harassment to express their disapproval of women's power positions in the military. Because of their abiding loyalty to the "chain of command," these men were not about to overtly disobey orders from a superior officer. Nor were they likely to use traditional forms of harassment, such as blatant sexual comments or sexual advances. Instead, they often used what sociologists refer to as *weapons of the weak*—strategies that subordinates employ to resist oppression from above. Such techniques include foot-dragging, feigned ignorance, gossip and rumors, and sabotage. According to one male officer interviewed by Miller, most soldiers at one time or another try to undermine the authority of their female superiors.

Because of the recent rash of publicity concerning sexual harassment, the military has taken steps to control such behaviors and has shown, through publicized sanctions against offenders, a decreasing tolerance of this problem. However, these improvements do not mean that female military personnel now work in a supportive environment.

Gender harassment is more subtle, and therefore more difficult to trace, than sexual harassment. Furthermore, this study shows us that positions of power are not sufficient to guarantee respect and authority. Rather, it shows that harassment lies at the cross-roads of power and gender.

Violence Against Women

The epitome of sexual domination expressed at the personal level is sexual violence. Forcible rape and other forms of sexual assault exist throughout the world, in the most democratic societies as well as in the most repressive.

In the United States, rape is the most frequently committed but least reported violent crime (U.S. Department of Justice, 2001). According to the National Crime Victimization Survey—an annual assessment of crime victimization carried out by the U.S. Bureau of Justice Statistics (2003)—more than 248,000 women over the age of 12 report being raped or sexually assaulted annually, close to three times the roughly 90,000 incidents of rape that are officially reported to the police each year (U.S. Bureau of the Census, 2004a).

Rape is the most personal of violent crimes. In 63% of rapes and 70% of attempted rapes, the victim knew the attacker (U.S. Bureau of Justice Statistics, 2003). On college campuses, where about 3% of college women experience a completed or attempted rape during a typical college year, 90% of the victims knew their attackers (U.S. Bureau of Justice Statistics, 2001).

Rape also has one of the lowest conviction rates of any violent crime. According to a report by the Senate Judiciary Committee (1993), 98% of rape victims never see their attacker caught, tried, and imprisoned. Of those rapists who are convicted, close to 25% never go to prison and another 25% receive sentences in local jails, where the average stay is 11 months.

Rape as a Means of Social Control

According to the conflict perspective, stratification along sex and gender lines has long distorted our understanding of rape. Throughout history, women have been viewed socially and legally as the property of men, as either daughters or wives. Thus in the past rape was seen as a crime against men or, more accurately, against men's property (Siegel, 2004). Any interest a husband took in a sexual assault on his wife probably reflected a concern with his own status, the loss of his male honor, and the devaluation of his sexual property. Globally, rape is a time-tested wartime tactic of terror, revenge, and intimidation, not only against female victims but also against husbands, sons, and fathers whose idea of honor is connected to their ability to protect "their" women (Amnesty International, 2004b; Enloe, 1993; Sengupta, 2004).

According to some feminist sociologists, men have also used rape and the threat of rape throughout history to exert control over women (Brownmiller, 1975). The mere existence of rape limits women's freedom of social interaction, denies them the right of self-determination, and makes them dependent on and ultimately subordinate to men (S. Griffin, 1986). All forms of oppression—whether against ethnic Darfurians in

Sudan, peasants in Bolivia, or women in the United States—employ the threat of violence to ensure compliance. The subordination of women depends on the power of men to intimidate and punish them sexually.

The fear of rape goes beyond simply making life terrifying and uncomfortable for women. It also can restrict their economic opportunities. Women may avoid some neighborhoods with affordable housing because of potential danger. If a woman has a job that requires night work, she may be forced to buy a car to avoid walking at night or using public transportation. The threat of sexual assault limits where and when she is able to work, thereby limiting her money-earning choices and perhaps keeping her financially dependent on others.

Women are also harmed by the larger cultural ideology surrounding rape and rapists. I think most of us are inclined to believe that men who rape must be insane or abnormally violent. All one has to do to avoid being raped, then, is to avoid strange guys. However, rapists as a group have not been shown to be any more disturbed or crazy than nonrapists (S. Griffin, 1986; Warshaw, 1988). In fact, most rapists are quite "normal" by usual societal standards. As I mentioned earlier, about two-thirds of them are friends, acquaintances, or relatives of their victims (U.S. Bureau of the Census, 2004a). But when rape is perceived to be perpetrated by psychologically defective strangers, it doesn't implicate the dominant culture or established social arrangements. In other words, rape isn't considered the fault of society; it's the fault of flawed individuals who can't abide by society's rules. This assumption may explain why date or acquaintance rape, marital rape, and other forms of sexual violence that don't fit the typical image have, until quite recently, been ignored or trivialized.

We must therefore examine the crime of rape within a broader cultural context that encourages certain types of behavior between men and women (S. Jackson, 1995). When we do so, rape becomes less an act of deviance and more an act of overconformity to cultural expectations; less an act of abnormal individuals and more an act of "normal" men taking cultural messages about power and assertiveness to their violent extreme. As one author wrote, rape is the "All-American crime," involving precisely those characteristics traditionally regarded as desirable in American men: strength, power, domination, and control (S. Griffin, 1989).

Victim Blaming

Globally, cultural beliefs about gender, sexuality, and intimacy influence societal and legal responses to rape and rape victims (Morgan, 1996):

- In Peru and Colombia, a man who rapes a woman—whether he knows her or not—can be absolved of all charges if he offers to marry her.
- In Senegal, single women who are rape victims may be killed by their families because as nonvirgins they can no longer command a high dowry; a married woman who's been raped may be killed by her "dishonored" husband.
- In Iran, because Islamic tradition forbids the execution of virgins, any woman condemned to die must first lose her virginity through forced rape.
- About 60% of Pakistani women who file rape charges—which require two witnesses for a conviction—are later criminally charged themselves for having sex outside of marriage (cited in Fisher, 2002).

Arguably, the United States has a more sympathetic reaction to rape victims. But the legal response here still tends to be consistent with men's interests, focusing on women's complicity or blameworthiness. In rape cases, unlike any other crime, victims typically must prove their innocence rather than the state having to prove the guilt of the defendant. Many women who have been victimized arrive at the conclusion that reporting their experiences would, at best, be embarrassing and useless (Sanday, 1996). No wonder that more than 70% of the rape victims in one study said they were concerned about their families discovering they had been raped, and about 66% worried that they might be blamed (cited in Johnston, 1992).

The conflict perspective provides one explanation for the widespread tendency to hold women responsible for their own victimization: The common definition of rape is based on a traditional model of sexual intercourse—penile-vaginal penetration—rather than on the violent context within which the act takes place. The primary focus on the sexual component of the crime requires that information about the intimate circumstances of the act and about the relationship between the people involved be taken into consideration—all of which tends to put female rape victims at a disadvantage during criminal proceedings. Research consistently shows that observers attribute more blame to victims and minimize the seriousness of the assault when the perpetrator is an acquaintance, date, or steady partner (S.T. Bell, Kuriloff, & Lottes, 1994). One study of convicted rapists found that those who assaulted strangers received longer prison sentences than rapists who were acquaintances or partners of their victims, regardless of the amount of force used or physical injury to the victim (McCormick, Maric, Seto, & Barbaree, 1998).

Consider also situations where husbands are accused of raping their wives. Only 17 states treat marital rape cases as they do other rape cases. Thirty-three states sometimes exempt husbands from rape prosecutions, usually when the degree of violence is minimal or when the couple is not living apart or separated at the time of the incident. Four states—Connecticut, Iowa, Minnesota, and West Virginia—extend these privileges to unmarried cohabitors (Bergen, 1999). With rare exception, courts have validated state laws protecting marital rape (Hasday, 2000).

Moreover, public attitudes toward rape and rapists continue to be influenced by the marital status of the people involved. One study of college students found that some people (mostly men) still believe it is acceptable for a man to force his wife to have sex with him and that when compared to other types of violent offenses, marital rape is considered less serious than rape committed by a previously unknown assailant (Kirkwood & Cecil, 2001).

Even when rape victims are not married to their attackers, they are expected to provide clear evidence that they were "unwilling" and tried to resist. No other serious crime requires that the victim prove lack of consent. People aren't asked if they wanted their car broken into or if they enticed someone to steal their wallet. Yet if women cannot prove that they resisted or cannot find someone to corroborate their story, consent (or even latent desire) may be presumed (Siegel, 2004). Anything short of vigorous and repeated resistance can call the victim's motives into question. Indeed, research suggests that police, prosecutors, and juries are less likely to believe allegations of rape if there is no evidence of violence (McEwan, 2005). In 1992, a man in Austin, Texas, forcibly entered a woman's apartment. The woman fled and locked herself in the bathroom. He broke down the door, held a knife to her, and demanded sex. Fearing for her life, not only because of the knife but also because of the chances of contracting a sexually transmitted disease, she begged the man to put on a condom. He agreed and went on to assault her for over an hour. The next day he was arrested for burglary with intent to commit sexual assault. In a sworn deposition he admitted that he had held a knife to her and had had sex with her. But the grand jury originally refused to indict the man because the victim's act of providing a condom was taken to mean consent. Only after widespread public outrage was the man tried, convicted, and sentenced to 40 years in prison.

Certain states are reconsidering the issue of what constitutes consent. In California, for example, a lower court initially ruled that a teenage boy, who was charged with rape after the girl he was having sex with consented but changed her mind during the act, was not guilty for refusing to stop. The California Supreme Court disagreed and allowed the boy to be charged; he was later convicted. In 2003, Illinois revised its legal definition of rape to include situations where the attacker refuses to stop when someone first agrees to have sex but then changes her or his mind (McKinney, 2003).

Public perceptions are still resistant to change, however. Many people regard situations in which a woman places herself at risk—by hitchhiking, attending a wild party, acting seductively, wearing "provocative" clothing, or telling dirty jokes—as a form of victim-precipitated rape. In one study, male and female high school students were given a list of statements and asked to indicate the extent to which they agreed with them (Kershner, 1996). Of the male and female subjects, 52% agreed that most women fantasize about being raped by a man, 46% felt that women encourage rape by the way they dress, and 53% said they felt that some women provoke men into raping them. Moreover, 31% agreed that many women falsely report rapes, and 35% felt that the victim should be required to prove her innocence during a rape trial. Research has linked such attitudes to an increased likelihood of holding rape victims responsible (Frese, Moya, & Megías, 2004) as well as a heightened risk of rape and sexual assault on college campuses (Ching & Burke, 1999).

The important sociological point of these findings is that many men and even some women don't always define violent sexual assault as a form of victimization. They think it is either something women bring upon themselves or something men are expected to do under certain circumstances. These views have become so entrenched that many women have internalized the message, blaming themselves to some degree when they are assaulted. Outside of fear, self-blame is the most common reaction to rape and is more frequent than anger (Janoff-Bulman, 1979). When rape victims say such things as "I shouldn't have walked alone," "I should have locked my windows," or "I shouldn't have worn that dress to the party," they are at least partly taking the blame for a crime they didn't commit. Such guilt and self-blame make recovery all the more difficult and tend to increase rates of depression, posttraumatic stress, shame, anxiety, and even suicidal thoughts (Kubany, Abueg, Owens, Brennan, Kaplan, & Watson, 1995).

As a consequence of victim blaming, women must bear much of the responsibility for preventing rape. I frequently pose this question to students in my Introduction to Sociology class: What can people do to stop rape from occurring? Their responses always echo the standard advice: Don't hitchhike. Don't walk alone at night. Don't get drunk at parties where men are present and if you do drink, know where your drink is at all times. Don't initiate sex play. Don't engage in foreplay if you have no intention of "going all the way." Don't miscommunicate your intentions. Don't wear revealing clothes. Don't accept invitations from strangers. All these safety measures are smart, sensible things to do. But note how all of these suggestions focus exclusively on things that *women* should avoid in order to prevent rape and say nothing about the things *men* can do to stop it. Confining discussions of rape prevention to women's behavior suggests that if a woman doesn't take these precautions, she is "inviting trouble." And "inviting trouble" implies that violent male behavior either is a natural response to provocation or is likely to happen if precautions aren't taken to discourage it.

Some progress is being made regarding cultural perceptions of rape. Myths are being debunked, the violent sexual exploitation of women in the media is being protested, and the rules governing admissible evidence in rape trials are being changed. The recent increase in attention paid to rape, particularly to rape between acquaintances and intimate partners, has increased public awareness of the problem. Rates of reported rapes and attempted rape dropped steadily throughout the 1990s, although they have stabilized somewhat in recent years (see Exhibit 12.1). However, as long as we live in a culture that objectifies women and glorifies male assertiveness, so, too, will we have sexual violence.

Exhibit 12.1   Trends in Forcible Rape

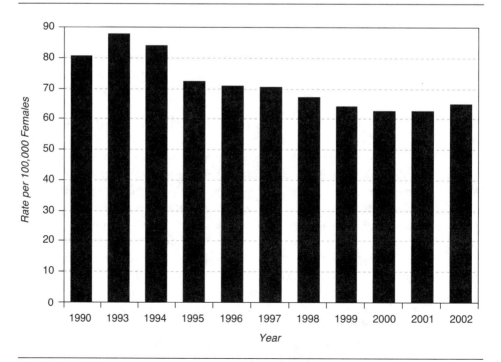

Source: U.S. Bureau of the Census, 2004a.

The Ideology of Sexism: Biology as Destiny

The domination of one group over another is always endorsed by a set of beliefs that explains and justifies that domination. You saw in the previous chapter that racism is often justified by the belief in innate racial inferiority. With sexism, it is the belief that men and women are biologically, naturally different.

For 19th- and early 20th-century physicians, few facts were more incontestable than the fact that women were the products and prisoners of their anatomy. One French scientist noted that women have smaller brains than men, which explained their "fickleness, inconstancy, absence of thought and logic, and incapacity to reason" (quoted in Angier & Chang, 2005, p. A1). Women's reproductive systems have been the object of scientific attention and concern for centuries (Scull & Favreau, 1986). Everything supposedly known about women that made them different from men—their subordinate place in society, their capacity for affection, their love of children and aptitude for child rearing, their "preference" for domestic work, and so on—could be explained by the existence and functioning of their uterus and ovaries (Ehrenreich & English, 1979; Scull & Favreau, 1986). Scholars in the past warned that young women who studied too much were struggling against nature, would badly damage their reproductive organs, and would perhaps even go insane in the process (Fausto-Sterling, 1985). So the exclusion of women from higher education was not only justifiable but necessary for health reasons and for the long-term good of society.

Some structural-functionalist sociologists have also used the observable physical differences between men and women to explain gender inequality. The fact that men tend to be physically stronger and that women bear and nurse children has created many culturally recognized and necessary sex-segregated social roles, especially at work and in the family (Parsons & Bales, 1955). This specialization of roles is the most effective way to maintain societal stability, structural-functionalists believe. By giving birth to new members, by socializing very young children, and by providing affection and nurturing, women make invaluable contributions to the reproduction of society. The common occupations that women have traditionally had outside the home—teacher, nurse, day care provider, maid, social worker, and so on—tend simply to be extensions of their "natural" tendencies.

Similarly, men's physical characteristics have been presumed to better suit them for the roles of economic provider and protector of the family. If it's true that men are "naturally endowed" with such traits as strength, assertiveness, competitiveness, and rationality, then they are best qualified to enter the serious and competitive world of work and politics (Kokopeli & Lakey, 1992). Sociologist Steven Goldberg (1999) argues that because male rule and male dominance seem to characterize the vast majority of human societies, this gender difference must be rooted in evolutionary biology. In 2005, the president of Harvard University created quite a stir when he suggested publicly that innate sex differences may explain why more men than women succeed in science and math careers (Dillon, 2005).

The problem with depicting masculinity and femininity as natural, biological phenomena is that it confuses sex with gender. The underlying assumption of sexist ideology—that gender is as unchangeable as sex—overlooks extensive similarities between the sexes and extensive variation within each sex. The distributions of men and women on most personality and behavioral characteristics generally overlap. For instance, men as a group do tend to be more aggressive than women as a group. Yet some women are much more aggressive than the average man, and some men are much less aggressive than the average woman. Indeed, social circumstances may have a greater impact on aggressive behavior than any innate, biological traits. Some studies show that when women are rewarded for behaving aggressively, they can be just as violent as men (Hyde, 1984).

Furthermore, the reliance on biology ignores the wide cultural and historical variation in conceptions of masculinity and femininity. For instance, although every known society has a division of labor based on sex, what's considered "men's work" and "women's work" differs. In most societies, men fish, hunt, clear land, and build boats and houses; but in some societies women regularly perform these tasks. In most societies, women do the cooking; but in some societies cooking is typically a male responsibility (Eitzen & Baca-Zinn, 1991).

Although women have become prominent in the U.S. workforce, many people still believe that they are less capable than men in performing certain tasks outside the home (Wagner, Ford, & Ford, 1986). Some people in the United States still may find female doctors or dentists unusual. Legislators and military officials continue to debate the role of female soldiers in direct ground combat. The controversy in several churches over whether or not women should be ordained as ministers and priests illustrates the depth and intensity of people's feelings about gender-appropriate career pursuits.

Moreover, the qualities we consider naturally feminine are usually seen as less socially valuable than those considered masculine. Girls do suffer sometimes when their behavior is considered "boylike." But a boy being accused of acting like a girl is the ultimate schoolyard insult. Even when they get older, many men can be easily whipped into aggressive responses by accusations of femininity, as when platoon leaders or coaches call their male troops or players "girls" or "ladies."

This devaluation of femininity even influences the cultural value of certain emotions. We think of love as involving emotional expressiveness, verbal self-disclosure, and affection (Cancian, 1987). These are qualities typically associated with feminity. Desirable masculine traits—independence, competitiveness, emotional inexpressiveness—usually imply the antithesis of love. Not coincidentally, U.S. society tends to glorify achievement and to downplay emotional expression as overly sentimental and foolish. Women are encouraged to specialize in and be emotionally responsible for romantic relationships, whereas men are expected to specialize in work activities, which are more highly regarded in society. When love is perceived in such a way, men's power over women is strengthened.

The biological rationale for gender inequality is difficult to justify. Technological advances—including bottled baby formula, contraceptives that give women control over their childbearing and child-rearing responsibilities, and innovations that lessen the need for sheer physical strength—have made it possible for women and men to fulfill many of the same responsibilities. Nevertheless, as long as people believe that gender-linked roles and societal contributions are determined by nature, they will continue to accept inequality in women's and men's opportunities, expectations, and outcomes.

If people consider it "natural" for women to play nurturing, weak, and dependent roles, then limiting women to such positions seems neither unfair nor oppressive.

Institutions and Sexual Inequality

The subordination of women that is part of the everyday workings of social institutions (or **institutional sexism**) has far greater consequences for women as a group than do personal expressions of sexism. When sexism in social institutions becomes part of the ongoing operation of large-scale organizations, it perpetuates and magnifies women's disadvantages, making social equality all the more difficult to attain. But not only are social institutions sexist, they are also gendered. In other words, institutions and organizations segregate, exploit, and exclude women solely on the basis of their physical characteristics and then compound the impact of their sexism by incorporating values and practices based on traditional expectations for women and men (Kimmel, 2004).

More often than not, institutions incorporate masculine values—which is not surprising because, historically, men have developed, dominated, and interpreted most institutions. Take competitive sports, for example. Most of us would agree that to be successful an athlete must be aggressive, strong, and powerful—attributes typically associated with masculinity. By celebrating these traits, a sport such as football symbolically declares itself an arena that women cannot or should not enter (except, of course as spectators or cheerleaders). But even such sports as gymnastics and figure skating that have traditionally valued more "feminine" traits, like grace, beauty, and balance, have now made their judging criteria more masculine. For a woman to be a world-class gymnast or skater these days, she must also be physically strong and exhibit explosive acrobatic power. Indeed, the popularity of women's team sports in this country (basketball, soccer, softball, and so on) coincides with the increasing presence of such traditionally male traits as physical strength and competitive vigor in female athletes.

Similarly, most bureaucracies in institutional areas such as business, politics, and the military operate according to taken-for-granted masculine principles. Successful leaders and organizations are usually portrayed as aggressive, goal oriented, competitive, and efficient—all characteristics associated with masculinity in this society. Rarely are strong governments, prosperous businesses, or efficient military units described as supportive, nurturing, cooperative, kind, and caring (Acker, 1992). This sort of bias pervades other institutions as well.

❖
Micro-Macro Connection
Women, Men, and Medicine

Sex and gender inequality has created some interesting discrepancies in the way the medical establishment treats men and women. In general, men tend to have more health problems than women. They occupy more physically demanding jobs and engage in riskier physical activity. Hence they've historically been at greater risk for various bodily injuries and stress-related ailments. According to figures from the U.S. Bureau of the Census (2004a), men have higher rates of most cancers and lower overall life expectancy than women. Yet women have historically been the focus of medical attention more than men (Rothman, 1984). Women are far more likely than men to undergo surgical and diagnostic procedures. Indeed, the three most common short-stay surgical procedures for women—repair of lacerations during childbirth, cesarean section, and hysterectomy—all deal with exclusively female anatomy and physiology. The three most common short-stay procedures for men—cardiac catheterization, removal of coronary obstruction, and coronary bypass—are not sex-specific. Similarly, physicians commonly specialize in *women's* health care—but rarely do they specialize in *men's*. Obstetricians and gynecologists deal exclusively with the reproductive and sexual matters of female patients. There are no comparable specialties of medicine devoted to men's reproductive health.

Normal biological events in women's lives—menstruation, pregnancy, childbirth, and menopause—have long been considered problematic conditions in need of medical intervention. For instance, the Board of Trustees of the American Psychiatric Association continues to debate the inclusion of a psychiatric diagnosis called "Premenstrual Dysphoric Disorder" in its official manual of mental disorders. Indisputably, women around the world experience irritability, moodiness, and other symptoms related to hormonal cycles. The issue, however, is whether these symptoms ought to be labeled as a medical and/or mental problem (Lander, 1988). To do so not only promotes the selling of drugs to healthy women (C. A. Bailey, 1993; Figert, 1996) but fosters the belief that women, biologically frail and emotionally erratic because of their hormones, cannot be allowed to work too hard or be trusted in positions of authority (Fausto-Sterling, 1985).

Given the special attention women's health problems receive, it's ironic that, outside of obstetrics and gynecology, research on women's general health needs has been rather limited. Twenty years ago, the U.S. Public Health Service reported that a lack of medical research on women limited our understanding of their health concerns (Rothman & Caschetta, 1999). The reason often given for their exclusion from medical studies was that their menstrual cycles made the interpretation of research findings complicated. In addition, medical researchers have historically been reluctant to perform research on women of childbearing age because of fears that exposing them to experimental manipulations might harm their reproductive capabilities. In fact, in the 1970s and 1980s, federal policies and guidelines actually called for the blanket exclusion of women of childbearing potential from certain types of drug research. That meant that any woman who was physically capable of becoming pregnant, regardless of her own desires to do or not to do so, could be excluded. Concerns were less with threats to women's health than with the possibility of liability if reproductive damage due to exposure to the experimental drug occurred (Hamilton, 1996).

The exclusion of women from medical research became so problematic that Congress passed a law in 1993 stipulating that women must be included in clinical trials in numbers sufficient to provide evidence of the different ways men and women respond to drugs, surgical treatments, and changes in diet or behavior. Nevertheless, a 2000 study found that many researchers were not complying with the law (cited in Pear, 2000). In 2003, the Agency for Healthcare Research and Quality reported that recent research on coronary heart disease (CHD) still either excludes women entirely or includes them only in limited numbers. Consequently, the therapies used to treat women with CHD—a disease that kills 250,000 women a year—are still based on studies conducted primarily on middle-aged men (cited in "Research Findings Affirm," 2003).

Interestingly, there is one popular area of research these days that cannot be generalized to women: male sexual performance. Male impotence can best be characterized as an embarrassment or an inconvenience, certainly not a grave, life-threatening illness. Still, a significant proportion of medical research today is devoted to developing impotence treatments—"lifestyle" drugs that improve the social lives of generally healthy men. Drugs to treat erectile dysfunction are a $2 billion a year industry (S. Elliott, 2004). About 6 million American men have taken Viagra since its introduction in 1998, and about a million more have taken either of its prime competitors, Cialis and Levitra (Tuller, 2004). Drug companies don't seem nearly as concerned with the sexual performance problems of older women, demonstrating once again the way that institutional decision makers cater to the interests of the dominant group.

Gender Inequality in the Media

You saw in Chapter 5 that the media's portrayal of men and women contributes to gender socialization. But the media as an institution can also contribute to the cultural devaluation of women and perpetuate gender inequality.

Worldwide, men tend to control the creation and production of media images. The upper levels of corporate media organizations and top newspaper management positions are also almost entirely male (Croteau & Hoynes, 2000). In key behind-the-scenes roles like creators, producers, directors, writers, editors, directors of photography, and the like, men outnumber women four to one (Media Report to Women, 2003). Such an imbalance in productive and creative control means that what we see in theaters and on television is likely to reflect men's perspectives.

Hence, aside from the occasional powerful female character—like Xena the Warrior Princess or Sydney Bristow on the popular TV show *Alias*—the portrayal of women on prime-time television remains rather traditional and stereotypical. Although fewer women are portrayed as housewives than in the past, men are still more likely than women to be shown working outside the home (D. Smith, 1997). Women express emotions much more easily and are significantly more likely to use sex and charm to get what they want than are men. An analysis of 18 prime-time television situation comedies found that female characters are significantly more likely than male characters to receive derogatory comments about their appearance from other characters. These comments are typically reinforced by audience laughter (Fouts & Burggraf, 2000). Similarly, an analysis of over 1,600 television commercials showed that female characters were less prevalent, more likely to be shown in families, and less likely to be employed outside the home than male characters (Coltrane & Adams, 1997).

A glimpse at the portrayal of modern women in U.S. advertising, fashion, television, music videos, and films further reveals a double-edged stereotype. On the one hand, we see the successful woman of the 21st century: the perfect wife/mother/career woman, the triumphant professional who leaps gracefully about the pages of fashion magazines. She is the high-powered lawyer or surgeon that we commonly see on prime-time television, outgoing, bright, and assertive. No occupation is beyond her reach.

Coexisting with this image, though, is the stereotypical image of the "exhibited" woman: the seductive sex object displayed in beer commercials, magazine advertisements, soap operas, and the swimsuit issue of *Sports Illustrated*. Perhaps the most memorable media event of 2004 was the exposure of Janet Jackson's breast during a halftime musical number at the Super Bowl, although many viewers missed it because they were watching the "Lingerie Bowl" on pay-per-view TV—a halftime "game" between teams of underdressed actresses and models. More generally, television continues to present stereotypes that show women as shallow, vain, and materialistic characters whose looks overshadow all else. Popular reality TV shows, like *Extreme Makeover* and *The Swan,* perpetuate the belief that without beauty (attainable through extensive plastic surgery), women are doomed to a lonely life of romantic heartache and occupational failure. Dating-themed shows like *The Bachelor* go one step further, reinforcing the belief that sexual charm and physical attractiveness are lures that women can use to attract men.

The image of beauty presented by the exhibited woman is artificial and largely unattainable, however. The average American woman is 5'4" tall and weighs 140 pounds. The average American fashion model is 5'11" tall and weighs 117 pounds and thus is thinner than 98% of American women (National Eating Disorders Association, 2004). Researchers at Johns Hopkins University compiled data on the heights and weights of Miss America pageant winners between 1922 and 1999. They found that the weights of these women have been steadily decreasing, reaffirming the cultural value of thinness (Rubinstein & Caballero, 2000). Recent winners have had a height-to-weight ratio that places them in a range of what the World Health Organization defines as "undernourished."

Nonetheless, these images continue to appeal to young women. A study of Canadian girls between 10 and 14 found that 30% of them were currently trying to lose weight (McVey, Tweed, & Blackmore, 2004). And perhaps as many as two thirds of all American high school girls are either on a diet or planning to start one (cited in Thomsen, Weber, & Brown, 2002). Dieting has become so common among young women that some researchers now believe that what was once considered disordered eating behavior is now considered "normal" adolescent eating. Ultra-thin, media-driven standards of beauty continue to be an ideal that many young women are willing to starve themselves to attain.

In sum, young women today are not only expected to achieve educationally and economically at unprecedented levels, they also must look sexy doing it. These images, created mainly by men, produce the illusion that success or failure is purely a personal, private achievement and ignore the complex social, economic, and political forces that continue to prevent real-life women from achieving success.

Gender Inequality in the Law

Historically, women have been denied many of the legal rights that men take for granted. For instance, in the 18th century, when women got married, they lost many of the rights they enjoyed as single women, such as legal title to their property and the right to enter binding contracts. A married woman's legal identity was submerged into that of her husband; she literally didn't exist as an independent citizen (Crittenden, 2001). Husbands were allowed by law to chastise their wives, force them to stay at home, and even force sex upon them without legal sanction.

To counteract a long history of legal inequality, the U.S. Congress has passed many laws aimed at improving the situation of women. In addition to its central focus on eliminating racial segregation, the 1964 Civil Rights Act contained provisions forbidding sex discrimination in employment. The 1972 Educational Amendments Act included a section forbidding sex discrimination in all federally funded institutions of education. Obstacles to equality have also been removed in other areas, such as housing, eligibility for credit, and hiring practices. The 1993 Family and Medical Leave Act, described in Chapter 7, guarantees some working mothers (as well as fathers) up to 12 weeks of unpaid sick leave per year to care for a new child or a sick relative.

Courts in the United States have also made several noteworthy decisions that address women's concerns. In 1993 the U.S. Supreme Court ruled that victims of workplace harassment could win lawsuits without having to prove that the offensive behavior left them psychologically damaged—which in the past meant either a documented nervous breakdown or psychiatric hospitalization—or unable to do their jobs. Now workers need prove only that as a result of harassment the workplace environment "would reasonably be perceived as hostile or abusive" (Greenhouse, 1993). In 1996 the Court ruled that all-male public colleges and universities have to admit women.

But laws and court decisions haven't been entirely effective in improving the status of women. In the United States and elsewhere, occupations are still highly segregated along gender lines. Female workers still earn significantly less than male workers. And a woman's right to control her own body through legal contraception and abortion continues to be challenged in the courts.

Such lack of progress extends from home and workplaces to educational institutions and sports arenas. Three decades ago, Title IX of the Educational Amendments Act mandated that women's athletic programs in schools receiving federal money should be equitable with men's. Since then, women's sports have become much more visible and legitimate. In 2001–2002, on average, 208 female students per Division I college participated in intercollegiate sports, up from 143 in 1995–1996 (cited in Giegerich, 2003). Nevertheless, women's athletics still lag behind men's. From 1992 to 1997, funding for women's athletics programs rose from an average of $263,000 a year to $663,000 a year. But during that same span, funding for men's programs increased from an average of $1.5 million to more than $2.4 million (Chambers, 1997). Women represent 53% of the students at Division I colleges, but they receive only 43% of sport scholarship dollars and 36% of operating budgets (Hogshead-Makar, 2003).

Even laws explicitly designed to protect women's rights have created unforeseen disadvantages. Divorce laws in the United States were revised in the 1970s to make the termination of marriages less combative and more equitable. However, divorced husbands typically experience an increase in their standard of living, while divorced wives—who are likely to have physical custody of children—suffer a decrease (P.G. Peterson, 1996). In California, for instance, after no-fault divorce laws were enacted only 13% of mothers with preschool children received spousal support (cited in Tavris, 1992). The situation was so bad that in 1990 Congress passed the Displaced Home-makers Self-Sufficiency Assistance Act, which provides funds to local communities so they can establish vocational training and other support programs for divorced women.

Gender Inequality in Families

Much of the inequality found in the law revolves around the traditional view of women's family role: keepers of the household and producers, nurturers, and socializ-ers of children. Although in other times and places women have had different levels of responsibility for homemaking, they have always been responsible for reproduction.

Reproductive Rights and Responsibilities

Motherhood has traditionally been considered the pinnacle of a woman's social iden-tity and her God-given and socially expected duty. This role can be the source of pride, joy, and comfort, but it can also be the source of pain, exploitation, and discrimination.

Consider how our society allocates responsibility for preventing pregnancy. Birth control techniques have been around for centuries (condoms, withdrawal, abortion, and so on) (P. Schwartz & Rutter, 1998). But not until the 1960s did innovations such as the intrauterine device (IUD) and the birth control pill give women themselves significant control over reproduction. This gain in control, however, was tempered by a parallel increase in responsibility. Women have always borne the burden of unwanted pregnancy, but now they also have almost exclusive responsibility for taking steps to prevent it. Women have become the gatekeepers of sexuality. Hence the issue of reproductive control has come to be seen as a women's issue and not a human issue (P. Schwartz & Rutter, 1998).

Women's right to choose *not* to bear children, through universal access to safe, legal contraception and abortion, has been the most visible aspect of the fight over reproductive rights. However, the issue of reproductive choice is much more com-plicated. Although most cultures continue to hold reproduction in high esteem and encourage most married women to "be fruitful and multiply," the reproductive capac-ities of some women—namely, poor women of color—are often blamed by politicians and social critics for an increase in poverty and an alleged rise in immorality in society (S. L. Thomas, 1998). Poor women—both married and nonmarried—may be accused of bearing children for the purpose of increasing a welfare check, of being sexually out of control, and of causing their own poverty (Murray, 1994).

In several states, lawmakers have passed or attempted to pass legislation requiring poor women to use certain contraceptives, sterilization, or family planning services as a condition for receiving public assistance (S.L. Thomas, 1998). In 1990, a Kansas representative introduced a bill to authorize free Norplant implants (a contraceptive device that consists of tiny rods surgically implanted under the skin of a woman's arm, which remains effective for five years) and $500 "insertion bonuses" for all poor women on welfare. By 1995, 70 similar bills had been proposed in 35 states, most offer-ing financial incentives to women on welfare who use Norplant or making its use a condition of receiving welfare payments.

Technological advances in infertility treatments have also complicated the issue of reproductive rights for women. Developments such as fertility drugs, artificial insemination, in vitro fertilization, and surrogate motherhood have allowed thousands of infertile women to conceive children. Although access to such procedures is limited primarily to the affluent—costs for these procedures range from about $2,000 for fertility pills to $35,000 for in vitro fertilization and are typically not covered by insurance (Kolata, 2004c)—these techniques have the potential of increasing reproductive choices and opportunities (B. K. Rothman, 1987; Rowland, 1990). Ironically, such advances, coupled with the U.S. culture's stigmatization of infertility, may actually take reproductive control away from women who choose not to have children. If infertility is seen as a "curable" condition, those who don't enthusiastically pursue all possible "cures" can be looked at with suspicion.

Because of the cultural value placed on having children, fertility research has faced virtually no criticism and has been allowed to expand with little community debate (Rowland, 1990). After all, who would criticize research that could provide infertile couples with the miracle of a baby? Consequently, the field of high-tech fertility treatment is flourishing. In only a decade the industry grew from 30 clinics to more than 400 and is worth over $2 billion ("Adoption/Infertility Industry," 2000). The number of women seeking fertility treatment increased by 68% between 1996 and 2001 (Kolata, 2004c). Moreover, this industry is largely exempt from government regulation and immune to the downward pressure on costs that insurance companies exert (Gabriel, 1996). At some hospitals, fertility doctors earn more than the hospitals' presidents.

Unfortunately, women serve as experimental subjects in this research. Instead of being seen as individual people, they often become objects, "alternative reproductive vehicles," "human incubators," or "uterine environments" within which "harvested" eggs can be planted (Raymond, 1993). Women must also face most of the emotional and physical risks, including infection, painful side effects, high-risk multiple births, permanent injury, and the heartbreak of failure.

Another reproductive issue that affects women disproportionately is the growing institutional emphasis on the protection of fetal rights. Women, far more than men, are seen to have a moral, societal, and legal responsibility to ensure a healthy birth. Consequently, pregnant women are sometimes denied the rights of bodily integrity and self-determination that all other competent adults in this society have (Tavris, 1992). Twenty-eight states presently criminalize harm to a fetus (cited in Rosenberg, 2003). For example, a South Carolina woman was sentenced to 12 years in prison for killing her unborn fetus by smoking crack cocaine. The jury deliberated 15 minutes before convicting her. In an earlier case, the South Carolina Supreme Court had ruled that a viable fetus could be considered a person under the state's criminal code (Firestone, 2001). Since the late 1980s, hundreds of women have been prosecuted for behavior while pregnant that posed a danger to their fetuses, the vast majority of cases involving the use of illegal drugs (Terry, 1996). Even more have been jailed during pregnancy (referred to as "protective incarceration") or deprived of custody of their newborns (D. E. Roberts, 1991).

From an institutional perspective, making pregnant women solely responsible for the well-being of fetuses allows us to ignore the threats to children that lie outside the mother's body—poor nutrition, inadequate health care, limited access to prenatal care, dilapidated housing, environmental hazards, and racism.

Housework and the Domestic Division of Labor

One of the major consequences of the industrial revolution of the 18th and 19th centuries was the separation of the workplace and the home. Prior to industrialization, most countries were primarily agricultural. People's lives centered around the farm, where husbands and wives were partners not only in making a home but also in making a living (Vanek, 1980). The farm couple was interdependent; each needed the other for survival. It was taken for granted that women provided for the family along with men (Bernard, 1981). Although the relationship between husbands and wives on the farm was never entirely equal—wives still did most if not all of the housekeeping and family care—complete male dominance was offset by women's indispensable contributions to the household economy (Vanek, 1980).

With the advent of industrialization, things began to change. New forms of technology and the promise of new financial opportunities and a good living drew people (mostly men) away from the farms and into cities and factories. For the first time in history, the family economy in some societies was based outside the household. Women no longer found themselves involved in the day-to-day supervision of the family's business as they had once been. Instead, they were consigned to the only domestic responsibilities that remained necessary in an industrial economy: the care and nurturing of children and the maintenance of the household. Because this work was unpaid and because visible goods were no longer being produced at home, women quickly found that their work was devalued (Hareven, 1992).

However, as we saw in Chapter 7, men weren't the only ones who left home each day to work in factories. At the turn of the century, hundreds of thousands of children worked in mines, mills, and factories (Coontz, 1992). And contrary to popular belief, one fifth of U.S. women worked outside the home in 1900, especially women of color (Staggenborg, 1998).

Today, the devaluation of "women's work" is the result of a separation of the public and private spheres (Sidel, 1990). As long as men dominate the public sphere—the marketplace and the government—they will wield greater economic and political power within society and also be able to translate that power into authority at home. "Women's work" within the relatively powerless private sphere of the home will continue to be hidden and undervalued.

According to the conflict perspective, the problem is not that housewives don't work; it's that they work for free outside the mainstream economy, in which work is strictly defined as something one is paid to do (Ciancanelli & Berch, 1987; Voyandoff, 1990). Ironically, however, domestic work is actually invaluable to the entire economic system. If a woman was paid the minimum going rate for all her labor as mother and housekeeper—child care, transportation, housecleaning, laundry, cooking, bookkeeping, grocery shopping, and so on—her yearly salary would be over $35,000, about the average salary of male full-time workers ("Mom's Market Value," 1998). But because societal and family power is a function of who brings home the cash, such work does not afford women the prestige it might if it were paid labor.

Despite significant shifts in American attitudes toward gender roles and the accelerated entry of women into the paid labor force in the past few decades, housework continues to be predominantly female (Baxter, 1997; Brines, 1994). Husbands do play a more prominent role in the raising of children than they did just two decades ago, and they've increased their contribution to housework somewhat (Bianchi, Milkie, Sayer, & Robinson, 2000), especially when compared to men in other industrialized countries (Fuwa, 2004). But the household work that husbands do tends to be quite different from the work that wives do. Women's tasks tend to be essential to the daily functioning of the household (Fuwa, 2004); men's chores are typically infrequent, irregular, or optional:

> They take out the garbage, they mow the lawns, they play with children, they occasionally go to the supermarket or shop for household durables, they paint the attic or fix the faucet; but by and large, they do not launder, clean, or cook, nor do they feed, clothe, bathe, or transport children. These . . . most time-consuming activities . . . are exclusively the domain of women. (Cowan, 1991, p. 207)

From a structural-functionalist perspective, one could argue that traditional gendered household responsibilities actually reflect an equitable, functional, interdependent division of labor. That is, the husband works in the paid labor force and supports the family financially; the wife takes care of the household work and child care. Each person provides essential services in exchange for those provided by the other. But research in this area indicates that the gender discrepancy in housework responsibilities does not diminish when women work full time outside the home. On average, women employed full time spend about 19 hours per week on housework, while men spend only about 10 hours (cited in Glazer, 2003). To be sure, the hours that working women spend on housework are down from 32 hours in the mid-1960s, and men have increased their contribution from 4 hours per week, but still men contribute only half as much time as women do to the maintenance of the household. According to a survey conducted by the U.S. Bureau of Labor Statistics (2004b), employed women spend about an hour a day more than employed men caring for young children. When they have older children, these women spend six hours a day in so-called "secondary care," like shopping with children in tow, while men spend only four hours a day in such activities.

Because working women continue to be primarily responsible for housework, they often end up working what amounts to two full-time jobs. Even when a husband is unemployed, he does less housework than a wife who puts in a 40-hour week. The dynamics of retirement, too, are a factor. Because wives, in general, are younger than their husbands, millions of women continue to work for pay after their husbands have retired. These women sometimes come to resent retired husbands who have lots of free time on their hands but who don't contribute much more around the house than they did while they were employed. One recent study of retirement-aged men and women found that working women whose husbands are retired were the least happy with their marriages of all types of couples; working men whose wives stayed home were the happiest (cited in Leland, 2004a).

Interestingly, couples who profess egalitarian, nonsexist values also experience discrepancies in the division of household labor (Blumstein & Schwartz, 1983). Husbands who say that all the housework should be shared still spend significantly less time doing it than their wives (Institute for Policy Research, 2002). The fact that housework is still predominantly women's work gives us some sense of how pervasive and powerful our sexist ideology continues to be.

Gender Inequality in Education

Another institutional setting in which gender inequality exists is education. In elementary school and beyond, teachers are likely to treat their male and female students differently:

- ◆ Girls receive less teacher attention and less useful feedback than boys.
- ◆ Girls talk significantly less in class than boys and when they do speak up, they are more likely than boys to be reminded to raise their hands.
- ◆ Students rarely see mention of the contributions of women in their textbooks, which continue to emphasize male accomplishments.
- ◆ Girls are more likely than boys to be the focus of unwanted sexual attention in school (Sadker, Sadker, Fox, & Salata 2004).

Over the course of their school careers such differential treatment takes its toll on girls. Since it is sometimes quite subtle, most people are unaware of the secret sexist lessons and quiet losses it creates (Sadker & Sadker, 1999).

In the early grades, girls outperform boys on almost every standard measure of academic achievement. Boys are more likely than girls to repeat a grade, drop out, be put in special education, or be diagnosed as having an emotional problem, a learning disability, or attention-deficit disorder (Lewin, 1998). Yet boys have higher expectations and higher self-esteem than girls, a gap that widens with each passing year in the school system. According to one study, around the ages of eight and nine about two-thirds of both boys and girls report feeling confident and positive about themselves. By high school, however, the percentage drops to 29% for young women (Freiberg, 1991). As girls make the transition from childhood to adolescence, they are faced with a conflict between the way they see themselves and the way others, particularly teachers, see them (Gilligan, 1990).

These gender-typed patterns pervade high school. Teenage boys' sense of their own masculinity tends to be derived primarily from participation in organized sports (Messner, 2002). Boys are also likely to be encouraged by counselors and teachers to formulate ambitious career goals. In contrast, prestige and popularity for teenage girls are still likely to come largely from their physical appearance and from having a boyfriend (Lott, 1987). Not surprisingly, by the end of high school boys perform better than girls. For instance, though 54% of all SAT takers are girls, boys' average total score is higher (1049 for boys versus 1005 for girls) (National Center for Fair and Open Testing, 2004).

Sexual inequality is evident in postsecondary education, too. Since 1980, more women than men have been enrolled in U.S. colleges (although more men than women go on for advanced degrees) (U.S. Bureau of the Census, 2004a). However, males are more likely to take rigorous courses geared for math and science majors and achieve higher grades in those courses than women (College Board, 1998). Many of the majors that lead to high-paying or high-prestige careers remain male dominated (engineering, economics, mathematics, earth sciences, and so on), whereas women are concentrated in such fields as nursing, literature, education, and library science (Brint, 1998).

To overcome the cumulative impact of this differential treatment, some educational reformers have advocated sex-segregated private schools as well as single-sex classrooms in coeducational public schools. They argue that girls who go to single-sex schools are more assertive, more confident, and more likely to take classes in math, computer science, and physics than girls in coeducational schools. They also have higher career aspirations than girls who attend coeducational schools (Watson, Quatman, & Edler, 2002). Boys in single-sex environments are less likely to get into trouble and more likely to pursue interests in art, music, and drama than their counterparts in coeducational schools (National Association for Single-Sex Public Education, 2004). In addition, graduates of single-sex high schools—both girls and boys—are more likely to go to prestigious colleges and more likely to attend graduate or professional school than graduates of coeducational high schools (Lee & Marks, 1990). Today there are about three dozen single-sex public schools in the country, almost all established after 1996. Another 72 coeducational schools offer single-sex classes in subjects like math and science (cited in Mendez, 2004). Some private schools now offer a combination of mixed-sex and single-sex education, with boys and girls learning together in elementary school and high school but being taught separately during the turbulent middle school years. As one prominent educator put it, "Girls who are 'confident at 11 and confused at 16' will more likely be creative thinkers and risk-takers as adults if educated apart from boys in middle school" (quoted in Gross, 2004b, p. A16).

Programs like these are hopeful signs. Trends in college enrollments and innovation in educational policy give us reason to believe that in the future sex and gender might become less significant factors in determining people's educational tracks.

Gender Inequality in the Economy

Because of their difficulty converting educational achievements into high pay, women have historically been prevented from taking advantage of the occupational opportunities and rewards to which most men have had relatively free access. Today, women continue to have much less earning power in the labor market than men (P.N. Cohen & Huffman, 2003). Consequently, although the size of the gap varies, women have higher rates of poverty than men in most countries around the world (Casper, McLanahan, & Garfinkel, 1994).

The unequal economic status of women not only results from the personal sexism of potential employers but is tied to larger economic structures and institutional forces. The standard assumptions that drive the typical workplace often work against women. Think of the things one generally has to do to be considered a good worker by a boss: work extra hours, travel to faraway business meetings, go to conferences, attend training programs, be willing to work unpopular shifts, or entertain out-of-town clients. These activities assume employees have the time and the freedom from familial obligations to do them. Because women, especially mothers, still tend to have the lion's share of responsibility at home, they are less able than their male colleagues to "prove" to management that they are good, committed employees. Even if women are able to commit extra time to work, employers frequently assume that, because they are women, they won't.

Consider the different reactions employers commonly have toward their male and female employees getting married. For a man, marriage is likely to be seen as a "stabilizing" influence. From the point of view of management, "settling down" will make him a better, more dependable worker. But for women, marriage is still likely to be seen as disruptive to their careers. The employer may jump to the conclusion that a newly married woman will soon be seeking maternity leave or quitting altogether. Rather than making her a more dependable worker, marriage actually may make her less dependable in the eyes of her employer. Beliefs like these can subtly influence hiring and promotion decisions even in those employers who advocate gender equality (Reskin & Hartmann, 1986).

Segregation in the Workplace

U.S. women have made remarkable progress in overcoming traditional obstacles to employment. In 1950 a little over 30% of adult women were employed in the paid labor force; today, that figure is around 60%, and it increases to 69.2% for married mothers and 73.1% for single mothers (U.S. Bureau of the Census, 2004a). Close to half of all U.S. workers today are female.

The increase in female labor force participation has been particularly dramatic in such traditionally male-dominated fields as engineering, medicine, law, and administration. For instance, in 1983 15% of lawyers and 16% of physicians in the United States were women; by 2003 those figures had nearly doubled (U.S. Bureau of the Census, 2004a). Exhibit 12.2 shows the increase in the percentages of U.S. women holding positions in a variety of professional occupations.

Although such figures are encouraging, segregation in the workplace on the basis of sex is still the rule. According to the U.S. Bureau of Labor Statistics (2005b), women constitute 96.9% of all secretaries, 92.2% of all registered nurses, 94.5% of all child care workers, 98.8% of all dental hygienists, and 98.1% of all preschool and kindergarten teachers. Despite their increased presence in traditionally male occupations, women are still underrepresented among dentists (22%), physicians (29.4%), engineers and architects (13.8%), lawyers (29.4%), police officers (13.3%), and firefighters (5.1%).

Most of the changes that have taken place in the sex distribution of different occupations have been the result of women entering male lines of work. Although women have entered traditionally male occupations at a steady clip since the 1970s, men have not noticeably increased their representation in female-dominated occupations. The number of male nurses, kindergarten teachers, librarians, and secretaries has increased only minimally, if at all (U.S. Bureau of the Census, 2004a). One study found that some men would rather suffer unemployment than accept "women's jobs," even high-paying ones, because of the potential damage to their sense of masculinity (Epstein, 1989).

This kind of "one-way" occupational shift may cause problems in the long run. Historically, when large numbers of women enter a particular occupation previously closed to them, the number of men in that occupation decreases. Given the fact that greater value is usually awarded to male pursuits, such occupations become less prestigious as men leave them. In fact, the higher the proportion of female workers in an

Exhibit 12.2   U.S. Women in Managerial and Professional Jobs

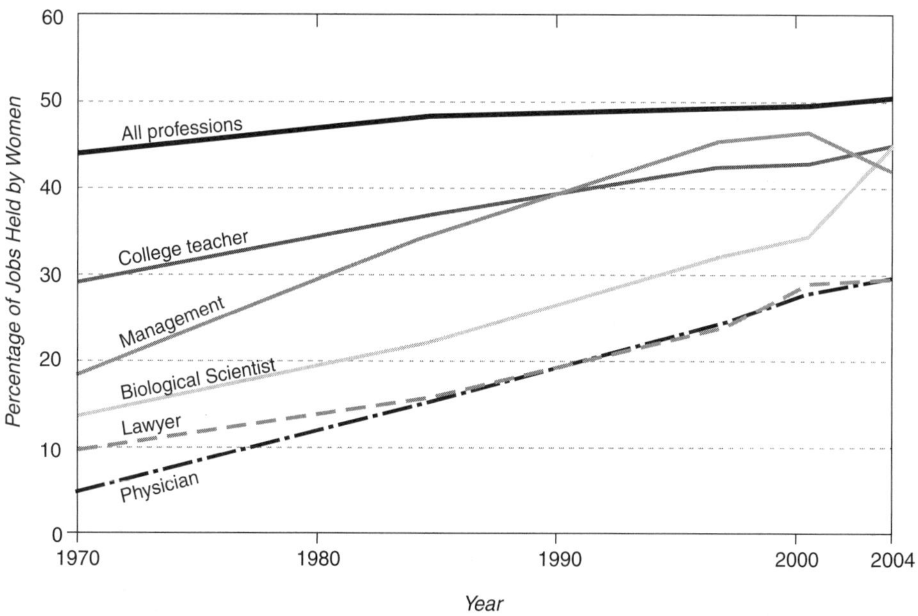

Sources: U.S. Bureau of Labor Statistics, 2005b; U.S. Bureau of the Census, 2002.

occupation, the less both male and female workers earn in that occupation (Padavic & Reskin, 2002).

Greater female entry into traditionally male lines of work doesn't necessarily mean gender equality either. A report by the American Bar Association states that the average annual income of female lawyers is significantly lower than that of male lawyers at every level of experience and in all types of legal practice (cited in N. Bernstein, 1996). Female lawyers are often given low-status projects to work on, which are not only less interesting but also a professional dead end. Hence they are promoted at a lower rate than their male counterparts, and they remain underrepresented in private practice, law firm partnerships, and in such high positions as judges on the federal courts, district courts, and circuit courts of appeals. Furthermore, women are more likely than men to enter the legal profession in relatively low-paying positions in the government or in public interest firms, hampering the trajectory of their careers. Their odds of landing a position as a law firm partner in private practice are less than one third of men's odds (Hull & Nelson, 2000).

In addition, sex segregation in jobs within occupations is still strong. For instance, in the field of medicine female physicians are substantially overrepresented in such specialties as family practice, pediatrics, and obstetrics and gynecology and underrepresented in more prestigious and lucrative areas such as neurosurgery. Sixty- eight percent of pediatric residents and 74% of obstetrics/gynecology residents today are women (Women Physicians Congress, 2004). Similarly, women who work as salesclerks in department stores are likely to be in the lower-paying departments (for example, clothing and housewares), whereas men are likely to be in the more lucrative departments (for example, furniture and large appliances). In 1997, Home Depot, the home improvement discount chain, paid $87.5 million to settle a lawsuit brought by female employees who claimed they were systematically relegated to cash register jobs rather than given higher-paying sales positions.

Such within-occupation segregation reinforces gender stereotypes. A study of jobs in a McDonald's restaurant found that despite roughly the same number of male and female workers, most of the women worked at the counter or the drive-up window and most of the men worked at the grill. Many of the workers found this arrangement unremarkable. They simply assumed that women were more interested in working with people and that the job requirements of smiling and showing deference to customers were best suited to a feminine style of interaction (Leidner, 1991).

In sum, although more women than ever work in the paid labor force, we continue to have some jobs that employ almost exclusively women and others that employ almost exclusively men. When people are allocated jobs on the basis of sex rather than ability to perform the work, chances for self-fulfillment are limited (Reskin & Hartmann, 1986). Society also loses, because neither men nor women are free to do the jobs for which they might best be suited. However, segregation is most harmful to individual women, because the occupations they predominantly hold tend to be less prestigious and to pay lower wages than those held predominantly by men.

The Wage Gap

> The Lord spoke to Moses and said, "When a man makes a special vow to the Lord which requires your valuation of living persons, a male between twenty and sixty years old shall be valued at fifty silver shekels. If it is a female, she shall be valued at thirty shekels." (Leviticus 27:1–4)

You don't have to go back to biblical times to find evidence of the practice of setting women's pay at about three fifths that of men's. Even though the 1963 Equal Pay Act guaranteed equal pay for equal work in the United States, and Title VII of the 1964 Civil Rights Act banned job discrimination on the basis of sex (as well as race, religion, and national origin), a sex-based gap in earnings persists. According to the U.S. Bureau of the Census (2004a), the median annual earnings for all U.S. men working full-time, year-round is $39,429. All women working full-time, year-round, earn an average $30,203 per year. To put it another way, for every dollar a full-time working man earns, a woman earns only about 76 cents. The differences are even more pronounced for African American women, who earn 67 cents for every dollar a man earns, and Latina women, who earn just 54 cents.

I should point out that the wage gap is a global phenomenon. To varying degrees, in every country around the world, men earn more than women. In the developing countries of Latin America, Africa, and Asia, women commonly earn 25% or less of what men earn (Tiano, 1987). In some countries, however, such as Australia, New Zealand, the United Kingdom, Sweden, Denmark, and France the wage gap is actually narrower than it is in the United States, with women earning 80% to 90% of what men earn (Lips, 2002).

Multinational corporations frequently export a wage gap abroad by paying female factory workers in developing countries as little as half of what they pay men. In many countries, more than three quarters of unskilled assembly workers are women. This preference for women is sometimes attributed to their supposedly high tolerance for monotonous work, inherent dexterity well suited to tasks involving tiny parts, and docile nature that allows them to withstand the pressure of closely supervised production (Tiano, 1987).

There have been efforts to narrow the wage gap. In 2004, a federal judge ruled that a class action, sex-discrimination lawsuit against Wal-Mart, the nation's largest employer, could proceed because of evidence that it had systematically paid female workers less than male workers and had given them fewer promotions. The suit could eventually include as many as 1.6 million current and former female employees. The pay disparities at Wal-Mart had become institutionalized, existing in every region of the country and in most job categories. And the salary gap widens over the span of workers' careers, even for men and women hired at the same time in the same job (Joyce, 2004). For instance, a female assistant manager in one California store made $23,000 a year less than a male assistant manager with the same seniority. Although 65% of all Wal-Mart employees are women, only 33% of managers are women (S. Greenhouse & Hays, 2004). The outcome of such a high-profile case could prompt many other companies to pursue greater equity for male and female employees.

But for now, the wage gap continues to exist. Why? One reason, of course, is occupational segregation and the types of jobs women are most likely to have. One study of workers in major U.S. metropolitan areas found that women in female-dominated jobs earn the lowest wages (less than $6.95 per hour) while men in male-dominated jobs earn the highest wages ($11.60 per hour) (P.N. Cohen & Huffman, 2003). For five of the "most female" jobs in the United States (that is, those more than 95% female)—which are preschool teacher, secretary, child care worker, dental assistant, and private house cleaner and/or servant—the average weekly salary is $407. For the five "most male" jobs (those more than 95% male)—which are airplane pilot, firefighter, aircraft engine mechanic, construction worker, and miner—the average weekly salary is $886 (U.S. Department of Labor, 2003).

Some economists and policymakers argue that the wage gap is essentially an institutional by-product that exists because men on the whole have more work experience and training, work more hours per year, and are more likely to work a full-time schedule than women (U.S. General Accounting Office, 2003). Twenty-eight percent of employed women work part time, compared to only 13% of employed men (U.S. Bureau of Labor Statistics, 2004c). Not only do part-time workers earn less, but during hard times, they are usually the first ones pushed out of employment—not because they're women but because their jobs are the most expendable.

However, gender differences in education, labor force experience, and seniority—factors that might justify discrepancies in salary—account for less than 15% of the wage gap between men and women (National Committee on Pay Equity, 1999). For instance, the average income of female workers in the United States is significantly lower than that of men with the same level of education or training. In fact, women with a bachelor's degree can expect to earn only slightly more than men with only a high school diploma (with median annual earnings of $32,394 for college-educated women compared to $28,827 for high school–educated men). Similarly, women with doctoral degrees (with mean annual earnings of $56,186) don't earn substantially more than men with only bachelor's degrees (with mean annual earnings of $50,527) (U.S. Bureau of the Census, 2005b). These statistics are depicted in Exhibit 12.3.

One possible remedy for the wage gap is increasing women's access to occupations that have traditionally been closed to them. As I noted earlier, this is already happening, to a certain degree, although sex segregation is still the rule.

A second solution is symbolized by the commonly heard phrase "equal pay for equal work." This approach seeks to overcome situations in which men and women in the same job, with the same seniority, performing the same work equally well, are paid differently. Such gaps would seem easy enough to spot and address. However, they still persist. For instance, female servers in restaurants make about $50 a week less than

Exhibit 12.3   The Gap Between Women's and Men's Pay

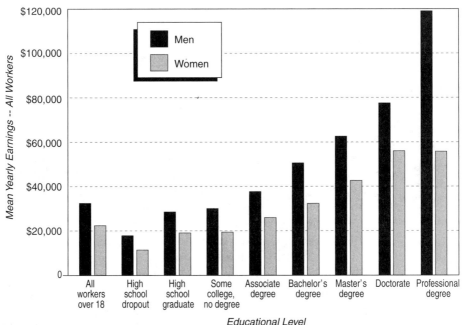

Source: U.S. Bureau of the Census, 2005b.

male servers; female secretaries make about $100 less per week than male secretaries (National Committee on Pay Equity, 1999). The median weekly income for male lawyers is $1,619, but female lawyers with the same seniority earn only $1,413 a week. Likewise, female physicians and surgeons make, on average, $688 a week less than male physicians and surgeons (U.S. Department of Labor, 2003).

A third, more controversial, approach is **comparable worth,** or **pay equity.** The principle behind this remedy is that the pay for particular jobs shouldn't be less simply because those jobs happen to be filled predominantly by women. Unlike "equal pay for equal work," comparable worth advocates claim that *different* jobs that are of equal value to society and require equal levels of training ought to have equal pay. This principle rejects the premise that women's work is inherently worth less than men's. The ultimate goal is to raise the wages of underpaid, female-dominated occupations (England, 1999). Various states have established job evaluation formulas to determine the comparability of certain occupations and whether wage disparities are discriminating against women. But political opposition to comparable worth policies has seriously weakened such initiatives on the national level, and it remains a strategy with mixed results.

The Global Devaluation of Women

At first glance, women may seem to be making tremendous advances worldwide—becoming better educated, more economically independent, and more involved in national politics than ever before. Over the past several decades, women in most regions of the world have increased their representation in most sectors of the paid labor force.

Nevertheless, anthropologists agree that women remain economically and physically disadvantaged in most societies around the world (Stockard & Johnson, 1992). Sociological research supports that view. In most countries, girls are less likely than boys to be enrolled in school (Dervarics, 2004c). Consequently, women have a higher rate of illiteracy worldwide than men (Population Reference Bureau, 2005a), leading to almost certain economic disadvantage later on. Women represent 70% of the 1.3 billion people living in poverty worldwide, even though they work an average of 13% more hours than men in every country, not to mention their unpaid labor in the home ("Vital Signs," 1995). In Africa, women make up close to 60% of all HIV-infected adults (Population Reference Bureau, 2005a). About 529,000 women around the world die each year in pregnancy and childbirth, an astounding 527,000 (or 99.6%) of them living in poor, less developed countries. The chances of a woman in a developed country dying from maternal causes is 1 in 2,800; for a woman in a less developed country it's 1 in 61 (Ashford, 2005). Women make up the vast majority of global factory workers in multinational corporations, often working under unsafe and unhealthy conditions at extremely low pay. And violence against women and girls—from sexual abuse and wife battering in the United States to wife burning in India and "honor killings" of rape victims in Turkey, Kenya, and Iraq—remains a global epidemic.

In many countries, women lack the same legal, familial, and physical protections that men enjoy:

◆ The Iranian constitution states that the value of a woman's life and her testimony in court is half that of a man's. An Iranian woman cannot travel anywhere without her husband's permission (I. Watson, 2005).

◆ In Kenya, when a woman's husband dies she loses her land, her livestock, and all household property. In addition, widows are transferred to a male relative of her deceased husband, who takes control of the property (Lacey, 2003). Land laws in many other places dictate that a family's property can be passed down only through males. On her marriage, a daughter's inheritance automatically goes to her husband (Owen, 1996).

◆ In Kyrgyzstan, it's estimated that more than half of all married women were abducted by their soon-to-be husbands in a centuries-old legal custom known as *ala kachuu* (which literally means "grab and run"). If the woman is kept in the man's home overnight, her virginity becomes suspect, her name disgraced, and her future marriage chances destroyed. So most women (about 80% according to estimates) eventually relent and marry their abductor, often with the urging of their own families (C.S. Smith, 2005).

◆ In Sri Lanka, an estimated 600,000 women are forced by economic need to abandon their own families and migrate to affluent Persian Gulf countries, where they work as maids for wealthy families. Saudi Arabians refer to Sri Lanka as "the country of housemaids" (Waldman, 2005). These women are considered heroines at home because of their economic contributions to their families, but they are often subjected to severe beatings and mistreatment at the hands of their foreign employers.

◆ In the southern African country of Lesotho, men make all sexual decisions, including the use of contraceptives. One out of every two women in Lesotho is HIV-positive. Nevertheless, poverty can force a woman to engage in what is sometimes called "transactional sex," risky secret relationships with four or five men who help her out financially in exchange for sex (Wines, 2004).

The cultural devaluation of women worldwide takes even more violent forms in a number of other societies:

◆ In Bangladesh, some men—usually spurned suitors—throw acid on the faces of women. Those who survive the attacks are typically left hideously deformed. One woman was forced by her parents to marry her attacker because they felt no one else would want to marry her. Most attackers are never arrested, and most who are arrested are never tried (Bearak, 2000).

◆ In India, about 7,000 wives—an average of 19 a day—were killed by their husbands in 1998 for not providing adequate dowries ("Bridal Dowry in India," 2000). Even though dowry (gifts that a woman receives from her parents upon marriage) was officially banned in 1961, it is still an essential part of premarital negotiations and now encompasses the wealth that the bride's family pays the groom. Young brides, who by custom live with their new husbands' parents, are commonly subjected to severe abuse if promised money is not paid. Sometimes dowry harassment ends in suicide or murder.

♦ In many Arab countries, women accused of sexual misconduct are often jailed, not to punish them but to protect them from being killed by their own families who seek to cleanse the family's honor (Jehl, 1999). In Pakistan, women are sometimes killed for marrying against their father's wishes.

The public devaluation of women can sometimes hide a very different private reality. For instance, Japanese women have historically occupied a visibly subservient position in society and in families. Wives are still legally prohibited from using different surnames than their husbands. Women in the workforce suffer discrimination in hiring, salary, and promotion despite equal opportunity laws there. Only 40% of women currently work outside the home, even though many economists argue that their inclusion could help boost an economy that has been slumping for over a decade (French, 2003). They are expected to clean, cook, and tend to the needs of their husbands within the home.

Yet many Japanese wives dominate their husbands completely. Typically, they control the household finances, giving their husbands monthly allowances as they see fit. If a man wants to withdraw money from the family account, the savings bank will usually phone the wife to get her approval. Japanese men are even starting to take on some of the housework responsibilities, which would have been unthinkable a couple of decades ago.

To some extent, the improvement of women's lives in some parts of the world can be attributed to the forces of globalization, which are spreading democratic values and humanitarian principles (Giddens, 2005). However, the globalization of the world economy also helps create a market for the international exploitation of women. In many poor countries, one of the fastest-growing criminal enterprises is forcing naïve and desperately poor women to work as prostitutes in other countries. In many of these receiving countries, prostitution is not illegal; in others it may be illegal, but enforcement is inconsistent and punishment light. Without any other means of support and often without knowledge of the native language, these women become completely dependent on men who are perfectly willing to exploit them.

A more positive example of the effects of globalization on women's lives is the international movement for women's rights. In India, for instance, although rural, lower-caste women still occupy the bottom rungs of the social ladder, approximately one million of them have been elected in recent years to the 500,000 or so *panchayat,* or village councils, that were established in 1993 to help rural villages deal with local political issues (Dugger, 1999b). In the past few years, several countries (for example, Egypt) have outlawed the traditional practice of female genital mutilation. Ironically, the United States is the only developed country in the world that has not ratified the U.N. Convention on the Elimination of All Forms of Discrimination Against Women, despite its advocacy of human rights worldwide. Opponents in the United States feel that such a treaty would set a dangerous precedent by overruling local, state, and federal law.

Conclusion

Inequality based on sex and gender goes beyond the degrading media and cultural images of women, the face-to-face interactions that reinforce the devaluation of women, and the stereotypical beliefs of individual people. It is woven into the institutional and cultural fabric of societies around the world. In the United States, it is as much a part of the social landscape as baseball, apple pie, and Fourth of July fireworks. Every woman has felt sexism at some level, whether as personal violence, annoying harassment, sexually suggestive leers and comments, fear of going out at night, job discrimination, legal obstacles, or subtle encouragement toward "appropriate" sports, hobbies, and careers.

Men tend to benefit from living in a society where language, identity, intimacy, history, culture, and social institutions are built on gender distinctions, even if the men themselves do not support such inequality. Like most people whose interests are being served by the system, men are largely unaware of the small and large advantages the social structure provides them (W. J. Goode, 1981). Thus most men don't see sex and gender inequality as their problem—it's a "women's issue"—and they are less likely than women to see a need for large-scale social change.

So the first step toward gender equality is that men will have to come to understand their role in the process, even in the absence of blatant, personal sexism. All men are tacitly involved in the oppression of women each time they automatically giggle at sexist jokes, mistake female doctors for nurses, see women in purely physical terms, expect less from women on the job or in school, or expect more of them at home.

The next step will require a fundamental transformation of institutional patterns and cultural values. Such a solution sounds too massive to be possible. But today we are seeing early steps in that direction: changing conceptions of family roles, women's increasing (though not yet equal) labor force participation, their growing (but not yet equal) political power, and greater awareness of sexual exploitation and violence worldwide. How far these changes will take us in the future remains to be seen.

❖

YOUR TURN

To understand how beliefs are translated into action, examine how sexism influences people's activities. One fruitful area of examination is the home. Locate a few of each of the following types of couples in which both partners work full time outside the home:

- ◆ Newly married without children (married less than 1 year)
- ◆ Married without children (married 10 years or more)
- ◆ Married (older or younger) with at least one child living at home
- ◆ Cohabiting (heterosexual or homosexual)
- ◆ Remarried

Ask each person in the couple to make a list of all the household chores that need to be done during the course of a week. Ask each to be as specific and exhaustive as possible (for example, "cleaning windows" rather than "cleaning the house"). After the lists are completed, ask each person to indicate which of these tasks he or she is primarily responsible for, which his or her partner is responsible for, and which are shared. Ask the participants also to estimate the total amount of time spent each week on all these tasks combined. Finally, ask them if they work for pay as well and, if so, about how many hours they work during a typical week. (*Note:* To ensure that you're gauging each individual's perceptions, interview each partner separately.)

Compare people's responses to see if you can find any differences—in terms of time spent doing housework and the number of tasks for which each one is responsible—between

- Partners in the same couple
- Men and women
- Younger and older couples
- Married and cohabiting couples
- Couples with and without children at home
- Married and remarried couples
- Heterosexual and homosexual couples

Do women who work outside the home still bear the primary responsibility for housework? Is the traditional gender division of labor absent in certain types of couples? How does the presence of children affect the household division of labor? If partners in the same couple have different ideas about housework responsibilities, to what do you attribute this lack of agreement? Describe the tensions that men and women experience when trying to balance work and home responsibilities.

CHAPTER HIGHLIGHTS

- Personal sexism is most apparent during the course of everyday interaction in the form of communication patterns and gestures. It can be particularly dangerous when expressed in the form of sexual harassment and sexual violence.

- Gender stratification is perpetuated by a dominant cultural ideology that devalues women on the basis of inherent biological differences between men and women. This ideology overlooks the equally important role of social forces in determining male and female behavior.

- Institutional sexism exists in the media, in the law, in the family, in the educational system, and in the economy. Women have entered the paid labor force in unprecedented numbers but they still tend to occupy jobs that are typically considered "female" and still earn significantly less than men.

- Not only are social institutions sexist in that women are systematically segregated, exploited, and excluded, they are also "gendered." Institutions themselves are structured along gender lines so that traits associated with success are usually stereotypically male characteristics: tough-mindedness, rationality, assertiveness, competitiveness, and so forth.

- Despite recent advances worldwide, women still tend to suffer physically, psychologically, economically, and politically in most societies.

KEY TERMS

comparable worth (pay equity) Principle that women and men who perform jobs that are of equal value to society and that require equal training ought to be paid equally

institutional sexism Subordination of women that is part of the everyday workings of economics, law, politics, and other social institutions

matriarchy Female-dominated society that gives higher prestige and value to women than to men

objectification Practice of treating people as objects

patriarchy Male-dominated society in which cultural beliefs and values give higher prestige and value to men than to women

sexism System of beliefs that asserts the inferiority of one sex and that justifies gender-based inequality

STUDY SITE ON THE WEB

Don't forget the interactive quizzes and other learning aids at www.pineforge.com/newman 6study. In the Resource Files for this chapter, you will also find more on sex and gender inequality, including:

Sociologists at Work

♦ Richard Levinson: Uncovering Sex Discrimination in Jobs

♦ Margaret Mead: Sex and Temperament

Micro-Macro Connection

♦ Tokenism in the Workplace

13

The Global Dynamics of Population

Demographic Trends

I admit it. I said those seven words people over 40 have been saying for centuries. The ones I once vowed I'd never say. The ones that, when uttered, permanently tag you as an over-the-hill relic: "*I just don't understand you kids today!*"

It all started several years ago when I was arguing with my two sons—one 16 at the time, the other 13—over what to watch on television. They wanted to watch the X Games on ESPN; I wanted to watch a rerun of the sixth game of the 1975 World Series on ESPN Classic. I told them that my choice was a priceless piece of U.S. sports history, the best World Series game ever played, according to most experts. Besides, I didn't understand the allure of the X Games. I know it's an annual alternative sports festival that began in the 1990s as a sort of anti-Olympics novelty based on obscure recreational sports such as skateboarding, in-line skating, stunt biking, snowboarding, and so on. But I don't care to know the difference between an "acid drop" and a "backside disaster." To me, "grinding" is what you do with coffee beans in the morning; a "McTwist" is a pastry you'd buy after eating a Big Mac, and "getting clean air" means moving out of Los Angeles.

They told me that I was a dinosaur and that I had better wake up and smell the 21st century if I knew what was good for me. The X Games, they claimed, was the future. And you know, they turned out to be right. "Extreme" sports, as they have come to be called, are part of a broader youth subculture with its own hard-edged language, fashion, and music. Even Hollywood films (*Blue Crush, The Fast and the Furious, XXX, Supercross, Lords of Dogtown,* and *Into the Blue,* to name a few), now cater to the "extreme" interests and tastes of many of the 70 or so million young people born between the late 1970s and the early 1990s. In fact, the word "extreme" has become a modifying adjective for any activity that pushes beyond what's commonly accepted: extreme camping, extreme bartending, extreme paintball, extreme pumpkin carving, extreme science, extreme chess, even extreme childbirth. Microsoft's online encyclopedia, *Encarta,* now has an entry for "extreme sports."

The X Games itself has grown from a quirky cable TV event into an international extravaganza, drawing hundreds of athletes from all over the world who compete in dozens of events. The spectacle—often set to a pounding rock 'n' roll soundtrack—is now broadcast to more than 200 countries, on several television networks, including

ESPN, ESPN2, and ABC. In addition to the original X Games—both summer and winter versions—there are now Asian X Games, European X Games, Latin American X Games, and the X Games Global Championship (Clarey, 2002). Other networks air spinoffs of the X Games such as the Gravity Games and the Gorge Games. There are now X Games summer camps, countless extreme sports Web sites, and even a cable network—the Extreme Sports Channel—devoted entirely to these pursuits. Halfpipe skiing is already a regular Olympic sport, and snowboard cross—a race with four snowboarders on the course at the same time—will make its debut at the 2006 Winter Olympics (B. Weber, 2005).

Extreme sports are self-consciously thrilling, dangerous, subversive, and rebellious. At a time when the trend in society is to eliminate risk (for instance, many communities have removed swings and monkey bars from playgrounds to avoid liability in the event of an injury), the appeal of extreme sports lies not so much in grace, strategy, or face-to-face competition as in the chance of disaster striking. Extreme athletes have tired of a bland and sometimes timid environment where individual expression is suppressed. As one early X Games slogan used to say, "If you're not living on the edge, you're taking up too much room."

For the most part, extreme athletes bear little resemblance to athletes in more traditional sports. They tend to despise rules, regulations, and standard conceptions of the competitive spirit. Indeed, many extreme sports don't have objective measures of success—like finishing first in a race—but are instead judged on their degree of risk and danger. The athletes take pride in their antiteam, individualistic attitude. They compete not only to win but to have fun. "We hate the jock mentality," said one early X Games participant. "And I think there are lots of kids who can relate more to snowboarders, surfers, and skaters than to some of the millionaire big-sport types" (quoted in Black, 1996, p. 56). A recent survey found that more teens and preteens prefer watching extreme sports on television than watching college basketball, college football, auto racing, hockey, tennis, or golf. Indeed, more Americans today skateboard than play baseball (Bennett, Henson, & Zhang, 2003). Tens of millions of people now regularly participate in such other extreme sports as inline skating, wall climbing, mountain biking, and wakeboarding ("Extreme Facts," 2005).

However, many of today's top extreme athletes have become more mainstream, training year-round, competing on professional circuits, and profiting from the financial support of corporate sponsors. One of the original pioneers of extreme sports, the skateboarder Tony Hawk, is now a multimillionaire with numerous commercial endorsements and his own line of clothing and video games.

Ironically, although extreme sports appear solidly antiestablishment, they have clearly become a marketing gold mine, generating $8 to $10 billion a year (Longman & Higgins, 2005). Such corporate giants as Verizon, Nokia, T Mobile, Walt Disney Company, Ford Motor Company, Pepsi/Mountain Dew, Activision, Coors Brewing Company, and Warner Brothers all prominently display their logos at X Games events or saturate TV commercial breaks with their advertisements. Corporate America has been scrambling to co-opt the language, image, and culture of extreme athletes in order to tap into a market that is booming. The popularity of snowboarding, for example, has entirely reshaped the ski equipment and ski resort industries (B. Weber, 2005).

What my sons didn't realize (they were too busy laughing at my middle-aged ignorance) was that they had identified one of the most crucial dividing lines in society today. They and I may be members of the same family. We may share the same genes, ethnicity, religion, social class, and political views. But we're also members of two extremely different, sometimes antagonistic, social groups that are distinguished by one simple and unchangeable fact: our ages. We are members of different **birth cohorts**—sets of people who were born during the same time period and who must face similar societal circumstances brought about by their position in the age structure of the population.

In the past several chapters, I examined various interconnected sources of social stratification: class, race and ethnicity, and gender. You have seen that the distance between the haves and the have-nots—both locally and globally—continues to grow wider as a result of their different levels of access to important cultural, economic, and political resources. But within the United States, as well as most other societies, imbalances between various age groups will also be a defining feature of social life in the decades to come. This chapter examines the relationship between broad population trends—which include not only changing age structure but also population growth and migration—and everyday life. How are these changes affecting the ability to provide people with the resources they need for a comfortable life? How are important social institutions functioning as a result of these population shifts?

The Influence of Birth Cohorts

If you're like most college students, you've no doubt asked yourself questions like, What career will I pursue after I graduate? Where will I live? Will I be able to afford a house? Will I have a spouse or lifetime partner? Will I ever be a parent? The answers to these questions are obviously influenced by your personal desires, traits, values, ambitions, and abilities. And as you've already read in this book so far, your social class, gender, race, religion, and ethnicity will shape the answers too. But they will also be influenced by your birth cohort, your place in the population at a given point in time.

Birth cohorts influence the everyday lives of individuals in two fundamental ways (Riley, 1971):

♦ People born at roughly the same time tend to experience life course events or social rites of passage—such as puberty, marriage, childbearing, graduation, entrance into the workforce, and death—at roughly the same time. Sociologists call these experiences **cohort effects**. The size of your birth cohort, relative to other cohorts, can have a significant impact on your life experiences. It can determine the availability of affordable houses, high-paying jobs, attractive potential mates, and so on. It can also affect how satisfied you feel with your own life. One study found that large cohorts in developed countries tend to have higher rates of suicide than small cohorts because people face more economic disadvantage and have more difficulty integrating into their communities when there are large numbers of people in the same age range competing for limited resources (Stockard & O'Brien, 2002).

♦ Members of the same birth cohort also share a common history. A cohort's place in time tells us a lot about the opportunities and constraints placed on its members. Historical events (wars, epidemics, natural disasters, economic depressions, and so on) and major social trends, called **period effects**, contribute to the unique shape and outlook of each birth cohort. Many historians, for instance, believe that a period of drought and famine caused the people of the Mayan civilization to abandon their great cities nearly a thousand years ago. Those who were young when this period began enjoyed comfortable lives, reveled in the high culture of the Mayans, and had tremendous prospects for the future. But for their children, born just a generation later, starvation, death, and social dislocation were basic facts of life (Clausen, 1986).

Cohort and period effects combine to profoundly influence the lives of individuals and give each birth cohort its distinctive properties, such as ethnic composition, average life expectancies, and age-specific birth rates. For instance, the birth cohort that experienced the Great Depression during its peak childbearing years had the lowest birth rate of any cohort in the 20th century. Therefore, people born between 1900 and 1910 tended as a group to have smaller families to rely on in their old age, which for them occurred roughly between 1970 and 1990. These experiences contrast sharply with those of people born a mere 10 years later, who were too young to have children during the Great Depression but entered adulthood during the prosperous years after World War II. They tended to have large families (Soldo & Agree, 1988).

Cohort and period effects also influence your worldview and self-concept. Think how different your goals and ambitions would be had you experienced childhood during a time of economic uncertainty as opposed to a period of relative affluence, such as the late 1990s. Rights and privileges considered unattainable dreams by one cohort are likely to be taken for granted by a different one. Similarly, the differences in attitudes and values between people who became adults during the Vietnam War and people who have become adults during the current war in Iraq are a function not only of simple age differences but also of differences in prevailing social and historical conditions. Imagine how different your perceptions of the world and your ideas about solving international conflicts would be if your most vivid teenage memory was one of angry crowds jeering soldiers going off to fight an unpopular war, as opposed to an image of supportive crowds with magnetic ribbons on the backs of their cars cheering soldiers going off to "fight terrorism."

As we grow older, we develop and change in a society that itself is developing and changing. We start our lives in one historical period with a distinct age pattern of behavior and set of social norms, and we end our lives in another. Early in the 20th century, for example, most people went to school for only six or seven years, which yielded an adequate education for the sorts of jobs their parents and older siblings held. Today, 85% of Americans go to school for at least 12 years (U.S. Bureau of the Census, 2004a). As a result, older cohorts on the whole tend to score substantially lower on standardized intelligence tests than do younger cohorts. Because of such test results, social scientists long assumed that intelligence declines markedly with age. But we now know that these differences are the result not of aging but of changing societal values regarding education (Clausen, 1986).

Even the way people personally experience the aging process is affected by the character of their birth cohort and by the social, cultural, and environmental changes to which their cohort is exposed in moving through the life course. Because of advances in nutrition, education, sanitation, medical treatment, working conditions, transportation safety, and environmental quality, people are living longer. As a result, cohorts experience the physical consequences of development in different ways (Riley, Foner, & Waring, 1988). For instance, the average age of menarche (a girl's first menstrual period) in the U.S. has dropped from about 14 a century ago to under 13 today (Chumlea et al., 2003; Darton, 1991). Combined with changing social norms, values, and cultural beliefs, such a change inevitably speeds up the point at which young women become sexually curious and explorative, putting pressure on relevant social institutions—like education, religion, and family—to catch up.

As you can see, birth cohorts are more than just a collection of individuals born within a few years of each other; they are distinctive generations tied together by historical circumstances, population trends, and societal changes. However, we must also realize that when many individuals in the same cohort are affected by social events in similar ways, the changes in their collective lives can produce changes in society. Each succeeding cohort leaves its mark on the prevailing culture. Each helps create and is shaped by its own *zeitgeist*—the intellectual, moral, and cultural spirit of the time (Mannheim, 1952). In other words, cohorts are not only affected by social changes but contribute to them as well (Riley et al., 1988).

Baby Boomers

The birth cohort that has received the most national attention is, without a doubt, the Baby Boom generation, those 80 million or so people born between 1946 and 1964. They now make up about 30% of the entire U.S. population (U.S. Bureau of the Census, 2004a). Preceded and followed by much smaller cohorts, they stand in sharp political, economic, and cultural contrast to those around them:

> They grew up as the first standardized generation, drawn together by the history around them, the intimacy of television, and the crowding that came from the sheer onslaught of other Baby Boomers. They shared the great economic expectations of the 1950's and the fears that came with *Sputnik* and the dawn of the nuclear era. They shared the hopes of John F. Kennedy's New Frontier and Lyndon Johnson's Great Society, and the disillusionment that came with the assassinations [of John Kennedy, Robert Kennedy, and Martin Luther King], Viet Nam, Watergate, and the resignation [of President Richard Nixon]. (Light, 1988, p. 10)

The passing of this massive cohort through the life course has been described metaphorically as "a pig in a python." If you've ever seen one of those nature shows on TV where snakes devour and digest small animals, you can see how apt the metaphor is. In 1980, the largest age group in the United States consisted of people between 15 and 24 years of age. In 1990, the largest group was 25- to 34-year-olds. In 2003, it was people between 40 and 44 (U.S. Bureau of the Census, 2004a). As this cohort bulge works its way through the life course, it stretches the parameters of the relevant social institutions at each stage. Baby Boomers packed hospital nurseries as infants; school classrooms as children; and college campuses, employment lines, and the housing market as young adults (Light, 1988). In middle age, they are prime movers in the burgeoning markets for adventure travel, diet, nutrition, and wellness products, relaxed-fit fashion, high-tech gadgets, financial services, and durable household goods such as furniture and appliances.

The trend will continue into the future. By the year 2030, there will be over 71 million Baby Boomers of retirement age, about twice the number of retirees today (U.S. Bureau of the Census, 2004a). As they reach their golden years, those programs concerned with later life—pension plans, Social Security, medical and personal care—will be seriously stressed. At the same time, though, they will represent a potentially lucrative market for many businesses. Several publishing companies, for instance, have begun issuing new paperbacks in bigger sizes with larger print so that aging Baby Boomers can read them (Wyatt, 2005). Similarly, the automobile industry has been looking for ways to make vehicles that suit the needs of older people, such as larger and lower doors, swiveling seats, and easy-to-use handles (Bradsher, 1999a). And sometime in the middle of the 21st century, there will no doubt be a huge surge in business for the funeral industry as this generation reaches the end of its collective life cycle (Schodolski, 1993).

People born during the Baby Boom have left a particularly influential mark on the institution of family. Their generation was the first to redefine families to include a variety of living arrangements, such as cohabitation, domestic partnerships, and never-married women with dependent children (Wattenberg, 1986). They were also the first to acknowledge the expectation of paid work as a central feature of women's lives. And they were the first to grow up with effective birth control, enabling delayed childbearing, voluntary childlessness, and low birth rates.

Consequently, as the Baby Boomers reach old age they will have fewer children to turn to for the kind of help they gave their own grandparents and parents (Butler, 1989). Thus Baby Boom elders will be more likely than previous generations were to turn to social service and health care organizations to care for them.

Generation X

Although Baby Boomers have dominated the cultural spotlight for decades, U.S. society has also taken notice of the next generation to follow them, known in the media as "Generation X." Today there are roughly 60 million U.S. residents who were born between 1965 and 1979 (U.S. Bureau of the Census, 2005b). The birth rate during the 1970s, when most of these individuals were born, was about half what it was during the post–World War II years of the Baby Boomers.

More Generation Xers—roughly 40% of them—experienced the divorce of their parents than any previous generation. As a result, they are emotionally conflicted about marriage. They are less likely to get married than older generations and more likely to delay marriage if they do. In addition, they're more likely to be single—with or without children—than previous generations (Sayer, Casper, & Cohen, 2004).

Even more Generation Xers were so-called latchkey children, the first generation of children to experience the effects of having two working parents while growing up.

For many of these children, childhood was marked by dependence on secondary relationships—teachers, friends, day care.

Many members of this cohort are angry that they have inherited a variety of gargantuan crises, from the national debt and the looming Social Security crisis to the degradation of the natural environment and growing urban decay. Resentful of the wasteful excesses of their elders, they are experiencing unprecedented apprehension about their own futures and their own families.

The Millennium Generation

The 70 to 80 million individuals born between 1980 and the late 1990s make up the next noticeable generation, known variously as the Millennium Generation, Generation Y, or Echo Boomers. This generation rivals the Baby Boom in size but differs in almost every other way. For one thing, unlike the Baby Boomers, this cohort is not evenly distributed across the nation. Those states that have large minority and immigrant populations (for example, California, Florida, and Texas) account for a relatively high proportion of the Millennium Generation (Faust, Gann, & McKibben, 1999). Consequently, according to the 2000 census, this cohort is more ethnically diverse than previous generations. For instance, over 35% of this group are people of color, compared to 24% of Baby Boomers (Howe & Strauss, 2000). They are also more likely than preceding cohorts to grow up in a nontraditional family. One in four lives in a single-parent household; three in four have working mothers.

The Millennium Generation is the most media connected of any generation. According to a Kaiser Family Foundation report (Rideout, Roberts, & Foehr, 2005), children between the ages of 8 and 18 spend over eight hours a day with some kind of communication or entertainment medium: watching TV, listening to CDs or MP3 players, playing video games, interacting with friends on computers or cell phones. Sixty-eight percent have a television in their bedrooms, and two thirds have portable CD or MP3 players.

The Millennium Generation is the first to claim computers as a birthright. Two thirds use them on a regular basis. Whereas the Baby Boomers and even some Generation Xers struggle to understand the basics of Windows XP, these kids became computer literate in nursery school. The Internet has become a universal presence in their lives. Two thirds of children between 8 and 18 use instant messaging and download music from the Internet; half listen to the radio through the Internet; 38% have made Internet purchases; and about a third have created a personal Web site or Web page (Rideout et al., 2005). Although this preoccupation with computers may create a generation less socially adept than generations of the past, the exposure to other cultures that the Internet provides will make these individuals significantly more worldly than any generation in history. And as the Millennium Generation enters and exits college, it will come to the workforce with unprecedented technological savvy.

Having done much of their growing up in the affluent 1990s, many people in this generation have positive feelings about their futures, despite recent economic downturns. Two thirds of teenage respondents in one national survey indicated that they were very optimistic about their chances of having a good job, and many are confident that problems such as sexual harassment and economic discrimination against women are on their way out. But their optimism isn't just about personal interest. Asked to identify the most important concept that will guide their working lives, the most common response was "to help others who need help" (Mogelonsky, 1998). This sort of altruism, if maintained into adulthood, could significantly alter the business environment of the future.

Members of the Millennium Generation may also be more socially conservative than prior generations. For instance, a nationwide study found that close to 70% of young people today support so-called zero tolerance policies against drugs in high school (cited in Howe & Strauss, 2000). In 1972, 10% of 18- to 24-year-olds in a national survey said that premarital sex was "always wrong"; by 1998, the figure for that age group had more than doubled. Similarly, the proportion of high school students who have had sexual intercourse within the preceding three months decreased from 37.5% in 1991 to 34.3% in 2003 (Child Trends Databank, 2004). And teenage boys and girls are significantly more likely to be virgins today than they were 15 years ago (cited in Bernstein, 2004). Indeed, rates of pregnancy, abortion, and births for girls between 15 and 17 have all declined since 1990 (U.S. Bureau of the Census, 2004a). At the same time though, members of the Millennium Generation seem even less eager to get married when in their early 20s than either Generation Xers or the Baby Boomers (see Exhibit 13.1).

Exhibit 13.1 Marriage Delay Among Baby Boomers, Generation Xers, and the Millennium Generation

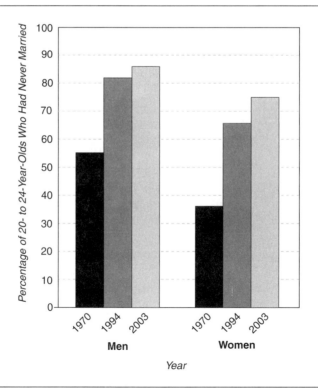

Sources: U.S. Bureau of the Census, 1995, 2004a.

As this cohort ages and begins to control important social institutions, these attitudes and behaviors will shape reality for other cohorts in U.S. society.

Demographic Dynamics

Many aspects of our personal lives are influenced by our birth cohort, but our lives are also affected by societywide and worldwide population trends. Sociologists who study fluctuations in population characteristics are called **demographers**. Demographers examine several important and interrelated population processes to explain current social problems or to predict future ones: birth or fertility rates (changes in the number of children people are having), death or mortality rates (changes in people's life expectancy), and patterns of migration (the movement of people from one society to another). These three processes influence a population's growth, overall age structure, and geographic distribution.

Population Growth

The most fundamental population characteristic is, of course, size. No other phenomenon has the ability to touch the lives of everyone on the planet as profoundly as the growth of the human population. Changes in population size are mostly a function of birth and death rates. As long as people are dying and being born at similar rates, the size of the population stabilizes (barring large changes caused by migration). But when birth rates increase and death rates decrease, the population grows.

It took hundreds of thousands of years, from the beginning of humanity to the early 19th century, for Earth's human population to reach 1 billion. However, it took only an additional hundred years to reach 2 billion. Then, 3 billion was reached 30 years later; 4 billion, 16 years later; and 5 billion, a little over 10 years after that. Today's population is over 6.4 billion and will likely reach about 9 billion by 2050 (United Nations, 2004; U.S. Bureau of the Census, 2004a). Exhibit 13.2 charts world population growth since 7000 B.C.E.

Undeniably, the global population is growing at unprecedented speed. However, people disagree about the consequences of that growth. In the past, large numbers of people were seen as a precious resource. The Bible urged humanity to be fruitful and multiply. One 18th-century British scholar, referring to the strategic importance of a large population, called a high birth rate "the never-failing nursery of Fleets and Armies" (quoted in Mann, 1993, p. 49).

Although few people today sing the praises of massive population growth, some argue that it isn't particularly troublesome. A larger population creates greater division of labor and a larger market to support highly specialized services. More people are available to contribute to the production of needed goods and services.

Others, however, haven't been so optimistic. When a particular population is excessively large, individuals are forced to compete for limited food, living space, jobs, and salaries. Thousands of years ago, philosophers in ancient China worried about the need to shift the masses to underpopulated areas. The ancient Greek philosopher Plato

Exhibit 13.2 World Population Growth Since 7000 B.C.E.

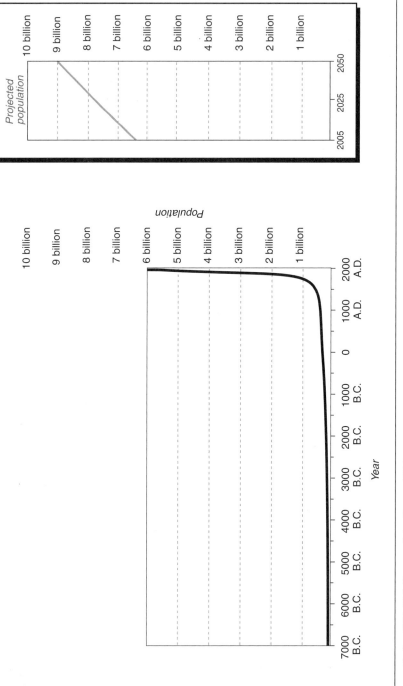

Sources: Farley, 1991; U.S. Bureau of the Census, 2004a.

said that cities with more than 5,040 landholders were too large (Mann, 1993). According to some contemporary demographers, population growth can compound, magnify, or even create a wide variety of social problems, such as pollution, housing shortages, high inflation, energy shortages, illiteracy, and the loss of individual freedom (Weeks, 1995). People's ability to achieve the standard of living they feel they are entitled to is hampered by the size of the population.

On a global scale, population growth could widen the gap between rich and poor nations; perpetuate social and economic inequality within nations; give rise to racial and ethnic separatism, and increase already high levels of world hunger and unemployment (Ehrlich & Ehrlich, 1993). Environmental threats are growing too: According to the World Wildlife Fund (2002), humanity's use of natural resources is now 20% higher than Earth's biologically productive capacity. Excessive population growth threatens to destroy the one-time bonanza of such environmental resources as fossil fuel, rich soil, and certain plant and animal species (Ehrlich & Ehrlich, 1993).

The problem, however, is not just that the overall population is growing rapidly but also that different countries are experiencing vastly different rates of growth. Populations in poor, developing countries are rapidly expanding, whereas those in wealthy, developed countries have either stabilized or are declining. The annual rate of growth of the world's population is approximately 1.22% (United Nations, 2004). But that figure masks dramatic regional differences that will exist for several decades to come (see Exhibit 13.3). Consider these facts:

♦ In Africa, the rate of natural population increase (that is, without taking migration into consideration) is about 2.3% each year; Europe, in contrast, sees a 0.1% *decline* in population each year. If current trends continue, by the middle of the 21st century, the population of Italy will be 11% smaller and Russia's population will be 23% smaller than they are today. In contrast, Mali's population will be 211% bigger and Niger's will be 259% bigger (Population Reference Bureau, 2005b).

♦ In 2000, all the countries of the European Union combined showed an increase of 343,000 people; India's population increased that much in the first week of 2001 (cited in Crossette, 2001).

♦ In 1950, half of the 10 most populous nations were in the industrialized world. By 2050, demographers predict that the United States will be the only developed country among the world's 10 most populous nations. The rest will be developing countries in Asia, Africa, and South America (Crossette, 2001; Population Reference Bureau, 2005b).

♦ Between 1995 and 2002, five countries accounted for close to half the world's population growth, all in the less developed areas of Asia and Africa: India, China, Pakistan, Bangladesh, and Nigeria. India and China alone accounted for 33% of the increase (United Nations Population Division, 2003).

♦ In 1950, over 28% of the world's population lived in North America and Europe. By 2050, about 12% will live in these regions. The rest of the world's population will reside in the developing countries of Africa, Asia, and Latin America (United Nations Population Division, 2005).

These imbalances will influence how people view one another; affect global and domestic policies; and determine the availability of food, energy, and adequate living space (Kennedy, 1993). When the most highly industrialized and economically

Exhibit 13.3   World Population Growth by Region

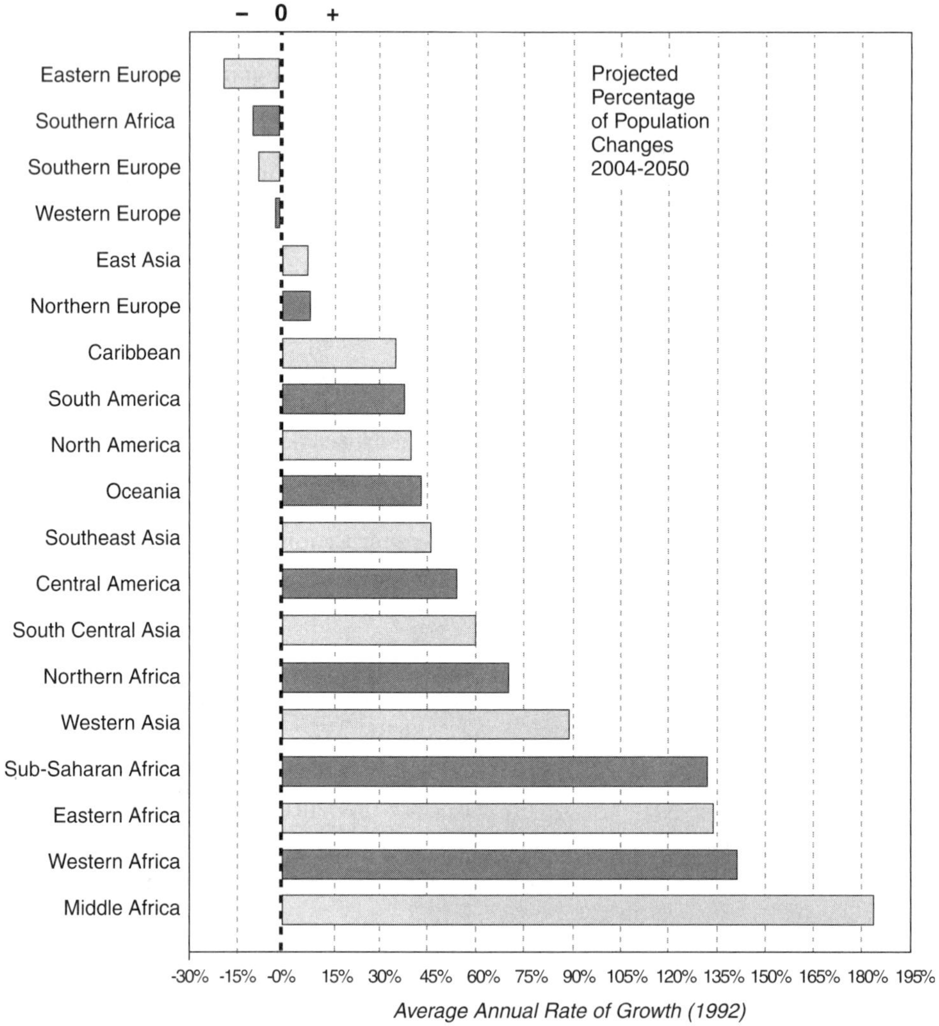

Average Annual Rate of Growth (1992)

Source: Population Reference Bureau, 2004a.

productive societies begin to experience shrinking populations, their role as major global producers and consumers of goods is thrown into doubt. The result can be economic and political turmoil as other societies jockey for global advantage.

The Demographic Transition

In 1972, a group of researchers at the Massachusetts Institute of Technology predicted that because of rapid population growth, the world would run out of gold by 1981, oil by 1992, and usable farmland by 2000; civilization itself would collapse by

2075 (Mann, 1993). Needless to say, none of these things has happened yet. Population growth slowed enough to prevent catastrophe. But why?

The 1972 prediction was based on a theory formulated by an 18th-century English clergyman named Thomas Malthus. He argued that populations always grow faster than food supplies. As the gap widens, starvation ensues. Famines, combined with wars, plagues, diseases, and the like, eventually act as natural limits to population growth. Malthus assumed that food supplies were the ultimate population check.

But Malthus couldn't have foreseen the ability of trade and technology to solve the food supply problem. Japan's population, for instance, would have started dying off long ago if it had to rely on its own food production instead of imports from other countries. In addition, agricultural progress over the last three decades has enabled societies to produce food more abundantly and more efficiently than was possible during Malthus's time. According to the World Resources Institute (2001), croplands and pasturelands support 1.5 billion more people today than they were able to support in 1970. People in developing countries now consume almost a third more calories than they did in the early 1960s, meaning that fewer people die from starvation and malnutrition than ever before. The famines that we've heard so much about in recent years—in Ethiopia, Somalia, or Sudan, for example—have been largely the result of war and civil unrest rather than a scarcity of food (Cooper, 1998b). In fact, many nations that experience famines actually have food surpluses (Keyfitz, 1989).

Given the inability of Malthus's theory to correctly predict population growth and contraction, demographers now give more weight to the theory of the **demographic transition**. Underlying this model is the assumption that all societies go through similar stages of economic and social development. During the first, preindustrial stage of development, both birth rates and death rates tend to be quite high. People have lots of children during this stage, but life expectancy is so low that roughly the same number of people die as are born each year. Hence, the size of the population remains fairly stable.

The second stage occurs when societies begin to industrialize and living conditions improve. The first demographic indicator to improve is usually the death rate. New technology often means better food supplies and increased knowledge about disease. Societies learn how to keep their water supplies clean and how to dispose of garbage and sewage. But for a considerable time after the death rate begins to fall, the birth rate remains high. The result is a dramatic increase in the size of the population. Many demographers feel that most of the world's developing countries are in this second stage of demographic transition. In these countries women will bear an average of 3.5 children in their lifetimes, and the number is above 7.0 in Guinea-Bissau, Mali, Niger, and Somalia. By comparison, the fertility rate in the United States is 2.0; in Canada it's 1.5, in Japan, it's 1.3; and in virtually all the countries of Eastern Europe, it's a minuscule 1.2 (Population Reference Bureau, 2005b).

Why would poor parents in developing countries, who already face enormous difficulties, continue to produce more mouths to feed? Part of the reason is the lack of access to effective birth control. In less developed countries (not including China), only 40% of women use some form of modern contraception compared to 58% in the developed world (Population Reference Bureau, 2005b). In most West African countries, that figure is below 10%. In contrast, 72% of American women and 78% of Swiss women use contraception. In addition, established laws, customs, and religious norms often continue to exert strong influences on people's reproductive behavior. In developing nations, children are likely to be perceived as productive assets and "social security" for old age (Mann, 1993).

As countries modernize, they reach the third and final stage, which is marked by a reduced birth rate to accompany the low death rate. People moving into crowded cities soon begin to realize that large families are an economic liability rather than an asset. Traditional beliefs become weaker as a result. In addition, driven by relative prosperity and freedom, women stay in school longer, put more emphasis on paid work, and marry later than women in developing countries. All these factors limit childbearing.

Although the demographic transition model is useful in understanding the unequal rates of population growth, it has drawbacks. The model is based on processes of urbanization and modernization that characterized Western societies a century ago but may not apply to developing countries today. Death rates fall at a much more accelerated rate in today's developing countries than they did 100 years ago because immunizations, antibiotics, pesticides, and other health technologies are likely to be imported from more advanced countries instead of arising from economic and scientific development within a country. As a result, declining mortality is not always associated with an increase in the standard of living, as it was in the past. And because birth rates don't tend to fall unless standards of living increase, the social pressures that drive down birth rates are also less of a factor in developing countries today. Hence, developing countries may be stalled in the second stage of the model, with less chance of moving to the final stage.

Signs indicate, however, that this assessment may be a bit pessimistic. Many people are beginning to seek more active ways to curb the global population explosion. More than 10 years ago, representatives from 179 nations and about 1,200 nongovernmental organizations attended the landmark International Conference on Population and Development in Cairo. Despite opposition from some Islamic countries and the Vatican, they agreed that promoting health care and reproductive education—particularly for women—is the best way to keep populations in developing countries in check (F. Ching, 1994).

This call to action may be working. Access to family planning is growing in many less developed countries. In Kenya, for instance, 4% of married women used modern contraception in 1978. Today that figure is 32%. In Bangladesh, modern contraceptive use has increased from 5% to 43% over the last three decades. Colombian women have increased their use from 9% to 64% over the same time period (Population Reference Bureau, 2004b). A survey by the Population Crisis Committee (now called Population Action International) found that of the 87 developing countries studied, 40% had decreased their average family size by a third, and another 42% exhibited smaller but still noticeable differences ("World Progress in Birth Control," 1993). What's interesting sociologically is that much of this decrease has occurred in countries where there is no official national family planning policy. Women in developing countries—in both rural villages and densely populated urban areas—have taken it upon themselves to regularly practice birth control (Crossette, 2002).

We must keep in mind, however, that although the rate of population growth may be declining, absolute numbers of people continue to mount in many countries and will continue to be large for several decades to come. When a country has a large and young population base, several generations may pass before a declining rate of growth can offset the sheer number of people produced by the high rates of the past, a process demographers call **population momentum.** Even though individual people may be producing fewer children, so many of them are having kids that the population continues to grow anyway. For instance, 44% of the people living in sub-Saharan Africa are 15 years old or younger, more than twice the percentage of Americans under 15 (Population Reference Bureau, 2005b). With so many young people about to reach childbearing age, population growth will likely continue in the next several decades, even if the overall birth rate is low.

Politics, Culture, and Population Growth

You may be getting the impression that population growth is a "natural" process working relentlessly and inevitably on unsuspecting populations. Yet human intervention—government intervention, more specifically—has at times purposefully altered the size or even the configuration of a population for political or economic reasons.

Take China, for example. Because of its massive population of more than 1.3 billion and its limited resources, China's leadership has been struggling for decades to limit family size. One of every five humans alive today is Chinese, but China has only 7% of Earth's farmland, much of it of poor quality. In response, the government enacted a strict birth policy in the early 1970s. Couples had to wait until their mid-20s to marry. Provinces and cities were assigned yearly birth quotas. Neighborhood committees determined which married couples could have a baby and when they could start trying. The committees also oversaw contraceptive use and even recorded women's menstrual cycles (Ignatius, 1988). In the 1990s, more than 80% of all Chinese couples of childbearing age were sterilized (Crossette, 1997a). Couples who had only one child were rewarded with salary bonuses, educational opportunities, and housing priorities. Penalties were imposed on couples who had more than one child, such as fines of more than a year's salary, lost access to apartments and schools, or dismissals from their jobs (Ignatius, 1988).

The effectiveness of China's birth policy has amazed demographers. Population targets were reached that weren't expected until 2010. The average number of births per woman has decreased from more than 7 in the 1960s to 1.7 in 2004 (Population Reference Bureau, 2005b). In contrast, the average number of births per woman in India, a country with similar population problems, is 3.1. Without the policy, there would be 300 million more Chinese citizens than there are now (Kahn, 2004).

But the success of China's birth policy has created some serious problems. So few babies are being born now—and so many more elderly people are living longer—that the overall age of the population is growing steadily. In 1950, there were eight working-age Chinese people for every one elderly person; today there are less than two. It's estimated that by 2040, China will have an older population than the United States but with only about one fourth the average per capita income (Kahn, 2004). Retirement funds and pension plans are scarce, and the social networks that once supported aging Chinese are no longer there.

Like China, officials in many other countries are now starting to worry that their populations aren't growing enough. In Taiwan, for instance, where the fertility rate dropped dramatically from 5.3 births per woman in 1963 to 1.3 in 2004 (Population Reference Bureau, 2005b; Weeks, 1995), the government adopted a "pro-baby" policy that, among other things, encourages early marriage and procreation and offers inexpensive specialist advice to infertile couples ("Taiwan's Little Problem," 1993). In other low-fertility countries, like Italy, Sweden, and Scotland, government officials are debating whether to offer would-be parents large tax breaks or even outright bonuses for having children. One town in Quebec pays couples $75 for their first child, $150 for their second child, and $750 for each child after that. In addition, it reimburses families with three or more children 50% of the costs for their children's music lessons and other cultural activities (Krauss, 2004). In South Korea, the national health plan now pays the entire cost for procedures to reverse vasectomies and tubal ligations (Onishi, 2005b). And in Japan, some companies will pay their employees bonuses—as much as $10,000—for each child they have (Sims, 2000).

Cultural tradition also continues to play a powerful role in people's decisions about having children. Some cultures express a deep preference for male children because only they can perpetuate the family line. In societies where women's earning power is minimal, sons represent an economic asset to families and a source of security for parents when they get older (Heise, 1989). For instance, even with its restrictive birth policy, China allows its poor, rural residents to have a second child if their first either is a girl or has a disability. If the second child is also a girl, the parents sometimes try to sell her. In 2003, police in Guangxi Province found 28 unwanted baby girls, between the ages of two and five months, stuffed in the back of a long-haul bus that was transporting them to be sold in another province (Rosenthal, 2003).

Such devaluation of female children can lead to extreme acts. Some time ago, I was stunned by the following passage in a newspaper article:

> At least 60 million females in Asia are missing and feared dead, victims of nothing more than their sex. Worldwide, research suggests, the number of missing females may top 100 million. (Kristof, 1991, p. C1)

If tens of millions of people were missing because of a war, earthquake, tidal wave, or plague, we surely would have heard something about it. How could something so massive and hideous happen so quietly?

Before I address this question, let me describe how demographers arrive at such an estimate. These figures are based on a few fundamental facts about human populations. Worldwide, 5% or 6% more male babies are born than female babies. But under normal circumstances males die at higher rates at every age thereafter. In the United States and Europe, the number of men and women evens out by the time a birth cohort reaches its 20s or 30s (Kristof, 1991). Later in life, though, the number of women is higher because women tend to live longer than men. The overall adult sex ratio in developed countries is approximately 105 women for every 100 men.

The figures in many developing countries contrast sharply with these demographic expectations. In India, for instance, the figure is only 92 females for every 100 males

(Dugger, 2001). In China, it is about 90 females for every 100 males (Rosenthal, 2003), and in some provinces, it's as low as 74 females for every 100 males (Yardley, 2005). Similar shortages of women have been found in South Korea, Pakistan, Bangladesh, Nepal, and Papua New Guinea. Hence, the estimate of 100 million missing females represents the difference between the actual number of females in the world and the number that would be expected under normal demographic circumstances.

The "missing" females may include children who have been aborted; killed at birth; abandoned, neglected, given up for foreign adoption; or hidden (Kristof, 1993). In some countries, girls die because they are given less food than boys or because family members view a sick daughter as a nuisance but view a sick son as a medical crisis requiring immediate attention. More commonly couples determine the sex of their fetus through sonograms and, if it's a girl, have an abortion. In South Korea, for instance, 1 out of 12 female fetuses—or 30,000 girls a year—is aborted because of its sex, even though disclosure of the sex of a fetus and abortion are against the law (WuDunn, 1997).

Alongside its concern about population growth, the Chinese government has now become quite concerned as well over the impending shortage of young people. As a result, selective abortions of female fetuses are now a criminal offense. Such abortions are already technically illegal, but there is a long tradition of doctors accepting bribes from parents who want to guarantee that they have a boy (Yardley, 2005).

Age Structure

In addition to population growth, demographers also study the **age structure** of societies, the balance of old and young people. Age structure, like the size of a population, is determined by birth rates and life expectancy.

The proportion of the world's population over the age of 60 has been growing steadily for decades. In 2000, 606 million of the world's people were aged 60 and older. In 2050, that number is projected to triple to about 1.9 billion. During that same period, the proportion of the "oldest old" (those people over 80) will increase more than five times, from 69 million to 377 million (United Nations Population Division, 2003).

But as we saw with population growth in general, the global growth of the elderly population is not currently spread evenly across countries. For developing countries where recent population growth is exceedingly rapid and where life expectancy remains low—as in most countries in Southeast Asia, Latin America, the Indian subcontinent, the Middle East, and especially Africa—the age structure tends to be dominated by young people. The average age of the male population in the four youngest countries in the world (Chad, the Republic of Congo, Uganda, and the Gaza Strip) is between 15 and 16 years (Geographic.org, 2005).

In contrast, those countries that are experiencing low birth rates coupled with increasing life expectancy have a very different age structure, as Exhibit 13.4 shows. More old people are living, and fewer young people are being born. The average age of the population in the world's four oldest countries (Italy, Japan, Germany, and Finland) is over 40 years. Demographers project that by 2050 the median age in Europe will be an unprecedented 52.3 years (cited in R. Bernstein, 2003).

Exhibit 13.4 Changing Age Distributions in Less Developed and Developed Countries

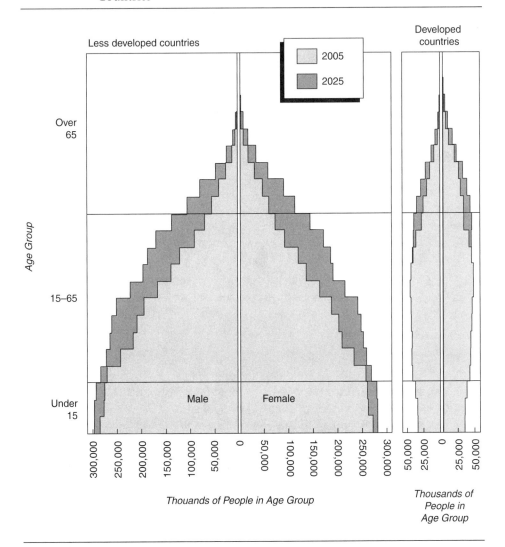

Source: United Nations Population Division, 2005.

The global implications of these different age structures cannot be understated. In Germany, Austria, France, and other European countries, a decreasing number of young people are paying into a pension system that must support a growing number of older people (R. Bernstein, 2003). Governments have reacted to the aging of their populations by reducing social services, including the pensions that millions of retirees had been counting on.

In contrast, when young people outnumber the elderly in a particular country, they are likely to overwhelm labor markets and educational systems (K. Davis, 1976).

The result is a steady decline in living standards, which usually means growing political unrest. That unrest can have an impact not only on the country's residents but also on the people who live in countries that depend on the troubled country for certain resources, goods, or services.

When combined with a skewed sex ratio—due to a shortage of young females and an overabundance of young males—the security of other countries may be threatened as well. Over half the populations of Egypt, Syria, Saudi Arabia, Iraq, and Iran are now under 25 years of age; in Pakistan and Afghanistan, the number is over 60% (cited in Sciolino, 2001). Since aggression is disproportionately associated with young, unemployed, single men, the potential for violent social upheaval both within and outside these countries is likely to increase. Some even go so far as to predict that if these young men cannot find spouses or jobs, they will pose such a threat to the internal stability of these countries that their governments may decide they have to go to war with other countries simply to occupy the surplus male population (Hudson & den Boer, 2004).

The obvious consequence of today's trends is that developing nations will have the burden of trying to accommodate populations dominated by young people, whereas developed nations will have the burden of trying to support millions of people over the age of 65.

Geographic Distribution

In response to these kinds of problems, many people will be motivated to escape through **migration,** or moving to another place where prospects for a comfortable life are brighter. Throughout history, humans have always had a tendency to move. Most scientists today believe that the first humans evolved in Africa and spread to all corners of the globe from there. Down through the centuries, migration has played a crucial role in history as people have contended for territory and the resources that go with it ("Workers of the World," 1998). Today, global television and the Internet expose people more quickly and more consistently than ever to appealing lifestyles elsewhere. Large-scale migration, the third major demographic process, includes both in-country movement and cross-border movement.

Migration Within a Society

Migration trends within a country can have a considerable effect on social life. Consider the so-called Great Migration of African Americans from the rural South to the industrial North following the Civil War. Many former slaves, convinced there was no future for them in the Jim Crow South, migrated to the northern cities of New York, Philadelphia, Boston, Chicago, Detroit, Cleveland, and St. Louis, seeking a better life. In 1865, more than 90% of all African Americans lived in the South. By 1960 nearly 50% lived in the urban North (Smallwood, 1998). In Chicago alone, the black population rose from 44,000 in 1910 to 110,000 in 1920 (P. Johnson, 1997). Blacks in the North were able to take advantage of opportunities unavailable to them in the South and establish the stable economic communities and strong political organizations that aided the civil rights movement of the 1950s and 1960s. By 1980, however, many southern Blacks were no longer seeing the decaying industrial centers of the

North as an economic "promised land" and were choosing to remain in the South. And recently, northern Blacks have begun to move back to the South, bringing their urban sensibilities and political savvy into everyday southern life.

That is not the only internal migration pattern in the United States today. For instance, there's a trend for people to relocate from the so-called Rust Belt of the industrial North to Sunbelt cities in the West, like Las Vegas and Phoenix. Economic issues have also motivated many people to move from desirable locales where the cost of living is high, like San Francisco and Seattle, to less developed areas where the cost of living is lower, such as coastal regions of Oregon or the Midwest.

Migration within developing countries is having an equally profound impact. In 1950, less than 30% of the world's population lived in cities. Today, that figure is 47% (Population Reference Bureau, 2005b), and it's estimated that by 2030, 61% of the world's population will be urban dwellers (Torrey, 2004). In 1950, 83 cities in the world had over a million inhabitants. By 2000, that figure had increased to 411 (Population Reference Bureau, 2003). Of the 10 largest "megacities"—urban areas with populations over 17 million—8 are in the developing world: Bombay, Lagos, Dhaka, São Paulo, Karachi, Mexico City, Delhi, and Jakarta (Brockerhoff, 2000).

This transformation has changed our assumptions about what urban living means worldwide. In the past, cities were meccas of commerce and culture. Cities tended to have higher standards of living and better health conditions than rural areas. But when cities grow rapidly, as many are in the developing world, their economies and infrastructures can't keep up. As a result, contemporary urban life is associated with environmental and social devastation. In developing countries, 90% of raw sewage from urban areas pours into streams and oceans. Of India's 3,000 cities, only 8 had full water-treatment plants in the mid-1990s (Crossette, 1996). Cities have much higher rates of poverty, crime, violence, and sexually transmitted diseases than do rural areas.

Migration From One Country to Another

Population movement from one country to another is equally significant. According to the United Nations, more than 120 million people worldwide—or 2% of the global population—live outside their countries of birth ("Workers of the World," 1998). Most have left their homelands in search of a better life somewhere else. In the process, they bring together an extraordinary diversity of ethnicities and cultures:

> A woman gynecologist from Romania sells bananas in a downtown supermarket [in the United States]. Polish engineers pick grapes in Swiss alpine vineyards. . . . Thai bar girls in Tokyo ride the Japanese economic boom together with 700,000 workers from Korea. . . . Among the 2.8 million foreign workers. . . . in the Middle East last year were 17,000 Vietnamese. Hundreds of thousands of Indonesians harvest rubber and copra in Malaysia for the same pocketbook reasons that Mexicans pump gasoline in Los Angeles. In Germany, there are more than 1,000 mosques for resident Turkish workers. (McMichael, 1996, p. 187)

International migration is encouraged by disparities in opportunities. Poverty, political instability, war, famine, environmental deterioration, high unemployment, and the lure of high wages in richer countries continue to drive the world's poorest people to give up their life savings and risk death to find a better life in more prosperous nations. According to the United Nations, each year, hundreds of thousands of illegal immigrants from poor countries in Africa, Central Asia, and the Middle East try to enter the wealthy nations of Western Europe (cited in Cowell, 2002).

You might think that when people migrate from underdeveloped, overcrowded countries to more developed, technologically advanced countries, everyone would benefit. After all, migration lowers population pressures and unemployment at home while offsetting the problems of negative population growth and an aging workforce in developed destination countries. Indeed, the only way Japan and Western Europe will be able to sustain a stable population is through immigration. For example, the United Nations estimates that through 2025 Italy will have to admit about 300,000 immigrants a year, Germany about 500,000, and Japan about 600,000 simply to maintain their current workforces (Crossette, 2000; French, 2000b).

From a sociological point of view, however, international migration often creates conflict. People seeking opportunities can no longer move to uncharted areas but rather must push into territories where other people already live. Instead of seeing immigrants for their contribution to the overall economy, the people already in residence see immigrants as an immediate and personal threat. The immigrants require jobs, housing, education, and medical attention, all of which are in limited supply. They also bring with them foreign habits, traditions, norms, and cultural ways.

Immigration creates a variety of cultural fears: fear that a nation can't control its own boundaries; fear that an ethnically homogeneous population will be altered through intermarriage; fear of an influx of a "strange" way of life; fear that newcomers will encroach on property, clog the educational system, and suck up social benefits owned and largely paid for by "natives" (Kennedy, 1993). Many people also express concern that immigrants are responsible for outbreaks of such diseases as AIDS, tuberculosis, measles, and cholera, which strain health care systems and thus create even more resentment. Above all, they fear that immigrants and their offspring may one day become a statistical majority, rendering the "natives" powerless in their own country.

Even though laws in most countries ban discrimination against foreigners, resentment and prejudice are global phenomena. In Great Britain, the antipathy is often directed against immigrants from India and Pakistan; in France, against Algerians and Moroccans; in Germany, Turks; in Sweden, Iraqis and Kurds; in Australia, South and East Asians; in the United States, immigrants from Latin America and Asia; and in Japan, almost anyone not Japanese.

Despite the economic necessity of immigrants, many industrialized countries have tried to close their gates. In France, mounting resentment against Muslim Arab immigrants a decade ago forced the government to place tight restrictions on immigration (Levin, 1993). In Australia, the navy routinely escorts boats filled with asylum seekers from Afghanistan and Iraq to offshore territories where they are kept in detention camps (Perlez, 2002). Even Sweden, a country that has always preached ethnic tolerance, has developed segregated communities in the suburbs of Stockholm for many of its 800,000 immigrants (Hoge, 1998).

It's important to note, though, that such hostility is not inevitable. Peaceable contact with immigrants at work, at school, or in the community can reduce feelings of threat and the willingness to expel legal immigrants from the country (McLaren, 2003). In any case, the trend toward greater immigration is unlikely to slow down as long as communication and transportation technologies continue to shrink the globe and economic disparities between countries continue to exist.

The Impact of Population Trends in the United States

How are all these demographic processes affecting the population in the United States? Talking about common effects is difficult, because different ethnoracial, religious, and gender groups experience population trends differently. Latino/as, for instance, have a significantly higher birth rate than do non-Hispanic Whites. Catholics and Mormons have higher birth rates than people of other religions (Weeks, 1995). U.S. women, on average, can expect to live longer than U.S. men.

Nevertheless, two important demographic trends in the United States will exert a profound effect on the entire population in years to come: the growing proportion of nonwhite, non–English-speaking immigrants and their children, and the shifting age structure of the population, marked by a growing proportion of elderly and a shrinking proportion of young people. These two trends together will strain the social fabric, raising questions about the fair distribution of social resources.

Immigration and the Changing Face of the United States

Because the U.S. population is currently growing at a manageable rate, U.S. residents may have trouble understanding the impact of population explosions in other countries on their everyday lives here. But as populations burst the seams of national boundaries elsewhere, many of those seeking better opportunities end up in the United States. Some arrive legally by plane, boat, or train. Others arrive illegally by foot or are smuggled in the backs of trucks or the holds of cargo ships.

The Immigrant Surge

In the mid-1980s the U.S. Bureau of the Census predicted that by the year 2050 the United States would have a population of 300 million (Pear, 1992). But that number was reached in 2005. Subsequently, the bureau has revised its estimate to 419 million by 2050 (U.S. Bureau of the Census, 2004a).

Part of the reason this projection was adjusted upward is that immigration increased more than had been anticipated. Since the early 1990s, over a million documented immigrants have entered the country each year (U.S. Bureau of the Census, 2004a). In addition, according to the Urban Institute, there are approximately 9.3 million undocumented immigrants currently living in the U.S. today (Passel, Capps, & Fix, 2004). About 11% of U.S. residents today (33 million people) were born somewhere else (U.S. Bureau of the Census, 2004a). In California, more than a quarter of all residents are foreign born (U.S. Bureau of the Census, 2004a).

(Text continues on page 491)

Immigrant Nation

Liz Grauerholz and Rebecca Smith

All around the world, immigration is a function of economic imbalances and political conflict. Gaps between rich people and poor people are increasing in most countries, and the gaps between rich and poor countries are growing as well. Wars and oppression are never-ending. These forces keep people moving across national borders in search of a better life.

Immigration has shaped American society since its beginning. The United States is a land of immigrants. In the early 20th century, a large influx of immigrants, mostly from Europe, enriched American culture and provided the labor to fuel America's rise as an industrial powerhouse. At the time, the need to incorporate so many new Americans was considered a societal problem, but today we take for granted the Italian, Polish, Irish, Jewish, and other once-foreign names and faces in our midst.

In the early 20th century, most immigrants arrived by boat, ferried across the Atlantic Ocean to Ellis Island in New York. There they were processed in massive numbers, sometimes for days or weeks, before leaving for their new homes in the United States.

❖ More recent immigrants are like earlier arrivals in their keen desire for a better life. But they are also different in some important ways. For one thing, they are likely to be from Latin America or Asia rather than Europe. For another, they typically make the trip in a fraction of the time that it took early 20th-century arrivals. Many simply book a flight to the United States. An airport processing area is their first stop, but as soon as their papers are determined to be in order, they're on their way.

❖ Poor immigrants who have difficulty obtaining the proper documentation often take a more harrowing route, however. Cubans and Haitians may cross the ocean in small boats and attempt to sneak ashore in Florida. Many Mexicans and other Latin Americans try to cross the southwestern U.S. border on foot. So common were accidents involving these pedestrians that signs like this one were posted on many highways leading from the border.

❖ Undocumented immigrants face many difficulties. Not the least is the U.S. law enforcement system and the antagonism of many U.S. citizens. Illegal immigration is considered by many Americans to be a threat to national security, especially since the attacks of September 11, 2001. Beefed-up security at airports is a hurdle for many would-be immigrants.

❖ But the porous southern border seems to be a greater concern. So many illegal immigrants come from Mexico that government officials use an acronym, OTM, to describe illegal immigrants "other than Mexicans" (OTMs). The men at this holding center in Brownsville, Texas, are all OTMs who have crossed the U.S.-Mexico border illegally. Mexican detainees are far more numerous.

❖ The legitimate path, of course, is to seek naturalization. Tens of thousands of immigrants take their oath as U.S. citizens each year, after a period in which they contribute to the social fabric and learn how to be Americans.

Among the roughly 2,000 people naturalized in this 2002 ceremony are immigrants who joined the armed forces and pledged to sacrifice their lives for their adopted country before they were even citizens.

❖ In the past, intermittent amnesty programs have allowed long-time undocumented residents to become citizens, but given current security concerns, this policy has become controversial. Meanwhile, babies born in the United States to illegal immigrants are considered U.S. citizens from birth and therefore enjoy all the privileges associated with citizenship. Many Mexican women deliberately seek to give birth in the United States, despite the hardships they face themselves as illegal immigrants.

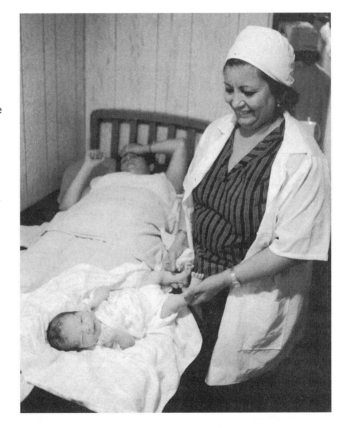

❖ The sheer number of new immigrants—both legal and illegal—strains the capacity of many social institutions to function adequately. Schools in some communities are struggling to educate students who need to learn not only reading, writing, arithmetic, science, and social studies but also English.

❖ Businesses and governments have to provide information in a variety of languages, as in this Chicago street sign.

❖ Poverty is another possible consequence of large-scale immigration, as the economy struggles to accommodate the influx of new workers. Unemployed immigrants strain the government's already dwindling ability to house, feed, and clothe those who are at a disadvantage in the competitive, individualistic American system.

487

❖ Anti-immigrant sentiment tends to be fueled by this sort of competition over scarce resources, as well as fear of outsiders and perhaps even outright racism. Many people regard immigrants, legal and illegal alike, with suspicion or outright hostility. During harsh economic times, social conflict over immigration issues may intensify.

Still, not all sentiment is anti-immigrant. Immigrants serve important economic functions in the labor market. First, they become servants, gardeners, cooks, and nannies, providing the middle class with the accoutrements of the rich. Second, they compete with the most disadvantaged groups for the least desirable jobs, thereby keeping wages (and prices) low and lessening the pressure to address other economic problems. In the process, consumers have the benefit of products made with cheap labor.

Despite concerns, immigration is likely to continue as long as the United States remains a vibrant and open society. In fact, cultural diversity keeps things lively. Fifty or so years ago, who knew that American culture would embrace these once-foreign artifacts and many others?

❖ New ideas: Buddhism and other eastern religions

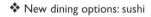

❖ New dining options: sushi

❖ New holidays: Cinco de Mayo

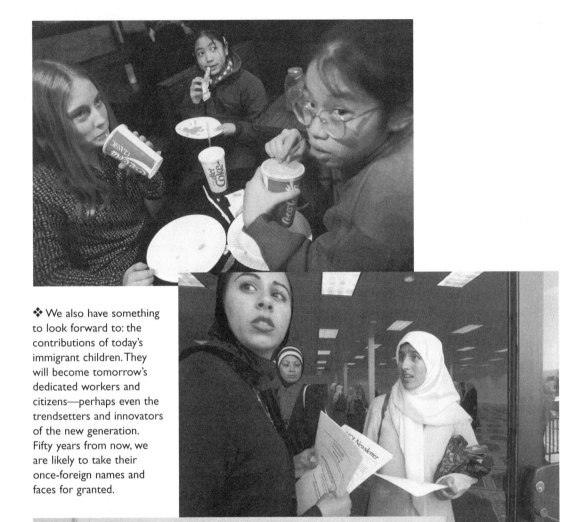

❖ We also have something to look forward to: the contributions of today's immigrant children. They will become tomorrow's dedicated workers and citizens—perhaps even the trendsetters and innovators of the new generation. Fifty years from now, we are likely to take their once-foreign names and faces for granted.

This isn't the first time the U.S. population has been radically increased by a surge of immigration. In the first decade of the 20th century, nearly 9 million immigrants entered the country. What makes contemporary immigration different, though, is that relatively few of today's newcomers are of European descent (see Exhibit 13.5). In the late 19th century, 90% of the immigrants who came to the United States were from northern and southern Europe. But in 2002 only 16.3% were from Europe; 32.2% were from Asia and 43% from Latin America and the Caribbean (U.S. Bureau of the Census, 2004a). Eighty percent of undocumented immigrants who enter the country each year come from Latin America; more than half come from Mexico alone (Passel et al., 2004).

Not surprisingly, then, the racial and ethnic composition of the United States has changed dramatically over the past century. In 1900, one out of every eight U.S. residents was of a race other than white; by 2000, the ratio was one in four (Hobbs &

Exhibit 13.5   Shifting Sources of Legal Immigrants to the United States

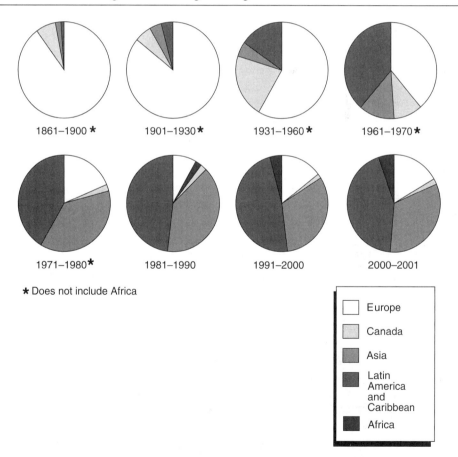

1861–1900 ★   1901–1930★   1931–1960 ★   1961–1970★

1971–1980★   1981–1990   1991–2000   2000–2001

★ Does not include Africa

- Europe
- Canada
- Asia
- Latin America and Caribbean
- Africa

Sources: Daniels, 1990; U.S. Bureau of the Census, 2000, 2004a.

Stoops, 2002). Experts estimate that by the year 2050 only one out of every two people in the U.S. will be white (U.S. Bureau of the Census, 2004b). That same year, one out of four Americans are projected to be Latino/a, and by 2100, one out of three will be Latino/a (Saenz, 2004).

Until quite recently, the non-European immigrant population was not spread equally across the country. Immigrants tended to settle in large urban areas that serve as ports of entry (New York, Los Angeles, Chicago, San Francisco, Houston, Miami, and so on). More than half of all Latino/as live in California and Texas. Of the 20 metropolitan areas with the largest proportion of Asian residents, 8 are in California and 6 are cities in the eastern corridor that runs from Boston to Washington, DC. (Zhao, 2002).

However, figures from the 2000 U.S. Census show that Latino/a and Asian immigrants are now settling in towns and cities all across the United States. Over the past decade, the need for people to teach English as a second language has grown most rapidly in school districts in the South, Midwest, and Northwest. In North Carolina, the number of students who speak little if any English has grown from 8,900 in 1993 to 52,500 today. The numbers of such students in Idaho, Nebraska, Tennessee, and Georgia have tripled (Zhao, 2002). Questions of how to integrate immigrants are now being debated all over the country.

The immigrant experience in the United States has changed in other ways, too. Advances in technology and cheaper travel fares mean that many immigrants today can base themselves in the United States—getting a job, finding a place to live, and so on—but maintain vital ties to their homelands. Those with the economic means travel back and forth frequently between their country of origin and the United States.

High immigration levels are likely to continue for some time. Most people who immigrate to the United States are pulled by the lure of employment and a better life. Until population and economic pressures ease in other regions of the world, the United States will remain an appealing destination.

Social Responses to Immigrants

U.S. residents have always had a love-hate relationship with immigrants. In good times immigrants have been welcome contributors to the economy. Early in the 20th century, their labor helped build roads and the U.S. rail system. Immigrants have filled unwanted jobs, opened businesses, and improved the lives of many U.S. residents by working cheaply as housekeepers, dishwashers, and gardeners.

When times are bad, however, or when the political winds shift, many U.S. residents are inclined to shut the door and blame immigrants for many of the country's economic and social woes. During these periods, people often describe the influx of immigrants as a "flood," subtly equating their arrival with disaster. As in Europe, immigrants to the United States often find they are the targets of a variety of social anxieties, from economic tension to outright anger (Sontag, 1992). Hatred directed toward Middle Eastern immigrants, for instance, reached a peak in the months following the September 11 attacks in 2001.

❖
Micro-Macro Connection
The Peculiar Politics of Immigration

In 1996, the conservative Republican Pat Buchanan ran his unsuccessful but influential presidential campaign on the theme that immigrants were overrunning the country and would soon "dilute" its European character. He called for the immediate deportation of all illegal aliens and advocated an impenetrable barrier along the border between the United States and Mexico to keep them out. Even today, anti-immigrant blogs and Web sites with racist overtones saturate the Internet.

Harsh anti-immigrant rhetoric is not the exclusive domain of conservative politicians or racists, however. For instance, in 2004 both major presidential candidates supported some limits on immigration. Some liberal politicians have periodically called on the government to seal the U.S. borders. Their primary concern is that foreign immigrants, both legal and illegal, hurt poor U.S. residents by directly competing with them for low-level jobs and settling for lower wages (Danziger & Gottschalk, 2004). According to some estimates, there are approximately 6 million undocumented immigrants employed in the United States—or about 5% of the entire labor force (Passel et al., 2004). Between 2001 and 2004, the number of new immigrants who found employment in the United States increased by 2.06 million. At the same time, the number of native-born and longer-term immigrant workers declined by over 1.3 million (cited in Herbert, 2004).

In addition, some members of liberal environmentalist groups, like the Sierra Club, oppose unlimited immigration. They believe that it will tax already limited natural resources and render an already overcrowded country unable to protect its environment (Barringer, 2004).

In 1996, the U.S. Senate passed a bill, the Immigration and Financial Responsibility Act, that authorized the hiring of an additional 4,700 U.S. border patrol agents, made it more difficult for those in the country illegally to gain employment, and set limits on social services available to illegal immigrants (W. Graham, 1996). Other legislation has been directed toward limiting the rights of immigrants who are in this country legally. Welfare reforms in 1996 slashed the number of legal immigrants who could use government services such as prenatal care, job training, college loans, Medicaid, and supplemental security income (Schmitt, 1996).

Recently, immigration has been linked to concerns over national security, and immigrants, especially those from the Middle East, have been perceived as imminent threats. In 2003, the Immigration and Naturalization Service (now called the Bureau of Citizenship and Immigration Services) became part of the U.S. Department of Homeland Security, reflecting a shift in the way immigration issues are defined. A relatively minor violation of immigration law—such as having an expired visa—is now commonly used as a quick, easy way to detain people suspected of being threats to national security (Sheridan, 2005).

Not everyone involved in politics is anti-immigrant. For many civil rights organizations and advocates for ethnic minorities, immigration is a human rights issue, and hostility toward immigrants is seen as fundamentally racist (Holmes, 1995).

In addition, rather odd coalitions of groups at vastly different ends of the political spectrum lobby on behalf of immigrants, though with their own agendas in mind. Some Christian fundamentalists, for instance, assert that proposals to restrict immigration for parents and siblings of naturalized U.S. citizens are "antifamily." The National Rifle Association and the American Civil Liberties Union are both opposed to proposals that immigrants be required to carry a national identification card containing a photograph and fingerprints.

In addition, many people see the economic benefits of immigrants, both legal and illegal. In a 1993 Gallup poll, 26% of respondents said that immigrants help the economy; 64% said they hurt it. By 2000, 44% said that immigrants help the economy and only 40% said they hurt it (cited in Schmitt, 2001a). Indeed, according to the National Academy of Sciences, immigration produces substantial economic benefits for the United States, outweighing the slight reduction in wages and job opportunities it creates for low-skilled U.S. workers (cited in Pear, 1997). The academy estimates that immigration adds perhaps $10 billion a year to the nation's output. Some economists even argue that Social Security would go broke without the $7 billion or so in annual payments from undocumented workers, many of whom—contrary to popular perceptions—pay their share of income taxes (Murphy, 2004; Porter, 2005).

Furthermore, many wealthy owners of manufacturing facilities and agricultural businesses that employ large numbers of workers believe that the free flow of people across national borders leads to prosperity. Easily exploited undocumented workers are particularly valued as abundant, cheap labor (W. Graham, 1996). As one journalist put it, without them:

> Fruit and vegetables would rot in fields. Toddlers in Manhattan would be without nannies. Towels at hotels in states like Florida, Texas, and California would go unlaundered. Commuters at airports from Miami to Newark would be stranded as taxi cabs sat driverless. Home improvement projects across the Sun Belt would grind to a halt. And bedpans and lunch trays at nursing homes in Chicago, New York, Houston, and Los Angeles would go uncollected. (Murphy, 2004, p. 1)

However, the overall benefits they provide to the economy are not necessarily reflected in personal well-being. Immigrants, in general, fare worse economically than native-born Americans. They tend to have lower educational achievement, higher levels of poverty and near-poverty, higher percentages of families without health insurance, and higher percentages of families receiving government assistance (Camarota, 2004).

The immigration issue illustrates a clash of political and economic forces. To politicians of all stripes, immigration is a hot-button campaign issue. But as long as powerful business interests see a need for a pool of cheap, mobile labor that is willing to work outside union and regulatory constraints, attempts to "close the borders" will remain ineffective (R. L. Clark & Passel, 1993). Unless U.S. laws barring the employment of illegal immigrants are fully enforced, poor foreigners will continue to come here seeking a better life.

The "Graying" of the United States

At the same time that the United States must deal with the changing ethnic and racial configuration of its population, it also must address its shifting age structure. The age structure of a society is one of the key factors determining the need for various social resources. Very young people require physical care and protection. Use of educational resources is based, in large part, on the age of individuals. Workers at the beginning and end of their careers are more susceptible to unemployment than those at midcareer. And old age is associated with higher medical costs.

The age structure can even influence certain social problems in ways that are not immediately apparent. Take violent crime, for instance. According to the FBI, almost 50% more arrests were made in the United States in 1980 than in 1970. To some, this statistic showed that society had fallen apart. To others, it was proof that the country had turned into a police state. Actually, neither was true. The large Baby Boom cohort had reached its late teens and early 20s, a period in the life course when criminal activity is most common (L. E. Cohen & Land, 1987). The crime rates went up not because crime became a more desirable pursuit or because U.S. residents as a whole became less respectful of the law, but simply because more people were at the age when criminal activity is statistically more likely to take place. Not surprisingly, rates of violent crime have been declining over the past decade as this cohort grows older. But at the same time, there has been a marked increase in accounting, corporate, and securities fraud, the "crimes of choice" among middle-aged perpetrators (Labaton, 2002).

Perhaps the most important and most problematic demographic trend in the United States today involves the increasing average age of the population. Two hundred years ago, the median age for U.S. residents was 16; in 1980 it was 30; today it is about 35.2. It is expected to be close to 40 by the middle of this century, as the massive Baby Boom cohort reaches old age (U.S. Bureau of the Census, 2004a).

Two developments in the past few decades have conspired to change the age structure of the United States (Preston, 1984). The first has been a decrease in the number of children being born. In 1960, there were approximately 24 births per 1,000 people in the population. By 2004, the rate had dropped to 14 per 1,000 (Population Reference Bureau, 2005b). In some vibrant cities, like San Francisco and Seattle, there are more dogs than children (Egan, 2005). Like many countries in the developed world, the U.S. fertility rate is below the level necessary to replace the current population in the next generation. Most of the conditions that have helped lower fertility—improved work conditions for women and more effective contraception, for example—are not likely to reverse in the future.

The other development has been a rapid increase in the number of people surviving to old age. Technological advances in medicine and nutrition have extended the lives of countless U.S. residents whose historical counterparts would have routinely died several decades ago. Life expectancy has risen from 67.1 for males and 74.7 for females born in 1970 to 74.9 for males and 80.7 for females born in 2005 (U.S. Bureau of the Census, 2004a). By 2030, the United States will have more old people than children (see Exhibit 13.6). The number of people over 85, an age group for which health care costs are exceptionally high, will grow fastest of all, increasing from 5.1 million today to 8 million by 2025 and soaring to over 20 million by 2050 (U.S. Bureau of the Census, 2004a).

Some demographers project that by 2050 there will be 10 times the number of centenarians (people living to 100) than we have today (cited in Dominus, 2004).

Why should we be concerned about the "graying" of the U.S. population? The answer is that a society with an aging population will inevitably experience increased demands for pensions, health care, and other social services for the elderly (OECD, 1988). The ability and willingness of society, and in particular the working population, to bear the additional burden of caring for the growing number of elderly people is an open question.

This concern has led demographers to look at the statistical relationship between the elderly and the rest of the population (Kart, 1990). As you can see in Exhibit 13.7, a declining number of tax-paying workers aged 18 to 64 will be available to support each Social Security recipient. On average, 40 or so years from now each worker may have to support twice as many older people (P.G. Peterson, 1996). This figure is probably exaggerated, however. Not all people over 65 are retired, nor are they all in poor health. And not all people between the ages of 18 and 64 are working, nor are they all in good health (Friedland, 1989). Nevertheless, the retirements of older people will be directly or indirectly financed by the working-age population through Social Security and other pension programs.

Exhibit 13.6 Changing Age Makeup of the U.S. Population

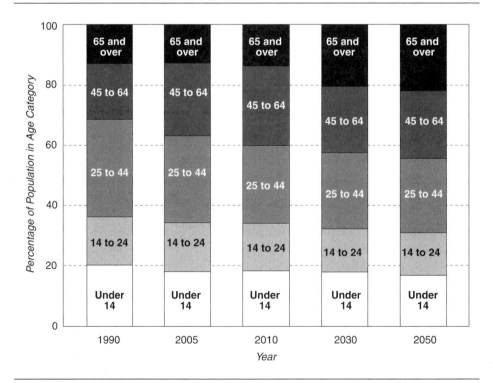

Source: U.S. Bureau of the Census, 2004a.

Exhibit 13.7 Declining Sources of Support for U.S. Retirees

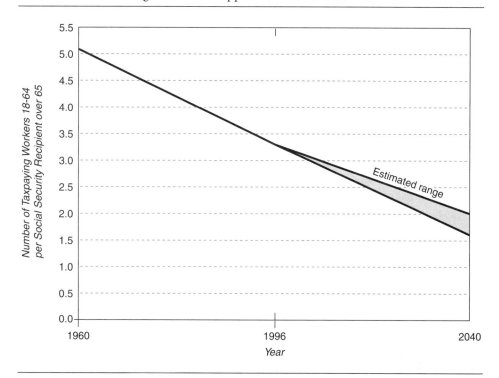

Source: R.R. Peterson, 1996.

Political debate rages today over how—or even whether—the Social Security system should be transformed to accommodate the growing number of people who will turn 65 in the coming years. A recent survey found that 20% of Americans feel that the Social Security system is in crisis, 40% believe it is in serious trouble, and 34% feel it is in some trouble. And 68% said they find it difficult to save money for retirement on their own (Toner & Connelly, 2005). Unless elderly Americans are better able to support themselves financially in the future than they are today, the government will have to play an even larger role in providing health care and other services. To do that, it will have to devote more tax dollars to the needs of older citizens.

The graying of the United States is also challenging employers to restructure the workplace. Already, fewer young workers are available to replace retiring workers. Some employers will be forced to pay more or add benefits to attract new workers or will be forced to focus more attention on employee productivity, perhaps turning to machines to replace workers.

On the positive side, however, employers will have to find innovative ways to keep older workers interested in the job. Business owners are beginning to realize that older workers are much less likely than younger workers to leave after a few years. Indeed, the turnover rate for workers under 30 is 10 times higher than the rate for workers over

50. So employers are developing new strategies to recruit older employees. Home Depot, for example, now offers their older workers "snowbird specials"—winter jobs in warm-climate regions like Florida and summer jobs in cooler states like Maine. Borders bookstores regularly recruit retired teachers to sales positions by promising reading and discussion groups (Freudenheim, 2005). Employers may also have to keep older workers interested in continuing to work by offering substantial bonuses or by creating prestigious and well-paid part-time positions. Once again, we see that structural forces and private experiences are interconnected.

Conclusion

In discussing current and future demographic trends, I can't help but think about my own children. Their Millennium Generation cohort is the first to reach the teen years during the 21st century. I wonder what kind of impact being born in the late 1980s and growing up in the 1990s and early 2000s will have on their lives. Will the world's population reach the predicted catastrophic proportions, or will we figure out a way to control population growth and enable all people to live quality lives? Will the growing ethnic diversity of U.S. society continue to create tension and conflict, or will Americans eventually learn how to be a truly multicultural nation? What will be the single, most definitive "punctuating" event for my sons' cohort: a war, an assassination, a severe economic depression, a terrorist attack, a natural disaster, a political scandal, or some other unimaginable catastrophe? Or will it be world peace, an end to hunger and homelessness, a cure for AIDS?

I also wonder how well social institutions will serve my children's generation. What will their experience in higher education be like? Will jobs be waiting for them when they're ready to go to work? What will be their share of the national debt? How will they perceive family life? Will marriage be an outdated mode of intimacy by the time they reach adulthood? What will be a desirable family size?

As a parent, of course, I'm more than a little curious about how these questions will be answered. I want to know the answers right now! But as a sociologist I realize that they will emerge only from the experiences and interactions of my kids, and others their age, as they progress through their lives. Herein lies the unique and fundamental message of the sociological perspective. As powerful and relentless as the demographic and generational forces described in this chapter are in determining my children's life chances, the responsibility for shaping and changing this society in the 21st century ultimately rests in the hands of their generation. This topic—the ability of individuals to change and reconstruct their society—is the theme of the final chapter.

◆

YOUR TURN

Demographers often use population pyramids (refer back to Exhibit 13.4) to graphically display the age and sex distributions of a population. These pictures are often used to draw conclusions about a population's most pressing economic, educational, and social needs. To see what these pyramids look like for different countries, visit the U.S. Bureau of the Census Web site (www.census.gov/ipc/www/idbpyr.html).

Using information from the most recent U.S. census (available in the government documents section of your school's library or at www.census.gov), construct population pyramids for several different types of U.S. cities:

- A college town (for example, Ann Arbor, Michigan; Princeton, New Jersey)
- A military town (for example, Norfolk, Virginia; Annapolis, Maryland)
- A large urban city (for example, New York City, Chicago, Los Angeles)
- A small rural town
- An affluent suburb
- A city with a large elderly retirement community (for example, St. Petersburg, Florida; Sun City, Arizona)

Exhibit 13.8 is a form you can copy and then use to construct your population pyramids.

Exhibit 13.8 Population Pyramid Form

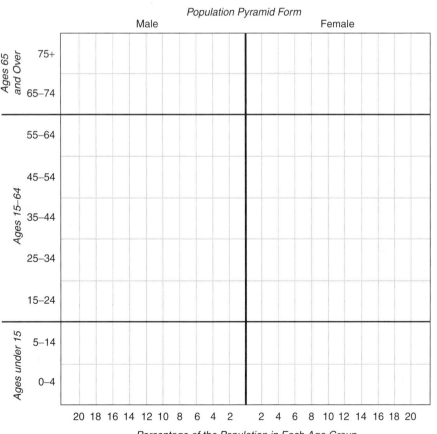

After constructing your population pyramids, describe how the age and sex profiles of these cities differ. What other characteristics of these cities would be different as a result of the shape of their populations? Consider the following:

- The nature of the educational system
- The types of businesses that would succeed or fail
- The sorts of recreational opportunities available
- Political issues considered important and the degree of citizen involvement in political activity
- Important health care issues
- Crime rates
- Divorce rates
- Suicide rates

From these differences, draw some general conclusions about how people's lives are influenced by the age and sex distribution of the population where they live.

CHAPTER HIGHLIGHTS

- Often overlooked in our quest to identify the structural factors that shape our everyday experiences are the effects of our birth cohort. Birth cohorts are more than just a collection of individuals born within a few years of each other; they are distinctive generations tied together by historical events, national and global population trends, and large-scale societal changes.

- Earth's population is growing at an unprecedented rate. But different countries experience different rates of growth. Poor, developing countries are expanding rapidly, whereas the populations in wealthy, developed countries have either stabilized or, in some cases, declined.

- When the population of a country grows rapidly, the age structure is increasingly dominated by young people. In slow-growth countries with low birth rates and high life expectancy, the population is much older, on average.

- As conditions in developing countries grow worse, pressures to migrate increase, creating a variety of cultural, political, and economic fears in countries experiencing high levels of immigration.

- The changing age structure of the U.S. population—more older people and fewer younger people—suggests that a number of adjustments will have to be made in both employment policies and social programs.

KEY TERMS

age structure Population's balance of old and young people

birth cohort Set of people who were born during the same era and who face similar societal circumstances brought about by their shared position in the overall age structure of the population

cohort effect Phenomenon in which members of a birth cohort tend to experience a particular life course event or rite of passage—puberty, marriage, childbearing, graduation, entry into the workforce, death—at roughly the same time

demographer Sociologist who studies trends in population characteristics

demographic transition Stage of societal development in unindustrialized countries marked by growing life expectancy and high birth rates; concept used to explain why populations in less developed countries grow faster than those in more developed countries

migration Movement of populations from one geographic area to another

period effect Phenomenon in which a historical event or major social trend contributes to the unique shape and outlook of a birth cohort

population momentum Tendency for populations to continue to grow despite lower birth rates because of the sheer numbers of people of childbearing age.

❖

STUDY SITE ON THE WEB

Don't forget the interactive quizzes and other learning aids at www.pineforge.com/newman 6study. In the Resource Files for this chapter, you will also find more on demographic trends, including:

Sociologist at Work

◆ Ruth Sidel: Generation X Women on Their Own

Micro-Macro Connection

◆ Graying of America

14 Architects of Change
Reconstructing Society

Social Change

Social Movements

The Sociological Imagination Revisited

Jonathan Simms, a 17-year-old A-level student from a working-class family in Belfast, Northern Ireland, was a gifted soccer player who some felt had a chance of playing professionally. In September 2001, however, things began to change. He seemed to lose interest in soccer and his play suffered. Around the house he became clumsy, falling down, dropping things, and so on. He slurred his words. His parents suspected that he was drinking or taking drugs.

Within weeks Jonathan became so weak that he had to be rushed to the hospital. He was diagnosed with a condition called variant Creutzfeldt-Jakob disease, popularly known as mad cow disease. This malady is a debilitating condition that results from eating infected beef. It can incubate in the body for years, even decades, before manifesting itself by attacking the brain (Belkin, 2002). By the middle of 2002, Jonathan could no longer walk or talk. His parents had to bathe him. Soon he became totally unresponsive, lying in bed in a vegetative state.

Doctors told Jonathan's parents that there was no hope and that he wouldn't live more than a year. But his father, Don, refused to accept the prognosis. And so he set out on a single-minded mission: To save his son's life. Don quit his job and spent all day on the Internet trying to find doctors, researchers, anybody who could commute his son's death sentence.

Don Simms eventually found a researcher, Steven Dealler, who had been experimenting with a powerful and sometimes lethal new drug called pentosan polysulphate (PPS). PPS had shown some effectiveness in treating animals suffering from a similar disease called scrapie but had never been tested on humans. The problem with PPS is that the molecules are so big that it can't be administered by pill or intravenously. Instead, the drug has been injected directly into the brains of the animals it's been used to treat. Most doctors were convinced that injecting this drug directly into a human's brain would be fatal.

So Don embarked on another quest, to find someone who would be willing to use this technique on his son. He found Dr. Nikolai Rainov, a neurosurgeon who was an expert on delivering cancer drugs directly to the brain. Dr. Rainov agreed to treat Jonathan, but the Board of Neurosurgery at Rainov's hospital refused to approve the treatment plan, stating that it was simply too dangerous (Belkin, 2002). Britain's

Committee on Safety of Medicines entered the fray, saying that there was no rational basis for prescribing the drug ("Family of VCJD Victim," 2003).

Don didn't give up. He found a hospital in Germany that would allow the PPS treatment. He chartered a medical transport plane—at his own expense—and prepared his son for the trip. But days before the family was set to leave, the German Department of Health blocked them. Germany had no cases of mad cow disease and wanted to keep it that way.

Again, Don refused to give up. He hired a lawyer and took the case to court in Great Britain. There were numerous legal battles. But in December 2002, 15 months after the initial diagnosis, a High Court judge ruled that the family could proceed with the treatment.

Jonathan began PPS treatments in February 2003. After several months, his doctors noticed that his heart rhythms were improving, that he had regained his ability to swallow, and that he was more responsive to light and pain. There were none of the adverse side effects that critics had predicted. By all accounts, the disease has been brought under control. In 2005, he was declared no longer terminally ill. It's doubtful that Jonathan will ever be fully "cured," but he is still alive, something no one—except his father—thought possible at the time of his diagnosis.

The message of the Jonathan Simms case is sociologically compelling: An individual was able to overcome the institutional obstacles of a massive international medical establishment to find a solution to a seemingly insoluble problem. As we have seen throughout this book, institutions must operate in a highly structured, standardized, and impersonal way, at a level above the interests and personalities of the individual people they are created to serve. Imagine the chaos that would ensue if the system were set up so that any parent with a terminally ill child could compel researchers, physicians, and hospitals to concoct unique treatments. The entire health care system would quickly collapse. From an institutional perspective, new drugs must be tested meticulously to determine their effectiveness and to identify all potentially dangerous side effects before they are made available to the public. A sharp line must be drawn between the need to satisfy the principles of sound scientific method and the desire to help people who are suffering (D.J. Rothman & Edgar, 1992). Indeed, in 2005, the Food and Drug Administration slowed down its drug approval process in response to several reports of unsafe drugs on the market (Harris, 2005). But Jonathan's story shows that individuals can overcome bureaucratic lethargy and actually change a part of the social structure. As a result of Don Simms's actions, the standard medical approach to treating people infected with mad cow disease will probably never be the same again.

In the past, only the most dedicated individuals, such as Don Simms, were able to become highly involved in medical decisions. Today, however, when a doctor mentions a diagnosis or prescribes a drug, patients can immediately go online to find information at over 100,000 medical Web sites now offering information (some of it more trustworthy than others) on everything from common colds to exotic diseases. And when they visit their doctors, more and more patients arrive with reams of printout bearing information downloaded from Web sites (Kolata, 2000).

By working together, individuals with the same illnesses or medical concerns have also been able to rise above institutional obstacles and act as their own best advocates.

For instance, in the early 1990s AIDS deaths were mounting while the slow progress of the government drug-approval process kept drugs out of the hands of the people who needed them. But AIDS activists succeeded in changing the way AIDS drugs are developed and regulated. Potentially helpful treatments are now being produced more quickly and are making an impact. The mother-to-child transmission of HIV/AIDS in the United States, for example, has been all but eliminated (Santora, 2005). AIDS activists have also successfully pressured pharmaceutical companies to allow developing countries in sub-Saharan Africa to import cheaper, generic anti-AIDS drugs (Swarns, 2001). These activists have worked together to magnify the power none of them could have had acting individually. The scope of their achievements reaches beyond sick individuals to global institutions and concerns.

This theme—the power of individuals acting collectively to change the structural elements of their society—guides this final chapter of the book. I have spent the previous 13 chapters discussing how our society and everything in it is socially constructed and how these social constructions, in turn, affect the lives of individuals. You may well feel a little helpless when considering how much control culture, bureaucracies, institutions, and systems of social stratification have over our lives. It's only fitting, then, to end this book on a more encouraging note, with a discussion of social change and the ways individuals can reconstruct their society.

Social Change

The world in which you are living at this precise moment is undoubtedly different from the one I experienced when I finished writing this book. Our personal perspectives are different, of course. But much can change in even a year. Change is the preeminent characteristic of modern human societies, whether it occurs in personal relationships, cultural norms and values, systems of stratification, or institutions. Everywhere you look—your school, your job, your home, your government, every aspect of your very way of life—institutional and cultural change is the rule, not the exception.

As a result of substantive changes affecting many social institutions simultaneously, the United States and other technologically advanced societies have become what sociologists call **postindustrial societies.** Economies that once centered around farms or factories and the production of material goods now revolve around information and service industries, including communication, mass media, research and development, tourism, insurance, banking and finance, and computer systems. The everyday lives of ordinary people in these societies are qualitatively different from the lives of those in agricultural or industrial societies.

Change is clear when we look at specific institutions. Consider how the nature of education has changed. If you had taken this sociology course 30 years ago, your instructor would have needed only a few tools: a good collection of books on the subject, a manual typewriter, some pencils, a ditto machine, a stack of carbon paper, and a love of the discipline. Good instructors today still need a love of the discipline (I hope), but it's becoming difficult to teach interestingly, effectively, and efficiently without taking advantage of state-of-the-art technology: a high-speed desktop or laptop computer, classroom access to the Internet, e-mail, online databases, computerized test banks, a video library, and access to photocopy and fax machines. My university goes so far as to offer financial incentives to professors who want to revise their courses to incorporate the latest technology. Indeed, technological advances have made similar inroads into almost every occupation—as well as almost every social institution.

U.S. family life has also changed considerably over the past 50 years. Divorce rates skyrocketed, then stabilized. Women have entered the workforce in unprecedented numbers. People are waiting longer to get married, and once they do, they are having fewer children. Cultural concerns about gender equality have altered the way men and women relate to one another inside and outside the home. Social and sexual rules that once seemed permanent have disintegrated: Unmarried couples can live openly together, unmarried women can have and keep their babies without community condemnation, and remaining single and remaining childless have become acceptable lifestyle options (Skolnick & Skolnick, 1992). In short, today's American family bears little resemblance to the cultural ideal of the 1950s.

These changes have, in turn, affected other institutions. Because so many families are headed by dual-earner couples these days, children spend less time with their parents than they did in the past, forcing families to depend on others to care for their children: paid caregivers, friends, teachers. More parents than ever before now rely on professional day care centers to watch their preschool-age children. Many of these centers require that children be toilet trained before they enroll, forcing many parents to exert premature pressure on their children to comply. As a result, many pediatricians report they are seeing more children with toilet training problems, such as lack of daytime and nighttime urine control (E. Goode, 1999).

Schools are also being called on to address many of the problems that families used to deal with at home. They now routinely provide students with training in moral values, technological and financial "literacy," adequate nutrition, and practical instruction to help them avoid drug and alcohol abuse, teen pregnancy, and sexually transmitted diseases.

Not surprisingly, the very nature of childhood is also changing. Contemporary social critics argue that childhood has all but disappeared in the modern world. In the United States, children are exposed to events, devices, and ideas that would have been inconceivable to their Baby Boom or Generation X parents when they were young. Parents and school officials place unprecedented pressures on children to perform and succeed:

> Preschoolers read, fifth graders take S.A.T.'s for admission to summer college programs and high school juniors are told they need three advanced-placement or college-level courses for Ivy League consideration. And they are urged to build a curriculum vitae that includes sports, student government, music, volunteer work, summer courses and internships. Children are drowning, up until midnight. (J. Gross, 1997, p. 22)

More seriously, children are increasingly having trouble getting along in society. A 2005 nationwide study found that about 7 out of every 1,000 3- and 4-year-old preschoolers are expelled each year for misbehavior, a rate more than three times as high as that for K–12 students (Gilliam, 2005). We read about 12-year-olds becoming pregnant and 7-year-olds being tried for such crimes as rape and drug smuggling.

In Pensacola, Florida, a 5-year-old girl faced assault charges for beating a 51-year-old school counselor. In Columbus, Ohio, an 8-year-old girl was charged with attempted murder for allegedly pouring poison into her great-grandmother's drink because the two didn't get along. A 6-year-old in Michigan shot and killed a classmate. A 7-year-old boy in Tampa beat his 7-month-old sister to death with a two-by-four (Chachere, 2005).

The National Longitudinal Study of Adolescent Health found that one in four young people between the ages of 12 and 17 has used a gun or knife—or has been in a situation where someone was injured by a weapon—in the past year ("Study Finds Increase in Weapons Use," 2000). Between 1998 and 2002, some 90,000 teachers nationwide were the victims of violent crimes and about one out of every ten elementary and secondary school teachers was threatened with injury by a student (DeVoe et al., 2004). No wonder that since the late 1980s, 44 states have adopted new laws enabling courts to try more children as adults. Each year over 6,000 children are sent to adult prisons (Bradsher, 1999b).

The situation is even worse in other parts of the world. For instance, a growing number of children are being drawn into combat as soldiers. According to the United Nations, more than 300,000 children under 18—some as young as 7—are taking part in armed conflicts in places such as the Sudan, Colombia, Angola, Iraq, and Afghanistan ("UN to Protect Children," 1999). Clearly children's lives are no longer as carefree as we might hope for them to be.

❖ ───────────────────────────

Micro-Macro Connection
Parental Pressure in Childhood Sports

In the past, childhood sports were simply for fun and recreation. But sports are now a multibillion-dollar business (Greene, 2004). A few years ago, Nike signed Freddie Adu, at the time a 13-year-old soccer player, to a $1 million endorsement deal. Another 13-year-old, a snowboarder, signed a multiyear contract with Mountain Dew. Nice Skateboards sponsored a 4-year-old skateboarding prodigy from Louisville. And Reebok created a commercial campaign built around a 3-year-old basketball player (Talbot, 2003). With the promise of lucrative careers looming large, young children who show some promise are being encouraged to hone their skills early on. For instance, gymnasts and figure skaters must start training for their athletic futures when they're toddlers, if they have any desire to compete and succeed later on.

At local communities all across the country, parents encourage or sometimes force their children—who may be as young as nine—to specialize in one sport and play it year-round, making sports look, for all intents and purposes, like work. When asked how long the baseball season is for his team of nine-year-olds, one coach replied, "Labor Day to Labor Day" (quoted in Pennington, 2003, p. C16). Ironically, such early specialization is making children less athletically well rounded and more prone to injury.

Furthermore, it has become rather common for children to be turned over to professionals for training for future athletic careers. Some affluent towns have youth soccer clubs that are run by paid directors and coached by professionals rather than parent volunteers. Many parents go even further. At IMG Academies, in Bradenton, Florida, for instance, potential sports prodigies—in team sports like baseball, basketball, and soccer as well as individual sports like tennis and golf—practice their sport over four hours a day for five days a week from September to May. In addition, they participate in hours of intense physical and mental conditioning each week. Tuition plus room and board can cost over $30,000 a year, and that's not counting other extras like private coaching sessions, which can go for an additional $500 an hour. In the end, some parents end up investing hundreds of thousands of dollars in their children's athletic futures (Sokolove, 2004).

Parents who pressure their children to succeed athletically defend their actions by citing studies that show that adolescents involved in sports are less likely to use drugs and are more likely to be good students than children who aren't involved. The ultra-organized model of sports teams, they believe, is a valuable way to teach children qualities they will need down the road, like teamwork, responsibility, and self-reliance.

But not everyone is in favor of specialized, pressurized sports experiences for children. In Montclair, New Jersey, for example, parents were successful in persuading local officials to sponsor a fall-only soccer team so their children could play other sports during the other seasons. At one middle school in La Jolla, California, administrators imposed a requirement that athletes play at least two sports (Pennington, 2003). And some communities have established "Silent Saturdays," days in which soccer coaches are asked not to coach their players and parents are asked not to cheer or guide their children in any way. There is no shouting, swearing, or yelling at referees and, according to supporters, no pressure on children. They are free to have fun (Powell, 2004).

As we saw in Chapter 9, the pressure on children to excel at younger and younger ages reflects a growing concern with young people's ability to compete in an increasingly tight economic marketplace. In the pressure-packed world of childhood sports we see the interconnections of large-scale social forces and everyday life.

The Speed of Social Change

In the distant past, societies tended to change slowly, almost imperceptibly, during the course of one's lifetime. Family and community traditions typically spanned many generations. Although the traditional societies that exist today still change relatively slowly, change in postindustrial societies is particularly fast paced. Just in writing this book, I've had to revise several examples at the last minute because some things changed so abruptly. The 1990s already seem like a long gone era.

Because we live in a world that seems to be in a constant state of flux, we're often tempted to believe that rapid social change is an exclusively contemporary issue. Keep in mind, however, that sociologists and other scholars have long expressed deep concern over the effects that social change has on people. The 19th-century sociologist Émile Durkheim argued that rapid social change creates a vacuum in norms, which he called **anomie**, where the old cultural rules no longer apply. When things change quickly—through sudden economic shifts, wars, natural disasters, population explosions, or rapid transitions from a traditional to a modern society—people become disoriented and experience anomie as they search for new guidelines to govern their lives.

Widespread anomie affects the larger society as well. When rapid change disrupts social norms, it unleashes our naturally greedy impulses. Without norms to constrain our unlimited aspirations and with too few resources to satisfy our unlimited desires, we are in a sense doomed to a frustrating life of striving for unattainable goals (Durkheim, 1897/1951). The result, Durkheim felt, is higher rates of suicide and criminal activity as well as weakened ties to family, neighborhood, and friends.

But rapid change isn't always bad. Sometimes rapid change is necessary to effectively address shifting social conditions. For instance, over the span of a few years in the late 1990s, school districts around the country drastically modified their curricula in response to the sudden ascendancy of the Internet in students' everyday lives, forever changing the face of U.S. education. In the wake of the September 11, 2001 attacks, universities around the country scrambled to offer more courses on Islam and the politics of the Middle East.

The velocity of change today has affected the way sociologists go about their work, too. When U.S. society was understood to be relatively stable, sociological study was fairly straightforward. Most social researchers in the 1950s believed that one could start a 5- or 10-year study of some social institution, such as the family or higher education, and assume that the institution would still be much the same when the study ended (A. Wolfe, 1991). Today, such assumptions about the staying power of institutions are dubious at best. There is no such thing as a permanent social institution. Thus sociologists, like everyone else in contemporary society, have had to adjust their thinking and their methods to accommodate the rapid pace of social change.

Causes of Social Change

The difficulty of pinning down any aspect of society when change is so rapid has led sociologists to study change itself. Following in the footsteps of Durkheim, they ask, What causes all these technological, cultural, and institutional changes? On occasion, massive social change—from the private lives of individuals to entire social institutions—can result from a single dramatic historical event, such as the attacks of September 11, 2001 or Hurricane Katrina. We can be thankful that such colossal events are relatively rare. Sociologists who focus on change, however, tell us that change is more likely to be caused over time by a variety of social forces, including environmental and population pressures, cultural innovation, and technological and cultural diffusion.

Environmental and Population Pressures

As you saw in Chapter 13, the shifting size and shape of the population—globally and locally—is enough by itself to create change in societies. As populations grow, more and more people move either into urban areas where jobs are easier to find or into previously uninhabited areas where natural resources are plentiful.

Environmental sociologists note the complex interplay among people, social structure, and natural resources as previously undeveloped territories are settled. For instance, one social scientist has argued that many civilizations throughout history—such as the Easter Islanders, the Mayans, and the Norse colony on Greenland—collapsed because deforestation led to soil erosion, which led to food shortages and ultimately political and social collapse (Diamond, 2005).

Even when new areas are developed for food production, environmental damage often occurs. Of course, improved food supplies have had obvious benefits for societies around the world. Fewer and fewer people are dying from famine and malnutrition than ever before. But the positive effects of a growing global food supply have been tempered by the serious environmental harm that new production techniques have caused. For instance, pesticide use has increased seventeen-fold over the past several decades, threatening the safety of water supplies. Some insects have developed resistances, which leads to increased pesticide use. New crop varieties often require more irrigation than old varieties, which has been accompanied by increased erosion and water runoff. As demand for meat products increases, cattle ranches expand, destroying natural habitats, displacing native animal species, and polluting water sources. Modern factory farming practices have helped spread mad cow disease throughout England (Cowley, 2003). The burning of forests to make room for farmland—not to mention the increasing consumption of coal, oil, and natural gas—has been implicated as one of the chief causes of global warming (M.H. Cooper, 1998b; Revkin, 1997).

But more positive social change has also accompanied environmental pressures. For example, natural disasters such as earthquakes, hurricanes, and tornadoes often inspire improvements in emergency response technology, home safety products, and architectural design that improve everyone's lives. Likewise, concerns about pollution have fostered innovative changes in behavior (such as recycling and conserving energy) and the development of environmentally safe products and services (low-watt light bulbs, low-flow shower heads, biodegradable detergent, and so on). Evidence of global warming and dwindling oil supplies are encouraging the development of nonpolluting energy sources, such as solar power and wind power. The result is felt not only on an individual level but also on a societal level, as eco-efficient and environmentally sustainable businesses grow around these innovations and attract investors.

Cultural Innovation

Sometimes change is spurred by scientific discoveries and technological inventions within the material culture of a society. Improvements in motor vehicle safety, such as air bags, safety belts, child safety seats, and motorcycle helmets have contributed to large reductions in motor vehicle deaths and fundamentally changed the way we drive. Water fluoridation is credited for a 40% to 60% reduction in tooth loss in adults. Safer and healthier foods have all but eliminated such nutritional deficiency diseases as rickets, goiter, and pellagra in the United States (Centers for Disease Control, 1999).

Often revolutionary cultural innovations seem small and insignificant at first. Imagine what life would be like without the invention of corrective eyeglasses, which dramatically extended the activities of near- and far-sighted people and fostered the belief that physical limitations could be overcome with a little ingenuity. The invention of indoor plumbing, the internal combustion engine, television, the microchip, nuclear fusion, antibiotics, and effective birth control have been instrumental in determining the course of human history. Sometimes the smallest innovation has the largest impact: According to one author, without the machine-made precision screw—the most durable way of attaching one object to another—entire fields of science would have languished, routine maritime commerce would have been impossible, and there would have been no machine tools and hence no industrial products and no industrial revolution (Rybczynski, 1999).

But social institutions can sometimes be slow to adjust to scientific and technological innovations. Consider, for instance, the medical treatment of infertility. Artificial insemination, in vitro fertilization, surrogate motherhood, and other medical advances have increased the number of previously infertile people who can now bear and raise children. Yet these technological developments were changing the face of parenthood well before society began to recognize and address the ethical, moral, and legal issues raised by them. For instance, surrogacy technology has divided motherhood into three distinct roles, which can now be occupied by three separate people—the *genetic* mother (the one who supplies the egg from which the fetus develops), the *gestational* mother (the one who carries the fetus and gives birth), and the *social* mother (the one who raises the child)—making legal parenthood unclear in some cases. Controversy arose recently in a case involving a lesbian couple in which one partner provided the eggs that were then fertilized with sperm from an anonymous donor and implanted into the other partner's uterus. Twin girls were born. But when the women broke up six years later, a battle ensued over who was entitled to custody of the children. The judge ruled in favor of the gestational mother, though the case is under appeal (P. Orenstein, 2004).

Technological innovations can also change people's behavior in unanticipated ways, as in the following cases (Hafner, 2002; Kolata, 1997; Tenner, 1996):

- ◆ Low-tar, low-nicotine cigarettes encourage people to continue smoking.
- ◆ Using home entertainment technology (VCRs, TiVo, DVD players, 500-channel satellite television receivers) now requires a complicated array of digital commands that can take hours to master, turning what was once a mindless form of relaxation into another form of stressful and time-consuming work.
- ◆ The distractions caused by technological devices used in cars—cell phones, on-board navigation systems, e-mail systems, entertainment centers, even fax machines—may be responsible for as many as 1.5 million crashes each year.
- ◆ The emphasis on antibacterial cleanliness in wealthy, technologically advanced countries has been accompanied by an increase in asthma, hay fever, eczema, and other allergic diseases (Morse, 1998). Some scientists argue that, without contact with dirt and germs—which contain helpful microbes—people's immune systems don't develop properly.

Similar problems have been created by advances in computer technology. The Internet, in particular, has revolutionized our lives by making purchasing, communicating, and information gathering easy and efficient. It has all but eliminated the constraints of time and place, whether we're conversing with friends, researching a topic of interest for a school paper, or conducting everyday business. Experts predict that within 10 years it will utterly transform news publishing, education, the workplace, health care, politics, art, international relations, neighborhoods, and private family life (Fox, Anderson, & Rainie, 2005).

But the convenience and unprecedented access to information that the Internet provides us have come at a steep price. At the level of personal well-being, the spread of computers has been implicated in increased rates of "Internet addiction" and carpal tunnel syndrome (a nerve disorder in the hands caused by too much keyboard use). Sitting at a computer too long can cause E-Thrombosis, the formation of blood clots in legs that can be fatal if they travel to the lungs (Aldridge, 2003).

Our reliance on computer technology has also made us much more vulnerable to identity theft and government surveillance. Hackers, viruses, worms, spam, spyware and phishing sites have become so common that it's virtually impossible to use a computer these days without falling victim to them. At the time I was writing this book, the computer security firm, Symantec, had catalogued over 11,000 computer vulnerabilities (Cha, 2005). Technology experts warn that in the coming decade the Internet will become such a crucial part of people's lives worldwide that the entire network itself will turn into an inviting target for attack (Fox et al., 2005).

And it's not just the Internet. Electric passes that allow drivers to have bridge or road tolls deducted automatically from their accounts let them proceed more quickly through toll booths, but they also allow the government to track drivers' movements (Clymer, 2002). Since September 11, 2001, there has been a huge increase in the use of surveillance cameras—some run by law enforcement, others by private businesses—in airports, stores, banks, schools, hospitals, busy urban sidewalks, and quiet suburban neighborhoods (Murphy, 2002). In 2004, the Food and Drug Administration approved the manufacture of under-the-skin computer chips that would provide access to individuals' medical information. Although supporters believe access to such information will improve medical care and save lives, opponents fear that the chips will further erode our personal privacy (Feder & Zeller, 2004).

Furthermore, although high-tech electronic and telecommunications gadgets have had breathtaking effects on the way we communicate with others, they've also blurred the traditional boundary between home and work. Cell phones, pagers, and wireless e-mail have created a workday and a workweek that never end (Hafner, 2000). With all these devices, the unspoken expectation is that a person will always be reachable. Hence we no longer have any excuse to be "away" from work, not even while on vacation. If such technological intrusion continues, institutions such as the family are almost certain to change.

Diffusion of Technologies and Cultural Practices

Another cause of social change is **cultural diffusion**: the process by which beliefs, technology, customs, and other cultural items are spread from one group or society to another. You may not realize it, but most of the taken-for-granted aspects of our daily lives originally came from somewhere else. For instance, pajamas, clocks, toilets, glass, coins, newspapers, and soap were initially imported into Western cultures from other cultures (Linton, 1937). Even a fair amount of the English language has been imported; for example,

Algebra (Arabic)	*Dynamite* (Swedish)
Anatomy (Greek)	*Ketchup* (Chinese)
Bagel (Yiddish)	*Medicine* (Latin)
Barbecue (Taino)	*Safari* (Swahili)
Boondocks (Filipino Tagalog)	*Sherbet* (Turkish)
Caravan (Arabic)	*Tycoon* (Chinese)
Catamaran (Tamil)	*Vogue* (French)
Coyote, poncho (Spanish)	*Zero* (Arabic)

Diffusion often occurs because one society considers the culture or technology of another society to be useful. However, the diffusion process is not always friendly, as you may recall from the discussion of colonization in Chapter 10. When one society's territory is taken over by another society, the indigenous people may be required to adapt to the customs and beliefs of the invaders. When the Europeans conquered the New World, Native American peoples were forced to abandon their traditional ways of life and become more "civilized." Hundreds of thousands of Native Americans died in the process, not only from violent conflict but also from malnutrition and new diseases inadvertently brought by their conquerors. Whether diffusion is invited or imposed, the effect is the same: a chain reaction of social changes that affect both individuals and the larger social structure.

Social Movements

One danger of talking about the structural sources of social change or its cultural, environmental, and institutional consequences is that we then tend to see change as a purely macro-level, structural phenomenon, something that happens to us rather than something we create. But social change is not some huge, invisible hand that descends from the heavens to arbitrarily alter our routine way of life. It is, in the end, a phenomenon driven by human action.

Collective action by large numbers of people has always been a major agent of social change, whether it takes the form of mothers marching on Washington, D.C. to demand gun control legislation, people holding a pray-in outside the Capitol building to encourage lawmakers to pass a budget "that is more reflective of the moral values of our nation" ("Religious groups gather," 2005), or a sit-in by students in the Harvard University president's house to demand higher wages for the school's blue-collar workers. When people organize and extend their activities beyond the immediate confines of the group, they may become the core of a **social movement** (Zurcher & Snow, 1981).

Underlying all social movements is a concern with social change: the desire to enact it, stop it, or reverse it. That desire may be expressed in a variety of ways, from such peaceful activities as signing petitions, participating in civil demonstrations, donating money, protesting in the streets, and campaigning during elections to such violent activities as rioting and overthrowing a government.

Types of Social Movements

Social movements can be categorized, depending on the magnitude of their goals, as either reform movements or revolutionary movements. A **reform movement** attempts to change limited aspects of a society but does not seek to alter or replace major social institutions. Take the U.S. civil rights movement of the 1960s. It did not call for an overhaul of the U.S. economic system (capitalism) or the political system (two-party democracy). Instead, it advocated a more limited change: opening up existing institutions to full and equal participation by members of minority groups (DeFronzo, 1991). Similarly, the anti–Vietnam War movement questioned government policy (and in the process brought down two presidents—Lyndon Johnson and Richard Nixon), but it didn't seek to change the form of government itself (Fendrich, 2003). Other recent examples of reform movements include the women's movement, the nuclear freeze movement, the labor union movement, the school prayer movement, and the environmental movement.

Because reform movements seek to alter some aspect of existing social arrangements, they are usually opposed by some people and groups. **Countermovements** are designed to prevent or reverse the changes sought or accomplished by an earlier movement. A countermovement is most likely to emerge when the reform movement against which it is reacting becomes large and effective in pursuing its goals and therefore comes to be seen as a threat to personal and social interests (Chafetz & Dworkin, 1987; Mottl, 1980).

For instance, the emergence in the 1980s and 1990s of a conservative social countermovement often called the "religious right" or the "Christian right" was provoked by a growing perception among its members of enormous social upheaval in U.S. society: a breakdown of traditional roles and values and a concerted challenge to such existing institutions as education, religion, and the family. Although members of the religious right blame these changes on the civil rights, antiwar, student, and women's movements of the 1960s and 1970s (Klatch, 1991), they perceive the women's movement as particularly corrosive. Indeed, the leaders of the religious right were the first, in modern times, to articulate the notion that the push for women's equality is responsible for the unhappiness of many individual women and the weakening of the American family (Faludi, 1991). Access to legal abortion, the high divorce rate, and the increased number of working mothers are often mentioned as proof that the moral bases of family life are eroding (Klatch, 1991).

Over the last few decades, the religious right has successfully shifted the political and social mood of the country. It first gained legitimacy in 1980, when presidential candidate Ronald Reagan and several Senate candidates it supported won election. It reasserted its influence in 1994 with the takeover of Congress by conservative Republicans. And it gained even more power and visibility with the election and reelection of George W. Bush, who promotes many religious right themes. At one point, the seven highest ranking Republican senators in the U.S. Senate were all staunch supporters of the religious right (Theocracy Watch, 2005).

In the 2000s, the religious right has turned its focus to opposing the increasing visibility of homosexuality in American society. It was mobilized, in particular, by a U.S. Supreme Court decision that deemed laws banning homosexual contact unconstitutional and by legislative actions in Massachusetts and the city of San Francisco that for a while allowed same-sex couples to marry. Through organizations such as the Eagle Forum, the Christian Coalition, the Family Research Council, the National Right to Life Committee, the Traditional Values Coalition, Concerned Women for America, Focus on the Family, the Alliance for Marriage and many smaller groups around the United States, it has achieved some notable triumphs at the state and local levels. It has succeeded in influencing public school curricula as well as promoting antigay rights legislation and defense of marriage acts.

Over the years, the religious right has been especially effective in limiting access to abortion. Even though the majority of U.S. citizens still favor the legal right to abortion, virtually every state in the nation has enacted new restrictions on abortion since 1996. In Montgomery, Alabama, for example, teenage girls who want an abortion without a parent's permission must go to court to get permission from a particular judge who is a member of the religious right. During the hearing, the girls face cross-examination by an attorney appointed by the court to represent the fetus (Holmes, 2003). In addition, abortion clinics have been picketed, blockaded, vandalized, and on occasion firebombed. Given such an environment, it's not surprising that rates of abortion have declined steadily over the past two decades (Finer & Henshaw, 2003). About 87% of all U.S. counties (and 97% of rural counties) have no abortion provider and the number of hospitals providing abortions decreased by 57% between 1982 and 2000 (Henshaw, 2003). By 1995, only 12% of obstetrics and gynecology residents were routinely trained in abortion techniques. The percentage remains low today, although pressure from medical student advocacy groups has led some programs to reinstate abortion in the curriculum (cited in T.M. Edwards, 2001).

The women's movement, the gay rights movement, and the religious right all remain quite active today, creating numerous colorful conflicts in the national political arena. However, it is important to remember that all these movements are pursuing their interests within the existing social system—as do all reform movements and countermovements. In contrast, **revolutionary movements** attempt to overthrow the entire system itself, whether it is the government or the existing social structure, in order to replace it with another (Skocpol, 1979). The American Revolution of 1776, the French Revolution of 1789, the Russian Revolution of 1917, the Iranian Revolution of 1979, and the Afghan Revolution of 1996 are examples of movements that toppled existing governments and created a new social order.

Revolutionary change in basic social institutions can be brought about through nonviolent means, such as peaceful labor strikes, democratic elections, and civil disobedience. However most successful revolutions have involved some level of violence on the part of both movement participants and groups opposing revolution (DeFronzo, 1991).

Elements of Social Movements

Whatever type they are, social movements occur when dissatisfied people see their condition as resulting from society's inability to meet their needs. Movements typically develop when certain segments of the population conclude that society's resources—access to political power, higher education, living wages, legal justice, medical care, a clean and healthy environment, and so on—are distributed unequally and unfairly (R. Brown, 1986). People come to believe that they have a moral right to the satisfaction of their unmet expectations and that this satisfaction cannot or will not occur without some effort on their part. This perception is often based on the experience of past failures of working within the system.

As individuals and groups who share this sense of frustration and unfairness interact, the existing system begins to lose its perceived legitimacy (Piven & Cloward, 1977). Individuals who ordinarily might have considered themselves helpless come to believe that they have the capacity to change things and significantly alter their lives and the lives of others. For example, in the early 2000s, tens of thousands of janitors all around the country went on strike to demand health insurance and better wages. Typically, janitors are among the most invisible and least appreciated workers. But in Chicago they banded together to block downtown traffic. In Los Angeles, they walked off their jobs. In New York, they marched down Park Avenue. In San Diego, some went on a hunger strike. In several cities, the janitors won new contracts.

Ideology

Any successful social movement must have an **ideology**, a coherent system of beliefs, values, and ideas that justifies its existence (R. W. Turner & Killian, 1987; Zurcher & Snow, 1981). An ideology fulfills several functions. First, it helps frame the issue in moral terms. Once people perceive the moral goodness of their position, they become willing to risk arrest, personal financial costs, or worse for the good of the cause; to *not* act is perceived as immoral. Second, the ideology defines the group's interests and helps to identify people as either supporters or enemies, creating identifiable groups of "good guys" and "villains." Finally, an ideology provides participants with a collective sense of what the specific goals of the movement are or should be.

Consider the antiabortion movement. Its ideology rests on several assumptions about the nature of childhood and motherhood (Luker, 1984). For instance, it assumes that each conception is an act of God, and so abortion violates God's will. The ideology also states that life begins at conception, the fetus is an individual who has a constitutional right to life, and every human life should be valued (Michener, DeLamater, & Schwartz, 1986). This ideology reinforces the view among adherents that abortion is immoral, evil, and self-indulgent.

The power of an ideology to mobilize support for a social movement often depends on the broader cultural and historical context in which the movement exists. For instance, it would have seemed, in the 2003 build up to the invasion of Iraq, that antiwar activists would be able to make a strong case against going to war by using an ideology based on a portrayal of the United States as a hostile aggressor. After all, the country we were set to invade, Iraq, posed no direct threat to the United States, hadn't undertaken a large-scale military mobilization, wasn't involved in planning or carrying out the 9/11 attacks that precipitated our military action, and wasn't harboring those who were involved. Internationally, the sympathetic response that we received from other countries immediately after the attacks was short-lived, replaced by a growing reputation of the United States as a global bully whose policies ignore the interests of people in other countries (Pew Research Center, 2005). The vast majority of nations around the world—foes and allies alike—were strongly opposed to the invasion.

But the post-9/11 cultural atmosphere in this country was a mixture of anger, fear, lingering shock, and heightened patriotism that made military restraint intolerable to many Americans. Enduring memories of earlier antiwar protestors' hostility toward soldiers returning from Vietnam during the late 1960s and early 1970s complicated the task. Reluctant to disrespect those individuals in Iraq who were willing to put their lives at risk, antiwar activists had to walk a thin line between opposing American aggression and expressing support for the young men and women who were being asked to carry out that aggression on the front lines. Against such a backdrop, the ideology of the antiwar movement—which advocated a diplomatic, reflective, and measured approach—sounded weak and inadequate, not to mention disloyal to the thousands who died in the 9/11 attacks. Not surprisingly, the movement failed to prevent the onset of war.

Although ideology might be what attracts people to a movement, the ideology must be spread through social networks of friends, family, coworkers, and other contacts (Zurcher & Snow, 1981). For some people, in fact, the ideology of the movement is secondary to other social considerations. Potential participants are unlikely to join without being introduced to the movement by someone they know. The ideological leaders of a social movement might want to believe that participants are there because of "the cause," but chances are that participants have a friend or acquaintance who convinced them to be there (Gerlach & Hine, 1970; Stark & Bainbridge, 1980).

Sometimes the activities required to promote or sustain a particular movement run counter to the ideological goals of the movement itself. The leaders of successful political revolutions, for example, soon realize that to run the country they now control, they must create highly structured bureaucracies not unlike the ones they have overthrown.

Individuals in reform movements may also have to engage in behaviors that conflict with the ideological tenets of the movement. The religious right movement's profamily, promotherhood positions are clearly designed to turn back the feminist agenda. However, early in the movement it became clear that to be successful it would have to enlist high-profile women to campaign against feminist policies. Women on the religious right frequently had to leave their families, travel the country to make speeches, and display independent strength—characteristics that were anything but the models of traditional womanhood they were publicly promoting.

Ironically, social movements sometimes require the involvement of individuals from outside the group of people whose interests the movement represents. For example, many of the people who fought successfully for Blacks' voting rights in Alabama and Mississippi during the civil rights movement of the 1950s and 1960s were middle-class white college students from the North. Similarly, it wasn't until mainstream religious organizations, labor groups, and college students got involved that the living wage movement—an effort to require cities and counties to pay its low-wage workers an amount above the federal minimum wage—became successful. Since 1994, over 100 cities have passed living-wages laws and close to that many are currently considering such ordinances (Tanner, 2002).

The ideology of a social movement gains additional credibility when voiced by those whose interests seem contrary to its goals. The movement against the war in Iraq gained traction not because people took a second look at its original ideology but because some American soldiers who fought there and saw the conditions firsthand started speaking out in opposition, often under the threat of disciplinary action (Houppert, 2005). Some even spoke out while on the front lines, posting daily Web blogs that criticized the condition of military equipment and resources, our lack of understanding of Iraqi insurgents, and ultimately our very involvement in the war (Finer, 2005). Membership in organizations with names like Operation Truth, Veterans for Peace, and Iraq Veterans Against the War has grown over the last few years (Banerjee, 2005). It remains to be seen whether an alliance between war veterans and civilian activists will ultimately achieve the movement's singular goal: to stop the war.

Furthermore, people who are already disadvantaged by particular social conditions may not be as effective as others in promoting their cause, because they lack the money, time, skills, and connections that successful movements require. For instance, the people who would stand to benefit the most from environmental improvement—individuals in poor, polluted communities—have historically been uninvolved in the environmental movement. They also often suspect that environmentalists are taking away their jobs rather than protecting their interests. Recently, however, many members of poor communities have joined the environmental movement, motivated not by a desire to "save the earth" but by an ideology that is more relevant to their everyday lives.

❖
Robert Bullard and Beverly Wright
The Environmental Justice Movement

In Chapter 11, I mentioned that environmental degradation disproportionately affects minority communities. Urban black ghettoes, rural Latino/a "poverty pockets," and economically destitute Native American reservations face the worst environmental devastation in the United States. In Los Angeles, more than 71% of African Americans and 50% of Latino/as live in areas with the most polluted air, compared to only 34% of the white population (Bullard, 1993). A report by the Commission for Racial Justice (1987) concluded that the racial makeup of a community is the best predictor of where toxic waste sites in the United States are located.

For the most part, African Americans and other people of color have been underrepresented in the mainstream environmental movement. The ideological supporters of this movement tend to be middle- and upper-middle-class Whites whose own neighborhoods are relatively unpolluted. They are likely to focus on such goals as wilderness and wildlife preservation, wise resource management, and population control (Bullard, 1993). The environmental degradation of poor, minority communities has been largely overlooked.

The most polluted communities are often on the brink of economic catastrophe, places where providing jobs for residents is of utmost concern. But in many instances bringing jobs to the community has been achieved only at great risk to the health of the workers and people in the surrounding area. For instance, in 1998 the Louisiana chapter of the National Association for the Advancement of Colored People (NAACP) supported the construction of a $700 million plastics plant in St. James Parish, which it knew could pose dangerous health risks to the neighborhoods nearby. Blacks made up 81% of the residents within four miles of the proposed site (Hines, 2001). At the time, the region suffered an unemployment rate of 12% and a poverty rate of 44%. The average income among black residents was less than $5,000 a year. So the possibility of a steady source of employment, no matter how dangerous, was quite attractive. The president of the NAACP said, "Poverty has been the No. 1 crippler of poor people, not chemical plants" (quoted in M.H. Cooper, 1998a, p. 532).

Nobody wants garbage dumps, landfills, incinerators, or polluting factories in their backyards. But if these are the only ventures that will provide steady employment for residents, poor communities are left with little choice but to support them. The result has been a form of blackmail: You can get a job, but only if you're willing to do work that will harm you, your family, and your neighbors (Bullard, 1993).

This issue is not limited to the United States. In the developing world, the desire for clean air and water to protect public health often conflicts with the need for jobs to help struggling workers survive. In 2000, for instance, thousands of people in New Delhi, India, took to the streets in violent protests, demanding that polluting local factories remain open after the Indian Supreme Court took steps to close them. Many of the protestors were sole breadwinners who were barely able to support their families on the $35 to $50 a month they earned in the local factories (Dugger, 2000).

Hence one of the biggest obstacles to getting people in poor, minority communities involved in the environmental movement has been an economic one: the fear of job loss or plant closure. How do you get people to protest against a polluting factory when that factory is their only hope for economic survival? To answer this question, sociologists Robert D. Bullard and Beverly H. Wright (1992) examined environmental activism within African American communities in the South, the region of the United States with the largest ecological disparities between black and white communities. They interviewed activist leaders in five communities involved in environmental disputes: Institute, West Virginia; Alsen, Louisiana; Emelle, Alabama; and black neighborhoods in Houston and Dallas, Texas. In addition, they examined newspaper articles, editorials, and feature stories concerning the disputes.

In the 1980s and early 1990s, communities such as these began to challenge both the industrial polluters and the often indifferent mainstream environmental movement by actively fighting environmental threats in their neighborhoods. The key, according to Bullard and Wright, was that these challenges framed environmental degradation within a social justice ideology rather than an exclusively ecological one. In other words, they were able to band together to fight for their own interests by painting pollution and environmental danger as a form of racial discrimination. The communities argued that environmental quality was a basic civil right of all individuals. Consequently, they adopted the confrontational strategies of the earlier civil rights movement. For instance, all the communities used local protest demonstrations, petitions, and press lobbying to publicize their plight.

Bullard and Wright found that all these movements were spearheaded by local people—church leaders, community improvement workers, and civil rights activists—who had very little previous experience with environmental issues. Many had worked in other organizations that fought discrimination in housing, employment, and education. Local people played a pivotal role in organizing, planning, and mobilizing opposition activities. Mainstream environmental leaders, referred to as "outside elites," played only a minor role. Indeed, many residents were suspicious of the motives of outside environmentalists and the largely white national environmental movement.

All the environmental justice movements that Bullard and Wright examined achieved some level of success:

♦ In West Dallas, people were able to convince the city and state to join in a lawsuit against an industrial polluter that pumped more than 269 tons of lead particles into the air each year. The plant was eventually shut down, and some residents won a $20 million out-of-court settlement against the company.

♦ In Houston, the city council, after intense pressure from the African American community, passed a resolution opposing the placement of a garbage dump nearby. However, a federal court ruled against the plaintiffs, and the dump was eventually built. Nevertheless, the city council passed ordinances that prohibited city-owned solid waste trucks from dumping at the controversial site and regulated the distance between the landfill and schools, parks, and playgrounds.

♦ In Alsen, Emelle, and Institute, protesting residents convinced government officials to fine facilities for pollution and safety violations. In addition, they extracted some concessions from the firms, such as technical modifications, updated pollution monitoring systems, and reduced emission levels.

More recently, residents in Anniston, Alabama, filed a class action suit against Monsanto for contaminating the black community there with polychlorinated biphenyls (PCBs), a highly toxic carcinogen. They reached an out-of-court settlement with the company for $42.8 million. In 2002, citizens of Norco, Louisiana, forced Shell Oil Company to agree to a buyout that allowed residents to relocate. The black community was practically encircled by oil refineries. As one Norco resident put it,

> I am surrounded by 27 petrochemical companies and oil refineries. My house is located only three meters away from the 15-acre Shell chemical plant. We are not treated as citizens with equal rights according to U.S. law and international human rights law. (quoted in Bullard, 2003, p. 26)

The movement has had some national success as well. In 1994 President Bill Clinton issued an executive order calling on each federal agency to identify and address the disproportionately high and adverse health effects of its programs, policies, and activities on minority and low-income populations. Environmental justice advocates say that even though the new policy didn't change any laws, it was a major step forward in protecting the civil rights of poor, minority communities.

We're unlikely to see a massive influx of people of color into national environmental groups in the near future. However, multiracial, grassroots environmental groups have been the fastest-growing segment of the environmental movement over the past decade. These groups are increasingly forming alliances with one another and with other community-based groups to increase their power (Bullard, 1993). The days are long gone when minority communities would remain silent or refuse to question the promise of new jobs by companies manufacturing dangerous products (D. E. Taylor, 1993). And the successes of these groups have caught the attention of mainstream environmental organizations, which now provide support in the form of technical advice, expert testimony, direct financial assistance, fund-raising, research, and legal assistance. The environmental community and the social justice community are beginning to take steps toward reducing the artificial barriers that have historically kept them apart.

❖ ❖

Rising Expectations

You might think that major social movements, particularly revolutionary ones, would be most likely to occur when many people's lives were at their lowest and most desperate point. Certainly huge numbers of disadvantaged people who see little chance that things will improve, and who perceive the government as unwilling or unable to meet their needs, are necessary for any massive movements for change (Tilly, 1978).

But some sociologists argue that social movements are actually more likely to arise when social conditions are beginning to improve than when they are at their worst (Brinton, 1965; Davies, 1962). Constant deprivation does not necessarily make people want to revolt. Instead, they are more likely to be preoccupied with daily survival than with demonstrations and street protests. Improvements in living conditions, however, show those who are deprived that their society is capable of being different, raising their expectations and sparking a desire for large-scale change. When these expectations aren't met, deprived people become angry. The gap between what they expect and what they have now seems intolerable. Although they may actually be somewhat better off than in the past, their situation relative to their expectations now appears much worse (Davies, 1962). Such frustration makes participation in protest or revolutionary activity more likely.

Consider the short-lived prodemocracy movement in China in 1989. During the early 1980s, the Chinese government began to introduce economic reforms that opened up markets and created faster growth. It also enacted political reforms that provided citizens with more freedom. The lives of ordinary Chinese were improving, but only slightly and not quickly enough. Because they could now imagine even greater freedom and democracy, young people began to actively protest for more reforms. The result was a wide-scale student movement. The government quickly and violently squashed the movement, although after a while it did continue to gradually liberalize Chinese society.

Resource Mobilization

At any given point, numerous problems in a society need fixing, and people's grievances remain more or less constant from year to year. Yet relatively few major social movements exist at any one time. If widespread dissatisfaction and frustration were all that is needed to sustain a social movement, "the masses would always be in revolt" (Trotsky, 1930/1959). What else is needed for a social movement to get started, gain support, and achieve its goals?

According to *resource mobilization theory,* the key ingredient is effective organization. No social movement can exist unless it has an organized system for acquiring needed resources: money, labor, participants, legal aid, access to the media, and so on (McCarthy & Zald, 1977). How far a movement goes in attaining its goals depends on its ability to expand its ranks, build large-scale public support, and transform those who join into committed participants (Zurcher & Snow, 1981).

Most large, long-term social movements involve a national, even international coalition of groups. Such widespread organization makes the movement more powerful by making recruiting and fund-raising more efficient. For example, most of us first heard of the movement against corporate globalization in 1999 when thousands of people in Seattle protested a meeting of the World Trade Organization (WTO). News reports of the event gave the impression that the protesters were a bunch of renegade anarchists who spontaneously took to the streets to vandalize local outlets of corporate giants such as McDonald's and Starbucks. Although a few of the protesters were, in fact, destructive, the vast majority were long-time nonviolent supporters of the movement. The mobilization that was required to get so many people involved was accomplished by various established organizations, such as the AFL-CIO, Sierra Club, Humane Society, Global Exchange, Public Citizen, and Rainforest Action Network. In fact, more than 1,200 labor, environmental, consumer, religious, farm, academic, and human rights groups from over 90 nations had already been working to halt the expansion of the WTO long before the Seattle protest took place (Nichols, 2000; Rothschild, 2000).

Moreover, those movements that historically have lasted longest—the women's movement, the antiabortion movement, the civil rights movement, the environmental movement—are those that are supported by large organizations. The National Organization for Women, the Christian Coalition, the NAACP, the Sierra Club, and the like have full-time lobbyists or political action committees in Washington that connect them to the national political system. Few movements can succeed without such connections because achieving social change often requires changing laws or convincing courts to interpret laws in particular ways.

Another important feature of highly organized social movements is an established network of communication (McCarthy & Zald, 1977). Movements need an effective system both for getting information to all participants and for recruiting and fund-raising (Tarrow, 1994). The ability to quickly mobilize large numbers of people for, say, a march on the nation's capital depends on the ability to tell them what is going to happen and when and where it will happen. Web sites, phone systems, direct mailing systems, and networked computers are all used by modern movements. In recent years, the religious right, for example, has launched several successful e-mail and phone campaigns to influence public opinion and mobilize people to act on such political issues as the Clinton impeachment hearings, the presidential election of 2004, congressional debates over abortion laws, the war in Iraq, and same-sex marriage.

The mass media play an equally important part in the success of a social movement by helping validate and enlarge the scope of its cause. In other words, the media play a key role in constructing a particular social reality useful to the movement. The media spotlight sends the message that the movement's concerns are valid and that the movement is an important force in society. A protest march with no media coverage at all is, for the most part, a nonevent. Media recognition is often a necessary condition before those who are the targets of influence respond to the movement's claims and demands (Gamson & Wolfsfeld, 1993).

In sum, movements that succeed in enacting substantial social change are not necessarily those with the most compelling ideological positions or the greatest emotional appeal (Ferree, 1992). Instead, they are the ones with the necessary high-level organization and communication networks to mobilize supporters and the necessary media access to neutralize the opposition and transform the public into sympathizers.

Bureaucratization

It makes sense that the most successful social movements are the ones that are the best organized. However, high-level organization can backfire if it leads to the rigidity and turf wars common to any bureaucracy. When organizations within a movement differ in their philosophies and tactics, tremendous infighting and bickering may break out among organizations ostensibly working toward the same goal.

For instance, the U.S. civil rights movement during the 1950s and 1960s included many diverse, seemingly incompatible organizations. The National Association for the Advancement of Colored People (NAACP) was large, racially integrated, legalistic, and bureaucratic in form; the Student Non-Violent Coordinating Committee (SNCC) was younger and more militant in its tactics and after a while excluded Whites from participation; the Southern Christian Leadership Conference (SCLC) was highly structured, had a religious ideology, and was dominated by male clergy; the Black Muslims and the Black Panthers advocated violent methods to achieve civil rights. The ideologies and methods of these diverse civil rights groups often conflicted, which arguably slowed down the extension of civil rights to African Americans.

No matter what their shape, size, or motive, social movements require sustained activity over a long period (R. W. Turner & Killian, 1987). Thus unlike riots, which are of limited duration, social movements may become permanent fixtures in the political and social environment. Ironically, a social movement whose goal is the large-scale alteration of some aspect of society can, in time, become so large and bureaucratic itself that it becomes part of the establishment it seeks to change. For instance, Sinn Féin was a movement founded in 1905 to end British rule in Ireland. Among its offshoots over the years was the Irish Republican Army, which carried out a bombing and terror campaign in Northern Ireland and England. In recent years, most of the violence has been stopped and the people of Ireland have won some autonomy. Sinn Féin is now the third largest political party in Ireland, with its own news organization, a highly structured network of local branches, and representatives in both the Irish Parliament and the European Parliament.

In addition, people who devote their lives to a movement come to depend on it for their own livelihood. Hence social movements organized for the purposes of enacting social change actually provide structure and order for the lives of their members, acting as sources of opportunities, careers, and rewards (Hewitt, 1988).

Political Opportunity Structure

Social movements also depend on conditions outside their reach. One such condition is the structure of existing political institutions. Political systems are more or less vulnerable and more or less receptive to challenge at different times (McAdam, McCarthy, & Zald, 1988). These ebbs and flows of political opportunities produce cycles of protest and movement activity. When political systems are firm, unyielding, and stable, people have to deal individually with their problems or air their grievances through existing channels. But when a system opens up and people realize it is vulnerable—that they can actually make a difference—movements are likely to develop.

Sometimes these opportunities are unintentional and exist quite independently from the actions of movement members. For instance, similar antinuclear movements arose about the same time in the 1970s in (what was then West) Germany and France. The movements had similar ideologies and used similar techniques. However, the German movement flourished and remains highly influential in German politics today. The French movement was weak and quickly died off. Why were the outcomes of these two movements so different? In West Germany, the government procedure for reviewing nuclear power facilities provided opportunities for those opposed to nuclear power to legally intervene. The procedure in place in France was closed and unresponsive to public sentiment (Nelkin & Pollack, 1981). Similarly, the emergence in the 1970s of the contemporary environmental movement in the United States was possible because government agencies were already sympathetic to environmental concerns (Gale, 1986).

The idea that unintentional political opportunities can encourage social movements for change was dramatically supported by the 1989 prodemocracy movement in the former Soviet Union and Eastern Europe. In the mid-1980s, the Soviet government under Mikhail Gorbachev embarked on a massive program of economic and structural reforms (*perestroika*) as well as a relaxation of constraints on freedom of expression (*glasnost*). The ensuing liberties encouraged open criticism of the political order and created new opportunities for political action (Tarrow, 1994). Protest movements took advantage of these opportunities, leading to the sometimes violent struggles for independence on the part of small, ethnically homogeneous republics that we saw during the 1990s and continue to see today in a few remaining areas. In other words, only when the political structure became less repressive could these monumental changes take place.

Political instability can sometimes spawn less dramatic reform movements. The changing fortunes of a government can create uncertainty among supporters and encourage challengers to try to take advantage of the situation. Consider once more the civil rights movement in the United States in the 1950s and 1960s. During the 1950s, as the first, early calls for racial equality were being heard, many conservative southern Democrats defected to the Republican Party, where their segregationist leanings met with more sympathy. The ensuing decline of southern white support for the Democratic Party, coupled with the movement of African Americans to large cities in the North, where they were more likely to vote, forced the Democrats to seek black support in the presidential election of 1960. The black vote is widely credited with John Kennedy's narrow victory that year (McAdam, 1982). Hence the Kennedy administration (and later the Johnson administration) felt compelled to campaign for civil rights (Tarrow, 1994). Increased political power, in turn, enhanced the bargaining position of civil rights forces, culminating in two landmark pieces of legislation: the Civil Rights Act of 1964 and the Voting Rights Act of 1965.

At other times, existing political regimes intentionally create or actively support structural opportunities for change. For example, from the beginning the George W. Bush administration accepted political and financial support from Christian fundamentalist groups and organizations. In return, it made some efforts to support things like school prayer, the teaching of "intelligent design" in science classes, and funding for faith-based organizations as well as efforts to limit abortion access and prohibit same-sex marriage. The success of these initiatives further fortified the growth and development of the religious groups and organizations and cemented their political power on the national scene.

Similarly, the U.S. anti–drunk driving movement is strong and influential today because it enjoys substantial support from federal, state, and local governments; state and federal highway agencies; and state and local police departments (McCarthy & Wolfson, 1992). When in the 1980s the movement advocated a national drinking age of 21, many state legislatures balked, fearing a backlash from powerful alcohol producers, distributors, and retailers. However, the federal government enacted legislation threatening to withhold significant amounts of federal highway funds from states that didn't establish the drinking age of 21—a strong incentive for states to pass such a law.

Political opportunities provide the institutional frame within which social movements operate. Movements form when ordinary citizens respond to changes in the opportunity structure that lower the costs of involvement and reveal where the authorities are vulnerable. Unlike money and power, these conditions are external to the movement. If political opportunities exist, then even groups with fairly mild grievances or few resources can develop a successful movement (see also Jenkins & Perrow, 1977). In contrast, groups with deep grievances and ample resources—but few political opportunities—may never get their movements off the ground (Tarrow, 1994).

The Sociological Imagination Revisited

In the summer of 1981 with my brand new bachelor's degree in hand, I had the good fortune to visit Florence, Italy. While there, I made a point of visiting the Galleria dell' Accademia, the museum where one of my favorite works of art, Michelangelo's statue of David, resides. To my eye it is truly a masterpiece of sculpture, nearly flawless in its detail. I stood there admiring this amazing work of art for close to two hours. Afterward, I noticed several sculptures that had escaped my attention when I first entered the museum. I soon discovered that they, too, were created by Michelangelo. What made them particularly interesting was that they were all unfinished. Some were obviously near completion, but others looked to me like shapeless blocks of granite. As I looked closer, I could see the actual chisel marks that the great sculptor had made. I imagined the plan Michelangelo had in his head as he worked. I envisioned him toiling to bring form to the heavy stone.

(Text continues on page 531)

The Coal Miners' Struggle

Eric Margolis

Americans have a long history of using conflict (sometimes violent) to bring about social change, beginning with the American Revolution and continuing through the abolitionist struggle to make slavery illegal, women's suffrage, the civil rights movement, and the movement against the war in Vietnam. One of the longest-lasting and most violent of those movements has been the movement to protect workers' rights, which began not long after the Civil War.

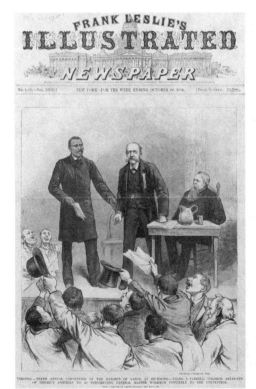

❖ In 1869 a group of Philadelphia tailors organized the Knights of Labor. Borrowing tactics from the abolitionists, the Knights sought nationwide political changes, including an eight-hour workday, an end to child labor, equal pay for women, a graduated income tax, and an end to prison labor contracts. The Knights sought to build an inclusive and diverse organization. This vintage newspaper shows Frank Farrell, an African American delegate to the 1886 Knights of Labor convention, introducing Terrence Powderly, who had risen from machinist to the organization's highest office, Grand Master Workman.

An early member of the Knights was John Mitchell, first president of the United Mine Workers of America (UMW). Coal miners have always had a reputation as radicals in the vanguard of labor organizing. In fact, a century after the Knights was formed, coal miners in Poland and Russia were instrumental in bringing down the Soviet Union. In the 19th and early 20th centuries in America, coal miners organized some of the strongest and most militant unions.

When the UMW was founded, coal mining was the most dangerous occupation in the country (it still is in places like China). Miners' grievances included safety issues as well as long hours, low pay, "fair weight" (an important issue when paid by the ton), and payment in scrip that had to be spent in company stores.

The mines employed many children, often as "breaker boys" separating coal from rock and slate and as mule drivers. Children routinely worked 12-hour shifts underground. In addition, companies could get away with paying children less than adults, and so child labor depressed the miners' wages. Between 1908 and 1912, the crusading photographer Lewis Hine took many photographs of children in the mines on behalf of the National Child Labor Committee (NCLC). The NCLC was founded in 1904 to seek legislation prohibiting child labor.

Mines tended to be in isolated rural areas where companies constructed company towns and rented houses to their employees. The town of Tabasco, Colorado, for instance, was owned by CF&I Corporation, which processed coal from the Tabasco and Berwind mines into coke for the huge steel mill in Pueblo, Colorado. Note the coal washery and coke ovens on the right side of the canyon and the miners' houses in the foreground.

Colorado coal miners went on strike every decade from 1877 to 1927. The 1913–1914 strike was an important event in labor history.

The UMW intended to shut down the mines until the union was recognized as the bargaining agent for the coal diggers; the companies were just as determined to keep the union out.

When the strike was called, the miners and their families had to move off company property and into tents that the union had furnished. Strikers' tent colonies functioned as picket lines, blocking entrance to the canyons where the coal was mined. The largest tent colony, called Ludlow, was a couple of miles from Tabasco and had about 1500 people, including miners and their families.

The battle was waged on the ground in Colorado but also in the court of American public opinion. One of the most effective organizers was 89-year-old Mother Jones. Her husband and children had died in a yellow fever epidemic, and she dedicated her life to the labor movement. "Pray for the dead," she said, "and fight like hell for the living!" Dressed in her customary black, she visited the Ludlow tent colony in 1913.

❖ During a volatile strike, when a confrontation between marching miners and an armed militia and deputies could easily have led to violence, Mother Jones led marches of women and children. It is said that she was the first to put a flower in the barrel of a National Guardsman's gun, a feat replicated during antiwar marches in the 1960s.

The strike dragged on through a long Colorado winter. Deep snows collapsed the miners' tents several times. On April 20, 1914, the tent colony was attacked by militia units that included a number of mine guards formerly employed by the coal companies.

❖ As violence began to escalate, the Colorado National Guard was called in to keep the two sides apart. The militia took a position on Water Tank Hill near Ludlow. Although it was not to take sides, it helped to suppress the strikers.

❖ As the militia raked the tents with machine gun fire, the miners hid in cellars that they had dug beneath the tents. On horseback, the militia raced up and down the rows of tents on horseback, setting fire to them with flaming coal oil. When the fires of Ludlow cooled, the bodies of eleven children and two women were found in one of the cellars.

In a fury, the miners grabbed their guns and attacked mines up and down Colorado's front range. They burned the buildings and killed any militia guards or strikebreakers that they found. The United States Army had to be called in to stop what locals called "The Ten Days War."

Despite public sentiment and political appeals, however, the strike ended without any concessions from the companies. No one was ever held accountable for the deaths of the Ludlow women and children, but strike leaders were arrested and tried, and strikers were prevented from ever working again in the coal industry.

In the nation's mines, mills, and factories, union recognition was finally achieved in 1935 when the National Labor Relations Act became law. The NLRA guaranteed workers the right to form a union by the simple democratic process of voting. The act also required employers to allow union organizing and to negotiate labor contracts with unions.

In the decades since Ludlow, workers have used strikes, picket lines, sit-down strikes, marches, demonstrations, and boycotts to try to achieve their goals. The federal government has stepped in with some regulations and litigation (particularly regarding health, safety, and the environment) that have reduced the occurrences of mine cave-ins, black-lung disease, and environmental degradation. But companies still react to labor unrest by hiring strikebreakers and armed guards to break strikes and by using the power of the state to force workers back to work. Lives and fortunes have been lost in the continuing conflict between workers and the companies they work for.

❖ At the River Rouge Ford plant in Dearborn, Michigan, in 1941, a worker votes in an election for union representation overseen by the National Labor Relations Board. The labor movement continues its struggle, however, as employers use their economic and political clout to limit union power.

These imperfect slabs of rock showed evidence of human creation in a way that the perfect, finished statue of David never could. At that moment, I saw Michelangelo as a real person who fashioned beauty from formlessness. I began to admire the genius of the creator and not just the creation. I went back to look at David again with a newfound appreciation.

Society isn't nearly as perfect as Michelangelo's David, yet we can still fall into the trap of seeing social structure as a product that exists on its own and not as something that people have collectively chiseled. We sometimes forget that many of the realities of our lives that we take for granted were the result, at some point in history, of the handiwork of individuals. One generation's radical changes become another's common features of everyday life. The fact that you can't be forced to work 70 or 80 hours a week, can't be exposed to dangerous working conditions without your knowledge, and are entitled to a certain number of paid holidays a year are a result of the actions of real people in early labor union movements.

Because we take many of our freedoms, rights, and desires for granted, we may not only overlook the struggles of those who came before us but also downplay the extent to which inequities and injustices existed in the past. For instance, many young women today have never even considered that they are only a generation or so removed from a time when they might have been prohibited from attending the college or pursuing the career of their choice; when they might have been expected to abandon their own dreams and ambitions to provide the support their husbands needed to succeed; or when they might have had to take sole responsibility for household chores and their children's daily care while their husbands focused on work and the outside world. The majority of young women polled in a recent survey indicated that they didn't know abortion was once illegal (Zernike, 2003). Like most beneficiaries of past movements, young women today simply take their freedoms and opportunities for granted, sometimes even expressing contempt for the women's movement responsible for the rights they so casually enjoy (Stacey, 1991). The irony of social movements, then, is that the more profound and far-reaching their accomplishments, the more likely we are to eventually forget the original inequities that fostered them and the efforts of the individuals who produced them.

Fundamentally, societies remain stable because enough individuals define existing conditions as satisfactory, and societies change because enough individuals define situations that were once tolerable as problems that must be acknowledged and solved. As one author wrote regarding the antiwar movement of the 1960s and 1970s:

> Ten years and 12 days after the first busloads of demonstrators rolled into Washington to protest U.S. involvement in Indochina, the last planeloads of Americans left Saigon. . . . The standard American histories of the Vietnam War, when they are culled from the memoirs of the generals and politicians . . . are unlikely to record this coincidence. But the decisions about the pursuit of those generals' and politicians' objectives in Indochina were not made only in their carpeted offices. They were also made in the barracks, in the schools, in the streets, by the millions of Americans—Blacks and whites, students, workers, nuns and priests, draftees and draft resisters—who made up the Anti-War Movement. (Cluster, 1979, p. 131)

Some influential acts of individuals may at first blush appear rather insignificant. Early in 1960, four black students at North Carolina Agricultural & Technical State University in Greensboro engaged in a series of discussions in their dormitory rooms about the state of the civil rights movement. They came to the conclusion that things weren't progressing quickly enough in the still-segregated South and that it was time for action. They decided to go to the lunch counter at the local Woolworth's store and order coffee and doughnuts. In the early 1960s South, public eating facilities that weren't reserved for Blacks were forbidden by law to serve Blacks.

After purchasing some school supplies in another part of the store, the four students sat down at the lunch counter and placed their orders. As anticipated, the reply was "I'm sorry, we don't serve you here" (McCain, 1991, p. 115). They remained seated for 45 minutes, citing the fact that they had been served in another part of the store without any difficulty. They were subjected to the verbal taunts, racial slurs, and even violence of angry Whites in the store.

Their actions attracted the attention of area religious leaders, community activists, and students from other local colleges, both black and white. Despite the abuses they knew awaited them, these four young men returned to Woolworth's a few days later, only this time with more demonstrators. At one point they and their fellow protestors occupied 63 of the 65 seats available at the lunch counter. This was the first social movement covered by television too, so word of their actions spread quickly. They received endorsements from religious organizations like the North Carolina Council of Churches. Within weeks, young African Americans and sympathetic Whites had engaged in similar acts in nine states and 54 cities in the South as well as several areas in the North, where stores were picketed. After several months of protests, Woolworth's integrated its lunch counter.

Some historians argue that many of the political movements for change that burst onto the scene in the 1960s—including the women's movement, the antiwar movement, and the student free speech movement—could trace their philosophical and tactical roots to this small act by four students (Cluster, 1979). More recently, college students have staged sit-ins to protest the working conditions in clothing and footwear factories overseas, with some success (Greenhouse, 2000). Admittedly, the participants in all these movements might have developed the sit-in as a tactic on their own, even if in 1960 the four students *had* been served coffee and doughnuts at Woolworth's. The point is, though, that the collective movement that arose from the actions of these seemingly insignificant individuals in 1960 had an enormous impact on the massive changes that occurred in the United States over the next 40 years and probably beyond.

We recreate society not only through acts of defiance and organized social movements but also through our daily interactions. The driving theme throughout this book has been that society and its constituent elements are simultaneously human creations and phenomena that exist independently of us, influencing and controlling our private experiences at every turn.

Organizations and institutions exist and thrive because they implicitly or explicitly discourage individuals from challenging the rules and patterns of behavior that characterize them. Imagine what would happen to the system of higher education if you and others like you challenged the authority of the university. You could establish a new order in which students would dictate the content of courses, take control of the classroom, abolish grading or any other evaluative mechanism used for assessing student performance, do away with tuition, and so on. But because you have an education and a career to gain from the institutional structure as it stands, you're not very likely to do something to jeopardize it.

Are we then to believe that we are all leaves in the wind, buffeted here and there by the powerful and permanent forces of a structure that dwarfs us? To some extent the answer is yes. I subscribe to the sociological imagination and strongly believe that to fully understand our lives we must acknowledge that processes larger than ourselves determine some of our private experiences. Along the way, though, we sometimes lose sight of our important role as shapers of society. Although society presents itself as largely unchangeable, U.S. culture is based at least in part on the "can do" attitude. I recall, as a child in 1969, sitting in a darkened living room with my parents on a warm July evening. The only light in the room came from the gray-blue glow of our little black and white television. I watched with great amazement the fuzzy, almost imperceptible image of astronaut Neil Armstrong taking the first tentative steps on the moon and stating, "That's one small step for man, one giant leap for mankind." I didn't realize at the time how far beyond the space program the power of that statement stretched. But since then I have come to realize that people do indeed leave footprints on the world in which they live.

Conclusion and Farewell

Sociology is not one of those disciplines that draws from a long-standing body of scientific facts and laws. We do have some good explanations for why certain important social phenomena happen, and we can make reasonable predictions about future developments. But sociology is not inherently a discipline of answers. It's a discipline of questions, one that provides a unique and useful method for identifying the puzzles of your life and your society.

This discipline scrutinizes, analyzes, and dissects institutional order and its effects on our thinking. It exposes the vulnerable underbelly of both objective and official reality and, by doing so, prods us into taking a closer look at ourselves and our private worlds, not an easy thing to do. Sociology makes life an unsafe place. I don't mean that it makes people violent or dangerous, I mean that it makes perceptions of social stability unstable or at least fair game for analysis. It's not easy to admit that our reality may be a figment of our collective minds and just one of many possible realities. We live under a belief system that tells us that our unchallenged assumptions are simply the way things are.

Sociology is thus a "liberating" perspective (Liazos, 1985). It forces us to look at the social processes that influence our thoughts, perceptions, and actions and helps us see how social change occurs and the impact we can have on others. In doing so, sociology also points out the very limits of liberation. We become aware of the chains that restrict our "movements." But sociology also gives us the tools to break those chains. The sociological imagination gives us a glimpse of the world both as it is and as it could be. To be a sociologically astute observer of the world as it is, you must be able to strip away fallacies and illusions and see the interconnected system underneath. Only then can you take full advantage of your role as a co-creator of society.

I leave you with one final thought: If you now look at your life and the lives of those around you differently, if you now question things heretofore unquestionable, if you now see where you fit in the bigger societal picture, if you now see orderly patterns in areas you previously thought were chaotic, or chaos in areas you previously thought were orderly, then you are well on your way to understanding the meaning—and the promise—of sociology.

YOUR TURN

Reading about people taking an active role in reconstructing a part of their personal lives or of their society is one thing, but it's quite another to see such people in action. Most communities contain people who were at one time active in a major movement for social change: the labor movement, the antiwar movement, the women's movement, the civil rights movement, the antiabortion movement, and so forth. Find a few people who were involved in one such movement. Ask them to describe their experiences. What was their motive for joining the movement? What sorts of activities did they participate in? What were the goals they wanted to accomplish? Looking back, do they feel the movement accomplished those goals? If not, why not? What else needs to be done?

For purposes of historical comparison, see if you can identify a movement that is currently under way in your community. It might be a drive in support of a broad societal concern, such as environmental or drunk-driving awareness, or a group organized to address an issue of local interest, such as the construction of a new skate park or an attempt to stop the construction of a factory or business.

Try to attend a gathering in which the movement is involved. It might be an organizational meeting, a town council meeting, a protest march, a fund-raiser, or a demonstration. What happened at the gathering? What seemed to be the overall atmosphere? Was it festive, solemn, angry, businesslike? Was any opposition present?

Interview some of the participants. Ask them the same questions you asked the participants who were in past movements. Do people get involved in social movements for the same reasons they did in the past?

Most social movement organizations now have their own Web sites on the Internet. Visit some of these sites to get a sense of the kinds of information these organizations provide. Do they tend to be primarily informational, focusing on the history and current state of the issue at hand, or are they primarily recruitment tools, designed to attract new participants and financial donors? How are these sites presented? Do they appeal to emotions, or do they rely on factual argument? Do these Web sites contain links to the sites of other organizations that have similar ideologies?

Relate your observations from the interviews and the Internet to the discussion of social movements in this chapter. What are the most effective tactics and strategies? How are resources mobilized? Why do some movements succeed and others fail?

CHAPTER HIGHLIGHTS

♦ Whether at the personal, cultural, or institutional level, change is the preeminent feature of modern societies.

♦ Social change is not some massive, impersonal force that arbitrarily disrupts our routine way of life; it is a human creation.

♦ Social change has a variety of causes: adaptation to environmental pressures, internal population changes, technological discoveries and innovations, and the importation of cultural practices from other countries.

♦ Social movements are long-term collective actions that address an issue of concern to large numbers of people.

♦ Societies remain stable because enough people define existing conditions as satisfactory, and they change because enough people define once-accepted conditions as problems that must be solved.

KEY TERMS

anomie Condition in which rapid change has disrupted society's ability to adequately regulate and control its members and the old rules that governed people's lives no longer seem to apply

countermovement Collective action designed to prevent or reverse changes sought or accomplished by an earlier social movement

cultural diffusion Process by which beliefs, technology, customs, and other elements of culture spread from one group or society to another

ideology Coherent system of beliefs, values, and ideas

postindustrial society Society in which knowledge, the control of information, and service industries are more important elements of the economy than agriculture or manufacturing and production

reform movement Collective action that seeks to change limited aspects of a society but does not seek to alter or replace major social institutions

revolutionary movement Collective action that attempts to overthrow an entire social system and replace it with another

social movement Continuous, large-scale, organized collective action motivated by the desire to enact, stop, or reverse change in some area of society

STUDY SITE ON THE WEB

Don't forget the interactive quizzes and other learning aids at www.pineforge.com/newman6study. In the Resource Files for this chapter, you will also find more on reconstructing society, including:

Sociologist at Work

♦ Douglas Murray: The Abolition of the Short-Handled Hoe

Micro-Macro Connection

♦ Collective Action

References

Abrams, K. K., Allen, L., & Gray, J. J. 1993. Disordered eating attitudes and behaviors, psychological adjustment and ethnic identity: A comparison of black and white female college students. *Journal of Eating Disorders, 14,* 49–57.

Acitelli, L. 1988. When spouses talk to each other about their relationship. *Journal of Social and Personal Relationships, 5,* 185–199.

Acker, J. 1978. Issues in the sociological study of women's work. In A. H. Stromberg & S. Harkees (Eds.), *Women working.* Palo Alto, CA: Mayfield.

Acker, J. 1992. From sex roles to gendered institutions. *Contemporary Sociology, 21,* 565–569.

Aday, D. P. 1990. *Social control at the margins.* Belmont, CA: Wadsworth.

Adler, P. 1985. *Wheeling and dealing.* New York: Columbia University Press.

Adoption/Infertility industry worth $3.65B. 2000, November 17. *Research Alert.*

AFL-CIO. 2002. Ask a working woman survey 2002. www.aflcio.org/issuespolitics/women/report/upload/aaww.pdf. Accessed June 1, 2005.

Ahrons, C. R., & Rodgers, R. H. 1987. *Divorced families: A multidisciplinary developmental view.* New York: Norton.

Ainlay, S. C., Becker, G., & Coleman, L. M. 1986. *The dilemma of difference.* New York: Plenum.

AIS Health. 2004. Medco says pediatric drug costs soar, driven by ADHD, Depression. www.aishealth.com/DrugCosts/DCMRMedcoPediatricCosts.html. Accessed June 3, 2005.

Al-Attab, M. 2005, February 5. Parents, children complicit in human trafficking. *Yemen Observer.* www.yobserver.com. Accessed June 7, 2005.

Aldridge, S. 2003. New computer-related health hazard. www.healthandage.com. Accessed June 30, 2003.

Allport, G. 1954. *The nature of prejudice.* Reading, MA: Addison-Wesley.

Alon, N. 1982. The stigma of overweight in everyday life. In B. B. Wolman (Ed.), *Psychological aspects of obesity.* New York: Van Nostrand Reinhold.

Alter, J. 2005, February 7. The end of "pay to praise." *Newsweek.*

Altman, D. 2003, April 26. Does a dollar a day keep poverty away? *New York Times.*

Alvidrez, J., & Areán, P. A. 2002. Psychosocial treatment research with ethnic minority populations: Ethical considerations in conducting clinical trials. *Ethics and Behavior, 12,* 103–116.

Amato, P. R. 2000. The consequences of divorce for adults and children. *Journal of Marriage and the Family, 62,* 126–288.

Amato, P. R., & Sobolewski, J. M. 2001. The effects of divorce and marital discord on adult children's psychological well-being. *American Sociological Review, 66,* 900–921.

American Association of University Women. 2001. Hostile hallways: Teasing and sexual harassment in school. www.aauw.org/research/girls_education/hostile.cfm. Accessed July 31, 2004.

American Psychiatric Association. 2000. *Diagnostic and statistical manual of mental disorders-IV-TR.* Washington, DC: American Psychiatric Association.

American Religion Data Archive. 2002. Religious groupings: Full U.S. report. www.thearda.com. Accessed May 27, 2005.

American Society of Plastic Surgeons. 2005a. 2004 quick facts. www.plasticsurgery.org/public_education/2004statistics.cfm. Accessed May 28, 2005.

American Society of Plastic Surgeons. 2005b. Cosmetic surgery telephone survey. www .plasticsurgery.org/public_education/statistics_phone_survey.cfm. Accessed May 28, 2005.

American Sociological Association. 2002. Statement of the American Sociological Association on the importance of collecting data and doing social scientific research on race. www .asanet.org/governance/racestmt.htm. Accessed June 18, 2003.

Ammerman, N. T. 1987. *Bible believers: Fundamentalists in the modern world.* New Brunswick, NJ: Rutgers University Press.

Amnesty International. 2004a. Death penalty facts. www.amnestyusa.org/abolish/racialprejudices .html. Accessed July 25, 2004.

Amnesty International. 2004b. Rape as a tool of war: A fact sheet. www.amnesty.usa.org/ stopviolence/factsheets/rapeinwartime.html. Accessed July 29, 2004.

Anderson, D. J. 2003. The impact on subsequent violence of returning to an abusive partner. *Journal of Comparative Family Studies, 34,* 93–112.

Anderson, E. 1990. *Streetwise: Race, class and change in an urban community.* Chicago: University of Chicago Press.

Andriote, J-M. 2005, March. HIV/AIDS and African Americans: A "state of emergency." Population Reference Bureau Report. www.prb.org. Accessed March 16, 2005.

Ang, A. 2004, December 13. Pageant is paean to plastic surgery. *Indianapolis Star.*

Angier, N. 1997a, May 13. New debate over surgery on genitals. *New York Times.*

Angier, N. 1997b, March 14. Sexual identity not pliable after all, report says. *New York Times.*

Angier, N., & Chang, K. 2005, January 24. Gray matter and the sexes: Still a scientific gray area. *New York Times.*

Ansell, A. E. 2000. The new face of race: The metamorphosis of racism in the post-civil rights era United States. In P. Kivisto & G. Rundblad (Eds.), *Multiculturalism in the United States.* Thousand Oaks, CA: Pine Forge Press.

Anti-Muslim incidents increase. 2004, May 4. *New York Times.*

Appelbaum, E., Berg, P., Frost, A., & Preuss, G. 2003. The effects of work restructuring on low-wage, low-skilled workers in U.S. hospitals. In E. Applebaum, A. Bernhardt, & R. J. Murname (Eds.), *Low wage America.* New York: Russell Sage Foundation.

Applebome, P. 1996, April 10. Holding parents legally responsible for the misbehavior of their children. *New York Times.*

Archer, D. 1985. Social deviance. In G. Lindzey & E. Aronson (Eds.), *Handbook of social psychology* (3rd ed., Vol. 2). New York: Random House.

Arendell, T. 1995. *Fathers and divorce.* Thousand Oaks, CA: Sage.

Argyle, M. 2000. The laws of looking. In J. Spradley & D. W. McCurdy (Eds.), *Conformity and conflict.* Boston: Allyn & Bacon.

Ariès, P. 1962. *Centuries of childhood: A social history of family life.* New York: Vintage.

Armstrong, P. J., Goodman, J. F. B., & Hyman, J. D. 1981. *Ideology and shop-floor industrial relations.* London: Croom Helm.

Ashford, L. S. 2005, April. Good health still eludes the poorest women and children. Population Reference Bureau Report. www.prb.org. Accessed April 23, 2005.

Astbury, J. 1996. *Crazy for you: The making of women's madness.* Melbourne: Oxford University Press.

Auletta, K. 1982. *The underclass.* New York: Random House.

Averett, S., & Korenman, S. 1999. Black and white differences in social and economic consequences of obesity. *International Journal of Obesity, 23,* 166–173.

Babbie, E. 1986. *Observing ourselves: Essays in social research.* Belmont, CA: Wadsworth.

Babbie, E. 1992. *The practice of social research.* Belmont, CA: Wadsworth.

Baca-Zinn, M., & Eitzen, D. S. 1996. *Diversity in families* (4th ed.). New York: HarperCollins.

Bach, P. B., Cramer, L. D., Warren, J. L., & Begg, C. B. 1999. Racial differences in the treatment of early-stage lung cancer. *New England Journal of Medicine, 341,* 119–205.

Bagdikian, B. H. 1991. Missing from the news. In J. H. Skolnick & E. Currie (Eds.), *Crisis in American institutions.* New York: HarperCollins.

Bagdikian, B. H. 2000. *The media monopoly* (6th ed.). Boston: Beacon Press.

Bailey, B. L. 1988. *From front porch to back seat: Courtship in 20th century America.* Baltimore: Johns Hopkins University Press.

Bailey, C. A. 1993. Equality with difference: On androcentrism and menstruation. *Teaching Sociology, 21,* 121–129.

Bailey, H., Wolffe, R., & Lipper, T. 2005, March 14. Tricks of the trade. *Newsweek.*

Bailey, W. C. 1990. Murder, capital punishment, and television: Execution publicity and homicide rates. *American Sociological Review, 55,* 628–633.

Bainbridge, W. L. 2005, February 5. Longer school year would benefit students. *Columbus Dispatch.*

Bakalar, N. 2005, May 3. Ugly children may get parental short shrift. *New York Times.*

Baker, P. L. 1997. And I went back: Battered women's negotiation of choice. *Journal of Contemporary Ethnography, 26,* 55–74.

Bald, M. 2000, December. Disputed dams. *World Press Review.*

Ballard, C. 1987. A humanist sociology approach to teaching social research. *Teaching Sociology, 15,* 7–14.

Bandura, A., & Walters, R. H. 1963. *Social learning and personality development.* New York: Holt, Rinehart & Winston.

Banerjee, N. 2005, January 23. Aided by elders and Web, Iraq veterans turn critics. *New York Times.*

Banfield, E. 1970. *The unheavenly city.* Boston: Little, Brown.

Baptists seek to "convert" Mormons. 2000, January 22. *New York Times.*

Barber, B. 1992, March. Jihad vs. McWorld. *Atlantic Monthly,* pp. 53–65.

Barker, C. 1997. *Global television.* Oxford, UK: Blackwell.

Barker, O. 2002. 8 minutes to a love connection in this rush-rush culture, "speed dating" is fast route to everlasting romance. *USA Today Online.* www.usatoday.com/usatonline/20021212/4694919s.htm. Accessed December 13, 2002.

The Barna Group. 2005. Church attendance. www.barna.org/FlexPage.aspx?PageCMD=Print. Accessed May 25, 2005.

Barringer, F. 2004, March 16. Bitter division for Sierra Club on immigration. *New York Times.*

Barro, R. J., & McCleary, R. M. 2003. Religion and economic growth across countries. *American Sociological Review, 68,* 760–781.

Barry, D. 2000, February 27. What to do if you're stopped by the police. *New York Times.*

Barstow, D. 2003, December 22. U.S. rarely seeks charges for deaths in workplace. *New York Times.*

Barstow, D., & Stein, R. 2005, March 13. Is it news or public relations? Under Bush, lines are blurry. *New York Times.*

Baxter, J. 1997. Gender equality and participation in housework: A cross-national perspective. *Journal of Comparative Family Studies, 28,* 220–247.

Beaman, A. L., Klentz, B., Diener, E., & Svanum, S. 1979. Objective self-awareness and transgression in children: A field study. *Journal of Personality and Social Psychology, 37,* 1835–1846.

Bearak, B. 2000, June 24. Women are defaced by acid and Bengali society is torn. *New York Times.*

Becker, E. 2004, December 8. Number of hungry rising, U.N. says. *New York Times.*

Becker, H. 1963. *The outsiders*. New York: Free Press.

Becker, H. S., & Geer, B. 1958. The fate of idealism in medical school. *American Sociological Review, 23,* 50–56.

Bedard, M. 1991. Captive clientele of the welfare supersystem: Breaking the cage wide open. *Humanity and Society, 15,* 23–48.

Belkin, L. 2002, May 11. Why is Jonathan Simms still alive? *New York Times Magazine.*

Bell, I., & McGrane, B. 1999. *This book is not required.* Thousand Oaks, CA: Pine Forge Press.

Bell, S. T., Kuriloff, P. J., & Lottes, I. 1994. Understanding attributions of blame in stranger rape and date rape situations: An examination of gender, race, identification, and students' social perceptions of rape victims. *Journal of Applied Social Psychology, 24,* 171–734.

Bellah, R., Madsen, R., Sullivan, W. M., Swidler, A., & Tipton, S. M. 1985. *Habits of the heart.* New York: Harper & Row.

Bell-Rowbotham, B., & Lero, D. 2001. Responses to extension of parental leaves. Centre for Families, Work, and Well-Being. www.uoguelph.ca/cfww/response.htm. Accessed July 10, 2001.

Belluck, P. 1998, March 20. Black youths' rate of suicide rising sharply. *New York Times.*

Belluck, P. 2001, January 20. A nation's voices: Concern and solace, resentment and redemption. *New York Times.*

Belluck, P. 2002, January 15. Doctors' new practices offer deluxe service for deluxe fee. *New York Times.*

Belluck, P. 2004, November 14. To avoid divorce, move to Massachusetts. *New York Times.*

Belson, K. 2004, June 27. I want to be alone. Please call me. *New York Times.*

Bennett, G., Henson, R. K., & Zhang, J. 2003. Generation Y's perceptions of the action sports industry segment. *Journal of Sports Management, 17,* 95–115.

Benokraitis, N. V., & Feagin, J. R. 1993. Sex discrimination: Subtle and covert. In J. Henslin (Ed.), *Down-to-earth sociology* (7th ed.). New York: Free Press.

Ben-Yehuda, N. 1990. *The politics and morality of deviance.* Albany: State University of New York Press.

Berenson, A. 2005, May 31. Despite vow, drug makers still withhold data. *New York Times.*

Berg, B. 1992. The guilt that drives working mothers crazy. In J. Henslin (Ed.), *Marriage and family in a changing society.* New York: Free Press.

Bergen, R. K. 1999. Marital rape. Violence Against Women Online Resources. www.vaw.umn.edu/documents/vawnet/mrape/mrape.html#id75958. Accessed June 13, 2005.

Berger, D. L., & Williams, J. E. 1991. Sex stereotypes in the United States revisited: 1972–1988. *Sex Roles, 24,* 413–423.

Berger, J. 2004, October 24. Pressure to live by an outmoded tradition is still felt among Indian immigrants. *New York Times.*

Berger, P. L. 1963. *Invitation to sociology.* Garden City, NY: Anchor.

Berger, P. L., & Kellner, H. 1964. Marriage and the construction of reality: An exercise in the micro-sociology of knowledge. *Diogenes, 46,* 1–23.

Berger, P. L., & Luckmann, T. 1966. *The social construction of reality.* Garden City, NY: Anchor.

Bernard, J. 1972. *The future of marriage.* New York: Bantam.

Bernard, J. 1981. The good provider role: Its rise and fall. *American Psychologist, 36,* 1–12.

Berndt, T. J., & Heller, K. A. 1986. Gender stereotypes and social inferences. *Journal of Social and Personality Psychology, 50,* 889–898.

Bernstein, N. 1996, January 8. Equal opportunity recedes for most female lawyers. *New York Times.*

Bernstein, N. 2004, March 7. In a culture of sex, more teenagers are striving for restraint. *New York Times.*

Bernstein, R. 2003, June 29. Aging Europe finds its pension is running out. *New York Times.*

Bertenthal, B. I., & Fischer, K. W. 1978. Development of self-recognition in the infant. *Developmental Psychology, 14,* 44–50.

Berthelsen, C. 1999, July 28. Suit says advanced-placement classes show bias. *New York Times.*

Bhattacharya, J., DeLeire, T., Haider, S., & Currie, J. 2003. Heat or eat? Cold-weather shocks and nutrition in poor American families. *American Journal of Public Health, 93,* 1149–1154.

Bianchi, S. M., Milkie, M. A., Sayer, L. C., & Robinson, J. P. 2000. Is anyone doing the housework? Trends in the gender division of household labor. *Social Forces, 79,* 191–228.

Bird, L. 2004. Bird: NBA "a black man's game." ESPN Online. http://sports.espn.go.com/nba/news/story?id=1818396. Accessed June 10, 2004.

Bird, P. 2005, May 13. Jury convicts parents in baby's death. *Indianapolis Star.*

Birenbaum, A., & Sagarin, E. 1976. *Norms and human behavior.* New York: Praeger.

Black, K. 1996, September 5. Extreme prejudice. *Rolling Stone.*

Black Health Care.com. 2003. Sickle-cell anemia—Description. www.blackhealthcare.com/BHC/SickleCell/Description.asp. Accessed June 17, 2003.

Blakeslee, S. 1998, October 13. Placebos prove so powerful even experts are surprised. *New York Times.*

Blau, P. M., & Duncan, O. D. 1967. *The American occupational structure.* New York: Wiley.

Blau, P. M., & Meyer, M. W. 1987. The concept of bureaucracy. In R. T. Schaeffer & R. P. Lamm (Eds.), *Introducing sociology.* New York: McGraw-Hill.

Blauner, R. 1992. The ambiguities of racial change. In M. L. Anderson & P. H. Collins (Eds.), *Race, class and gender: An anthology.* Belmont, CA: Wadsworth.

Blumstein, P., & Schwartz, P. 1983. *American couples.* New York: Morrow.

Blustein, P. 2005, June 12. Debt cut is set for poorest nations. *Washington Post.*

Bonilla-Silva, E. 2003. *Racism without racists: Color-blind racism and the persistence of racial inequality in the United States.* Lanham, MD: Rowman & Littlefield.

Bonner, R., & Fessenden, F. 2000, September 22. States with no death penalty share lower homicide rates. *New York Times.*

Bonner, R., & Lacey, M. 2000, September 12. Pervasive disparities found in the federal death penalty. *New York Times.*

Bonnie, R. J., & Whitebread, C. H. 1974. *The marijuana conviction.* Charlottesville: University of Virginia Press.

Booth, A., Johnson, D. R., Branaman, A., & Sica, A. 1995. Belief and behavior: Does religion matter in today's marriage? *Journal of Marriage and the Family, 57,* 661–671.

Boshara, R. 2002, September 29. Poverty is more than a matter of income. *New York Times.*

Boston Archdiocese closing 65 parishes. 2004, May 25. *New York Times.*

Bowker, L. H. 1993. A battered woman's problems are social, not psychological. In R. J. Gelles & D. R. Loeske (Eds.), *Current controversies on family violence.* Newbury Park, CA: Sage.

Bowles, S., & Gintis, H. 1976. *Schooling in capitalist America: Educational reform and the contradictions of economic reform.* New York: Basic Books.

Bradshaw, Y. W., & Wallace, M. 1996. *Global inequalities.* Thousand Oaks, CA: Pine Forge Press.

Bradsher, K. 1993, July 22. Mark Twain would understand the water crisis that's corrupting Iowans. *New York Times.*

Bradsher, K. 1995, April 17. Gap in wealth in U.S. called widest in West. *New York Times.*

Bradsher, K. 1999a, March 1. As buyers age, car designers make subtle shifts. *New York Times.*

Bradsher, K. 1999b, November 21. Fear of crime trumps fear of lost youth. *New York Times.*

Bragg, R. 1998, January 4. Proposal to ban sofas from porches creates culture clash. *Indianapolis Star.*

Bramlett, M. D., & Mosher, W. D. 2001. First marriage dissolution, divorce, and remarriage: United States. Centers for Disease Control and Prevention Advance Data 323. www.cdc .gov/nchs/data/ad/ad323.pdf. Accessed September 8, 2005.

Braun, D. 1997. *The rich get richer: The rise of income inequality in the United States and the world.* Chicago: Nelson-Hall.

Breaking the rules of engagement. 2002, July/August. *American Demographics.*

Bridal dowry in India. 2000. Morning Edition, National Public Radio. www.npr.org/ programs/morning. Accessed June 19, 2000.

Brines, J. 1994. Economic dependency, gender and the division of labor at home. *American Journal of Sociology, 100,* 652–688.

Brinkley, J. 2000, April 2. C.I.A. depicts a vast trade in forced labor. *New York Times.*

Brint, S. 1998. *Schools and societies.* Thousand Oaks, CA: Pine Forge Press.

Brinton, C. 1965. *The anatomy of revolution.* New York: Vintage.

Brockerhoff, M. P. 2000. An urbanizing world. *Population Bulletin, 55,* 1–4.

Bronner, E. 1998a, January 10. Inventing the notion of race. *New York Times.*

Bronner, E. 1998b, April 1. U of California reports big drop in black admission. *New York Times.*

Brooke, J. 2004, October 18. Strangers in life join hands in death as the Web becomes a tool for suicide in Japan. *New York Times.*

Brouillette, J. R., & Turner, R. E. 1992. Creating the sociological imagination on the first day of class: The social construction of deviance. *Teaching Sociology, 20,* 276–279.

Broverman, I., Vogel, S., Broverman, D., Clarkson, F., & Rosenkrantz, P. 1972. Sex role stereotypes: A current appraisal. *Journal of Social Issues, 28,* 59–78.

Brown, L. R., & Flavin, C. 1999. A new economy for a new century. In L. R. Brown, C. Flavin, & H. French (Eds.), *State of the world: A Worldwatch Institute report on progress toward a sustainable society.* New York: Norton.

Brown, P. 1998. Biology and the social construction of the "race" concept. In J. Ferrante & P. Brown (Eds.), *The social construction of race and ethnicity in the United States.* New York: Longman.

Brown, P. L. 2002, May 8. Jazzercise relents to plus-size pressure. *New York Times.*

Brown, P. L. 2003, February 8. In California, S.U.V. owners have guilt, but will travel. *New York Times.*

Brown, R. 1986. *Social psychology.* New York: Free Press.

Browne, B. A. 1998. Gender stereotypes in advertising on children's television in the 1990s: A cross-national analysis. *Journal of Advertising, 27,* 8–7.

Brownmiller, S. 1975. *Against our will: Men, women, and rape.* New York: Simon & Schuster.

Brutus, D. 1999. Africa 2000 in the new global context. In T. J. Gallagher (Ed.), *Perspectives: Introductory sociology.* St. Paul, MN: Coursewise.

Bullard, R. D. 1993. Anatomy of environmental racism and the environmental justice movement. In R. D. Bullard (Ed.), *Confronting environmental racism.* Boston: South End Press.

Bullard, R. D. 2001. Decision making. In L. Westra & B. E. Lawson (Eds.), *Faces of environmental racism: Confronting issues of global justice.* Lanham, MD: Rowman & Littlefield.

Bullard, R. D. 2003, January–February. Environmental justice for all. *Crisis.*

Bullard, R. D., & Wright, B. H. 1992. The quest for environmental equity: Mobilizing the African-American community for social change. In R. E. Dunlap & A. G. Mertig (Eds.), *American environmentalism: The U.S. environmental movement, 1970–1990.* Philadelphia: Taylor & Francis.

Bullington, B. 1993. All about Eve: The many faces of United States drug policy. In F. Pearce & M. Woodiwiss (Eds.), *Global crime connections.* Toronto: University of Toronto Press.

Bumiller, E. 2003, May 16. Keepers of Bush image lift stagecraft to new heights. *New York Times.*

Butler, R. 1989. A generation at risk: When the baby boomers reach Golden Pond. In W. Feigelman (Ed.), *Sociology full circle.* New York: Holt, Rinehart & Winston.

Butterfield, F. 1995, October 5. More Blacks in their 20's have trouble with the law. *New York Times.*

Butterfield, F. 1999, January 10. Eliminating parole boards isn't a cure-all, experts say. *New York Times.*

Butterfield, F. 2000, April 26. Racial disparities seen as pervasive in juvenile justice. *New York Times.*

Butterfield, F. 2005, February 13. In rural America, guns and a "culture of suicide." *New York Times.*

Cahill, S. 1999. Emotional capital and professional socialization: The case of mortuary science students (and me). *Social Psychology Quarterly, 62,* 10–16.

Caldwell, C. 2005, January 23. The triumph of gesture politics. *New York Times.*

Camarota, S. A. 2004. Economy slowed, but immigration didn't: The foreign-born population, 2000–2004. Center for Immigration Studies. www.cis.org/articles/2004/back1204.html. Accessed June 9, 2005.

Cameron, D. 1999, April 28. You don't have to be nice here, but it helps to pretend: Language, gender, and emotional labor in the new workplace. Paper presented at DePauw University Colloquium Series, Greencastle, Indiana.

Campbell, A. 1987. Self-definition by rejection: The case of gang girls. *Social Problems, 34,* 451–466.

Campbell, A., Converse, P. E., & Rodgers, W. L. 1976. *The quality of American life.* New York: Russell Sage Foundation.

Campbell, J. C. 2003. Risk factors for femicide in abusive relationships: Results from a multisite case control study. *American Journal of Public Health, 93,* 1089–1097.

Campo-Flores, A., & Fineman, H. 2005, May 30. A Latin power surge. *Newsweek.*

Canadian Broadcasting Company. 2003. What border? The Americanization of Canada. www.tv.cbc.ca/national/pgminfo/border/culture.html. Accessed May 27, 2003.

Cancian, F. 1987. *Love in America: Gender and self-development.* New York: Cambridge University Press.

Caplan, P. J. 1995. *They say you're crazy: How the world's most powerful psychiatrists decide who's normal.* Reading, MA: Addison-Wesley.

Carey, B. 2005a, June 7. Most will be mentally ill at some point, study says. *New York Times.*

Carey, B. 2005b, June 21. Some politics may be etched in genes. *New York Times.*

Carey, K. 2005. One step from the finish line: Higher college graduation rates are within our reach. Education Trust Report. www2.edtrust.org/EdTrust/Press+Room/college+results .htm. Accessed January 26, 2005.

Carnevale, A. P., & Rose, S. J. 2003. Socioeconomic status, race/ethnicity, and selective college admissions. Century Foundation Paper. www.tcf.org/publications/white_papers/carnevale_rose .pdf. Accessed April 9, 2003.

Carr, D. 2004. Improving the health of the world's poorest people. Health Bulletin 1. Washington, DC: Population Reference Bureau.

Carr, J. 1988. *Crisis in intimacy.* Pacific Grove, CA: Brooks/Cole.

Carter, H., & Glick, P. C. 1976. *Marriage and divorce: A social and economic study.* Cambridge, MA: Harvard University Press.

Casper, L. M., McLanahan, S. S., & Garfinkel, I. 1994. The gender-poverty gap: What we can learn from other countries. *American Sociological Review, 59,* 594–605.

Cast, A. D. 2004. Role taking and interaction. *Social Psychology Quarterly, 67,* 296–309.

Catalyst. 2002. 2002 Catalyst census of women corporate officers and top earners in the Fortune 500. www.catalystwomen.org. Accessed June 11, 2003.

Cellular Telecommunications & Internet Association. 2005. Background on CTIA's semi-annual wireless industry survey. http://files.ctia.org/pdf/CTIAYearend2004survey.pdf. Accessed May 25, 2005.

Center for the Advancement of Health. 2003. The forgotten population: Health disparities and minority men. www.cfah.org/factsoflife/vol8no5.cfm. Accessed May 11, 2003.

Centers for Disease Control and Prevention. 1999. Ten great public health achievements in the United States, 1900–1999. *Mortality and Morbidity Weekly Report, 48,* 241–243.

Centers for Disease Control and Prevention. 2004. Tobacco-related mortality [Fact sheet]. www.cdc.gov/tobacco/factsheets/Tobacco_Related_Mortality_factsheet.htm. Accessed June 4, 2005.

Cha, A. E. 2005, June 26. Viruses, security issues undermine Internet. *Washington Post.*

Chachere, V. 2005, June 3. Young killers a quandary for states. *Indianapolis Star.*

Chafetz, J. S. 1978. *A primer on the construction and testing of theories in sociology.* Itasca, IL: Peacock.

Chafetz, J. S., & Dworkin, A. G. 1987. In the face of threat: Organized anti-feminism in comparative perspective. *Gender and Society, 1,* 33–60.

Chambers, M. 1997, June 18. For women, 25 years of Title IX has not leveled the playing field. *New York Times.*

Chambliss, D. F. 1989. The mundanity of excellence: An ethnographic report on stratification and Olympic swimmers. *Sociological Theory, 7,* 70–86.

Chambliss, W. 1964. A sociological analysis of the law of vagrancy. *Social Problems, 12,* 66–77.

Chambliss, W., & Nagasawa, R. H. 1969. On the validity of official statistics: A comparative study of white, black and Japanese high-school boys. *Journal of Research in Crime and Delinquency, 6,* 71–77.

Charon, J. 1992. *Ten questions: A sociological perspective.* Belmont, CA: Wadsworth.

Charon, J. 1998. *Symbolic interactionism.* Upper Saddle River, NJ: Prentice Hall.

Chase-Dunn, C., & Rubinson, R. 1977. Toward a structural perspective on the world system. *Politics and Society, 7,* 453–476.

Chen, D. W. 2004, September 22. U.S. seeking cuts in rent subsidies for poor families. *New York Times.*

Cherlin, A. 1992. *Marriage, divorce, remarriage.* Cambridge, MA: Harvard University Press.

Cherlin, A., Furstenberg, F. F., Chase-Landale, P. L., Kiernan, K. E., Robins, P. K., Morrison, D. R., & Teitler, J. O. 1991. Longitudinal studies of effects of divorce on children in Great Britain and the United States. *Science, 252,* 1386–1389.

Cherry, R. 1989. *Discrimination: Its economic impact on Blacks, women and Jews.* Lexington, MA: Lexington Books.

CHILD, Inc. 2005. Religious exemptions from health care for children. www.childrenshealthcare .org. Accessed May 24, 2005.

Child Trends Databank. 2004. Sexually active teens. www.chidtrendsdatabank.org/pdf. 23_PDF.pdf. Accessed July 23, 2005.

Ching, C. L., & Burke, S. 1999. An assessment of college students' attitudes and empathy toward rape. *College Student Journal, 33,* 573–584.

Ching, F. 1994, October 6. Talking sense on population. *Far Eastern Economic Review.*

Christian faith in the age of Prozac. 1995, December. *Harper's.*

Chumlea, W. C., Schubert, C. M., Roche, A. F., Kulin, H. E., Lee, P. A., Himes, J. H., & Sun, S. S. 2003. Age at menarche and racial comparisons in US girls. *Pediatrics, 111,* 110–113.

Ciancanelli, P., & Berch, B. 1987. Gender and the GNP. In B. B. Hess & M. M. Ferree (Eds.), *Analyzing gender: A handbook of social science research.* Newbury Park, CA: Sage.

Citrin, J. 1996, Winter. Affirmative action in the people's court. *Public Interest,* pp. 39–48.

Clarey, C. 2002, November 24. Ask the athletes what's in a name. *New York Times.*

Clarity, J. F. 1999, March 14. Lost youth in Ireland: Suicide rate is climbing. *New York Times.*

Clark, B. 1960. The "cooling out" function in higher education. *American Journal of Sociology, 65,* 569–576.

Clark, C. 1997. *Misery and company: Sympathy in everyday life.* Chicago: University of Chicago Press.

Clark, M. A. 2003. Trafficking in persons: An issue of human security. *Journal of Human Development, 4,* 247–263.

Clark, R. L., & Passel, J. S. 1993, September 3. Studies are deceptive. *New York Times.*

Clausen, J. A. 1986. *The life course: A sociological perspective.* Englewood Cliffs, NJ: Prentice Hall.

Clear Channel Communications. 2003. Clear Channel Radio. www.clearchannel.com/radio. Accessed July 3, 2003.

Clifford, M. M., & Walster, E. 1973. The effect of physical attractiveness on teacher expectations. *Sociology of Education, 46,* 248–258.

Clinard, M. B., & Meier, R. F. 1979. *Sociology of deviant behavior.* New York: Holt, Rinehart & Winston.

Cluster, D. 1979. *They should have served that cup of coffee.* Boston: South End Press.

Clymer, A. 2002, August 26. Bay area traffic tracking creates concern for privacy. *New York Times.*

Cobb, N. J., Stevens-Long, J., & Goldstein, S. 1982. The influence of televised models on toy preference in children. *Sex Roles, 8,* 1075–1080.

Coe, R. M. 1978. *Sociology of medicine.* New York: McGraw-Hill.

Cohen, A. K. 1955. *Delinquent boys: The culture of the gang.* New York: Free Press.

Cohen, A. K. 1966. *Deviance and control.* Englewood Cliffs, NJ: Prentice Hall.

Cohen, F. G. 1986. *Treaties on trial: The continuing controversy over Northwest Indian fishing rights.* Seattle: University of Washington Press.

Cohen, L. E., & Land, K. C. 1987. Age structure and crime: Symmetry vs. asymmetry and the projection of crime rates through the 1990's. *American Sociological Review, 52,* 170–183.

Cohen, P. 2003, April 5. Visions and revisions of child-raising experts. *New York Times.*

Cohen, P. N., & Huffman, M. L. 2003. Occupational segregation and the devaluation of women's work across U.S. labor markets. *Social Forces, 81,* 881–908.

The College Board. 1998. SAT and gender differences. Research Summary RS-04. www.college board.com/repository/rs04_3960.pdf. Accessed July 1, 2004.

Collins, C., & Williams, D. R. 1999. Segregation and mortality: The deadly effects of racism. *Sociological Forum, 14,* 49–23.

Collins, R. 1971. Functional and conflict theories of educational stratification. *American Sociological Review, 36,* 1002–1019.

Collins, R. 1981. On the microfoundations of macro-sociology. *American Journal of Sociology, 86,* 984–1014.

Coltrane, S., & Adams, M. 1997. Work–family imagery and gender stereotypes: Television and the reproduction of difference. *Journal of Vocational Behavior, 50,* 32–47.

Comer, J. P., & Poussaint, A. F. 1992. *Raising black children.* New York: Plume.

Commission for Racial Justice. 1987. *Toxic waste and race.* New York: United Church of Christ.

Connelly, M. 2004, November 7. How Americans voted: A political portrait. *New York Times.*

Connolly, C. 2005, July 13. Data show scourge of hospital infections. *Washington Post.*

Conrad, P. 1975. The discovery of hyperkinesis: Notes on the medicalization of deviant behavior. *Social Problems, 23,* 12–21.

Conrad, P., & Schneider, J. W. 1992. *Deviance and medicalization: From badness to sickness.* Philadelphia: Temple University Press.

Cookson, P., & Persell, C. 1985. *Preparing for power*. New York: Basic Books.

Cooley, C. H. 1902. *Human nature and social order*. New York: Scribner's.

Coolidge, S. 2005, August 20. Parents must pay $7M. *Cincinnati Enquirer*.

Coontz, S. 1992. *The way we never were*. New York: Basic Books.

Coontz, S. 2005. *Marriage, a history: From obedience to intimacy, or how love conquered marriage*. New York: Viking.

Cooper, K. J. 1999. Admissions models for inclusion. *Black Issues in Higher Education, 16*, 3–5.

Cooper, M. H. 1994, August 19. Prozac controversy. *CQ Researcher* [Special issue].

Cooper, M. H. 1998a, June 19. Environmental justice. *CQ Researcher* [Special issue].

Cooper, M. H. 1998b, July 17. Population and the environment. *CQ Researcher* [Special issue].

Corcoran, K. 2005, May 26. Judge: Parents can't teach pagan beliefs. *Indianapolis Star*.

Corcoran, M. 2001. Mobility, persistence, and the consequences of poverty for children: Child and adult outcomes. In S. H. Danziger & R. H. Haveman (Eds.), *Understanding poverty*. New York: Russell Sage Foundation.

Cose, E. 1993. *The rage of the privileged class*. New York: HarperCollins.

Cose, E. 1999, June 7. The good news about black America. *Newsweek*.

Coser, L., & Coser, R. 1993. Jonestown as a perverse Utopia. In K. Finsterbusch & J. S. Schwartz (Eds.), *Sources: Notable selections in sociology*. Guilford, CT: Dushkin.

Coser, R. L. 1960. Laughter among colleagues: A study of the social functions of humor among staff of a mental hospital. *Psychiatry, 23*, 81–95.

Coulson, M. A., & Riddell, C. 1980. *Approaching sociology*. London: Routledge & Kegan Paul.

Cowan, R. 1991. More work for Mother: The postwar years. In L. Kramer (Ed.), *The sociology of gender*. New York: St. Martin's Press.

Cowell, A. 2002, April 28. Migrants feel chill in a testy Europe. *New York Times*.

Cowley, G. 1997, May 9. Gender limbo. *Newsweek*.

Cowley, G. 2003, May 5. How progress makes us sick. *Newsweek*.

Cowley, G. 2005, Summer. Chasing black fever. *Newsweek* [Special issue].

Cowley, G., & Murr, A. 2004, December 6. The new face of AIDS. *Newsweek*.

Coyle, M. 2003. Race and class penalties in crack cocaine sentencing. The Sentencing Project Report No. 5077. www.sentencingproject.org/policy/mc-crackcocaine.pdf. Accessed June 20, 2003.

Crandall, C. S., & Martinez, R. 1996. Culture, ideology, and antifat attitudes. *Personality and Social Psychology Bulletin, 22*, 1165–1176.

Cranz, G. 1998. *The chair: Rethinking culture, body, and design*. New York: Norton.

Crary, D. 2003, June 1. Internet can speed up divorces. *Indianapolis Star*.

Critser, G. 2000, March. Let them eat fat: The heavy truths about American obesity. *Harper's*.

Crittenden, A. 2001. *The price of motherhood: Why the most important job in the world is still the least valued*. New York: Owl Books.

Cross, G. 1997. *Kids' stuff: Toys and the changing world of American childhood*. Cambridge, MA: Harvard University Press.

Cross, J., & Guyer, M. 1980. *Social traps*. Ann Arbor: University of Michigan Press.

Crossette, B. 1996, June 3. Hope, and pragmatism, for U.N. cities conference. *New York Times*.

Crossette, B. 1997a, November 2. How to fix a crowded world: Add people. *New York Times*.

Crossette, B. 1997b, July 27. What modern slavery is, and isn't. *New York Times*.

Crossette, B. 2000, January 2. Europe stares at a future built by immigrants. *New York Times*.

Crossette, B. 2001, February 28. Against a trend, U.S. population will bloom, UN says. *New York Times*.

Crossette, B. 2002, March 10. Population estimates fall as poor women assert control. *New York Times*.

Croteau, D., & Hoynes, W. 2000. *Media/Society: Industries, images, and audiences.* Thousand Oaks, CA: Pine Forge Press.

Crowley, G. 1994, February 7. The culture of Prozac. *Newsweek.*

Crystal, D. 2003. *English as a global language.* Cambridge, UK: Cambridge University Press.

Cummings, B. 1992. *War and television,* London: Verso.

Curra, J. 2000. *The relativity of deviance.* Thousand Oaks, CA: Sage.

Curtin, J. S. 2004. Suicide also rises in land of rising sun. *Asia Times Online.* www.atimes .com/atimes/Japan/FG28Dh01.html. Accessed November 19, 2004.

Cushing, R., & Bishop, B. 2005, July 20. The rural war. *New York Times.*

Cushman, J. H. 1993, November 19. U.S. to weigh Blacks' complaints about pollution. *New York Times.*

Dahrendorf, R. 1959. *Class and class conflict in industrial society.* Stanford, CA: Stanford University Press.

Daley, S. 1996, May 9. A new charter wins adoption in South Africa. *New York Times.*

Daley, S. 2000, April 9. More and more, Europeans find fault with U.S. *New York Times.*

Daniels, R. 1990. *Coming to America.* New York: HarperCollins.

Danziger, S., & Gottschalk, P. 2004, December. Diverging fortunes: Trends in poverty and inequality. Population Reference Bureau Report. www.prb.org. Accessed January 19, 2005.

Darton, N. 1991, Summer. The end of innocence. *Newsweek* [Special issue].

Davey, M. 2004, September 9. For 1,000 troops, there is no going home. *New York Times.*

Davies, J. C. 1962. Toward a theory of revolution. *American Sociological Review, 27,* 5–19.

Davis, F. J. 1991. *Who is black?* University Park: Pennsylvania State University Press.

Davis, J. A., & Smith, T. 1986. *General social survey cumulative file 1972–1982.* Ann Arbor, MI: Inter-University Consortium for Political and Social Research.

Davis, K. 1937. The sociology of prostitution. *American Sociological Review, 2,* 744–755.

Davis, K. 1976. The world's population crisis. In R. K. Merton & R. Nisbett (Eds.), *Contemporary social problems.* New York: Harcourt Brace Jovanovich.

Davis, K., & Moore, W. 1945. Some principles of stratification. *American Sociological Review, 10,* 242–247.

Davis, S. 2003. Sex stereotypes in commercials targeted toward children: A content analysis. *Sociological Spectrum, 23,* 407–424.

Death Penalty Information Center. 2005. Time on death row. www.deathpenaltyinfo.org/article.php?&did=1397. Accessed June 4, 2005.

Deaton, A., & Paxson, C. 1999. Mortality, education, income, and inequality among American cohorts. National Bureau of Economic Research Working Paper 7140. www.nber.org/papers/w7140. Accessed June 7, 2005.

Deaux, K., & Kite, M. E. 1987. Thinking about gender. In B. B. Hess & M. M. Ferree (Eds.), *Analyzing gender: A handbook of social science research.* Newbury Park, CA: Sage.

Declaration of Sentiments and Resolutions, Seneca Falls Convention, 1848. 2001. In P. S. Rothenberg (Ed.), *Race, class, and gender in the United States.* New York: Worth.

DeFronzo, J. 1991. *Revolutions and revolutionary movements.* Boulder, CO: Westview.

De Leire, T. 2000. The unintended consequences of the Americans with Disabilities Act. *Regulation, 23,* 21–24.

DeNavas-Walt, C., Proctor, B. D., & Lee, C. H. 2005. Income, poverty, and health insurance coverage in the United States: 2004. *Current Population Reports, P60-229.* U.S. Census Bureau. www.census.gov/prod/2005pubs/p60-229.pdf. Accessed September 21, 2005.

DeNavas-Walt, C., Proctor, B. D., & Mills, R. J. 2004. Income, poverty, and health insurance coverage in the United States. *Current Population Reports, P60–226.* U.S. Census Bureau. www.census.gov/prod/2004pubs/p60–226.pdf. Accessed August 27, 2004.

Denzin, N. 1977. *Childhood socialization: Studies in the development of language, social behavior, and identity.* San Francisco: Jossey-Bass.

Denzin, N. 1989. *The research act: A theoretical introduction to sociological methods.* Englewood Cliffs, NJ: Prentice Hall.

DePalma, A. 1996, January 13. For Mexico's Indians, new voice but few gains. *New York Times.*

Derber, C. 1979. *The pursuit of attention.* New York: Oxford University Press.

Dervarics, C. 2004a, March. Conspiracy beliefs may be hindering HIV prevention among African Americans. Population Reference Bureau Report. www.prb.org. Accessed March 16, 2005.

Dervarics, C. 2004b, August. Minorities overrepresented among America's "disconnected" youth. Population Reference Bureau Report. www.prb.org. Accessed June 10, 2005.

Dervarics, C. 2004c, March. Tiny successes in bid to close male-female gap in schooling worldwide. Population Reference Bureau Report. www.prb.org. Accessed July 15, 2004.

DeSouza, R-M. 2004, October. In harm's way: Hurricanes, population trends, and environmental change. Population Reference Bureau Report. www.prb.org. Accessed December 30, 2004.

Deutsch, K. W. 1966. *Nationalism and social communication.* Cambridge, MA: MIT Press.

DeVoe, J. F., Peter, K., Kaufman, P., Miller, A., Noonan, M., Snyder, T. D., & Baum, K. 2004. Indicators of school crime and safety: 2004. www.ojp.usdoj.gov/bjs/pub/pdf/iscs04ex.pdf. Accessed June 21, 2005.

Diamond, J. 2005. *How societies choose to succeed or fail.* New York: Viking.

Diekman, A. B., & Murnen, S. K. 2004. Learning to be little women and little men: The inequitable gender equality of nonsexist children's literature. *Sex Roles, 50,* 373–385.

Diekmann, A., & Engelhardt, H. 1999. The social inheritance of divorce: Effects of parent's family type in postwar Germany. *American Sociological Review, 64,* 78–93.

Diller, L. H. 1998. *Running on Ritalin.* New York: Bantam.

Dillon, S. 2005, January 18. Harvard chief defends his talk on women. *New York Times.*

DiMaggio, P. J., & Powell, W. W. 1983. The iron cage revisited: Institutional isomorphism and collective rationality in organizational fields. *American Sociological Review, 48,* 147–160.

DiMaggio, P. J., & Powell, W. W. 1991. Introduction. In W. W. Powell & P. J. DiMaggio (Eds.), *The new institutionalism in organizational analysis.* Chicago: University of Chicago Press.

Dion, K. 1972. Physical attractiveness and evaluations of children's transgressions. *Journal of Personality and Social Psychology, 24,* 207–213.

Dion, K., Berscheid, E., & Walster, E. 1972. What is beautiful is good. *Journal of Personality and Social Psychology, 24,* 285–290.

Dixon, T. L., & Linz, D. 2000. Race and the misrepresentation of victimization on local television news. *Communication Research, 27,* 547–573.

Dobash, R. E., & Dobash, R. P. 1979. *Violence against wives: A case against the patriarchy.* New York: Free Press.

Doctors implicated in Tutsi genocide. 1996. *Lancet, 347,* 684.

Domhoff, G. W. 1983. *Who rules America now? A view from the eighties.* Englewood Cliffs, NJ: Prentice Hall.

Domhoff, G. W. 1998. *Who rules America? Power and politics in the year 2000.* Mountain View, CA: Mayfield.

Domino's. 2005. Inside Domino's. www.dominos.com. Accessed May 25, 2005.

Dominus, S. 2004, February 22. Life in the age of old, old age. *New York Times Magazine.*

Drucker, S. 1996, March 10. Who is the best restaurateur in America? *New York Times Magazine.*

D'Souza, D. 1995. *The end of racism.* New York: Free Press.

Dugger, C. W. 1996, February 29. Immigrant cultures raising issues of child punishment. *New York Times.*

Dugger, C. W. 1999a, April 25. India's poorest are becoming its loudest. *New York Times.*

Dugger, C. W. 1999b, May 3. Lower-caste women turn village rule upside down. *New York Times.*

Dugger, C. W. 2000, November 24. A cruel choice in New Delhi: Jobs vs. a safer environment. *New York Times.*

Dugger, C. W. 2001, April 22. Abortion in India is tipping scales sharply against girls. *New York Times.*

Dugger, C. W. 2004a, July 16. Devastated by AIDS, Africa sees life expectancy plunge. *New York Times.*

Dugger, C. W. 2004b, December 28. Supermarket giants crush Central American farmers. *New York Times.*

Dugger, C. W. 2004c, July 28. World Bank challenged: Are the poor really helped? *New York Times.*

Dugger, C. W. 2005, January 18. U.N. proposes doubling of aid to cut poverty. *New York Times.*

Duke, S. B. 1994. Casualties of war. *Reason, 25,* 20–27.

DuLong, J. 2002, April 16. Rosie's crusade. *The Advocate.*

Duncan, G. J. 1984. *Years of poverty, years of plenty.* Ann Arbor: University of Michigan Press.

Durkheim, É. 1947. *The division of labor in society.* G. Simpson (Trans.). Glencoe, IL: Free Press. (Original work published in 1893)

Durkheim, É. 1951. *Suicide.* New York: Free Press. (Original work published 1897)

Durkheim, É. 1954. *The elementary forms of religious life.* J. Swain (Trans.). New York: Free Press. (Original work published 1915)

Durkheim, É. 1958. *Rules of sociological method.* G. E. G. Catlin (Ed.); A. Solovay & J. H. Mueller (Trans.). Glencoe, IL: Free Press. (Original work published 1895)

Duster, T. 1997. Pattern, purpose, and race in the drug war. In C. Reinarman & H. G. Levine (Eds.), *Crack in America.* Berkeley: University of California Press.

Ebaugh, H. R. F. 1988. *Becoming an ex.* Chicago: University of Chicago Press.

Eckholm, E. 2001, February 18. Psychiatric abuse by China reported in repressing sect. *New York Times.*

Economic Policy Institute. 2004. The state of working America 2004/2005. www.epinet.org. Accessed December 2, 2004.

Edidin, P. 2005, March 6. How to shake hands or share a meal with an Iraqi. *New York Times.*

Edney, J. 1979, August. Free riders en route to disaster. *Psychology Today,* pp. 80–102.

Edney, J. J., & Harper, C. S. 1978. The commons dilemma: A review of contributions from psychology. *Environmental Management, 2,* 491–507.

Education Trust, The. 2002. The funding gap: Low-income and minority students receive fewer dollars. www.edtrust.org. Accessed January 16, 2003.

Edwards, H. 1971, November. The sources of black athletic superiority. *Black Scholar.*

Edwards, T. M. 2000, August 28. Flying solo. *Time.*

Edwards, T. M. 2001, May 7. How med students put abortion back in the classroom. *Time.*

Egan, T. 1999, February 28. The war on crack retreats, still taking prisoners. *New York Times.*

Egan, T. 2005, March 24. Vibrant cities find one thing missing: Children. *New York Times.*

Ehrenreich, B. 1990. Is the middle class doomed? In B. Ehrenreich (Ed.), *The worst years of our lives.* New York: Harper & Row.

Ehrenreich, B. 2002, June 30. Two-tiered morality. *New York Times.*

Ehrenreich, B., & English, D. 1979. *For her own good: 150 years of the experts' advice to women.* Garden City, NY: Anchor.

Ehrlich, P. R., & Ehrlich, A. H. 1993. World population crisis. In K. Finsterbusch & J. S. Schwartz (Eds.), *Sources: Notable selections in sociology.* Guilford, CT: Dushkin.

Eichengreen, B. 2001. U.S. foreign economic policy after September 11. *Social Science Research Council Archive.* www.ssrc.org/Sept11/essays. Accessed May 18, 2003.

Eitzen, D. S., & Baca Zinn, M. 1989. *Social problems.* Boston: Allyn & Bacon.

Eitzen, D. S., & Baca Zinn, M. 1991. *In conflict and order: Understanding society.* Boston: Allyn & Bacon.

Elder, G. H., & Liker, J. K. 1982. Hard times in women's lives: Historical influences across 40 years. *American Journal of Sociology, 88,* 241–269.

Elliot, C. 2003, June. American bioscience meets the American dream. *American Prospect.*

Elliott, S. 2004, June 30. With its Viagra under attack by new rivals, Pfizer chooses a new agency for ads in the United States. *New York Times.*

England, P. 1999. The case for comparable worth. *Quarterly Review of Economics and Finance, 39,* 74–55.

English, C. 1991. Food is my best friend: Self-justifications and weight loss efforts. *Research in the Sociology of Health Care, 9,* 335–345.

English, D. J. 1998. The extent and consequences of child maltreatment. *Future of Children, 8,* 39–53.

Enloe, C. 1993. *The morning after: Sexual politics at the end of the cold war.* Berkeley: University of California Press.

Entine, J. 2000. *Taboo: Why black athletes dominate sports and why we're afraid to talk about it.* New York: Public Affairs.

Epstein, C. F. 1989. Workplace boundaries: Conceptions and creations. *Social Research, 56,* 571–590.

Equal Employment Opportunity Commission. 2005. Sexual harassment charges EEOC & FEPAs combined: FY1992-FY2004. www.eeoc.gov/stats/harass.html. Accessed June 13, 2005.

Erikson, K. 1966. *Wayward Puritans.* New York: Wiley.

Erlanger, S. 2000, April 2. Across a new Europe, a people deemed unfit for tolerance. *New York Times.*

Evans, L., & Davies, K. 2000. No sissy boys here: A content analysis of the representation of masculinity in elementary school reading textbooks. *Sex Roles, 42,* 255–270.

Evans-Pritchard, E. E. 1937. *Witchcraft, oracles and magic among the Azande.* Oxford, UK: Oxford University Press.

Evered, R. 1983. The language of organizations: The case of the Navy. In L. R. Pondy, P. J. Frost, G. Morgan, & T. C. Dandridge (Eds.), *Organizational symbolism.* Greenwich, CT: JAI Press.

Ewing, W. 1992. The civic advocacy of violence. In M. S. Kimmel & M. A. Messner (Eds.), *Men's lives.* New York: Macmillan.

Extreme facts. 2005, June 4. *Indianapolis Star.*

Faludi, S. 1991. *Backlash: The undeclared war against women.* New York: Crown.

Family of VCJD victim claim untried treatment is a success. 2003. www.vegsource.com/talk/madcow/messages/422.html. Accessed June 30, 2003.

Farb, P. 1983. *Word play: What happens when people talk.* New York: Bantam.

Farley, J. 1982. *Majority-minority relations.* Englewood Cliffs, NJ: Prentice Hall.

Farley, J. 1991. *Sociology.* Englewood Cliffs, NJ: Prentice Hall.

Farley, R. 2002. *Identifying with multiple races: A social movement that succeeded but failed?* Population Studies Center Research Report No. 01–491. Ann Arbor: Institute for Social Research, University of Michigan.

Farley, R., & Frey, W. H. 1994. Changes in the segregation of whites from Blacks during the 1980s: Small steps toward a more integrated society. *American Sociological Review, 59,* 23–45.

Farmer, R. 2002, Spring. Same sex couples face post-September 11 discrimination. *National NOW Times.*

Faust, K., Gann, M., & McKibben, J. 1999. The boomlet goes to college. *American Demographics, 21,* 4–5.

Fausto-Sterling, A. 1985. *Myths of gender: Biological theories about women and men.* New York: Basic Books.

Fausto-Sterling, A. 2000. *Sexing the body: Gender politics and the construction of sexuality.* New York: Basic Books.

FBI (Federal Bureau of Investigation). 2003. Hate crimes statistics, 2002. www.fbi.gov/ucr/hatecrime2002.pdf. Accessed July 29, 2004.

Feagin, J. R. 1975. *Subordinating the poor.* Englewood Cliffs, NJ: Prentice Hall.

Feagin, J. R. 1991. The continuing significance of race: Anti-black discrimination in public places. *American Sociological Review, 56,* 101–116.

Feagin, J. R., & O'Brien, E. 2003. *White men on race: Power, privilege, and the shaping of cultural consciousness.* Boston: Beacon Press.

Fears, D., & Deane, C. 2001, July 5. Biracial couples report tolerance. *Washington Post.*

Feder, B. J., & Zeller, T. 2004, October 14. Identity badge worn under skin approved for use in health care. *New York Times.*

Feldman, L., Marlantes, L., & Bowers, F. 2003, March 14. The impact of Bush linking 9/11 and Iraq. *Christian Science Monitor.*

Felmlee, D., Sprecher, S., & Bassin, E. 1990. The dissolution of intimate relationships: A hazard model. *Social Psychology Quarterly, 53,* 13–30.

Fendrich, J. M. 2003. The forgotten movement: The Vietnam antiwar movement. *Sociological Inquiry, 73,* 338–358.

Ferguson, N. 2004, April 4. Eurabia? *New York Times Magazine.*

Ferree, M. M. 1992. The political context of rationality. In A. D. Morris & C. M. Mueller (Eds.), *Frontiers in social movement theory.* New Haven, CT: Yale University Press.

Festinger, L., Riecken, H., & Schacter, S. 1956. *When prophecy fails.* New York: Harper & Row.

Feuer, A. 2004, May 15. Vatican discourages marriage with Muslims for Catholic women. *New York Times.*

Fields, J. 2003. Children's living arrangements and characteristics: March 2002. *Current Population Reports, P20–547.* U.S. Census Bureau. Washington, DC: U.S. Government Printing Office.

Fields, J. 2004. America's families and living arrangements: 2003. *Current Population Reports, P20–553.* U.S. Census Bureau. Washington, DC: U.S. Government Printing Office.

Fields, J., & Casper, L. M. 2001. America's families and living arrangements: March 2000. *Current Population Reports, P20–537.* U.S. Census Bureau. Washington, DC: U.S. Government Printing Office.

FIFA. 2003. 2002 FIFA World Cup TV coverage. www.fifa.com/en/marketing/newmedia/index/0,3509,10,00.html. Accessed June 5, 2005.

Figert, A. 1996. *Women and the ownership of PMS.* New York: Aldine de Gruyter.

Fincham, F., & Bradbury, T. N. 1987. The impact of attributions in marriage: A longitudinal analysis. *Journal of Personality and Social Psychology, 53,* 510–517.

Fine, G. A. 1990. *Talking sociology.* Boston: Allyn & Bacon.

Finer, J. 2005, August, 12. The new Ernie Pyles: Sgtlizzie and 67shdocs. *Washington Post.*

Finer, L. B., & Henshaw, S. K. 2003. Abortion incidence and services in the United States in 2000. *Perspectives on Sexual and Reproduction Health, 35,* 6–15.

Finnegan, W. 1998. *Cold new world: Growing up in a harder country.* New York: Random House.

Firestone, D. 2001, May 18. Woman is convicted of killing her fetus by smoking cocaine. *New York Times.*

Fischer, M. J., & Massey, D. S. 2000. Residential segregation and ethnic enterprise in U.S. metropolitan areas. *Social Problems, 47,* 40–24.

Fisher, I. 2002, July 28. Seeing no justice, a rape victim chooses death. *New York Times.*

Fleischaker, D. T. 2004. Dead man pausing: The continuing need for a nationwide moratorium on executions. *Human Rights, 31,* 14–18.

Forbes, H. D. 1997. *Ethnic conflict: Commerce, culture and the contact hypothesis.* New Haven, CT: Yale University Press.

Fortune Magazine. 2005. The 2005 Global 500. www.fortune.com/fortune/global500/fulllist/0,24394,1,00.html. Accessed September 27, 2005.

Fountain, H. 2005, June 5. Unloved, but not unbuilt. *New York Times.*

Fouts, G., & Burggraf, K. 2000. Television situation comedies: Female weight, male negative comments, and audience reactions. *Sex Roles, 42,* 925–932.

Fox, S., Anderson, J. Q., & Rainie, L. 2005. The future of the Internet. Pew Internet and American Life Project. www.pewinternet.org/pdfs/PIP_Future_of_Internet.pdf. Accessed January 20, 2005.

Frank, A. G. 1969. *Capitalism and under-development in Latin America.* New York: Monthly Review Press.

Frank, N. 2004. Gays and lesbians at war: Military service in Iraq and Afghanistan under "Don't Ask, Don't Tell." Center for the Study of Sexual Minorities in the Military. www.gaymilitary.ucsb.edu/publications/Frank091504_GaysAtWar.doc. Accessed September 26, 2004.

Frankenberg, E., Lee, C., & Orfield, G. 2003. A multiracial society with segregated schools: Are we losing the dream? The Civil Rights Project. www.civilrightsproject.harvard.edu/research/reseg03/reseg03_full.php. Accessed January 21, 2003.

Franklin, C. W., II. 1988. *Men and society.* Chicago: Nelson-Hall.

Free the Children. 2005. About Craig Kielburger. www.freethechildren.com/aboutus/about_craig.htm. Accessed May 23, 2005.

Freedman, V. A., Martin, L. G., & Schoeni, R. F. 2004. Disability in America. *Population Bulletin, 59,* 1–32.

Freeman, M. 2002, April 15. Fewer series feature black-dominant casts. *Electronic Media.*

Freiberg, P. 1991. Self-esteem gender gap widens in adolescence. *APA Monitor, 22,* 29.

French, H. W. 1999a, November 15. "Japanese only" policy takes body blow in court. *New York Times.*

French, H. W. 1999b, October 12. Japan's troubling trend: Rising teen-age crime. *New York Times.*

French, H. W. 2000a, May 3. Japan unsettles returnees, who yearn to leave again. *New York Times.*

French, H. W. 2000b, March 14. Still wary of outsiders, Japan expects immigration boom. *New York Times.*

French, H. W. 2002, September 23. Educators try to tame Japan's blackboard jungles. *New York Times.*

French, H. W. 2003, July 25. Japan's neglected resource: Female workers. *New York Times.*

Frese, B., Moya, M., & Megías, J. L. 2004. Social perception of rape: How rape myth acceptance modulates the influence of situational factors. *Journal of Interpersonal Violence, 19,* 143–161.

Freudenheim, M. 2005, March 23. More help wanted: Older workers please apply. *New York Times.*

Freund, P. E. S., & McGuire, M. B. 1991. *Health, illness, and the social body: A cultural sociology.* Englewood Cliffs, NJ: Prentice Hall.

Friedland, R. 1989. Questions raised by the changing age distribution of the U.S. population. *Generations, 13,* 11–13.

Friedman, T. L. 2005, April 3. It's a flat world after all. *New York Times Magazine.*

Frieze, I. H., Parsons, J. E., Johnson, P. B., Ruble, D. N., & Zellman, G. L. 1978. *Women and sex roles: A social psychological perspective.* New York: Norton.

Furstenberg, F. F., & Cherlin, A. J. 1991. *Divided families.* Cambridge, MA: Harvard University Press.

Furstenberg, F. F., & Nord, C. 1985. Parenting apart: Patterns of childrearing after marital disruption. *Journal of Marriage and the Family, 47,* 893–904.

Fuwa, M. 2004. Macro-level gender inequality and the division of household labor in 22 countries. *American Sociological Review, 69,* 751–767.

Gabriel, T. 1996, January 7. High-tech pregnancies test hope's limit. *New York Times.*

Gale, R. P. 1986. Social movements and the state: The environmental movement, countermovement and governmental agencies. *Sociological Perspectives, 29,* 202–240.

Galles, G. M. 1989, June 8. What colleges really teach. *New York Times.*

Galliher, J. M., & Galliher, J. F. 2002. A "commonsense" theory of deterrence and the "ideology" of science: The New York State death penalty debate. *Journal of Criminal Law and Criminology, 92,* 307–333.

Gamson, W. A., Fireman, B., & Rytina, S. 1982. *Encounters with unjust authority.* Homewood, IL: Dorsey Press.

Gamson, W. A., & Wolfsfeld, G. 1993. Movements and media as interactive systems. *Annals of the American Academy of Political and Social Science, 528,* 114–125.

Gans, H. 1971, July/August. The uses of poverty: The poor pay for all. *Social Policy,* pp. 20–24.

Gans, H. 1996. Positive functions of the undeserving poor: Uses of the underclass in America. In J. Levin & A. Arluke (Eds.), *Snapshots and portraits of society.* Thousand Oaks, CA: Pine Forge Press.

Gardner, G. 2005, March/April. Yours, mine, ours—or nobody's? *World Watch.*

Gardner, P. D. 2005. Recruiting trends, 2004–2005. Collegiate Employment Research Institute. www.csp.msu.edu/pages/misc/ceri/pub/rectrends.cfm#exec0405. Accessed April 12, 2005.

Garfinkel, J. 2003, February 24. Boutique medical practices face legal, legislative foes. *Cincinnati Business Courier.* www.bizjournals.com/cincinnati/stories/2003/02/24/focus2.html. Accessed July 12, 2004.

Garment, L. 1996, June 27. Holier than us? *New York Times.*

Garson, B. 1988. *The electronic sweatshop.* New York: Penguin.

Gates, H. L. 1992. TV's black world turns—but stays unreal. In M. L. Anderson & P. H. Collins (Eds.), *Race, class and gender: An anthology.* Belmont, CA: Wadsworth.

Gaubatz, K. T. 1995. *Crime in the public mind.* Ann Arbor: University of Michigan Press.

Gee, H. 2004. From *Bakke* to *Grutter* and beyond: Asian Americans and diversity in America. *Texas Journal on Civil Liberties & Civil Rights, 9,* 129–158.

Gelles, R. J., & Straus, M. A. 1988. *Intimate violence.* Thousand Oaks, CA: Sage.

Genocchio, B. 2004, April 4. For Japanese girls, black is beautiful. *New York Times.*

Geographic.org. 2005. Median age—Total 2004. www.photius.com/rankings/population/median_age_total_2004_1.html. Accessed June 19, 2005.

Gergen, K. J. 1991. *The saturated self.* New York: Basic Books.

Gerlach, P., & Hine, V. H. 1970. *People, power, change: Movements of social transformation.* Indianapolis: Bobbs-Merrill.

Gerson, K. 1993. *No man's land: Men's changing commitments to family and work.* New York: Basic Books.

Getlin, J., & Wilkinson, T. 2003, April 3. "Embedded" reporters are mixed blessing for the military. *Seattle Times.*

Gibbons, D. C. 1992. *Society, crime and criminal behavior.* Englewood Cliffs, NJ: Prentice Hall.

Giddens, A. 1984. *The construction of society: Outline of the theory of structuration.* Berkeley: University of California Press.

Giddens, A. 2000. *Runaway world: How globalization is reshaping our lives.* New York: Routledge.

Giddens, A. 2005. The global revolution in family and personal life. In A. S. Skolnick & J. H. Skolnick (Eds.), *Family in transition.* Boston: Allyn & Bacon.

Giegerich, S. 2003, July 22. College sports see narrowing of gender gap. *Indianapolis Star.*

Gillen, B. 1981. Physical attractiveness: A determinant of two types of goodness. *Personality and Social Psychology Bulletin, 7,* 277–281.

Gilliam, W. S. 2005. Prekindergarteners left behind: Expulsion rates in state prekindergarten systems. Foundation for Child Development. www.fcd-us.org/PDFs/NationalPreKExpulsion Paper03.02_new.pdf. Accessed May 17, 2005.

Gilligan, C. 1990. Teaching Shakespeare's sister: Notes from the underground of female adolescence. In C. Gilligan, N. P. Lyons, & T. J. Hanmer (Eds.), *Making connections.* Cambridge, MA: Harvard University Press.

Gilliom, J. 2001. *Overseers of the poor: Surveillance, resistance, and the limits of privacy.* Chicago: University of Chicago Press.

Gilman, S. 2004. *Fat boys.* Lincoln: University of Nebraska Press.

Ginzel, L. E., Kramer, R. M., & Sutton, R. I. 2004. Organizational impression management as a reciprocal influence process: The neglected role of the organizational audience. In M. J. Hatch & M. Schultz (Eds.), *Organizational identity.* New York: Oxford University Press.

Gitlin, T. 1979. Prime time ideology: The hegemonic process in television entertainment. *Social Problems, 26,* 251–266.

Gladwell, M. 1996, April 29 & May 6. Black like them. *New Yorker.*

Glazer, S. 2003. Mothers' movement. *CQ Researcher, 13,* 297–320.

Gleason, H. A. 1961. *An introduction to descriptive linguistics.* New York: Holt, Rinehart & Winston.

Glick, P., & Fiske, S. T. 1996. The ambivalent sexism inventory: Differentiating hostile and benevolent sexism. *Journal of Personality and Social Psychology, 70,* 49–12.

Godson, R., & Olson, W. J. 1995. International organized crime. *Society, 32,* 18–29.

Goffman, E. 1952. On cooling the mark out: Some aspects of adaptation to failure. *Psychiatry, 15,* 451–463.

Goffman, E. 1959. *The presentation of self in everyday life.* Garden City, NY: Doubleday.

Goffman, E. 1961. *Asylums.* Garden City, NY: Anchor.

Goffman, E. 1963. *Stigma: Notes on the management of spoiled identity.* Englewood Cliffs, NJ: Prentice Hall.

Goffman, E. 1967. *Interaction ritual.* Chicago: Aldine-Atherton.

Goldberg, C. 2001, April 22. In some states, sex offenders serve more than their time. *New York Times.*

Goldberg, S. 1999. The logic of patriarchy. *Gender Issues, 17,* 53–69.

Goleman, D. 1989, October 10. Sensing silent cues emerges as key skill. *New York Times.*

Goleman, D. 1990, December 25. The group and the self: New focus on a cultural rift. *New York Times.*

Goleman, D. 1993, May 4. Therapists find some patients are just hateful. *New York Times.*

Golway, T. 2004, August 2–9. Redrafting America. *America.*

Goode, E. 1989. *Drugs in American society.* New York: McGraw-Hill.

Goode, Erica. 1999, January 12. Pediatricians renew battle over toilet training. *New York Times.*

Goode, Erica. 2002, June 30. Antidepressants lift clouds, but lose "miracle drug" label. *New York Times.*

Goode, Erich. 1994. *Deviant behavior.* Englewood Cliffs, NJ: Prentice Hall.

Goode, W. J. 1971. World revolution and family patterns. *Journal of Marriage and the Family, 33,* 624–635.

Goode, W. J. 1981. Why men resist. In B. Thorne & M. Yalom (Eds.), *Rethinking the family: Some feminist questions.* New York: Longman.

Goode, W. J. 1993. *World changes in divorce patterns.* New Haven, CT: Yale University Press.

Goodnough, A. 2005, April 27. Florida expands right to use deadly force in self-defense. *New York Times.*

Goodstein, L. 2003a, June 11. Louisville archdiocese to pay $25 million abuse settlement. *New York Times.*

Goodstein, L. 2003b, September 11. Survey finds slight rise in Jews' intermarrying. *New York Times.*

Goodwin, J. 2003. The ultimate growth industry: Trafficking in women and girls. In E. Disch (Ed.), *Reconstructing gender: A multicultural anthology.* New York: McGraw-Hill.

Gordon, M. M. 1964. *Assimilation in American life.* New York: Oxford University Press.

Gott, N. 2004, November 6. Textbooks ok'd after marriage redefined. *Indianapolis Star.*

Gould, S. J. 1981. *The mismeasure of man.* New York: Norton.

Gould, S. J. 1997, June. Dolly's fashion and Louis's passion. *Natural History.*

Gove, W., Hughes, M., & Geerkin, M. R. 1980. Playing dumb: A form of impression management with undesirable effects. *Social Psychology Quarterly, 43,* 89–102.

Gove, W., Style, C. B., & Hughes, M. 1990. The effect of marriage on the well-being of adults. *Journal of Family Issues, 11,* 34–35.

Gracey, H. L. 1991. Learning the student role: Kindergarten as academic boot camp. In J. Henslin (Ed.), *Down-to-earth sociology.* New York: Free Press.

Grady, D. 2002, April 4. Few risks seen to the children of 1st cousins. *New York Times.*

Graham, L. O. 1999. *Our kind of people: Inside America's black upper class.* New York: HarperCollins.

Graham, W. 1996, July. Masters of the game. *Harper's.*

Gray, H. 1995. Television, black Americans, and the American dream. In G. Dines & J. M. Humez (Eds.), *Gender, race and class in media.* Thousand Oaks, CA: Sage.

Greeley, A. M., & Hout, M. 1999. Americans' increasing belief in life after death: Religious competition and acculturation. *American Sociological Review, 64,* 813–835.

Green, J. C., Smidt, C. E., Guth, J. L., & Kellstedt, L. A. 2005. The American religious landscape and the 2004 presidential vote: Increased polarization. Pew Forum on Religion and Public Life. http://pewforum.org/publications/surveys/postelection.pdf. Accessed May 27, 2005.

Greenberg, J. 1998, December 20. Israel battles new foreign foe: Music. *New York Times.*

Greencastle Banner Graphic. 1992, March 7. Letter to the editor.

Greene, M. F. 2004, November 28. Sandlot summer: Hyperscheduled, overachieving children learn how to play. *New York Times Magazine.*

Greenhouse, L. 1993, November 10. Court, 9–0, makes sex harassment easier to prove. *New York Times.*

Greenhouse, L. 2000, January 26. Anti-sweatshop movement is achieving gains overseas. *New York Times.*

Greenhouse, L. 2003, April 11. Refusal to fire unattractive saleswoman led to dismissal, suit contends. *New York Times.*

Greenhouse, L. 2005a, June 7. Justices say U.S. may prohibit the use of medical marijuana. *New York Times.*

Greenhouse, L. 2005b, June 14. Supreme Court rules for Texan on death row. *New York Times.*

Greenhouse, S. 2004a, November 19. Forced to work off the clock, some fight back. *New York Times.*

Greenhouse, S. 2004b, March 7. If you're a waiter the future is rosy. *New York Times.*

Greenhouse, S., & Hays, C. L. 2004, June 23. Wal-Mart sex-bias suit given class-action status. *New York Times.*

Greider, W. 1997. *One world, ready or not: The manic logic of global capitalism.* New York: Simon & Schuster.

Griffin, S. 1986. *Rape: The power of consciousness.* New York: Harper & Row.

Griffin, S. 1989. Rape: The all-American crime. In L. Richardson & V. Taylor (Eds.), *Feminist frontiers II.* New York: Random House.

Griswold, W. 1994. *Cultures and societies in a changing world.* Thousand Oaks, CA: Pine Forge Press.

Gross, E. 1984. Embarrassment in public life. *Society, 21,* 48–53.

Gross, E., & Etzioni, A. 1985. *Organizations and society.* Englewood Cliffs, NJ: Prentice Hall.

Gross, E., & Stone, G. P. 1964. Embarrassment and the analysis of role requirements. *American Journal of Sociology, 70,* 1–15.

Gross, J. 1997, October 5. Wall Street's frenetic? Try the eighth grade. *New York Times.*

Gross, J. 2004a, February 24. Older women team up to face future together. *New York Times.*

Gross, J. 2004b, May 31. Splitting up boys and girls, just for the tough years. *New York Times.*

Grossman, C. L. 2003, October 6. Public opinion is divided on gay marriages. *USA Today.*

Gusfield, J. R. 1963. *Symbolic crusade: Status politics and the American temperance movement.* Urbana: University of Illinois Press.

Hacker, A. 1992. *Two nations: Black and white, separate, hostile, unequal.* New York: Scribner's.

Hacker, A. 1994, October 31. White on white. *New Republic.*

Hafferty, F. W. 1991. *Into the valley: Death and socialization of medical students.* New Haven, CT: Yale University Press.

Hafner, K. 2000, March 30. For the well-connected, all the world's an office. *New York Times.*

Hafner, K. 2002, April 28. A tyranny of digital controls invades the comfort of home. *New York Times.*

Hagan, J. 1985. *Modern criminology: Crime, criminal behavior and its control.* New York: McGraw-Hill.

Hagan, J. 2000. The poverty of a classless criminology: The American Society of Criminology 1991 presidential address. In R. D. Crutchfield, G. S. Bridges, J. G. Weis, & C. Kubrin (Eds.), *Crime readings.* Thousand Oaks, CA: Pine Forge Press.

Hakim, D. 2005, June 8. G.M. will reduce hourly workers in U.S. by 25,000. *New York Times.*

Halbfinger, D. M., & Holmes, S. A. 2003, March 30. Military mirrors a working-class America. *New York Times.*

Hall, P. 1990. The presidency and impression management. In J. W. Heeren & M. Mason (Eds.), *Sociology: Windows on society.* Los Angeles: Roxbury.

Hall, W. 1986. Social class and survival on the *S.S. Titanic. Social Science and Medicine, 22,* 687–690.

Hallin, D. C. 1986. We keep America on top of the world. In T. Gitlin (Ed.), *Watching television.* New York: Pantheon.

Hamilton, B. E., Martin, J. A., & Sutton, P. D. 2003. Births: Preliminary data for 2002. *National Vital Statistics Report, 51,* 1–20.

Hamilton, D. L. 1981. *Cognitive processes in stereotyping and intergroup behavior.* Hillsdale, NJ: Erlbaum.

Hamilton, J. A. 1996. Women and health policy: On the inclusion of women in clinical trials. In C. F. Sargent & C. B. Brettell (Eds.), *Gender and health: An international perspective.* Upper Saddle River, NJ: Prentice Hall.

Hamilton, V. L., & Sanders, J. 1995. Crimes of obedience and conformity in the workplace: Surveys of Americans, Russians, and Japanese. *Journal of Social Issues, 51,* 67–88.

Haney López, I. F. 1996. *White by law: The legal construction of race.* New York: New York University Press.

Hankiss, E. 2001. *Symbols of destruction.* After September 11. Social Science Research Council. www.ssrc.org/Sept11/essays/hankiss.html. Accessed May 17, 2003.

Harden, B. 2000, April 6. Africa's gems: Warfare's best friend. *New York Times.*

Harden, B. 2001, August 12. The dirt in the new machine. *New York Times Magazine.*

Hardin, G., & Baden, J. 1977. *Managing the commons.* New York: Freeman.

Hareven, T. K. 1978. *Transitions: The family and the life course in historical perspective.* New York: Academic Press.

Hareven, T. K. 1992. American families in transition: Historical perspectives on change. In A. S. Skolnick & J. H. Skolnick (Eds.), *Family in transition* (7th ed.). New York: HarperCollins.

Harris, D. R., & Sim, J. J. 2002. Who is multiracial? Assessing the complexity of lived race. *American Sociological Review, 67,* 614–627.

Harris, G. 2003, December 7. If shoe won't fit, fix the foot? Popular surgery raises concern. *New York Times.*

Harris, G. 2005, August 6. F.D.A. responds to criticism with new caution. *New York Times.*

Harris, J. R. 1998. *The nurture assumption.* New York: Free Press.

Harrison, P. M., & Karberg, J. C. 2004. Prison and jail inmates at midyear 2003. Bureau of Justice Statistics Bulletin NCJ 203947. www.ojp.usdoj.gov/bjs/pub/pdf/pjim03.pdf. Accessed July 25, 2004.

Hartmann, H., Kraut, R. E., & Tilly, L. A. 1989. Job content: Job fragmentation and the deskilling debate. In D. S. Eitzen & M. Baca-Zinn (Eds.), *The reshaping of America.* Englewood Cliffs, NJ: Prentice Hall.

Harvard Mental Health Letter. 2005. The nocebo response. March, pp. 6–7.

Hasday, J. E. 2000. Contest and consent: A legal history of marital rape. *California Law Review, 88,* 1373–1506.

Hass, N. 1995, September 10. Margaret Kelly Michaels wants her innocence back. *New York Times Magazine.*

Hass, N. 1998, February 22. A TV generation is seeing beyond color. *New York Times.*

Hayward, M. D., & Heron, M. 1999. Racial inequality in active life among adult Americans. *Demography, 36,* 77–91.

Health Grades. 2004. Health Grades quality study: Patient safety in American hospitals. www.healthgrades.com/media/english/pdf/HG_Patient_Safety_Study_Final.pdf. Accessed June 5, 2005.

Heise, L. 1989, April 9. The global war against women. *Washington Post Magazine.*

Helmreich, W. B. 1992. The things they say behind your back: Stereotypes and the myths behind them. In H. F. Lena, W. B. Helmreich, & W. McCord (Eds.), *Contemporary issues in sociology.* New York: McGraw-Hill.

Henderson, J. J., & Baldasty, G. J. 2003. Race, advertising, and prime-time television. *The Howard Journal of Communication, 14,* 97–112.

Henley, N. 1977. *Body politics.* Englewood Cliffs, NJ: Prentice Hall.

Henriques, D. B. 1999, August 24. New take on perpetual calendar. *New York Times.*

Henshaw, S. K. 2003, January–February. Abortion incidence and services in the United States, 2000. *Family Planning Perspectives.*

Henslin, J. 1991. *Down-to-earth sociology.* New York: Free Press.

Henwood, D. 2001, April 9. Wealth report. *The Nation.*

Herbert, B. 2004, July 23. Who's getting the new jobs? *New York Times.*

Herman, N. J. 1993. Return to sender: Reintegrative stigma-management strategies of ex-psychiatric patients. *Journal of Contemporary Ethnography, 22,* 29–30.

Herrnstein, R. J., & Murray, C. 1994. *The bell curve: Intelligence and class structure in American life.* New York: Free Press.

Hewitt, J. P. 1988. *Self and society: A symbolic interactionist social psychology.* Boston: Allyn & Bacon.

Hewitt, J. P., & Hewitt, M. L. 1986. *Introducing sociology: A symbolic interactionist perspective.* Englewood Cliffs, NJ: Prentice Hall.

Hewitt, J. P., & Stokes, R. 1975. Disclaimers. *American Sociological Review, 40,* 1–11.

Higginbotham, E., & Weber, L. 1992. Moving up with kin and community: Upward social mobility for black and white women. *Gender & Society, 6,* 416–440.

Hill, M. E. 2000. Color differences in the socioeconomic status of African American men: Results from a longitudinal study. *Social Forces, 78,* 1437–1460.

Hill, N. E. 1997. Does parenting differ based on social class? African American women's perceived socialization for achievement. *American Journal of Community Psychology, 25,* 67–97.

Hiller, E. T. 1933. *Principles of sociology.* New York: Harper & Row.

Hills, S. 1980. *Demystifying social deviance.* New York: McGraw-Hill.

Hines, R. I. 2001. African Americans' struggle for environmental justice and the case of the Shintech plant: Lessons learned from a war waged. *Journal of Black Studies, 31,* 777–789.

Hirschi, T. 1969. *Causes of delinquency.* Berkeley: University of California Press.

Hitt, J. 2005, August 21. The new Indians. *New York Times Magazine.*

Hobbs, F., & Stoops, N. 2002. *Demographic trends in the 20th century.* Census 2000 Special Reports, Series CENSR-4. Washington, DC: U.S. Government Printing Office.

Hochschild, A. R. 1983. *The managed heart.* Berkeley: University of California Press.

Hochschild, A. R. 1997. *The time bind: When work becomes home and home becomes work.* New York: Metropolitan Books.

Hodson, R. 1991. The active worker: Compliance and autonomy at the workplace. *Journal of Contemporary Ethnography, 20,* 47–78.

Hodson, R. 1996. Dignity in the workplace under participative management: Alienation and freedom revisited. *American Sociological Review, 61,* 719–738.

Hodson, R. 2001. *Dignity at work.* New York: Cambridge University Press.

Hoffman, J. 1997, January 16. Crime and punishment: Shame gains popularity. *New York Times.*

Hoffman, J. 2005, January 25. Sorting out ambivalence over alcohol and pregnancy. *New York Times.*

Hoge, W. 1998, August 10. Sweden, the world's role model, now drifting as currents change. *New York Times.*

Hogshead-Makar, N. 2003, July. The ongoing battle over Title IX. *USA Today Magazine.*

Holmes, S. A. 1995, December 31. The strange politics of immigration. *New York Times.*

Holmes, S. A. 1998, November 20. Klan case transcends racial divide. *New York Times.*

Holmes, S. A. 2000, March 11. New policy on census says those listed as white and minority will be counted as minority. *New York Times.*

Holmes, S. A. 2003, January 20. Courts put girls on the stand in Alabama. *New York Times.*

Holtzworth-Munroe, A., & Jacobson, N. S. 1985. Causal attributions of married couples: When do they search for causes? What do they conclude when they do? *Journal of Personality and Social Psychology, 48,* 1398–1412.

Hooks, G., & Smith, C. L. 2004. The treadmill of destruction: National sacrifice areas and Native Americans. *American Sociological Review, 69,* 558–575.

Horon, I. L., & Cheng, D. 2001. Enhanced surveillance for pregnancy-associated mortality—Maryland, 1993–1998. *Journal of the American Medical Association, 285,* 1455–1459.

Horwitz, A. V. 2002. *Creating mental illness.* Chicago: University of Chicago Press.

Houppert, K. 2005, March 28. The new face of protest? *The Nation.*

House, J. 1981. Social structure and personality. In M. Rosenberg & R. H. Turner (Eds.), *Social psychology: Sociological perspectives.* New York: Basic Books.

Hout, M., & Lucas, S. R. 2001. Narrowing the income gap between rich and poor. In P. Rothenberg (Ed.), *Race, class, and gender in the United States.* New York: Worth.

Howard, J. A., & Hollander, J. 1997. *Gendered situations, gendered selves.* Newbury Park, CA: Sage.

Howe, N., & Strauss, W. 2000. *Millennials rising: The next great generation.* New York: Vintage.

Huber, J., & Form, W. H. 1973. *Income and ideology.* New York: Free Press.

Hubert, C. 2005, June 7. Cell phone addictive for users. *Indianapolis Star.*

Hudson, V. M., & den Boer, A. 2004. *Bare branches: The security implications of Asia's surplus male population.* Cambridge, MA: MIT Press.

Hughes, D., & Chen, L. 1997. When and what parents tell children about race: An examination of race-related socialization among African American families. *Applied Developmental Science, 1,* 200–214.

Hull, K. E., & Nelson, R. L. 2000. Assimilation, choice, or constraint? Testing theories of gender differences in the careers of lawyers. *Social Forces, 79,* 229–264.

Human Rights Watch. 2001. *Caste discrimination: A global concern.* www.hrw.org/reports/2001/globalcaste. Accessed June 16, 2004.

Humphreys, L. 1970. *The tearoom trade: Impersonal sex in public places.* Chicago: Aldine-Atherton.

Hunt, J. 1985. Police accounts of normal force. *Urban Life, 13*(4), 315–341.

Hunter, J. D. 1991. *Culture wars: The struggle to define America.* New York: Basic Books.

Hurst, C. 1979. *The anatomy of social inequality.* St. Louis: Mosby.

Hutchens, T. 2002, December 21. Coverdale gives IU its heart and soul. *Indianapolis Star.*

Hyde, J. S. 1984. How large are gender differences in aggression? A developmental meta-analysis. *Developmental Psychology, 20,* 722–736.

Ignatieff, M. 2005, June 26. Who are Americans to think that freedom is theirs to spread? *New York Times Magazine.*

Ignatius, A. 1988, July 14. China's birthrate is out of control again as one-child policy fails in rural areas. *Wall Street Journal.*

Inciardi, J. A. 1992. *The war on drugs II.* Mountain View, CA: Mayfield.

Initiative Media North America. 2002. Proprietary study reveals TV networks winning African American viewers. *IMsight News, 2,* 1–2. www.im-na.com/news/img/IMsightsv2n4.pdf. Accessed August 1, 2003.

Institute for Policy Research. 2002. Housework in double-income marriages still divides unevenly. *Institute for Policy Research News, 24,* 1–2. www.northwestern.edu/ipr/publications/newsletter/iprn0212/housework.html. Accessed August 2, 2003.

Institute of Medicine. 1999a. *To err is human: Building a safer health care system.* Committee on Quality of Health Care in America. Washington, DC: National Academy Press.

Institute of Medicine. 1999b. The unequal burden of cancer: An assessment of NIH research and programs for ethnic minorities and the medically underserved. www2.nas.edu .whatsnew/29aa.html. Accessed January 20, 2000.

Institute of Medicine. 2003. Preparing for the psychological consequences of terrorism: A public health strategy. National Academies Press. www.nap.edu. Accessed June 10, 2003.

Ioannidis, J. P. A. 2005. Contradicted and initially stronger effects in highly cited clinical research. *JAMA, 294,* 218–228.

Is selfish routing causing a "tragedy of the commons"? 2003, March 3. *Science Letter.*

Is there a Santa Claus? 1897, September 21. *New York Sun.*

It can't happen here. 2002, May–June. *Utne Reader.*

Jackall, R. 1988. *Moral mazes: The world of corporate managers.* New York: Oxford University Press.

Jackman, T., & Eggen, D. 2002, June 20. "Combatants" lack rights, U.S. argues. *Washington Post.*

Jackson, J., & Hart, P. 2001. Fear & Favor 2001: How power shapes the news. Fairness & Accuracy in Reporting. www.fair.org/reports/ff2001.html. Accessed January 16, 2003.

Jackson, S. 1995. The social context of rape: Sexual scripts and motivation. In P. Searles & R. J. Berger (Eds.), *Rape and society.* Boulder, CO: Westview Press.

Janoff-Bulman, R. 1979. Characterological versus behavioral self-blame: Inquiries into depression and rape. *Journal of Personality and Social Psychology, 37,* 1798–1809.

Jefferson, T. 1955. *Notes on the State of Virginia.* Chapel Hill: University of North Carolina Press. (Original work published 1781)

Jehl, D. 1999, June 20. Arab honor's price: A woman's blood. *New York Times.*

Jencks, C., & Phillips, M. 1998. *The black-white test score gap.* Washington, DC: Brookings Institute.

Jenkins, H. 1999, July. Professor Jenkins goes to Washington. *Harper's.*

Jenkins, J. C., & Perrow, C. 1977. Insurgency of the powerless: Farm worker movements (1946–1972). *American Sociological Review, 42,* 249–268.

Jensen, C., & Project Censored. 1995. *The news that didn't make the news—and why.* New York: Four Walls Eight Windows.

Jha, A. K., Varosy, P. D., Kanaya, A. K., Hunninghake, D. B., Hlatky, M. A., Waters, D. D., Furberg, C. D., & Shlipak, M. G. 2003. Differences in medical care and disease outcomes among black and white women with heart disease. *Circulation, 108,* 1089–1094.

Jimmy Swaggart. Just. Shut. Up. 2004. www.brutallyhonest.org/brutally_honest/2004/09/ jimmy_swaggart_.html. Accessed June 2, 2005.

Johnson, P. 1997. *A history of the American people.* New York: HarperCollins.

Johnson, R. 1987. *Hard time: Understanding and reforming the prison.* Pacific Grove, CA: Brooks/Cole.

Johnston, D. 1992, April 24. Survey shows number of rapes far higher than official figures. *New York Times.*

Johnston, D. 2002a, April 7. Affluent avoid scrutiny on taxes even as I.R.S. warns of cheating. *New York Times.*

Johnston, D. 2002b, July 10. Big names but no authority to prosecute. *New York Times.*

Johnston, D. 2005, June 5. Richest are leaving even the rich far behind. *New York Times.*

Jones, A. 1980. *Women who kill.* New York: Fawcett Columbine.

Jones, E. E., Farina, A., Hastorf, A. H., Markus, H., Miller, D. T., & Scott, R. A. 1984. *Social stigma: The psychology of marked relationships.* New York: Freeman.

Jones, E. E., & Pittman, T. S. 1982. Toward a general theory of strategic self-presentation. In J. Suls (Ed.), *Psychological perspectives on the self* (Vol. 1). Hillsdale, NJ: Erlbaum.

Jones, J. M. 1986. The concept of racism and its changing reality. In B. P. Bowser & R. G. Hunt (Eds.), *Impacts of racism on white Americans.* Beverly Hills, CA: Sage.

Jost, K. 2002. Sexual abuse and the clergy. *CQ Researcher, 12,* 393–416.

Joyce, A. 2004, June 23. Wal-Mart bias case moves forward. *Washington Post.*

Joyce, A. 2005, June 6. Workplace improves for gay, transgender employees, rights group says. *Washington Post.*

Juergensmeyer, M. 1996, November. Religious nationalism: A global threat? *Current History.*

Justice Policy Institute. 2002. Cellblocks or classrooms? The funding of higher education and corrections and its impact on African American men. www.justicepolicy.org/coc1/corc .htm. Accessed January 15, 2003.

Kagay, M. R., & Elder, J. 1992, August 9. Numbers are no problem for pollsters. Words are. *New York Times.*

Kahn, J. 2004, May 30. The most populous nation faces a population crisis. *New York Times.*

Kain, E. 1990. *The myth of family decline.* Lexington, MA: Lexington Books.

Kalmijn, M. 1994. Assortive mating by cultural and economic occupational status. *American Journal of Sociology, 100,* 422–452.

Kanter, R. M. 1977. *Men and women of the corporation.* New York: Basic Books.

Kanter, R. M., & Stein, B. A. 1979. *Life in organizations: Workplaces as people experience them.* New York: Basic Books.

Karabel, J. 1972. Community colleges and social stratification. *Harvard Educational Review, 42,* 521–559.

Kariya, T., & Rosenbaum, J. E. 1987. Self-selection in Japanese junior high schools: A longitudinal study of students' educational plans. *Sociology of Education, 60,* 168–180.

Karp, D. A., & Yoels, W. C. 1976. The college classroom: Some observations on the meanings of student participation. *Sociology and Social Research, 60,* 421–439.

Karraker, K. H., Vogel, D. A., & Lake, M. A. 1995. Parents' gender stereotyped perceptions of newborns: The eye of the beholder revisited. *Sex Roles, 33,* 687–701.

Kart, C. S. 1990. *The realities of aging.* Boston: Allyn & Bacon.

Katz, J. 1975. Essences as moral identities: Verifiability and responsibility in imputations of deviance and charisma. *American Journal of Sociology, 80,* 1369–1390.

Katz, N. 2003. Rapes/sexual assault at the Air Force Academy. http://womensissues.about.com/cs/ militarywomen/a/aaairforcerapes.htm. Accessed August 2, 2003.

Kearl, M. C. 1980. Time, identity and the spiritual needs of the elderly. *Sociological Analysis, 41,* 172–180.

Kearl, M. C., & Gordon, C. 1992. *Social psychology.* Boston: Allyn & Bacon.

Keister, L. A., & Moller, S. 2000. Wealth inequality in the United States. *Annual Review of Sociology, 26,* 63–81.

Keith, V. M., & Herring, C. 1991. Skin tone and stratification in the black community. *American Journal of Sociology, 97,* 760–778.

Kelly, K. 2002, February 18. Gay parents get endorsed by kids' docs. *US News & World Report.*

Kennedy, P. 1993. *Preparing for the 21st century.* New York: Random House.

Kerbo, H. R. 1991. *Social stratification and inequality.* New York: McGraw-Hill.

Kershaw, S. 2004, July 21. It's a long, lonely search for men looking for love in Alaska. *New York Times.*

Kershaw, S. 2005, January 26. Old law shielding a woman's virtue faces an updating. *New York Times.*

Kershner, R. 1996. Adolescent attitudes about rape. *Adolescence, 31,* 29–33.

Kessler, S. J., & McKenna, W. 1978. *Gender: An ethnomethodological approach.* Chicago: University of Chicago Press.

Kessler-Harris, A. 1982. *Out to work: A history of wage-earning women in the United States.* New York: Oxford University Press.

Keyfitz, N. 1989, September. The growing human population. *Scientific American.*

Khalema, N. E., & Wannas-Jones, J. 2003. Under the prism of suspicion: Minority voices in Canada post-September 11. *Journal of Muslim Minority Affairs, 23,* 25–39.

Kilborn, P. T. 1999, September 16. Bias worsens for minorities buying homes. *New York Times.*

Kimmel, M. S. 2004. *The gendered society.* New York: Oxford University Press.

King, M. L., Jr. 1991. Letter from Birmingham City jail. In C. Carson, D. J. Garrow, G. Gill, V. Harding, & D. Clark Hine (Eds.), *The eyes on the prize civil rights reader.* New York: Penguin.

Kirkwood, M. K., & Cecil, D. K. 2001. Marital rape: A student assessment of rape laws and the marital exemption. *Violence Against Women, 7,* 1234–1253.

Kirn, W. 2004, July 18. Cursing Casanova. *New York Times Magazine.*

Kishor, S., & Johnson, K. 2004. Profiling domestic violence: A multi-country study. www.measuredhs.com/pubs/pdf/OD31/DV.pdf. Accessed June 1, 2005.

Klatch, R. 1991. Complexities of conservatism: How conservatives understand the world. In A. Wolfe (Ed.), *America at century's end.* Berkeley: University of California Press.

Klawitter, M. M. 1994. Who gains, who loses from changing U.S. child support policies? *Policy Sciences, 27,* 197–219.

Kleck, R. 1968. Physical stigma and nonverbal cues emitted in face-to-face interaction. *Human Relations, 21,* 19–28.

Kleck, R., Ono, H., & Hastorf, A. 1966. The effects of physical deviance and face-to-face interaction. *Human Relations, 19,* 425–436.

Klinenberg, E. 2002. *Heat wave: A social autopsy of disaster in Chicago.* Chicago: University of Chicago Press.

Kluckholm, C. 2000. Queer customs. In G. Massey (Ed.), *Readings for sociology.* New York: Norton.

Knuckey, J., & Orey, B. D. 2000. Symbolic racism in the 1995 Louisiana gubernatorial election. *Social Science Quarterly, 81,* 1027–1035.

Kobrin, F. E. 1976. The fall in household size and the rise of the primary individual in the United States. *Demography, 31,* 127–138.

Koch, K. 1999, October 22. Rethinking Ritalin. *CQ Researcher* [Special issue].

Kocieniewski, D. 1999, April 29. New Jersey's state police enlist hotel workers in war on drugs. *New York Times.*

Koeppel, B. 1999, November 8. Cancer Alley, Louisiana. *The Nation.*

Kohlberg, L. A. 1966. A cognitive-developmental analysis of children's sex-role concepts and attitudes. In E. Maccoby (Ed.), *The development of sex differences.* Stanford, CA: Stanford University Press.

Kohn, H. 1994, November 6. Service with a sneer. *New York Times Magazine.*

Kohn, M. L. 1979. The effects of social class on parental values and practices. In D. Reiss & H. A. Hoffman (Eds.), *The American family: Dying or developing.* New York: Plenum Press.

Kohut, A. 1999, December 3. Globalization and the wage gap. *New York Times.*

Kokopeli, B., & Lakey, G. 1992. More power than we want: Masculine sexuality and violence. In M. L. Anderson & P. H. Collins (Eds.), *Race, class and gender: An anthology.* Belmont, CA: Wadsworth.

Kolata, G. 1997, February 13. Accidents much more likely when drivers hold a phone. *New York Times.*

Kolata, G. 2000, March 6. Web research transforms visit to the doctor. *New York Times.*

Kolata, G. 2004a, July 13. Experts set a lower low for cholesterol levels. *New York Times.*

Kolata, G. 2004b, September 30. Health and money issues arise over who pays for weight loss. *New York Times.*

Kolata, G. 2004c, May 11. The heart's desire. *New York Times.*

Korean girls take poison to aid kin. 1989, March 3. *Hartford Courant.*

Kosmin, B. A., & Mayer, E. 2001. American religious identification survey. Exhibit 3. www.gc .cuny.edu/studies/key_findings.htm. Accessed July 22, 2003.

Kovel, J. 1980. The American mental health industry. In D. Ingleby (Ed.), *Critical psychiatry.* New York: Pantheon.

Kramer, P. 1997. *Listening to Prozac.* New York: Penguin.

Krauss, C. 2004, March 2. In aging Quebec, town pays to keep the babies coming. *New York Times.*

Kreider, R. M. 2005. Number, timing, and duration of marriages and divorces: 2001. *Current Population Reports, P70–97.* U.S. Census Bureau. Washington, DC: U.S. Government Printing Office.

Kress, M. 2005, April 20. Mormonism is booming in the U.S. and overseas. *Ft. Wayne News-Sentinel.*

Kristof, N. D. 1991, November 5. Stark data on women: 100 million are missing. *New York Times.*

Kristof, N. D. 1993, July 21. Peasants of China discover new way to weed out girls. *New York Times.*

Kristof, N. D. 2002, November 22. China's super kids. *New York Times.*

Kristof, N. D. 2003, August 15. Believe it or not. *New York Times.*

Krueger, A. B. 2002, November 14. The apple falls close to the tree, even in the land of opportunity. *New York Times.*

Kubany, E. S., Abueg, F. R., Owens, J. A., Brennan, J. M., Kaplan, A. S., & Watson, S. B. 1995. Initial examination of a multidimensional model of trauma-related guilt: Applications to combat veterans and battered women. *Journal of Psychopathology and Behavioral Assessment, 17,* 353–376.

Kuczynski, A. 2004, May 2. A lovelier you, with off-the-shelf parts. *New York Times.*

Kulick, D., & Machado-Borges, T. 2005. Leaky. In D. Kulick & A. Meneley (Eds.), *Fat: The anthropology of an obsession.* New York: Tarcher/Penguin.

Kurtz, L. R. 1995. *Gods in the global village.* Thousand Oaks, CA: Pine Forge Press.

Kusmer, K. 2005, July 10. Catholic group: Abuse scandal could cost up to $3 billion. *Indianapolis Star.*

Labaton, S. 1996, September 15. The packaging of a perpetrator. *New York Times.*

Labaton, S. 2002, June 2. Downturn and shift in population feed boom in white collar crime. *New York Times.*

Labaton, S. 2005, April 15. House passes bankruptcy bill; overhaul now awaits president's signature. *New York Times.*

Lacey, M. 2003, March 5. Rights group calls for end to inheriting African wives. *New York Times.*

Lakoff, R. 1975. *Language and woman's place.* New York: Harper & Row.

Lakshmi, R. 2005, February 27. India call centers suffer storm of 4-letter words. *Washington Post.*

Lalasz, R. 2005, January. Full-time work no guarantee of livelihood for many U.S. families. Population Reference Bureau Report. www.prb.org. Accessed January 19, 2005.

Lamont, M. 1992. *Money, morals & manners: The culture of the French and American upper middle class.* Chicago: University of Chicago Press.

Lander, L. 1988. *Images of bleeding: Menstruation as ideology.* New York: Orlando.

Landesman, P. 2004, January 25. The girls next door. *New York Times.*

Landler, M. 1996, September 10. Corporate insurer to cover cost of spin doctors. *New York Times.*

Landler, M. 2002, December 1. For Austrians, Ho-Ho-Ho is no laughing matter. *New York Times.*

Lang, S. 1998. *Men as women, women as men: Changing gender in Native American cultures.* Austin: University of Texas Press.

Langan, P. A., & Levin, D. J. 2002. Recidivism of prisoners released in 1994. Bureau of Justice Statistics Bulletin NCJ 193427. www.ojp.usdoj.gov/bjs/abstract/rpr94.htm. Accessed January 20, 2003.

Langman, L. 1988. Social stratification. In M. B. Sussman & S. K. Steinmetz (Eds.), *Handbook of marriage and the family.* New York: Plenum Press.

Langston, D. 1992. Tired of playing monopoly? In M. L. Anderson & P. H. Collins (Eds.), *Race, class and gender: An anthology.* Belmont, CA: Wadsworth.

Lapchick, R. E. 2003. Racial and gender report card. Institute for Diversity and Ethics in Sport. www.bus.ucf.edu/sport/public/downloads/media/ides/release_05.pdf. Accessed June 10, 2005.

Lareau, A. 2003. *Unequal childhoods: Class, race, and family life.* Berkeley: University of California Press.

Larew, J. 2003. Why are droves of unqualified, unprepared kids getting into our top colleges? Because their dads are alumni. In K. E. Rosenblum & T. C. Travis (Eds.), *The meaning of difference: American constructions of race, sex and gender, social class, and sexual orientation.* New York: McGraw-Hill.

Larson, L. E., & Goltz, J. W. 1989. Religious participation and marital commitment. *Review of Religious Research, 30,* 387–400.

Lasch, C. 1977. *Haven in a heartless world.* New York: Basic Books.

Lauer, R., & Handel, W. 1977. *Social psychology: The theory and application of symbolic interactionism.* Boston: Houghton Mifflin.

Lawson, C. 1993, February 11. Stereotypes unravel, but not too quickly, in new toys for 1993. *New York Times.*

Leape, L. L., & Bates, D. W. 1995. Systems analysis of adverse drug events. *JAMA, 274,* 35–43.

LeBesco, K. 2004. *Revolting bodies? The struggle to redefine fat identity.* Amherst: University of Massachusetts Press.

Lee, F. R. 2003, January 18. Does class count in today's land of opportunity? *New York Times.*

Lee, S. M. 1993. Racial classifications in the U.S. Census: 1890–1990. *Ethnic and Racial Studies, 16,* 75–94.

Lee, S. M., & Edmonston, B. 2005. New marriages, new families: U.S. racial and Hispanic intermarriage. *Population Bulletin, 60,* 1–36.

Lee, V., & Marks, H. M. 1990. Sustained effects of the single-sex secondary school experience on attitudes, behaviors and values in college. *Journal of Educational Psychology, 82,* 578–592.

Leidner, R. 1991. Serving hamburgers and selling insurance: Gender work and identity in interactive service jobs. *Gender and Society, 5,* 154–177.

Leinberger, P., & Tucker, B. 1991. *The new individualists: The generation after the organization man.* New York: HarperCollins.

Lekachman, R. 1991. The specter of full employment. In J. H. Skolnick & E. Currie (Eds.), *Crisis in American institutions.* New York: HarperCollins.

Leland, J. 1996, February 19. Tightening the knot. *Newsweek.*

Leland, J. 2004a, March 23. He's retired, she's working, they're not happy. *New York Times.*

Leland, J. 2004b, June 13. Why America sees the silver lining. *New York Times.*

Leland, J. 2005, July 7. Just a minute, Boss. My cellphone is ringing. *New York Times.*

Lemert, E. 1972. *Human deviance, social problems, and social control.* Englewood Cliffs, NJ: Prentice Hall.

Leonhardt, D. 2000, April 16. Executive pay drops off the political radar. *New York Times.*

Leonhardt, D. 2002, May 1. Blacks' mortgage costs exceed whites' of like pay. *New York Times.*

Leonhardt, D. 2003a, January 12. Defining the rich in the world's wealthiest nation. *New York Times*.

Leonhardt, D. 2003b, May 14. Graduates lowering their sights in today's stagnant job market, *New York Times*.

Leonhardt, D. 2005, May 24. The college dropout boom: Working class and staying that way. *New York Times*.

Leonnig, C. D. 2005, June 8. Tobacco escapes huge penalty. *New York Times*.

Lerner, M. 1970. The desire for justice and reactions to victims. In J. Macauley & L. Berkowitz (Eds.), *Altruism and helping behavior*. New York: Academic Press.

Lester, W. 2005, January 8. Poll: 29% in U.S. give tsunami aid. *Indianapolis Star*.

Levin, J. 1993. *Sociological snapshots*. Newbury Park, CA: Pine Forge Press.

Levine, H. G. 1992. Temperance cultures: Concern about alcohol problems in Nordic and English-speaking cultures. In M. Lader, G. Edwards, & D.C. Drummond (Eds.), *The nature of alcohol and drug-related problems*. New York: Oxford University Press.

Levinson, D. 1989. *Family violence in cross-cultural perspective*. Newbury Park, CA: Sage.

Lewin, T. 1994, October 21. Outrage over 18 months for man who killed his wife in "heat of passion." *New York Times*.

Lewin, T. 1998, December 13. How boys lost out to girl power. *New York Times*.

Lewin, T. 2000, April 11. Disabled student is suing over test-score labeling. *New York Times*.

Lewin, T. 2001, October 21. Shelters have empty beds; Abused women stay home. *New York Times*.

Lewis, M. 1978. *The culture of inequality*. New York: New American Library.

Lewis, M. M. 1948. *Language in society*. New York: Social Science Research Council.

Lewis, N. A. 2004, November 30. Red Cross finds detainee abuse in Guantánamo. *New York Times*.

Lewis, O. 1968. The culture of poverty. In D. P. Moynihan (Ed.), *On understanding poverty: Perspectives from the social sciences*. New York: Basic Books.

Lewis, P. H. 1998, August 15. Too late to say "extinct" in Ubykh, Eyak or Ona. *New York Times*.

Liazos, A. 1985. *Sociology: A liberating perspective*. Boston: Allyn & Bacon.

Lichtblau, E. 2003, March 18. U.S. lawsuit seeks tobacco profits. *New York Times*.

Lichtblau, E. 2004, May 4. Cracker Barrel agrees to plan to address reports of bias. *New York Times*.

Light, P. 1988. *Baby boomers*. New York: Norton.

Lindesmith, A. R., Strauss, A. L., & Denzin, N. K. 1991. *Social psychology*. Englewood Cliffs, NJ: Prentice Hall.

Link, B. G., Mirotznik, J., & Cullen, F. T. 1991. The effectiveness of stigma coping orientations: Can negative consequences of mental illness labeling be avoided? *Journal of Health and Social Behavior, 32*, 302–320.

Linton, R. 1937. One hundred percent American. *American Mercury, 40*, 427–429.

Lippmann, L. W. 1922. *Public opinion*. New York: Harcourt Brace Jovanovich.

Lips, H. M. 1993. *Sex and gender: An introduction*. Mountain View, CA: Mayfield.

Lips, H. M. 2002. Wage inequities confronting, undervaluing women: A worldwide phenomenon. www.runet.edu/~gstudies/sources/wage_gaps/wageinequities.htm. Accessed July 21, 2003.

Liptak, A. 2003, June 3. For jailed immigrants, a presumption of guilt. *New York Times*.

Loe, V. 1997, September 21. New nuptial license gets cool reception. *Indianapolis Star*.

Lofland, L. H. 1973. *A world of strangers: Order and action in urban public space*. New York: Basic Books.

Lohr, S. 2005a, June 24. Cutting here, but hiring over there. *New York Times*.

Lohr, S. 2005b, June 4. How to exorcise a corporate scandal. *New York Times*.

Longman, J., & Higgins, M. 2005, August 3. Rad dudes of the world, unite. *New York Times.*

Lorber, J. 1989. Dismantling Noah's Ark. In B. J. Risman & P. Schwartz (Eds.), *Gender in intimate relationships: A microstructural approach.* Belmont, CA: Wadsworth.

Lorber, J. 2000. *Gender and the social construction of illness.* Walnut Creek, CA: AltaMira Press.

Lott, B. 1987. *Women's lives: Themes and variations in gender learning.* Pacific Grove, CA: Brooks/Cole.

Luker, K. 1984. *Abortion and the politics of motherhood.* Berkeley: University of California Press.

Lyall, S. 2000, July 8. Irish now face the other side of immigration. *New York Times.*

Lyall, S. 2004, February 15. In Europe, lovers now propose: Marry me, a little. *New York Times.*

Lyman, R. 2005, April 4. Gay couples file suit after Michigan denies benefits. *New York Times.*

Lytton, H., & Romney, D. M. 1991. Parents' differential socialization of boys and girls: A meta-analysis. *Psychology Bulletin, 109,* 267–296.

MacAndrew, C., & Edgerton, R. B. 1969. *Drunken comportment: A social explanation.* Chicago: Aldine-Atherton.

MacDonald, K., & Parke, R. D. 1986. Parent-child physical play: The effects of sex and age on children and parents. *Sex Roles, 15,* 367–378.

Macgillivray, I. K. 2000. Educational equity for gay, lesbian, bisexual, transgendered, and queer/questioning students: The demands of democracy and social justice for America's schools. *Education and Urban Society, 32,* 303–323.

Maharidge, D. 2004. *Homeland.* New York: Seven Stories Press.

Mann, C. C. 1993, February. How many is too many? *Atlantic Monthly.*

Mannheim, K. 1952. The problem of generations. In P. Kecskemeti (Ed. and Trans.), *Essays on the sociology of knowledge.* London: Routledge & Kegan Paul.

Mannon, J. 1997. *Measuring up.* Boulder, CO: Westview.

Mansnerus, L. 2003, August 13. Great haven for families, but don't bring children. *New York Times.*

Marger, M. N. 1994. *Race and ethnic relations: American and global perspectives.* Belmont, CA: Wadsworth.

Marla Olmstead. 2004. www.marlaolmstead.com. Accessed November 23, 2004.

Marmot, M. 2004. *The status syndrome: How social standing affects our health and longevity.* New York: Times Books.

Marsh, B. 2005, January 2. The vulnerable become more vulnerable. *New York Times.*

Martin, C. L., & Ruble, D. 2004. Children's search for gender cues. *Current Directions in Psychological Science, 13,* 67–70.

Martin, D. 1997, June 1. Eager to bite the hands that would feed them. *New York Times.*

Martin, K. A. 1998. Becoming a gendered body: Practices of pre-schools. *American Sociological Review, 63,* 494–511.

Martin, T. C., & Bumpass, L. L. 1989. Recent trends in marital disruption. *Demography, 26,* 37–51.

Marx, K. 1963. *The 18th Brumaire of Louis Bonaparte.* New York: International Publishers. (Original work published 1869)

Marx, K., & Engels, F. 1982. *The communist manifesto.* New York: International Publishers. (Original work published 1848)

Massey, D. 1990. American apartheid: Segregation and the making of the underclass. *American Journal of Sociology, 96,* 329–357.

Massey, D., & Fischer, M. J. 1999. Does rising income bring integration? New results for Blacks, Hispanics, and Asians in 1990. *Social Science Research, 28,* 316–326.

Mastrilli, T., & Sardo-Brown, D. 2002. Pre-service teachers' knowledge about Islam: A snapshot post September 11, 2001. *Journal of Institutional Psychology, 4,* 159–173.

Mathews, L. 1996, July 6. More than identity rides on a new racial category. *New York Times*.

Mauro, J. 1994. And Prozac for all . . . . *Psychology Today, 27,* 44–52.

MBA vs. prison. 1999, May–June. *American Prospect*.

McAdam, D. 1982. *Political process and the development of black insurgency, 1930–1970*. Chicago: University of Chicago Press.

McAdam, D., McCarthy, J. D., & Zald, M. N. 1988. Social movements. In N. J. Smelser (Ed.), *Handbook of sociology*. Newbury Park, CA: Sage.

McCain, F. 1991. Interview with Franklin McCain. In C. Carson, D. J. Garrow, G. Gill, V. Harding, & D. Clark Hine (Eds.), *The eyes on the prize civil rights reader*. New York: Penguin.

McCall, G. J., & Simmons, J. L. 1978. *Identities and interactions*. New York: Free Press.

McCarthy, J. D., & Wolfson, M. 1992. Consensus movements, conflict movements, and the cooptation of civic and state infrastructures. In A. D. Morris & C. M. Mueller (Eds.), *Frontiers in social movement theory*. New Haven, CT: Yale University Press.

McCarthy, J. D., & Zald, M. N. 1977. Resource mobilization and social movements: A partial theory. *American Journal of Sociology, 82,* 1212–1241.

McCarthy, T. 2001, May 14. He makes a village. *Time*.

McCormick, J. S., Maric, A., Seto, M. C., & Barbaree, H. E. 1998. Relationship to victim predicts sentence length in sexual assault cases. *Journal of Interpersonal Violence, 13,* 41–20.

McDonald's Corporation. 2003, June 6. McDonald's reports May 2003 sales and provides second quarter update [Press release]. www.mcdonalds.com/corporate/press/financial/2003/06062003/index.htm. Accessed June 10, 2003.

McEwan, J. 2005. Proving consent in sexual cases: Legislative change and cultural evolution. *International Journal of Evidence and Proof, 9,* 1–28.

McGinn, A. P. 1997, July–August. The nicotine cartel. *World Watch*.

McHugh, P. 1968. *Defining the situation*. Indianapolis: Bobbs-Merrill.

McIntosh, P. 2001. White privilege: Unpacking the invisible knapsack. In P. Rothenberg (Ed.), *Race, class, and gender in the United States*. New York: Worth.

McKenry, P. C., & Price, S. J. 1995. Divorce: A comparative perspective. In B. B. Ingoldsby & S. Smith (Eds.), *Families in multicultural perspective*. New York: Guilford Press.

McKinney, D. 2003, July 29. Clarification of rape law signed quietly by governor. *Chicago Sun-Times*.

McLaren, L. M. 2003. Anti-immigrant prejudice in Europe: Contact, threat perception, and preferences for the exclusion of migrants. *Social Forces, 81,* 909–936.

McLean, R. 2005, January 12. Spaniards dare to question the way the day is ordered. *New York Times*.

McLoyd, V. C., Cauce, A. M., Takeuchi, D., & Wilson, L. 2000. Marital processes and parental socialization in families of color: A decade review of research. *Journal of Marriage and the Family, 62,* 1070–1094.

McMichael, P. 1996. *Development and social change: A global perspective*. Thousand Oaks, CA: Pine Forge Press.

McNeil, D. G. 2000, May 21. Drug companies and the third world: A case study of neglect. *New York Times*.

McNeil, D. G. 2004a, June 2. Large study on mental illness finds a global problem. *New York Times*.

McNeil, D. G. 2004b, May 23. When real food isn't an option. *New York Times*.

McPhee, J. 1971. *Encounters with the archdruid*. New York: Noonday.

McVey, G., Tweed, S., & Blackmore, E. 2004. Dieting among preadolescent and young adolescent females. *Canadian Medical Association Journal, 170,* 1559–1561.

Mead, G. H. 1934. *Mind, self and society.* Chicago: University of Chicago Press.

Meckler, L. 1999, July 9. Millions living close to the edge of a financial precipice. *Indianapolis Star.*

Media Awareness Network. 2005. Gender stereotyping. www.media-awareness.ca/english/parents/video_games/concerns/gender_videogames.cfm. Accessed January 8, 2005.

Media Report to Women, 2003. Boxed in: Women still outnumbered behind scenes and on screen in prime time. www.mediareporttowomen.com/issues/314.htm. Accessed June 30, 2004.

Meertens, R. W., & Pettigrew, T. F. 1997. Is subtle prejudice really prejudice? *Public Opinion Quarterly, 61,* 54–71.

Mehan, H., & Wood, H. 1975. *The reality of ethnomethodology.* New York: Wiley.

Mehren, E. 2005, May 17. More backlash than bliss 1 year after marriage law. *Los Angeles Times.*

Meier, B. 2004, June 15. Group is said to seek full drug-trial disclosure. *New York Times.*

Mendez, T. 2004, May 25. Separating the sexes: A new direction for public education? *Christian Science Monitor.*

Merton, R. 1948. The self-fulfilling prophecy. *Antioch Review, 8,* 193–210.

Merton, R. 1957. *Social theory and social structure.* New York: Free Press.

Messick, D. M., & Brewer, M. B. 1983. Solving social dilemmas: A review. In L. Wheeler & P. Shaver (Eds.), *Review of personality and social psychology.* Beverly Hills, CA: Sage.

Messner, M. 2002. Boyhood, organized sports, and the construction of masculinities. In D. M. Newman & J. O'Brien (Eds.), *Sociology: Exploring the architecture of everyday life (Readings).* Thousand Oaks, CA: Pine Forge Press.

Meyer, J. W., & Rowan, B. 1977. Institutionalized organizations: Formal structure as myth and ceremony. *American Journal of Sociology, 83,* 340–363.

Miall, C. E. 1989. The stigma of involuntary childlessness. In A. S. Skolnick & J. H. Skolnick (Eds.), *Family in transition.* Boston: Little, Brown.

Michaels, K. 1993. Eight years in Kafkaland. *National Review, 45,* 36–38.

Michener, H. A., DeLamater, J. D., & Schwartz, S. H. 1986. *Social psychology.* San Diego: Harcourt Brace Jovanovich.

Microsoft offers MyDoom reward. 2004, January 30. CNN/*Money* Online. http://money.cnn.com/2004/01/28/technology/mydoom_costs/. Accessed May 10, 2005.

Milbank, D., & Deane, C. 2003, September 6. Hussein link to 9/11 lingers in many minds. *Washington Post.*

Milgram, S. 1974. *Obedience to authority.* New York: Harper & Row.

Miller, A. G., Collins, B. E., & Brief, D. E. 1995. Perspectives on obedience to authority: The legacy of the Milgram experiments. *Journal of Social Issues, 51,* 1–19.

Miller, C. L. 1987. Qualitative differences among gender-stereotyped toys: Implications for cognitive and social development. *Sex Roles, 16,* 473–488.

Miller, L. 1997. Not just weapons of the weak: Gender harassment as a form of protest for army men. *Social Psychology Quarterly, 60,* 32–51.

Miller, M. V. 1985. Poverty and its definition. In R. C. Barnes & E. W. Mills (Eds.), *Techniques for teaching sociological concepts.* Washington, DC: American Sociological Association.

Miller, S. M., & Ferroggiaro, K. M. 1995. Class dismissed? *American Prospect, 21,* 10–04.

Millman, M. 1980. *Such a pretty face.* New York: Norton.

Mills, C. W. 1940. Situated actions and vocabularies of motive. *American Sociological Review, 5,* 904–913.

Mills, C. W. 1956. *The power elite.* New York: Oxford University Press.

Mills, C. W. 1959. *The sociological imagination.* New York: Oxford University Press.

Mills, J. L. 1985, February. Body language speaks louder than words. *Horizons.*

Mishel, L., Bernstein, J., & Allegretto, S. 2004. *The state of working America: 2004/2005.* Economic Policy Institute. Ithaca, NY: Cornell University Press.

Mishel, L., Bernstein, J., & Schmitt, J. 1997. *The state of working America 1996–1997.* Armonk, NY: Sharpe.

Modelminority.com. 2003. About ModelMinority.com: A guide to Asian American Empowerment. www.modelminority.com. Accessed June 19, 2003.

Moffatt, M. 1989. *Coming of age in New Jersey.* New Brunswick, NJ: Rutgers University Press.

Mogelonsky, M. 1998. Teens' working dreams. *American Demographics, 20,* 14.

Mokhiber, R. 1999, July–August. Crime wave! The top 100 corporate criminals of the 1990s. *Multinational Monitor,* pp. 1–9.

Mokhiber, R. 2000, July–August. White collar crime spree. *Multinational Monitor,* p. 38.

Mokhiber, R., & Weissman, R. 2004, December. The ten worst corporations of 2004. *Multinational Monitor,* pp. 8–21.

Molloy, B. L., & Herzberger, S. D. 1998. Body image and self-esteem: A comparison of African-American and Caucasian women. *Sex Roles, 38,* 631–643.

Molotch, H., & Lester, M. 1974. News as purposive behavior: On the strategic use of routine events, accidents, and scandals. *American Sociological Review, 39,* 101–112.

Molotch, H., & Lester, M. 1975. Accidental news: The great oil spill as local occurrence and national event. *American Journal of Sociology, 81,* 235–260.

Mom's market value. 1998, March–April. *Utne Reader.*

Moore, R. B. 1992. Racist stereotyping in the English language. In M. L. Anderson & P. H. Collins (Eds.), *Race, class and gender: An anthology.* Belmont, CA: Wadsworth.

Morgan, G. 1986. *Images of organizations.* Newbury Park, CA: Sage.

Morgan, M. 1982. Television and adolescents' sex role stereotypes: A longitudinal study. *Journal of Personality and Social Psychology, 48,* 1173–1190.

Morgan, M. 1987. Television sex role attitudes and sex role behavior. *Journal of Early Adolescence, 7,* 269–282.

Morgan, R. 1996. *Sisterhood is global.* New York: Feminist Press at the City University of New York.

Morrongiello, B. A., & Hogg, K. 2004. Mothers' reactions to children misbehaving in ways that can lead to injury: Implications for gender differences in children's risk taking and injuries. *Sex Roles, 50,* 103–118.

Morse, M. 1998, January–February. Get down and dirty. *Utne Reader.*

Moss, R. F. 2001, February 25. The shrinking lifespan of the black sitcom. *New York Times.*

Mottl, T. L. 1980. The analysis of countermovements. *Social Problems, 27,* 620–635.

Mulrine, A. 2003, May 5. Echoes of a scandal. *US News & World Report.*

Murdock, G. P. 1949. *Social structure.* New York: Macmillan.

Murdock, G. P. 1957. World ethnography sample. *American Anthropologist, 59,* 664–687.

Murguia, E., & Telles, E. E. 1996. Phenotype and schooling among Mexican Americans. *Sociology of Education, 69,* 276–289.

Murphy, D. E. 2002, September 29. As security cameras sprout, someone's always watching. *New York Times.*

Murphy, D. E. 2004, January 11. Imagining life without illegal immigrants. *New York Times.*

Murray, C. 1994, December. What to do about welfare. *Commentary,* pp. 26–34.

Mydans, S. 1995, February 12. A shooter as vigilante, and avenging angel. *New York Times.*

MyDoom virus "biggest in months." 2004, January 27. BBC News Online. www.bbc.co.uk/1/hi/technology/3432639.stm. Accessed May 10, 2005.

Nanda, S. 1994. *Cultural anthropology.* Belmont, CA: Wadsworth.

Nanda, S. 2003. Hijra and Sādhin: Neither man nor woman in India. In S. LaFont (Ed.), *Constructing sexualities: Readings in sexuality, gender, and culture.* Upper Saddle River, NJ: Prentice Hall.

Nasar, S., & Mitchell, K. B. 1999, May 23. Booming job market draws young black men into the fold. *New York Times.*

National Alliance to End Homelessness. 2005. Frequently asked questions. www.endhomelessness .org/disc/index.htm#three. Accessed June 8, 2005.

National Association for Single Sex Public Education. 2004. Single sex education. www.single sexschools.org. Accessed July 10, 2004.

National Association of Colleges and Employers. 2005. College hiring up 13 percent for class of 2005. www.naceweb.org/press/display.asp?year=&prid=214. Accessed May 23, 2005.

National Center for Education Statistics. 2004. Highlights from the Trends in International Mathematics and Science Study (TIMSS) 2003. www.nces.ed.gov/pubs2005/2005005.pdf. Accessed June 6, 2005.

National Center for Fair and Open Testing. 2004. 2004 college bound seniors test scores: SAT. www.fairtest.org. Accessed December 6, 2004.

National Center for Health Statistics. 2003. Health, United States, 2003. www.cdc.gov/nchs/ products/pubs/pubd/hus/trendtables.htm. Accessed September 23, 2004.

National Center for Health Statistics. 2005. Self-inflicted injury/suicide. Tables 46 & 58. www.cdc .gov/nchs/data/hus/hus04trend.pdf#059. Accessed April 11, 2005.

National Coalition of Anti-Violence Programs. 2002. *Lesbian, gay, bisexual, and transgender domestic violence in 2001.* www.avp.org. Accessed June 6, 2003.

National Committee on Pay Equity. 1995. The wage gap: Myths and facts. In P. S. Rothenberg (Ed.), *Race, class and gender in the United States.* New York: St. Martin's Press.

National Committee on Pay Equity. 1999. *The wage gap: 1998.* www.feminist.com/fairpay. Accessed July 1, 2000.

National Conference of State Legislatures. 2005. Same sex marriage. www.ncsl.org/programs/ cyf/samesex.htm#DOMA. Accessed June 3, 2005.

National Eating Disorders Association. 2004. Statistics: Eating disorders and their precursors. www.nationaleatingdisorders.org. Accessed July 21, 2004.

National Fair Housing Alliance. 2004. 2004 fair housing trends report. www.nationalfairhousing .org. Accessed August 31, 2004.

National Labor Committee for Worker and Human Rights. 2001. Shah Haksdum Garments Factor, Dhaka, Bangladesh. www.nlcnet.org/campaigns/shahmakhdum/0502/sm0201.shtml. Accessed June 16, 2003.

National Low Income Housing Coalition. 2003. Out of reach 2003: America's housing wage climbs. www.nlihc.org/oor_current/. Accessed October 27, 2004.

National Mental Health Association. 2005. Why mental health parity makes economic sense. www.nmha.org/state/parity/parity_economy.cfm. Accessed June 3, 2005.

National Partnership for Women and Families. 2005. Expecting better: A state-by-state analysis of parental leave programs. www.nationalpartnership.org/portals/p3/library/PaidLeave/ ParentalLeaveReportMay05.pdf. Accessed June 1, 2005.

National Public Radio. 2005a. Debating the Patriot Act. http://www.npr.org/templates/story/ story.php?storyId=4759727&sourceCode=gaw. Accessed July 27, 2005.

National Public Radio. 2005b, March 19. Jobless with a college degree: The numbers rise. www.npr.org/templates/story/story.php?storyId=4542578. Accessed May 20, 2005.

National Urban League. 2004. The state of black America 2004. www.nul.org/pdf/sobaexec.pdf. Accessed April 6, 2005.

Nationmaster.com. 2005. Encyclopedia: Sesame Street. www.nationmaster.com/encyclopedia/ Sesame-Street#Regional_variations_of_the_show. Accessed June 6, 2005.

Nelkin, D., & Pollack, M. 1981. *The atom besieged.* Cambridge, MA: MIT Press.

Nestle, M. 2002. *Food politics.* Berkeley: University of California Press.

Neubeck, K. 1986. *Social problems: A critical approach.* New York: Random House.

Neuman, W. L. 1994. *Social research methods: Qualitative and quantitative approaches.* Boston: Allyn & Bacon.

Newman, D. 2007. *Identities and inequalities: Exploring the intersections of race, class, gender, and sexuality.* New York: McGraw-Hill.

Newman, K. 2005. Family values against the odds. In A. S. Skolnick & J. H. Skolnick (Eds.), *Family in transition* (13th ed.). Boston: Allyn & Bacon.

Nichols, J. 2000, January. Now what? Seattle is just a start. *Progressive.*

Niebuhr, G. 1996, December 16. Shift on rabbis is voted down by lay leaders. *New York Times.*

Niebuhr, G. 1998a, August 2. As the old-line Anglican churches wilt, those in Africa flower profusely. *New York Times.*

Niebuhr, G. 1998b, April 12. Makeup of American religion is looking more like a mosaic, data say. *New York Times.*

Nielsen Media Research. 2002. The African-American audience: Weekly TV usage. www.nielsen-media.com/ethnicmeasure/african-american/AAweeklyusage.html. Accessed June 19, 2003.

Nord, M., Andrews, M., & Carlson, S. 2003. Household food security in the United States, 2002. U.S. Department of Agriculture, Food Assistance and Nutrition Research Report No. 35. www.ers.usda.gov/publications/fanrr35/fanrr35.pdf/. Accessed July 19, 2004.

"Normal" blood pressure now risky. 2003, May 15. *Indianapolis Star.*

Norris, F. 2004, December 7. U.S. students fare badly in international survey of math skills. *New York Times.*

Nugman, G. 2002. World divorce rates. www.divorcereform.org/gul.html. Accessed July 6, 2003.

Nunberg, G. 2004, July 11. How much wallop can a simple word pack? *New York Times.*

OECD (Organization for Economic Co-operation and Development). 1988. *Aging populations: The social policy implications.* Washington, DC: Author.

Oldenburg, R., & Brissett, D. 1982. The third place. *Qualitative Sociology, 5,* 265–284.

Olsen, M. 1965. *The logic of collective action.* Cambridge, MA: Harvard University Press.

Omi, M., & Winant, H. 1992. Racial formations. In P. S. Rothenberg (Ed.), *Race, class and gender in the United States.* New York: St. Martin's Press.

Onishi, N. 2002, October 3. Globalization of beauty makes slimness trendy. *New York Times.*

Onishi, N. 2003, September 21. Taboo against divorce weakens in South Korea. *New York Times.*

Onishi, N. 2004a, March 30. On U.S. fast food, more Okinawans grow super-sized. *New York Times.*

Onishi, N. 2004b, December, 16. Tokyo's flag law: Proud patriotism, or indoctrination? *New York Times.*

Onishi, N. 2005a, April 27. In Japan crash, time obsession may be culprit. *New York Times.*

Onishi, N. 2005b, August 21. South Korea, in a turnabout, now calls for more babies. *New York Times.*

Ordóñez, J. 2005, May 30. Speak English. Live Latin. *Newsweek.*

Orenstein, C. 2004, June 9. Stepford is us. *New York Times.*

Orenstein, P. 2004, July 25. The other mother. *New York Times Magazine.*

Orfield, G., & Yun, J. T. 1999. Resegregation in American schools. Cambridge, MA: The Civil Rights Project, Harvard University.

Organ Procurement and Transplant Network. 2004. National data. www.optn.org/latestData/rptData.asp. Accessed July 18, 2004.

O'Sullivan-See, K., & Wilson, W. J. 1988. Race and ethnicity. In N. Smelser (Ed.), *Handbook of sociology.* Newbury Park, CA: Sage.

Owen, M. 1996. *A world of widows.* London: Zed Books.

Padavic, I., & Reskin, B. 2002. *Women and men at work* (2nd ed.). Thousand Oaks, CA: Sage.

Pager, D. 2003. The mark of a criminal record. *American Journal of Sociology, 108,* 937–975.

Parenti, M. 1986. *Inventing reality.* New York: St. Martin's Press.

Parenti, M. 1995. *Democracy for the few.* New York: St. Martin's Press.

Parker, S., Nichter, M., Nichter, M., Vuckovic, N., Sims, C., & Ritenbaugh, C. 1995. Body image and weight concerns among African American and white adolescent females: Differences that make a difference. *Human Organization, 54,* 103–114.

Parlee, M. B. 1989. Conversational politics. In L. Richardson & V. Taylor (Eds.), *Feminist frontiers II.* New York: Random House.

Parsons, T. 1951. *The social system.* New York: Free Press.

Parsons, T. 1971. Kinship and the associational aspect of social structure. In F. L. K. Hsu (Ed.), *Kinship and culture.* Chicago: Aldine-Atherton.

Parsons, T., & Bales, R. F. 1955. *Family, socialization and interaction process.* Glencoe, IL: Free Press.

Parsons, T., & Smelser, N. 1956. *Economy and society.* New York: Free Press.

Passel, J. S., Capps, R., & Fix, M. 2004. Undocumented immigrants: Facts and figures. www.urban.org/UPLoadedPDF/1000587_undoc_immigrants_facts.pdf. Accessed April 6, 2005.

Pattillo-McCoy, M. 1999. *Black picket fences: Privilege and peril among the black middle class.* Chicago: University of Chicago Press.

Payer, L. 1988. *Medicine and culture.* New York: Penguin.

Pear, R. 1992. December 4. New look at U.S. in 2050: Bigger, older and less white. *New York Times.*

Pear, R. 1997, May 18. Academy's report says immigration benefits the U.S. *New York Times.*

Pear, R. 2000, April 30. Studies find research on women lacking. *New York Times.*

Pear, R. 2003, February 14. House endorses stricter work rules for poor. *New York Times.*

Pearce, D. 1979. Gatekeepers and homeseekers: Institutional patterns in racial steering. *Social Problems, 26,* 325–342.

Pearce, L. D., & Axinn, W. G. 1998. The impact of family religious life on the quality of mother-child relations. *American Sociological Review, 63,* 81–28.

Pennington, B. 2003, November 12. As team sports conflict, some parents rebel. *New York Times.*

Perez-Peña, R. 2003, April 19. Study finds asthma in 25% of children in central Harlem. *New York Times.*

Perin, C. 1988. *Belonging in America.* Madison: University of Wisconsin Press.

Perlez, J. 1991. August 31. Madagascar, where the dead return, bringing joy. *New York Times.*

Perlez, J. 2002, May 8. Deep fears behind Australia's immigration policy. *New York Times.*

Perlin, S. A., Sexton, K., & Wong, D. W. S. 1999. An examination of race and poverty for populations living near industrial sources of air pollution. *Journal of Exposure Analysis and Environmental Epidemiology, 9,* 29–48.

Perlman, D., & Fehr, B. 1987. The development of intimate relationships. In D. Perlman & S. Duck (Eds.), *Intimate relationships: Development, dynamics and deterioration.* Newbury Park, CA: Sage.

Perrow, C. 1986. *Complex organizations: A critical essay.* New York: Random House.

Pescosolido, B. A. 1986. Migration, medical care and the lay referral system: A network theory of role assimilation. *American Sociological Review, 51,* 523–540.

Pescosolido, B. A., Grauerholz, E., & Milkie, M. A. 1997. Culture and conflict: The portrayal of Blacks in U.S. children's picture books through the mid- and late-twentieth century. *American Sociological Review, 62,* 443–464.

Peterson, I. 2005, March 14. Casino with weight policy finds boon in controversy. *New York Times.*

Peterson, J., & Kim, P. 1991. *The day America told the truth*. Englewood Cliffs, NJ: Prentice Hall.

Peterson, P. 1991. The urban underclass and the poverty paradox. In C. Jencks & P. Peterson (Eds.), *The urban underclass*. Washington, DC: Brookings Institution.

Peterson, P. G. 1996, May. Will America grow up before it grows old? *Atlantic Monthly*.

Peterson, R. D., & Bailey, W. C. 1991. Felony murder and capital punishment: An examination of the deterrence question. *Criminology, 29*, 367–395.

Peterson, R. R. 1996. A re-evaluation of the economic consequences of divorce. *American Sociological Review, 61*, 528–536.

Peterson, S. B., & Lach, M. A. 1990. Gender stereotypes in children's books: Their prevalence and influence in cognitive and affective development. *Gender and Education, 2*, 185–197.

Petrunik, M., & Shearing, C. D. 1983. Fragile facades: Stuttering and the strategic manipulation of awareness. *Social Problems, 31*, 125–138.

Pettit, B., & Western, B. 2004. Mass imprisonment and the life course: Race and class inequality in U.S. incarceration. *American Sociological Review, 69*, 151–169.

Pew Forum on Religion and Public Life. 2002. Americans struggle with religion's role at home and abroad. Survey report. http://people-press.org/reports. Accessed January 18, 2003.

Pew Forum on Religion and Public Life. 2004. The American religious landscape and politics, 2004. www.pewforum.org/publications/surveys/green.pdf. Accessed December 31, 2004.

Pew Research Center. 2005. Pew Global Attitudes Project. http://pewglobal.org/reports/display.php?PageID=800. Accessed June 24, 2005.

Pfohl, S. J. 1994. *Images of deviance and social control*. New York: McGraw-Hill.

Phillips, K. 2002. *Wealth and democracy*. New York: Broadway Books.

Phillips, P., & Project Censored. 1997. *The news that didn't make the news—and why*. New York: Seven Stories Press.

Phillips, P., & Project Censored. 2000. *Censored 2000: The year's top 25 censored stories*. New York: Seven Stories Press.

Physical traits affect earning power, study says. 1994, July 13. *New York Times*.

Piore, A. 2003, March 17. Home alone. *Newsweek*.

Piper, A. 1992. Passing for white, passing for black. *Transition, 58*, 4–32.

Piven, F. F., & Cloward, R. A. 1977. *Poor people's movements: Why they succeed, how they fail*. New York: Vintage.

Pizza Hut. 2005. About Pizza Hut: Our story. www.pizzahut.com/about/. Accessed May 25, 2005.

Pizza must go through: It's the law in San Francisco. 1996, July 14. *New York Times*.

Plastic Surgery Research.info 2004. Cosmetic plastic surgery research. www.cosmeticplasticsurgerystatistics.com/statistics.html. Accessed January 2, 2005.

Polgreen, L. 2003, July 27. For mixed-race South Africans, equity is elusive. *New York Times*.

Pope exalts women for roles as wife, mom. 2003, June 7. *Indianapolis Star*.

Popenoe, D. 1993. American family decline, 1960–1990: A review and appraisal. *Journal of Marriage and the Family, 55*, 527–555.

Popenoe, R. 2005. Ideal. In D. Kulick & A. Meneley (Eds.), *Fat: The anthropology of an obsession*. New York: Tarcher/Penguin.

Population Reference Bureau. 2003. Human population: Fundamentals of growth patterns of world urbanization. www.prb.org/Content/NavigationMenu/PRB/Educators/Human_Population/Urbanization2/Patterns_of_World_Urbanization1.htm. Accessed August 4, 2003.

Population Reference Bureau. 2004a. 2004 World population data sheet. www.prb.org. Accessed June 1, 2005.

Population Reference Bureau. 2004b. Transitions in world population. *Population Bulletin, 59*, 1–41.

Population Reference Bureau. 2004c, May. The wealth gap in health. *Population Reference Bureau Report.* www.prb.org. Accessed July 15, 2004.

Population Reference Bureau. 2005a, February. Women of our world. *Population Reference Bureau Report.* www.prb.org. Accessed June 14, 2005.

Population Reference Bureau. 2005b. World population data sheet. www.prb.org/pdf05/05WorldDataSheet_Eng.pdf. Accessed August 27, 2005.

Porter, E. 2004, July 18. Hourly pay in U.S. not keeping pace with price rises. *New York Times.*

Porter, E. 2005, April 5. Illegal immigrants are bolstering Social Security with billions. *New York Times.*

Powell, R. A. 2004, November 5. No yelling, no cheering. Shhhhh! It's silent Saturday. *New York Times.*

Pratkanis, A., & Aronson, E. 1991. *Age of propaganda.* New York: Freeman.

President's Council on Bioethics. 2003. *Beyond therapy: Biotechnology and the pursuit of happiness.* Washington, DC: U.S. Government Printing Office.

Preston, S. H. 1984, December. Children and the elderly in the U.S. *Scientific American,* pp. 44–49.

Price, S. L. 1997, December 8. Whatever happened to the white athlete? *Sports Illustrated.*

Proctor, B. D., & Dalaker, J. 2002. Poverty in the United States: 2001. *Current Population Reports, P60-219.* Washington, DC: U.S. Government Printing Office.

Project Censored. 2003. The top 25 censored media stories of 2001–2002. www.projectcensored.org/publications/2003/index.html. Accessed May 23, 2003.

Project Censored. 2005. Censored 2005: The top 25 censored media stories of 2003–2004. www.projectcensored.org/publications/2005/index.html. Accessed January 2, 2005.

Project for Excellence in Journalism. 2005. Embedded reporters: What are Americans getting? www.journalism.org/resources/research/reports/war/embed/pejembedreport.pdf. Accessed May 25, 2005.

Provine, R. R. 2000. *Laughter: A scientific investigation.* New York: Penguin.

Pugliesi, K. 1987. Deviation in emotion and the labeling of mental illness. *Deviant Behavior, 8,* 79–102.

Putnam, R. D. 1995. Bowling alone: America's declining social capital. *Journal of Democracy, 6,* 65–78.

Quinney, R. 1970. *The social reality of crime.* Boston: Little, Brown.

Raymond, J. 1998, September 14. Say what? Preserving endangered languages. *Newsweek.*

Raymond, J. G. 1993. *Women as wombs.* New York: HarperCollins.

Redstone, J. 2003. *The language of war.* Worldwatch. www.omegastar.org/worldwatch/America/Language_of_War.html. Accessed May 23, 2003.

Reiman, J. 2004. *The rich get richer and the poor get prison.* Boston: Allyn & Bacon.

Reinharz, S. 1992. *Feminist methods in social research.* New York: Oxford University Press.

Relethford, J. H., Stern, M. P., Caskill, S. P., & Hazuda, H. P. 1983. Social class, admixture, and skin color variation in Mexican Americans and Anglo Americans living in San Antonio, Texas. *American Journal of Physical Anthropology, 61,* 97–102.

Religious groups gather for "Justice Wednesday" pray in. 2005, April 26. www.wfn.org/2005/04/msg00274.html. Accessed July 24, 2005.

Rennison, C. M. 2003. Intimate partner violence, 1993–2001. United States Bureau of Justice Statistics Crime Data Brief NCJ 197838. Washington, DC: U.S. Government Printing Office.

Rennison, C. M., & Welchans, S. 2000. Intimate partner violence. United States Bureau of Justice Statistics Special Report No. NCJ 178247. Washington, DC: U.S. Government Printing Office.

Renzetti, C. M., & Curran, D. J. 2003. *Women, men and society: The sociology of gender.* Boston: Allyn & Bacon.

Research findings affirm health of women hinges on reform of clinical research. 2003, August 14. *Women's Health Weekly.*

Reskin, B., & Hartmann, H. 1986. *Women's work, men's work: Sex segregation on the job.* Washington, DC: National Academy Press.

Revkin, A. C. 1997, December 1. Who cares about a few degrees? *New York Times.*

Reyes, L., & Rubie, P. 1994. *Hispanics in Hollywood: An encyclopedia of film and television.* New York: Garland Press.

Rhea County officials seek change in law to ban gays. 2004. www.wkrn.com/global/story.asp?s=1718183&ClientType=Printable. Accessed March 26, 2004.

Richtel, M. 2004, June 26. For liars and loafers, cellphones offer an alibi. *New York Times.*

Rideout, V., Roberts, D. F., & Foehr, U. G. 2005. Generation M: Media in the lives of 8–18 year olds. http://profile.kff.org/entmedia/loader.cfm?url=/commonspot/security/getfile/cfm&PageID=51805. Accessed June 16, 2005.

Riesman, D. 1950. *The lonely crowd.* New Haven, CT: Yale University Press.

Riley, M. W. 1971. Social gerontology and the age stratification of society. *Gerontologist, 11,* 79–87.

Riley, M. W., Foner, A., & Waring, J. 1988. Sociology of age. In N. J. Smelser (Ed.), *Handbook of sociology.* Newbury Park, CA: Sage.

Rimer, S. 2002, June 4. Suspects lacking lawyers are freed in Atlanta. *New York Times.*

Rimer, S., & Arenson, K. W. 2004, June 24. Top colleges take more blacks, but which ones. *New York Times.*

Ritzer, G. 2000. *The McDonaldization of society.* Thousand Oaks, CA: Pine Forge Press.

Rivoli, P. 2005. *The travels of a t-shirt in the global economy.* New York: Wiley.

Robert Wood Johnson Foundation. 2005. Characteristics of the uninsured: A view from the states. www.rwjf.org/files/research/Full_SHADAC.pdf. Accessed May 20, 2005.

Roberts, D. E. 1991. Punishing drug addicts who have babies: Women of color, equality and the right of privacy. *Harvard Law Review, 104,* 1419–1482.

Roberts, J. L., 2005, June 6. World tour. *Newsweek.*

Roberts, S. 1995, December 24. Alone in the vast wasteland. *New York Times.*

Robinson, B. A. 1999. Facts about inter-faith marriages. www.religioustolerance.org/ifm_fact.htm. Accessed July 6, 2003.

Robinson, R. V., & Bell, W. 1978. Equality, success and social justice in England and the United States. *American Sociological Review, 43,* 125–143.

Robinson, R. V., & Kelley, J. 1979. Class as conceived by Marx and Dahrendorf: Effects on income inequality and politics in the United States and Great Britain. *American Sociological Review, 44,* 38–58.

Rodin, J. 1985. The application of social psychology. In G. Lindzay & E. Aronson (Eds.), *The handbook of social psychology.* New York: Random House.

Rodriguez, C. E., & Cordero-Guzman, H. 2004. Placing race in context. In C. A. Gallagher (Ed.), *Rethinking the color line: Readings in race and ethnicity.* New York: McGraw-Hill.

Rodriguez, G. 2002, April 7. The overwhelming allure of English. *New York Times.*

Roehling, M. V. 1999. Weight-based discrimination in employment: Psychological and legal aspects. *Personnel Psychology, 52,* 969–1017.

Roethlisberger, F. J., & Dickson, W. J. 1939. *Management and the worker.* Cambridge, MA: Harvard University Press.

Rohter, L. 2004, December 29. Learn English, says Chile, thinking upwardly global. *New York Times.*

Rohter, L. 2005, January 30. Divorce ties Chile in knots. *New York Times.*

Roland, A. 1988. *In search of self in India and Japan.* Princeton, NJ: Princeton University Press.

Romero, S. 1999, July 24. Cashing in on security woes. *New York Times.*

Rosato, D. 2004, August. Flights of fancy. Part 2: Airlines class warfare. *Money.*

Roscigno, V. J., & Hodson, R. 2004. The organizational and social foundations of worker resistance. *American Sociological Review, 69,* 14–39.

Rose, M. 2004. *The mind at work.* New York: Viking.

Rosen, J. 1997, March 30. Abraham's drifting children. *New York Times Book Review.*

Rosenbaum, D. E. 2005, April 14. True to ritual, house votes for full repeal of estate tax. *New York Times.*

Rosenberg, D. 2003, June 9. The war over fetal rights. *Newsweek.*

Rosenblatt, P. C., Karis, T. A., & Powell, R. D. 1995. *Multiracial couples.* Thousand Oaks, CA: Sage.

Rosenthal, E. 2002, November. Study links rural suicides in China to stress and ready poisons. *New York Times.*

Rosenthal, E. 2003, July 20. Bias for boys leads to sale of baby girls in China. *New York Times.*

Rosenthal, R., & Jacobson, L. 1968. *Pygmalion in the classroom.* New York: Holt, Rinehart & Winston.

Ross, C. E., Mirowsky, J., & Goldstein, K. 1990. The impact of family on health: The decade in review. *Journal of Marriage and the Family, 52,* 1059–1078.

Rossi, A. 1968. Transition to parenthood. *Journal of Marriage and the Family, 30,* 26–39.

Rossi, P., Waite, E., Bose, C. E., & Berk, R. E. 1974. The seriousness of crimes: Normative structure and individual differences. *American Sociological Review, 39,* 224–237.

Rothenberg, P. S. (Ed.). 1992. *Race, class and gender in the United States.* New York: St. Martin's Press.

Rothman, B. K. 1984. Women, health and medicine. In J. Freeman (Ed.), *Women: A feminist perspective.* Palo Alto: Mayfield.

Rothman, B. K. 1987. Reproduction. In B. B. Hess & M. M. Ferree (Eds.), *Analyzing gender: A handbook of social science research.* Newbury Park, CA: Sage.

Rothman, B. K., & Caschetta, M. B. 1999. Treating health: Women and medicine. In S. J. Ferguson (Ed.), *Mapping the social landscape: Readings in sociology.* Mountain View, CA: Mayfield.

Rothman, D. J., & Edgar, H. 1992. Scientific rigor and medical realities: Placebo trials in cancer and AIDS research. In E. Fee & D. M. Fox (Eds.), *AIDS: The making of a chronic disease.* Berkeley: University of California Press.

Rothschild, M. 2000, January. Soothsayers of Seattle. *Progressive.*

Rothstein, R. 2001, December 12. An economic recovery will tell in the classroom. *New York Times.*

Rowland, R. 1990. Technology and motherhood: Reproductive choice reconsidered. In C. Carlson (Ed.), *Perspectives on the family: History, class and feminism.* Belmont, CA: Wadsworth.

Roy, S. 2003. KTSF-TV: Bringing in-language news to Asian Americans. New California Media Online. crm.ncmonline.com/news/view_article.html?article_id=72fd29857745210ab13a 81464f50990f. Accessed July 21, 2005.

Rubin, J. Z., Provenzano, F. J., & Luria, Z. 1974. The eye of the beholder: Parents' views on sex of newborns. *American Journal of Orthopsychiatry, 44,* 512–519.

Rubin, L. 1994. *Families on the fault line.* New York: HarperCollins.

Rubinstein, S., & Caballero, B. 2000. Is Miss America an undernourished role model? *Journal of the American Medical Association, 283,* 1569.

Ruethling, G. 2005, June 22. Chicago police put arrest photos of prostitution suspects online. *New York Times.*

Rusbult, C. E., Zembrodt, I. M., & Iwaniszek, J. 1986. The impact of gender and sex-role orientation on responses to dissatisfaction in close relationships. *Sex Roles, 15,* 1–20.

Russell Sage Foundation. 2000. Multi-city study of urban inequality. www.russellsage.org/special_interest/point_5_residential.htm. Accessed May 31, 2000.

Rutenberg, J. 2004, October 6. Spinning out clear winner even before debate begins. *New York Times.*

Rybczynski, W. 1999, April 18. One good turn. *New York Times Magazine.*

Ryckaert, V. 2005, June 1. ICLU sues over prayers read at statehouse. *Indianapolis Star.*

Sack, K. 1997, November 12. Blacks strip slaveholders' names off schools. *New York Times.*

Sack, K., & Elder, J. 2000, July 11. Poll finds optimistic outlook but enduring racial division. *New York Times.*

Sadker, M., & Sadker, D. 1999. Failing at fairness: Hidden lessons. In S. Ferguson (Ed.), *Mapping the social landscape.* Mountain View, CA: Mayfield.

Sadker, M., Sadker, D., Fox, L., & Salata, M. 2004. Gender equity in the classroom: The unfinished agenda. In M. S. Kimmel (Ed.), *The gendered society reader.* New York: Oxford University Press.

Saenz, R. 2004, August. Latinos and the changing face of America. Population Reference Bureau Report. www.prb.org. Accessed September 3, 2004.

Safer, D. J., Zito, J. M., & dosReis, S. 2003. Concomitant psychotropic medication for youths. *American Journal of Psychiatry, 160,* 438–449.

Safire, W. 1995, July 17. News about Jews. *New York Times.*

Sage, G. H. 2001. Racial equality and sport. In D. S. Eitzen (Ed.), *Sport in contemporary society.* New York: Worth.

Sanday, P. R. 1996. *A woman scorned: Acquaintance rape on trial.* New York: Doubleday.

Santora, M. 2005, January 30. U.S. is close to eliminating AIDS in infants, officials say. *New York Times.*

Sapir, E. 1929. The status of linguistics as a science. *Language, 5,* 207–214.

Sapir, E. 1949. *Selected writings.* D. G. Mandelbaum (Ed.). Berkeley: University of California Press.

Saul, L. 1972. Personal and social psychopathology and the primary prevention of violence. *American Journal of Psychiatry, 128,* 1578–1581.

Saul, S. 2005, April 3. Drug makers race to cash in on nation's fight against fat. *New York Times.*

Saunders, J. M. 1991. Relating social structural abstractions to sociological research. *Teaching Sociology, 19,* 270–271.

Sayer, L., Casper, L., & Cohen, P. 2004, October. Women, men, and work. Population Reference Bureau Report. www.prb.org. Accessed December 30, 2004.

Scalia, J. 2001. Federal drug offenders, 1999 with trends 1984–1999. Bureau of Justice Statistics Special Report No. NCJ 187285. www.ojp.usdoj.gov/bjs/pub/pdf/fd099.pdf. Accessed June 2, 2005.

Schacter, S. 1951. Deviation, rejection, and communication. *Journal of Abnormal and Social Psychology, 46,* 190–207.

Schemo, D. J. 2001, February 17. Head of U. of California seeks to end SAT use in admissions. *New York Times.*

Schlesinger, A. 1992. *The disuniting of America.* New York: Norton.

Schlosser, E. 2001. *Fast food nation.* New York: Houghton Mifflin.

Schmitt, E. 1996, May 28. Provisions on legal immigrants jeopardize bill on illegal aliens. *New York Times.*

Schmitt, E. 2001a, January 14. Americans (a) love (b) hate immigrants. *New York Times.*

Schmitt, E. 2001b, March 13. For 7 million people in census, one race category is not enough. *New York Times.*

Schmitt, E. 2004, February 26. Military women reporting rapes by U.S. soldiers. *New York Times.*

Schmitt, E., & Shanker, T. 2005, July 25. New name for "War on Terror" reflects wider U.S. campaign. *New York Times.*

Schodolski, V. J. 1993, December 26. Funeral industry, pitching videos, 2-for-1 specials to baby boomers. *Indianapolis Star.*

Schooler, C. 1996. Cultural and social structural explanations of cross-national psychological differences. *Annual Review of Sociology, 22,* 323–349.

Schor, J. B. 1991. *The overworked American: The unexpected decline of leisure.* New York: Basic Books.

Schuman, H., & Krysan, M. 1999. A historical note on whites' beliefs about racial inequality. *American Sociological Review, 64,* 84–55.

Schuman, H., Steeh, C., Bobo, L., & Krysan, M. 1997. *Racial attitudes in America: Trends and interpretations.* Cambridge, MA: Harvard University Press.

Schur, E. M. 1984. *Labeling women deviant: Gender, stigma and social control.* New York: Random House.

Schwartz, J. 2004, January 3. That parent-child conversation is becoming instant, and online. *New York Times.*

Schwartz, J., Revkin, A. C., & Wald, M. L. 2005, September 12. In reviving New Orleans, a challenge of many tiers. *New York Times.*

Schwartz, P., & Rutter, V. 1998. *The gender of sexuality.* Thousand Oaks, CA: Sage.

Schwartz, R. D., & Skolnick, J. H. 1962. Two studies of legal stigma. *Social Problems, 10,* 133–138.

Sciolino, E. 2001, December 9. Radicalism: Is the devil in the demographics? *New York Times.*

Scott, J., & Leonhardt, D. 2005, May 15. Class in America: Shadowy lines that still divide us. *New York Times.*

Scott, L. D. 2003. The relation of racial identity and racial socialization to coping with discrimination among African American adolescents. *Journal of Black Studies, 33,* 520–538.

Scott, L. D. 2005, May 16. Life at the top in America isn't just better, it's longer. *New York Times.*

Scott, M., & Lyman, S. 1968. Accounts. *American Sociological Review, 33,* 46–62.

Screen Actors Guild. 2004. Casting data report, 2003. www.sag.org/sagWebApp/index.jsp. Accessed June 10, 2005.

Scull, A., & Favreau, D. 1986. A chance to cut is a chance to cure: Sexual surgery for psychosis in three nineteenth-century societies. In S. Spitzer & A. T. Scull (Eds.), *Research in law, deviance and social control* (Vol. 8). Greenwich, CT: JAI Press.

Seelye, K. Q., & Elder, J. 2003, December 21. Strong support is found for ban on gay marriage. *New York Times.*

Segal, D. R., & Segal, M. W. 2004. America's military population. *Population Bulletin, 59,* 1–44.

Senate Judiciary Committee. 1993. The response to rape: Detours on the road to equal justice. www.inform.umd.edu/EdRes/Topic/WomensStudies/GenderIssues/Violence+Women/ResponsetoRape/full-text. Accessed January 18, 2001.

Sengupta, S. 2002, April 29. Child traffickers prey on Bangladesh. *New York Times.*

Sengupta, S. 2004, October 26. Relentless attacks on women in West Sudan draw an outcry. *New York Times.*

Sennett, R. 1984. *Families against the city: Middle-class homes in industrial Chicago.* Cambridge, MA: Harvard University Press.

Sennett, R., & Cobb, J. 1972. *Hidden injuries of class.* New York: Vintage.

Sex offender's case denied in court. 2001, January 16. *Associated Press Online.* Accessed January 30, 2001.

Sexual harassment statistics in the workplace and in education. 2004. http://womensissues .about.com/cs/goverornews/a/sexharassstats.htm. Accessed July 31, 2004.

Shah, A. 2004. Causes of poverty: Poverty facts and statistics. www.globalissues.org/TradeRelated/ Facts.asp?p=1. Accessed November 11, 2004.

Shakin, M., Shakin, D., & Sternglanz, S. H. 1985. Infant clothing: Sex labeling for strangers. *Sex Roles, 12,* 955–964.

Shanker, T. 2004, December 8. Inquiry faults commanders in assaults on cadets. *New York Times.*

Sheridan, M. B., 2005, June 13. Immigration law as anti-terrorism tool. *Washington Post.*

Sherraden, M. 1988, Winter. Rethinking social welfare: Toward assets. *Social Policy,* pp. 37–43.

Shibutani, T. 1961. *Society and personality: An interactionist approach to social psychology.* Englewood Cliffs, NJ: Prentice Hall.

Shipler, D. K. 2004. *The working poor: Invisible in America.* New York: Knopf.

Shorto, R. 1997, December 7. Belief by the numbers. *New York Times Magazine.*

Shotland, R. L., & Straw, M. K. 1976. Bystander response to an assault: When a man attacks a woman. *Journal of Personality and Social Psychology, 34,* 990–999.

Shugart, H. A. 2003. She shoots, she scores: Mediated construction of contemporary female athletes in coverage of the 1999 US Women's soccer team. *Western Journal of Communication, 67,* 1–31.

Shweder, R. A. 1997, March 9. It's called poor health for a reason. *New York Times.*

Sidel, R. 1986. *Women and children last.* New York: Penguin.

Sidel, R. 1990. *On her own: Growing up in the shadow of the American dream.* New York: Penguin.

Siegel, R. B. 2004. A short history of sexual harassment. In C. A. MacKinnon & R. B. Siegel (Eds.), *Directions in sexual harassment law.* New Haven: Yale University Press.

Signorielli, N. 1990. Children, television, and gender roles. *Journal of Adolescent Health Care, 11,* 50–58.

Silverman, D. 1982. *Secondary analysis in social research: A guide to data sources and methods with examples.* Boston: Allen & Unwin.

Silverstein, K. 1999, July 19. Millions for Viagra, pennies for the poor. *The Nation.*

Simmel, G. 1950. *The sociology of Georg Simmel.* K. Wolff (Ed.). New York: Free Press. (Original work published 1902)

Simons, M. 2001, April 30. An awful task: Assessing 4 roles in death of thousands in Rwanda. *New York Times.*

Simpson, I. H. 1979. *From student to nurse: A longitudinal study of socialization.* Cambridge, UK: Cambridge University Press.

Sims, C. 2000, May 30. Japan's employers are giving bonuses for having babies. *New York Times.*

Sinclair Broadcast Group. 2005. Company profile. www.sbgi.net/about/profile.shtml. Accessed May 24, 2005.

Singleton, R., Straits, B. C., & Straits, M. M. 1993. *Approaches to social research.* New York: Oxford University Press.

Site warns of new neighbors who are sex offenders. 2001, June 13. News Bytes News Network. www.findarticles.com/p/articles/mi_m0NEW/is_2001_June_13/ai_75497990. Accessed September 10, 2005.

Skocpol, T. 1979. *States and social revolutions: A comparative analysis of France, Russia and China.* New York: Cambridge University Press.

Skolnick, A. S. 1991. *Embattled paradise.* New York: Basic Books.

Skolnick, A. S., & Skolnick, J. H. (Eds.). 1992. *Family in transition* (7th ed.). New York: HarperCollins.

Sloan, A. 2005, February 7. A new way on CEO pay. *Newsweek.*

Smallwood, A. D. 1998. *The atlas of African-American history and politics: From the slave trade to modern times* New York: McGraw-Hill.

Smith, C. S. 2002, May 5. Risking limbs for height and success in China. *New York Times.*

Smith, C. S. 2005, April 30. Abduction, often violent, a Kyrgyz wedding rite. *New York Times.*

Smith, D. 1997, May 1. Study looks at portrayal of women in media. *New York Times.*

Smith, D. A. 1993. Technology and the modern world system: Some reflections. *Science, Technology and Human Values, 18,* 186–195.

Smith, W. 2002, April 5. Eroica trio offers beauty of more than one kind. *Indianapolis Star.*

Sniderman, P. M., & Tetlock, P. E. 1986. Symbolic racism: Problems of motive attribution in political analysis. *Social Forces, 42,* 129–150.

Snipp, C. M. 1986. American Indians and natural resource development. *American Journal of Economics and Sociology, 45,* 457–474.

Snow, D. A., & Machalek, R. 1982. On the presumed fragility of unconventional beliefs. *Journal for the Scientific Study of Religion, 21,* 15–26.

Sokolove, M. 2004, November 28. Constructing a teen phenom. *New York Times Magazine.*

Sokolove, M. 2005, February 13. Clang! *New York Times Magazine.*

Soldo, B. J., & Agree, E. M. 1988. America's elderly. *Population Bulletin, 43,* 1–45.

Sontag, D. 1992, December 11. Across the U.S., immigrants find the land of resentment. *New York Times.*

Sontag, S. 2004, May 23. Regarding the torture of others. *New York Times Magazine.*

Soukup, E. 2004, August 2. Till blog do us part. *Newsweek.*

South, S. J., & Lloyd, K. M. 1995. Spousal alternatives and marital dissolution. *American Sociological Review, 60,* 21–35.

Squadron, D. 2005, June 1. United we stand (in line). *New York Times.*

Squires, G. D. 1980, May. Runaway factories are also a civil rights issue. *In These Times,* pp. 14–20.

Srikameswaran, A. 2002, July 23. Minorities lag in receiving transplants and heart surgeries. *Pittsburgh Post-Gazette.*

Stacey, J. 1991. Backward toward the postmodern family. In A. Wolfe (Ed.), *America at century's end.* Berkeley: University of California Press.

Staggenborg, S. 1998. *Gender, family, and social movements.* Thousand Oaks, CA: Pine Forge Press.

Stagnitti, M. N. 2005. Antidepressant use in the U.S. civilian noninstitutionalized population, 2002. Medical Expenditure Panel Survey. Brief No. 77. www.meps.ahrq.gov/papers/st77/stat77.pdf. Accessed June 3, 2005.

Staples, B. 1999, July 6. The final showdown on interracial marriage. *New York Times.*

Staples, R. 1992. African American families. In J. M. Henslin (Ed.), *Marriage and family in a changing society.* New York: Free Press.

Starbucks. 2005. Starbucks coffee international. www.starbucks.com/aboutus/international.asp. Accessed May 25, 2005.

Stark, R., & Bainbridge, W. S. 1980. Networks of faith: Interpersonal bonds and recruitment in cults and sects. *American Journal of Sociology, 85,* 1376–1395.

Starr, P. 1982. *The social transformation of American medicine.* New York: Basic Books.

Stein, R., & Connolly, C. 2004, July 16. Medicare changes policy on obesity; some treatments may be covered. *Washington Post.*

Steinberg, J. 2002, May 2. More family income committed to college. *New York Times.*

Steinberg, J. 2003, February 2. The new calculus of diversity on campus. *New York Times.*

Steiner, A. 1998, January–February. As the world turns. *Utne Reader.*

Steinhauer, J. 2005, May 29. When the Joneses wear jeans. *New York Times.*

Steinmetz, S. K., Clavan, R., & Stein, K. F. 1990. *Marriage and family realities: Historical and contemporary perspectives.* New York: Harper & Row.

Stephan, C. W., & Stephan, W. G. 1989. After intermarriage: Ethnic identity among mixed-heritage Japanese-Americans and Hispanics. *Journal of Marriage and the Family, 51,* 507–519.

Stephens, G. 1994. The global crime wave. *Futurist, 28,* 22–28.

Stephens, W. N. 1963. *The family in cross-cultural perspective.* New York: University Press of America.

Stewart, A. J., Copeland, A. P., Chester, A. L., Malley, J. E., & Barenbaum, N. B. 1997. *Separating together: How divorce transforms families.* New York: Guilford Press.

Stewart, J. E. 1980. Defendant's attractiveness as a factor in the outcome of criminal trials: An observational study. *Journal of Applied Social Psychology, 10,* 348–361.

Stille, A. 2001, December 15. Grounded by an income gap. *New York Times.*

Stille, A. 2002, June 29. Textbook publishers learn to avoid messing with Texas. *New York Times.*

Stinnett, N., & DeFrain, J. 1985. *Secrets of strong families.* Boston: Little, Brown.

Stockard, J., & Johnson, M. M. 1992. *Sex and gender in society.* Englewood Cliffs, NJ: Prentice Hall.

Stockard, J., & O'Brien, R. M. 2002. Cohort effects on suicide rates: International variation. *American Sociological Review, 67,* 854–872.

Stokes, R., & Hewitt, J. P. 1976. Aligning actions. *American Sociological Review, 41,* 837–849.

Stolberg, S. G. 1998a, March 13. New cancer cases decreasing in U.S. as deaths do, too. *New York Times.*

Stolberg, S. G. 1998b, April 5. Live and let die over transplants. *New York Times.*

Stolberg, S. G. 2002, August 8. Patient deaths tied to lack of nurses. *New York Times.*

Stolberg, S. G. 2004, March 21. When spin spins out of control. *New York Times.*

Stone, G. P. 1981. Appearance and the self: A slightly revised version. In G. P. Stone & H. A. Farberman (Eds.), *Social psychology through symbolic interaction.* New York: Wiley.

Straus, M. A. 1977. A sociological perspective on the prevention and treatment of wife beating. In M. Roy (Ed.), *Battered women.* New York: Van Nostrand Reinhold.

Straus, M. A. 1991. Physical violence in American families: Incidence, rates, causes, and trends. In D. Knudsen & J. Miller (Eds.), *Abused and battered.* Chicago: Aldine-Atherton.

Straus, M. A., & Gelles, R. J. 1990. How violent are American families? Estimates from the National Family Violence Resurvey and other studies. In M. A. Straus & R. J. Gelles (Eds.), *Physical violence in American families.* New Brunswick, NJ: Transaction.

Strom, S. 2003, November 16. In middle class, health benefits become luxury. *New York Times.*

Strom, S. 2005, January 13. U.S. charity overwhelmed by disaster aid. *New York Times.*

Strube, M. J., & Barbour, L. S. 1983. The decision to leave an abusive relationship: Economic dependence and psychological commitment. *Journal of Marriage and the Family, 45,* 785–793.

Stryker, J. 1980. *Symbolic interactionsim.* Menlo Park, CA: Benjamin/Cummings.

Stryker, J. 1997, July 13. The age of innocence isn't what it once was. *New York Times.*

Study finds increase in weapons use. 2000, November 30. *New York Times.*

Suarez, Z. 1998. The Cuban-American family. In C. H. Mindel, R. W. Habenstein, & R. Wright (Eds.), *Ethnic families in America: Patterns and variations.* Upper Saddle River, NJ: Prentice Hall.

Sudarkasa, N. 2001. Interpreting the African heritage in Afro-American family organization. In S. J. Ferguson (Ed.), *Shifting the center: Understanding contemporary families.* Mountain View, CA: Mayfield.

Sudnow, D. 1965. Normal crimes: Sociological features of the penal code in a public defender's office. *Social Problems, 12,* 255–264.

Sutherland, E., & Cressey, D. 1955. *Criminology.* Philadelphia: Lippincott.

Swanson, G. 1992. Doing things together: On some basic forms of agency and structuring in collective action and on some explanations for them. *Social Psychology Quarterly, 55,* 94–117.

Swarns, R. L. 2001, April 20. Drug makers drop South Africa suit over AIDS medicines. *New York Times.*

Swarns, R. L. 2004, October 24. Hispanics resist racial grouping by census. *New York Times.*

Sykes, G., & Matza, D. 1957. Techniques of neutralization: A theory of delinquency. *American Sociological Review, 22,* 664–670.

Tahan, R. 1997, November 16. Realtors to receive cultural training. *Indianapolis Star.*

Taiwan's little problem. 1993, June 5. *The Economist.*

Takayama, H. 2003, January 13. The Okinawa way. *Newsweek.*

Talbot, M. 2000a, February 27. A mighty fortress. *New York Times Magazine.*

Talbot, M. 2000b, January 9. The placebo prescription. *New York Times Magazine.*

Talbot, M. 2002, October 13. Men behaving badly. *New York Times Magazine.*

Talbot, M. 2003, September 21. Why, isn't he just the cutest brand-image enhancer you've ever seen? *New York Times Magazine.*

Tannen, D. 1990. *You just don't understand: Women and men in conversation.* New York: Ballantine.

Tanner, J. 2002. Living wage movement. *CQ Researcher, 12,* 769–792.

Tarnished gold. 1999, October. *Harper's.*

Tarrow, S. 1994. *Power in movement.* New York: Cambridge University Press.

Taub, E.A. 2001, November 22. Cell yell: Thanks for (not) sharing. *New York Times.*

Tauber, M. A. 1979. Parental socialization techniques and sex differences in children's play. *Child Development, 50,* 225–234.

Tavris, C. 1992. *The mismeasure of woman.* New York: Touchstone.

Tavris, C., & Offir, C. 1984. *The longest war: Sex differences in perspective.* New York: Harcourt Brace Jovanovich.

Taylor, D. E. 1993. Environmentalism and the politics of inclusion. In R. D. Bullard (Ed.), *Confronting environmental racism.* Boston: South End Press.

Taylor, S. J., & Bogdan, R. 1980. Defending illusions: The institution's struggle for survival. *Human Organization, 39,* 209–218.

Teachman, J. D. 1991. Contributions to children by divorced fathers. *Social Problems, 38,* 358–371.

Telles, E. E., & Murguia, E. 1990. Phenotypic discrimination and income differences among Mexican Americans. *Social Science Quarterly, 71,* 682–696.

Tenner, E. 1996. *Why things bite back.* New York: Knopf.

Terry, D. 1996, August 17. In Wisconsin, a rarity of a fetal-harm case. *New York Times.*

Theocracy Watch. 2005. The rise of the religious right in the Republican Party. www.theocracy watch.org. Accessed June 22, 2005.

Thoits, P. 1985. Self-labeling process in mental illness: The role of emotional deviance. *American Journal of Sociology, 91,* 221–249.

Thomas, C. B., & Healy, R. 2003, March 10. Conduct unbecoming. *Time.*

Thomas, S. L. 1998. Race, gender and welfare reform: The antinatalist response. *Journal of Black Studies, 28,* 419–446.

Thompson, G. 2003, February 13. Behind roses' beauty, poor and ill workers. *New York Times.*

Thompson, T. L., & Zerbinos, E. 1995. Gender roles in animated cartoons: Has the picture changed in 20 years? *Sex Roles, 32,* 651–673.

Thomsen, S. R., Weber, M. M., & Brown, L. B. 2002. The relationship between reading beauty and fashion magazines and the use of pathogenic dieting methods among adolescent females. *Adolescence, 37,* 1–18.

Thomson, D. S. 2000. The Sapir-Whorf hypothesis: Worlds shaped by words. In J. Spradley & D. W. McCurdy (Eds.), *Conformity and conflict.* Boston: Allyn & Bacon.

Thorne, B., & Yalom, M. 1982. *Rethinking the family: Some feminist questions.* New York: Longman.

Thornton, A. 1989. Changing attitudes toward family issues in the United States. *Journal of Marriage and the Family, 51,* 873–893.

Thornton, M. 1997. Strategies of racial socialization among black parents: Mainstreaming, minority, and cultural messages. In R. Taylor, J. Jackson, & L. Chatters (Eds.), *Family life in black America.* Thousand Oaks, CA: Sage.

Thurlow, C. 2001. Naming the "outsider within": Homophobic pejoratives and the verbal abuse of lesbian, gay, and bisexual high-school pupils. *Journal of Adolescence, 24,* 25–38.

Tiano, S. 1987. Gender, work and world capitalism: Third world women's role in development. In B. B. Hess & M. M. Ferree (Eds.), *Analyzing gender: A handbook of social science research.* Newbury Park, CA: Sage.

Tilly, C. 1978. *From mobilization to revolution.* Reading, MA: Addison-Wesley.

Timms, E., & McGonigle, S. 1992, April 5. Psychological warfare. *Indianapolis Star.*

Tjaden, P., & Thoennes, N. 2000. Extent, nature, and consequences of intimate partner violence. Bureau of Justice Statistics Bulletin NCJ 181867. www.ncjrs.org/pdffiles1/nij/181867.pdf. Accessed October 12, 2004.

Tobin, J. J., Wu, D. Y. H., & Davidson, D. H. 1989. *Preschool in three cultures: Japan, China and the United States.* New Haven, CT: Yale University Press.

Toner, R., & Connelly, M. 2005, June 19. Poll finds broad pessimism on Social Security benefits. *New York Times.*

Tönnies, F. 1957. *Community and society (Gemeinschaft und Gesellschaft).* C. P. Loomis (Ed.). East Lansing: Michigan State University Press. (Original work published 1887)

Torrey, B. B. 2004, April. Urbanization: An environmental force to be reckoned with. Population Reference Bureau Report. www.prb.org. Accessed June 25, 2004.

Toymakers study troops, and vice versa. 2003, March 30. *New York Times.*

Triandis, H. C., McCusker, C., & Hui, C. H. 1990. Multimethod probes of individualism and collectivism. *Journal of Personality and Social Psychology, 59,* 1006–1020.

Trotsky, L. 1959. *The history of the Russian Revolution.* F. W. Dupee (Ed.). Garden City, NY: Doubleday. (Original work published 1930)

Trudgill, P. 1972. Sex, covert prestige and linguistic change in the urban British English of Norwich. In B. Thorne & N. Henley (Eds.), *Language and society.* Cambridge, UK: Cambridge University Press.

Tsushima, T., & Gecas, V. 2001. Role taking and socialization in single-parent families. *Journal of Family Issues, 22,* 267–288.

Tuller, D. 2004, June 21. Gentlemen, start your engines? *New York Times.*

Tumin, M. 1953. Some principles of stratification: A critical analysis. *American Sociological Review, 18,* 387–393.

Turner, J. H. 1972. *Patterns of social organization.* New York: McGraw-Hill.

Turner, R. W., & Killian, L. M. 1987. *Collective behavior.* Englewood Cliffs, NJ: Prentice Hall.

Turning Point Project. 1999, November 15. Global monoculture. *New York Times.*

Ubel, P., Zell, M. M., Miller, D. J., Fischer, G. S., Peters-Stefani, D., & Arnold, R. M. 1995. Elevator talk: Observational study of inappropriate comments in a public space. *American Journal of Medicine, 99,* 190–194.

Uchitelle, L. 2005, January 13. College degree still pays, but it's leveling off. *New York Times.*

Uggen, C., & Blackstone, A. 2004. Sexual harassment as a gendered expression of power. *American Sociological Review, 69,* 64–92.

Uggen, C., & Manza, J. 2002. Democratic contraction? Political consequences of felon disenfranchisement in the United States. *American Sociological Review, 67,* 777–803.

UN to protect children in conflicts. 1999, August 26. *New York Times.*

UN/AIDS. 2004. 2004 report on the global AIDS epidemic. www.unaids.org/bangkok2004/report.html. Accessed July 20, 2004.

United Nations. 2004. World population to 2300. www.un.org/esa/population/publications/longrange2/WorldPop2300final.pdf. Accessed June 16, 2005.

United Nations Population Division. 2003. World population prospects: The 2002 revision. www.un.org/esa/population/publications/wpp2002/wpp2002-highlightsrev1.pdf. Accessed June 26, 2003.

United Nations Population Division. 2005. World population prospects: The 2004 revision population database. http://esa.un.org/unpp/index.asp?panel=2. Accessed July 15, 2005.

United States [U.S.] Bureau of Justice Statistics. 2001. The sexual victimization of college women [Press release]. 222.ojp.usdoj.gov/bjs/pub/press/svcw.pr. Accessed January 28, 2001.

United States [U.S.] Bureau of Justice Statistics. 2002. Sourcebook of criminal justice statistics. Tables 4.10 and 5.45. www.albany.edu/sourcebook. Accessed June 2, 2005.

United States [U.S.] Bureau of Justice Statistics. 2003. Criminal victimization in the United States, 2002 statistical tables. Bureau of Justice Statistics Bulletin NCJ 200561. www.ojp.usdoj.gov/bjs/pub/pdf/cvus02.pdf. Accessed July 28, 2004.

United States [U.S.] Bureau of Justice Statistics. 2004a. Criminal victimization in the United States, 2002 statistical tables, Table 27. Bureau of Justice Statistics Bulletin NCJ 200561. www.ojp.usdoj.gov/bjs/pub/pdf/cvus02.pdf. Accessed May 24, 2005.

United States [U.S.] Bureau of Justice Statistics. 2004b. Homicide trends in the U.S. www.ojp.usdoj.gov/bjs/homicide/gender.htm. Accessed May 24, 2005.

United States [U.S.] Bureau of Justice Statistics. 2004c. Capital punishment statistics. www.ojp.usdoj.gov/bjs/cp.htm. Accessed June 2, 2005.

United States [U.S.] Bureau of Justice Statistics. 2005. Nation's prison and jail population grew by 932 inmates per week; Number of female inmates reached more than 100,000. www.ojp.usdoj.gov/bjs/pub/press/pjim04pr.htm. Accessed May 17, 2005.

United States [U.S.] Bureau of Labor Statistics. 2004a. Consumer expenditures in 2002. Report No. 974. www.bls.gov/cex/csxann02.pdf. Accessed October 7, 2004.

United States [U.S.] Bureau of Labor Statistics. 2004b. Time-use survey—First results announced by BLS. News Release No. USDL04–1797. www.bls.gov/tus/. Accessed September 15, 2004.

United States [U.S.] Bureau of Labor Statistics. 2004c. Work experience of the population: 2003. www.bls.gov/news/release/pdf/work.pdf. Accessed June 14, 2005.

United States [U.S.] Bureau of Labor Statistics. 2005a. The employment situation: March 2005. www.bls.gov/news.release/pdf/empsit.pdf. Accessed April 12, 2005.

United States [U.S.] Bureau of Labor Statistics. 2005b. Women in the labor force: A databook. www.bls.gov/cps/wlf-table11–2005.pdf. Accessed June 14, 2005.

United States [U.S.] Bureau of the Census. 1995. *Statistical abstract of the United States.* Washington, DC: U.S. Government Printing Office.

United States [U.S.] Bureau of the Census. 1998. *Statistical abstract of the United States.* Washington, DC: U.S. Government Printing Office.

United States [U.S.] Bureau of the Census. 1999. *Statistical abstract of the United States.* Washington, DC: U.S. Government Printing Office.

United States [U.S.] Bureau of the Census. 2000. *Statistical abstract of the United States.* Washington, DC: U.S. Government Printing Office.

United States [U.S.] Bureau of the Census. 2002. *Statistical abstract of the United States.* Washington, DC: U.S. Government Printing Office.

United States [U.S.] Bureau of the Census. 2003. Children's living arrangements and characteristics: March 2002. *Current Population Reports, P20–547.* www.census.gov/population/www/socdemo/hh-fam/cps2002.html. Accessed July 6, 2003.

United States [U.S.] Bureau of the Census. 2004a. Statistical abstract of the United States. www.census.gov/prod/www/statistical-abstract-04.html. Accessed June 15, 2005.

United States [U.S.] Bureau of the Census. 2004b. U.S. interim projections by age, sex, race, and Hispanic origin, Table 1a. www.census.gov/ipc/www/usinterimproj/Accessed June 10, 2005.

United States [U.S.] Bureau of the Census. 2005a. Current population survey (CPS)—Definitions and explanations. www.census.gov/population/www/cps/cpsdef.html. Accessed September 21, 2005.

United States [U.S.] Bureau of the Census. 2005b. Educational attainment in the United States: 2004, Table 9. www.census.gov/population/www/socdemo/education/cps2004.html. Accessed June 14, 2005.

United States [U.S.] Commission on Human Rights. 1992. Indian tribes: A continuing quest for survival. In P. S. Rothenberg (Ed.), *Race, class and gender in the United States.* New York: St. Martin's Press.

United States Conference of Mayors. 2004. Hunger and homelessness survey. www.usmayors.org/uscm/hungersurvey/2004/onlinereport/HungerAndHomelessnessReport 2004.pdf. Accessed June 8, 2005.

United States [U.S.] Department of Agriculture. 2001. USDA estimates child rearing costs. USDA News Release No. 0097.01. www.usda.gov/news/releases/2001/06/0097.htm. Accessed June 17, 2001.

United States [U.S.] Department of Health and Human Services. 2004. *Child maltreatment 2002.* Washington, DC: U.S. Government Printing Office.

United States [U.S.] Department of Health and Human Services. 2005. 2003 state estimates of substance use. www.oas.samhsa.gov/2k3state/ch4.htm#4.2. Accessed May 24, 2005.

United States [U.S.] Department of Justice. 2001. Criminal victimization in United States, 1999 statistical tables. Bureau of Justice Statistics Bulletin NCJ 184938. www.ojp.usdoj.gov/bjs/pub/pdf/cvus99.pdf. Accessed January 28, 2001.

United States [U.S.] Department of Labor. 2001. FMLA survey. www.dol.gov/asp/fmla/toc.htm. Accessed June 7, 2003.

United States [U.S.] Department of Labor. 2003. Household data, annual averages, Table 39. www.bls.gov/cps/cpsaat39.pdf. Accessed August 18, 2004.

United States [U.S.] Department of Labor. 2004a. The Americans with Disabilities Act of 1990. www.dol.gov/esa/regs/statutes/ofccp/ada.htm. Accessed December 14, 2004.

United States [U.S.] Department of Labor. 2004b. Characteristics of minimum wage workers: 2003, Table 1. www.bls.gov/cps/minwage2003tbls.htm. Accessed August 23, 2004.

United States [U.S.] Department of State. 2005. Victims of Trafficking and Violence Protection Act of 2000: Trafficking in persons report 2005. www.state.gov/g/tip/rls/tiprpt/2005. Accessed June 7, 2005.

United States General Accounting Office. 2003. Women's earnings: Work patterns partially explain difference between men's and women's earnings. Report to Congressional Requesters No. GAO-04–35. Washington, DC: U.S. Government Printing Office.

United States [U.S.] Network for Global Economic Justice. 2000. False profits: Who wins, who loses when the IMF, World Bank, and WTO come to town. www.50years.org/april16/booklet .html. Accessed June 22, 2000.

United States [U.S.] Sentencing Commission, 1998. Sourcebook of federal sentencing statistics. www. ussc.gov./ANNRPT/1998/Sbtoc98.htm. Accessed June 20, 2001.

United States [U.S.] Sentencing Commission. 2004. Fifteen years of guidelines sentencing: An assessment of how well the federal criminal justice system is achieving the goals of sentencing reform. www.ussc.gov/15_year/15year.htm. Accessed November 27, 2004.

Van Ausdale, D., & Feagin, J. R. 2001. *The first R: How children learn race and racism.* Lanham, MD: Rowman & Littlefield.

van den Haag, E. 1975. *Punishing criminals: Concerning a very old and painful question.* New York: Basic Books.

Vanek, J. 1980. Work, leisure and family roles: Farm households in the United States: 1920–1955. *Journal of Family History, 5,* 422–431.

Vaughan, D. 1986. *Uncoupling.* New York: Vintage.

Vedantam, S. 2005, June 26. Patients' diversity is often discounted. *Washington Post.*

Viets, E. 1992, November 29. Give a whistle, he'll love it. *St. Louis Post-Dispatch.*

Villarosa, L. 2004, August 7. Patients with H.I.V. seen as separated by a racial divide. *New York Times.*

Vital signs. 1995, September 11. *The Nation.*

Vogeler, I. 2003. Maquiladoras. University of Wisconsin—Eau Claire. www.uwec.edu/geography/Ivogeler/w188/border/maquil.htm. Accessed July 6, 2003.

Vojdik, V. K. 2002. Gender outlaws: Challenging masculinity in traditionally male institutions. *Berkeley Women's Law Journal, 17,* 68–122.

Von Zielbauer, P. 2005, June 17. Race a factor in job offers for ex-convicts. *New York Times.*

Voyandoff, P. 1990. Economic distress and family relations: A review of the eighties. *Journal of Marriage and Family, 52,* 1099–1115.

Wade, N. 2002, July 30. Race is seen as real guide to track roots of disease. *New York Times.*

Wagner, D. G., Ford, R. S., & Ford, T. W. 1986. Can gender inequalities be reduced? *American Sociological Review, 51,* 47–61.

Wahl, O. 1999. *Telling is risky business.* New Brunswick, NJ: Rutgers University Press.

Waite, L. J., & Gallagher, M. 2000. *The case for marriage: Why married people are happier, healthier, and better off financially.* New York: Doubleday.

Waldman, A. 2003, March 28. Broken taboos doom lovers in an Indian village. *New York Times.*

Waldman, A. 2005, May 8. Sri Lankan maids' high price for foreign jobs. *New York Times.*

Wal-Mart. 2003. U.S. operations and International operations. www.walmartstores.com. Accessed July 3, 2003.

Walton, J. 1990. *Sociology and critical inquiry.* Belmont, CA: Wadsworth.

Warshaw, R. 1988. *I never called it rape.* New York: Harper & Row.

Wartik, N. 2003, September 9. Muting the obsessions over perceived flaws. *New York Times.*

Watson, C. M., Quatman, T., & Edler, E. 2002. Career aspirations of adolescent girls: Effects of achievement level, grade, and single-sex school environment. *Sex Roles, 46,* 323–335.

Watson, I. 2005, June 13. As elections near, Iranian women stage protest. NPR Morning Edition. www.npr.org/templates/story/story.php?storyID=4700486. Accessed June 13, 2005.

Wattenberg, E. 1986. The fate of baby boomers and their children. *Social Work, 31,* 20–28.

Watzlawick, P. 1976. *How real is real?* Garden City, NY: Doubleday.

Watzlawick, P. 1984. Self-fulfilling prophecies. In P. Watzlawick (Ed.), *The invented reality: How do we know what we believe we know? Contributions to constructivism.* New York: Norton.

Webb, E. J., Campbell, D. T., Schwartz, R. D., Sechrest, L., & Grove, J. B. 1981. *Nonreactive measures in the social sciences.* Boston: Houghton Mifflin.

Weber, B. 2005, January 29. Extreme is becoming more mainstream. *New York Times.*

Weber, M. 1946. Bureaucracy. In H. H. Gerth & C. W. Mills (Eds.), *From Max Weber: Essays in sociology* (pp. 196–244). New York: Oxford University Press.

Weber, M. 1947. *The theory of social and economic organization.* New York: Free Press.

Weber, M. 1970. *From Max Weber: Essays in sociology.* H. H. Gerth & C. W. Mills (Eds.). New York: Oxford University Press.

Weber, M. 1977. *The Protestant ethic and the spirit of capitalism.* New York: Macmillan. (Original work published 1904)

Weeks, J. 1995. *Population: An introduction to concepts and issues* (updated 5th ed.). Belmont, CA: Wadsworth.

Wehrfritz, G., & Cochrane, J. 2005, January 17. Charity and chaos. *Newsweek.*

Weismantel, M. 2005. White. In D. Kulick & A. Meneley (Eds.), *Fat: The anthropology of an obsession.* New York: Tarcher/Penguin.

Weitzman, L., Eifler, D., Hodada, E., & Ross, C. 1972. Sex-role socialization in picture books for preschool children. *American Journal of Sociology, 77,* 1125–1150.

Whalen, C. K., & Henker, B. 1977. The pitfalls of politicization: A response to Conrad's "The discovery of hyperkinesis: Notes on the medicalization of deviance." *Social Problems, 24,* 590–595.

What is coltan? 2002, January 21. ABCNews.com. http://abcnews.go.com/sections/nightline/DailyNews/coltan_explainer.html. Accessed June 11, 2003.

White, J. E. 1997, May 5. Multiracialism: The melding of America. *Time.*

White, L., & Brinkerhoff, D. 1981. The sexual division of labor: Evidence from childhood. *Social Forces, 60,* 170–181.

Whorf, B. 1956. *Language, thought and reality.* Cambridge, MA: MIT Press.

Whyte, M. K. 1990. *Dating, mating and marriage.* New York: Aldine de Gruyter.

Whyte, W. H. 1956. *The organization man.* Garden City, NY: Doubleday.

Wildman, S. M., & Davis, A. D. 2002. Making systems of privilege visible. In P. S. Rothenberg (Ed.), *White privilege: Essential readings on the other side of racism.* New York: Worth.

Wilgoren, J. 2001, January 10. Calls for change in the scheduling of the school day. *New York Times.*

Wilgoren, J. 2002, June 9. Cutting class on Fridays to cut school budgets. *New York Times.*

Wilgoren, J. 2003, January 12. Governor assails system's errors as he empties Illinois death row. *New York Times.*

Wilkinson, L. C., & Marrett, C. B. 1985. *Gender influences in classroom interaction.* Orlando, FL: Academic Press.

Will, G. 2003, May 12. The stiletto's sharp idea. *Newsweek.*

Williams, B. 2004, June 28. The "n-word." Minnesota Public Radio. http://news.minnesota.publicradio.org/features/2004/06–28_williamsb_nword/. Accessed October 14, 2004.

Williams, L. 1991, April 30. When blacks shop bias often accompanies sale. *New York Times.*

Williams, W. L. 1992. *The spirit and the flesh: Sexual diversity in American Indian culture.* Boston: Beacon Press.

Williamson, R. C. 1984. A partial replication of the Kohn-Gecas-Nye thesis in a German sample. *Journal of Marriage and the Family, 46,* 971–979.

Wilmer, F. 2002. *The social construction of man, the state, and war: Identity, conflict, and violence in former Yugoslavia.* New York: Routledge.

Wilson, W. J. 1980. *The declining significance of race.* Chicago: University of Chicago Press.

Wilson, W. J. 1987. *The truly disadvantaged.* Chicago: University of Chicago Press.

Wines, M. 2004, July 20. Women in Lesotho become easy prey for H.I.V. *New York Times.*

Winter, G. 2002, May 19. Workers say Coke sold old soda. *New York Times.*

Winter, G. 2003, June 24. Ruling provides relief, but less than hoped. *New York Times.*

Wise, T. 2002. Membership has its privileges: Thoughts on acknowledging and challenging whiteness. In P. S. Rothenberg (Ed.), *White privilege: Essential readings on the other side of racism.* New York: Worth.

Wisotsky, S. 1998. A society of suspects: The war on drugs and civil liberties. In H. A. Widdison (Ed.), *Social problems 98/99*. Guilford, CT: Dushkin.

Wolfe, A. 1991. *America at century's end*. Berkeley: University of California Press.

Wolfe, A. 1998. *One nation, after all*. New York: Viking.

Wolfe, A. 1999, September 22. The new politics of inequality. *New York Times*.

Women Physicians Congress. 2004. Women residents by specialty—2003, Table 4. www.ama-assn .org/ama/pub/category/12915.html. Accessed June 15, 2005.

Wood, N. 2005, February 6. Eight nations agree on plan to lift status of Gypsies. *New York Times*.

Word, C. O., Zanna, M. P., & Cooper, J. 1974. The nonverbal mediation of self-fulfilling prophecies in interracial interaction. *Journal of Experimental Social Psychology, 10*, 109–120.

Workers of the world. 1998, January 30. *Economist*.

World Bank. 2003. Global poverty monitoring. www.worldbank.org/research/povmonitor. Accessed August 24, 2004.

World Bank. 2004. Global economic prospects 2004. www.worldbank.org/prospects/gep2004/ index.htm. Accessed June 6, 2005.

World Health Organization. 1999. Tobacco—health facts (Fact sheet no. 221) and Tobacco dependence (Fact sheet no. 222). www.who.int/inf-fs/en. Accessed June 16, 2003.

World progress in birth control. 1993, August. *Futurist*.

World Resources Institute. 2001. *Feeding the world*. Sustainable Development Information Service. www.wri.org/trends/feeding.html. Accessed February 3, 2001.

World Wildlife Fund. 2002. Living planet report 2002. www.panda.org/downloads/general/ LPR_2002.pdf. Accessed June 29, 2003.

Worsnop, R. 1996, February 23. Getting into college. *CQ Researcher*.

Wright, E. O. 1976. Class boundaries in advanced capitalist societies. *New Left Review, 98*, 3–41.

Wright, E. O., Costello, C., Hachen, D., & Sprague, J. 1982. The American class structure. *American Sociological Review, 47*, 709–726.

Wright, E. O., & Perrone, L. 1977. Marxist class categories and income inequality. *American Sociological Review, 42*, 32–55.

Wright, J. D., & Wright, S. R. 1976. Social class and parental values for children: A partial replication and extension of the Kohn thesis. *American Sociological Review, 41*, 52–37.

Wrong, D. 1988. *Power: Its forms, bases, and uses*. Chicago: University of Chicago Press.

WuDunn, S. 1996, January 23. In Japan, even toddlers feel the pressure to excel. *New York Times*.

WuDunn, S. 1997, January 14. Korean women still feel demands to bear a son. *New York Times*.

Wuthnow, R. 1994. *Sharing the journey*. New York: Free Press.

Wyatt, E. 2005, August 10. Books, not tales, get taller before baby boomers' eyes. *New York Times*.

Wynia, M. K., VanGeest, J. B., Cummins, D. S., Wilson, I. B. 2003. Do physicians not offer useful services because of coverage restrictions. *Health Affairs, 22*, 190–198.

Xiao, H. 2000. Class, gender, and parental values in the 1990s. *Gender & Society, 14*, 785–803.

Yardley, J. 2000, March 25. Unmarried and living together, till the sheriff do us part. *New York Times*.

Yardley, J. 2005, January 31. Fearing future, China starts to give girls their due. *New York Times*.

Yi, C-C., Chang, C-F., & Chang, Y-H. 2004. The intergenerational transmission of family values: A comparison between teenagers and parents in Taiwan. *Journal of Comparative Family Studies, 35*, 523–545.

Young, L. M., & Powell, B. 1985. The effects of obesity on the clinical judgments of mental health professionals. *Journal of Health and Social Behavior, 26*, 233–246.

Zaldivar, R. A. 1998, August 2. Balancing the "good" life with the risk. *Indianapolis Star*.

Zeller, T. 2004, January 11. Of fuzzy math and "food security." *New York Times.*

Zernike, K. 2003, January 20. 30 years after Roe v. Wade, new trends but the old debate. *New York Times.*

Zernike, K. 2004, December 19. Does Christmas need to be saved? *New York Times.*

Zhao, Y. 2002, August 5. Wave of pupils lacking English strains schools. *New York Times.*

Zola, I. 1986. Medicine as an institution of social control. In P. Conrad & R. Kern (Eds.), *The sociology of health and illness.* New York: St. Martin's Press.

Zoll, R. 2005, June 7. Poll reveals U.S. leads in religious devotion. *Indianapolis Star.*

Zuckoff, M. 2000, June 8. Lawsuit accuses drug maker Eli Lilly of concealing Prozac data from trial. *Boston Globe.*

Zuger, A. 1999, April 30. Take some strychnine and call me in the morning. *New York Times.*

Zurcher, L. A., & Snow, D. A. 1981. Collective behavior: Social movements. In M. Rosenberg & R. H. Turner (Eds.), *Social psychology: Sociological perspectives.* New York: Basic Books.

Zweigenhaft, R. L. 1987. Minorities and women of the corporation. In G. W. Domhoff & T. R. Dye (Eds.), *Power elites and organizations.* Newbury Park, CA: Sage.

Zwingle, E. 1999, August. A world apart. *National Geographic.*

Photo Credits

"The Old Ball Game," p. 36

Photo p. 36, Cal Ripkin, © Reuters NewMedia, Inc./CORBIS; photo p. 38, © Reuters NewMedia, Inc./CORBIS; photo p. 39, © Reuters NewMedia, Inc./CORBIS

"Personal Billboards," p. 72

Photo p. 72, American Nazis, © Owen Franken/CORBIS; photo p. 72, Wavy Gravy in Tie-Dye, © Lynn Goldsmith/CORBIS; photo p. 73, Young Girl Gazing, © Mark Petersen/CORBIS SABA; photo p. 73, Bumper Stickers, ©Phil Schermeister/CORBIS; photo p. 74, Bumper Sticker on a Rancher's Truck, © Tom Bean/CORBIS; photo p. 74, Hawaiian Bumper Sticker, © Robert Holmes/CORBIS; photo p. 75, American Flag Bumper Sticker, © Bob Rowan, Progressive Images/CORBIS; photo, p. 75, Pakistan Muslim Cleric, © AFP/CORBIS; photo p. 76, 1993 Gay Freedom Day Parade, © Robert Holmes/CORBIS; photo p. 76, Native American Bumper Sticker, © Ed Eckstein/CORBIS; photo p. 76, Looking AIDS in the Face, © Gideon Mendel/CORBIS; photo p. 77, Aboriginal Rights T-Shirt, © Penny Tweedle/CORBIS; photo p. 77, Man Leaning on his Cyclo; photo p. 77, Kurdistan Workers Party Protester, © CORBIS; photo p. 78, Anti-Abortion Woman, © Robert Maass/CORBIS; photo p. 78, Pro-Abortion Demonstrators, © CORBIS; photo p. 79; Sinn Fein Conference Demonstrators, © CORBIS

"Becoming a Mariner," p. 156

Photo p. 156, Ships on Icy Lake Superior, © James L. Amos/CORBIS; photo p. 157, "Let's Finish the Job!" © Swim Ink/CORBIS; photo p. 157, Trainees, © CORBIS; photos p. 158, Freshman Students, © Judy Griesedieck/CORBIS; photos p. 158-161, Merchant Marine Students, © Michael S. Yamashita/CORBIS

"Looking Cool," p. 177

Photo p. 177, Woman followed by two men, © Underwood & Underwoood/CORBIS; photo p. 177, Teenage girls in Central Park, © Bettmann/CORBIS; photo p. 178, Greenwich Village Beatniks, © Bettmann/CORBIS; photo p. 178, Hippie Woman Getting Her Face Painted, © Bettmann/CORBIS; Photo p. 178, Punk Teenagers Pose, © Bettmann/CORBIS; photo p. 179, Hip-Hop Teenager, © Fotosearch; photo p. 179, Russian Teenager, © CORBIS; photo p. 179, Models on Runway, © Reuters NewMedia, Inc./CORBIS; photo p. 180, High School Student, © Bill Ross/CORBIS; photo p. 181, Teenage Skateboarder Couple, © Image 100/Royalty-Free/CORBIS; photo p. 181, Students on their Way to the Prom, © John-Marshall

Mantel/CORBIS; photo p. 181, Trendy Teenage Couple, © Image 100/Royalty-Free/ CORBIS; photo p. 182, Young Man Holding Drink, © Gary Houlder/CORBIS; photo p. 182, Hacker with Dreadlocks, © Jonathan Torgovnik/CORBIS; photo p. 182, Teen Couple Wearing Ripped Jeans, © Image 100/Royalty-Free/CORBIS; photo p. 183, Tahitian Man, © Charles & Josette Lenars/CORBIS; photo p. 183, Teen Boy with Tattoo, © Philip Wallick/CORBIS; photo p. 183, Sun Tattoo on Woman's Neck, © Henry Diltz/CORBIS; photo p. 184, Nomad Man in Pushkar, © Brian Vikander/CORBIS; photo p. 184, Man Wearing Nose and Eyebrow Rings, © Lawrence Manning/CORBIS; photo p. 184, Man with Pierced Tongue, © Jose Luis Pelaez, Inc./CORBIS

"Family Friendly," p. 219

Photo p. 219, Family at the Beach, © Julian Hirshowitz/CORBIS; photo p. 220, Couple on Beach, © Tony Arruza/CORBIS; photo p. 220, Young Woman on Telephone, © Dennis Degnan/CORBIS; photo p. 220, Gay Couple, © Royalty-Free/CORBIS; photo p. 221, People with Mickey Mouse, © David Butow/CORBIS SABA; photo p. 222, Children Sitting in Honda, © Peter Yates/CORBIS; photo, p. 222, kids playroom, © Fotosearch.com; photo p. 223, Baby Changing Station, © Fotosearch; photo p. 223, Family Biking Together, © Raoul Minsart/CORBIS; photo p. 224, Breakfast Together, © Jose Luis Pelaez, Inc./CORBIS; photo p. 224, Children at Playground, © Image 100/Royalty-Free/CORBIS; photo p. 225, Pedestrians in San Francisco, © Sandy Felsenthal/CORBIS; photo p. 225, Mother Nursing Infant, © Owen Franken/CORBIS; photo p. 225, RV's Welcome, © Fotosearch; photo, p. 226, emergency room, © CORBIS; photo p. 226, College Students Studying, © Royalty-Free/CORBIS

"A Culture of Tramps," p. 256

Photos by Douglas Harper.

"The Trail of the Tomato," p. 312

Photos by Deborah Barndt.

"Images of Social Class," p. 333

Photo p. 335, Businessmen in Limousine, © George Shelley, Inc./CORBIS; photo p. 335, Students Watching Science Experiment, © Jim Cummins/CORBIS; photo p. 335, Garbage Collectors, © Gideon Mendel/CORBIS; photo p. 336, Girl Having a Tea Party, © Ariel Skelley/CORBIS; photo p. 339, Father and Kids Washing the Dog, © Ariel Skelley/CORBIS; photo p. 339, Homeless Man with Dog, © Gideon Mendel/CORBIS

"Immigrant Nation," p. 483

Photo p. 483, Immigrants Arriving at Ellis Island, © Bettmann/CORBIS; photo p. 484, Ugandan Immigrants Arriving, © Hulton-Deutsch Collection/CORBIS; photo p. 484, Immigrant Crossing Highway Sign, © Royalty-Free/CORBIS; photo p. 485, Holding Center, © Danny Lehman/CORBIS; photo p. 485, Illegal Immigrants Held at Border, © David Turnley/CORBIS; photo p. 486, Naturalization, © CORBIS; photo p. 486, Midwife with Newborn, © Danny Lehman/CORBIS; photo p. 487, Elementary School Students, © Kim Kulish/CORBIS SABA; photo p. 487, Street Sign in San Francisco, © CORBIS; photo p. 487, Columbian Family, © James Marshall/CORBIS; photo p. 488, Immigration Protesters, © AFP/CORBIS; photo p. 488, Protesters, © Najlah Feanny/CORBIS; photo p. 489, Monks in Chinatown, © David Turnley/CORBIS; photo p. 489, Business People Eating Sushi, © Gerhard Steiner/CORBIS; photo p. 489, Girls in Cinco de Mayo Parade, © Catherine Karnow/CORBIS; photo p. 490, Girls Eating Lunch at Mimi's, © Mark Peterson/CORBIS SABA; photo p. 490, Afghanistan Immigrants, © Julie Plasencia/San Francisco Chronicle/Corbis; photo p. 491, Gale Community Academy, © Ralf-Finn Hestoft/CORBIS SABA

"The Coal Miners' Struggle," p. 525

Photo p. 525, Courtesy of the Library of Congress; photos p. 526, Courtesy of the Smithsonian and the National Archives; photos pp. 527-528, Harvey Phelps Margolis Collection; photo p. 529, Denver Public Library

Glossary/Index